ACKNOWLEDGEMENTS

Every summer, when this book is finished, I vow never to do another edition. But every fall and winter, I admit to a thrill when I see the *Hockey Scouting Report* on the bookstore shelves, or, even better, in the hands of a fan. I hope we've succeeded in making this year's edition lively and informative.

The people who make this book possible remain anonymous, but the cast is enormous. Players past and present, pro and junior scouts, coaches, general managers, directors of player personnel — all contribute to the opinions you'll find in these pages. Not all of the assessments will be popular, but they are honest, and that's the reason for the secrecy. They have one thing in common, and that is a love for the game. Thanks again for your time and patience.

Great thanks also to the team public relations directors throughout the league for their help all year, with a special nod to the New Jersey Devils' Mike Levine and the San Jose Sharks' Ken Arnold — and their staffs — for the endless and enormously helpful supply of clips and statistics.

Thanks also to the National Hockey League's media relations staff for their clips and statistics. Andy McGowan did a terrific job with a weekly newsletter, which was a great source of information. Also, my gratitude to Rob Sanders and Robert Clements at Douglas & McIntyre Ltd.; the staff at ProPhase Systems Inc.; and editors Anne Rose and Kerry Banks. They have one thing in common, and that is a love for the game. Thanks again for your time and patience.

And, a special mention to Michael ("Wayne's World") Myers for giving the book a plug on "Late Show with David Letterman." But you still owe my pals at Skyrink $30 for ice time.

Finally, thanks to my family, friends and temporarily neglected pets for their patience through this project.

Sherry Ross
West Orange, N.J.
July 1995

CONTENTS

ANAHEIM MIGHTY DUCKS

Players' Statistics 1994-95

POS	NO.	PLAYER	GP	G	A	PTS	+/-	PIM	PP	SH	GW	GT	S	PCTG
L	9	*PAUL KARIYA	47	18	21	39	-17	4	7	1	3	1	134	13.4
C	22	SHAUN VAN ALLEN	45	8	21	29	-4	32	1	1	1		68	11.8
C	47	STEPHAN LEBEAU	38	8	16	24	6	12	1		2		70	11.4
L	25	TODD KRYGIER	35	11	11	22	1	10	1		1		90	12.2
R	16	PETER DOURIS	46	10	11	21	4	12			4		69	14.5
R	21	PATRIK CARNBACK	41	6	15	21	-8	32					58	10.3
D	2	BOBBY DOLLAS	45	7	13	20	-3	12	3	1	1		70	10.0
C	19	BOB CORKUM	44	10	9	19	-7	25			1	1	100	10.0
R	14	JOE SACCO	41	10	8	18	-8	23	2				77	13.0
C	20	*STEVE RUCCHIN	43	6	11	17	7	23			1		59	10.2
R	26	MIKE SILLINGER	28	4	11	15	4	8	2				39	10.3
D	10	*OLEG TVERDOVSKY	36	3	9	12	-6	14	1	1			26	11.5
L	11	*VALERI KARPOV	30	4	7	11	-4	6					48	8.3
D	7	*MILOS HOLAN	25	2	8	10	4	14	1		1		93	2.2
D	3	*JASON YORK	24	1	9	10	2	10					28	3.6
L	18	GARRY VALK	36	3	6	9	-4	34					53	5.7
D	24	TOM KURVERS	22	4	3	7	-13	6	1		1		44	9.1
D	29	RANDY LADOUCEUR	44	2	4	6	2	36					42	4.8
D	15	DAVE KARPA	28	1	5	6	-1	91					33	3.0
C	27	*JOHN LILLEY	9	2	2	4	2	5	1				10	20.0
D	4	DAVID WILLIAMS	21	2	2	4	-5	26				1	30	6.7
L	42	*DENNY LAMBERT	13	1	3	4	3	4					14	7.1
D	5	ROBERT DIRK	38	1	3	4	-3	56					15	6.7
L	8	TIM SWEENEY	13	1	1	2	-3	2					11	9.1
L	12	*DAVID SACCO	8		2	2	-3						5	
D	48	*DARREN VAN IMPE	1		1	1		4						
D	3	*JASON MARSHALL	2		1	1		4					1	
D	6	DON MCSWEEN	2										1	
G	35	M. SHTALENKOV	18					2						
R	36	TODD EWEN	24				-2	90					14	
G	31	GUY HEBERT	39					2						

GP = games played; G = goals; A = assists; PTS = points; +/- = goals-for minus goals-against while player is on ice; PIM = penalties in minutes; PP = power play goals; SH = shorthanded goals; GW = game-winning goals; GT = game-tying goals; S = no. of shots; PCTG = percentage of goals to shots; * = rookie

PATRIK CARNBACK

Yrs. of NHL service: 2
Born: Goteberg, Sweden; Feb. 1, 1968
Position: right wing
Height: 6-0
Weight: 187
Uniform no.: 21
Shoots: left

Career statistics:

GP	G	A	TP	PIM
122	18	26	44	88

1992-93 statistics:

GP	G	A	TP	+/-	PIM	PP	SH	GW	GT	S	PCT
6	0	0	0	-4	2	0	0	0	0	4	0.0

1993-94 statistics:

GP	G	A	TP	+/-	PIM	PP	SH	GW	GT	S	PCT
72	12	11	23	-8	54	3	0	2	0	81	14.8

1994-95 statistics:

GP	G	A	TP	+/-	PIM	PP	SH	GW	GT	S	PCT
41	6	15	21	-8	32	0	0	0	0	58	10.3

LAST SEASON

Fifth on team in points.

THE FINESSE GAME

Carnback was the number one centre by default last season. Anaheim was desperate for someone to play with Paul Kariya, and after six years of playing in Sweden and one year in the NHL, Carnback at least had some hockey sense. Carnback is clever with the puck, but isn't highly skilled. His skating was the best part of his game, and he was able to at least stay within hailing distance of Kariya. He has some quickness and is agile in his turn and acceleration.

Carnback got off to a very fast start, and was able to keep the momentum going through the short season. He was fair on face-offs.

THE PHYSICAL GAME

Carnback has very little physical presence. He gets in the way and because of his strong balance isn't easy to knock off the puck, but he does very little battling in front of the net. He prefers to jump in and out of holes.

THE INTANGIBLES

As Anaheim improves its overall talent, Carnback will slide down to the third or fourth line.

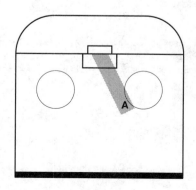

2

BOB CORKUM

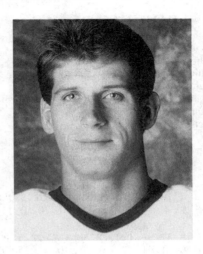

Yrs. of NHL service: 3
Born: Salisbury, Mass.; Dec. 18, 1967
Position: centre/right wing
Height: 6-2
Weight: 212
Uniform no.: 19
Shoots: right

Career statistics:

GP	G	A	TP	PIM
216	43	45	88	104

1991-92 statistics:

GP	G	A	TP	+/-	PIM	PP	SH	GW	GT	S	PCT
20	2	4	6	-9	21	0	0	0	0	23	8.7

1992-93 statistics:

GP	G	A	TP	+/-	PIM	PP	SH	GW	GT	S	PCT
68	6	4	10	-3	38	0	1	1	0	69	8.7

1993-94 statistics:

GP	G	A	TP	+/-	PIM	PP	SH	GW	GT	S	PCT
76	23	28	51	+4	18	3	3	0	1	180	12.8

1994-95 statistics:

GP	G	A	TP	+/-	PIM	PP	SH	GW	GT	S	PCT
44	10	9	19	-7	25	0	0	1	1	100	10.0

LAST SEASON

Second on team in shots on goal.

THE FINESSE GAME

Corkum is the prime example of a player with average skills taking full advantage of a situation with an expansion team and adding a new facet to his game.

He has good overall speed, balance and acceleration. He drives to the net for short-range shots and likes to use a strong wrist shot, though he doesn't get it away quickly. Because of his point production in Anaheim's inaugural season, he got some playing time with Paul Kariya, but Corkum is not a true number one centre.

Corkum likes to use a short, sure pass. He will pass off rather than carry the puck. He anticipates well and will hit the open man. He is not terribly clever with the puck, but he'll make the bread-and-butter play with confidence. Most of Corkum's skills are average. Anything he achieves is the result of his hard work and desire.

THE PHYSICAL GAME

Corkum stands tough in front of the net and works hard along the boards. He is a strong fore-checker who likes to take the body. He relishes the physical game and makes big hits — anyone hit by Corkum knows it. He works hard and uses his size and strength well. He takes draws and kill penalties.

THE INTANGIBLES

As the Mighty Ducks get mightier, Corkum will go from the first line to a third-line checking role, which is really his métier. Corkum was never a scorer at any level of hockey in his career — maybe he scored more than 20 in Nintendo hockey — but now he's done it at the NHL level (he came close again last season, with his goals that were prorated). His future as a checking centre who can pop in 15 goals or so seems secure in Anaheim; his leadership was noted last year when he was given an "A" for his jersey.

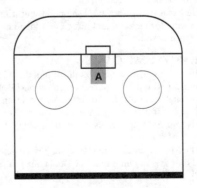

BOBBY DOLLAS

Yrs. of NHL service: 5
Born: Montreal, Que.; Jan. 31, 1965
Position: right defense
Height: 6-2
Weight: 212
Uniform no.: 2
Shoots: left

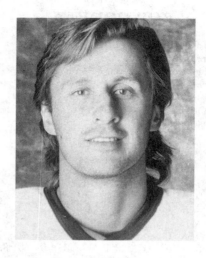

Career statistics:

GP	G	A	TP	PIM
292	22	38	60	193

1991-92 statistics:

GP	G	A	TP	+/-	PIM	PP	SH	GW	GT	S	PCT
27	3	1	4	+4	20	0	1	0	0	0	11.5

1992-93 statistics:

GP	G	A	TP	+/-	PIM	PP	SH	GW	GT	S	PCT
6	0	0	0	-1	2	0	0	0	0	5	0.0

1993-94 statistics:

GP	G	A	TP	+/-	PIM	PP	SH	GW	GT	S	PCT
77	9	11	20	+20	55	1	0	1	0	121	7.4

1994-95 statistics:

GP	G	A	TP	+/-	PIM	PP	SH	GW	GT	S	PCT
45	7	13	20	-3	12	3	1	1	0	70	10.0

LAST SEASON

Led team defensemen in scoring. Career high in assists. Tied career high in points.

THE FINESSE GAME

Much was expected of Dollas when he was a first-round draft pick of Winnipeg in 1983, but he was never able to bring to the NHL the same blend of offense and defense he had shown in junior.

Dollas is a very good skater with speed, mobility and agility, and he is strong on his feet. He doesn't like to get involved too much in the offense, preferring to make a smart, quick pass to start a teammate off. He makes poised plays out of the defensive zone, but has become more and more conservative.

Dollas gets a lot of ice time, and can handle it because he doesn't wear himself out racing up and down the ice. He will take the offensive chance when it is a high percentage play, and he is skilled enough to handle point work on the second unit.

He has a strong shot from the point, but it takes him awhile to release it and more often than not the shot gets blocked.

THE PHYSICAL GAME

Because of his size, Dollas was thrust into the role of an enforcer with three different organizations. Dollas is not tough, doesn't like to fight and got an unfair label as a soft player when the Red Wings (his last club before Anaheim) accused him of shirking when he had a back injury.

The Mighty Ducks knew what they were getting and didn't ask anything more of Dollas than to play steady defensive hockey. That he does. He uses his size to tie up rather than rub out players around the net. Dollas doesn't scare people, but he won't be intimidated.

THE INTANGIBLES

Dollas is content in his role, and Anaheim seems happy with a defenseman who is a stabilizing force. Anaheim can bring in offensive defensemen like Milos Holan and Oleg Tverdovsky, and anchor either one of them with Dollas. His work ethic is strong.

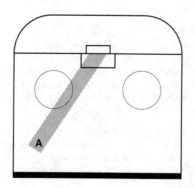

PETER DOURIS

Yrs. of NHL service: 5
Born: Toronto, Ont.; Feb. 19, 1966
Position: right wing
Height: 6-1
Weight: 195
Uniform no.: 16
Shoots: right

Career statistics:

GP	G	A	TP	PIM
289	46	60	106	71

1991-92 statistics:

GP	G	A	TP	+/-	PIM	PP	SH	GW	GT	S	PCT
54	10	13	23	+9	10	0	0	1	0	107	9.3

1992-93 statistics:

GP	G	A	TP	+/-	PIM	PP	SH	GW	GT	S	PCT
19	4	4	8	+5	4	0	1	0	0	33	12.1

1993-94 statistics:

GP	G	A	TP	+/-	PIM	PP	SH	GW	GT	S	PCT
74	12	22	34	-5	21	1	0	1	0	142	8.5

1994-95 statistics:

GP	G	A	TP	+/-	PIM	PP	SH	GW	GT	S	PCT
46	10	11	21	+4	12	0	0	4	0	69	14.5

LAST SEASON

Led team in game-winning goals. Fourth on team in points.

THE FINESSE GAME

Douris has never been special enough to make an impact, but he has a lot of nice little skills and is a quick skater with a somewhat unusual style. He's smart around the net, offering a decent touch but not a great release. He's also an intelligent player, and if asked to play a system or a specific role, he'll do it.

Douris scored a big goal here and there for Anaheim last season (game-winning goals can be deceptive, but one of his was scored in overtime). He looked like a much more confident player offensively, but never lost sight of his defensive duties. He was always quick to come back in his own zone.

THE PHYSICAL GAME

Douris is not especially strong and doesn't get involved much in the physical end, though he does forecheck diligently and will block shots.

THE INTANGIBLES

Douris is one of a legion of journeymen players who have been given new life by expansion, and he is making the best of it. He has a shot at 20 goals this season, but much will depend on the development of Anaheim's younger forwards.

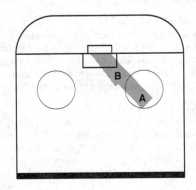

GUY HEBERT

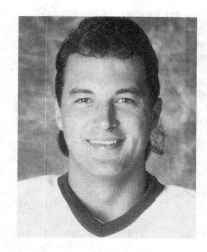

Yrs. of NHL service: 3
Born: Troy, N.Y.; Jan. 7, 1967
Position: goaltender
Height: 5-11
Weight: 180
Uniform no.: 31
Catches: left

Career statistics:

GP	MINS	GA	SO	GAA	A	PIM
128	7031	360	5	3.07	1	6

1991-92 statistics:

GP	MINS	GAA	W	L	T	SO	GA	S	SAPCT	PIM
13	738	2.93	5	5	1	0	36	393	.908	0

1992-93 statistics:

GP	MINS	GAA	W	L	T	SO	GA	S	SAPCT	PIM
24	1210	3.67	8	8	2	1	74	630	.883	2

1993-94 statistics:

GP	MINS	GAA	W	L	T	SO	GA	S	SAPCT	PIM
52	2991	2.83	20	27	3	2	141	1513	.907	2

1994-95 statistics:

GP	MINS	GAA	W	L	T	SO	GA	S	SAPCT	PIM
39	2092	3.13	12	20	4	2	109	1132	.904	2

self he belongs. Hebert faltered just after Ron Tugnutt was traded, as if realizing "Oh my God, I'm the guy," but he finished well and seems ready to carry the number one role. He was challenged slightly by Mikhail Shtalenkov last season, and may have to face that challenge again.

LAST SEASON
Matched season high in shutouts.

THE PHYSICAL GAME
Hebert combines good angle play with quick reflexes. He keeps his feet well and doesn't get flustered when he sees a lot of shots. He deadens pucks with his pads and doesn't leave big rebounds.

He uses his stick well around the net to control rebounds and deflect passes, but he doesn't handle the puck aggressively outside his net. He will probably be asked to do more stickhandling to help out his defense. Hebert doesn't have to whip the puck up ice like Ron Hextall, but he should be secure enough to make little passes to avoid fore-checkers.

Hebert needs to improve his lateral movement. He takes away a lot of the net low and forces shooters to go high. Since he is a small goalie, shooters expect him to go down and scramble, but he stands his ground effectively.

THE MENTAL GAME
The best thing about Hebert is his consistency. His weak stretches seldom last long. He has good intensity and concentration. His attitude and work ethic are sound. Playing for an expansion team can wear on a goalie, but Hebert maintains a positive attitude.

THE INTANGIBLES
Hebert has paid his dues to get here, first coming out of a small college (Div. II Hamilton College), getting no attention from the American developmental program, and then ending up four goalies deep in the St. Louis farm system. No doubt he had to convince him-

MILOS HOLAN

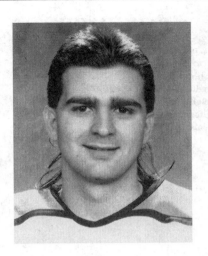

Yrs. of NHL service: 1
Born: Bilovec, Czechoslovakia; April 22, 1971
Position: defense
Height: 5-11
Weight: 196
Uniform no.: 7
Shoots: left

Career statistics:

GP	G	A	TP	PIM
33	3	9	12	18

1993-94 statistics:

GP	G	A	TP	+/-	PIM	PP	SH	GW	GT	S	PCT
8	1	1	2	-4	4	1	0	0	0	26	3.8

1994-95 statistics:

GP	G	A	TP	+/-	PIM	PP	SH	GW	GT	S	PCT
25	2	8	10	+4	14	1	0	1	0	93	2.2

LAST SEASON

First NHL season. Acquired from Philadelphia for Anatoli Semenov.

THE FINESSE GAME

Holan has a huge shot, combined with a sliding lateral move that allows him to get the puck through a crowd. His shot is tough to block, even for a defender brave enough to throw his body in front of it. Holan gets a lot of shots on goal (he averaged four shots per game).

Holan is very good skater, with bursts of speed and agility. His play is heavily tilted to the offensive side. He is a good passer from the blueline in, but he has to pay more attention to his own end of the ice. Still, his offensive skills compensate for his defensive shortcomings.

THE PHYSICAL GAME

Holan will never get an "A" on his report card for physical play, but he won't get pushed around. He is definitely happier in open ice, where he can scoot away from contact.

THE INTANGIBLES

Holan has waited a long time, and not patiently, to get his crack at an NHL job. Along with Oleg Tverdovsky, he could be part of one of the best power play point combinations in the league, once he and his young partner gain more experience.

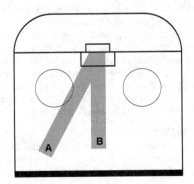

7

PAUL KARIYA

Yrs. of NHL service: 1
Born: North Vancouver, B.C.; Oct. 16, 1974
Position: left wing
Height: 5-10
Weight: 157
Uniform no.: 9
Shoots: left

Career statistics:

GP	G	A	TP	PIM
47	18	21	39	4

1994-95 statistics:

GP	G	A	TP	+/-	PIM	PP	SH	GW	GT	S	PCT
47	18	21	39	-17	4	7	1	3	1	134	13.4

LAST SEASON

Only rookie to lead his team in scoring. Led team and NHL rookies in goals. Tied for team lead and second among NHL rookies in assists. Led team and second among NHL rookies in power play goals. Scored one of team's three shorthanded goals. Led team and NHL rookies in shots. Led team in shooting percentage. Worst plus-minus on team. Finalist for 1995 Calder Trophy. Named to 1995 NHL All-Rookie Team.

THE FINESSE GAME

A silky skater, so smooth and fluid his movement appears effortless, Kariya is also explosive, with a good change of direction, and he can turn a defender inside out on a one-on-one rush. His speed is a weapon, since he forces defenders to play off him for fear of being burnt, and that opens the ice for his playmaking options. He combines his skating with no-look passes that are uncanny. Anyone playing with him has to be prepared, because Kariya can slip them a pass when they're not even sure he sees them.

Kariya is smart; some would say cerebral. He is a magician with the puck and can make a play when it looks as if there are no possible options. Linemates always have to be ready, because they may not think they're open, but Kariya will make them open. He likes to use the net for protection, like his idol Wayne Gretzky, and make passes from behind the goal line.

His overall positional play is well advanced for a youngster. He has been tested at high levels of competition and has excelled. He has a tendency to hang a little near the neutral zone looking for the breakout pass, and needs to come back and help out more defensively. He is learning that playing hard 90 per cent of the time, or on 90 per cent of the ice, isn't enough — that other 10 per cent can kill your team.

THE PHYSICAL GAME

No doubt his size is a question mark because he cannot get into any physical confrontations at the NHL level, but his skill levels are so high it's worth the trade-off. Kariya is more ready physically than he was in his draft year. He has very strong legs and has improved his upper body.

THE INTANGIBLES

With the Europeans, everyone is willing to make allowances for their small stature because of their skill level, but few seem as willing to grant North Americans the same licence. Well, Kariya deserves that much. His game has suffered a bit because the Mighty Ducks haven't found a number one centre to go with him, nor the ideal finishing right wing. He is doing a lot himself now, and while it's good, it won't become great without more support.

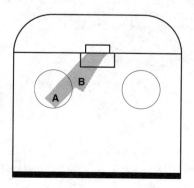

VALERI KARPOV

Yrs. of NHL service: 1
Born: Chelyabinsk, Russia; Aug. 5, 1971
Position: right wing
Height: 5-10
Weight: 190
Uniform no.: 11
Shoots: left

Career statistics:

GP	G	A	TP	PIM
30	4	7	11	6

1994-95 statistics:

GP	G	A	TP	+/-	PIM	PP	SH	GW	GT	S	PCT
30	4	7	11	-4	6	0	0	0	0	48	8.3

LAST SEASON
First NHL season.

THE FINESSE GAME
Karpov is an above average skater. He doesn't have outstanding breakaway speed, but he has a nice change of pace and handles the puck well. He has great hands. He goes to the net and gets his shots away quickly, more in the manner of Valeri Zelepukin than Pavel Bure.

The Mighty Ducks are desperate for a finisher, and while Karpov is not the power forward everyone covets, he creates chances with his quickness and has the hand skills and clever shots to put his opportunities away. He had a strong training camp but seemed to lose his momentum with the lockout and played briefly in the minors once the season got underway.

THE PHYSICAL GAME
Karpov's size may hold him back, but he has gotten stronger since his draft year. He still doesn't have a great knack for handling physical play, and will try to play his game in open ice.

THE INTANGIBLES
Karpov went through a period of adjustment to the NHL and life in North America, and was just starting to feel comfortable near the end of the shortened season. He is projected as a linemate for Paul Kariya and will get a share of prime ice time. We predicted a possible 25-goal rookie season for Karpov, which was wildly optimistic (even prorated, his total would only be 11). But he could easily top the 20-goal mark this year if his progress continues.

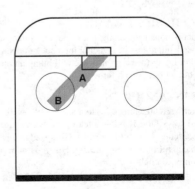

TODD KRYGIER

Yrs. of NHL service: 6
Born: Chicago Heights, Mich.; Oct. 12, 1965
Position: left wing
Height: 5-11
Weight: 180
Uniform no.: 25
Shoots: left

Career statistics:

GP	G	A	TP	PIM
375	78	87	165	384

1991-92 statistics:

GP	G	A	TP	+/-	PIM	PP	SH	GW	GT	S	PCT
67	13	17	30	-1	107	1	0	1	0	127	10.2

1992-93 statistics:

GP	G	A	TP	+/-	PIM	PP	SH	GW	GT	S	PCT
77	11	12	23	-13	60	0	2	0	1	133	8.3

1993-94 statistics:

GP	G	A	TP	+/-	PIM	PP	SH	GW	GT	S	PCT
66	12	18	30	-4	60	0	1	3	0	146	8.2

1994-95 statistics:

GP	G	A	TP	+/-	PIM	PP	SH	GW	GT	S	PCT
35	11	11	22	+1	10	1	0	1	0	90	12.2

LAST SEASON

Fourth on team in points. Missed two games with a groin injury.

THE FINESSE GAME

Krygier may be too fast for his own good. He has blazing speed and anticipation, which gets him his share of breakaways and odd-man rushes. But when it comes time to shoot or move the puck to a teammate, he can't do it. He has to slow down in order to do something constructive with the puck.

Most of his successful shots come with his hard wrist shot, but he doesn't beat many goalies cleanly. He needs someone screening in front, but he doesn't know how to time his plays to use an opposing defenseman in that manner.

Krygier plays with enthusiasm, and is a strong penalty killer. His speed allows him to back-check and badger the puck carrier from behind, lifting the stick and stealing the puck.

THE PHYSICAL GAME

Krygier is not strong on the puck. He intimidates with his speed, but unless he is racing for a puck in open ice he is not likely to scrap for it. He will bump an opponent, but without much ferocity.

THE INTANGIBLES

Krygier overcame long odds to make it to the NHL (he played for a Div. II NCAA team, the University of Connecticut, on an outdoor rink). His speed and work ethic keep him in a team's lineup. His maximum production is 20 goals.

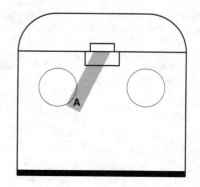

RANDY LADOUCEUR

Yrs. of NHL service: 12
Born: Brockville, Ont.; June 30, 1960
Position: left defense
Height: 6-2
Weight: 220
Uniform no.: 29
Shoots: left

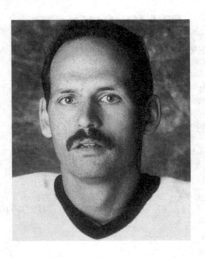

Career statistics:

GP	G	A	TP	PIM
867	29	123	152	1275

1991-92 statistics:

GP	G	A	TP	+/-	PIM	PP	SH	GW	GT	S	PCT
74	1	9	10	-1	127	0	0	0	0	59	1.7

1992-93 statistics:

GP	G	A	TP	+/-	PIM	PP	SH	GW	GT	S	PCT
62	2	4	6	-18	109	0	0	0	0	37	5.4

1993-94 statistics:

GP	G	A	TP	+/-	PIM	PP	SH	GW	GT	S	PCT
81	1	9	10	+7	74	0	0	0	0	66	1.5

1994-95 statistics:

GP	G	A	TP	+/-	PIM	PP	SH	GW	GT	S	PCT
44	2	4	6	+2	36	0	0	0	0	42	4.8

LAST SEASON

Missed four games with an ankle injury.

THE FINESSE GAME

Ladouceur is limited in his stick and skating skills, but not in his heart and smarts. He has a championship attitude and plays about as sound a stay-at-home style as you can find in the NHL. There is nothing fancy about him, but he is a rock on defense.

He will ice the puck when he has to, or shoot it off the glass near the end of a game when he doesn't want to risk a turnover in his own end. He is always very aware of the game situation and the appropriate play, and he's a useful player when protecting a lead.

Ladouceur's offensive involvement is limited to a slap shot from the point. One or two will sneak through every season, but he generates little on the attack.

THE PHYSICAL GAME

Ladouceur is a clean, solid hitter. His skating limits his range, but he will win one-on-one battles along the boards or in front of the net by sheer force of will. He is very strong and competes every single shift. He does what it takes to win. He is a great guy for younger defensemen to learn from.

THE INTANGIBLES

Ladouceur has been a captain in Hartford and now in Anaheim. He is greatly respected by his coaches and teammates. He is an important role player and can probably contribute for another season or two in his usual quiet manner.

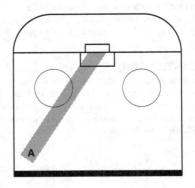

STEVE RUCCHIN

Yrs. of NHL service: 1
Born: London, Ont.; July 4, 1971
Position: centre
Height: 6-3
Weight: 210
Uniform no.: 20
Shoots: left

Career statistics:

GP	G	A	TP	PIM
43	6	11	17	23

1994-95 statistics:

GP	G	A	TP	+/-	PIM	PP	SH	GW	GT	S	PCT
43	6	11	17	+7	23	0	0	1	0	59	10.2

LAST SEASON
First NHL season. Led team in plus-minus.

THE FINESSE GAME
Rucchin expected to be in grad school last season, not in the NHL, but the 1994 Supplemental Draft pick exceeded not only management's expectations, but his own. A centre with good size and range, Rucchin gained the confidence to try a move on a defender and found his moves worked. He is an older rookie, and his defensive game is advanced.

Rucchin's offensive skills were the unexpected bonus. A bit in awe of the league at first (he played in front of more fans in the home opener at Anaheim than he did his entire career at the University of Western Ontario), Rucchin has good hockey sense that makes the most of his above-average skating, passing and shooting skills. His team-leading plus-minus was a true indication of his all-around play. He had a very good last month, once he started believing in his ability.

THE PHYSICAL GAME
Rucchin can become a real force. He's strong and balanced, willing to fore-check hard and fight for the puck along the boards and in the corners. When he wins the puck, he is able to create a smart play with it. He has long arms and a long reach for holding off defenders and working the puck one-handed, or reaching in defensively to knock the puck away from an attacker.

THE INTANGIBLES
Rucchin is an ideal number two centre for the Mighty Ducks. He started the season as a third- or fourth-line centre, but as he gained more confidence in his skills became more of an offensive force. A sleeper. He may jump from 17 to 70 points.

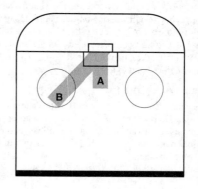

JOE SACCO

Yrs. of NHL service: 2
Born: Medford, Mass.; Feb. 4, 1969
Position: left/right wing
Height: 6-1
Weight: 195
Uniform no.: 14
Shoots: right

Career statistics:

GP	G	A	TP	PIM
185	40	39	79	98

1991-92 statistics:

GP	G	A	TP	+/-	PIM	PP	SH	GW	GT	S	PCT
17	7	4	11	+8	4	0	0	1	0	40	17.5

1992-93 statistics:

GP	G	A	TP	+/-	PIM	PP	SH	GW	GT	S	PCT
23	4	4	8	-4	8	0	0	0	0	38	10.5

1993-94 statistics:

GP	G	A	TP	+/-	PIM	PP	SH	GW	GT	S	PCT
84	19	18	37	-11	61	3	1	2	1	206	9.2

1994-95 statistics:

GP	G	A	TP	+/-	PIM	PP	SH	GW	GT	S	PCT
41	10	8	18	-8	23	2	0	0	0	77	13.0

could be capable of 25 goals, though 20 is more likely his limit.

LAST SEASON

Missed seven games with a thumb injury, ending club record of 93 consecutive games.

THE FINESSE GAME

Sacco got his training on the big international rinks with the U.S. Olympic Team in 1992; his outside speed is his greatest asset. A left-handed shot, he played primarily on his off-wing and scored most of his goals driving cross-ice to the net from the right side. There is nothing creative or dazzling about Sacco's moves. He just goes full-tilt. When he does score, it's highlight material.

His skating ability earned him some playing time on Paul Kariya's line, but he's not a great finisher. He loves to shoot, but isn't always in the best spot to do so.

If Sacco learned to use his teammates better, such as finding an open man after he has forced the defense back, he would be a more dangerous threat, but he has tunnel vision with the puck. Basically, he's just not a very smart player.

He has never been a prolific scorer at the pro level (minors or NHL). He is solid defensively, good in his own zone and keeps the game simple.

THE PHYSICAL GAME

Sacco does not play an involved game physically. He has a decent size to at least bang around a bit, but he is better with the puck than trying to obtain it.

THE INTANGIBLES

Sacco is becoming more aware of how he can use his speed as a weapon to drive the defense back, and

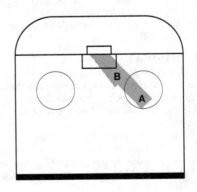

OLEG TVERDOVSKY

Yrs. of NHL service: 1
Born: Donetsk, Ukraine; May 18, 1976
Position: defense
Height: 6-0
Weight: 183
Uniform no.: 10
Shoots: left

1993-94 statistics:

GP	G	A	TP	PIM
36	3	9	12	14

1994-95 statistics:

GP	G	A	TP	+/-	PIM	PP	SH	GW	GT	S	PCT
36	3	9	12	-6	14	1	1	0	0	26	11.5

LAST SEASON

First NHL season. Second among NHL rookie defensemen in points. Second among team defensemen in points. Named to 1995 All-Rookie Team.

THE FINESSE GAME

Tverdovsky is an impressive talent. A weakness in the offensive zone is tough to find because this defenseman passes the puck well and shoots bullets. While he's clearly going to be primarily an offensive defenseman, Tverdovsky also settled down in his own zone after a stumbling start. If anything, he was guilty of trying to do too much instead of keeping the game simple. Once he realized that, he played a much more solid all-around game.

Tverdovsky is such a good passer he doesn't feel the need to carry the puck all the time. And he doesn't just get the puck and go, he knows when to go. There were several nights last season when he was simply brilliant, but he hasn't achieved consistency yet. He is so quick at coming back, getting the puck and moving it, that he spends precious little time in his own zone.

Tverdovsky has Brian Leetch potential. He is an explosive skater and can carry the puck at high tempo. He works the point on the power play and kills penalties. He sees his options and makes his decisions at lightning speed. Tverdovsky was bothered by groin and foot injuries (the latter kept him out of the World Junior Championships), so he wasn't 100 per cent until late last season.

THE PHYSICAL GAME

Some of Tverdovsky's defensive weaknesses can be attributed to the fact that he sometimes plays the puck instead of the man, or tries to poke-check without backing it up with his body. However, to date, he has been pretty much a boy playing against men.

Tverdovsky is a devoted practice player who almost has to be wrestled off the ice. He loves to play and is very enthusiastic and extremely competitive. He's added about 15 pounds since his draft year and is looking to get stronger.

THE INTANGIBLES

So much is asked of top draft picks, especially by weaker teams, people often forget they are only 18 or 19 years old when they step in. Factor in a player like Tverdovsky coming to a new country and learning a new language, and the transition is even harder. He is on the right track, though. He wants to play and his character and personality should speed his continued development.

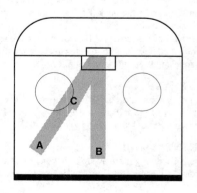

GARRY VALK

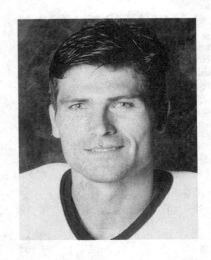

Yrs. of NHL service: 4
Born: Edmonton, Alberta; Nov. 27, 1967
Position: left wing
Height: 6-1
Weight: 205
Uniform no.: 18
Shoots: left

Career statistics:

GP	G	A	TP	PIM
286	45	68	113	334

1991-92 statistics:

GP	G	A	TP	+/-	PIM	PP	SH	GW	GT	S	PCT
65	8	17	25	+3	56	2	1	2	0	93	8.6

1992-93 statistics:

GP	G	A	TP	+/-	PIM	PP	SH	GW	GT	S	PCT
48	6	7	13	+6	77	0	0	2	1	46	13.0

1993-94 statistics:

GP	G	A	TP	+/-	PIM	PP	SH	GW	GT	S	PCT
78	18	27	45	+8	100	4	1	5	0	165	10.9

1994-95 statistics:

GP	G	A	TP	+/-	PIM	PP	SH	GW	GT	S	PCT
36	3	6	9	-4	34	0	0	0	0	53	5.7

And, like Corkum, Valk will find as the team gets deeper, he can find a niche as a third-line checking forward, though his production is starting to slump.

LAST SEASON

Missed 10 games with a sprained left knee.

THE FINESSE GAME

Not much about Valk's game is pretty, but it is gritty. He is a defensive specialist, with a knock-kneed stance (the opposite of the many bowlegged skaters in the league). Through determination, Valk gets to where he has to go. He had knee surgery two seasons ago and another knee problem this year, but he still has a great deal of drive in his skating. He is strong on his skates but not fast.

Very streaky, he will go forever without getting a goal, then will pop home several in a week. Valk goes to the net hard, but he doesn't have great hands. Most of his goals come from second and third efforts around the net.

Valk is a defensive forward. He kills penalties well and has good jump fore-checking. He keeps himself in excellent physical condition and mentally accepts his role as a checker.

THE PHYSICAL GAME

Valk has a strong work ethic and likes to get out on the ice and provide a spark for his team. He throws his body around with enthusiasm and will get into altercations. He can be very annoying to play against. Nothing Valk does is flashy, but he gets the job done in a blue-collar (well, OK, teal-collar) fashion.

THE INTANGIBLES

Like Bob Corkum, Valk was once a spare part on an established team (Vancouver), who found ice time and scoring chances in Anaheim and took advantage.

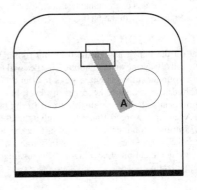

SHAUN VAN ALLEN

Yrs. of NHL service: 2
Born: Shaunavon, Sask.; Aug. 29, 1967
Position: centre
Height: 6-1
Weight: 200
Uniform no.: 22
Shoots: left

Career statistics:

GP	G	A	TP	PIM
148	17	50	59	102

1992-93 statistics:

GP	G	A	TP	+/-	PIM	PP	SH	GW	GT	S	PCT
21	1	4	5	-2	6	0	0	0	0	19	5.3

1993-94 statistics:

GP	G	A	TP	+/-	PIM	PP	SH	GW	GT	S	PCT
80	8	25	33	0	64	2	2	1	0	104	7.7

1994-95 statistics:

GP	G	A	TP	+/-	PIM	PP	SH	GW	GT	S	PCT
45	8	21	29	-4	32	1	1	1	0	68	11.8

LAST SEASON

Tied for team lead in assists. Second on team in points.

THE FINESSE GAME

Van Allen always posted huge numbers in the minors, but like a lot of minor league stars, he couldn't transfer his scoring to the majors. The flaw in Van Allen's case is his skating, which is marginally NHL calibre and has forced him to change his strategy to that of a positional, defensive player.

When Van Allen does accomplish things offensively, like on the power play, it's because of his smarts. He is the best face-off man on the Mighty Ducks. If he controls the draw in the offensive zone, he knows how to set up an attack. Van Allen also kills penalties. He seldom plays a poor game because he is aware of his limitations.

THE PHYSICAL GAME

Van Allen's solid, intelligent play is enhanced by his work ethic. He's not a banger but he will get in the way. He knows he would have been a career minor leaguer but for this chance, and he doesn't forget what he has to do to stay in the NHL.

THE INTANGIBLES

Great on the bench and in the dressing room, Van Allen will always be on the bubble. Coaches will keep trying younger, more talented guys in Van Allen's spot, but he'll probably keep getting back into the lineup because he's too valuable to sit in the press box. Anaheim rewarded Van Allen with a three-year, $1.275-million contract at the end of last season, even though he had a year left on his old contract, which gives some indication of how highly he is regarded by the organization.

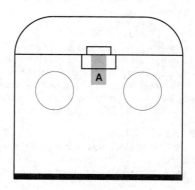

JASON YORK

Yrs. of NHL service: 0
Born: Ottawa, Ont.; May 20, 1970
Position: defense
Height: 6-1
Weight: 192
Uniform no.: 3
Shoots: right

Career statistics:

GP	G	A	TP	PIM
33	2	11	13	12

1992-93 statistics:

GP	G	A	TP	+/-	PIM	PP	SH	GW	GT	S	PCT
2	0	0	0	0	0	0	0	0	0	1	0.0

1993-94 statistics:

GP	G	A	TP	+/-	PIM	PP	SH	GW	GT	S	PCT
7	1	2	3	0	2	0	0	0	0	9	11.1

1994-95 statistics:

GP	G	A	TP	+/-	PIM	PP	SH	GW	GT	S	PCT
24	1	9	10	+2	10	0	0	0	0	28	3.6

LAST SEASON

First NHL season. Acquired from Detroit with Mike Sillinger for Stu Grimson, Mark Ferner and a sixth-round draft pick in 1996.

THE FINESSE GAME

York is about ready to hit his defensive prime. He is a smart, all-around defenseman who was able to put up some decent numbers at the AHL level, but is now concentrating more on his defensive play.

York's finesse skills are fine. He is a good skater with a very hard point shot. He could get some power play time in Anaheim, but it is likely to be on the second unit. York is a fine penalty killer. He reads plays well and has the skating ability to spring some short-handed chances.

THE PHYSICAL GAME

York is not very physical. He is not a big checker, but like New Jersey's Bruce Driver he employs positional play to angle attackers to the boards, using his stick to sweep-check or poke pucks. And once he gains control of the puck, he moves it quickly with no panicky mistakes.

THE INTANGIBLES

York got caught in a numbers game in Detroit, where he was not flashy enough to move ahead of players such as Paul Coffey and Nicklas Lidstrom, nor enough of a banger to merit much playing time. But a lot of teams were interested in acquiring York before Anaheim won his services. In another year, he will be a reliable two-way defenseman, who could have a long and useful NHL career.

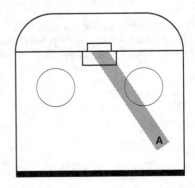

BOSTON BRUINS

Players' Statistics 1994-95

POS	NO.	PLAYER	GP	G	A	PTS	+/-	PIM	PP	SH	GW	GT	S	PCTG
C	12	ADAM OATES	48	12	41	53	-11	8	4	1	2		109	11.0
D	77	RAY BOURQUE	46	12	31	43	3	20	9		2		210	5.7
R	8	CAM NEELY	42	27	14	41	7	72	16		5	1	178	15.2
C	20	BRYAN SMOLINSKI	44	18	13	31	-3	31	6		5		121	14.9
R	19	*MARIUSZ CZERKAWSKI	47	12	14	26	4	31	1		2		126	9.5
L	26	MATS NASLUND	34	8	14	22	-4	4	2		1		48	16.7
D	32	DON SWEENEY	47	3	19	22	6	24	1		2		102	2.9
C	21	TED DONATO	47	10	10	20	3	10	1		1		71	14.1
R	22	JOZEF STUMPEL	44	5	13	18	4	8	1		2		46	10.9
R	23	STEVE HEINZE	36	7	9	16		23		1			70	10.0
D	6	ALEXEI KASATONOV	44	2	14	16	-2	33		1			50	4.0
L	18	BRENT HUGHES	44	6	6	12	6	139					75	8.0
R	27	STEPHEN LEACH	35	5	6	11	-3	68	1		1		82	6.1
D	38	*JON ROHLOFF	34	3	8	11	1	39			1	1	51	5.9
L	17	DAVE REID	38	5	5	10	8	10				1	47	10.6
R	45	*SANDY MOGER	18	2	6	8	-1	6	2				32	6.3
R	44	GLEN MURRAY	35	5	2	7	-11	46			2		64	7.8
D	34	DAVID SHAW	44	3	4	7	-9	36	1				58	5.2
D	28	JAMIE HUSCROFT	34		6	6	-3	103					30	
D	36	*JOHN GRUDEN	38		6	6	3	22					30	
L	48	*FRED KNIPSCHEER	16	3	1	4	1	2				1	20	15.0
R	42	MIKKO MAKELA	11	1	2	3			1				10	10.0
C	40	*BRETT HARKINS	1		1	1							1	
R	29	MARC POTVIN	6		1	1	1	4					4	
G	31	*BLAINE LACHER	35		1	1		4						
D	49	JEFF SEROWIK	1				1							
L	13	GRIGORI PANTELEEV	1											
C	16	CAMERON STEWART	5					2					2	
G	37	VINCENT RIENDEAU	11					2						
G	1	CRAIG BILLINGTON	17					4						

GP = games played; G = goals; A = assists; PTS = points; +/- = goals-for minus goals-against while player is on ice; PIM = penalties in minutes; PP = power play goals; SH = shorthanded goals; GW = game-winning goals; GT = game-tying goals; S = no. of shots; PCTG = percentage of goals to shots; * = rookie

RAY BOURQUE

Yrs. of NHL service: 16
Born: Montreal, Que.; Dec. 28, 1960
Position: right defense
Height: 5-11
Weight: 210
Uniform no.: 77
Shoots: left

Career statistics:

GP	G	A	TP	PIM
1146	323	908	1231	877

1991-92 statistics:

GP	G	A	TP	+/-	PIM	PP	SH	GW	GT	S	PCT
80	21	60	81	+11	56	7	1	2	0	334	6.3

1992-93 statistics:

GP	G	A	TP	+/-	PIM	PP	SH	GW	GT	S	PCT
78	19	63	82	+38	40	8	0	7	0	330	5.8

1993-94 statistics:

GP	G	A	TP	+/-	PIM	PP	SH	GW	GT	S	PCT
72	20	71	91	+26	58	10	3	1	1	386	5.2

1994-95 statistics:

GP	G	A	TP	+/-	PIM	PP	SH	GW	GT	S	PCT
46	12	31	43	+3	20	9	0	2	0	210	5.7

LAST SEASON

Became only second defenseman in history to record 900 assists. Tied for second in scoring among NHL defensemen. Second on team in scoring. Led NHL in shots on goal. Second in NHL in power play points (29). Missed two games with back spasms.

THE FINESSE GAME

Bourque has tremendous defensive instincts, though his offensive skills usually get the headlines. His defensive reads are almost unmatched in the NHL, and he is an excellent transition player. He is not afraid to make the simple play, if it is the right one, instead of making a flashy play. If he is under pressure and his team is getting scrambly, Bourque is not too proud to simply flip the puck over the glass for a face-off.

As a passer, Bourque can go tape-to-tape as well as anybody in the league. He has the touch and the vision of a forward, and eagerly makes what for anyone else would be a low-percentage play, because his passes and skating are so sure.

Bourque is adept at keeping the puck in the zone at the point. He is a key player on special teams units. On the point, he has a low, heavy shot with a crisp release. He is an excellent skater who will also shoot from mid-range with a handy snap shot, or in close with a wrist shot. He does not squander his scoring chances and is a precise shooter down low. Bourque is able to go top shelf to either corner, which few other defensemen, let alone forwards, can match.

Willing to lead a rush or jump up into the play, he is a balanced skater, with speed, agility and awesome balance. It takes a bulldozer to knock Bourque off the puck.

THE PHYSICAL GAME

Bourque plays a physical game when he has to. It's amazing what kind of punishment he has been able to absorb over the years without missing time with a serious injury, since he is not very big by today's standards for defensemen (or forwards, for that matter). Most other teams try to eliminate him physically, and he has paid a big price because of it.

He devotes much of his off-season to conditioning, and it pays off because of all of the ice time he logs. He's tough to beat one-on-one in open ice or in the trenches. Only twice in his 16 seasons has he failed to play more than 60 games (one of those an asterisk due to the lockout), and he is no perimeter player.

Bourque is a team leader who demands the same effort from his teammates. No one is more deserving of a captain's "C."

THE INTANGIBLES

Bourque has been the highest impact defenseman in the NHL for the last 12 years. He is approaching the beginning of his downturn, only because the seasons and hits are starting to take their toll. Still one of the top five defensemen in the league, he could go down in league history as the best player never to win the Cup.

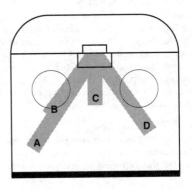

MARIUSZ CZERKAWSKI

Yrs. of NHL service: 1
Born: Radomsko, Poland; Apr. 13, 1973
Position: left wing
Height: 5-11
Weight: 185
Uniform no.: 19
Shoots: right

Career statistics:

GP	G	A	TP	PIM
51	14	15	29	31

1993-94 statistics:

GP	G	A	TP	+/-	PIM	PP	SH	GW	GT	S	PCT
4	2	1	3	-2	0	0	1	0	0	11	18.2

1994-95 statistics:

GP	G	A	TP	+/-	PIM	PP	SH	GW	GT	S	PCT
47	12	14	26	+4	31	1	0	2	0	126	9.5

LAST SEASON

First NHL season. Second among NHL rookies in shots. Third among NHL rookies in power play assists (7).

THE FINESSE GAME

Although Czerkawski is a right-handed shot, the Bruins moved him to his off-wing for much of last season, and he had the hand skills to make the position work. Czerkawski likes to use all of the ice (he should be happy when the Bruins move to their big new home rink this season), and will cut across the middle or to the right side to make the play. He is a very shifty skater, not one with great straightaway speed, but he puts the slip on a defender with a lateral move and is off. Czerkawski is hard to defend one-on-one because of the jitterbugging his body does, all while in full control of the puck.

Virtually a self-taught player in his native Poland, Czerkawski loves to shoot. His quick wrist shot is his best weapon. With the extra room on the power play, he is at his best. He has soft hands for passes and good vision. He needs to play with someone who will get him the puck, since he will not go into the corners for it.

THE PHYSICAL GAME

Czerkawski has to get better at protecting the puck and perform at least a willing game along the boards. He uses his body in the offensive zone, but in a perfunctory manner, and he doesn't like to get involved too much in the defensive zone. He is quick enough to peel back and help out with back-checking since he is very smart at anticipating passes, but he will rarely knock anyone off the puck.

THE INTANGIBLES

Czerkawski still has some growing to do, since his rookie season was lockout-shortened. We said in last year's *HSR* that he would make a good linemate for Bryan Smolinski (because of the latter's defensive play and ability to get Czerkawski the puck). Smolinski, Czerkawski and Jozef Stumpel formed an effective second line for the Bruins during the regular season. Expect another half-season of adjustment before Czerkawski can be too harshly graded, but the early indications are promising, as long as he remains teamed with the same kind of linemates.

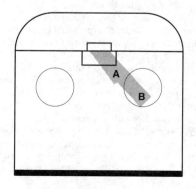

TED DONATO

Yrs. of NHL service: 3
Born: Dedham, Mass.; Apr. 28, 1969
Position: centre
Height: 5-10
Weight: 170
Uniform no.: 21
Shoots: left

Career statistics:

GP	G	A	TP	PIM
223	48	64	112	138

1991-92 statistics:

GP	G	A	TP	+/-	PIM	PP	SH	GW	GT	S	PCT
10	1	2	3	-1	8	0	0	0	0	13	7.7

1992-93 statistics:

GP	G	A	TP	+/-	PIM	PP	SH	GW	GT	S	PCT
82	15	20	35	+2	61	3	2	5	0	118	12.7

1993-94 statistics:

GP	G	A	TP	+/-	PIM	PP	SH	GW	GT	S	PCT
84	22	32	54	0	59	9	2	1	1	158	13.9

1994-95 statistics:

GP	G	A	TP	+/-	PIM	PP	SH	GW	GT	S	PCT
47	10	10	20	+3	10	1	0	1	0	71	14.1

LAST SEASON

Has not missed a game due to injury in the past two seasons (131 games).

THE FINESSE GAME

Donato is a small man who is able to survive in a big man's game because of his hockey sense. He is an excellent power play man, though he didn't see much power play time last season. As a member of the second unit, Donato seldom got on the ice since the first unit was either scoring or staying on for almost the entire two minutes. When Donato gets the chance, he can work down low or use a shot from the point.

Donato has always had the knack for scoring big goals at every level he has played. He scored the winning goal in the NCAA Championship game when Harvard beat Minnesota, and he scored the winning goal for his high school to win the championships in Massachusetts.

He is also a strong penalty killer, especially working with Steve Heinze (they were teammates with the U.S. Olympic team in 1992 and began killing penalties together then). He can thrive as a forward on the shorthanded team because opponents are more concerned about getting the puck than hitting, and he is usually in the middle part of the ice. He gets a lot of defensive assignments but creates offense with his anticipation.

Donato is like a quarterback, very aware of what is going on around him and always communicating with his teammates so they know what is going on, too. He has good hands and makes hard or soft passes as the occasion warrants.

THE PHYSICAL GAME

Donato is cunning and doesn't allow himself to get into situations where he's close to the boards and could get taken out. He is a very elusive skater. Donato can be outmuscled, but he hustles for the puck and often manages to keep it alive along the boards.

THE INTANGIBLES

There is a recent trend among teams such as Boston, Montreal, Quebec and now Toronto to emphasize hometown boys — not to sell tickets, but because playing in your hometown can bring out the best in players who can stand the pressure. Donato seems to thrive on it. He has a solid future as a third-line defensive centre who can also score 10-15 goals a season.

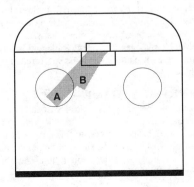

STEVE HEINZE

Yrs. of NHL service: 3
Born: Lawrence, Mass.; Jan. 30, 1970
Position: right wing
Height: 5-11
Weight: 190
Uniform no.: 23
Shoots: right

Career statistics:

GP	G	A	TP	PIM
200	38	37	75	85

1991-92 statistics:

GP	G	A	TP	+/-	PIM	PP	SH	GW	GT	S	PCT
14	3	4	7	-1	6	0	0	2	0	29	10.3

1992-93 statistics:

GP	G	A	TP	+/-	PIM	PP	SH	GW	GT	S	PCT
73	18	13	31	+20	24	0	2	4	0	146	12.3

1993-94 statistics:

GP	G	A	TP	+/-	PIM	PP	SH	GW	GT	S	PCT
77	10	11	21	-2	32	0	2	1	0	183	5.5

1994-95 statistics:

GP	G	A	TP	+/-	PIM	PP	SH	GW	GT	S	PCT
36	7	9	16	0	23	0	1	0	0	70	10.0

LAST SEASON

Did not miss any games due to injury.

THE FINESSE GAME

Heinze is a traditional grinding Bruins forward who skates up and down his wing. Nothing special — which is probably why he was benched for 12 games last season. He has surprisingly good hands for a grinder, with a quick snap shot. He seems to get goals that go in off his legs, arms and elbows from his work in front of the net.

Heinze is smart at trailing plays along the way and digging out loose pucks, which he either takes to the net himself or, more often, passes off.

He has a good first step to the puck, which helps in his penalty killing as he forces the puck carrier. Heinze was part of the Bruins' top-ranked penalty-killing unit last season, and had one of the team's three shorthanded goals.

He was a big scorer at Boston College with David Emma and Marty McInnis (the HEM Line), but he succeeded at that level mainly because he was able to overpower people; he doesn't have that same edge in the pros. He plays an intelligent game and is a good playmaker with passing skills on his forehand and backhand.

THE PHYSICAL GAME

Heinze is hampered by his lack of size and strength. His probable future is as a third-line checking winger, but he doesn't have the power to line up against other teams' top power forwards. He is willing to get in the way and force people to go through him. The trouble is, they usually do.

THE INTANGIBLES

Heinze faces another season on the bubble. Outmuscled by New Jersey in the 1995 playoffs, the Bruins will be looking to beef up their lineup. Heinze could still find a spot on the roster as a role player, but it will be a reduced role.

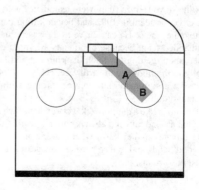

BRENT HUGHES

Yrs. of NHL service: 5
Born: New Westminster, B.C.; Apr. 5, 1966
Position: left wing
Height: 5-11
Weight: 194
Uniform no.: 18
Shoots: left

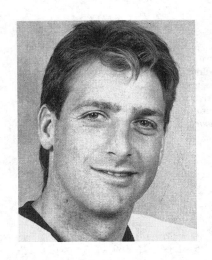

Career statistics:

GP	G	A	TP	PIM
230	29	26	55	626

1991-92 statistics:

GP	G	A	TP	+/-	PIM	PP	SH	GW	GT	S	PCT
8	1	1	2	+1	38	0	0	1	0	10	10.0

1992-93 statistics:

GP	G	A	TP	+/-	PIM	PP	SH	GW	GT	S	PCT
62	5	4	9	-4	191	0	0	0	0	54	9.3

1993-94 statistics:

GP	G	A	TP	+/-	PIM	PP	SH	GW	GT	S	PCT
77	13	11	24	+10	143	1	0	1	0	100	13.0

1994-95 statistics:

GP	G	A	TP	+/-	PIM	PP	SH	GW	GT	S	PCT
44	6	6	12	+6	139	0	0	0	0	75	8.0

LAST SEASON

Led team in PIM. Missed three games with a back injury. Served automatic one-game suspension for incurring third game misconduct of season.

THE FINESSE GAME

Hughes just won't go away. Lord knows, the Bruins have tried. He always seems to be on the bubble or on waivers at the start of a season, but is a regular in the lineup once the playoffs roll around. Opponents have an even harder time ridding themselves of this pesky forward.

Hughes is infused with a work ethic, a quality prized above all else in Beantown. Other than that, his skills are moderate. He has some quickness, but is not very agile. He is a strong skater.

Most of his goals come from close range and just plain cussedness around the net. He can kill penalties because of his fore-checking.

THE PHYSICAL GAME

Hughes crease-crashed and took advantage of the relaxed rules in that area last season. He is unafraid to take on the biggest, meanest guy on the other team, even though he seldom wins a fight. He should not be a team's penalty leader, but no one else on the Bruins is willing to do what he does. If that's the price for playing in the NHL, Hughes will willingly pay it.

THE INTANGIBLES

No doubt Hughes will be on the bubble again this fall in Boston. No doubt by the end of the season he will have worked his way into a regular's role. He seldom fails to add some intensity when he's on the ice.

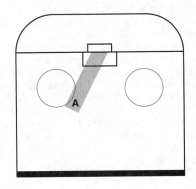

AL IAFRATE

Yrs. of NHL service: 11
Born: Dearborn, Mich.; Mar. 21, 1966
Position: left defense
Height: 6-3
Weight: 220
Uniform no.: 43
Shoots: left

Career statistics:

GP	G	A	TP	PIM
740	144	295	439	1182

1991-92 statistics:

GP	G	A	TP	+/-	PIM	PP	SH	GW	GT	S	PCT
78	17	34	51	+1	180	6	0	1	1	151	11.3

1992-93 statistics:

GP	G	A	TP	+/-	PIM	PP	SH	GW	GT	S	PCT
81	25	41	66	+15	169	11	1	4	0	289	8.7

1993-94 statistics:

GP	G	A	TP	+/-	PIM	PP	SH	GW	GT	S	PCT
79	15	43	58	+16	163	6	0	4	0	299	5.0

1994-95 statistics:

P	G	A	TP	+/-	PIM	PP	SH	GW	GT	S	PC
				Did not play in NHL							

LAST SEASON

Missed entire season with a right knee injury.

THE FINESSE GAME

Welcome to the Planet Iafrate. The Bruins endured a full season of will he?/won't he?/where is he? as Iafrate rehabilitated his right knee following surgery. Iafrate sought out differing opinions, and his own assessment of his physical progress varied wildly, often on a day-to-day basis.

We can only assess the pre-surgery Iafrate, and wonder whether he will return to his former frightening self. He has a big-time slap shot, he can leave a defender flat-footed with his skating, and he has one of the spookiest stares in the NHL. Iafrate can play an all-out offensive game, which is his strength, or settle back and provide some solid defense.

It's unlikely Iafrate will be the skater he was before his injury, which is unfortunate; he was fast and agile for a large man. He is capable of rushing end to end but is better at jumping up into the play. He moves the puck quickly out of his own zone, often taking it himself. He can stickhandle and uses all of the ice.

Iafrate can play either point on the power play. He has a deadly one-timer. His point shot is intimidating, and he will fake the shot, freeze the defense, then move around for a snap shot or slide the puck in deep. There isn't much he can't do as far as finesse skills are concerned. The combination of Iafrate and Ray Bourque on the points is about as good as a power play gets, but who knows at this stage if they'll be reunited in Boston?

THE PHYSICAL GAME

For a big guy, Iafrate does not hit with much intensity. He can, but he is more intent on playing the offensive game. He does not enjoy the one-on-one battles. He will be a booming open-ice hitter when the spirit moves him, but just as often he will be wiped out along the boards.

THE INTANGIBLES

Iafrate's major weakness has always been his intensity and inconsistency — and his mettle was under fire last season. He remains an enormous question mark for 1995-96.

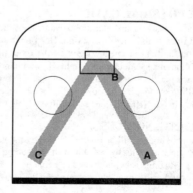

FRED KNIPSCHEER

Yrs. of NHL service: 0
Born: Ft. Wayne, Ind.; Sept. 3, 1969
Position: centre/left wing
Height: 5-11
Weight: 185
Uniform no.: 48
Shoots: left

Career statistics:

GP	G	A	TP	PIM
27	6	3	9	16

1993-94 statistics:

GP	G	A	TP	+/-	PIM	PP	SH	GW	GT	S	PCT
11	3	2	5	+3	14	0	0	1	0	15	20.0

1994-95 statistics:

GP	G	A	TP	+/-	PIM	PP	SH	GW	GT	S	PCT
16	3	1	4	+1	2	0	0	1	0	20	15.0

LAST SEASON

Will be entering first full NHL season. Missed four games with a shoulder injury. Was second in team scoring for Providence (AHL) with 29 goals and 34 assists in 71 games.

THE FINESSE GAME

Knipscheer is a classic Boston Bruins find. A scrappy free agent signing, Knipscheer is a player who gets his scoring chances through sheer effort. Now all he has to do is learn to put those chances away, and he could carve out a living as a third-line centre or wing. He has been a scorer at the college and minor league levels and has shown a decent touch in his brief NHL stints.

Knipscheer's skating is limited. He isn't fast and he needs to learn anticipation and timing to be in better position. He also tends to go all-out and becomes undisciplined, but he plays with so much energy he's hard to ignore.

THE PHYSICAL GAME

Knipscheer could become a Steve Kasper-type player for the Bruins. And just the luck, Kasper, who coached Knipscheer at Providence, is now the Bruins head coach.

If Kasper works closely enough with Knipscheer and teaches him to do the little things well, Knipscheer's hard work will pay dividends. He is not very physical but he gets involved in battles for the puck in the corners and along the boards.

THE INTANGIBLES

Knipscheer has the kind of work ethic that impresses coaches. He will have to battle for his spot in training camp, but with the change in the coaching staff he may have an edge.

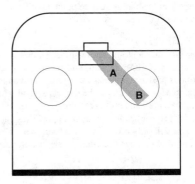

BLAINE LACHER

Yrs. of NHL service: 1
Born: Medicine Hat, Alta.; Sept. 5, 1970
Position: goaltender
Height: 6-1
Weight: 205
Uniform no.: 31
Catches: left

Career statistics:

GP	MINS	G	SO	AVG	A	PIM
35	1965	79	4	2.41	1	4

1994-95 statistics:

GP	MINS	GAA	W	L	T	SO	GA	S	SAPCT	PIM
35	1965	2.41	19	11	2	4	79	805	.902	4

LAST SEASON

First NHL season. Tied for third among NHL goalies in shutouts. Tied for fifth among NHL goalies in wins. Missed four games with a hamstring injury.

THE PHYSICAL GAME

Lacher looked to have solid fundamentals in college (where he played for Lake Superior State), but there he seldom faced second shots and seldom got backdoored. His fundamentals aren't as impressive at the NHL level and they won't improve, unless he gets some goalie coaching. The Bruins have not had a full-time goalie coach for several seasons, but with players such as Lacher and Evgeny Ryabchikov in their system, they're unlikely to get much production out of them without help.

Boston has a tradition of making average goalies (such as Jon Casey two seasons ago) among the league leaders in categories because of the team's style of play, which raises a goalie's play to a certain level, rather than vice versa.

Lacher is big and when he stays on his feet he takes up a lot of net. He has to play his angles and let the puck hit him — to make the game as simple as possible. As it is, Lacher often makes the easy saves look difficult, and the difficult ones become impossible to stop. He needs work handling the puck, not just moving it but using his stick to break up plays around the net.

THE MENTAL GAME

Lacher is confident and competitive. He has an edge of cockiness to him as well, and he stood up under enormous pressure last season. Few goalies can make the jump as successfully as he did last season without falling to pieces under the pressure.

Lacher must be aware that youth, reflexes and enthusiasm will only take him to a certain point. His future as a true number one goalie is a question mark.

THE INTANGIBLES

Lacher was a surprise for the Bruins last season, but showed signs of crumbling in the playoffs. The Bruins have never seemed willing to pay for high-priced goalie talent, but it wouldn't be a shock to see them go after a well-established goalie.

Their confidence in Lacher isn't as great as his confidence in himself.

GLEN MURRAY

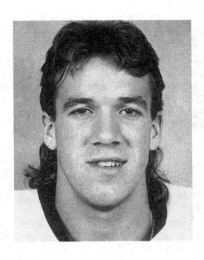

Yrs. of NHL service: 3
Born: Halifax, N.S.; Nov. 1, 1972
Position: right wing
Height: 6-2
Weight: 210
Uniform no.: 44
Shoots: right

Career statistics:

GP	G	A	TP	PIM
148	29	20	49	102

1991-92 statistics:

GP	G	A	TP	+/-	PIM	PP	SH	GW	GT	S	PCT
5	3	1	4	+2	0	1	0	0	0	20	15.0

1992-93 statistics:

GP	G	A	TP	+/-	PIM	PP	SH	GW	GT	S	PCT
27	3	4	7	-6	8	2	0	1	0	28	10.7

1993-94 statistics:

GP	G	A	TP	+/-	PIM	PP	SH	GW	GT	S	PCT
81	18	13	31	-1	48	0	0	4	2	114	15.8

1994-95 statistics:

GP	G	A	TP	+/-	PIM	PP	SH	GW	GT	S	PCT
35	5	2	7	-11	46	0	0	2	0	64	7.8

LAST SEASON

Missed three games with a sinus infection.

THE FINESSE GAME

Nothing seemed to go right for Murray last season. Coaches tried the bad cop/good cop routine on him, first benching him and then boosting him to the number one line. The problem with the promotion was that while it put Murray on the big line with Adam Oates and Cam Neely, it also put him on the left wing, on his backhand, and Murray isn't deft enough with the puck to do much with passes coming onto his backhand.

Murray has good size and a good short game that had fans in Boston calling him the "Mini Cam" — as in Neely, which is part of the curse of expectation Murray has to cope with.

He does have a quick release, and like a lot of great goal scorers he just plain shoots. He doesn't even have to look at the net because he feels where the shot is going. He protects the puck well with his body.

Murray is a little fragile confidence-wise, but when he gets hot he'll be a super streaky scorer.

THE PHYSICAL GAME

On nights when he's playing well, Murray is leaning on people and making his presence felt. He likes to bang, but on some nights he doesn't want to pay the price and prefers to rely on his shot. When he sleepwalks, he is useless. When he's ready to rock and roll, he is effective.

Murray isn't the fighter that Neely was early in his career, either, so he doesn't get as much room as Neely does.

THE INTANGIBLES

Murray is an enigma. He clearly hasn't found his role on this team. By rights he should be the number two right wing behind Neely, but the Bruins used Bryan Smolinski in that role last season. Murray will have to scramble to find his spot in training camp and he might be the odd man out unless he comes into camp smoking.

Early indications peg him as a 20-goal man.

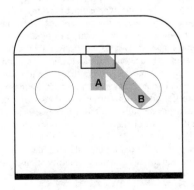

CAM NEELY

Yrs. of NHL service: 12
Born: Comox, B.C.; June 6, 1965
Position: right wing
Height: 6-1
Weight: 210
Uniform no.: 8
Shoots: right

Career statistics:

GP	G	A	TP	PIM
677	369	279	648	1210

1991-92 statistics:

GP	G	A	TP	+/-	PIM	PP	SH	GW	GT	S	PCT
9	9	3	12	+9	16	1	0	2	0	30	30.0

1992-93 statistics:

GP	G	A	TP	+/-	PIM	PP	SH	GW	GT	S	PCT
13	11	7	18	+4	25	6	0	1	0	45	24.4

1993-94 statistics:

GP	G	A	TP	+/-	PIM	PP	SH	GW	GT	S	PCT
49	50	24	74	+12	54	20	0	13	1	185	27.0

1994-95 statistics:

GP	G	A	TP	+/-	PIM	PP	SH	GW	GT	S	PCT
42	27	14	41	+7	72	16	0	5	1	178	15.2

LAST SEASON

Led team and ninth in the NHL in goals. Led NHL in power play goals. Third on team in points. Tied for team lead in game-winning goals. PIM four-season high. Missed five games with a hip injury.

THE FINESSE GAME

Considering what Neely's body and psyche have gone through during the past few seasons, his effective return to nearly full-time duty — albeit during a lockout-shortened season — was remarkable. Neely went from contemplating retirement at the start of 1993-94 to the game's premier power play forward.

Neely has a big-time goal-scoring release. Get the puck to him, as partner Adam Oates usually does, and the shot is away quickly and on net. He is the best in the NHL at going to the net and keeping goal-scoring simple. Neely has excellent scoring instincts and is a terror down low on the power play. His point totals for his limited ice time last season are nothing short of amazing. Neely scores where other players don't simply because he goes into the trenches where many players won't. The work required to rehabilitate his knee has made Neely a faster, stronger skater. Nearly impossible to budge once he plants himself around the net, Neely was more effective than ever in open ice and created some chances off the rush. Defensemen have to get all of him, otherwise they will simply bounce off as he bulls past them. Once he establishes himself in front of the net, especially on the power play, Neely is always facing the shooter and watching the shot or the incoming pass. He has the hand-eye coordination for tip-ins and the determination to get to loose pucks and rebounds.

THE PHYSICAL GAME

Few players have ever combined legitimate heavyweight toughness and scoring ability as well as Neely. He is the prototype NHL power forward. Strong mentally and physically, Neely endured a long summer of Claude Lemieux questions after the Devils forward effectively shut him down in the playoffs. He has fought so hard for his career that he can be expected to come back more determined than ever. How will playing on a larger ice surface at the new Fleet Center affect him? He scored 17 of his 27 goals at home last season on the cozy old Garden ice surface.

THE INTANGIBLES

Although he missed limited time due to his dicey physical condition, Neely's health remains a question mark. He didn't respond to ex-Bruins coach Brian Sutter (who split up the Oates-Neely combo under checking pressure in the playoffs), but may have a new and improved attitude with Steve Kasper.

There is the little matter of a contract to clear up. Neely played out his option last year, and was asking for a salary of around $3.5 million.

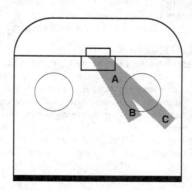

ADAM OATES

Yrs. of NHL service: 10
Born: Weston, Ont.; Aug. 27, 1962
Position: centre
Height: 5-11
Weight: 189
Uniform no.: 12
Shoots: right

Career statistics:

GP	G	A	TP	PIM
676	211	611	822	231

1991-92 statistics:

GP	G	A	TP	+/-	PIM	PP	SH	GW	GT	S	PCT
80	20	79	99	-9	22	6	0	4	2	191	10.5

1992-93 statistics:

GP	G	A	TP	+/-	PIM	PP	SH	GW	GT	S	PCT
84	45	97	142	+15	32	24	1	11	0	254	17.7

1993-94 statistics:

GP	G	A	TP	+/-	PIM	PP	SH	GW	GT	S	PCT
77	32	80	112	+10	45	16	2	3	0	197	16.2

1994-95 statistics:

GP	G	A	TP	+/-	PIM	PP	SH	GW	GT	S	PCT
48	12	41	53	-11	8	4	1	2	0	109	11.0

LAST SEASON

Led team and tied for fourth in league in assists. Led team in points. Tied for worst plus-minus on team. Only Bruin to appear in all 48 games. Scored 600th career assist.

THE FINESSE GAME

Oates uses a shorter than average blade (the result of a happy accident several years ago), which he finds results in better control of the puck. In addition, Oates uses a minimal curve. This gives him great control on the backhand, making him an even better backhand passer than forehand. It's no surprise that he has had his greatest success teamed with two right wings (Brett Hull in St. Louis and Cam Neely in Boston), even though he is a righty shooter.

Use of the backhand gives Oates a tremendous edge against all but the rangiest of NHL defensemen. By shielding the puck with his body, he forces defenders to reach in and frequently draws penalties when he is hooked or tripped. If defenders don't harrass him, then Oates has carte blanche to work his passing magic. He will even drive to the net on his backhand, and may try a shot though he will look for his passing options first.

He still doesn't shoot enough. It doesn't matter how hard you shoot the puck when you have the jeweller's precision of Oates. Taking more shots makes him a less predictable player, since the defense cannot back off and anticipate the pass. Oates is one of the best playmakers in the league because of his passing ability and his creativity. He is most effective down low where he can open up more ice, especially on the power play. He has outstanding timing and vision.

Yet Oates isn't stubborn to a fault. He will also play a dump-and-chase game if he is being shadowed closely, throwing the puck smartly into the opposite corner and with just the right velocity to allow his wingers to get in on top of the defense.

He is among the top five players in the league on face-offs, which makes him a natural on penalty killing (Boston ranked first in the league in that department), because a successful draw eats up 10-15 seconds on the clock, minimum. He is not a great skater, but he is quick and agile enough.

THE PHYSICAL GAME

Under deposed coach Brian Sutter, Oates saw a lot of ice time over the past two years, and each year in the playoffs he looked worn and weary. He is not a physical player, but he doesn't avoid contact. He's smart enough at this stage of his career to avoid the garbage, he plays in traffic and he'll take a hit to make the play.

Oates is an intense player and has a wiry strength. He is durable and can play a lot of minutes, but may be more judiciously used by new coach Steve Kasper in order to keep him fresh in the post-season. Oates underwent surgery on his right hand during the off-season, and his marvellous touch may be affected at the start of the season.

THE INTANGIBLES

Oates was rewarded with a new five-year, $10-million contract during the season. The Bruins need to find a left wing to complement the Oates-Neely combination (the team held a 48-game audition last year with no winner). Depth on the team would also help take some of the heat off Oates, who tends to get checked into the ground by defensive specialists in the playoffs. During the regular season, expect Oates to reign among the league's top assist men once again.

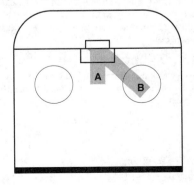

DAVE REID

Yrs. of NHL service: 9
Born: Toronto, Ont.; May 15, 1964
Position: left wing
Height: 6-1
Weight: 205
Uniform no.: 17
Shoots: left

Career statistics:

GP	G	A	TP	PIM
540	99	124	223	160

1991-92 statistics:

GP	G	A	TP	+/-	PIM	PP	SH	GW	GT	S	PCT
43	7	7	14	+5	27	2	1	0	0	70	10.0

1992-93 statistics:

GP	G	A	TP	+/-	PIM	PP	SH	GW	GT	S	PCT
65	20	16	36	+12	10	1	5	2	0	116	17.2

1993-94 statistics:

GP	G	A	TP	+/-	PIM	PP	SH	GW	GT	S	PCT
83	6	17	23	+10	25	0	2	1	0	145	4.1

1994-95 statistics:

GP	G	A	TP	+/-	PIM	PP	SH	GW	GT	S	PCT
38	5	5	10	+8	10	0	0	0	1	47	10.6

LAST SEASON

Led team in plus-minus. Missed two games with a hip pointer.

THE FINESSE GAME

Reid is a defensive forward and penalty-killing specialist. Opposition power plays always have to be aware of taking away Reid's space if they lose the puck, because he has the ability to blow the puck by the goalie from a lot of places on the ice. Possessing an underrated, accurate shot with a quick release, he can freeze a lot of goalies with his unexpected shot.

Reid is a good skater with surprising straight-ahead speed, especially for a big player. He has proven he can play regularly in the league and contribute. All of his moderate skills are enhanced by his hard work and hustle.

THE PHYSICAL GAME

Reid can create a little maelstrom on the ice. A big guy who can get his skating revved up, he causes problems once he is in motion. He isn't a big hitter, though, and there is no nasty side to him. He is just an honest checker.

THE INTANGIBLES

Reid is a checking winger who lost what little scoring punch he has and now seems relegated to the 10-15 goals range.

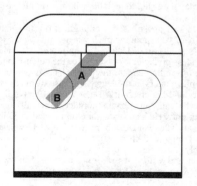

JON ROHLOFF

Yrs. of NHL service: 1
Born: Mankato, Minn.; Oct. 3, 1969
Position: right defense
Height: 5-11
Weight: 220
Uniform no.: 38
Shoots: right

Career statistics:

GP	G	A	TP	PIM
34	3	8	11	39

1994-95 statistics:

GP	G	A	TP	+/-	PIM	PP	SH	GW	GT	S	PCT
34	3	8	11	+1	39	0	0	1	1	51	5.9

LAST SEASON

First NHL season. Missed eight games with a groin injury. Missed one game with the flu.

THE FINESSE GAME

Rohloff is an older rookie, having completed four years at Minnesota-Duluth and a season in the minors before earning a spot with the Bruins last season. He has a mature, polished game. He is good enough to play on his off side, which is something few defensemen can handle.

Rohloff has a big shot, and an ability to score from anywhere. He has to develop more confidence in his shooting and scoring ability. Once he does, a lot of people are going to wonder why they've never heard of him before. You're hearing it now. He is also a smart passer. He can skate or move the puck out of his own end.

THE PHYSICAL GAME

Rohloff has come back all the way from major knee surgery. He is a fine skater, and defends well one-on-one. He eliminates the body well and does a great job in his own end taking away space. He competes every night, every shift.

THE INTANGIBLES

Rohloff is on his way to becoming a solid two-way defenseman. He didn't get as much playing time as his talent deserved last season. Depending on Al Iafrate's status, he could move up to the number three defense spot, right behind Ray Bourque and Don Sweeney. Not bad company.

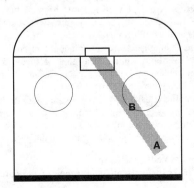

BRYAN SMOLINSKI

Yrs. of NHL service: 2
Born: Toledo, Ohio; Dec. 27, 1971
Position: centre/right wing
Height: 6-1
Weight: 195
Uniform no.: 20
Shoots: right

Career statistics:

GP	G	A	TP	PIM
136	50	36	86	117

1992-93 statistics:

GP	G	A	TP	+/-	PIM	PP	SH	GW	GT	S	PCT
9	1	3	4	+3	4	0	0	0	0	10	10.0

1993-94 statistics:

GP	G	A	TP	+/-	PIM	PP	SH	GW	GT	S	PCT
83	31	20	51	+4	82	4	3	5	0	179	17.3

1994-95 statistics:

GP	G	A	TP	+/-	PIM	PP	SH	GW	GT	S	PCT
44	18	13	31	-3	31	6	0	5	0	121	14.9

LAST SEASON

Tied for team lead in game-winning goals. Second on team in goals. Missed four games with a charley horse.

THE FINESSE GAME

Moving Smolinski from centre (a position he played in college and in his rookie NHL season) to wing made better use of his size and power, and as a result he produced bigger games, bigger goals and fewer mistakes. Playing with Mariusz Czerkawski and Jozef Stumpel, Smolinski helped give the Bruins a legitimate second line through the regular season, though the young trio failed to produce in the playoffs.

It wouldn't hurt the Bruins to give Smolinski another look at centre, however, since the team is lacking in depth at that position. He has excellent vision and hockey sense; some scouts have compared him to a budding Jean Ratelle for his crafty play. He has a quick release and an accurate shot, and works to get himself into quality shooting areas. Confidence is a big factor, and Smolinski is, at this stage of his career, one of those streak-or-slump players, though his game is maturing. His play away from the puck has improved to where he can contribute even when the points aren't forthcoming.

His skating is adequate, but it could improve with some lower body work. He has good balance and lateral movement but is not very quick. He has a railroad track skating base.

Smolinski has the smarts to be an asset on both special teams once he gains more experience. He has good defensive awareness, and his play away from the puck is sound. He is good in tight with the puck.

THE PHYSICAL GAME

Smolinski inadvertently threw one of the hardest checks of the 1995 playoffs when he caught burly New Jersey defenseman Scott Stevens with his head down and rattled him. Smolinski needs to make more of those plays on purpose. He is sturdy and strong enough to make an impact, but hasn't shown much of a taste for it. Should he get moved back to centre, improved conditioning and a bit of a mean streak (if he's got one) would improve his play. He is showing signs of becoming a determined penalty killer, with good pursuit of the puck, but needs to be more diligent in his own end.

THE INTANGIBLES

Smolinski's goal production, pro-rated over an 84-game season, would have been 35 — very satisfactory for a second-line forward in his second season. Expect Steve Kasper's arrival to help Smolinski, who needs a confidence boost now and again.

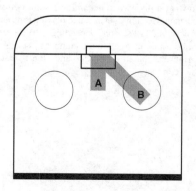

JOZEF STUMPEL

Yrs. of NHL service: 2
Born: Nitra, Czechoslavkia; June 20, 1972
Position: centre/right wing
Height: 6-1
Weight: 190
Uniform no.: 22
Shoots: right

Career statistics:

GP	G	A	TP	PIM
120	15	31	46	26

1991-92 statistics:

GP	G	A	TP	+/-	PIM	PP	SH	GW	GT	S	PCT
4	1	0	1	+1	0	0	0	0	0	3	33.3

1992-93 statistics:

GP	G	A	TP	+/-	PIM	PP	SH	GW	GT	S	PCT
13	1	3	4	-3	4	0	0	0	0	8	12.5

1993-94 statistics:

GP	G	A	TP	+/-	PIM	PP	SH	GW	GT	S	PCT
59	8	15	23	+4	14	0	0	1	0	62	12.9

1994-95 statistics:

GP	G	A	TP	+/-	PIM	PP	SH	GW	GT	S	PCT
44	5	13	18	+4	8	1	0	2	0	46	10.9

LAST SEASON

Second NHL season. Missed four games with a sprained knee.

THE FINESSE GAME

Stumpel's best attribute is his skating. He has speed and agile, quick moves that can shake a defender, and he has a long reach with good puck control.

Stumpel took a big step forward last season, taking over as the Bruins' second-line centre (with Mariusz Czerkawski and Bryan Smolinski). Although the point production wasn't as consistent as the Bruins had hoped — he was a much less effective player on the road — he showed good chemistry with his new linemates. The Czech has a deft scoring touch and is also a passer with a good short game. He had been considered a disappointment but is starting to show some improvement.

Stumpel has good hockey sense and is still adjusting to a full-time role. Given more time on the power play, he could respond to the responsibility.

THE PHYSICAL GAME

Stumpel is not an overly physical player, and can be intimidated. He goes into the corners and bumps, and he protects the puck with his body.

THE INTANGIBLES

Stumpel has to learn to play with more emotion every night. He has solid games and then nights when he is a non-factor. This will be a key season for him, with a new coach coming into Boston and a potential change again in his role, just as he was starting to get comfortable for perhaps the first time in his career.

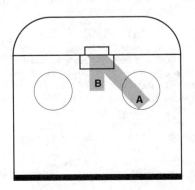

DON SWEENEY

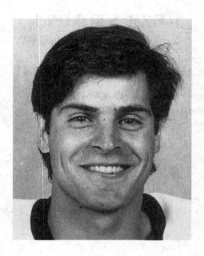

Yrs. of NHL service: 7
Born: St. Stephen, N.B.; Aug. 17, 1966
Position: left defense
Height: 5-11
Weight: 170
Uniform no.: 32
Shoots: left

Career statistics:

GP	G	A	TP	PIM
452	33	95	128	361

1991-92 statistics:

GP	G	A	TP	+/-	PIM	PP	SH	GW	GT	S	PCT
75	3	11	14	-9	74	0	0	1	0	92	3.3

1992-93 statistics:

GP	G	A	TP	+/-	PIM	PP	SH	GW	GT	S	PCT
84	7	27	34	+34	68	0	1	0	0	107	6.5

1993-94 statistics:

GP	G	A	TP	+/-	PIM	PP	SH	GW	GT	S	PCT
75	6	15	21	+29	50	1	2	2	0	136	4.4

1994-95 statistics:

GP	G	A	TP	+/-	PIM	PP	SH	GW	GT	S	PCT
47	3	19	22	+6	24	1	0	2	0	102	2.9

LAST SEASON

Second among team defensemen in scoring. Missed one game with a sore back.

THE FINESSE GAME

Sweeney has found a niche for himself in the NHL. He's mobile, physical and greatly improved in the area of defensive reads. He has good hockey sense for recognizing offensive situations as well.

He mostly stays at home and out of trouble, but he is a good enough skater to get involved in the attack and take advantage of the open ice when opposing teams overload on Ray Bourque's side. He is a good passer and has an adequate shot, and he has developed more confidence in his skills. He skates his way out of trouble and moves the puck well.

Sweeney is also an intelligent player who knows his strengths and weaknesses. He didn't get much playing time in his first two seasons in Boston, but, despite being a low draft pick (166th overall), he wouldn't let anyone overlook him.

THE PHYSICAL GAME

Sweeney is built like a little human Coke machine. He is tough to play against, and while wear and tear is a factor, he never hides. He is always in the middle of physical play. He utilizes his lower body drive and has tremendous leg power. He is also shifty enough to avoid a big hit when he sees it coming, and many a large fore-checking forward has sheepishly picked himself up off the ice after Sweeney has scampered away from the boards with the puck.

Sweeney is the ultimate gym rat, devoting a great deal of time to weightlifting and overall conditioning.

Pound for pound, he is one of the strongest defensemen in the NHL.

THE INTANGIBLES

Consistent pairing with Bourque has made Sweeney a better defenseman — it's almost impossible not to improve when playing alongside one of the game's greatest. But don't get the idea that Bourque is carrying Sweeney. Sweeney has speed, smarts and tons of heart, and is remarkably consistent. If he were three inches taller and 15 pounds heavier, he would be a Norris Trophy candidate. It's hard not to root for someone who works as hard as Sweeney does.

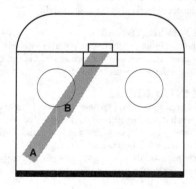

BUFFALO SABRES

Players' Statistics 1994-95

POS	NO.	PLAYER	GP	G	A	PTS	+/-	PIM	PP	SH	GW	GT	S	PCTG
R	89	ALEXANDER MOGILNY	44	19	28	47		36	12		2	1	148	12.8
R	28	DONALD AUDETTE	46	24	13	37	-3	27	13		7		124	19.4
D	3	GARRY GALLEY	47	3	29	32	4	30	2				97	3.1
C	16	PAT LAFONTAINE	22	12	15	27	2	4	6	1	3	1	54	22.2
L	13	YURI KHMYLEV	48	8	17	25	8	14	2	1	1		71	11.3
C	26	DEREK PLANTE	47	3	19	22	-4	12	2				94	3.2
D	8	DOUG BODGER	44	3	17	20	-3	47	2				87	3.4
R	18	WAYNE PRESLEY	46	14	5	19	5	41		5	2		90	15.6
C	10	DALE HAWERCHUK	23	5	11	16	-2	2	2		2		56	8.9
C	14	DAVE HANNAN	42	4	12	16	3	32		2			36	11.1
D	44	ALEXEI ZHITNIK	32	4	10	14	-6	61	3				66	6.1
L	43	JASON DAWE	42	7	4	11	-6	19		1	2		51	13.7
L	17	CRAIG SIMPSON	24	4	7	11	-5	26	1			1	20	20.0
D	42	RICHARD SMEHLIK	39	4	7	11	5	46		1	1		49	8.2
C	20	BOB SWEENEY	45	5	4	9	-6	18	1		2		47	10.6
L	29	SCOTT PEARSON	42	3	5	8	-14	74					40	7.5
D	22	CHARLIE HUDDY	41	2	5	7	-7	42	1				51	3.9
L	27	BRAD MAY	33	3	3	6	5	87	1				42	7.1
D	5	CRAIG MUNI	40		6	6	-4	36					32	
D	33	*MARK ASTLEY	14	2	1	3	-2	12					21	9.5
D	6	DOUG HOUDA	28	1	2	3	1	68					21	4.8
C	19	*BRIAN HOLZINGER	4		3	3	2						3	
L	32	ROB RAY	46		3	3	-4	173					7	
C	37	*CURTIS BROWN	1	1	1	2	2	2					4	25.0
L	36	MATTHEW BARNABY	23	1	1	2	-2	116					27	3.7
R	9	*VIKTOR GORDIOUK	10		2	2	-3						10	
C	76	*WAYNE PRIMEAU	1	1		1	-2				1		2	50.0
L	12	*PETER AMBROZIAK	12		1	1	-1						3	
L	44	*DOUG MACDONALD	2				-1							
D	3	*DEAN MELANSON	5				-1	4					1	
G	35	ROBB STAUBER	7											
G	39	DOMINIK HASEK	41					2						

GP = games played; G = goals; A = assists; PTS = points; +/- = goals-for minus goals-against while player is on ice; PIM = penalties in minutes; PP = power play goals; SH = shorthanded goals; GW = game-winning goals; GT = game-tying goals; S = no. of shots; PCTG = percentage of goals to shots; * = rookie

DONALD AUDETTE

Yrs. of NHL service: 4
Born: Laval, Que.; Sept. 23, 1969
Position: right wing
Height: 5-8
Weight: 175
Uniform no.: 28
Shoots: right

Career statistics:

GP	G	A	TP	PIM
238	100	70	170	198

1991-92 statistics:

GP	G	A	TP	+/-	PIM	PP	SH	GW	GT	S	PCT
63	31	17	48	-1	75	5	0	6	1	153	20.3

1992-93 statistics:

GP	G	A	TP	+/-	PIM	PP	SH	GW	GT	S	PCT
44	12	7	19	-8	51	2	0	0	0	92	13.0

1993-94 statistics:

GP	G	A	TP	+/-	PIM	PP	SH	GW	GT	S	PCT
77	29	30	59	+2	41	16	1	4	0	207	14.0

1994-95 statistics:

GP	G	A	TP	+/-	PIM	PP	SH	GW	GT	S	PCT
46	24	13	37	-3	27	13	0	7	0	124	19.4

LAST SEASON

Second on team in points. Led team in goals, power play goals and game-winning goals. Tied for second in league in power play goals and game-winning goals.

THE FINESSE GAME

Audette is a bustling forward who barrels to the net at every opportunity. He is eager and feisty down low and has good hand skills. He also has keen scoring instincts, along with the quickness to make good things happen. His feet move so fast (with a choppy stride) that he doesn't look graceful, but he can really get moving and he has good balance.

A scorer first, Audette has a great top-shelf shot, which he gets away quickly and accurately. He can also make a play, but he will do this at the start of a rush. Once he is inside the offensive zone and low, he wants the puck. His selfishness can be forgiven, considering his scoring ability.

Audette is at his best on the power play. He is smart enough not to just stand around and take his punishment, he times his jumps into the space between the left post and the bottom of the left circle. He didn't have much use for John Muckler's defensive system; a new coach may suit him even better.

THE PHYSICAL GAME

Opponents hate Audette, which he takes as a great compliment. He runs goalies, yaps and takes dives — then goes out and scores on the power play after the opposition takes a bad penalty.

He will fore-check and scrap for the puck but isn't as diligent coming back. He's not very big, but around the net he plays like he's at least a six-footer. He keeps jabbing and working away until he is bowled over by an angry defender.

THE INTANGIBLES

Audette has had to overcome a low draft (ninth round), two serious knee injuries and one shoulder separation. He lacks size, but not heart. He loves a challenge. If he fights to keep his place on the second line and the first power play unit, he could produce 40 goals.

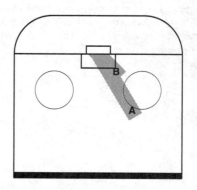

DOUG BODGER

Yrs. of NHL service: 11
Born: Chemainus, B.C.; June 18, 1966
Position: left defense
Height: 6-2
Weight: 210
Uniform no.: 8
Shoots: left

Career statistics:

GP	G	A	TP	PIM
762	89	360	449	780

1991-92 statistics:

GP	G	A	TP	+/-	PIM	PP	SH	GW	GT	S	PCT
73	11	35	46	+1	108	4	0	1	0	180	6.1

1992-93 statistics:

GP	G	A	TP	+/-	PIM	PP	SH	GW	GT	S	PCT
81	9	45	54	+14	87	6	0	0	1	154	5.8

1993-94 statistics:

GP	G	A	TP	+/-	PIM	PP	SH	GW	GT	S	PCT
75	7	32	39	+8	76	5	1	1	0	144	4.9

1994-95 statistics:

GP	G	A	TP	+/-	PIM	PP	SH	GW	GT	S	PCT
44	3	17	20	-3	47	2	0	0	0	87	3.4

LAST SEASON

Missed one game with the flu.

THE FINESSE GAME

Bodger is a smooth skater with good quickness, and he can make tight pivots while carrying the puck. He's among the better-skating defensemen in the league, though he lacks the dynamite speed of the more charismatic defensemen. He is the major puck carrier for the Sabres. It is Bodger who will collect the puck from the goalie behind the net, let his teammates wheel back and get ready to attack, then move out with the puck. He can either carry up, or feed one of the forwards with a smooth pass and then jump into the play. Bodger sees his passing options well and is very smart with the puck.

A natural on the point on the power play, he works the left point. He has a big slap that he keeps down for tips and scrambles in front. His best shot is a one-timer off a feed.

Bodger has great poise with the puck. He gives his team a sense of control when he is quarterbacking.

THE PHYSICAL GAME

Bodger takes the body when he absolutely must, but he is not by nature a hitter. He has never used his size as well as he should. Because his hand skills are so good, he prefers to position himself and try to poke- or sweep-check. He's a strong one-on-one defender because of his skating, but he will not clear people out from in front of his net as well as he should. He is aggressive stepping up into the neutral zone and challenges on penalty killing as well.

THE INTANGIBLES

Bodger is becoming more and more defensively oriented, and is a good two-way defenseman who can contribute at both ends of the ice. He has had some nagging injuries but he is still quietly effective and can help Buffalo's younger defensemen learn the game. Adding depth to the team's defense will allow him to play a more selective role, and actually increase his usefulness.

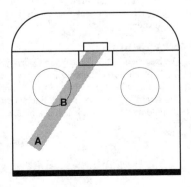

JASON DAWE

Yrs. of NHL service: 2
Born: North York, Ont.; May 29, 1973
Position: left wing
Height: 5-10
Weight: 195
Uniform no.: 43
Shoots: left

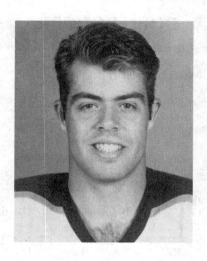

Career statistics:

GP	G	A	TP	PIM
74	13	11	24	31

1993-94 statistics:

GP	G	A	TP	+/-	PIM	PP	SH	GW	GT	S	PCT
32	6	7	13	+1	12	3	0	1	0	35	17.1

1994-95 statistics:

GP	G	A	TP	+/-	PIM	PP	SH	GW	GT	S	PCT
42	7	4	11	-6	19	0	1	2	0	51	13.7

LAST SEASON

Second NHL season. Missed six games with a knee injury.

THE FINESSE GAME

After taking his place on the team's top line with Pat LaFontaine and Alexander Mogilny late in the season, Dawe handled a rather difficult task well. He was supposed to do his job as a fore-checker, but also back-check well enough to free up his two linemates to do their freewheeling thing. Dawe did the job. His best scoring chances come not from fore-checking, but by trailing the play behind his two quick linemates. He has a quick release on his shot, usually from the top of the left circle in. He has the good sense to read the play and knows when to back off and support the defense as the third man high.

Dawe is a good skater with a fluid stride and good balance. He's shifty and didn't look out of place with the speedy LaFontaine and Mogilny, though he lacks their outright breakaway speed. Dawe handles the puck well at high tempo and in traffic. He is very effective on the power play.

THE PHYSICAL GAME

Dawe is willing to do the grunt work for his line. He is not big, but he is stocky and strong and will bang people off the puck. He is a diligent back-checker and has an aggressive streak.

THE INTANGIBLES

Dawe, who has been compared to Yvan Cournoyer, is ranked highly by the Sabres coaches for his work ethic and desire to improve. He will have to continue to compete to retain his spot on the top line. The only thing that could hold him back is his lack of size.

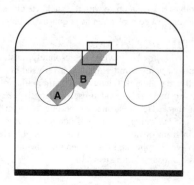

GARRY GALLEY

Yrs. of NHL service: 11
Born: Montreal, Que., Apr. 16, 1963
Position: left defense
Height: 6-0
Weight: 190
Uniform no.: 3
Shoots: left

Career statistics:

GP	G	A	TP	PIM
740	83	322	405	831

1991-92 statistics:

GP	G	A	TP	+/-	PIM	PP	SH	GW	GT	S	PCT
77	5	27	32	-2	117	3	0	1	0	125	4.0

1992-93 statistics:

GP	G	A	TP	+/-	PIM	PP	SH	GW	GT	S	PCT
83	13	49	62	+18	115	4	1	3	1	231	5.6

1993-94 statistics:

GP	G	A	TP	+/-	PIM	PP	SH	GW	GT	S	PCT
81	10	60	70	-11	91	5	1	0	1	186	5.4

1994-95 statistics:

GP	G	A	TP	+/-	PIM	PP	SH	GW	GT	S	PCT
47	3	29	32	+4	30	2	0	0	0	97	3.1

LAST SEASON

Acquired from Philadelphia for Petr Svoboda. Led team defensemen in scoring and led team in assists.

THE FINESSE GAME

Galley is a puck mover. He follows the play and jumps into the attack. He has decent speed to keep up with the play, though he won't be rushing the puck himself. He is mobile and has a good shot that he can get away on the fly. He will pinch aggressively, but he's also quick enough to get back if there is a counterattack.

He works well on the power play. His lateral movement allows him to slide away from the point to the middle of the blueline, and he keeps his shots low. He is a smart player and his experience shows. Galley helps any younger player he is teamed with because of his poise and communication.

THE PHYSICAL GAME

Galley has added a physical element to his game over the past few seasons, but he is not and will never be a big hitter. He will take his man, but not always take him out, and more physical forwards take advantage of him. Galley gets in the way, though, and does not back down. There are just times when he is simply overpowered.

Galley has a quick stick and uses sweep- and poke-checks well. He will also get a little chippy now and then, just to keep people guessing.

THE INTANGIBLES

For the past three seasons (two with Philadelphia, the last with the Flyers and Buffalo), Galley has led the team defensemen in scoring. He is not a true number one defenseman, but he served that role for the past two seasons and may have to again this season, though that is asking too much of him. He and Alexei Zhitnik will do some good things, but may have some nightmare nights as well.

Galley underwent off-season surgery on his left shoulder in 1994. The lockout gave him time to heal, but if he comes back with full confidence in the joint he may be more of a factor. His work ethic is seldom doubted.

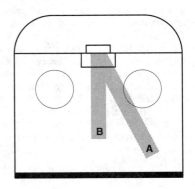

DOMINIK HASEK

Yrs. of NHL service: 4
Born: Pardubice, Czech Republic; Jan. 29, 1965
Position: goaltender
Height: 5-11
Weight: 165
Uniform no.: 39
Catches: left

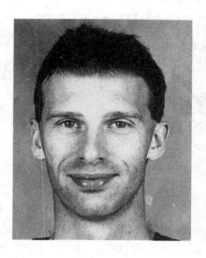

Career statistics:

GP	MINS	GA	SO	GAA	A	PIM
152	8412	321	13	2.29	3	16

1991-92 statistics:

GP	MINS	GAA	W	L	T	SO	GA	S	SAPCT	PIM
20	1014	2.60	10	4	1	1	44	413	.893	8

1992-93 statistics:

GP	MINS	GAA	W	L	T	SO	GA	S	SAPCT	PIM
28	1429	3.15	11	10	4	0	75	720	.896	0

1993-94 statistics:

GP	MINS	GAA	W	L	T	SO	GA	S	SAPCT	PIM
58	3358	1.95	30	20	6	7	109	1552	.930	6

1994-95 statistics:

GP	MINS	GAA	W	L	T	SO	GA	S	SAPCT	PIM
41	2416	2.11	19	14	7	5	85	1221	.930	2

LAST SEASON

Won 1995 Vezina Trophy. Finalist for Hart Trophy for second consecutive season. Tied for NHL lead in goals-against average and shutouts. Led NHL in save percentage for second consecutive season. Matched save percentage of 1993-94, which was the best since the NHL began keeping the statistic in 1982-93. Missed three games with a shoulder injury. Stopped Mark Recchi on penalty shot.

THE PHYSICAL GAME

What a mess! What a success! Nobody has worse technique nor better leg reflexes than Hasek. His foot speed is simply tremendous. He wanders and flops and sprawls. But he stops the puck.

Hasek tells his defensemen, "Let me see the puck," and they do. Sure, the shot clock may ring up numbers like a cash register on Christmas Eve, but Hasek has come away from games where he has seen every shot but one or two. And usually what Hasek sees, he stops. He is adept at directing his rebounds away from onrushing attackers. He prefers to hold pucks for face-offs, and the Sabres have a decent corps of centres so that tactic works fine for his team.

Hasek learned to come out of his net a little bit more, but he still doesn't cut down his angles well. He also has to work on his puckhandling. He has the single most bizarre habit of any NHL goalie we've seen in recent years. In scrambles around the net, he abandons his stick entirely and grabs the puck with his blocker hand. His work with the stick is brutal, which may be why he lets go of it so often.

THE MENTAL GAME

Hasek is unflappable. He is always prepared for tough saves early in a game, and has very lew lapses of concentration. His excitable style doesn't bother his teammates, who quickly developed faith in his ability.

THE INTANGIBLES

Hasek was a training camp holdout for a new contract, receiving a three-year extension worth $8 million plus massive bonuses. He suffered a slight knee injury in an auto accident during camp, and late in the season was arrested for driving while intoxicated. He was unfazed by the former, but the latter may have contributed to his dismal playoff performance. Hasek's no kid. He's proven himself as a number one goalie, but now has to handle the responsibility.

BRIAN HOLZINGER

Yrs. of NHL service: 0
Born: Parma, Ohio; Oct. 10, 1972
Position: centre
Height: 5-11
Weight: 180
Uniform no.: 19
Shoots: right

Career statistics:

GP	G	A	TP	PIM
4	0	3	3	0

1994-95 statistics:

GP	G	A	TP	+/-	PIM	PP	SH	GW	GT	S	PCT
4	0	3	3	+2	0	0	0	0	0	3	0.0

LAST SEASON

Will be entering first NHL season. Named CCHA Player of the Year. Won 1995 Hobey Baker Award.

THE FINESSE GAME

Holzinger is a scorer and a playmaker, and that combination will keep the defense guessing. He has a very good touch down low and patience with the puck to find the open passing lane. He will need to work with a grinder on one wing, because he is too small to do much effective work in the corners. It will help to have LaFontaine as a teammate; there is much Holzinger could learn from watching the veteran centre. Holzinger isn't quite as gritty as LaFontaine, nor does he have the latter's speed. He is more like Neal Broten (a former Hobey Baker winner), crafty and deceptively quick.

Like most players coming out of the college ranks, Holzinger will have to adapt to the size and speed of NHL players on a regular basis. He showed good sense and poise when thrown into the Stanley Cup playoffs on just four games' worth of regular-season experience, and scored two goals for Buffalo.

THE PHYSICAL GAME

Holzinger will have to work for his open ice in the NHL. He is not very big, nor very strong. Strength and conditioning work must figure in his summer vacation plans. The Sabres feel he is willing to work to achieve a regular role.

THE INTANGIBLES

Holzinger joined the Sabres following a four-year career at Bowling Green University, and by the playoffs had supplanted number two centre Derek Plante. With Hawerchuk gone to St. Louis, the door swings open for Holzinger, who should get an honest shot at cracking the Sabres' lineup. The Hobey Baker has been something of a curse in recent years, but Holzinger and Anaheim's Paul Kariya (the 1994 winner) may change that.

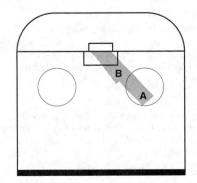

YURI KHMYLEV

Yrs. of NHL service: 3
Born: Moscow, Russia; Aug. 9, 1964
Position: left wing
Height: 6-1
Weight: 196
Uniform no.: 13
Shoots: right

Career statistics:

GP	G	A	TP	PIM
188	55	67	122	91

1992-93 statistics:

GP	G	A	TP	+/-	PIM	PP	SH	GW	GT	S	PCT
68	20	19	39	+6	28	0	3	3	0	122	16.4

1993-94 statistics:

GP	G	A	TP	+/-	PIM	PP	SH	GW	GT	S	PCT
72	27	31	58	+13	49	11	0	4	0	171	15.8

1994-95 statistics:

GP	G	A	TP	+/-	PIM	PP	SH	GW	GT	S	PCT
48	8	17	25	+8	14	2	1	1	0	71	11.3

LAST SEASON

Only Sabre to appear in all 48 games. Led team in plus-minus.

THE FINESSE GAME

Khmylev is a strong skater with outstanding balance. If his stick is tied up, he'll keep the puck going with his feet and make smart "soccer" passes. He doesn't worry much about the offensive zone, but he has a nice wrist shot and will work through traffic with the puck. He employs his long reach as a defensive weapon, to reach in around puck carriers to knock the puck free.

Khmylev kills penalties and is highly effective and aggressive. When a defenseman gambles deep, he will be the forward who drops back to cover the point.

Well-schooled in the eastern European system where the left winger is the most defensively responsible member of his line, Khmylev can be teamed with offensive players to act as a safety valve for their more freewheeling style. He has the skating and hand skills to complement almost anyone, but he won't dazzle with one-on-one play. He's a good support player.

THE PHYSICAL GAME

Khmylev is a tough, grinding winger who makes big checks. He will step up and create turnovers, and will bounce off checks and keep going. He is better suited to North American play than many Canadians and Americans.

THE INTANGIBLES

Khmylev is one of the new breed of players from the former Soviet Union. His skills aren't as dazzling as Alexander Mogilny's, but his overall ability and hockey sense are the right combination for a developing two-way winger.

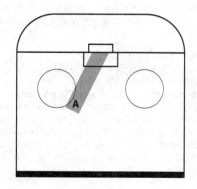

PAT LAFONTAINE

Yrs. of NHL service: 12
Born: St. Louis, Mo.; Feb. 22, 1963
Position: centre
Height: 5-10
Weight: 175
Uniform no.: 16
Shoots: right

Career statistics:

GP	G	A	TP	PIM
709	403	449	852	499

1991-92 statistics:

GP	G	A	TP	+/-	PIM	PP	SH	GW	GT	S	PCT
57	46	47	93	+10	98	23	0	5	1	203	22.7

1992-93 statistics:

GP	G	A	TP	+/-	PIM	PP	SH	GW	GT	S	PCT
84	53	95	148	+11	63	20	2	7	1	306	17.3

1993-94 statistics:

GP	G	A	TP	+/-	PIM	PP	SH	GW	GT	S	PCT
16	5	13	18	-4	2	1	0	0	0	40	12.5

1994-95 statistics:

GP	G	A	TP	+/-	PIM	PP	SH	GW	GT	S	PCT
22	12	15	27	+2	4	6	1	3	1	54	22.2

LAST SEASON

Missed 26 games rehabilitating a knee injury. Led team in shooting percentage. Won 1995 Masterton Trophy.

THE FINESSE GAME

LaFontaine missed 91 games over the past two seasons with major reconstructive knee surgery. There were whispers around Buffalo that he was too slow to come back and serious doubts about his ability to compete — which were thoroughly dispelled after the astounding numbers he put on the board in the last part of the season.

If LaFontaine were a baseball player, he would be like the midget Bill Veeck once sent up to the plate. With LaFontaine's skating crouch, there is no strike zone. He's a ball of fire on the ice, low to the ground and almost impossible to catch or knock off stride. He gears up in the defensive zone and simply explodes.

Inexhaustible, he is double-shifted almost every night and doesn't miss a call. Nor does he float: he's like a shark, always circling and in motion. He has great quickness and acceleration, with deep edges for turns. Few players can get as many dekes into a short stretch of ice at high speed as LaFontaine does when he is bearing down on a goalie. His favourite move is "patented" but still almost unstoppable. He streaks in, moves the puck to his backhand, then strides right with the puck on his forehand. A goalie's only hope is for LaFontaine to lose control. Slim chance.

LaFontaine takes almost all of the Sabres' offensive zone draws. He has quick hands and after winning the draw will burst past the opposing centre to the front of the net.

On the power play, LaFontaine likes to lurk behind the net, then burst out into the open ice at either side of the net for a pass and a scoring chance.

Opposing teams have to make the percentage play in their defensive zone against LaFontaine because of his anticipation and alertness in picking off passes.

THE PHYSICAL GAME

There were questions about whether LaFontaine would be the same player after his surgery. Much of the recovery process is mental, but the classy centre returned with his bold style intact. He is much less of a perimeter player than people think. He goes into high-traffic areas and crashes the net. He won't knock people down, and he won't run around making useless hits, but he will battle effectively in the neutral zone.

Strong on his skates and on his stick, LaFontaine will push off a defender with one arm and get a shot away one-handed. He is very disciplined and despite the abuse he takes, spends little time in the penalty box.

THE INTANGIBLES

LaFontaine's ability to endure a full schedule will be put to the test. With John Muckler moving upstairs, the team may move away from its trapping style (implemented, ironically enough, due to LaFontaine's lengthy absence). Nothing would make LaFontaine happier. This is a guy who loves wide-open offense, and he's one of the best in the league at it.

He may reclaim his spot among the NHL's elite forwards, but remains a risky proposition this season because of his injury.

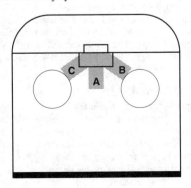

BRAD MAY

Yrs. of NHL service: 4
Born: Toronto, Ont.; Nov. 29, 1971
Position: left wing
Height: 6-0
Weight: 209
Uniform no.: 27
Shoots: left

Career statistics:

GP	G	A	TP	PIM
268	45	49	94	809

1991-92 statistics:

GP	G	A	TP	+/-	PIM	PP	SH	GW	GT	S	PCT
69	11	6	17	-12	309	1	0	3	0	82	13.4

1992-93 statistics:

GP	G	A	TP	+/-	PIM	PP	SH	GW	GT	S	PCT
82	13	13	26	+3	242	0	0	1	0	114	11.4

1993-94 statistics:

GP	G	A	TP	+/-	PIM	PP	SH	GW	GT	S	PCT
84	18	27	45	-6	171	3	0	3	0	166	10.8

1994-95 statistics:

GP	G	A	TP	+/-	PIM	PP	SH	GW	GT	S	PCT
33	3	3	6	+5	87	1	0	0	0	42	7.1

LAST SEASON

Missed 15 games with a broken right hand.

THE FINESSE GAME

May is better off trying to make the safe play instead of the big play, though he knows that, more often than not, the safe play leads to the big play. He has more than brute strength on his side and possesses nice passing skills and good hockey sense.

He is not much of a finisher, though as he becomes more relaxed and confident (he was neither last year) this may develop. He is certainly not a natural scorer; his goals will come off his hard work around the net.

May does have sound defensive instincts and was one of the few plus players on the Sabres. He is not a very fast or agile skater so he has to be conscious of keeping his position. He won't be able to race back to cover for an error in judgement.

THE PHYSICAL GAME

May is tough and rugged and he uses his size well. He is strong along the boards and in front of the net. A well-conditioned athlete, he is sturdy and durable. He has good balance and leg drive and is difficult to knock off his feet. He will take a hit to make a play and protects the puck well.

THE INTANGIBLES

A big paycheck can be a heavy burden to carry and May ($1.2 million per year, or what translates to $400,000 per goal) wasn't ready to handle it. He has to cope with the pressure and return to the Rick Tocchet-like path he was following before being sidetracked by the cash and sidelined by his injury.

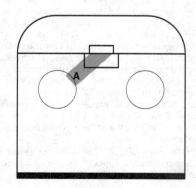

CRAIG MUNI

Yrs. of NHL service: 9
Born: Toronto, Ont.; July 19, 1962
Position: right defense
Height: 6-3
Weight: 200
Uniform no.: 5
Shoots: left

Career statistics:

GP	G	A	TP	PIM
643	26	107	133	608

1991-92 statistics:

GP	G	A	TP	+/-	PIM	PP	SH	GW	GT	S	PCT
54	2	5	7	+11	34	0	0	0	0	38	5.3

1992-93 statistics:

GP	G	A	TP	+/-	PIM	PP	SH	GW	GT	S	PCT
81	0	11	11	-14	75	0	0	0	0	60	0.0

1993-94 statistics:

GP	G	A	TP	+/-	PIM	PP	SH	GW	GT	S	PCT
82	2	12	14	+31	66	0	1	2	0	45	4.4

1994-95 statistics:

GP	G	A	TP	+/-	PIM	PP	SH	GW	GT	S	PCT
40	0	6	6	-4	36	0	0	0	0	32	0.0

LAST SEASON

Missed five games with a left hamstring injury.

THE FINESSE GAME

Muni is a defensive defenseman because there is no offense to his game. He doesn't have the skating range, hand skills or taste for it.

There is nothing wrong with that. A specialist is a specialist, and Muni's specialty is getting his team out of trouble. He can handle a night against the opposition's top offensive line or their toughest line. He is capable in any situation, but is an outstanding penalty killer (the Sabres were among the top three in the NHL in penalty killing over the past two seasons). He blocks shots well and is seldom beaten one-on-one because he holds his position and isn't fooled by fakes.

Muni has a long reach, which he uses to compensate for a fairly significant lack of range. He does not skate poorly, but he is not fast or mobile. Playing half his games on a smaller ice surface helps keep him from getting burned with outside speed.

THE PHYSICAL GAME

Muni is big, strong and tough, both mentally and physically, and he can hurt people with his checks.

THE INTANGIBLES

Muni is a blue-collar defenseman and a sturdy, steady defensive presence. Let other defenders do the fancy stuff. Muni will stay back on the doorstep.

SCOTT PEARSON

Yrs. of NHL service: 5
Born: Cornwall, Ont.; Dec. 19, 1969
Position: left wing
Height: 6-1
Weight: 205
Uniform no.: 29
Shoots: left

Career statistics:

GP	G	A	TP	PIM
220	49	36	85	472

1991-92 statistics:

GP	G	A	TP	+/-	PIM	PP	SH	GW	GT	S	PCT
10	1	2	3	-5	14	0	0	0	0	14	7.1

1992-93 statistics:

GP	G	A	TP	+/-	PIM	PP	SH	GW	GT	S	PCT
41	13	1	14	+3	95	0	0	1	0	45	28.9

1993-94 statistics:

GP	G	A	TP	+/-	PIM	PP	SH	GW	GT	S	PCT
72	19	18	37	-4	165	3	0	7	0	160	11.9

1994-95 statistics:

GP	G	A	TP	+/-	PIM	PP	SH	GW	GT	S	PCT
42	3	5	8	-14	74	0	0	0	0	40	7.5

LAST SEASON

Acquired from Edmonton for Ken Sutton. Worst plus-minus on team.

THE FINESSE GAME

All of Pearson's goals laid end-to-end wouldn't reach from the crease to the hash marks. His game is in tight, but he gets many more whacks at the puck than goals because he lacks the true goal-scorer's knack of following up the first shot. If the first shot goes in, fine, but Pearson will seldom pursue the rebound.

Since he doesn't add much else to a team, this lack of drive is what prevents him from being a more useful player. He has decent size — not big by NHL standards these days, but big enough — but doesn't exploit it to the utmost. If he's not scoring goals himself, Pearson has to drive to the net to screen the goalie for his teammate's shots. He did some of that well for Buffalo after his trade last season.

Pearson is a fair skater, not very agile but strong on his skates for work along the boards (which he performs in the attacking zone, rarely at the other end of the ice).

THE PHYSICAL GAME

Pearson should be more involved. There are occasional glimpses of what kind of player he can be when he mixes things up a little more. He will stand up to a challenge, but doesn't initiate enough.

THE INTANGIBLES

Pearson was a disappointment as a first-rounder with Quebec and Buffalo is his fourth NHL stop. Teams keep waiting for more intensity to show in his games every night, but that consistency eludes him. The Sabres are desperate for size up front, and he will be given every chance to earn his ice time.

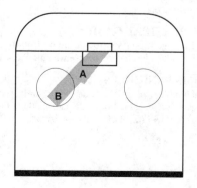

MIKE PECA

Yrs. of NHL service: 1
Born: Toronto, Ont.; March 26,
Position: right wing
Height: 5-11
Weight: 180
Uniform no.: 33
Shoots: right

Career statistics:

GP	G	A	TP	PIM
37	6	6	12	32

1993-94 statistics:

GP	G	A	TP	+/-	PIM	PP	SH	GW	GT	S	PCT
4	0	0	0	-1	2	0	0	0	0	5	0.0

1994-95 statistics:

GP	G	A	TP	+/-	PIM	PP	SH	GW	GT	S	PCT
33	6	6	12	-6	30	2	0	1	1	46	13.0

LAST SEASON

First NHL season. Missed 12 games with a fractured cheekbone. Acquired from Vancouver with Mike Wilson and a first-round draft pick in 1995 for Alexander Mogilny and a fifth-round pick in 1995.

THE FINESSE GAME

Peca is a strong, sure skater who plays every shift as if a pink slip will be waiting on the bench if he slacks off. He's good with the puck, but not overly creative. Peca just reads offensive plays well and does a lot of the little things, especially when fore-checking, that create turnovers and scoring chances. His goals come from his quickness and his effort. He will challenge anyone for the puck.

While Peca is known for his grit, he can be a useful offensive player. Defensively, though, his game needs work, and he seems willing to learn. He is only average on face-offs. Peca's hustle and attitude have earned him his NHL shot.

THE PHYSICAL GAME

Peca plays much bigger than his size. He's desperate to try to add five more pounds of muscle, but even at 175 pounds last season he was one of the league's best open-ice hitters. Peca drew the attention of the Winnipeg Jets with a jarring hit on Teemu Selanne — the collision in which Peca fractured his face — then in his first game in Winnipeg after the incident, he threw the biggest check of the game. Knowing he was a marked man and playing that kind of high-profile game showed Peca's hockey courage.

Peca will also drop the gloves and go after even the biggest foe. He is fearless.

THE INTANGIBLES

Peca doesn't know how good he can be yet. Right now, he is the spark plug guy whose hits fire up the home crowd and his teammates. He will have more of an impact playing with the right kind of big wingers and developing more confidence in his offensive ability. Peca won a gold medal with the 1995 Canadian World Junior team.

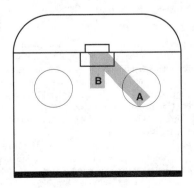

WAYNE PRESLEY

Yrs. of NHL service: 10
Born: Dearborn, Mich.; March 23, 1965
Position: right wing
Height: 5-11
Weight: 180
Uniform no.: 18
Shoots: right

Career statistics:

GP	G	A	TP	PIM
604	149	139	288	868

1991-92 statistics:

GP	G	A	TP	+/-	PIM	PP	SH	GW	GT	S	PCT
59	10	16	26	-27	133	3	0	1	0	135	7.4

1992-93 statistics:

GP	G	A	TP	+/-	PIM	PP	SH	GW	GT	S	PCT
79	15	17	32	+5	96	0	1	2	0	97	15.5

1993-94 statistics:

GP	G	A	TP	+/-	PIM	PP	SH	GW	GT	S	PCT
65	17	8	25	+18	103	1	5	1	0	93	18.3

1994-95 statistics:

GP	G	A	TP	+/-	PIM	PP	SH	GW	GT	S	PCT
46	14	5	19	+5	41	0	5	2	0	90	15.6

LAST SEASON

Led team and tied for second in NHL in shorthanded goals, both for second consecutive season. Missed one game with a groin injury.

THE FINESSE GAME

Presley has developed into a defensive specialist and penalty killer par excellance. He has adequate shooting skills in tight, where everything is reaction. When he has too much time to think, he will overhandle the puck and tighten up. He has soft hands for doing something with deflections and rebounds, and he is willing to pay the physical price to get himself into position for those opportunities.

Presley is a strong, determined skater and forechecker. He takes the body and creates chances by forcing turnovers. He is especially dogged in his pursuit when killing penalties and will never give up on the puck, which is how he get his shorthanded scoring chances. He is not much of a playmaker (note the ratio between goals and assists over the past two seasons).

THE PHYSICAL GAME

Presley crashes the net and is good at getting to the goalie, even right on top of the goalie since the interference rules started to relax last season. He is also good at making contact with the netminder and making it appear as if the defender forced him into the crease. (It is usually Presley dragging the defender along with him.) It's a great veteran play, and it drives goalies nuts.

Presley is annoying to play against. He takes the body consistently and rubs his gloves or stick into an opponent's face. He is able to goad rivals into taking bad penalties while he remains cool and creates a power play chance for his team.

THE INTANGIBLES

Presley is the ultimate checking winger who can net 15-20 goals a season.

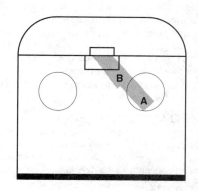

ROB RAY

Yrs. of NHL service: 6
Born: Stirling, Ont.; June 8, 1968
Position: left wing
Height: 6-0
Weight: 203
Uniform no.: 32
Shoots: left

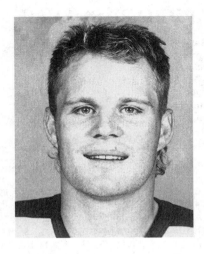

Career statistics:

GP	G	A	TP	PIM
352	21	21	42	1461

1991-92 statistics:

GP	G	A	TP	+/-	PIM	PP	SH	GW	GT	S	PCT
63	5	3	8	-9	354	0	0	0	0	29	17.2

1992-93 statistics:

GP	G	A	TP	+/-	PIM	PP	SH	GW	GT	S	PCT
68	3	2	5	-3	211	1	0	0	0	28	10.7

1993-94 statistics:

GP	G	A	TP	+/-	PIM	PP	SH	GW	GT	S	PCT
82	3	4	7	+2	274	0	0	0	0	34	8.8

1994-95 statistics:

GP	G	A	TP	+/-	PIM	PP	SH	GW	GT	S	PCT
46	0	3	3	-4	173	0	0	0	0	7	0.0

LAST SEASON

Led team in PIM for second consecutive season. Tied for fifth in the NHL in PIM. Missed one game with the flu.

THE FINESSE GAME

Ray is a good skater for a big guy, very mobile and surprisingly quick. He is a solid fore-checker and is learning to keep his gloves and stick down. There is nothing wrong with taking aggressive penalties, but Ray is big enough to check cleanly and effectively. His problem is one of the chicken-or-egg variety. Is Ray not getting enough ice time to allow him to improve his game, or is he merely a tough-guy winger that the team can't afford to have on the ice too often?

Ray has to work hard for his points. He has a nice wrist shot from in clsoe and a hard slap shot. He doesn't do much creatively but patrols up and down his wing. He has good balance and can plant himself in front of the net, but he doesn't have really quick hands for picking up loose pucks.

THE PHYSICAL GAME

Ray is one of those hitters who can galvanize a bench and a building. A defender with the puck knows Ray is coming and either has to be willing to stand up to the check or bail out — either way, Ray has a good shot at loosening a puck and getting a turnover. The problem is that he can't do much with the puck once he gets it and needs a clever linemate to trail in and pick up the pieces.

A good fighter who doesn't get challenged much anymore, Ray was the player chiefly responsible for a rule change last season that penalized a player for shucking his jersey before an altercation. Ray continued to fight on half-naked, since he has gotten very good at making it look like the opponent has pulled off his jersey, which he wears large and loose and with the protective equipment sewn onto it.

THE INTANGIBLES

There is still a place for a Rob Ray, especially on a team that has valuable players like Pat LaFontaine. But the Sabres look to be adding talent to go with their toughness, and Ray may find himself on the bubble if the team has enough players who can take care of themselves. If the Sabres don't want him, there will be plenty of teams that will.

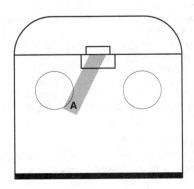

RICHARD SMEHLIK

Yrs. of NHL service: 3
Born: Ostrava, Czechoslovakia; Jan. 23, 1970
Position: right defense
Height: 6-3
Weight: 208
Uniform no.: 42
Shoots: left

Career statistics:

GP	G	A	TP	PIM
203	22	61	83	174

1992-93 statistics:

GP	G	A	TP	+/-	PIM	PP	SH	GW	GT	S	PCT
80	4	27	31	+9	59	0	0	0	0	82	4.9

1993-94 statistics:

GP	G	A	TP	+/-	PIM	PP	SH	GW	GT	S	PCT
84	14	27	41	+22	69	3	3	1	1	106	13.2

1994-95 statistics:

GP	G	A	TP	+/-	PIM	PP	SH	GW	GT	S	PCT
39	4	7	11	+5	46	0	1	1	0	49	8.2

LAST SEASON

Led team defensemen in plus-minus. Missed nine games with a shoulder injury.

THE FINESSE GAME

Skating well with a strong stride, Smehlik is not fast, but he's agile with good lateral movement and is very solid on his skates. Because his balance is so good, he is tough to knock down.

He has become much more involved in the offense. If he is paired with an offense-oriented partner, like Doug Bodger, Smehlik is more than willing to let the senior defenseman control the puck. But when he is the more skilled of a pairing he will take the offensive responsibility. He has good passing skills and fair hockey vision, and can spot and hit the breaking forward. Most of his assists will be traced back to a headman feed out of the defensive zone.

Smehlik is vulnerable to a strong fore-check. Teams are aware of his lack of experience and try to work his corner.

THE PHYSICAL GAME

Smehlik is still adapting to the North American game. He can use his body well but has to be more consistent and authoritative. He gained confidence through the season and was willing to step up aggressively, especially when killing penalties. He has to clean up his crease better, but he's not a mean hitter. He prefers to use his stick to break up plays, and he does this effectively. He has a long reach and is able to intercept passes or reach in around a defender to pry the puck loose.

THE INTANGIBLES

Smehlik will never be a team's chief offensive contributor, but he can become a solid number three or maybe even number two defenseman because of his skill level, depending on who he is paired with. Poised and intelligent, he will seldom shine as one of the stars of a game, but he will often emerge as the team's most reliable and consistent defenseman.

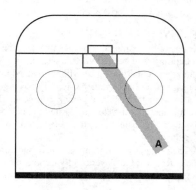

ALEXEI ZHITNIK

Yrs. of NHL service: 3
Born: Kiev, Ukraine; Oct. 10, 1972
Position: left defense
Height: 5-10
Weight: 178
Uniform no.: 44
Shoots: left

Career statistics:

GP	G	A	TP	PIM
191	28	86	114	242

1992-93 statistics:

GP	G	A	TP	+/-	PIM	PP	SH	GW	GT	S	PCT
78	12	36	48	-3	80	5	0	2	0	136	8.8

1993-94 statistics:

GP	G	A	TP	+/-	PIM	PP	SH	GW	GT	S	PCT
81	12	40	52	-11	101	11	0	1	1	227	5.3

1994-95 statistics:

GP	G	A	TP	+/-	PIM	PP	SH	GW	GT	S	PCT
32	4	10	14	-6	61	3	0	0	0	66	6.1

LAST SEASON

Acquired from Los Angeles with Robb Stauber and Charlie Huddy for Grant Fuhr, Philippe Boucher and Denis Tsygurov. Missed three games with a broken thumb. Missed four games with a ruptured calf muscle.

THE FINESSE GAME

Zhitnik has a bowlegged skating style that ex-coach, Barry Melrose, once compared to Bobby Orr's. Zhitnik is no Orr, but he was born with skates on. He has speed, acceleration and lateral mobility.

He plays the point on the power play with Garry Galley, moving to the right point to open up his forehand for the one-timer. Zhitnik likes to rush the puck and shoots well off the fly. He uses all of the blueline well on the power play. He has a good, hard shot, but needs to work on keeping it low for tips and deflections in front.

Zhitnik sees the ice well and is a good playmaker. He can snap a long, strong headman pass or feather a short pass on a give-and-go. He can also grab the puck and skate it out of danger. Consistency continues to elude him, but he has the ingredients to put a great game together.

THE PHYSICAL GAME

Zhitnik has an undisciplined side to his game. He makes wild, leaping checks that are borderline charges, but for the most part he plays sensibly and doesn't take bad penalties. Teams often target Zhitnik physically and try to take him out of a game early, and the tactic will work as he wears out. He has to get stronger and pay more attention to conditioning, since he may emerge as the Sabres' number one defenseman.

THE INTANGIBLES

Zhitnik is a well-kept secret. His second NHL season was spent in L.A. with a bad team and in a mental funk. Injuries and the trade disrupted last season.

He is a prototypical '90s defenseman: mobile, strong, a big shooter and adept at both ends of the ice. Buffalo is rebuilding, and he is a defenseman to build on.

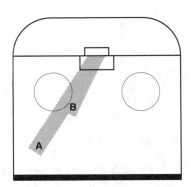

CALGARY FLAMES

Players' Statistics 1994-95

POS	NO.	PLAYER	GP	G	A	PTS	+/-	PIM	PP	SH	GW	GT	S	PCTG
R	14	THEOREN FLEURY	47	29	29	58	6	112	9	2	5		173	16.8
C	25	JOE NIEUWENDYK	46	21	29	50	11	33	3		4		122	17.2
D	6	PHIL HOUSLEY	43	8	35	43	17	18	3				135	5.9
C	26	ROBERT REICHEL	48	18	17	35	-2	28	5		2		160	11.3
D	33	ZARLEY ZALAPSKI	48	4	24	28	9	46	1		1		76	5.3
D	21	STEVE CHIASSON	45	2	23	25	10	39	1				110	1.8
C	13	GERMAN TITOV	40	12	12	24	6	16	3	2	3		88	13.6
C	29	JOEL OTTO	47	8	13	21	8	130		2	2	1	46	17.4
C	17	WES WALZ	39	6	12	18	7	11	4		1		73	8.2
L	12	PAUL KRUSE	45	11	5	16	13	141			2		52	21.2
R	23	SHELDON KENNEDY	30	7	8	15	5	45	1				44	15.9
R	22	RONNIE STERN	39	9	4	13	4	163	1				69	13.0
D	4	KEVIN DAHL	34	4	8	12	8	38					30	13.3
C	11	KELLY KISIO	12	7	4	11	2	6	5	1			26	26.9
C	32	MIKE SULLIVAN	38	4	7	11	-2	14			2		31	12.9
R	16	NIKOLAI BORSCHEVSKY	27		10	10	10						40	
D	5	JAMES PATRICK	43		10	10	-3	14					43	
R	15	SANDY MCCARTHY	37	5	3	8	1	101			2		29	17.2
D	28	LEONARD ESAU	15		6	6	-10	15					21	
D	39	DAN KECZMER	28	2	3	5	7	10					33	6.1
L	41	ALAN MAY	34	2	3	5	3	119					28	7.1
D	3	FRANK MUSIL	35		5	5	6	61					18	
L	10	GARY ROBERTS	8	2	2	4	1	43	2				20	10.0
L	19	*VESA VIITAKOSKI	10	1	2	3	-1	6	1				6	16.7
R	42	*ED WARD	2	1	1	2	-2	2					1	00.0
R	16	MARK GREIG	8	1	1	2	1	2					5	20.0
C	20	*CORY STILLMAN	10		2	2	1	2					7	
G	31	RICK TABARACCI	13		2	2		2						
D	18	TRENT YAWNEY	37		2	2	-4	108					20	
C	38	*TODD HLUSHKO	2		1	1	1	2					3	
L	24	JIM PEPLINSKI	6		1	1	-2	11					5	
C	92	MICHAEL NYLANDER	6		1	1	1	2					2	
G	37	TREVOR KIDD	43		1	1		2						
D	7	STEVE KONROYD	1											
G	36	*JASON MUZZATTI	1											
D	7	*JAMIE ALLISON	1											
D	34	*JOEL BOUCHARD	2											
C	35	NEIL EISENHUT	3										2	
L	28	BARRY NIECKAR	3					12						
L	27	*SCOTT MORROW	4										1	
G	1	*ANDREI TREFILOV	6											

GP = games played; G = goals; A = assists; PTS = points; +/- = goals-for minus goals-against while player is on ice; PIM = penalties in minutes; PP = power play goals; SH = shorthanded goals; GW = game-winning goals; GT = game-tying goals; S = no. of shots; PCTG = percentage of goals to shots; * = rookie

STEVE CHIASSON

Yrs. of NHL service: 8
Born: Barrie, Ont.; Apr. 14, 1967
Position: left defense
Height: 6-0
Weight: 205
Uniform no.: 21
Shoots: left

Career statistics:

GP	G	A	TP	PIM
471	67	200	267	886

1991-92 statistics:

GP	G	A	TP	+/-	PIM	PP	SH	GW	GT	S	PCT
62	10	24	34	+22	136	5	0	2	1	143	7.0

1992-93 statistics:

GP	G	A	TP	+/-	PIM	PP	SH	GW	GT	S	PCT
79	12	50	62	+14	155	6	0	1	0	227	5.3

1993-94 statistics:

GP	G	A	TP	+/-	PIM	PP	SH	GW	GT	S	PCT
82	13	33	46	+17	122	4	1	2	0	238	5.5

1994-95 statistics:

GP	G	A	TP	+/-	PIM	PP	SH	GW	GT	S	PCT
45	2	23	25	+10	39	1	0	0	0	110	1.8

THE INTANGIBLES

Chiasson is on the verge of becoming a complete two-way defenseman, maybe one of the most underrated blueliners in the NHL. He takes his leadership role to heart.

LAST SEASON

Third among team defensemen in scoring.

THE FINESSE GAME

Chiasson's finesse game has improved along with his skating. The two go hand in hand (or foot in skate), and Chiasson has dedicated himself to improving in this critical area. He still has a bit of a choppy stride, but he's quick and better at getting himself into position offensively. He has a cannon shot. He will get more power play time in Calgary, possibly working in tandem with Phil Housley if the latter stays healthy.

Chiasson is not afraid to gamble in deep, either, and has good instincts about when to pinch in. He handles the puck well down low and uses a snap or wrist shot. He is poised with the puck on the attack.

Defensively, he plays a solid positional game and reads rushes well. While not great in any one area (save, perhaps, his shot), he has a nice overall package of skills.

THE PHYSICAL GAME

Chiasson is a competitor. He will play hurt, he will defend his teammates, and he is prepared to compete every night. He lacked conditioning early in his career and it hurt him, but he has matured in his approach to his livelihood and it's paying off.

Chiasson never quite settled into his game in his first season in Calgary. He seemed afraid to hit, and he's the kind of player who just has to snap every 10 games or so and discipline be damned, or else he keeps too much emotion and intensity bottled up. He seemed to play last season in a straitjacket.

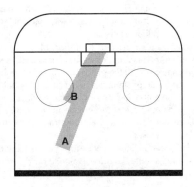

THEOREN FLEURY

Yrs. of NHL service: 6
Born: Oxbow, Sask.; June 29, 1968
Position: right wing/centre
Height: 5-6
Weight: 160
Uniform no.: 14
Shoots: right

Career statistics:

GP	G	A	TP	PIM
488	232	288	520	991

1991-92 statistics:

GP	G	A	TP	+/-	PIM	PP	SH	GW	GT	S	PCT
80	33	40	73	0	133	11	1	6	0	225	14.7

1992-93 statistics:

GP	G	A	TP	+/-	PIM	PP	SH	GW	GT	S	PCT
83	34	66	100	+14	88	12	2	4	0	250	13.6

1993-94 statistics:

GP	G	A	TP	+/-	PIM	PP	SH	GW	GT	S	PCT
83	40	45	85	+30	186	16	1	6	0	278	14.4

1994-95 statistics:

GP	G	A	TP	+/-	PIM	PP	SH	GW	GT	S	PCT
47	29	29	58	+6	112	9	2	5	0	173	16.8

LAST SEASON

Led team in power play goals for second consecutive season. Led team in goals, points, game-winning goals and shots. Tied for team lead in shorthanded goals. Named to Second All-Star Team.

THE FINESSE GAME

Fleury continues to prove that a small man can excel in a big man's game. Possessing great speed and quickness, he often seems to be dancing over the ice with his blades barely touching the frozen surface. He is always on the move, which is as much a tactic as an instinct for survival. You can't catch what you can't hit. He uses his outside speed to burn slower, bigger defensemen, or he can burst up the middle and split two defenders.

A better finisher than playmaker, Fleury is not at his best handling the puck; he's much better receiving the pass late and then making things happen. He always has his legs churning, and he draws penalties by driving to the net. He has a strong wrist shot that he can get away from almost anywhere. He can score even if he is pulled to his knees.

Fleury is a strong penalty killer, blocking shots and getting the puck out along the boards. He is very poised and cool with the puck under attack, holding it until he finds an opening instead of just firing blindly. His defensive play has improved, and he does a good job as a back-checker in holding up opposing forwards so his defensemen have extra time with the puck.

His hand quickness makes him very effective on draws, and he will take offensive-zone draws.

THE PHYSICAL GAME

Fleury can take a hit and not get knocked down because he is so solid and has a low centre of gravity. He uses his stick liberally (he was perhaps too feisty again last season). He no longer has to prove himself and needs to spend more time on the ice and less in the penalty box.

THE INTANGIBLES

Only his size prevents Fleury from being among the NHL's elite forwards. He is a gamer, and should flirt with the 100-point mark again, but the Flames are undergoing yet another coaching change, which may affect his or the team's style.

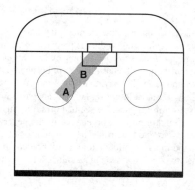

PHIL HOUSLEY

Yrs. of NHL service: 13
Born: St. Paul, Minn.; Mar. 9, 1964
Position: right defense
Height: 5-10
Weight: 185
Uniform no.: 6
Shoots: left

Career statistics:

GP	G	A	TP	PIM
909	257	625	882	584

1991-92 statistics:

GP	G	A	TP	+/-	PIM	PP	SH	GW	GT	S	PCT
74	23	63	86	-5	92	11	0	4	1	234	9.8

1992-93 statistics:

GP	G	A	TP	+/-	PIM	PP	SH	GW	GT	S	PCT
80	18	79	97	-14	52	6	0	2	0	249	7.2

1993-94 statistics:

GP	G	A	TP	+/-	PIM	PP	SH	GW	GT	S	PCT
26	7	15	22	-5	12	4	0	1	1	60	11.7

1994-95 statistics:

GP	G	A	TP	+/-	PIM	PP	SH	GW	GT	S	PCT
43	8	35	43	+17	18	3	0	0	0	135	5.9

LAST SEASON

Led team defensemen in scoring. Led team in assists and plus-minus. Third on team in scoring. Missed five games with a finger injury. Scored 600th career assist.

THE FINESSE GAME

Among the best-skating defensemen in the NHL, Housley, like Paul Coffey, takes a lot of heat for his defensive shortcomings, but his offensive skills are extraordinary.

Housley's skating fuels his game. He can accelerate in a heartbeat, and his edges are deep and secure, giving him the ability to avoid checks with gravity-defying moves. Everything he does is at high tempo. He intimidates with his speed and skills, forcing defenders back on their heels and opening up more ice for himself and his teammates.

He has an excellent grasp of the ice. On the power play he is a huge threat. His shots are low, quick and heavy, either beating the goalie outright or setting up a rebound for the forwards down deep. He will also set up low on the power play, and he doesn't mind shooting from an "impossible" angle that can catch a goalie napping on the short side.

Housley has great anticipation and can break up a rush by picking off a pass and turning the play into a counterattack. He is an excellent passer for a long headman or a short cup-and-saucer pass over a defender's stick.

THE PHYSICAL GAME

Housley is not the least bit physical. Who wants a player as gifted as Housley risking life and limb in routine plays along the boards when there are a dozen less gifted players who could do it for him? He is not strong enough to shove anyone out of the zone, so his defensive play is based on his pursuit of the puck. Fragile because of a recent back injury, he is even more likely to avoid traffic areas unless he feels he can get in and out with the puck quickly enough.

Success on a rush, even a two-on-one, against Housley is no guarantee, since he is so good a skater that he will position himself well and try to break up the play with his stick. He'll block shots at crunch time.

THE INTANGIBLES

Housley has resumed his slot among the league's top-scoring defensemen, but he has never been close to a Norris Trophy or a Stanley Cup.

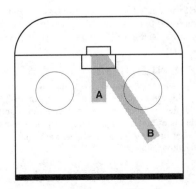

TREVOR KIDD

Yrs. of NHL service: 2
Born: Dugald, Man.; March 29, 1972
Position: goaltender
Height: 6-2
Weight: 190
Uniform no.: 37
Catches: left

Career statistics:

GP	MINS	G	SO	AVG	A	PIM
76	4197	200	3	2.86	5	6

1991-92 statistics:

GP	MINS	GAA	W	L	T	SO	GA	S	SAPCT	PIM
2	120	4.00	1	1	0	0	8	56	.857	0

1992-93 statistics:

P	MINS	GAA	W	L	T	SO	GA	S	SAPCT	PI
Did not play in NHL										

1993-94 statistics:

GP	MINS	GAA	W	L	T	SO	GA	S	SAPCT	PIM
31	1614	3.16	13	7	6	0	85	752	.887	4

1994-95 statistics:

GP	MINS	GAA	W	L	T	SO	GA	S	SAPCT	PIM
43	2463	2.61	22	14	6	3	107	1170	.909	2

LAST SEASON
Second in NHL in minutes played. Fifth in NHL in shots faced. Tied for second in NHL in wins.

THE PHYSICAL GAME
Kidd is a butterfly-style goalie who takes away the low part of the net well with his long legs. Most butterfly goalies tend to be smaller, which makes them susceptible on the high corners, but Kidd is so big that he has a better chance of covering those spots.

He is also athletic, with good mobility and agility. He concentrates well to keep his attention on the puck through screens. He plays his angles well and will challenge shooters. He moves the puck well.

Kidd has not been rushed. He had a stint with the Canadian Olympic team, followed by a season in the minors, before his solid rookie debut behind Mike Vernon a season ago. His progress (plus having Andrei Trefilov in the talent pool) allowed the Flames to make the Vernon deal.

He was drafted ahead of Martin Brodeur and Felix Potvin in 1990, but both of those goalies have come along faster, and have had more success in the playoffs.

THE MENTAL GAME
Kidd was not ready for the day-in, day-out pressure of being the number one goalie in the playoffs. He started playing a tentative, in-between game, getting caught out of his net when trying to decide whether to challenge or stand his ground. He went down early, and he allowed untimely goals.

THE INTANGIBLES
Kidd should bounce back strong from his playoff experience. He didn't have a very tough team (mentally or physically) in front of him, and still managed to put up some nice numbers during the regular season.

PAUL KRUSE

Yrs. of NHL service: 3
Born: Merritt, B.C.; March 15, 1970
Position: left wing
Height: 6-0
Weight: 202
Uniform no.: 12
Shoots: left

Career statistics:

GP	G	A	TP	PIM
157	19	17	36	439

1991-92 statistics:

GP	G	A	TP	+/-	PIM	PP	SH	GW	GT	S	PCT
16	3	1	4	+1	65	0	0	0	0	12	25.0

1992-93 statistics:

GP	G	A	TP	+/-	PIM	PP	SH	GW	GT	S	PCT
27	2	3	5	+2	41	0	0	0	0	17	11.8

1993-94 statistics:

GP	G	A	TP	+/-	PIM	PP	SH	GW	GT	S	PCT
68	3	8	11	-6	185	0	0	0	0	52	5.8

1994-95 statistics:

GP	G	A	TP	+/-	PIM	PP	SH	GW	GT	S	PCT
45	11	5	16	+13	141	0	0	2	0	52	21.2

LAST SEASON

Goals career high. Led team in shooting percentage. Led team forwards in plus-minus.

THE FINESSE GAME

Kruse is a prime example of a player who, with natural skating ability and a willingness to work and listen to his coaches, can develop an NHL career with just a modicum of other skills. Kruse spent considerable time in the minors to work on his defensive game. He has become a player who won't make the big game mistake. He will make the short outlet pass, or chip a puck off the boards if that is the safest play. He doesn't seek headlines, just playing time.

He understands defensive zone coverage and how to position himself for the outlet pass. He is fundamentally sound and gaining more confidence with increased playing time.

Kruse is fast in the flat and quick in the corners. A solid skater, he gets good leg drive to work the boards and fore-checks. He does not have great hands, and doesn't handle the puck well when moving, but is smart enough to know his limitations and doesn't try to do too much. Kruse's scoring chances come off forced turnovers and work around the net.

THE PHYSICAL GAME

Solid and sturdy, with a little mean streak, the rugged Kruse is starting to establish a reputation in the NHL and is a player who will have opponents looking over their shoulders. He has piled up the penalty minutes wherever he has played (313 PIM in 83 games with Salt Lake of the IHL in 1990-91, for example), so he has to learn to pick his spots. He is not a legitimate NHL heavyweight, but he will go toe-to-toe with the game's other big men and always acquits himself well.

THE INTANGIBLES

Kruse has to stay hungry to keep earning his spot in the lineup. He is a tough, reliable checking forward who can add 15-20 goals a season if he maintains his position on the third line.

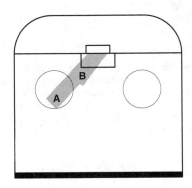

SANDY MCCARTHY

Yrs. of NHL service: 2
Born: Toronto, Ont.; June 15, 1972
Position: right wing
Height: 6-3
Weight: 224
Uniform no.: 15
Shoots: right

Career statistics:

GP	G	A	TP	PIM
116	10	8	18	274

1993-94 statistics:

GP	G	A	TP	+/-	PIM	PP	SH	GW	GT	S	PCT
79	5	5	10	-3	173	0	0	0	0	39	12.8

1994-95 statistics:

GP	G	A	TP	+/-	PIM	PP	SH	GW	GT	S	PCT
37	5	3	8	+1	101	0	0	2	0	29	17.2

LAST SEASON

Second NHL season. Missed games with a strained right knee.

THE FINESSE GAME

A surprisingly high draft pick in 1991 (52nd overall), McCarthy wasn't exactly singled out for his finesse skills. He does have some scoring instincts, however, enough to earn him more than a fourth-line role in the future.

He has a decent shot, but most of his chances will come from in close. A daring coach might even try using him up late on a power play, positioning his massive body to screen the goalie. He is hard to budge from in front of the net.

McCarthy has to work more on his defensive game to become a better all-around player.

THE PHYSICAL GAME

Yet another in the honoured Calgary tradition of drafting large appliances masquerading as hockey players, the massive McCarthy worked at improving his leg strength to get more power out of his stride and be more of a force around the net. McCarthy doesn't back down from any challenge (he accumulated 892 PIM in three seasons in junior, and another 220 with Salt Lake in 1992-93) and was a junior teammate of Gino Odjick, so he knows his way around a hockey fight.

THE INTANGIBLES

Enormous forwards who can also play are a rare and coveted commodity in the NHL. Calgary has added to its stable with McCarthy. He will have to continue to take another stride forward. With good work habits, he could become a 10-15 goal scorer and an intimidating physical presence.

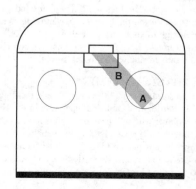

FRANK MUSIL

Yrs. of NHL service: 8
Born: Vysoké Myto, Czechoslovakia; Dec. 17, 1964
Position: left defense
Height: 6-3
Weight: 215
Uniform no.: 3
Shoots: left

Career statistics:

GP	G	A	TP	PIM
606	32	91	123	1052

1991-92 statistics:

GP	G	A	TP	+/-	PIM	PP	SH	GW	GT	S	PCT
78	4	8	12	+12	103	1	1	0	0	71	5.6

1992-93 statistics:

GP	G	A	TP	+/-	PIM	PP	SH	GW	GT	S	PCT
80	6	10	16	+28	131	0	0	0	0	87	6.9

1993-94 statistics:

GP	G	A	TP	+/-	PIM	PP	SH	GW	GT	S	PCT
75	1	8	9	+38	50	0	0	0	0	65	1.5

1994-95 statistics:

GP	G	A	TP	+/-	PIM	PP	SH	GW	GT	S	PCT
35	0	5	5	+6	61	0	0	0	0	18	0.0

LAST SEASON

Missed 13 games with knee injuries.

THE FINESSE GAME

A strong skater with good lateral movement, Musil is tough to beat one-on-one because he surrenders nothing, and he won't be fooled by head fakes. Poised and confident, he has a relaxed look even when he is working hard.

Musil moves well with the puck and can even turn with it on his backhand, but he employs this skill only to skate the puck out of danger in the defensive zone and does not get involved in the attack. He is not very fast and does not overcommit in the offensive zone.

In the neutral zone, he will often step up and challenge. He can start a transition play when he takes the puck away, as he is a smooth passer. His offensive contributions are limited.

THE PHYSICAL GAME

Musil is strong but doesn't play the type of physical game he should on a consistent basis. If anything is lacking, it is his intensity. He can be a presence when he steps up his play. He finishes his checks and is not above adding a little spice by jabbing with his stick.

THE INTANGIBLES

Musil is content to play a conservative game on the Flames' blueline and seldom pushes the envelope.

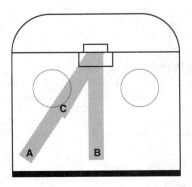

JOE NIEUWENDYK

Yrs. of NHL service: 8
Born: Oshawa, Ont.; Sept. 10, 1966
Position: centre
Height: 6-1
Weight: 195
Uniform no.: 25
Shoots: left

Career statistics:

GP	G	A	TP	PIM
577	314	302	616	316

1991-92 statistics:

GP	G	A	TP	+/-	PIM	PP	SH	GW	GT	S	PCT
69	22	34	56	-1	55	7	0	2	1	137	16.1

1992-93 statistics:

GP	G	A	TP	+/-	PIM	PP	SH	GW	GT	S	PCT
79	38	37	75	+9	52	14	0	6	0	208	18.3

1993-94 statistics:

GP	G	A	TP	+/-	PIM	PP	SH	GW	GT	S	PCT
64	36	39	75	+19	51	14	1	7	1	191	18.8

1994-95 statistics:

GP	G	A	TP	+/-	PIM	PP	SH	GW	GT	S	PCT
46	21	29	50	+11	33	3	0	4	0	122	17.2

LAST SEASON

Second on team in scoring and tied for second on team in assists.

THE FINESSE GAME

If a "puck tipping" contest is ever added to the NHL All-Star Game skills competition, Nieuwendyk would be one of the favourites. He has fantastic hand-eye coordination and not only gets his blade on the puck, he acts as if he knows where he's directing it.

He is aggressive, tough and aware around the net. He can finish or make a play down low. He has the good vision, poise and hand skills to make neat little passes through traffic. He is a better playmaker than finisher, but never doubt that he will convert his chances. Nieuwendyk has good anticipation in the neutral zone, and he uses his long reach to break up passes.

Those same hand skills serve him well on draws and he is defensively sound. Once a 50-goal scorer, knee surgery a few seasons ago robbed him of the necessary quickness to produce those numbers again. Nieuwendyk has become a better all-around player, though.

THE PHYSICAL GAME

He does not initiate, but he will take the punishment around the front of the net and stand his ground. He won't be intimidated, but he won't scare anyone else, either. Nieuwendyk would like to carry more weight, but recurring back and shoulder problems require him to stay on the lean side.

THE INTANGIBLES

Nieuwendyk battled back problems all season and missed only two games, though at one time it was thought he might need surgery. He has been a less effective player since being afflicted.

Once again, his name has cropped up in numerous trade rumours, and he is a likely candidate for a new uniform next season.

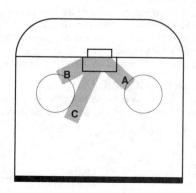

MICHAEL NYLANDER

Yrs. of NHL service: 2
Born: Stockholm, Sweden; Oct. 3, 1972
Position: centre
Height: 5-11
Weight: 184
Uniform no.: 92
Shoots: left

Career statistics:

GP	G	A	TP	PIM
138	24	65	89	68

1992-93 statistics:

GP	G	A	TP	+/-	PIM	PP	SH	GW	GT	S	PCT
59	11	22	33	-7	36	3	0	1	0	85	12.9

1993-94 statistics:

GP	G	A	TP	+/-	PIM	PP	SH	GW	GT	S	PCT
73	13	42	55	+8	30	4	0	1	2	95	13.7

1994-95 statistics:

GP	G	A	TP	+/-	PIM	PP	SH	GW	GT	S	PCT
6	0	1	1	+1	2	0	0	0	0	2	0.0

LAST SEASON

Missed 42 games with a broken wrist.

THE FINESSE GAME

A glimpse of what the Flames had lost almost all season with the injury to Nylander was provided in the playoffs. When he played with German Titov and Robert Reichel, Nylander helped form an excellent line. He has a very high skill level, but defects in his defensive game kept ex-coach Dave King from using him in a regular role. Nylander has to be forgiven for some of his flaws and given a looser rein, because he can make things happen.

An excellent skater with great composure with the puck, Nylander hangs onto the disk and looks at all the options to make a play. This is a gift — not a skill that any coach can teach. In a few seasons, he may rank among the best forwards in holding the puck until the last split second before making the pass (understandably, Wayne Gretzky is his idol). Nylander does things with the puck that are magical.

Nylander knows all about time and space. He is an open ice player, but is all right in perimeter grinding and can survive unless he faces a team with punishing defensemen.

He still needs to improve his shot. If anything, he is guilty of hanging onto the puck too long and passing up quality scoring chances to force a pass to a teammate who is not in as good a position for the shot.

THE PHYSICAL GAME

Nylander is on the small side and plays even smaller, but he is still filling out. He will use his body to protect the puck, though he won't fight hard to get it away from the opposition.

THE INTANGIBLES

Nylander has to show he has gained the maturity to go with his talent. He remains a question mark, but is still only 23. The right coach might bring out a startling season from him.

The young Swede has to realize that the game doesn't revolve around him. He has very good practice habits on ice, but his off-ice work habits need improvement. He is a stranger to the weight room and he needs to be stronger. He loves to play, but he won't get much of a chance until he proves he merits the ice time.

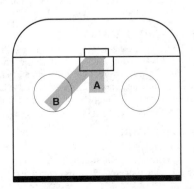

JOEL OTTO

Yrs. of NHL service: 10
Born: Elk River, Minn.; Oct. 29. 1961
Position: centre
Height: 6-4
Weight: 220
Uniform no.: 29
Shoots: right

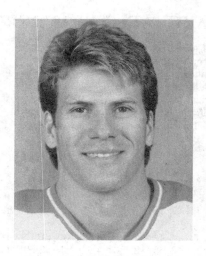

Career statistics:

GP	G	A	TP	PIM
730	167	261	428	1646

1991-92 statistics:

GP	G	A	TP	+/-	PIM	PP	SH	GW	GT	S	PCT
78	13	21	34	-10	163	5	1	3	0	105	12.4

1992-93 statistics:

GP	G	A	TP	+/-	PIM	PP	SH	GW	GT	S	PCT
75	19	33	52	+2	150	6	1	4	1	115	16.5

1993-94 statistics:

GP	G	A	TP	+/-	PIM	PP	SH	GW	GT	S	PCT
81	11	12	23	-17	92	3	1	1	0	108	10.2

1994-95 statistics:

GP	G	A	TP	+/-	PIM	PP	SH	GW	GT	S	PCT
47	8	13	21	+8	130	0	2	2	1	46	17.4

LAST SEASON

Tied for team lead in shorthanded goals. Finalist for 1995 Selke Trophy.

THE FINESSE GAME

Otto remains one of the game's best checking forwards. On draws, he doubles over his huge frame so that his head and shoulders prevent the opposing centre from seeing the puck drop. Helmets clash on Otto's face-offs. He has lost a little hand speed on the draws but is still among the best in the league.

Although he has the build to be a power centre, his production has always been a disappointment. In addition to bulk, power forwards have to have soft hands in deep for tips and rebounds, and Otto does not have the touch.

Otto is not very fast, but he is quite agile for a player of his size, and he is so strong and balanced on his skates that he has to be dynamited out of place. Even players close to his size bounce off him when they try to check him.

THE PHYSICAL GAME

A fierce and intelligent competitor, Otto is big, strong and involved. He knows he is a brute force, and he likes to make people scatter as he drives to the net. He also delivers bruising checks along the wall. He loves the hitting part of the game, and he has the work ethic to perform consistently to his own high level.

THE INTANGIBLES

Otto was overplayed by ex-coach Dave King last season, and used in a lot of situations that weren't his strong suit. Otto will go back to his defensive role this season, whether it's with the Flames or another team (Otto was a free agent). He will be valuable wherever he plays.

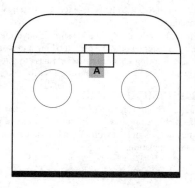

JAMES PATRICK

Yrs. of NHL service: 11
Born: Winnipeg, Man.; June 14, 1963
Position: right defense
Height: 6-2
Weight: 205
Uniform no.: 5
Shoots: right

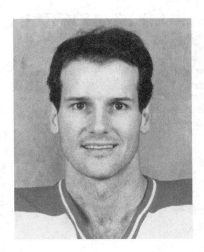

Career statistics:

GP	G	A	TP	PIM
776	114	395	509	593

1991-92 statistics:

GP	G	A	TP	+/-	PIM	PP	SH	GW	GT	S	PCT
80	14	57	71	+34	54	6	0	1	0	148	9.5

1992-93 statistics:

GP	G	A	TP	+/-	PIM	PP	SH	GW	GT	S	PCT
60	5	21	26	+1	61	3	0	0	0	99	5.1

1993-94 statistics:

GP	G	A	TP	+/-	PIM	PP	SH	GW	GT	S	PCT
68	10	25	35	-5	40	5	1	2	1	91	11.0

1994-95 statistics:

GP	G	A	TP	+/-	PIM	PP	SH	GW	GT	S	PCT
43	0	10	10	-3	14	0	0	0	0	43	0.0

LAST SEASON

Failed to score a goal for first time in career. Missed five games with back spasms. Suffered a fractured ankle in playoffs.

THE FINESSE GAME

Patrick is a gifted offensive defenseman, a wonderful, fluid skater. He skates backwards faster than many NHLers can skate forwards. He carries the puck out of the zone or makes the smart first pass and follows up on the play. Defensively he is tough to beat one-on-one, because he can stop on a dime and give six cents change.

The criticism of Patrick over the years is that he makes everything look easy — so easy it looks like he isn't challenging himself, never pushing the envelope to see if there is another level to his game. The flip side of that — the conservative side — is that he is aware of his limitations and plays within them. There will always be two camps of opinion as far as Patrick is concerned.

There is no doubt that Patrick is a better support player than star. He would rather pass than shoot, and if the pass isn't there he will take a stride over the redline and dump in the puck, always timing it well so that his mates are on the chase.

He plays the point on the power play and uses a strong, accurate wrist shot that he keeps low and on net. He will also cheat to the top of the circle for a one-timer.

THE PHYSICAL GAME

Patrick has never played to his size and isn't about to start now. He gets in the way. He bumps. He ties peo-ple up. But he doesn't bulldoze his crease or scrap one-on-one along the boards. He uses his finesse skills as his defense. With a dodgy back, he is even more reluctant to take the body, and he isn't a defenseman who should be on the ice late protecting a lead.

THE INTANGIBLES

Patrick is a class act and a gentleman, a grand addition to any team with young defensemen, since he will take the time and trouble to try to help their development. Patrick's own career is winding down and he has become increasingly fragile. He is not likely to play for Calgary this season, since the team has placed an emphasis on toughness, but he could play a nice number six role with a young team looking for specific offensive help. Since he's from Winnipeg, the Jets would be a nice fit.

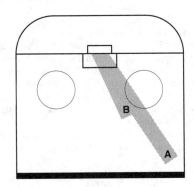

ROBERT REICHEL

Yrs. of NHL service: 5
Born: Litvinov, Czechoslovakia; June 25, 1971
Position: centre
Height: 5-10
Weight: 170
Uniform no.: 26
Shoots: left

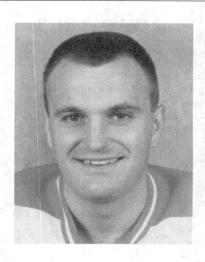

Career statistics:

GP	G	A	TP	PIM
355	137	174	311	196

1991-92 statistics:

GP	G	A	TP	+/-	PIM	PP	SH	GW	GT	S	PCT
77	20	34	54	+1	34	8	0	3	0	181	11.0

1992-93 statistics:

GP	G	A	TP	+/-	PIM	PP	SH	GW	GT	S	PCT
80	40	48	88	+25	54	12	0	5	0	238	16.8

1993-94 statistics:

GP	G	A	TP	+/-	PIM	PP	SH	GW	GT	S	PCT
84	40	53	93	+20	58	14	0	6	0	249	16.1

1994-95 statistics:

GP	G	A	TP	+/-	PIM	PP	SH	GW	GT	S	PCT
48	18	17	35	-2	28	5	0	2	0	160	11.3

LAST SEASON

One of two Flames to appear in all 48 games, Reichel has not missed a game in two seasons. Second on team in power play goals.

THE FINESSE GAME

The key to a great playmaker is how he makes a scoring opportunity materialize when there appears to be no avenue to the net. Reichel does this time and time again. He has great puck control in open ice or along the boards. A possession in the corner turns into a goal as he darts out with the puck, takes a quality shot, follows his own rebound, wheels behind the net and stuffs a wraparound. His pursuit of loose pucks makes you think they're made of platinum. Reichel is not breakaway fast, but he is quick spinning out of traffic.

For a smallish player, Reichel has an explosive shot and he is quick and accurate in its release. He does not fire away enough, but he is so creative with the puck that his playmaking can be as effective as his shot.

THE PHYSICAL GAME

Reichel is willing to play a contact game, though with his one-step quickness he usually tries to avoid a hit instead of absorbing punishment. His good anticipation and ability to stay in constant motion draw many penalties. He does get caught down low, since that's where he likes to work. He has to kick up his defensive game a bit more.

His conditioning has improved, and he can handle the extra ice time a player of his calibre is required to.

THE INTANGIBLES

Reichel's salary arbitration dragged on into the summer, and he may abandon the NHL to play in Germany this season. If he does, the Flames will be minus a player who has shown he is capable of a 100-point season.

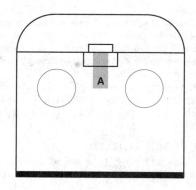

GARY ROBERTS

Yrs. of NHL service: 8
Born: North York, Ont.; May 23, 1966
Position: left wing
Height: 6-1
Weight: 190
Uniform no.: 10
Shoots: left

Career statistics:

GP	G	A	TP	PIM
550	235	228	463	1670

1991-92 statistics:

GP	G	A	TP	+/-	PIM	PP	SH	GW	GT	S	PCT
76	53	37	90	+32	219	15	0	2	3	196	27.0

1992-93 statistics:

GP	G	A	TP	+/-	PIM	PP	SH	GW	GT	S	PCT
58	38	41	79	+32	172	8	3	4	2	166	22.9

1993-94 statistics:

GP	G	A	TP	+/-	PIM	PP	SH	GW	GT	S	PCT
73	41	43	84	+37	145	12	3	5	1	202	20.3

1994-95 statistics:

GP	G	A	TP	+/-	PIM	PP	SH	GW	GT	S	PCT
8	2	2	4	+1	43	2	0	0	0	20	10.0

LAST SEASON

Missed 40 games with recurrence of a neck injury.

THE FINESSE GAME

Of all the many Calgary players sidelined by injury last season, Roberts is the one the Flames missed most desperately.

Roberts is one seriously tough player, and talented as well. He has excellent hands and instincts around the net. He works hard for loose pucks and when he gets control, he wastes little time trying to do anything fancy. As soon as the puck is on his blade, it's launched towards the net. He is not very creative with the puck as a playmaker, either. His theory is, throw it in front and see what happens. Frequently, he creates something good.

Roberts is not an agile skater. He can beat the defender one-on-one on the occasional rush, powered by his strong stride and his ability to handle the puck at a fair pace.

He sees the ice well and will spot an open teammate for a smart pass. He fore-checks well and creates turnovers with his persistent work. A scary sight when he's bearing down on a defenseman, he will force many a hurried pass. An excellent penalty killer, he anticipates well and turns mistakes into shorthanded chances.

Roberts is among the NHL's best at interfering with goalies. He is constantly barreling towards the net and he always makes it look as though the defenseman has pitchforked him into the crease. He's an impact player in more ways than one.

THE PHYSICAL GAME

Roberts has worked hard for his NHL success. In addition to two career-threatening injuries, he fights a constant battle with asthma. For Roberts, hockey is a job that lasts 12 months. He works on conditioning and nutrition, and the results have paid dividends on the ice.

He is strong and determined around the net. He creates a lot of room with his physical play and is respected around the league for his toughness. He works the boards and corners and wins most of his battles.

Roberts has a reputation as a stick man, which makes him feel like he has a target on the back of his jersey as far as the league office is concerned, and it sometimes cramps his aggressive style — but never for long.

THE INTANGIBLES

Roberts is the best on-ice leader on the Flames. He reformed himself from a pure goon into one of the NHL's premier power forwards, a player to go to war with. A healthy Roberts should flirt with the 100-point mark this season.

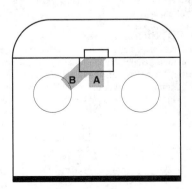

RONNIE STERN

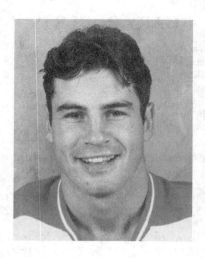

Yrs. of NHL service: 6
Born: Ste-Agathe, Que.; Jan. 11, 1967
Position: right wing
Height: 6-0
Weight: 195
Uniform no.: 22
Shoots: right

Career statistics:

GP	G	A	TP	PIM
362	47	57	104	1500

1991-92 statistics:

GP	G	A	TP	+/-	PIM	PP	SH	GW	GT	S	PCT
72	13	9	22	0	338	0	1	1	0	96	13.5

1992-93 statistics:

GP	G	A	TP	+/-	PIM	PP	SH	GW	GT	S	PCT
70	10	15	25	+4	207	0	0	1	0	82	12.2

1993-94 statistics:

GP	G	A	TP	+/-	PIM	PP	SH	GW	GT	S	PCT
71	9	20	29	+6	243	0	1	3	0	105	8.6

1994-95 statistics:

GP	G	A	TP	+/-	PIM	PP	SH	GW	GT	S	PCT
39	9	4	13	+4	163	1	0	0	0	69	13.0

LAST SEASON

Led team in PIM for second consecutive season. Missed games with a foot injury.

THE FINESSE GAME

Stern is a rugged, seek-and-destroy missile with modest skills. He is not a pretty skater or a good shooter, but he has the offensive instincts to make some smart plays in the attacking zone; his second effort often catches defenders napping. He has some quickness to the puck to get a jump on the defender, and looks for help from his linemates. He will drive to the cage and create his scoring chances off his physical involvement in front of the net.

Stern is not mesmerized by the puck. He doesn't make a lot of pretty plays but instead looks to get rid of the puck quickly with a pass or a shot.

He would be ideally suited as a checking winger but for his lack of skating ability. He also isn't as alert defensively as offensively, but he works hard at whatever task he is given.

THE PHYSICAL GAME

Stern makes his teammates feel a few inches taller and a few pounds heavier. He has no fear of anyone or any situation. He never bails out of a corner no matter what's coming. He's willing and able to go toe-to-toe with anybody. If he plays on a checking line, Stern is defensively aware and finishes every check. He will be on the ice at crunch time to protect a lead. If he plays on a fourth line, he will act as the catalyst, coming out with a strong shift to lift his bench.

THE INTANGIBLES

Stern's mission is to get momentum on the Flames' side. He is an effective fourth-liner. He plays with a sense of purpose now, and by cutting down on bad penalties he has become a more effective player. He just doesn't have the finishing skills to do much more than net 10 goals a season.

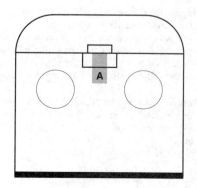

CORY STILLMAN

Yrs. of NHL service: 0
Born: Peterborough, Ont.; Dec. 20, 1970
Position: centre
Height: 6-0
Weight: 180
Uniform no.: 20
Shoots: left

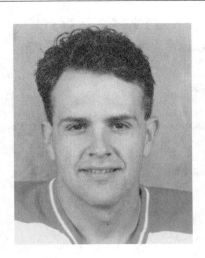

Career statistics:

GP	G	A	TP	PIM
10	0	2	2	2

1994-95 statistics:

GP	G	A	TP	+/-	PIM	PP	SH	GW	GT	S	PCT
10	0	2	2	+1	2	0	0	0	0	7	0.0

LAST SEASON

Will be entering first NHL season. Second on team in scoring for Saint John (AHL) with 28-53 — 81 in 63 games.

THE FINESSE GAME

Stillman is an offensive specialist, but doesn't provide much skill level in the other zones. His offensive talent may not be enough to compensate for his other deficiencies. He is quick and explosive at the minor league level, but doesn't have that next gear (or at least, didn't show it in his brief NHL stint) to make him a player who can burn NHL defensemen. He has good hands and a keen understanding of the game. He's smart and reads plays well. Dale Hawerchuk isn't a great skater, either, but possesses great patience and puckhandling skills, and is efficient in small areas. Stillman has the potential to be that kind of player, if he is supported by gifted wingers.

Stillman needs to play with finishers. He doesn't have a great shot, but he is a fine playmaker. He can run a power play.

Stillman has a one-dimensional game right now, and needs to develop his defensive play.

THE PHYSICAL GAME

Stillman is thick and sturdy enough to absorb some hard hits. He is not overly aggressive, but will protect the puck.

THE INTANGIBLES

Given the talent level and aging centres on the Flames, Calgary may be forced to give Stillman his shot. He is a little short on confidence, but if a new coach has some faith in him, he could show some jump and put up some numbers next season. He needs to be a number two centre.

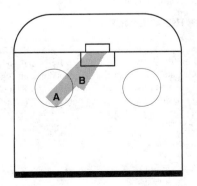

GERMAN TITOV

Yrs. of NHL service: 2
Born: Borovsk, Russia; Oct. 16, 1965
Position: centre/left wing
Height: 6-1
Weight: 190
Uniform no.: 13
Shoots: left

Career statistics:

GP	G	A	TP	PIM
116	39	30	69	44

1993-94 statistics:

GP	G	A	TP	+/-	PIM	PP	SH	GW	GT	S	PCT
76	27	18	45	+20	28	8	3	2	0	153	17.6

1994-95 statistics:

GP	G	A	TP	+/-	PIM	PP	SH	GW	GT	S	PCT
40	12	12	24	+6	16	3	2	3	0	88	13.6

LAST SEASON

Second NHL season. Tied for team lead in short-handed goals. Missed eight games with a groin injury.

THE FINESSE GAME

Whether he plays wing or centre (his preferred position), Titov never merely skates up and down his alley. He uses all of the ice, the way a creative centre does, and shows great hockey sense in both zones. He is very creative, but last season was a streaky scorer. It might help if he can find a comfortable role. He plays a strong one-on-one game, but is sometimes susceptible defensively because he is eagerly pursuing the action in the attacking zone.

Titov is an agile skater. Not outstandingly fast, he is very quick coming off the boards and driving to the circle for a shot. Strong on his skates, he is tough to knock down. He only adds to the Calgary Flames' depth on face-offs with his good hands on the draw.

THE PHYSICAL GAME

Titov uses his good size well. He takes a hit to make a play, blocks shots and sacrifices his body.

He protects the puck in an unusual way, by getting his left leg out to kick away the stick of a defender so that he can sweep- or poke-check him. It's a move that requires superb balance.

THE INTANGIBLES

Titov played his best hockey last season with Robert Reichel and Michael Nylander, and needs to be with the kind of linemates who play a European style of weaving and puck control rather than dump and chase. Titov seemed frustrated at times under ex-coach Dave King's system; the new coach may turn him loose.

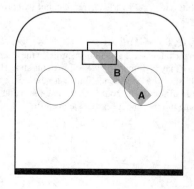

VESA VIITAKOSKI

Yrs. of NHL service: 0
Born: Lappeenranta, Finland; Feb. 13, 1971
Position: left wing
Height: 6-3
Weight: 215
Uniform no.: 19
Shoots: left

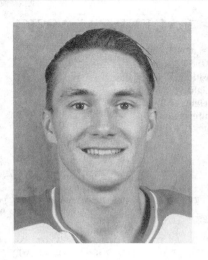

Career statistics:

GP	G	A	TP	PIM
18	2	4	6	6

1993-94 statistics:

GP	G	A	TP	+/-	PIM	PP	SH	GW	GT	S	PCT
8	1	2	3	0	0	1	0	0	0	15	6.7

1994-95 statistics:

GP	G	A	TP	+/-	PIM	PP	SH	GW	GT	S	PCT
10	1	2	3	-1	6	1	0	0	0	6	16.7

LAST SEASON

Will be entering first NHL season. Fourth in scoring for Saint John (AHL) with 17-26 — 43.

THE FINESSE GAME

Viitakoski is a tall, rangy winger who uses his reach well. His skating is only average, but his scoring touch is fine. He will shoot first and ask questions later, a departure from many internationally trained athletes who tend to turn away from the play. He has an excellent shot that he gets away quickly and accurately. Viitakoski is similar to Dave Andreychuk in build and reach, and, like Andreychuk, is a power play specialist: his next even-strength goal will be his first at the NHL level.

Viitakoski played in training camp on a line with Michael Nylander and Theo Fleury, an indication of how highly the Flames thought of him, but when the lockout began he was sent to Saint John, where he struggled. Disappointment may have been a factor, and his attitude may have prevented an immediate recall when the NHL season started. There is nothing fancy about his game. He simply likes to go to the net.

THE PHYSICAL GAME

Viitakoski is a former track and field competitor who is very fit. He needs to prove he is tough enough to play North American-style NHL hockey. He is very strong for work around the net, and is defensively responsible.

THE INTANGIBLES

Viitakoski should get another shot at training camp and if the Flames lose a lot of their free agents during the summer, he could get a slot on the number two line.

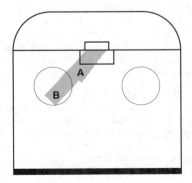

ZARLEY ZALAPSKI

Yrs. of NHL service: 7
Born: Edmonton, Alta.; Apr. 22, 1968
Position: right defense
Height: 6-1
Weight: 210
Uniform no.: 33
Shoots: left

Career statistics:

GP	G	A	TP	PIM
480	84	254	338	496

1991-92 statistics:

GP	G	A	TP	+/-	PIM	PP	SH	GW	GT	S	PCT
79	20	37	57	-7	116	4	0	3	1	230	8.7

1992-93 statistics:

GP	G	A	TP	+/-	PIM	PP	SH	GW	GT	S	PCT
83	14	51	65	-34	94	8	1	0	0	192	7.3

1993-94 statistics:

GP	G	A	TP	+/-	PIM	PP	SH	GW	GT	S	PCT
69	10	37	47	-6	74	1	0	1	0	156	6.4

1994-95 statistics:

GP	G	A	TP	+/-	PIM	PP	SH	GW	GT	S	PCT
48	4	24	28	+9	46	1	0	1	0	76	5.3

THE INTANGIBLES

Zalapski should have another 40-50 point season, while giving his new coach, Pierre Page, headaches.

LAST SEASON

Second among Flames defensemen in scoring. One of two Flames to appear in all 48 games.

THE FINESSE GAME

Zalapski is the ultimate tease. On any given night, he will elicit a "Wow!" and seem destined to be the next impact defenseman. The next night, he will make a mistake that costs his team the game. There is no level of consistency.

Zalapski has all-world offensive skills. He is a tremendous skater with speed and agility. He has great acceleration and scoring instincts to join or lead a rush, though his passing skills are overrated. The problem is that his vision of the ice is so weak that he might as well be hockey blind. He does not see any of his playmaking options, nor is he an intelligent shooter. He simply blasts away from the point. He has a good enough shot to get by, but he could do so much more, and that is what is so frustrating. He could take something off his shot to make it more tippable. He could fake a slap and slide a pass into an open area of the ice. But he does not keep anyone guessing.

Zalapski is not a very good back skater, either. He doesn't read plays coming at him well, which makes him just a mess in the defensive zone.

THE PHYSICAL GAME

Zalapski gets tremendous power from his upper legs and is well conditioned. But he has never established himself physically. He has the potential to be an absolutely dominating defenseman, but until he plays the body instead of the stick, he will never be thought of as more than an offensive defenseman.

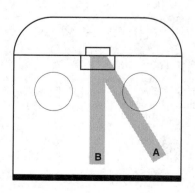

CHICAGO BLACKHAWKS

Players' Statistics 1994-95

POS	NO.	PLAYER	GP	G	A	PTS	+/-	PIM	PP	SH	GW	GT	S	PCTG
C	92	BERNIE NICHOLLS	48	22	29	51	4	32	11	2	5		114	19.3
R	17	JOE MURPHY	40	23	18	41	7	89	7		3		120	19.2
D	7	CHRIS CHELIOS	48	5	33	38	17	72	3	1			166	3.0
D	20	GARY SUTER	48	10	27	37	14	42	5				144	6.9
R	10	TONY AMONTE	48	15	20	35	7	41	6	1	3	1	105	14.3
C	27	JEREMY ROENICK	33	10	24	34	5	14	5		1		93	10.8
L	44	PATRICK POULIN	45	15	15	30	13	53	4		2		77	19.5
C	18	DENIS SAVARD	43	10	15	25	-3	18	2		1		82	12.2
R	25	*SERGEI KRIVOKRASOV	41	12	7	19	9	33	6		2	1	72	16.7
C	11	JEFF SHANTZ	45	6	12	18	11	33	2				58	10.3
C	12	BRENT SUTTER	47	7	8	15	6	51	1		1		65	10.8
R	33	DIRK GRAHAM	40	4	9	13	2	42	1	1			68	5.9
D	2	ERIC WEINRICH	48	3	10	13	1	33	1		2		50	6.0
D	5	STEVE SMITH	48	1	12	13	6	128					43	2.3
L	32	MURRAY CRAVEN	16	4	3	7	2	2	1		2		29	13.8
L	19	BRENT GRIEVE	24	1	5	6	2	23					30	3.3
R	15	JIM CUMMINS	37	4	1	5	-6	158			1		23	17.4
D	6	GERALD DIDUCK	35	2	3	5	-5	63	1				42	4.8
D	8	CAM RUSSELL	33	1	3	4	4	88					18	5.6
D	3	GREG SMYTH	22		3	3	2	33					10	
G	30	ED BELFOUR	42		3	3		11						
L	55	*ERIC DAZE	4	1	1	2	2	2					1	00.0
D	26	ROGER JOHANSSON	11	1		1	1	6					10	10.0
D	4	KEITH CARNEY	18	1		1	-1	11			1		14	7.1
L	34	TONY HORACEK	19		1	1	-4	25					6	
G	49	JIM WAITE	2											
L	23	*DANIEL GAUTHIER	5										4	
G	31	JEFF HACKETT	7											
R	29	DARIN KIMBLE	14				-5	30					2	
C	22	STEVE DUBINSKY	16				-5	8					16	

GP = games played; G = goals; A = assists; PTS = points; +/- = goals-for minus goals-against while player is on ice; PIM = penalties in minutes; PP = power play goals; SH = shorthanded goals; GW = game-winning goals; GT = game-tying goals; S = no. of shots; PCTG = percentage of goals to shots; * = rookie

TONY AMONTE

Yrs. of NHL service: 4
Born: Hingham, Mass.; Aug. 2, 1970
Position: left wing
Height: 6-0
Weight: 185
Uniform no.: 10
Shoots: left

Career statistics:

GP	G	A	TP	PIM
289	100	122	222	182

1991-92 statistics:

GP	G	A	TP	+/-	PIM	PP	SH	GW	GT	S	PCT
79	35	34	69	+12	55	9	0	4	0	234	15.0

1992-93 statistics:

GP	G	A	TP	+/-	PIM	PP	SH	GW	GT	S	PCT
83	33	43	76	0	49	13	0	4	0	270	12.2

1993-94 statistics:

GP	G	A	TP	+/-	PIM	PP	SH	GW	GT	S	PCT
79	17	25	42	0	37	4	0	4	0	195	8.7

1994-95 statistics:

GP	G	A	TP	+/-	PIM	PP	SH	GW	GT	S	PCT
48	15	20	35	+7	41	6	1	3	1	105	14.3

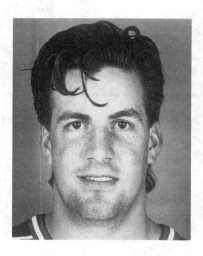

LAST SEASON

One of six Blackhawks to appear in all 48 games.

THE FINESSE GAME

Amonte is blessed with exceptional speed and acceleration. His timing is accurate and his anticipation keen. He has good balance and can carry the puck at a pretty good clip, though he is more effective when streaking down the wing and getting the puck late. Playing on the left side with high school teammate Jeremy Roenick, Amonte's forehand is open for one-timers. He has been called a young Yvan Cournoyer for the way he uses his speed to drive wide around the defense to the net.

He has a quick release on his wrist shot. He likes to go top-shelf, just under the crossbar, and can also go to the backhand shot or a wrist shot off his back foot, like a fadeaway jumper. Amonte is a top power play man, since he is always working himself into open ice. He is an accurate shooter, but is also creative in his playmaking. He passes very well, and is conscious of where his teammates are and usually makes the best percentage play.

Offensively, Amonte is a smart player away from the puck. He sets picks and creates openings for his teammates. Defensively, he still needs to improve his checking and his awareness down low.

THE PHYSICAL GAME

Amonte's speed and movement keep him out of a lot of trouble zones, but he will also drive to the front of the net and take the punishment there if that's the correct play. He loves to score, he loves to help his linemates score, and although he is outweighed by a lot of NHL defensemen, he is seldom outworked.

He takes a lot of abuse and plays through the checks. He seldom takes bad retaliatory penalties. He just keeps his legs driving and draws calls with his non-stop skating.

THE INTANGIBLES

Amonte has a lot of jump, and if Roenick is healthy this season he should be worth 70 points.

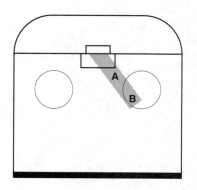

ED BELFOUR

Yrs. of NHL service: 5
Born: Carman, Man.; Apr. 21, 1965
Position: goaltender
Height: 5-11
Weight: 182
Uniform no.: 30
Catches: left

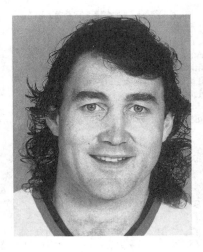

Career statistics:

GP	MINS	GA	SO	GAA	A	PIM
332	18760	824	28	2.64	13	180

1991-92 statistics:

GP	MINS	GAA	W	L	T	SO	GA	S	SAPCT	PIM
52	2928	2.70	21	18	10	5	132	1241	.894	40

1992-93 statistics:

GP	MINS	GAA	W	L	T	SO	GA	S	SAPCT	PIM
71	4106	2.59	41	18	11	7	177	1880	.906	28

1993-94 statistics:

GP	MINS	GAA	W	L	T	SO	GA	S	SAPCT	PIM
70	3998	2.67	37	24	6	7	178	1892	.906	61

1994-95 statistics:

GP	MINS	GAA	W	L	T	SO	GA	S	SAPCT	PIM
42	2450	2.28	22	15	3	5	93	990	.906	11

LAST SEASON

Won 1995 Jennings Trophy (with Jeff Hackett and Jim Waite). Finalist for 1995 Vezina Trophy. Fifth in NHL in GAA. Tied for second in NHL in wins. Tied for NHL shutout lead. Third in NHL in minutes played.

THE PHYSICAL GAME

We don't know this for a fact, but we suspect this is the way Belfour suits up for a game: the trainer strews his equipment all over the floor, then Belfour comes in and rolls around to put everything on. It helps him get warmed up for action.

Belfour is always on his belly, his side, his back. He may be the best goalie with the worst style in the NHL. But hey, it works, at least in the regular season.

He has great instincts and reads the play well in front of him. He plays with an inverted V, giving the five-hole but usually taking it away from the shooter with his quick reflexes. He is very aggressive and frequently comes so far out of his crease that he gets tangled with his own defenders — as well as running interference on the opponents. He knows he is well-padded and is not afraid to use his body.

In fact, Belfour uses his body more than his stick or glove, and that his part of his problem. He tries to make the majority of saves with his torso, thus making the routine saves more difficult.

He tends to keep his glove low and the book on him is to shoot high, but that's the case with most NHL goalies and a lot of NHL shooters have trouble picking that spot.

He sometimes gives up bad rebounds, but his defense is so good and so quick that they will swoop in on the puck before the opposition gets a second or third whack. When play is developing around his net, Belfour uses the odd-looking tactic of dropping his stick low along the ice to take away low shots and lunges at the puck. It's weird, but it's effective.

Belfour has a lot of confidence and an impressive ability to handle the puck, though he sometimes overdoes it. He will usually go for short passes, but can go for the home-run play as well. He uses his body to screen as he is handling the puck for a 15-foot pass.

THE MENTAL GAME

Belfour has to learn to channel his emotions, but it's difficult to put a lid on so intense a competitor. He takes fewer bad penalties, but his attitude isn't always, shall we say, sportsmanlike. After his team was ousted in five games by Detroit in the playoffs, he hustled off the ice and refused to join the traditional handshake line. Sure, Bill Smith used to do the same thing, but Smith was usually in the winning dressing room.

THE INTANGIBLES

Belfour has the no-win situation of playing behind a strong defense, so everyone says the credit belongs to the team instead of the goalie. The two obviously go hand in hand. But yet another dismal playoff collapse by the Hawks has started to raise doubts about Belfour's ability to win the big ones.

CHRIS CHELIOS

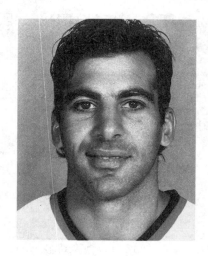

Yrs. of NHL service: 11
Born: Chicago, Ill.; Jan. 25, 1962
Position: right defense
Height: 6-1
Weight: 186
Uniform no.: 7
Shoots: right

Career statistics:

GP	G	A	TP	PIM
767	129	471	600	1786

1991-92 statistics:

GP	G	A	TP	+/-	PIM	PP	SH	GW	GT	S	PCT
80	9	47	56	+24	245	2	2	2	1	239	3.8

1992-93 statistics:

GP	G	A	TP	+/-	PIM	PP	SH	GW	GT	S	PCT
84	15	58	73	+14	282	8	0	2	0	290	5.2

1993-94 statistics:

GP	G	A	TP	+/-	PIM	PP	SH	GW	GT	S	PCT
76	16	44	60	+12	212	7	1	2	0	219	7.3

1994-95 statistics:

GP	G	A	TP	+/-	PIM	PP	SH	GW	GT	S	PCT
48	5	33	38	+17	72	3	1	0	0	166	3.0

LAST SEASON

Led team defensemen in scoring for second consecutive season. Tied for third in NHL in power play assists (20). One of six Blackhawks to appear in all 48 games. Led team in assists, plus-minus and shots. Third on team in points. Finalist for 1995 Norris Trophy. Named to NHL First All-Star Team.

THE FINESSE GAME

Chelios is among the top two-way defensemen in the league. Whatever the team needs they'll get from Chelios. He can become a top offensive defenseman, pinching boldly at every opportunity. He can create offense off the rush, make a play through the neutral zone or quarterback the power play from the point. He has a good, low, hard slap shot. He is not afraid to skate in deep, where he can handle the puck well and use a snap shot or wrist shot with a quick release.

If defense is needed, Chelios will rule in his own zone. He is extremely confident and poised with the puck and doesn't overhandle it. He wants to get the puck away from his net by the most expedient means possible. He is aggressive in forcing the puck carrier to make a decision by stepping up. Chelios also steps up in the neutral zone to break up plays with his stick.

Chelios is an instinctive player. When he is on his game, he reacts and makes plays few other defensemen can. When he struggles, which is seldom, he is back on his heels. He tries to do other people's jobs and becomes undisciplined.

He has excellent anticipation and is a strong penalty killer when he's not doing time in the box himself. He's a mobile, smooth skater with good lateral movement. He is seldom beaten one-on-one, and he's even tough facing a two-on-one. In his mind, he can do anything. He usually does.

THE PHYSICAL GAME

Chelios doesn't seem to tire, no matter how much ice time he gets, and he gets plenty. He is tough and physical, strong and solid on his skates, and has a mean streak the size of Lake Michigan. He plays very strong in front of the net for someone who is considered primarily an offensive defenseman. He is absolutely fearless. He has expressed an interest in playing a full 60 minutes some day. He could do it, too.

Chelios plays with the heart and toughness of a much bigger player. He toils on through adversity, and played in all 16 playoff games with a hairline fracture in his left foot.

THE INTANGIBLES

Chelios knows how much the Hawks rely on him and he relishes his leadership role. He is among the league's elite defensemen and has been for a number of years. Now his only goal is to lead the Hawks to the Stanley Cup, as he helped do in Montreal. But the Canadiens weren't Chelios's team. The Blackhawks are. He needs help, though. The playoffs once again proved that Chelios can't do it all himself, no matter how hard he tries.

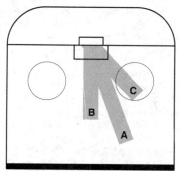

MURRAY CRAVEN

Yrs. of NHL service: 13
Born: Medicine Hat, Alta.; July 20, 1964
Position: left wing/centre
Height: 6-2
Weight: 185
Uniform no.: 32
Shoots: left

Career statistics:

GP	G	A	TP	PIM
801	224	408	632	429

1991-92 statistics:

GP	G	A	TP	+/-	PIM	PP	SH	GW	GT	S	PCT
73	27	33	60	-2	46	9	4	1	1	152	17.8

1992-93 statistics:

GP	G	A	TP	+/-	PIM	PP	SH	GW	GT	S	PCT
77	25	52	77	-1	32	6	3	2	0	151	16.6

1993-94 statistics:

GP	G	A	TP	+/-	PIM	PP	SH	GW	GT	S	PCT
78	15	40	55	+5	30	2	1	3	0	115	13.0

1994-95 statistics:

GP	G	A	TP	+/-	PIM	PP	SH	GW	GT	S	PCT
16	4	3	7	+2	2	1	0	2	0	29	13.8

LAST SEASON

Missed most of season awaiting ruling to determine contract status. Acquired from Vancouver for Christian Ruuttu. Missed games with a back injury.

THE FINESSE GAME

Craven was a mere blip on the NHL screen last season, as he had to wait while his salary figures were determined. He was a highly sought after commodity, because he can do so many things competently. He will check. He will score. He will play first unit on the power play or penalty killing. He will take draws. He will play right wing, left wing or centre. He's the ultimate fill-in forward.

Craven has never attained star status because, while he does a lot of things well, he isn't great at any one thing. He's a good skater, but doesn't have the hockey sense to use it as well he should. He isn't a natural scorer. He has to work hard for his 20 or so goals a season and scores most of them from close range. He does have a good slap shot, though, and can be used on the point on the power play.

Craven is unselfish and, poised down low, he will confidently slide a backhand pass across the goal mouth to a teammate. He goes to the net with determination and has good hands for picking up loose pucks. He has a long reach and can beat a defender one-on-one by using his speed and dangling the puck away from his body but under control. He's no speed demon, but he plays well positionally.

THE PHYSICAL GAME

Craven is wiry but not very big. He loses some one-on-one battles in tight, but he uses his body effectively in the defensive as well as the offensive zone. He never regained the conditioning he lost from missing so much playing time last year.

THE INTANGIBLES

Craven has become a very good defensive role player who can also produce upwards of 20 goals a season — a pretty formidable combination. He is a complete hockey player, one who fits nicely into a role as a number two or number three centre. His numbers dropped sharply last season, which may indicate a more defensive trend in his future.

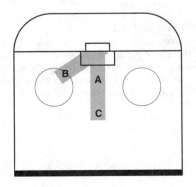

ERIC DAZE

Yrs. of NHL service: 0
Born: Montreal, Que.; July 2, 1975
Position: left wing
Height: 6-4
Weight: 202
Uniform no.: 55
Shoots: left

Career statistics:

GP	G	A	TP	PIM
4	1	1	2	2

1994-95 statistics:

GP	G	A	TP	+/-	PIM	PP	SH	GW	GT	S	PCT
4	1	1	2	+2	2	0	0	0	0	1	100.0

LAST SEASON

Will be entering first full NHL season.

THE FINESSE GAME

While the most impressive thing about Daze (pro-nounced da-ZAY) is his size, it is his skating ability that sets him apart from other lumbering big men. He isn't a speed demon, but he skates well at the NHL level and his playoff performance (coming in fresh out of junior with only four games' worth of NHL experience) was notable. He never looked out of place.

Daze has excellent hands for shooting or scoring, and is an adept stickhandler who can draw defenders to him and then slip a pass through to a teammate. He has good hockey vision and an innate understanding of the game, and is also advanced defensively, especially for a player from the Quebec League, which is generally known for producing one-way talent. He has a surprisingly complete game for a 19-year-old.

THE PHYSICAL GAME

Daze doesn't back down, but he didn't show much initiative, either. It might have been a case of being too green or too shy to throw his weight around. But he needs to make his presence felt. He is simply too big to play small. He will take a hit to make a play, but he is capable of bowling people over and should do so as he drives to the net.

THE INTANGIBLES

Scouts noted Daze's poise under pressure in the play-offs. He was a big scorer in junior (54-45 — 99 in 57 games with Beauport of the QMJHL last season), and if he's able to marry his scoring touch with his power, the Blackhawks will have potent scoring punch from the left side.

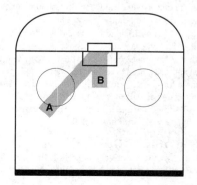

GERALD DIDUCK

Yrs. of NHL service: 10
Born: Edmonton, Alta.; Apr. 6, 1965
Position: right defense
Height: 6-2
Weight: 207
Uniform no.: 6
Shoots: right

Career statistics:

GP	G	A	TP	PIM
624	45	120	165	1215

1991-92 statistics:

GP	G	A	TP	+/-	PIM	PP	SH	GW	GT	S	PCT
77	6	21	27	-3	224	2	0	1	0	128	4.7

1992-93 statistics:

GP	G	A	TP	+/-	PIM	PP	SH	GW	GT	S	PCT
80	6	14	20	+32	171	0	1	0	0	92	6.5

1993-94 statistics:

GP	G	A	TP	+/-	PIM	PP	SH	GW	GT	S	PCT
55	1	10	11	+2	72	0	0	0	0	50	2.0

1994-95 statistics:

GP	G	A	TP	+/-	PIM	PP	SH	GW	GT	S	PCT
35	2	3	5	-5	63	1	0	0	0	42	4.8

LAST SEASON

Acquired from Vancouver for Bogdan Savenko and a third-round draft pick in 1995.

THE FINESSE GAME

One of the better skaters among the big defensemen in the league, Diduck gets a great deal of drive and power from his lower body. He has good balance, is mobile and likes to jump into the play to support the rush. He often gets too caught up in the excitement of the attack, when it would be wiser for him to be more conservative and not pinch.

Diduck makes a strong first pass out of the zone. He doesn't try to carry the puck himself but makes good use of his teammates. The puck travels much faster without him, and he's aware of that.

He has a powerful slap shot but needs a range-finder to get it on net. If he could master the strong, accurate wrist shot from the point, he wouldn't have to listen so often to the discouraging sound of the puck banging off the glass.

He kills penalties well. He doesn't overhandle the puck and he positions his body intelligently.

THE PHYSICAL GAME

Diduck fit in well as a support player on the Chicago defense. He cleans out the front of his crease well, but he falls into occasional lapses where he doesn't get involved physically. His defense has to be physical to be effective.

THE INTANGIBLES

Diduck isn't a dominating defenseman, but he can help make a defense squad deeper as a number five or sometimes a number four. He was a free agent during the summer and might be on the move, though he seems ideal for Chicago.

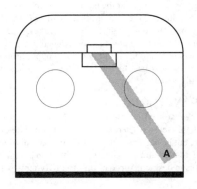

SERGEI KRIVOKRASOV

Yrs. of NHL service: 1
Born: Angarsk, Soviet Union; Apr. 15, 1974
Position: right wing
Height: 5-10
Weight: 174
Uniform no.: 25
Shoots: left

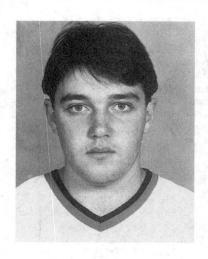

Career statistics:

GP	G	A	TP	PIM
54	13	7	20	39

1992-93 statistics:

GP	G	A	TP	+/-	PIM	PP	SH	GW	GT	S	PCT
4	0	0	0	-2	2	0	0	0	0	0	0.0

1993-94 statistics:

GP	G	A	TP	+/-	PIM	PP	SH	GW	GT	S	PCT
9	1	0	1	-2	4	0	0	0	0	7	14.3

1994-95 statistics:

GP	G	A	TP	+/-	PIM	PP	SH	GW	GT	S	PCT
41	12	7	19	+9	33	6	0	2	0	72	16.7

some power play time last season, and may do so again on the second unit this year.

LAST SEASON

First full NHL season. Tied for third among NHL rookies in power play goals.

THE FINESSE GAME

The Blackhawks were in desperate need of Krivokrasov's creativity last season, but his defensive play was not up to ex-coach Darryl Sutter's standards and the skilled right wing found himself in and out of the lineup.

Krivokrasov controls the puck well and reads offensive plays. He will shoot or pass and has good timing in both areas. He holds onto the puck, drawing defenders and opening up ice for a teammate, before dishing off and heading to the net himself for a give-and-go.

His skating needs to get a hair quicker. He is strong and will drive to the net. Like New Jersey's Valeri Zelepukin, he will score a lot of goals from in tight.

THE PHYSICAL GAME

Krivokrasov is not a physical player. He will use some body work in pursuit of the puck in the offensive zone, but he is not a strong fore-checker. He uses his stick to break up plays. Although strong on his skates, he will never be known as a physical force. There were nights last season when he did hit and on a couple of nights was the team's best forward, but he was inconsistent with his effort.

THE INTANGIBLES

Krivokrasov will have to prove himself to a new coach this season. There is a great deal of upside to his game, but he has to improve his skating and his defensive game to earn a regular role with the Hawks. The team is in desperate need of offense. Krivokrasov saw

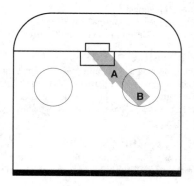

JOE MURPHY

Yrs. of NHL service: 8
Born: London, Ont.; Oct. 16, 1967
Position: right wing
Height: 6-1
Weight: 190
Uniform no.: 17
Shoots: left

Career statistics:

GP	G	A	TP	PIM
452	144	149	293	432

1991-92 statistics:

GP	G	A	TP	+/-	PIM	PP	SH	GW	GT	S	PCT
80	35	47	82	+17	52	10	2	2	2	193	18.1

1992-93 statistics:

GP	G	A	TP	+/-	PIM	PP	SH	GW	GT	S	PCT
19	7	10	17	-3	18	5	0	1	0	43	16.3

1993-94 statistics:

GP	G	A	TP	+/-	PIM	PP	SH	GW	GT	S	PCT
81	31	39	70	+1	111	7	4	4	0	222	14.0

1994-95 statistics:

GP	G	A	TP	+/-	PIM	PP	SH	GW	GT	S	PCT
40	23	18	41	+7	89	7	0	3	0	120	19.2

LAST SEASON

Led team in goals. Second on team in points and power play goals. Missed one game with a sprained knee. Missed three games with a groin injury.

THE FINESSE GAME

Murphy has tremendous speed and great hands. He is creative off the fore-check and has confidence with the puck. He is sometimes too selfish and single-minded when he has made the decision to shoot, even when a better option to pass suddenly presents itself.

He has a lot of zip on his slap and wrist shots. He gets both away quickly and through a crowd, and he's been a high-percentage shooter through much of his career.

Murphy is fairly keen defensively and can kill penalties and take defensive zone draws. He has become a more consistent player but remains below the elite level.

THE PHYSICAL GAME

Murphy makes preemptive hits when going for the puck in the corners — which is a nice way of saying he takes a lot of interference calls. He will use his size and strength in front of the net to establish position, and he'll fight along the wall and in the corners. He's not a big banger or crasher, but he does have a nasty streak.

THE INTANGIBLES

Murphy gets huge chunks of ice time on the top line with Jeremy Roenick and Tony Amonte, but that line faces a lot of checking pressure and Murphy doesn't consistently fight his way through the clinches. There will be enough nights when he can open it up and get his 30-35 goals, but he is not a gamer.

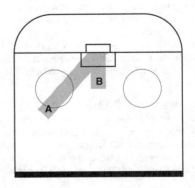

BERNIE NICHOLLS

Yrs. of NHL service: 14
Born: Haliburton, Ont.; June 24, 1961
Position: centre
Height: 6-0
Weight: 185
Uniform no.: 92
Shoots: right

Career statistics:

GP	G	A	TP	PIM
933	438	636	1074	1139

1991-92 statistics:

GP	G	A	TP	+/-	PIM	PP	SH	GW	GT	S	PCT
50	20	29	49	+4	40	7	0	2	0	117	17.1

1992-93 statistics:

GP	G	A	TP	+/-	PIM	PP	SH	GW	GT	S	PCT
69	13	47	60	-13	80	5	0	1	0	132	9.8

1993-94 statistics:

GP	G	A	TP	+/-	PIM	PP	SH	GW	GT	S	PCT
61	19	27	46	+24	86	3	0	1	1	142	13.4

1994-95 statistics:

GP	G	A	TP	+/-	PIM	PP	SH	GW	GT	S	PCT
48	22	29	51	+4	32	11	2	5	0	114	19.3

LAST SEASON

One of six Blackhawks to appear in all 48 games. Led team in points, power play goals and game-winning goals. Tied for team lead in shorthanded goals. Signed as free agent.

THE FINESSE GAME

A loose and loopy personality off the ice, Nicholls exhibits some of those same tendencies on the ice. Sometimes this is a plus, as Nicholls can be wonderfully inventive with the puck, especially when creating plays from behind the net. The downside comes on nights when it looks like his mind is elsewhere. Bad penalties and baffling decisions follow.

Nicholls is an excellent passer, equally deft on the forehand to his left wing or the backhand to his right wing. He has vision and touch. He is best down low. He will not plant himself in front of the net, being a bit too frail for that, but he will linger on the fringes and then move through the goalie's line of sight, either screening or picking a puck out of mid-air for a re-direct. He has quick reactions for picking caroms off the goalie's pads.

Nicholls has turned into an excellent penalty killer. He blocks shots better than many defensemen. While he is not fast, he does pay attention to his positioning.

THE PHYSICAL GAME

Nicholls is strong for his size and has a real nasty streak. When playing with the right bodyguard, he becomes an outrageous opponent. He needles, nettles and intimidates with his words (but he's so funny it's a wonder he doesn't just leave opponents doubled over in laughter). Nicholls is erratic on face-offs. He is fairly quick with his hands, but gets overpowered by bigger centres.

THE INTANGIBLES

Nicholls had a great first half as the Hawks number two centre, but his production vanished along with the injured Jeremy Roenick. He should probably be a third-line centre at this stage of his career, since his defensive play has improved and his production is unreliable.

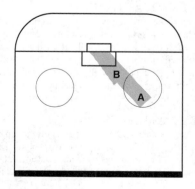

PATRICK POULIN

Yrs. of NHL service: 3
Born: Vanier, Que.; Apr. 23, 1973
Position: left wing
Height: 6-1
Weight: 208
Uniform no.: 44
Shoots: left

Career statistics:

GP	G	A	TP	PIM
194	49	60	109	143

1991-92 statistics:

GP	G	A	TP	+/-	PIM	PP	SH	GW	GT	S	PCT
1	0	0	0	-1	2	0	0	0	0	0	0.0

1992-93 statistics:

GP	G	A	TP	+/-	PIM	PP	SH	GW	GT	S	PCT
81	20	31	51	-19	37	4	0	2	0	160	12.5

1993-94 statistics:

GP	G	A	TP	+/-	PIM	PP	SH	GW	GT	S	PCT
67	14	14	28	-8	51	2	0	3	0	96	14.6

1994-95 statistics:

GP	G	A	TP	+/-	PIM	PP	SH	GW	GT	S	PCT
45	15	15	30	+13	53	4	0	2	0	77	19.5

LAST SEASON

Led team in shooting percentage. Led team forwards in plus-minus.

THE FINESSE GAME

Poulin has all of the tools — size, strength, speed, shot, hands — to be an elite player, and he finally started putting all the elements together last season. He is a dream to coach, since he is intelligent and attentive, but he is also high maintenance, since he gets down on himself and needs to be shored up mentally. As he matures, he has to take more of the burden upon himself to motivate his game. It's not an uncommon tendency for a player who starred at the junior level with little effort, as Poulin did, to try to cruise on talent alone his first season or two in the NHL. The honeymoon is over.

Possessing explosive speed, Poulin can peel off the wing and barrel in with a rifle shot from the circle. He has an excellent shot with a quick release, and his wrist shot is very strong; however, he does not skate well with the puck.

Poulin needs a great deal of work on his defensive game, but he has good hockey instincts and a grasp of positional play.

THE PHYSICAL GAME

Poulin is large in stature but not in on-ice presence. He does not use his body well, doesn't finish his checks and doesn't create the openings on the ice a player of his ability should. Floating should be something Poulin does in the pool, not on the ice.

In terms of conditioning, Poulin is a peak performer who has excellent cardiovascular endurance and can skate all day.

THE INTANGIBLES

Now that Poulin has shown the kind of player he can be, the next step will be to remain consistent and produce a 30-goal season this year. It's certainly within his range of ability physically, but Poulin's greatest question mark is his mental toughness. He did not have a great playoff.

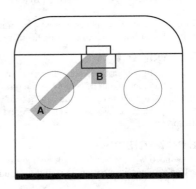

BOB PROBERT

Yrs. of NHL service: 7
Born: Windsor, Ont.; June 5, 1965
Position: right wing
Height: 6-3
Weight: 215
Uniform no.: 24
Shoots: left

Career statistics:

GP	G	A	TP	PIM
474	114	145	259	2090

1991-92 statistics:

GP	G	A	TP	+/-	PIM	PP	SH	GW	GT	S	PCT
63	20	24	44	+16	276	8	0	1	0	96	20.8

1992-93 statistics:

GP	G	A	TP	+/-	PIM	PP	SH	GW	GT	S	PCT
80	14	29	43	-9	292	6	0	3	0	128	10.9

1993-94 statistics:

GP	G	A	TP	+/-	PIM	PP	SH	GW	GT	S	PCT
66	7	10	17	-1	275	1	0	0	0	105	6.7

1994-95 statistics:

P	G	A	TP	+/-	PIM	PP	SH	GW	GT	S	PC
Did not play in NHL											

to live up to, but his biggest hurdles won't be the ones on the ice.

LAST SEASON

Missed full season with NHL-mandated alcohol rehabilitation. Signed as free agent.

THE FINESSE GAME

Probert is a slugger with a nice touch. He needs a little time to get away his shot, but let's face it, not too many brave souls play him that tight. In traffic, he can stickhandle and even slide a backhand pass down low. His shots aren't very heavy, but he is accurate and shoots mostly from close range.

He doesn't have open-ice speed, but in tight he has one-step quickness and can even pivot surprisingly well with the puck. He can be used up front on the power play because he parks himself right in front of the net; the goaltender looks like a bobble-head doll as he tries to peer around Probert's giant frame for a view of the puck. However, Probert was seldom used in this role during his last season with the Red Wings, and has been relied upon less and less as an offensive contributor.

Probert has to play with linemates who get him the puck since he can't help out in pursuing the disk.

THE PHYSICAL GAME

Still the best fighter in the NHL, Probert is strong, quick-fisted and mean, but he is slow to rile on some nights when the other teams decide it is best to let a sleeping dog lie. If he falls asleep on the ice, he is a non-factor.

THE INTANGIBLES

Just how much will Probert have left after sitting out the season? He has a four-year, $6.6-million contract

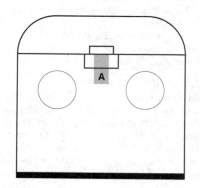

JEREMY ROENICK

Yrs. of NHL service: 7
Born: Boston, Mass.; Jan. 17, 1970
Position: centre
Height: 6-0
Weight: 200
Uniform no.: 27
Shoots: right

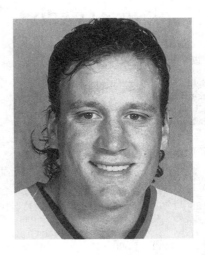

Career statistics:

GP	G	A	TP	PIM
458	235	294	529	461

1991-92 statistics:

GP	G	A	TP	+/-	PIM	PP	SH	GW	GT	S	PCT
80	53	50	103	+23	98	22	3	13	0	234	22.6

1992-93 statistics:

GP	G	A	TP	+/-	PIM	PP	SH	GW	GT	S	PCT
84	50	57	107	+15	86	22	3	3	3	255	19.6

1993-94 statistics:

GP	G	A	TP	+/-	PIM	PP	SH	GW	GT	S	PCT
84	46	61	107	+21	125	24	5	5	1	281	16.4

1994-95 statistics:

GP	G	A	TP	+/-	PIM	PP	SH	GW	GT	S	PCT
33	10	24	34	+5	14	5	0	0	1	93	10.8

LAST SEASON
Missed 15 games with a knee injury.

THE FINESSE GAME
Roenick is driven by an overwhelming desire to succeed. He has a palpable fear of not being respected or considered a winner. That fear pushes him to the max, every shift, every night.

He has great quickness and is tough to handle one-on-one. He won't make the same move or take the same shot twice in a row. He has a variety of shots and can score from almost anywhere on the ice. He can rifle a wrist shot from 30 feet away, or else wait until the goalie is down and lift in a backhand from in tight.

Roenick commands a lot of attention when he is on the ice. He has great acceleration and can turn quickly, change directions or burn a defender with outside speed. A defenseman who plays aggressively against him will be left staring at the back of his jersey as he skips by en route to the net. Roenick has to be forced into the high traffic areas, where his lack of size and strength are the only things that derail him.

He does have some defensive shortcomings once he leaves the fore-checking mode, and he needs to play with at least one defensively alert winger.

THE PHYSICAL GAME
Roenick plays with such a headlong style that injuries are routine, but last year's big hurt was a hit by Derian Hatcher that just caught Roenick wrong. He came back early in the playoffs to try to help his team, but obviously wasn't up to par. He has trouble keeping weight on. He came into camp last season at close to 200 pounds and probably finished around 180.

Roenick takes aggressive penalties — smashing people into the boards, getting his elbows up — and he never backs down. He plays through pain.

THE INTANGIBLES
Roenick was a winner in the power struggle with coach Darryl Sutter (who resigned) and now will be playing for Craig Hartsburg, who has no NHL head coaching experience. The pressure shifts to the player when he is perceived as being responsible for a coaching change (for reference, see Mark Messier after Roger Neilson got axed in New York). Will Hartsburg let Roenick play the kind of creative offensive game he prefers?

Roenick has long been a favourite in our pages. He represents everything that is right about a professional athlete. In an era of high-priced stars who think the world owes them a living, Roenick's first responsibility is to his teammates. He would never demand more from them than he himself would deliver. He is really going to have to come through.

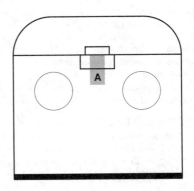

DENIS SAVARD

Yrs. of NHL service: 15
Born: Pointe Gatineau, Que.; Feb. 4, 1961
Position: centre
Height: 5-10
Weight: 175
Uniform no.: 18
Shoots: right

Career statistics:

GP	G	A	TP	PIM
1063	451	812	1263	1167

1991-92 statistics:

GP	G	A	TP	+/-	PIM	PP	SH	GW	GT	S	PCT
77	28	42	70	+12	73	12	1	5	0	174	16.1

1992-93 statistics:

GP	G	A	TP	+/-	PIM	PP	SH	GW	GT	S	PCT
63	16	34	50	+1	90	4	1	2	1	99	16.2

1993-94 statistics:

GP	G	A	TP	+/-	PIM	PP	SH	GW	GT	S	PCT
74	18	28	46	-1	106	2	1	2	0	181	9.9

1994-95 statistics:

GP	G	A	TP	+/-	PIM	PP	SH	GW	GT	S	PCT
43	10	15	25	-3	18	2	0	1	0	82	12.2

LAST SEASON

Acquired from Tampa Bay for a sixth-round pick in 1996.

THE FINESSE GAME

Savard, a former one-way offensive centre, is using his offensive gifts in a more defensive mode. Yes, the spin-o-rama is still there, but now Savard uses it killing penalties and not dazzling defenders.

Savard can still weave his magic when he is behind the net and is given a little time to set up a play. He has learned to rely more on his teammates and less on his diminishing skills. Instead of trying to stickhandle through three defenders, Savard might beat one man and make a play, or beat one man and send the puck deep. Few players work a give-and-go as skillfully as he does. Playing for a deep Chicago team, Savard can be well-spotted.

Great players hang on because they retain their skating ability, and Savard hasn't lost his legs. He is agile and dangerous from the area of the ice between the circles down to the left and right slots. A better playmaker than shooter, he is using his linemates better than he did earlier in his career. He can't beat defenders one-on-one on a consistent basis any more, so he needs the support.

He still depends on a very effective wrist shot — heavy, quick and accurate — as his major weapon.

THE PHYSICAL GAME

Savard does not push along the walls or in the corners. He is strong with the puck only because few people can catch up to him to try to take it away when he is dancing through the crowd. He uses his stick (he had an ugly stick-swinging incident last season). And he's a great actor, drawing frequent calls.

THE INTANGIBLES

Savard was thrilled with his return to Chicago and was one of the team's best playoff forwards. Obviously, he can't be expected to be a top-line centre anymore, but he could contribute another solid season in the right situation.

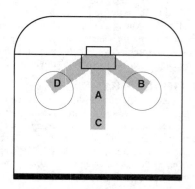

JEFF SHANTZ

Yrs. of NHL service: 2
Born: Duchess, Alta; Oct. 10, 1973
Position: centre
Height: 6-0
Weight: 184
Uniform no.: 11
Shoots: right

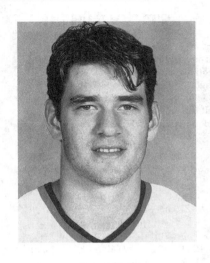

Career statistics:

GP	G	A	TP	PIM
97	9	25	34	63

1993-94 statistics:

GP	G	A	TP	+/-	PIM	PP	SH	GW	GT	S	PCT
52	3	13	16	-14	30	0	0	0	0	56	5.4

1994-95 statistics:

GP	G	A	TP	+/-	PIM	PP	SH	GW	GT	S	PCT
45	6	12	18	+11	33	0	2	0	0	58	10.3

LAST SEASON
Second NHL season. Tied for team lead in short-handed goals.

THE FINESSE GAME
Shantz doesn't excel in many technical areas, but he is one of the best Hawk prospects in terms of hockey sense. He is a smart, two-way centre who can take the crunch-time draws or provide a heady pass in the waning seconds of a game to set up a goal.

A good skater, Shantz is smooth in his turns with average quickness. He handles the puck well and sees his passing options. He won't be forced into many bad passes, preferring to eat the puck rather than toss it away.

He has a decent touch around the net, but he won't score many highlight goals. He has a heavy shot but doesn't have a quick release. Most of his scoring will come from in tight off his fore-checking efforts — perfect for Chicago's dump-and-chase style of attack.

THE PHYSICAL GAME
Shantz is gritty, doesn't take bad penalties and plays hard but clean. He works hard on his conditioning and lifts weights to improve his upper body strength.

THE INTANGIBLES
Shantz is the heir apparent to Brent Sutter as Chicago's best defensive centre. He is already superior to Sutter on draws (he might be the best on the team), and figures to have a future as a checking forward. He won't put big numbers on the board at the NHL level. Around 10-15 goals should be his output.

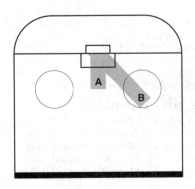

STEVE SMITH

Yrs. of NHL service: 10
Born: Glasgow, Scotland; Apr. 30, 1963
Position: left defense
Height: 6-4
Weight: 215
Uniform no.: 5
Shoots: left

Career statistics:

GP	G	A	TP	PIM
644	71	274	345	1900

1991-92 statistics:

GP	G	A	TP	+/-	PIM	PP	SH	GW	GT	S	PCT
76	9	21	30	+23	304	3	0	1	0	153	5.9

1992-93 statistics:

GP	G	A	TP	+/-	PIM	PP	SH	GW	GT	S	PCT
78	10	47	57	+12	214	7	1	2	0	212	4.7

1993-94 statistics:

GP	G	A	TP	+/-	PIM	PP	SH	GW	GT	S	PCT
57	5	22	27	-5	174	1	0	1	0	89	5.6

1994-95 statistics:

GP	G	A	TP	+/-	PIM	PP	SH	GW	GT	S	PCT
48	1	12	13	+6	128	0	0	0	0	43	2.3

LAST SEASON

One of six Blackhawks to appear in all 48 games. Finalist for 1995 Masterton Trophy.

THE FINESSE GAME

Smith is a tower of strength on the blueline, an aggressive, smart and confident defenseman who probably doesn't get the credit he deserves because he is a complementary player who always makes his partner looks better.

But don't sell Smith short. For one thing, he's huge. For another, he's mobile. And he's developed more confidence to get involved in the attack, which makes him scary in all three zones.

Smith is not a clever passer, but he's effective at getting the puck from point A to point B. He makes a great outlet pass from his defensive zone and can see the second option. He can carry the puck if he has to.

He does not have an overwhelming shot, but it is accurate and low from the point, and he can work on the power play. Defensively, Smith is tough to beat one-on-one. He has great balance, which allows him to drop to one knee, drag his back skate and place his stick flat along the ice while in motion. That shuts off a tremendous stretch of passing lane from the sideboards to the middle. He steps up in the neutral zone and plays aggressively to kill penalties.

THE PHYSICAL GAME

Smith is a powerful and punishing hitter whose only problem is that he's too tall. When he works along the boards, smaller players are sometimes able to wriggle free underneath him, if they're tenacious enough.

He's a force in front of the net and is an intimidat-ing presence. He doesn't get in many fights, but he will keep 90 per cent of the players wondering and worrying. Smith lost a little bit of power last year due to his recovery from a broken leg (in 1993-94) and the short conditioning period for last season.

THE INTANGIBLES

Smith has become the kind of reliable defenseman that his skills promised he would someday be. His head has caught up to the rest of him and he should have several more seasons of rating among the league's best. One thing he does not do is dominate the game. Despite his size, he is more effective in a quiet way.

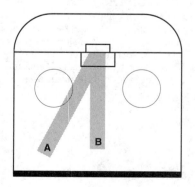

GARY SUTER

Yrs. of NHL service: 10
Born: Madison, Wisc.; June 24, 1964
Position: left defense
Height: 6-0
Weight: 190
Uniform no.: 20
Shoots: left

Career statistics:

GP	G	A	TP	PIM
681	140	467	607	930

1991-92 statistics:

GP	G	A	TP	+/-	PIM	PP	SH	GW	GT	S	PCT
70	12	43	55	+1	126	4	0	0	0	189	6.3

1992-93 statistics:

GP	G	A	TP	+/-	PIM	PP	SH	GW	GT	S	PCT
81	23	58	81	-1	112	10	1	2	1	263	8.7

1993-94 statistics:

GP	G	A	TP	+/-	PIM	PP	SH	GW	GT	S	PCT
41	6	12	18	-12	38	4	1	0	0	86	7.0

1994-95 statistics:

GP	G	A	TP	+/-	PIM	PP	SH	GW	GT	S	PCT
48	10	27	37	+14	42	5	0	0	0	144	6.9

LAST SEASON

One of six Blackhawks to appear in all 48 games. Second on team in plus-minus.

THE FINESSE GAME

Suter has great natural skills, starting with his skating. He is secure on his skates with a wide stance for balance. He has all of the components that make a great skater: acceleration, flat-out speed, quickness and mobility. He skates well backwards and can't be bested one-on-one except by the slickest skaters. He loves to jump into the attack, and he will key a rush with a smooth outlet pass or carry the puck and lead the parade.

Suter has a superb shot. It's not scary-hard, but Suter will keep his shot low. With his good friend, Chris Chelios, now working the points with him in Chicago, Suter will be given free rein to quarterback the team's power play, and he will help them improve.

Not a great playmaker, his creativity comes from his speed and his dangerous shot. He can handle some penalty-killing time, though it is not his strong suit.

THE PHYSICAL GAME

If Suter pays attention to off-ice conditioning, he will be able to play 30 minutes a game. He is a mean hitter (it was his check in the 1991 Canada Cup that was the source of Wayne Gretzky's back troubles). But he can get too carried away with the hitting game and will take himself out of position, even when penalty killing. He doesn't like to be hit; he'll bring his stick up at the last second before contact to protect himself. His defensive reads are average to fair, and he doesn't play hard consistently, though he did a better job last season than he has in years.

THE INTANGIBLES

Suter may be a notch below the league's elite defensemen, but he can handle a lot of responsibility. He was hampered by a hand injury in the playoffs and the Blackhawks missed him. Even when he did come back, he had to play with a cast that restricted his stickhandling.

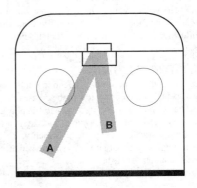

ERIC WEINRICH

Yrs. of NHL service: 5
Born: Roanoke, Va.; Dec. 19, 1966
Position: right defense
Height: 6-1
Weight: 210
Uniform no.: 2
Shoots: left

Career statistics:

GP	G	A	TP	PIM
362	27	129	156	258

1991-92 statistics:

GP	G	A	TP	+/-	PIM	PP	SH	GW	GT	S	PCT
76	7	25	32	+10	55	5	0	0	0	97	7.2

1992-93 statistics:

GP	G	A	TP	+/-	PIM	PP	SH	GW	GT	S	PCT
79	7	29	36	-11	76	0	2	2	0	104	6.7

1993-94 statistics:

GP	G	A	TP	+/-	PIM	PP	SH	GW	GT	S	PCT
62	4	24	28	+1	35	2	0	2	0	115	3.5

1994-95 statistics:

GP	G	A	TP	+/-	PIM	PP	SH	GW	GT	S	PCT
48	3	10	13	+1	33	1	0	2	0	50	6.0

LAST SEASON

One of six Blackhawks to appear in all 48 games.

THE FINESSE GAME

Being paired with Chris Chelios may be the best thing to ever happen to Weinrich. When he has to carry the mail himself, he is a less useful player. When the pressure is off and he is playing with a superior defenseman, his game comes through. He doesn't have to do anything fancy, just move the puck and move up into the play, and he can do this quite nicely.

Weinrich's skating is above average. He accelerates quickly and has good straightaway speed, but he doesn't have great balance for pivots or superior leg drive for power. He has worked to improve his skating but needs to get even better. He is not sturdy on his feet.

He is strong on the puck, shooting and passing hard. He works on the point on the first power play unit and has a low, accurate shot that he gets away quickly. He will not gamble down low, but will sometimes sneak into the top of the circle for a one-timer. His offensive reads are much better than his defensive reads.

THE PHYSICAL GAME

Weinrich is a good one-on-one defender, but he needs to take the body better down low in the crease area. He always has a high conditioning level and can play a lot of minutes. He is not a soft player (a criticism that dogged him early in his career). Weinrich will fight. It's not in his nature, but he won't get pushed around and will stand up for his teammates.

Lower-body strength and balance continue to be a weakness, causing him to lose some battles to smaller players.

THE INTANGIBLES

Weinrich is not the kind of player who will make others around him better, but he is a complementary defenseman. He can do a lot of nice things offensively, but will probably never burst out of the 35-40 point range.

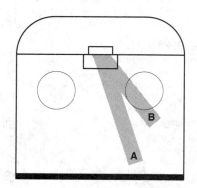

COLORADO

Players' Statistics 1994-95

POS	NO.	PLAYER	GP	G	A	PTS	+/-	PIM	PP	SH	GW	GT	S	PCTG
C	19	JOE SAKIC	47	19	43	62	7	30	3	2	5		157	12.1
C	21	*PETER FORSBERG	47	15	35	50	17	16	3		3		86	17.4
R	11	OWEN NOLAN	46	30	19	49	21	46	13	2	8		137	21.9
R	48	SCOTT YOUNG	48	18	21	39	9	14	3	3			167	10.8
C	9	MIKE RICCI	48	15	21	36	5	40	9		1	1	73	20.5
L	17	WENDEL CLARK	37	12	18	30	-1	45	5				95	12.6
L	13	VALERI KAMENSKY	40	10	20	30	3	22	5	1	5		70	14.3
C	28	BOB BASSEN	47	12	15	27	14	33		1	1		66	18.2
R	51	ANDREI KOVALENKO	45	14	10	24	-4	31	1		3		63	22.2
D	4	UWE KRUPP	44	6	17	23	14	20	3		1	1	102	5.9
R	18	*ADAM DEADMARSH	48	9	8	17	16	56			1		48	18.8
D	7	CURTIS LESCHYSHYN	44	2	13	15	29	20					43	4.7
D	2	SYLVAIN LEFEBVRE	48	2	11	13	13	17					81	2.5
C	47	CLAUDE LAPOINTE	29	4	8	12	5	41					40	10.0
L	12	CHRIS SIMON	29	3	9	12	14	106					33	9.1
L	25	MARTIN RUCINSKY	20	3	6	9	5	14					32	9.4
D	6	CRAIG WOLANIN	40	3	6	9	12	40					36	8.3
D	52	ADAM FOOTE	35		7	7	17	52					24	
L	15	BILL HUARD	33	3	3	6		77				1	21	14.3
R	23	PAUL MACDERMID	14	3	1	4	3	22		1			13	23.1
R	14	*DWAYNE NORRIS	13	1	2	3	1	2		1			7	14.3
D	5	ALEXEI GUSAROV	14	1	2	3	-1	6			1		7	14.3
L	20	*RENE CORBET	8		3	3	3	2					4	
D	31	*AARON MILLER	9		3	3	2	6					12	
D	22	*JANNE LAUKKANEN	11		3	3	3	4					12	
G	35	STEPHANE FISET	32		3	3		2						
D	29	STEVEN FINN	40		3	3	1	64					28	
D	24	*JON KLEMM	4	1		1	3	2					5	20.0
G	1	*GARTH SNOW	2											
G	41	JOCELYN THIBAULT	18											

GP = games played; G = goals; A = assists; PTS = points; +/- = goals-for minus goals-against while player is on ice; PIM = penalties in minutes; PP = power play goals; SH = shorthanded goals; GW = game-winning goals; GT = game-tying goals; S = no. of shots; PCTG = percentage of goals to shots; * = rookie

WENDEL CLARK

Yrs. of NHL service: 10
Born: Kelvington, Sask.; Oct. 25, 1966
Position: left wing
Height: 5-11
Weight: 195
Uniform no.: 17
Shoots: left

Career statistics:

GP	G	A	TP	PIM
500	220	164	538	1388

1991-92 statistics:

GP	G	A	TP	+/-	PIM	PP	SH	GW	GT	S	PCT
43	19	21	40	-14	123	7	0	4	0	158	12.0

1992-93 statistics:

GP	G	A	TP	+/-	PIM	PP	SH	GW	GT	S	PCT
66	17	22	39	+2	193	2	0	5	1	146	11.6

1993-94 statistics:

GP	G	A	TP	+/-	PIM	PP	SH	GW	GT	S	PCT
64	46	30	76	+10	115	21	0	8	0	275	16.7

1994-95 statistics:

GP	G	A	TP	+/-	PIM	PP	SH	GW	GT	S	PCT
37	12	18	30	-1	45	5	0	0	0	95	12.6

LAST SEASON

Missed 11 games with a thigh injury.

THE FINESSE GAME

To Clark, a goalie is a waving red flag and he is the bull. Two seasons ago, he lost a few inches off his stick and added a bushel of goals to his statistics. Before, his big shots were getting deflected too much. Now his hands are up higher on the stick, like Brett Hull's, and the results showed in a higher shot total, since he missed the net less often. He can still over-power a goalie from the blueline, even with his wrist shot, which has tremendous power.

Not a clever player, Clark rarely passes the puck. His effectiveness depends on him charging down the ice, wreaking havoc and letting his teammates trail in his wake, picking through the debris to make a play. When Clark gets the puck, he has to shoot in. He gets into trouble when he makes plays.

Clark is not a smart player positionally. Although a strong skater, he's not very agile, fast or mobile. When he's playing well, he uses his leg-drive like a linebacker in football to hit hard.

THE PHYSICAL GAME

Clark is just plain mean. He hits when it's least ex-pected, often well away from the play. He had to write a $1,000 check for an elbow to New York's Alexei Kovalev in the 1995 playoffs, but that didn't slow him a bit. He kept on head-hunting, and you can be sure he got his money's worth. Clark is a big, big hitter who hurts. He's a strong fore-checker, but gets frustrated when his scoring touch deserts him and will run around and take bad penalties.

THE INTANGIBLES

Although Clark has spent more time on maintenance and conditioning programs, injuries struck again late in the season and he failed to regain his confidence and scoring touch. He is a team leader by example, but his tendency to get injured makes him a risky prospect to count on for a full season.

Clark gives everything he's got, but who knows how much is left.

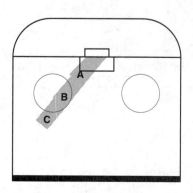

ADAM DEADMARSH

Yrs. of NHL service: 1
Born: Trail, B.C.; May 10, 1975
Position: right wing
Height: 6-0
Weight: 195
Uniform no.: 18
Shoots: right

Career statistics:

GP	G	A	TP	PIM
48	9	8	17	56

1994-95 statistics:

GP	G	A	TP	+/-	PIM	PP	SH	GW	GT	S	PCT
48	9	8	17	+16	56	0	0	0	1	48	18.8

LAST SEASON

First NHL season. One of four Nordiques to appear in all 48 games. Second among NHL rookies in plus-minus. Tied for fourth among NHL rookies in shooting percentage.

THE FINESSE GAME

Deadmarsh is a bigger version of Kevin Dineen. He's feisty and tough and can work in a checking role, but he can also score off the chances he creates with his defense. Despite his youth, he was probably the most consistent checker with Quebec last season. Deadmarsh has dangerous speed and quickness. He has a good scoring touch to convert the chances he creates off his fore-checking. He can play centre as well as both wings, so he is versatile. He doesn't play a very creative game. He's a basic up-and-down winger, a nice complement to all of the flash and dash on the Nordiques last season, and a dedicated penalty killer.

THE PHYSICAL GAME

Deadmarsh always finishes his checks. He has a strong work ethic with honest toughness. He never backs down from a challenge and issues some of his own.

THE INTANGIBLES

Finding ice time for Deadmarsh last season was a problem with a team so deep up front, but he is projected to become one of their top nine forwards in the next season or two. He was a good scorer at the junior level, but it's his diligent two-way game that will make him a regular in the NHL. Great character and toughness.

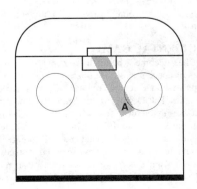

STEPHANE FISET

Yrs. of NHL service: 3
Born: Montreal, Que.; June 17, 1970
Position: goaltender
Height: 6-0
Weight: 175
Uniform no.: 35
Catches: left

Career statistics:

GP	MINS	G	SO	AVG	A	PIM
151	8277	472	5	3.43	8	18

1991-92 statistics:

GP	MINS	GAA	W	L	T	SO	GA	S	SAPCT	PIM
23	1133	3.76	7	10	2	1	71	646	.890	6

1992-93 statistics:

GP	MINS	GAA	W	L	T	SO	GA	S	SAPCT	PIM
37	1939	3.40	18	9	4	0	110	945	.884	2

1993-94 statistics:

GP	MINS	GAA	W	L	T	SO	GA	S	SAPCT	PIM
50	2798	3.39	20	25	4	2	158	1434	.890	8

1994-95 statistics:

GP	MINS	GAA	W	L	T	SO	GA	S	SAPCT	PIM
32	1879	2.78	17	10	3	2	87	968	.910	2

LAST SEASON

Career-best GAA. Missed four games with a back injury.

THE PHYSICAL GAME

Fiset plays a butterfly style and looks an awful lot like his former teammate, Ron Hextall, in the way he faces shooters. When he's on his game, Fiset appears enormous in the net.

With his very quick hands and feet, Fiset dares shooters to go for the upper corners, then snaps out a glove hand, which he normally carries a bit low. In close, he is especially good because of his reflexes.

Fiset's major weaknesses lie in his use of the stick and control of his rebounds, and the two are connected. He handles the puck well on hard-arounds and moves the puck well.

He could poke or sweep away the puck with a stronger stick. He has improved in angle play and lets in fewer soft goals. Fiset is starting to rely less on his reflexes and is becoming more of a student of the game.

THE MENTAL GAME

Fiset has become a better battler, but still suffers lapses of concentration. He doesn't control the puck and play with the kind of command that very successful goalies (Patrick Roy, Martin Brodeur) demonstrate when they are on form. His teammates have yet to develop the kind of confidence in him that the team needs to take its place among the NHL's elite, but that's not to say Fiset won't ever get to that stage. He is maturing, and doesn't get rattled so easily anymore.

Fiset was rushed to the NHL at 19 with a develop-

ing franchise. The damage has yet to be fully repaired.

THE INTANGIBLES

Fiset and Jocelyn Thibault may share the goaltending duties until one emerges as a true number one goalie — and the two of them will be pushed by minor leaguer Garth Snow. Fiset will probably benefit from the move to Colorado, since Thibault was the crowd favorite at Le Colisee and Fiset sulked because of it. He has to get over that to emerge as the number one netminder in Denver.

ADAM FOOTE

Yrs. of NHL service: 4
Born: Toronto, Ont.; July 10, 1971
Position: right defense
Height: 6-1
Weight: 202
Uniform no.: 52
Shoots: right

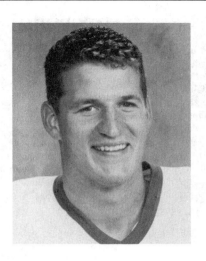

Career statistics:

GP	G	A	TP	PIM
207	8	29	37	331

1991-92 statistics:

GP	G	A	TP	+/-	PIM	PP	SH	GW	GT	S	PCT
46	2	5	7	-4	44	0	0	0	1	55	3.6

1992-93 statistics:

GP	G	A	TP	+/-	PIM	PP	SH	GW	GT	S	PCT
81	4	12	16	+6	168	0	1	0	0	54	7.4

1993-94 statistics:

GP	G	A	TP	+/-	PIM	PP	SH	GW	GT	S	PCT
45	2	6	8	+3	67	0	0	0	0	42	4.8

1994-95 statistics:

GP	G	A	TP	+/-	PIM	PP	SH	GW	GT	S	PCT
35	0	7	7	+17	52	0	0	0	0	24	0.0

LAST SEASON

Missed two games with a back injury and 11 games with groin injuries.

THE FINESSE GAME

Foote has great foot speed and quickness. Defensively, he's strong in his coverage and is a stay-at-home type. He is not creative with the puck, probably his biggest deficiency, but he was strong in that department as a junior player and there is hope he can recover some of that knack. Even if he doesn't, he is so competitive that he can always earn a spot on any team's roster.

Foote usually skates the puck out of his zone. He is less likely to find the man for an outlet pass. There are few defensemen in the league who can match him in getting the first few strides in and jumping out of the zone. He is an excellent penalty killer.

THE PHYSICAL GAME

Foote is big and solid and uses his body well. He is highly aggressive is his defensive zone, and anyone trying to get through Foote to the net will pay a price. He plays it smart and takes few bad penalties.

THE INTANGIBLES

Foote has a history of freakish injuries. He underwent back surgery in the off-season of 1994, so his conditioning last season wasn't at the level it should have been. A full, healthy season would allow him to contribute regularly to a team.

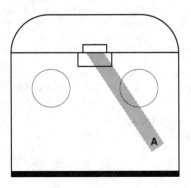

PETER FORSBERG

Yrs. of NHL service: 1
Born: Omskoldsvik, Sweden; July 20, 1973
Position: centre
Height: 5-11
Weight: 190
Uniform no.: 21
Shoots: left

Career statistics:

GP	G	A	TP	PIM
47	15	35	50	16

1994-95 statistics:

GP	G	A	TP	+/-	PIM	PP	SH	GW	GT	S	PCT
47	15	35	50	+17	16	3	0	3	0	86	17.4

LAST SEASON

First NHL season. Won 1995 Calder Trophy. Led NHL rookies in points, assists, power play assists (12) and plus-minus. Tied for NHL rookie lead in game-winning goals. Second on team in assists and points. Missed one game with the flu.

THE FINESSE GAME

Imagine being billed for three years as the best player not yet in the NHL, then finally arriving and not only meeting — but far exceeding — the advance hype.

That was the case with Forsberg last year. Given time early in the shortened season to feel his way around the league, he got better and better as the season progressed; by the end of the year he was among the team's leaders in ice time. Forsberg can be used in all game situations: power play, penalty killing and four-on-four. His skill level is amazing.

Forsberg protects the puck as well as anybody in the league. He is strong, tough, and his passing is nearly as good as teammate Joe Sakic's. In fact, Denver now has two of the top four or five playmakers in the league in Sakic and Forsberg, which is joyous news to their wingers, but should depress the heck out of the rest of the NHL.

Forsberg is a smooth skater with explosive speed (think Teemu Selanne) and can accelerate while carrying the puck. He has excellent vision of the ice and is an outstanding playmaker. One of the few knocks on him is that he doesn't shoot enough. He is best down between the circles with a wrist or backhand shot off the rush.

Defensively, his down-low coverage has to improve some, but he is well advanced for a rookie and he's a quick study. Forsberg is a complete package.

THE PHYSICAL GAME

Forsberg is better suited for the North American style than most Europeans — or many North Americans, for that matter. He is tough to knock down. He loves the game and dishes out more than he receives. He relishes contact. Just try to knock him off the puck. He has a wide skating base and great balance.

Forsberg has a cockiness that many great athletes carry about them like an aura, and he can expect to be challenged. His drive to succeed will help him handle the cheap stuff and keep going.

THE INTANGIBLES

Forsberg can easily take his place among the league's top three forwards. Over the next few seasons, it will be he, Eric Lindros and Jaromir Jagr dominating All-Star games and trophy balloting. (Just imagine if his rights hadn't been included in the package Philadelphia sent to Quebec for Lindros, then both studs would have been on the same team.) We predicted in last year's *HSR* that Forsberg would be in the top 20 scorers in his rookie year. He was tied for 14th. He's only going to get better. Next season, top ten.

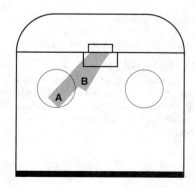

UWE KRUPP

Yrs. of NHL service: 9
Born: Cologne, West Germany; June 24, 1965
Position: right defense
Height: 6-6
Weight: 235
Uniform no.: 4
Shoots: right

Career statistics:

GP	G	A	TP	PIM
551	53	167	220	546

1991-92 statistics:

GP	G	A	TP	+/-	PIM	PP	SH	GW	GT	S	PCT
67	8	29	37	+13	49	2	0	0	0	128	6.3

1992-93 statistics:

GP	G	A	TP	+/-	PIM	PP	SH	GW	GT	S	PCT
80	9	29	38	+7	67	2	0	2	0	116	7.8

1993-94 statistics:

GP	G	A	TP	+/-	PIM	PP	SH	GW	GT	S	PCT
41	7	14	21	+11	30	3	0	0	0	82	8.5

1994-95 statistics:

GP	G	A	TP	+/-	PIM	PP	SH	GW	GT	S	PCT
44	6	17	23	+14	20	3	0	1	1	102	5.9

LAST SEASON

Led team defensemen in scoring. Scored first career hat trick. Missed four games with hip injuries.

THE FINESSE GAME

Krupp has a hard shot, but it takes him far too long to get his big slapper underway and it is often blocked. Because he is so tall and uses such a long stick, he doesn't one-time the puck well but instead must stop it and tee it up. He has a good wrist shot that he can use to better purpose, because he can get it away cleanly and with some velocity.

He reads plays well both offensively and defensively. He is a good skater for his size and makes sure to position himself well so he needs only a stride to cut off the attacker. He is very steady and has been moved more and more into a defensive role, though he has sharp offensive instincts and can quarterback a power play.

Krupp helped his team immeasurably by his ability to move the puck smartly out of the zone. He is a smooth passer and creates a lot of odd-man rushes by spotting the developing play and making the solid first pass.

Occasionally, Krupp will go coast-to-coast with the puck. He's not a great stickhandler, but he can fend off an attacker with one arm and protect the puck.

THE PHYSICAL GAME

Krupp is enormous and takes up a lot of space on the ice, but doesn't use his body as a weapon. It's more of a roadblock, and it's one heck of a detour to get around. Krupp blocks shots willingly and is a very good penalty killer. He plays with restraint and takes few bad penalties. Checkers seem to bounce off him. On the rare nights when he gets physical, he can dominate, but he doesn't often play that way. Krupp saw a lot of ice time, and seemed to tire late last season.

THE INTANGIBLES

Krupp is reliable and sensible and can be used to protect a lead. He has been used with a lot of partners and complements all of them well, especially younger defenseman. He is a steadying influence.

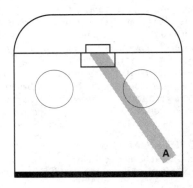

SYLVAIN LEFEBVRE

Yrs. of NHL service: 6
Born: Richmond, Que.; Oct. 14, 1967
Position: right defense
Height: 6-2
Weight: 204
Uniform no.: 2
Shoots: left

Career statistics:

GP	G	A	TP	PIM
413	17	74	91	368

1991-92 statistics:

GP	G	A	TP	+/-	PIM	PP	SH	GW	GT	S	PCT
69	3	14	17	+9	91	0	0	0	0	85	3.5

1992-93 statistics:

GP	G	A	TP	+/-	PIM	PP	SH	GW	GT	S	PCT
81	2	12	14	+8	90	0	0	0	0	81	2.5

1993-94 statistics:

GP	G	A	TP	+/-	PIM	PP	SH	GW	GT	S	PCT
84	2	9	11	+33	79	0	0	0	1	96	2.1

1994-95 statistics:

GP	G	A	TP	+/-	PIM	PP	SH	GW	GT	S	PCT
48	2	11	13	+13	17	0	0	0	0	81	2.5

LAST SEASON

One of four Nordiques to appear in all 48 games.

THE FINESSE GAME

Lefebvre is a good argument for instituting an NHL award for defensive defensemen (as opposed to the Norris Trophy, which in recent years has gone to offensive defensemen). If there were such a piece of hardware, Lefebvre would be a finalist, if not a winner. He's one of the best at one-on-one coverage. He's always in position and always square with his man. He reads the play well, makes good outet passes from out of his own end, and has a smidge of offensive ability to boot. Lefebvre even saw some power play time last season.

Lefebvre plays his position the way any coach would try to teach it to a youngster. Safe and dependable, Lefebvre makes the first pass and then forgets about the puck. He couldn't be any less interested in the attack. If he has the puck at the offensive blueline and doesn't have a lane, he just throws it into the corner. His game is defense first, and he is very basic and consistent in his limited role. He does it all playing his "wrong" side on defense and matching up against the other team's top lines on a nightly basis.

Lefebvre actually has below-average skills in speed and puckhandling, but by playing within his boundaries and within the system he is ultrareliable. His acquisition helped the Nordiques improve from 21st in team defense in 1993-94 to ninth last season.

THE PHYSICAL GAME

Tough without being a punishing hitter, Lefebvre patrols and controls the front of his net and plays a hard-nosed style. He plays a containment game.

THE INTANGIBLES

Lefebvre is a rock-solid defensive defenseman. He is a quiet leader, well respected by teammates and opponents.

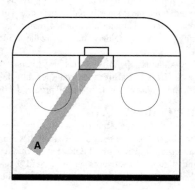

CURTIS LESCHYSHYN

Yrs. of NHL service: 7
Born: Thompson, Man.; Sept. 21, 1969
Position: left defense
Height: 6-1
Weight: 205
Uniform no.: 7
Shoots: left

Career statistics:

GP	G	A	TP	PIM
439	29	85	114	430

1991-92 statistics:

GP	G	A	TP	+/-	PIM	PP	SH	GW	GT	S	PCT
42	5	12	17	-28	42	3	0	1	0	61	8.2

1992-93 statistics:

GP	G	A	TP	+/-	PIM	PP	SH	GW	GT	S	PCT
82	9	23	32	+25	61	4	0	2	0	73	12.3

1993-94 statistics:

GP	G	A	TP	+/-	PIM	PP	SH	GW	GT	S	PCT
77	4	15	19	-7	143	0	2	1	0	66	6.1

1994-95 statistics:

GP	G	A	TP	+/-	PIM	PP	SH	GW	GT	S	PCT
44	2	13	15	+29	20	0	0	0	0	43	4.7

LAST SEASON

Led team and tied for second in NHL in plus-minus. Second among team defensemen in scoring. Missed four games with a groin laceration.

THE FINESSE GAME

Leschyshyn probably had his best NHL season last year and is the team's top all-around defenseman. He has excellent skills for a big man, especially his skating, which is strong forward and backward. He has great lateral movement and quickness.

Leschyshyn has finely tuned stick skills. His passes are soft, and he will jump into the rush by skating the puck out of the defensive zone, moving it off his forehand or backhand. He is not as effective with his passes out of the zone, as he tends to get flustered, so he will usually lug it out when he gets the chance.

He has a nice point shot. It's low and accurate, and he gets it away quickly. He will also make a foray into the circle on occasion and can utilize his quick wrist shot. He knows the importance of getting the shot on target and would rather take a little velocity off the puck to make sure his aim is true.

Leschyshyn is not overly creative, but works on the second power play unit. He does all the little things well, with a minimum of flash.

THE PHYSICAL GAME

Leschyshyn is very fit. He made a successful comeback from a potentially career-threatening knee injury, a challenge that is more mental than physical. And he provides consistency and strong defensive-zone coverage.

Leschyshyn needs to hit more. He lacks a mean streak to establish a presence, something he has been unable to do and which his team desperately needs. He will move out players and battle along the boards, but not with any authority.

THE INTANGIBLES

Leschyshyn is quietly developing into a solid defenseman. The team's improvement in defensive depth by the addition of Uwe Krupp and Sylvain Lefebvre last season helped him by reducing some of the burden.

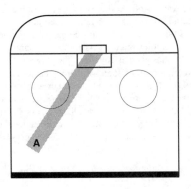

OWEN NOLAN

Yrs. of NHL service: 5
Born: Belfast, N. Ireland; Feb. 12, 1972
Position: right wing
Height: 6-1
Weight: 195
Uniform no.: 11
Shoots: right

Career statistics:

GP	G	A	TP	PIM
253	111	101	222	526

1991-92 statistics:

GP	G	A	TP	+/-	PIM	PP	SH	GW	GT	S	PCT
75	42	31	73	-9	183	17	0	0	1	190	22.1

1992-93 statistics:

GP	G	A	TP	+/-	PIM	PP	SH	GW	GT	S	PCT
73	36	41	77	-1	185	15	0	4	1	241	14.9

1993-94 statistics:

GP	G	A	TP	+/-	PIM	PP	SH	GW	GT	S	PCT
6	2	2	4	+2	8	0	0	0	0	15	13.3

1994-95 statistics:

GP	G	A	TP	+/-	PIM	PP	SH	GW	GT	S	PCT
46	30	19	49	+21	46	13	2	8	0	137	21.9

LAST SEASON

Tied for third in NHL in goals; one of only five players to reach 30-goal mark. Led team and tied for second in NHL in power play goals. Led NHL in game-winning goals. Led team forwards in plus-minus. Missed two games with a shoulder injury.

THE FINESSE GAME

Nolan came back strong off serious shoulder surgery. After a slow start — understandable, as he played only six games in 1993-94 — his timing and conditioning picked up and he took every advantage of playing with Swedish rookie sensation, Peter Forsberg.

Nolan rips one-timers from the circle with deadly speed and accuracy. He is a pure shooter with good hands; his game suffers when he tries to get too fancy and ventures away from a meat-and-potatoes game. When that happens, he holds onto the puck too long and tries to make plays instead of shooting. Nobody knows where Nolan's shot is going, except Nolan. He has an amazing knack for letting the puck go at just the right moment. He has a little move in tight to the goal with a forehand to backhand, and around the net he is about as good as anyone in the game.

Nolan is a strong skater with good balance and fair agility. He is quick straight ahead but won't split the defense when carrying the puck. He's better without the puck, driving into open ice for the pass and quick shot. Defensively, he has improved tremendously. He now takes it as a personal affront when he gets scored on.

THE PHYSICAL GAME

The mental part of recovery from a serious injury is possibly more important than the physical. Nolan got into a couple of fights early in the season and his shoulder stood up well. That gave him the confidence to start banging people and bulling his way to the net.

The addition of the fiery Wendel Clark inspired Nolan to become a more feisty, physical forward. Nolan has a mean streak and is unpredictable. That earns him more room around the net, and makes him a smaller version of Cam Neely. He is very competitive.

THE INTANGIBLES

If he stays healthy, Nolan could easily hit 50 goals over a full season. He meshed well with the great playmaker Forsberg, who is a left-handed shooter and most likely to feed his right-winger. Consistency over a full season is the only thing that has eluded him so far.

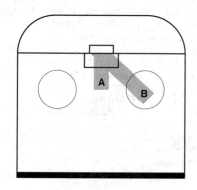

MIKE RICCI

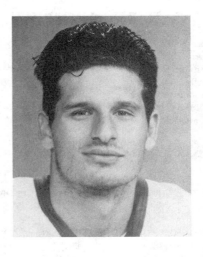

Yrs. of NHL service: 5
Born: Scarborough, Ont.; Oct. 27, 1971
Position: centre
Height: 6-0
Weight: 190
Uniform no.: 9
Shoots: left

Career statistics:

GP	G	A	TP	PIM
354	113	149	262	433

1991-92 statistics:

GP	G	A	TP	+/-	PIM	PP	SH	GW	GT	S	PCT
78	20	36	56	-10	93	11	2	0	0	149	13.4

1992-93 statistics:

GP	G	A	TP	+/-	PIM	PP	SH	GW	GT	S	PCT
77	27	51	78	+8	123	12	1	10	1	142	19.0

1993-94 statistics:

GP	G	A	TP	+/-	PIM	PP	SH	GW	GT	S	PCT
83	30	21	51	-9	113	13	3	6	1	138	21.3

1994-95 statistics:

GP	G	A	TP	+/-	PIM	PP	SH	GW	GT	S	PCT
48	15	21	36	+5	40	9	0	1	1	73	20.5

LAST SEASON

One of four Nordiques to appear in all 48 games. Second on team in power play goals.

THE FINESSE GAME

Ricci is a known quantity. He has terrific hand skills, combined with hockey sense and an outstanding work ethic. He always seems to be in the right place, ready to make the right play. He sees his passing options well and is a solid performer on the power play because of his patience with the puck. Ricci can rifle it as well. He has a good backhand shot from in deep and scores most of his goals from the slot by picking the top corners. His lone drawback is his speed. He's fast enough to not look out of place and he has good balance and agility, but his lack of quickness prevents him from being more of an offensive force.

Very slick on face-offs, he has good hand speed and hand-eye coordination for winning draws outright, or he can pick a bouncing puck out of the air. This serves him well in scrambles in front of the net, too, or he can deflect mid-air slap shots.

Ricci is a very good penalty killer, with poise and a controlled aggression for forcing the play.

THE PHYSICAL GAME

Ricci is not big, but he is so strong that it's not unusual to see him skate out from behind the net, dragging along or fending off a checker with one arm while he makes a pass or takes a shot with his other arm. He plays a tough game without being overly chippy. He is very strong in the corners and in front of the net. He plays bigger than he is.

Ricci will play hurt, and it takes a serious injury to knock him out of the lineup. He pays attention to conditioning and has a great deal of stamina.

THE INTANGIBLES

Badly handled by the previous Quebec braintrust, the hardworking Ricci responded to new coach Marc Crawford with a solid season. He is a budding Ron Francis, a player who will kill penalties, take face-offs, get you 80 points, drive the Zamboni, whatever. His quality, character, leadership and dedication to the game and his teammates are impeccable. We said in last year's *HSR* to expect a big bounce-back season from Ricci. His prorated point production would have been 63 points for last season. We think he can, and will, do even better. He was probably the best Quebec player in the playoffs.

Ice time would seem to be a bit of a problem with Joe Sakic and Peter Forsberg also in Denver, but all three get power play time, kill penalties and play four-on-four. Quebec didn't use a strict defensive line last season, but Ricci's trio (with Scott Young and an assortment of left wings) performed something akin to that role last season.

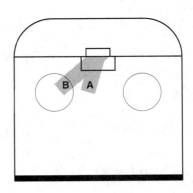

MARTIN RUCINSKY

Yrs. of NHL service: 3
Born: Most, Czechoslovkia; March 11, 1971
Position: left wing
Height: 6-0
Weight: 190
Uniform no.: 25
Shoots: left

Career statistics:

GP	G	A	TP	PIM
163	31	60	91	125

1991-92 statistics:

GP	G	A	TP	+/-	PIM	PP	SH	GW	GT	S	PCT
6	1	1	2	-2	2	0	0	0	0	5	20.0

1992-93 statistics:

GP	G	A	TP	+/-	PIM	PP	SH	GW	GT	S	PCT
77	18	30	48	+16	51	4	0	1	3	133	13.5

1993-94 statistics:

GP	G	A	TP	+/-	PIM	PP	SH	GW	GT	S	PCT
60	9	23	32	+4	58	4	0	1	0	96	9.4

1994-95 statistics:

GP	G	A	TP	+/-	PIM	PP	SH	GW	GT	S	PCT
20	3	6	9	+5	14	0	0	0	0	32	9.4

LAST SEASON

Missed 28 games with a separated shoulder and subsequent surgery.

THE FINESSE GAME

Rucinsky is very quick with hand skills to match at high tempo. He is most dangerous off the rush, where he can use his speed to intimidate the defense and then use the room they give him to fire his shot.

Rucinsky's flaw is that he is not overly patient. He has nice little moves, and can beat people one-on-one.

THE PHYSICAL GAME

Rucinsky is wiry, but isn't a big banger. His physical effectiveness will depend on his recovery from surgery. Confidence will allow him to continue to play in traffic and take hits to protect the puck.

THE INTANGIBLES

Rucinsky has the potential to become a game-breaking scorer. He was injured last season after getting off to a good start, playing with Mike Ricci and Scott Young.

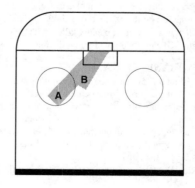

JOE SAKIC

Yrs. of NHL service: 7
Born: Burnaby, B.C.; July 7, 1969
Position: centre
Height: 5-11
Weight: 185
Uniform no.: 19
Shoots: left

Career statistics:

GP	G	A	TP	PIM
508	234	392	626	183

1991-92 statistics:

GP	G	A	TP	+/-	PIM	PP	SH	GW	GT	S	PCT
69	29	65	94	+5	20	6	3	1	1	217	13.4

1992-93 statistics:

GP	G	A	TP	+/-	PIM	PP	SH	GW	GT	S	PCT
78	48	57	105	-3	40	20	2	4	1	264	18.2

1993-94 statistics:

GP	G	A	TP	+/-	PIM	PP	SH	GW	GT	S	PCT
84	28	64	92	-8	18	10	1	9	1	279	10.0

1994-95 statistics:

GP	G	A	TP	+/-	PIM	PP	SH	GW	GT	S	PCT
47	19	43	62	+7	30	3	2	5	0	157	12.1

LAST SEASON

Led team in assists and points for second consecutive season. Fourth in NHL in points and third in assists. Second on team in goals.

THE FINESSE GAME

While Sakic's playmaking is considered world class, the rest of his skills are often underappreciated. With the puck, one-on-one, he's dangerous. Sakic has two or three gears, and is tremendously quick off the puck. He finds and hits the holes.

Sakic is gifted in that he has great patience with the puck. He will hold it until the last minute, when he has drawn the defenders to him and opened up ice, creating — as coaches love to express it — time and space for his linemates. This makes him a gem on the power play. He was used as a point man last season by the Nordiques, but he can also create opportunities when he cycles down low.

Sakic has started to use his shot more, which makes his attack even more unpredictable. He has an above average shot — not great, but underrated. He has quick hands for fast and accurate release, and a decent slap shot.

Sakic is a scoring threat every time he is on the ice, because he can craft a dangerous scoring chance out of a situation that looks innocent.

He doesn't have a great deal of speed, but he has enough quickness and mobility to be effective without being flashy. He appears to glide along, disappearing here, and then suddenly materializing in an open area of the ice in his quiet manner. He is lethal trailing the rush. He takes a pass in full stride without slowing, then dekes and shoots before the goalie can even flinch.

Sakic is a good face-off man and if he is tied up, he will use his skates to kick the puck free.

THE PHYSICAL GAME

Sakic is not a physical player. He's stronger than he looks, and, like Wayne Gretzky, will spin off his checks when opponents take runs at him. He uses his body to protect the puck when he is carrying deep; you have to go through him to get it away. He will try to keep going through traffic or along the boards with the puck, and often squirts free with it because he is able to maintain control and his balance. He creates turnovers with his quickness and his hands, but not by initiating contact.

THE INTANGIBLES

Sakic is a quiet leader. He didn't get the attention he deserved in Quebec because of the small market, and may get his due with the move to Denver. But he is soft-spoken and doesn't crave the lineup. Sakic is proud, however, and last season's first-round departure in the playoffs should rankle and drive him to new heights this season. Expect another 100 points.

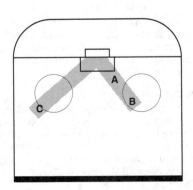

CHRIS SIMON

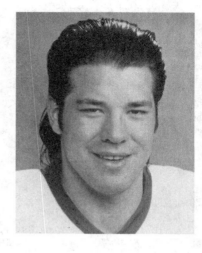

Yrs. of NHL service: 3
Born: Wawa, Ont.; Jan. 30, 1972
Position: left wing
Height: 6-3
Weight: 219
Uniform no.: 12
Shoots: left

Career statistics:

GP	G	A	TP	PIM
82	8	14	22	305

1992-93 statistics:

GP	G	A	TP	+/-	PIM	PP	SH	GW	GT	S	PCT
16	1	1	2	-2	67	0	0	1	0	15	6.7

1993-94 statistics:

GP	G	A	TP	+/-	PIM	PP	SH	GW	GT	S	PCT
37	4	4	8	-2	132	0	0	1	0	39	10.3

1994-95 statistics:

GP	G	A	TP	+/-	PIM	PP	SH	GW	GT	S	PCT
29	3	9	12	+14	106	0	0	0	0	33	9.1

to prove, but there is promise here.

LAST SEASON

Led team in PIM. Missed six games with a back injury. Missed 13 games with a shoulder injury.

THE FINESSE GAME

In many ways, Simon is the prototypical NHL fourth-line winger. He has made his reputation with his toughness, but has shown an added dimension in his ability to make plays that result in points. Whenever he does, jaws drop and observers wonder, "Where did that move came from?" But they shouldn't be so dumbfounded. After all, Simon gets a lot of room, which gives a player with modest skills more time to make a play.

Simon has decent hands for a big guy, but all of his successes come in tight. Lack of quickness is a major drawback. With any improvement in his skating he would earn more ice time and get the chance to develop confidence. If he gets a regular shift, he will answer the questions about his consistency and might produce some surprising numbers, but there are a couple of steps he has to take to reach that level.

THE PHYSICAL GAME

Simon is as tough as they come and has a wide streak of mean. He has already established himself as a player who can throw them when the time comes, and opponents have to keep a wary eye on him because they never know when he's going to snap.

THE INTANGIBLES

Simon has to overcome his propensity to get injured and improve his skill levels in order to become a full-time player. He also needs to step up his conditioning. The door is open for him, since a team full of finesse players needs some balance in grit, but there are questions about how badly he wants it. There is much left

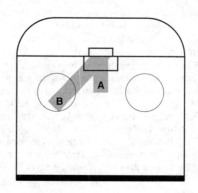

JOCELYN THIBAULT

Yrs. of NHL service: 2
Born: Montreal, Que.; Jan. 12, 1975
Position: goaltender
Height: 5-11
Weight: 170
Uniform no.: 41
Catches: left

Career statistics:

GP	MINS	G	SO	AVG	A	PIM
47	2402	118	1	2.95	0	2

1993-94 statistics:

GP	MINS	GAA	W	L	T	SO	GA	S	SAPCT	PIM
29	1504	3.31	8	13	3	0	83	768	.892	2

1994-95 statistics:

GP	MINS	GAA	W	L	T	SO	GA	S	SAPCT	PIM
18	898	2.34	12	2	2	1	35	423	.917	0

LAST SEASON

Career-best GAA. Missed 10 games with a sprained shoulder. Stopped Martin Straka on penalty shot.

THE PHYSICAL GAME

Thibault is a butterfly-style goalie. He plays his angles well and controls his rebounds. He doesn't leave many, and when he does they are usually away from the front of the net.

Thibault has a tendency to go down too quickly, losing the advantage that his big size gives him when he stays upright. His puck handling has to improve. Right now it's not sufficient for an NHL goalie.

Thibault has a good glove hand and challenges shooters. He has an efficient style that should help him handle a lot of ice time if he gets the opportunity.

THE MENTAL GAME

Thibault is very competitive and performs well in pressure situations. He shakes off bad goals. He is also mentally tough and maintains his concentration on the ice.

THE INTANGIBLES

Thibault will battle Stephane Fiset (and possibly Garth Snow) for the number one role in Denver this season. Thibault should thrive on the challenge. He is mature for being 20 years old and is smart and analytical in his approach to the game.

CRAIG WOLANIN

Yrs. of NHL service: 10
Born: Grosse Pointe, Mich.; July 27, 1967
Position: right defense
Height: 6-3
Weight: 205
Uniform no.: 6
Shoots: left

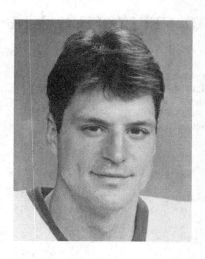

Career statistics:

GP	G	A	TP	PIM
572	33	109	142	817

1991-92 statistics:

GP	G	A	TP	+/-	PIM	PP	SH	GW	GT	S	PCT
69	2	11	13	-12	80	0	0	0	0	71	2.8

1992-93 statistics:

GP	G	A	TP	+/-	PIM	PP	SH	GW	GT	S	PCT
24	1	5	6	+9	49	0	0	0	0	17	5.9

1993-94 statistics:

GP	G	A	TP	+/-	PIM	PP	SH	GW	GT	S	PCT
63	6	10	16	+16	80	0	0	0	0	78	7.7

1994-95 statistics:

GP	G	A	TP	+/-	PIM	PP	SH	GW	GT	S	PCT
40	3	6	9	+12	40	0	0	0	0	36	8.3

LAST SEASON

Missed four games with a recurring groin injury. Missed four games with a knee injury.

THE FINESSE GAME

Wolanin stands up well defensively and has improved his reads. He lacks one-step quickness and can get burned by defenders in close, but once he is on stride he is fluid. He is not well balanced, though rehab work on his groin/thigh injury has added much-needed lower body strength for his work along the boards and clearing his crease.

Because he is not very shifty, Wolanin has to rely more on his positional play and use his burly body to take up as much ice as possible. He can be beaten wide, so he has to make sure he angles skaters to the boards and takes them out, and not let them slither past.

As Wolanin has concentrated more and more on defense, his offense has just about vanished. He could do a shade more. He has a heavy point shot. He makes good decisions with the puck and doesn't like to give it away.

THE PHYSICAL GAME

The team's most physical defenseman, Wolanin has become a nastier hitter. Improved lower-body conditioning has made him a more powerful checker. He also uses his stick well, breaking up plays and poking pucks off sticks. He has a long reach and can cover a lot of territory.

THE INTANGIBLES

Are the injuries finally a thing of the past for Wolanin? He made it through much of the lockout-shortened season and Quebec's brief playoff stint intact. Improved defensive depth on the Nordiques helped him last season, as he was usually partnered with the very steady Sylvain Lefebvre.

Wolanin is a very likable guy who has become more responsible about his life (a wife and new baby will do that) and his occupation. He has worked hard to overcome injuries to stay in the NHL. He also learned how to maintain his body better, and that bodes well for a healthier future. Wolanin is becoming a complete defenseman with a professional approach to the game.

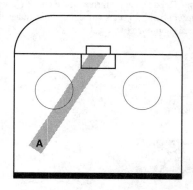

SCOTT YOUNG

Yrs. of NHL service: 6
Born: Clinton, Mass.; Oct. 1, 1967
Position: right wing
Height: 6-0
Weight: 190
Uniform no.: 48
Shoots: right

Career statistics:

GP	G	A	TP	PIM
446	134	181	315	165

1991-92 statistics:

Did not play in NHL

1992-93 statistics:

GP	G	A	TP	+/-	PIM	PP	SH	GW	GT	S	PCT
82	30	30	60	+5	20	9	6	5	0	225	13.3

1993-94 statistics:

GP	G	A	TP	+/-	PIM	PP	SH	GW	GT	S	PCT
76	26	25	51	-4	14	6	1	1	0	236	11.0

1994-95 statistics:

GP	G	A	TP	+/-	PIM	PP	SH	GW	GT	S	PCT
48	18	21	39	+9	14	3	3	0	0	167	10.8

LAST SEASON

One of four Nordiques to appear in all 48 games. Led team in shorthanded goals and shots. Fourth on team in points.

THE FINESSE GAME

Young is a hockey machine. A powerful, intelligent player with a great shot, he can take as much time up front as a coach is willing to give him. And, in a pinch, he can drop back and play his old college position on defense.

Young may have the hardest shot on the team. He loves to fire it off the wing or he can one-time the puck low on the face-off, or he will battle for pucks and tips in front of the net. Young is keen to score and always goes to the net with his stick down, ready for the puck.

With all of that in mind, his defensive awareness is even more impressive, because Young is basically a checking winger. He reads plays in all zones equally well and has good anticipation.

Young is a very fast skater, which, combined with his reads, makes him a sound fore-checker. He will often outrace defensemen to touch pucks and avoid icings, and his speed allows him to recover when he gets overzealous in the attacking zone.

THE PHYSICAL GAME

Young's lone drawback is that he is not a very physical player. He will do what he has to do in battles along the boards in the defensive zone, but he's more of a defensive force with his quickness and hand skills. He's not a pure grinder, but will bump and get in the way.

THE INTANGIBLES

A checking winger who can score 60 points is a rarity, and Young is that. He is a complete player and a model of consistency. Players with great wheels like his tend to last a long time, so expect him to display his veteran ability for many more seasons.

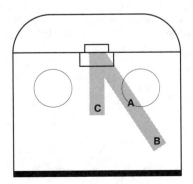

DALLAS STARS

Players' Statistics 1994-95

POS	NO.	PLAYER	GP	G	A	PTS	+/-	PIM	PP	SH	GW	GT	S	PCTG
C	15	DAVE GAGNER	48	14	28	42	2	42	7		2	1	138	10.1
C	9	MIKE MODANO	30	12	17	29	7	8	4	1			100	12.0
D	4	KEVIN HATCHER	47	10	19	29	-4	66	3		2	1	138	7.2
L	11	MIKE DONNELLY	44	12	15	27	-4	33	3		3		116	10.3
C	6	COREY MILLEN	45	5	18	23	6	36	1				74	6.8
R	22	TRENT KLATT	47	12	10	22	-2	26	5		3		91	13.2
L	23	GREG ADAMS	43	8	13	21	-3	16	3	2			72	11.1
C	10	*TODD HARVEY	40	11	9	20	-3	67	2		1		64	17.2
L	39	*MIKE KENNEDY	44	6	12	18	4	33	2				76	7.9
D	12	GRANT LEDYARD	38	5	13	18	6	20	4			1	79	6.3
R	21	PAUL BROTEN	47	7	9	16	-7	36				1	67	10.4
D	2	DERIAN HATCHER	43	5	11	16	3	105	2		2		74	6.8
C	16	DEAN EVASON	47	8	7	15	3	48	1				53	15.1
C	41	BRENT GILCHRIST	32	9	4	13	-3	16	1	3	1		70	12.9
D	14	PAUL CAVALLINI	44	1	11	12	8	28					69	1.4
C	25	PETER ZEZEL	30	6	5	11	-6	19			1		47	12.8
D	3	CRAIG LUDWIG	47	2	7	9	-6	61					55	3.6
D	5	DOUG ZMOLEK	42		5	5	-6	67					28	
R	27	SHANE CHURLA	27	1	3	4		186			1		22	4.5
R	11	*JARKKO VARVIO	5	1	1	2	1		1				9	11.1
D	24	RICHARD MATVICHUK	14		2	2	-7	14					21	
D	43	GORD DONNELLY	16	1		1	1	52					9	11.1
R	29	*GRANT MARSHALL	2		1	1	1							
G	35	ANDY MOOG	31		1	1		14						
R	37	*ZAC BOYER	1										1	
G	30	*EMMANUEL FERNANDEZ	1											
D	28	*TRAVIS RICHARDS	2										1	
R	38	*MARK LAWRENCE	2										3	
C	20	*JAMIE LANGENBRUNNER	2					2					1	
G	1	*MIKE TORCHIA	6											
D	18	MIKE LALOR	12					9					6	
G	34	DARCY WAKALUK	15					4						

GP = games played; G = goals; A = assists; PTS = points; +/- = goals-for minus goals-against while player is on ice; PIM = penalties in minutes; PP = power play goals; SH = shorthanded goals; GW = game-winning goals; GT = game-tying goals; S = no. of shots; PCTG = percentage of goals to shots; * = rookie

GREG ADAMS

Yrs. of NHL service: 11
Born: Nelson, B.C.; Aug. 1, 1963
Position: left wing
Height: 6-3
Weight: 185
Uniform no.: 23
Shoots: left

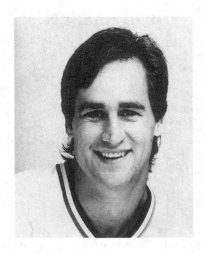

Career statistics:

GP	G	A	TP	PIM
687	249	271	520	221

1991-92 statistics:

GP	G	A	TP	+/-	PIM	PP	SH	GW	GT	S	PCT
76	30	27	57	+8	26	13	1	5	0	184	16.3

1992-93 statistics:

GP	G	A	TP	+/-	PIM	PP	SH	GW	GT	S	PCT
53	25	31	56	+31	14	6	1	3	0	124	20.2

1993-94 statistics:

GP	G	A	TP	+/-	PIM	PP	SH	GW	GT	S	PCT
68	13	24	37	-1	20	5	1	2	0	139	9.4

1994-95 statistics:

GP	G	A	TP	+/-	PIM	PP	SH	GW	GT	S	PCT
43	8	13	21	-3	16	3	2	0	0	72	11.1

LAST SEASON

Acquired from Vancouver with Dan Kesa and a fifth-round draft pick in 1995 for Russ Courtnall.

THE FINESSE GAME

Adams has terrific speed, but it is deceptive because his skating looks effortless.

He can shoot a hard slap shot on the fly off the wing, but most of his goals come from within five feet of the net. He drives fearlessly to the goal and likes to arrive by the most expedient route possible. If that means crashing through defensemen, then so be it. Adams has good shifty moves in deep and is an unselfish player. He played a lot of centre early in his career and is nearly as good a playmaker as finisher. One of the few knocks on him is that he doesn't shoot enough. One of his best scoring moves is a high backhand in tight. He always has his head up and is looking for the holes.

Adams has worked hard at improving his defensive awareness and has become a complete hockey player.

THE PHYSICAL GAME

Adams's crease-crashing style exacts a price, and he is nearly always wearing an ice pack or getting medical attention for a nick or bruise somewhere on his person. Yet he always comes right back for more. He is physical and tough without being an aggressor. He does not fight and, considering the checking attention he gets, he remains remarkably calm and determined, seldom taking bad retaliatory penalties. He just gets the job done. Adams is stronger than he looks.

THE INTANGIBLES

Adams is an underrated player. He always shows up for the opening face-off and is battling through the final buzzer. He was hampered by a lingering flu bug last season and was mentally affected by the trade. He is a candidate for a big bounce-back season, even at age 32, because his hand skills haven't deteriorated. He had a very strong finish to last season and decent playoffs, a positive sign.

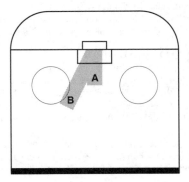

BOB BASSEN

Yrs. of NHL service: 9
Born: Calgary, Alta.; May 6, 1965
Position: centre/left wing
Height: 5-11
Weight: 170
Uniform no.: 28
Shoots: left

Career statistics:

GP	G	A	TP	PIM
556	76	129	205	801

1991-92 statistics:

GP	G	A	TP	+/-	PIM	PP	SH	GW	GT	S	PCT
79	7	25	32	+12	167	0	0	1	0	101	6.9

1992-93 statistics:

GP	G	A	TP	+/-	PIM	PP	SH	GW	GT	S	PCT
53	9	10	19	0	63	0	1	0	0	61	14.8

1993-94 statistics:

GP	G	A	TP	+/-	PIM	PP	SH	GW	GT	S	PCT
59	11	17	28	+2	70	1	1	1	0	73	15.1

1994-95 statistics:

GP	G	A	TP	+/-	PIM	PP	SH	GW	GT	S	PCT
47	12	15	27	+14	33	0	1	1	0	66	18.2

LAST SEASON

Despite the lockout-shortened season, recorded second-highest goal total of career. Missed one game with a back injury. Signed as a free agent.

THE FINESSE GAME

Bassen has average straightaway speed, and with the playing time missed due to injuries (for the second consecutive season), he looked even slower last season. But he does have quickness and agility when healthy, which he puts to work in close quarters to avoid hits from bigger players. Don't get us wrong: if Bassen has to take a hit, he will, but he's also smart enough to avoid unnecessary punishment.

Bassen doesn't have great hands or a great shot to go with his work ethic. All of his finesse skills are average at best. His few goals come from going for the puck in scrambles around the net.

Bassen is only so-so on face-offs. He's not big enough to tie up most opposing centres, and he lacks the hand speed to win draws outright. He does try to scrunch himself low on draws to get his head under the opposing centre's to block the sight of the puck.

THE PHYSICAL GAME

Bassen plays much bigger than his size, aware every night that if he isn't scrapping along the boards or in front of the net, someone might take his job. He is extremely fit. There isn't an ounce of body fat on him. He hates to lose and will do whatever he must to avoid it.

Bassen has a low centre of gravity, which makes it tough to knock him off his feet, and he's closer to the puck than a lot of other skaters. He often wins scrums just by being able to pry the puck loose from flailing feet.

THE INTANGIBLES

Bassen is a blood and guts competitor, a throwback to hockey's glory days with the skills of a '90s player. He will be a hot commodity on the (unrestricted) free agent market during the off-season, but given the promise of the team in Denver to be a force for the next decade, his old team would seem to have a good shot at keeping him.

Bassen is a reliable team man, one of those players who always delivers an honest effort. He matches up night after night against most of the league's bigger, better forwards, and makes them work for what they get. He is a valuable role player, and a role model as well. Unasked, Bassen goes out of his way to help younger players (such as Peter Forsberg and Adam Deadmarsh last year) acclimatize themselves to the NHL. Simply, Bassen is a coach's dream.

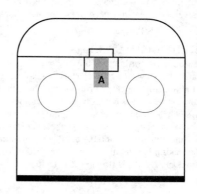

PAUL CAVALLINI

Yrs. of NHL service: 8
Born: Toronto, Ont.; Oct. 13, 1965
Position: defense
Height: 6-1
Weight: 210
Uniform no.: 14
Shoots: left

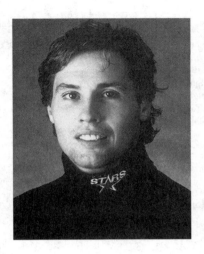

Career statistics:

GP	G	A	TP	PIM
556	56	177	233	744

1991-92 statistics:

GP	G	A	TP	+/-	PIM	PP	SH	GW	GT	S	PCT
66	10	25	35	+7	95	3	1	2	1	164	6.1

1992-93 statistics:

GP	G	A	TP	+/-	PIM	PP	SH	GW	GT	S	PCT
82	6	12	18	+6	56	1	0	0	0	99	6.1

1993-94 statistics:

GP	G	A	TP	+/-	PIM	PP	SH	GW	GT	S	PCT
74	11	33	44	+13	82	6	0	3	0	145	7.6

1994-95 statistics:

GP	G	A	TP	+/-	PIM	PP	SH	GW	GT	S	PCT
44	1	11	12	+8	28	0	0	0	0	69	1.4

LAST SEASON

Led team in plus-minus.

THE FINESSE GAME

Cavallini loves to get involved in the attack. A fine all-around skater with speed, agility and balance, he is extremely confident in his skating and tries to force a lot of plays. He will challenge at the blueline and will pinch in and fore-check in the attacking zone. He has improved his defensive reads and is smart about when to pinch, rather than recklessly dashing in and leaving his partner (often the steady Craig Ludwig) vulnerable.

Cavallini reads offensive plays very well. He has good hockey vision and will start plays out of his own end with a strong pass, or he will carry the puck, which he can do at high tempo. He trails into the play well. His best shot is a quick slapper from the point. He also has a good wrist shot from close range.

Experience and intelligence over the past few seasons have added a great deal to his natural skills. Cavallini is gifted enough that the Stars used him up front on occasion.

THE PHYSICAL GAME

Cavallini plays an effective and efficient take-out game. He is not a big or a mean hitter, though he is a willing checker. He does not clear out the front of his net well, so he is best paired with a more physical defenseman who will give him some support. Preferring to play the puck instead of the man, he goes for poke-checks that he can turn into quick breakouts. He competes hard and has a competitive edge.

THE INTANGIBLES

Cavallini makes a solid third or fourth defenseman who gives an honest effort every night. He won't do much to surprise you, but he will seldom disappoint. The question about his offense is: will he return to a double-digit goal total? Given the number of Hatchers on Dallas, it seems unlikely he'll get the kind of prime ice time to do so. He is an emotional competitor who doesn't hold much back every night. He gives what he has.

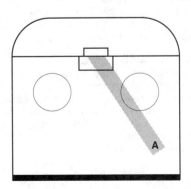

SHANE CHURLA

Yrs. of NHL service: 7
Born: Fernie, B.C.; June 24, 1965
Position: right wing
Height: 6-1
Weight: 200
Uniform no.: 27
Shoots: right

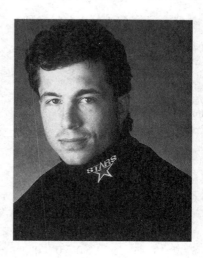

Career statistics:

GP	G	A	TP	PIM
388	22	38	60	1962

1991-92 statistics:

GP	G	A	TP	+/-	PIM	PP	SH	GW	GT	S	PCT
57	4	1	5	-12	278	0	0	0	0	42	9.5

1992-93 statistics:

GP	G	A	TP	+/-	PIM	PP	SH	GW	GT	S	PCT
73	5	16	21	-8	286	1	0	1	0	61	8.2

1993-94 statistics:

GP	G	A	TP	+/-	PIM	PP	SH	GW	GT	S	PCT
69	6	7	13	-8	333	3	0	0	1	62	9.7

1994-95 statistics:

GP	G	A	TP	+/-	PIM	PP	SH	GW	GT	S	PCT
27	1	3	4	0	186	0	0	1	0	22	4.5

LAST SEASON

Led team in PIM for fifth consecutive season. Second in NHL in PIM for second consecutive season. Served a four-game suspension. Missed 12 games with torn medial collateral ligament in left knee. Missed one game with the flu.

THE FINESSE GAME

Churla is among the new breed of physical role players. He brings more to his game than his fists. He can be effective with his checking and play without being a heavyweight fighter, and he has made himself more valuable. He doesn't have sharp scoring instincts but will go to the net and get his goals by thrashing around for loose pucks. The Stars even gave him an occasional stint up front on the power play.

Like a lot of players of his ilk, Churla gets a little too carried away by overhandling the puck. By keeping his game simple, he will be more effective.

Churla has gained more confidence with increased ice time, and he saw steady employment on a third line as a checker. He will continue to try to stretch his game and his offensive numbers will improve.

THE PHYSICAL GAME

Churla hits hard and loves it. He's a tenacious checker and isn't afraid of anyone. He moves to the front of the net with authority and power, and stays there. He can still use his dukes when he has to, but he has already earned a fair amount of respect around the league. Churla can change the emotional tide of a game with his adrenaline.

THE INTANGIBLES

Churla is among the best in the league at what he does. He will protect his teammates or help protect a lead. He doesn't look out of place on the ice as a player, not just a fighter. He plays with a lot of fire and often wears a letter on his jersey because of his leadership and intensity.

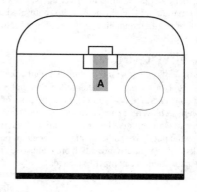

MIKE DONNELLY

Yrs. of NHL service: 8
Born: Detroit, Mich.; Oct. 10, 1963
Position: left wing
Height: 5-11
Weight: 185
Uniform no.: 11
Shoots: left

Career statistics:

GP	G	A	TP	PIM
438	112	116	228	243

1991-92 statistics:

GP	G	A	TP	+/-	PIM	PP	SH	GW	GT	S	PCT
80	29	16	45	+5	20	0	1	4	0	197	14.7

1992-93 statistics:

GP	G	A	TP	+/-	PIM	PP	SH	GW	GT	S	PCT
84	29	40	69	+17	45	8	1	2	0	244	11.9

1993-94 statistics:

GP	G	A	TP	+/-	PIM	PP	SH	GW	GT	S	PCT
81	21	21	42	+2	34	4	2	3	0	177	11.9

1994-95 statistics:

GP	G	A	TP	+/-	PIM	PP	SH	GW	GT	S	PCT
44	12	15	27	-4	33	3	0	3	0	116	10.3

LAST SEASON

Tied for team lead in game-winning goals. Missed one game with a concussion. Acquired from Los Angeles for a fourth-round draft pick in 1996.

THE FINESSE GAME

A digger who gets his goals from in close, Donnelly is tenacious around the net, using his quickness to dart in and out of holes. He has a good nose for the net and good hands for his shots. He has become more eager to shoot and is a more effective player because of it.

Donnelly can also work passes in tight areas. He has good open-ice speed to drive to the outside on a defenseman. Many of his scoring chances develop from two-on-one breaks that are created quickly just inside the blueline.

He can work on the second power play unit and is a savvy player who can work both special teams. He has worked hard to make himself into a reliable two-way winger.

THE PHYSICAL GAME

Donnelly plays bigger than his size. He is tenacious and uses his body as well as he can to get in people's way, but he is too small to do any damage. It's pretty remarkable, given the way he plays, that he hasn't done more damage to himself.

THE INTANGIBLES

Donnelly's small size is the only thing that limits him from being more of an impact player. He is not likely to toy with the 30-goal mark again, though 20 is a safe bet. His effort should earn him regular ice time in Dallas.

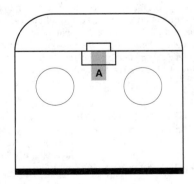

DEAN EVASON

Yrs. of NHL service: 11
Born: Flin Flon, Man.; Aug. 22, 1964
Position: centre
Height: 5-10
Weight: 180
Uniform no.: 16
Shoots: right

Career statistics:

GP	G	A	TP	PIM
736	132	226	358	960

1991-92 statistics:

GP	G	A	TP	+/-	PIM	PP	SH	GW	GT	S	PCT
74	11	15	26	-22	94	1	0	1	0	88	12.5

1992-93 statistics:

GP	G	A	TP	+/-	PIM	PP	SH	GW	GT	S	PCT
84	12	19	31	-35	132	3	0	1	1	107	11.2

1993-94 statistics:

GP	G	A	TP	+/-	PIM	PP	SH	GW	GT	S	PCT
80	11	33	44	-12	66	3	2	2	1	118	9.3

1994-95 statistics:

GP	G	A	TP	+/-	PIM	PP	SH	GW	GT	S	PCT
47	8	7	15	+3	48	1	0	0	0	53	15.1

LAST SEASON

Missed one game with bruised ribs.

THE FINESSE GAME

Evason is constantly in motion. Since he has lost a step over recent seasons, he is determined to keep up through sheer energy. He fore-checks hard, and smart. There is little wasted motion.

He doesn't generate much offense despite always being on the puck carrier and forcing turnovers. He creates scoring chances, but is incapable of finishing most plays. He is unselfish to a fault because he lacks confidence in his scoring touch. Even on a two-on-one, he will pass across to a teammate who is covered rather than take the open shot himself.

Evason kills penalties well. He is agile and doesn't give up in his pursuit. He is built low to the ground and takes his share of defensive draws.

THE PHYSICAL GAME

Evason can get mismatched in size and speed, but he has a sturdy build and can take a lot of bumps. He is durable and won't be intimidated, but his frustration is evident, since he can't win the one-on-one battles in front of the net and along the boards. That doesn't stop him from trying. He is tough and smart.

THE INTANGIBLES

Evason leads by example every night with his hard work and hustle. He is a reliable defensive forward who is still in the game because of his intensity. Other players are more skilled, but not as dedicated. His numbers aren't likely to top 35 points, but his value is measured in other ways.

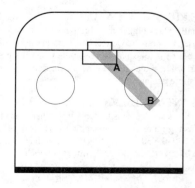

DAVE GAGNER

Yrs. of NHL service: 9
Born: Chatham, Ont.; Dec. 11, 1964
Position: centre
Height: 5-10
Weight: 180
Uniform no.: 15
Shoots: left

Career statistics:

GP	G	A	TP	PIM
644	244	290	534	747

1991-92 statistics:

GP	G	A	TP	+/-	PIM	PP	SH	GW	GT	S	PCT
78	31	40	71	-4	107	17	0	3	0	229	13.5

1992-93 statistics:

GP	G	A	TP	+/-	PIM	PP	SH	GW	GT	S	PCT
84	33	43	76	-13	141	17	0	5	1	230	14.3

1993-94 statistics:

GP	G	A	TP	+/-	PIM	PP	SH	GW	GT	S	PCT
76	32	29	61	+13	83	10	0	6	1	213	15.0

1994-95 statistics:

GP	G	A	TP	+/-	PIM	PP	SH	GW	GT	S	PCT
48	14	28	42	+2	42	7	0	2	1	138	10.1

one centre after Modano's injury, but he doesn't have the size and speed to do it over the course of a full season. His effort is admirable, though, and he should be a reliable 30-goal man again this season if slotted back into his proper number two role, where he can evade some heavy-duty checking attention.

LAST SEASON

Led team in goals, assists, points and power play goals. Tied for team lead in shots. Only Star to appear in all 48 games.

THE FINESSE GAME

Gagner can score from just about anywhere except way out by the blueline. He can score off the rush or set up other players. He will pick up garbage goals, scoop up clean ones, finish off an outnumbered attack, or score off a drive down the wing with just his shot. He doesn't overpower goalies with his shot, but he has a quick and cunning release. Defensemen will sometimes back off him on a rush, because he does have some moves to slip past them.

On the power play he can work down low, though he works better coming off the half-wall.

Gagner's speed isn't as noticeable as his quickness. In a 20-foot radius, he's pretty quick, and he can throw in several dekes low as he drives to the net.

He is not a good defensive player, though he has worked to improve this. He is only average on face-offs.

THE PHYSICAL GAME

Gagner plays a tenacious, in-your-face offensive style. For a smaller player, he is pretty resilient. He stays in the traffic and doesn't get bounced out too easily. He can get overmatched one-on-one, but he tries to avoid battles where he can't use his quickness. Gagner's hard work is an inspiration to his teammates.

THE INTANGIBLES

Gagner did the best job he could filling in as a number

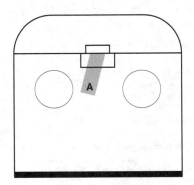

BRENT GILCHRIST

Yrs. of NHL service: 6
Born: Moose Jaw, Sask.; Apr. 3, 1967
Position: centre/left wing
Height: 5-11
Weight: 181
Uniform no.: 41
Shoots: left

Career statistics:

GP	G	A	TP	PIM
412	82	96	178	207

1991-92 statistics:

GP	G	A	TP	+/-	PIM	PP	SH	GW	GT	S	PCT
79	23	27	50	+29	57	2	0	3	2	146	15.8

1992-93 statistics:

GP	G	A	TP	+/-	PIM	PP	SH	GW	GT	S	PCT
68	10	11	21	-12	49	2	0	0	0	106	9.4

1993-94 statistics:

GP	G	A	TP	+/-	PIM	PP	SH	GW	GT	S	PCT
76	17	14	31	0	31	3	1	5	0	103	16.5

1994-95 statistics:

GP	G	A	TP	+/-	PIM	PP	SH	GW	GT	S	PCT
32	9	4	13	-3	16	1	3	1	0	70	12.9

THE INTANGIBLES

Because he plays so many different roles, it's difficult to tell where Gilchrist's top end is. He seems to be capable of a 25-goal season, but with much of his attention focused on a checking role, it's unlikely he'll produce more than 20.

LAST SEASON

Missed 16 games with surgery to repair torn cartilage in his wrist. Led team in shorthanded goals.

THE FINESSE GAME

Gilchrist is a versatile forward who can play all three positions up front. It would probably help him if he could find a niche (he has played centre throughout most of his career), because he is a good defensive player with some offensive flair. He was a scorer at the junior and AHL levels, but so far the best total he has been able to manage in the NHL was 57 points four seasons ago in Montreal.

He has the versatility to play on the top line in a scoring role in a pinch, but is better on the third line as a checker. Gilchrist has good knowledge of the ice. He anticipates well and is a smart and effective penalty killer.

Gilchrist will work hard around the net and generates most of his scoring chances there. He has good balance and quickness in small areas, but is not a great finisher.

THE PHYSICAL GAME

Gilchrist is a strong player, though he doesn't take command of the ice. His good skating helps him move around and create a little more havoc, and he's not afraid to stand in and take a drubbing around the net. He won't back down from a challenge. Gilchrist had a tough season physically. In addition to the wrist injury (which came from a hit into the boards), he suffered mouth lacerations and lost three teeth when he was hit from behind in a game against San Jose, but returned to finish the game.

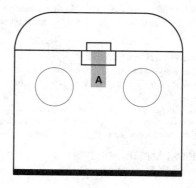

TODD HARVEY

Yrs. of NHL service: 1
Born: Hamilton, Ont.; Feb. 17, 1975
Position: centre/right wing
Height: 5-11
Weight: 200
Uniform no.: 10
Shoots: right

Career statistics:

GP	G	A	TP	PIM
40	11	9	20	67

1994-95 statistics:

GP	G	A	TP	+/-	PIM	PP	SH	GW	GT	S	PCT
40	11	9	20	-3	67	2	0	1	0	64	17.2

LAST SEASON

First NHL season. Led team in shooting percentage. One of only three NHL rookies to record a hat trick.

THE FINESSE GAME

Harvey has a competitive spirit that compensates for any shortfalls in his technical game. His skating is rough. In fact, it's pretty choppy, and as a result he lacks speed. To make up for that, Harvey has great anticipation and awareness. He's clever and his hands are very good. When he gets the puck, he has patience and strength with it.

Harvey saw a lot of power play time and works the front of the net with grit. He goes to the net and follows up shots with second and third effort. He always has his feet moving and he has good hand-eye coordination.

Harvey wasn't used in crucial situations, though he will be in the future, but it's unlikely he'll develop into a player who will be used to kill penalties. Although he played centre as a junior, the Stars plan to keep him on the right wing. Even though he is isn't big, he could be a number two winger or maybe even a number one with Mike Modano if those two players click.

THE PHYSICAL GAME

Size isn't everything. Harvey followed a fitness program during the lockout and it paid off. He will never thrash people, but he's tough in his way and sticks his nose in for battles around the net. He has added about 10 pounds since his rookie year and is solid. He bangs bodies and creates some room for himself around the net. Harvey has confidence in his physical game and that gives him a presence.

THE INTANGIBLES

Harvey was the captain of the champion Canadian World Junior Team and may be future "C" material at the NHL level as well. He is personable, and his effort and intensity won over the veterans in the Dallas dressing room. Harvey is athletic and will work to improve those areas of his game that are lacking.

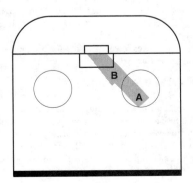

DERIAN HATCHER

Yrs. of NHL service: 4
Born: Sterling Heights, Mich.; June 4, 1972
Position: left defense
Height: 6-5
Weight: 205
Uniform no.: 2
Shoots: left

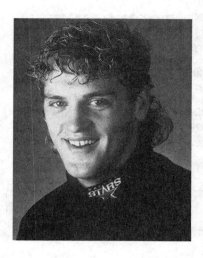

Career statistics:

GP	G	A	TP	PIM
236	28	50	78	582

1991-92 statistics:

GP	G	A	TP	+/-	PIM	PP	SH	GW	GT	S	PCT
43	7	5	12	+7	88	0	0	2	0	51	13.7

1992-93 statistics:

GP	G	A	TP	+/-	PIM	PP	SH	GW	GT	S	PCT
67	4	15	19	-27	178	0	0	1	1	73	5.5

1993-94 statistics:

GP	G	A	TP	+/-	PIM	PP	SH	GW	GT	S	PCT
83	12	19	31	+19	211	2	1	2	0	132	9.1

1994-95 statistics:

GP	G	A	TP	+/-	PIM	PP	SH	GW	GT	S	PCT
43	5	11	16	+3	105	2	0	2	0	74	6.8

LAST SEASON

Missed four games with a staph infection in little finger. Missed one game with a sprained ankle.

THE FINESSE GAME

The number one Hatcher in Dallas, Derian took another big step forward last season. He has developed to the stage that when he is not in the Stars' lineup, they are a much diminished team. He plays in all key situations and is developing a confidence in his decision-making process.

Hatcher's skating is laboured, but he understands the game well and lets the play come to him instead of, say, trying to chase Pavel Bure all over the ice. He is sturdy and well balanced. The fewer strides he has to take, the better.

He has very good hands for a big man, and he has a good head for the game. He sees the game and understands it, especially offensively. Hatcher is effective from the point — not because he has a big, booming slap shot, but because he has a good wrist shot and will get the puck on net quickly. He will join the rush eagerly and he handles the puck nicely.

Hatcher makes fewer mistakes and his game is becoming more low-risk.

THE PHYSICAL GAME

Hatcher is a big force. He has a mean streak when provoked and is a punishing hitter, but has a long enough fuse to stay away from bad penalties. He plays physically every night and demands respect and room. He is the player who injured Jeremy Roenick, and while Roenick himself absolved Hatcher of any dirty play, some of the Hawks coaches screamed for Hatcher's head. He was a bit ruffled by the fuss, but his play was not affected.

He is a big horse and eats up all the ice time Dallas gives him. The more work he gets, the better.

THE INTANGIBLES

After Mark Tinordi was traded, several players wore the "C" for Dallas until it was conferred upon Hatcher. It should stay on his shoulder for a long time. Hatcher carries the responsibility well, and wants to be the kind of player the team looks to for consistent effort and intensity. He is a fine role model for the younger Stars and the veterans reject him as well. He is a quiet player who wants to make a big impact.

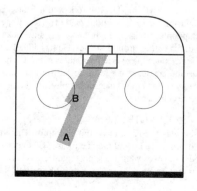

KEVIN HATCHER

Yrs. of NHL service: 10
Born: Detroit, Mich.; Sept. 9, 1966
Position: right defense
Height: 6-4
Weight: 225
Uniform no.: 4
Shoots: right

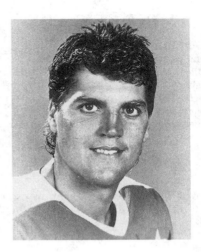

Career statistics:

GP	G	A	TP	PIM
732	159	296	455	1067

1991-92 statistics:

GP	G	A	TP	+/-	PIM	PP	SH	GW	GT	S	PCT
79	17	37	54	+18	105	8	1	2	1	246	6.9

1992-93 statistics:

GP	G	A	TP	+/-	PIM	PP	SH	GW	GT	S	PCT
83	34	45	79	-7	114	13	1	6	0	329	10.3

1993-94 statistics:

GP	G	A	TP	+/-	PIM	PP	SH	GW	GT	S	PCT
72	16	24	40	-13	108	6	0	3	0	217	7.4

1994-95 statistics:

GP	G	A	TP	+/-	PIM	PP	SH	GW	GT	S	PCT
47	10	19	29	-4	66	3	0	2	1	138	7.2

LAST SEASON

Acquired from Washington for Mark Tinordi and Rick Mrozik. Led team defensemen and tied for second on team in scoring. Tied for team lead in shots.

THE FINESSE GAME

Hatcher has wonderful anticipation in his own zone for picking off passes, which he then carries up the middle to start a counterattack. He has the speed and strength to elude checkers in the neutral zone, and he's solid enough on his skates that he seldom goes off-course or loses the puck if bumped. He can finish in close offensively. And he is smart about jumping into the play, but also smart enough to make the best play the situation dictates. He will drive it deep or take a shot from the point if a shot is open. Hatcher moves to the left point on the power play to open up his forehand for one-timers.

Hatcher has the puck so much during a game that there are times when he'll turn the puck over or carry it dangerously in front of his own net, but he makes a far greater number of intelligent plays than mistakes. He makes decisions quickly in all zones. If the heat is on him in his own zone, he is aware of his teammates' positions on the ice and makes the smart outlet pass or bangs the puck off the glass. He is constantly looking to see which attackers might be bearing in on him, but he is poised under pressure.

He is sometimes slow with his first step but achieves top speed quite quickly for a big skater.

THE PHYSICAL GAME

Hatcher was not in game shape when he started the season in Dallas after the trade, and didn't start play-

ing his best hockey until late in the season and into the playoffs. He was able to to handle 26-30 minutes of ice time.

Hatcher has to learn to play tough and mean without spending much time in the penalty box. He has to have a consistent physical element in his game. Afterall, who wants a finesse defenseman this big?

THE INTANGIBLES

Hatcher has had two lost seasons now, given his contract hassles in Washington. He has adapted to a new system and a new environment, was rewarded with a fat new contract, and now has to deliver the goods. The Stars were happy with him last year, but would like to be ecstatic, and Hatcher may have an 80-point season in him. But he has yet to prove he can be a dominating defenseman.

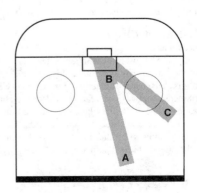

MIKE KENNEDY

Yrs. of NHL service: 1
Born: Vancouver, B.C.; April 13, 1972
Position: centre/left wing
Height: 6-1
Weight: 170
Uniform no.: 39
Shoots: right

Career statistics:

GP	G	A	TP	PIM
44	6	12	18	33

1994-95 statistics:

GP	G	A	TP	+/-	PIM	PP	SH	GW	GT	S	PCT
44	6	12	18	+4	33	2	0	0	0	76	7.9

LAST SEASON
First NHL season. Was leading Kalamazoo in scoring (20-28 — 48) and named to IHL All-Star Team before call-up.

THE FINESSE GAME
Kennedy is deceiving in all aspects of his game. His skating is better than it looks and his puck work is better than his statistics indicate.

He has a good head for the game and good hands. He is very patient with the puck and is always involved in high-traffic areas to gain control. When he gets it, Kennedy has a fine short game with his passes or shot. He played his off-side frequently last year and struggled a bit at times, especially in the defensive zone. He doesn't see much special teams duty, and spent a lot of time on the bench on nights when there were a lot of penalties called.

Kennedy shows signs of developing into a dependable two-way winger, along Mike McPhee lines.

THE PHYSICAL GAME
Kennedy isn't big, but he's strong in a rangy way. He's willing to go to war for the puck in the corners, along the boards and in front of the net. There can never be too many of these kinds of players in a team's system. Kennedy is consistent in his effort.

THE INTANGIBLES
Kennedy was a bubble player in the Stars' 1994 training camp, but he just refused to let the team keep him out of the lineup. His skills make his job vulnerable again this year, but if Kennedy is just as hungry and determined as he was last year, he will be wearing a Dallas jersey again. Unless he can be slotted on the more comfortable left side, it's unlikely he will post the kind of numbers he did in the minors, but his efforts should earn him 40 points.

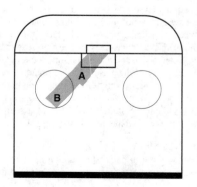

TRENT KLATT

Yrs. of NHL service: 3
Born: Robbinsdale, Minn.; Jan. 30, 1971
Position: right wing
Height: 6-1
Weight: 210
Uniform no.: 22
Shoots: right

Career statistics:

GP	G	A	TP	PIM
156	30	53	83	94

1992-93 statistics:

GP	G	A	TP	+/-	PIM	PP	SH	GW	GT	S	PCT
47	4	19	23	+2	38	1	0	0	0	69	5.8

1993-94 statistics:

GP	G	A	TP	+/-	PIM	PP	SH	GW	GT	S	PCT
61	14	24	38	+13	30	3	0	2	0	86	16.3

1994-95 statistics:

GP	G	A	TP	+/-	PIM	PP	SH	GW	GT	S	PCT
47	12	10	22	-2	26	5	0	3	0	91	13.2

LAST SEASON

Tied for team lead in game-winning goals. Second on team in power play goals.

THE FINESSE GAME

Klatt had a good start to last season, but then tailed off, hitting a streak of about 20 games where he couldn't have put the puck into a soccer net. It's all part of the learning process for a young player.

Klatt is a right-handed, right-wing Mike McPhee. A dependable player defensively, he also has a few offensive dimensions.

Klatt has a big shot off the wing, though he does not use it as often as he should. He needs to find some more offensive tenacity and finish with more authority. Confidence and playing time should bring out this asset. He hides the puck well with his large body and knows what to do with the puck. He is a good passer and uses other players well.

He is strong on his skates and has fair speed and quickness.

THE PHYSICAL GAME

Klatt is learning to play with his weight. He can control the corners and the front of the net. He will play through traffic to create offense. He takes his man out in the corners and along the boards, and he finishes his checks.

THE INTANGIBLES

For a stretch, he played on a line with Mike Modano, and perhaps thought the Stars expected 40 goals from him. Other times, he was a checking winger. Klatt needs to realize what he can do that will keep him in the NHL for 10 years, and that role should be a 20-25 goal scorer as a second- or third-line winger who does his defensive job as well.

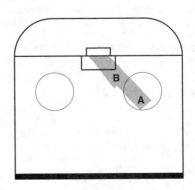

RICHARD MATVICHUK

Yrs. of NHL service: 3
Born: Edmonton, Alta.; Feb. 5, 1973
Position: left defense
Height: 6-2
Weight: 195
Uniform no.: 24
Shoots: left

Career statistics:

GP	G	A	TP	PIM
92	2	8	10	62

1992-93 statistics:

GP	G	A	TP	+/-	PIM	PP	SH	GW	GT	S	PCT
53	2	3	5	-8	26	1	0	0	0	51	3.9

1993-94 statistics:

GP	G	A	TP	+/-	PIM	PP	SH	GW	GT	S	PCT
25	0	3	3	+1	22	0	0	0	0	18	0.0

1994-95 statistics:

GP	G	A	TP	+/-	PIM	PP	SH	GW	GT	S	PCT
14	0	2	2	-7	14	0	0	0	0	21	0.0

LAST SEASON

Missed 34 games with knee surgery and rehab stint with Kalamazoo (IHL).

THE FINESSE GAME

Matvichuk is a good skater with a long stride, and he skates well backwards and pivots in either direction. He likes to come up-ice and get involved in the attack. He has the hand skills and instincts to develop into a solid two-way defenseman.

Matvichuk has a low, hard, accurate shot from the point. He makes smart, crisp passes and uses other players well. He could play either side defensively, but plays best on the left, which is where the Stars use him.

Matvichuk was having an impressive training camp when he suffered a knee injury that required surgery. He came back physically and mentally over the hurdle.

THE PHYSICAL GAME

Matvichuk is aware of the importance of strength and aerobic training, and wants to add even more muscle to stay competitive at the NHL level, since he is a little light by today's NHL standards. He's added five pounds since his draft year and is very solid, and he's still growing. He's not mean, but he will stand in and use his body. Matvichuk occasionally gets into a mode where he starts fishing for the puck.

THE INTANGIBLES

This will be like a second rookie year for Matvichuk, coming off the lost season. He could work his way up to carrying more weight (maybe as much as 210 pounds), and will be a more physical force. He should be one of the top five defensemen in Dallas.

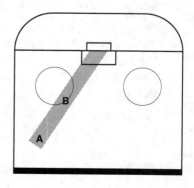

MIKE MODANO

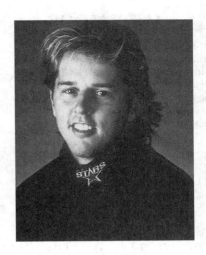

Yrs. of NHL service: 6
Born: Livonia, Mich.; June 7, 1970
Position: centre
Height: 6-3
Weight: 190
Uniform no.: 9
Shoots: left

Career statistics:

GP	G	A	TP	PIM
423	185	246	401	319

1991-92 statistics:

GP	G	A	TP	+/-	PIM	PP	SH	GW	GT	S	PCT
76	33	44	77	-9	46	5	0	8	2	256	12.9

1992-93 statistics:

GP	G	A	TP	+/-	PIM	PP	SH	GW	GT	S	PCT
82	33	60	93	-7	83	9	0	7	0	307	10.7

1993-94 statistics:

GP	G	A	TP	+/-	PIM	PP	SH	GW	GT	S	PCT
76	50	43	93	-8	54	18	0	4	2	281	17.8

1994-95 statistics:

GP	G	A	TP	+/-	PIM	PP	SH	GW	GT	S	PCT
30	12	17	29	+7	8	4	1	0	0	100	12.0

LAST SEASON

Tied for second on team in points. Missed four games with a bruised ankle. Missed 14 games with ruptured tendon in his left ankle.

THE FINESSE GAME

Modano's season ended early with a career-threatening ankle injury. That sobering reality is another hard-learned lesson on Modano's road to becoming a mature NHL star, and his recovery will determine whether he can make it to the game's elite class.

Modano was young in a lot of ways when he broke in six seasons ago, but he is hitting his prime and may not have come near the ceiling yet. He is a thrilling player to watch on nights when he decides the game is his to toy with. He has outstanding offensive instincts and great hands, and he is a smooth passer and a remarkable skater in all facets (though his flexibility and strength may be affected for the first half of the season).

Modano makes other players around him better, which is the mark of an elite player. His speed and movement with the puck mesmerizes defenders and opens up ice for his linemates. He hasn't found the ideal linemate yet. Right wing is his best passing side, and Todd Harvey may prove to be the answer.

Modano has become a better goal-scorer by fighting through checks to pick the third rebound in front of the net as well as scoring off his blazing solo efforts. He must better utilize players coming through the neutral zone and pick off an open lane to the top of the circle, as opposed to carrying it. His game is of-

fense and he has to develop a complete repertoire.

His defensive game has improved a great deal, and his anticipation and quick hands help him intercept passes. He needs work on his face-offs.

THE PHYSICAL GAME

Modano pays the price for his work around the net. He is strong and can lean on people. He doesn't play a physical game, but he has the size to earn some respect for himself. He can already create room with his speed. If he does it with his size as well, the ice will be his.

THE INTANGIBLES

Modano probably has more sheer talent than anyone else in his age group, with the exception of Teemu Selanne (both were drafted in 1988, along with Trevor Linden, Jeremy Roenick and Rod Brind'Amour). The drive and intensity that were question marks earlier in his career now seem to have become exclamation points. Modano's success this season will depend on his rehab from ankle surgery, but word during the off-season was that he would be ready to skate at training camp. He hasn't hit the 100-point mark yet, but with health and the right linemates, it could occur this season.

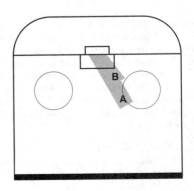

ANDY MOOG

Yrs. of NHL service: 14
Born: Penticton, B.C.; Feb. 18, 1960
Position: goaltender
Height: 5-8
Weight: 170
Uniform no.: 35
Catches: left

Career statistics:

GP	MINS	GA	SO	GAA	A	PIM
582	32854	1791	21	3.27	23	186

1991-92 statistics:

GP	MINS	GAA	W	L	T	SO	GA	S	SAPCT	PIM
62	3640	3.23	28	22	9	1	196	1727	.887	52

1992-93 statistics:

GP	MINS	GAA	W	L	T	SO	GA	S	SAPCT	PIM
55	3194	3.16	37	14	3	3	168	1357	.876	14

1993-94 statistics:

GP	MINS	GAA	W	L	T	SO	GA	S	SAPCT	PIM
55	3121	3.27	24	20	7	2	170	1604	.894	16

1994-95 statistics:

GP	MINS	GAA	W	L	T	SO	GA	S	SAPCT	PIM
31	1770	2.44	10	12	7	2	72	846	.915	14

LAST SEASON

Recorded best save percentage in at least four seasons. Missed one game with a hip injury. Missed five games with a hamstring injury. NHL leader among active goalies in wins.

THE PHYSICAL GAME

Moog is a fairly good technical goalie who has relied on his reflexes for most of his career, but at this veteran stage he has improved his technique. He is a butterfly goalie who stays well on the top of his crease.

He is aggressive and comes so far out of his net that most teams know enough to come down the wing, fake a shot, go around him and pass to an open man for a lot of gimme chip-ins. His five-hole is not as good as it should be for a technically sound goalie, and he is now more vulnerable high than he was earlier in his career when he had such a good glove hand.

Moog scrambles back to his feet quickly when he is down, but he keeps on his feet well and plays his angles.

Moog has adopted a stick with the "Curtis curve" (named for Curtis Joseph). It is a bent paddle that makes it easier for the goalie to get his stick to lie flat on the ice across the front of the net — to stop wraparounds and take away low shots. The drawback is that it is harder for a goalie to move his hand down the shaft to poke-check or otherwise use his stick defensively, but Moog was never that aggressive in those areas, anyway.

THE MENTAL GAME

Moog is the number one man in Dallas again (despite the previous challenge from Darcy Wakaluk), and that made him a more relaxed and reliable goaltender. He allowed very few soft goals.

THE INTANGIBLES

Moog is a tough competitor and a consummate pro. He needs to stay healthy and fit, because the Stars are relying on him for one, and possibly two, more seasons as their number one. The team is improving in front of him, which will help Moog's numbers even more this season.

DOUG ZMOLEK

Yrs. of NHL service: 3
Born: Rochester, Minn.; Nov. 3, 1970
Position: right defense
Height: 6-1
Weight: 195
Uniform no.: 5
Shoots: left

Career statistics:

GP	G	A	TP	PIM
201	6	19	25	429

1992-93 statistics:

GP	G	A	TP	+/-	PIM	PP	SH	GW	GT	S	PCT
84	5	10	15	-50	229	2	0	0	0	94	5.3

1993-94 statistics:

GP	G	A	TP	+/-	PIM	PP	SH	GW	GT	S	PCT
75	1	4	5	-8	133	0	0	0	0	32	3.1

1994-95 statistics:

GP	G	A	TP	+/-	PIM	PP	SH	GW	GT	S	PCT
42	0	5	5	-6	67	0	0	0	0	28	0.0

LAST SEASON

Acquired from San Jose with Mike Lalor for Ulf Dahlen.

THE FINESSE GAME

Playing on the same team with Craig Ludwig must make Zmolek feel as if he's looking at his future. Zmolek is, like Ludwig, an efficient, stay-at-home defenseman.

Zmolek is a fine skater with a strong stride. He has good balance and agility and he moves well laterally. His skating helps him angle attackers to the boards. He is a little awkward in his turning and can be victimized.

He has some nice offensive instincts. He moves the puck out of the zone well with quick, accurate passes, and he has soft hands for touch passes in tighter quarters. His understanding of the game is growing.

Zmolek is an excellent penalty killer. He is intelligent and alert, and stops and starts well forwards to backwards.

THE PHYSICAL GAME

Zmolek developed in college (University of Minnesota) where the physical element of the game is not as important, but he took a great step forward last season by incorporating more physical play in his game. He was defensively consistent, and he had some major battles with NHL heavyweights like Marty McSorley. He proved to himself that not only is he a game player, but he can also be effective with his body work.

THE INTANGIBLES

Zmolek was very pleased with his progress at establishing a more physical presence, and seems eager to pay the price to become that kind of defenseman. It's an important element to add to his already solid, conservative defensive style, and makes him a more valuable defenseman. His point totals will be neglible, but he is seriously tough.

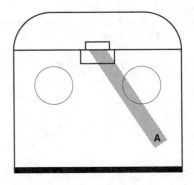

DETROIT RED WINGS

Players' Statistics 1994-95

POS	NO.	PLAYER	GP	G	A	PTS	+/-	PIM	PP	SH	GW	GT	S	PCTG
D	77	PAUL COFFEY	45	14	44	58	18	72	4	1	2		181	7.7
C	91	SERGEI FEDOROV	42	20	30	50	6	24	7	3	5		147	13.6
R	22	DINO CICCARELLI	42	16	27	43	12	39	6		3		106	15.1
L	55	KEITH PRIMEAU	45	15	27	42	17	99	1		3		96	15.6
R	26	RAY SHEPPARD	43	30	10	40	11	17	11		5	1	125	24.0
C	19	STEVE YZERMAN	47	12	26	38	6	40	4		1		134	9.0
C	13	VYACHESLAV KOZLOV	46	13	20	33	12	45	5		3		97	13.4
D	5	NICKLAS LIDSTROM	43	10	16	26	15	6	7				90	11.1
R	17	DOUG BROWN	45	9	12	21	14	16	1	1	2		69	13.0
L	21	BOB ERREY	43	8	13	21	13	58			1		72	11.1
D	44	VIACHESLAV FETISOV	18	3	12	15	1	2	3				37	8.1
L	11	SHAWN BURR	42	6	8	14	13	60			3		65	9.2
D	16	VLAD. KONSTANTINOV	47	3	11	14	10	101					57	5.3
R	25	DARREN MCCARTY	31	5	8	13	5	88	1		2		27	18.5
R	20	MARTIN LAPOINTE	39	4	6	10	1	73			1		46	8.7
C	23	GREG JOHNSON	22	3	5	8	1	14	2				32	9.4
C	33	KRIS DRAPER	36	2	6	8	1	22					44	4.5
D	3	BOB ROUSE	48	1	7	8	14	36			1		51	2.0
D	4	MARK HOWE	18	1	5	6	-3	10			1		14	7.1
C	18	MIKE KRUSHELNYSKI	20	2	3	5	3	6					20	10.0
C	37	*TIM TAYLOR	22		4	4	3	16					21	
D	2	TERRY CARKNER	20	1	2	3	7	21					9	11.1
D	15	MIKE RAMSEY	33	1	2	3	11	23					29	3.4
D	8	*AARON WARD	1		1	1	1	2						
D	27	MARK FERNER	17		1	1	-4	6					16	
L	32	STU GRIMSON	42		1	1	-11	147					18	
C	14	ANDREW MCKIM	2					2						
G	30	CHRIS OSGOOD	19					2						
G	29	MIKE VERNON	30					8						

GP = games played; G = goals; A = assists; PTS = points; +/- = goals-for minus goals-against while player is on ice; PIM = penalties in minutes; PP = power play goals; SH = shorthanded goals; GW = game-winning goals; GT = game-tying goals; S = no. of shots; PCTG = percentage of goals to shots; * = rookie

DOUG BROWN

Yrs. of NHL service: 8
Born: Southborough, Mass.; June 12, 1964
Position: right wing
Height: 5-10
Weight: 185
Uniform no.: 17
Shoots: right

Career statistics:

GP	G	A	TP	PIM
472	95	129	224	118

1991-92 statistics:

GP	G	A	TP	+/-	PIM	PP	SH	GW	GT	S	PCT
71	11	17	28	+17	27	1	2	1	0	140	7.9

1992-93 statistics:

GP	G	A	TP	+/-	PIM	PP	SH	GW	GT	S	PCT
15	0	5	5	+3	2	0	0	0	0	17	0.0

1993-94 statistics:

GP	G	A	TP	+/-	PIM	PP	SH	GW	GT	S	PCT
77	18	37	55	+19	18	2	0	1	0	152	11.8

1994-95 statistics:

GP	G	A	TP	+/-	PIM	PP	SH	GW	GT	S	PCT
45	9	12	21	+14	16	1	1	2	0	69	13.0

LAST SEASON

Acquired on waivers from Pittsburgh.

THE FINESSE GAME

Call him "Doug Brownov." This bread-and-butter right wing adapted to the caviar style of Russian linemates Sergei Fedorov and Vyacheslav Kozlov, serving as the safety valve for the risk-taking Kozlov and using his skating and passing skills to get involved in the attack.

Because Brown is always hustling, he gives the impression of being a fast skater. He's not, at least not straight ahead, though he does have real quickness side-to-side. He is sometimes too fast on his feet and wipes out frequently after losing his edges. Brown gets a lot of breakaways because of the quick jumps he gets on the opposition. The lack of a finishing touch prevents him from scoring as many goals as he should.

Brown offers a consistent effort night after night. He always attains his level of play but seldom surpasses it, which is why coaches often give younger players ice time ahead of Brown at the start of the season, then tend to go back to the old reliable redhead.

A determined penalty killer and shorthanded threat, he never quits around the net and comes up with tip-ins and stuffs. He blocks shots fearlessly and approaches the game with intelligence and enthusiasm.

THE PHYSICAL GAME

Brown is not a strong player, but he is one of the better grinders along the wall, since he will hang in there and not give up on a puck. He keeps the puck alive with his stick or feet. Brown won't fight, but he won't be intimidated, either.

THE INTANGIBLES

Brown is a chameleon. Despite lacking world-class skills, he fits in with world-class players. He hustles and grinds and does all of the little things it takes to win a hockey game. Brown has spent most of his career on the bubble (he was never drafted, but was signed as a free agent out of college; he was a free agent again, and then left unprotected in last year's waiver draft). Playing with a Presidents' Trophy winner and Stanley Cup finalist team may finally lend Brown the cachet of a winner.

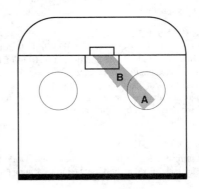

SHAWN BURR

Yrs. of NHL service: 10
Born: Sarnia, Ont,; July 1, 1966
Position: left wing
Height: 6-1
Weight: 200
Uniform no.: 11
Shoots: left

Career statistics:

GP	G	A	TP	PIM
659	148	214	362	765

1991-92 statistics:

GP	G	A	TP	+/-	PIM	PP	SH	GW	GT	S	PCT
79	19	32	51	+26	118	2	0	3	1	140	13.6

1992-93 statistics:

GP	G	A	TP	+/-	PIM	PP	SH	GW	GT	S	PCT
80	10	25	35	+18	74	1	1	2	0	99	10.1

1993-94 statistics:

GP	G	A	TP	+/-	PIM	PP	SH	GW	GT	S	PCT
51	10	12	22	+12	31	0	1	1	0	64	15.6

1994-95 statistics:

GP	G	A	TP	+/-	PIM	PP	SH	GW	GT	S	PCT
42	6	8	14	+13	60	0	0	3	0	65	9.2

the ice when he only produces 10 goals a year. Burr was benched in the Stanley Cup finals for an odd incident: the coaching staff believed he had given Scott Niedermayer back his stick after a clash behind the net, only to have Niedermayer go down the ice to score.

LAST SEASON

Games missed due to coaches' decision.

THE FINESSE GAME

Burr is an aggressive fore-checker with an in-and-out game. He's in the lineup one night, out the next, and it's tied to his effort. His skating isn't the best, but he is a diligent enough plugger to stick with all but the fastest NHL forwards. He goes hard to the nets and along the boards, trying to make up with energy what he lacks in acceleration.

Burr is a smart hockey player, which makes him a natural in the defensive role, either as a checker or as the safety valve on a scoring line (a role he played with Keith Primeau and Dino Ciccarelli). He creates turnovers with his aggressive checking, but lacks the finishing touch to bury his chances. He was a scorer at the junior and minor league level, but that touch has not manifested itself in the majors. Most of Burr's scoring chances come from scrums around the net. His shots scare no one.

THE PHYSICAL GAME

Burr has to be involved every night. He is lean but uses his muscle along the boards and in front of the net. He makes puck carriers rush their passes because he sticks to them tenaciously. Because he is not a very good skater and has limited range, he does not hit in open ice. He is scrappy and can be very annoying to play against.

THE INTANGIBLES

Burr is respected for his honest defensive work despite his lack of production, but he has to bring a lot to

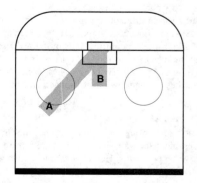

DINO CICCARELLI

Yrs. of NHL service: 15
Born: Sarnia, Ont.; Feb. 18, 1960
Position: right wing
Height: 5-10
Weight: 175
Uniform no.: 22
Shoots: right

Career statistics:

GP	G	A	TP	PIM
1015	529	528	1057	1113

1991-92 statistics:

GP	G	A	TP	+/-	PIM	PP	SH	GW	GT	S	PCT
78	38	38	76	-10	78	13	0	7	0	279	13.6

1992-93 statistics:

GP	G	A	TP	+/-	PIM	PP	SH	GW	GT	S	PCT
82	41	56	97	+12	81	21	0	8	0	200	20.5

1993-94 statistics:

GP	G	A	TP	+/-	PIM	PP	SH	GW	GT	S	PCT
66	28	29	57	+10	73	12	0	1	2	153	18.3

1994-95 statistics:

GP	G	A	TP	+/-	PIM	PP	SH	GW	GT	S	PCT
42	16	27	43	+12	39	6	0	3	0	106	15.1

LAST SEASON

Played 1,000th NHL game. Third on team in points. Missed one game with a groin injury. Missed one game with facial lacerations.

THE FINESSE GAME

For a smallish player, Ciccarelli casts a big shadow. Yapping and jabbing, he plays few invisible games. His attitude and aggressive style enhance his skills, which are highlighted by his quickness and his scoring knack.

Ciccarelli has great hands for finishing plays. Although he has a big slap shot, he is more effective down low. He creates havoc for goaltenders, digging for loose pucks, deflecting shots, screening the goaltender. His offensive game is straightforward. He's not a very creative playmaker, so he shoots first and asks questions later. Somehow, he always seems to get a piece of the puck.

A strong fore-checker, Ciccarelli takes the body well despite his small size, and he can do something with the puck when it does squirt free. He doesn't have breakaway speed and dazzling moves, but he is a strong and well-balanced skater who is very quick in small spaces.

THE PHYSICAL GAME

"Dino the Disturber." Ciccarelli is starved for attention and isn't happy unless he's got a goalie in a tizzy or a goal judge pushing that red-light button. He isn't a very good skater, so he can't afford to be a perimeter player. He has to be parked right on the paint in front of the net, his heels on the crease, taking the punishment and dishing it out. Intimidation is a huge part of his game. He will check goalies out of their crease and try to get a piece of them while they're still in it.

Ciccarelli plays as if he has to prove his courage every night; pound for pound he's as strong as most bigger players. He has a low centre of gravity and is difficult to move. Defensemen may think, "No problem, I can move this guy," only to find Ciccarelli impossible to budge. Punish him as much as you want. He'll keep coming back.

THE INTANGIBLES

Ciccarelli remains the quintessential hockey brat. Injuries and age have slowed him, but Dino was never known for his speed anyway. With sufficient power play time, he should be productive again. His desire and competitive nature is always a plus.

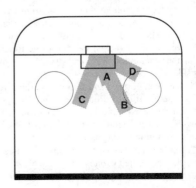

PAUL COFFEY

Yrs. of NHL service: 15
Born: Weston, Ont.; June 1, 1961
Position: right defense
Height: 6-0
Weight: 200
Uniform no.: 77
Shoots: left

Career statistics:

GP	G	A	TP	PIM
1078	358	978	1336	1546

1991-92 statistics:

GP	G	A	TP	+/-	PIM	PP	SH	GW	GT	S	PCT
64	11	58	69	+1	87	5	0	1	0	232	4.7

1992-93 statistics:

GP	G	A	TP	+/-	PIM	PP	SH	GW	GT	S	PCT
80	12	75	87	+16	77	5	0	0	0	254	4.7

1993-94 statistics:

GP	G	A	TP	+/-	PIM	PP	SH	GW	GT	S	PCT
80	14	63	77	+28	106	5	0	3	0	278	5.0

1994-95 statistics:

GP	G	A	TP	+/-	PIM	PP	SH	GW	GT	S	PCT
45	14	44	58	+18	72	4	1	2	0	181	7.7

LAST SEASON

Won 1995 Norris Trophy. Named to First All-Star Team. Led team defensemen in scoring for third consecutive season. Led team in assists, points, plus-minus and shots. Led NHL defensemen in scoring. Led NHL in power play assists (27) and power play points (31). Missed three games with a back injury.

THE FINESSE GAME

The rejuvenated Coffey is a joy to watch in open ice. He may be the best-skating defenseman of all-time. He doctors his skates so there is minimal hollow in the blades, and he just glides over the ice.

Coffey handles the puck while he is skating and whirling at top speed or changing directions. Few players are better at the long home-run pass, and Coffey has all the finesse skills of a forward when he works down low. He has tremendous vision to make a play, feather a pass or work a give-and-go. He understands the concept of time and space.

Coffey has a whole menu of shots, from wristers to slaps. He is a world-class point man on the power play, faking slaps and sending passes low, sliding the puck over to his point partner for a one-timer, or drilling the shot himself. He prefers to attack down the right side.

He has enough speed and skill to split the defense or beat a defender one-on-one. He is almost impossible to hit because he is so shifty and strong on his skates. He creates a lot of open ice for his teammates because he is intimidating as a skater.

Coffey's defensive lapses are often comical, or tragic. He was toasted in one memorable playoff goal

last season by Coffey wannabe Scott Niedermayer.

THE PHYSICAL GAME

Coffey has the size to hit and clear the slot, but he doesn't, and at this stage in his distinguished career that is not about to change. There will be times when he gets beaten coming out of the corner because he doesn't hit the opponent. Anyone who hires Coffey for his offensive gifts has to be willing to put up with his defensive shortcomings.

He will block shots when it counts (like in the playoffs), but most of his defense is based on his anticipation in picking off passes.

THE INTANGIBLES

Coffey makes good players better and very good players great, and he is excellent at working with younger defensemen (like potential Coffey clone Nicklas Lidstrom). Last year's *HSR* said Coffey was beginning to hit his downside (wrong), but that he would still be good for 65-70 points (right, but he nearly did it in essentially half a season). His back injuries will nag him, but Coffey was disappointed by his team's collapse in the 1995 finals and has something to prove.

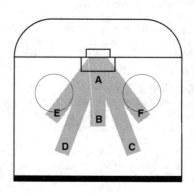

KRIS DRAPER

Yrs. of NHL service: 1
Born: Toronto, Ont.; May 24, 1971
Position: centre
Height: 5-11
Weight: 190
Uniform no.: 33
Shoots: left

Career statistics:

GP	G	A	TP	PIM
95	10	14	24	62

1991-92 statistics:

GP	G	A	TP	+/-	PIM	PP	SH	GW	GT	S	PCT
10	2	0	2	0	2	0	0	0	0	19	10.5

1992-93 statistics:

GP	G	A	TP	+/-	PIM	PP	SH	GW	GT	S	PCT
7	0	0	0	-6	2	0	0	0	0	5	0.0

1993-94 statistics:

GP	G	A	TP	+/-	PIM	PP	SH	GW	GT	S	PCT
39	5	8	13	+11	31	0	1	0	0	55	9.1

1994-95 statistics:

GP	G	A	TP	+/-	PIM	PP	SH	GW	GT	S	PCT
36	2	6	8	+1	22	0	0	0	0	44	4.5

LAST SEASON

Career high in games played, goals, assists and points.

THE FINESSE GAME

Draper has to work hard for his goals. They come off his fore-check and his anticipation when a linemate is doing the honours and forces a defender into a give-away. Draper is there to jump on the free puck and get a good scoring opportunity away quickly.

But the strength of Draper's game is his defense. He plays his position well and is proud of his checking role. A good skater, he is strong on his feet and well balanced, though not fast. His smart play makes him seem much quicker than he is.

Draper is unselfish and is a good passer, especially in traffic. He is an effective penalty killer and can handle time on the second power play unit because of his intelligent work around the net, but he doesn't have a great finishing touch.

THE PHYSICAL GAME

Draper is not big, but he has wiry strength and uses his body well. He works the boards and corners and relishes physical play. He is intense and ready to play every night. Draper completes his checks and is a no-frills defensive centre with a strong work ethic.

THE INTANGIBLES

Draper plays his best in big games and in key situations. While he might sit around on the bench for long stretches, due to the Red Wings' depth, he has the kind of character that a lot of more skilled players lack. He has a ton of heart, and with enough ice time could chip in 15-20 goals as well.

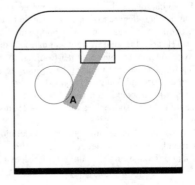

SERGEI FEDOROV

Yrs. of NHL service: 5
Born: Pskov, Russia; Dec. 13, 1969
Position: centre
Height: 6-1
Weight: 191
Uniform no.: 91
Shoots: left

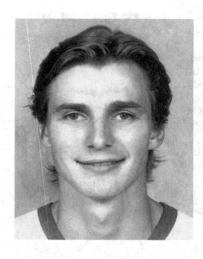

Career statistics:

GP	G	A	TP	PIM
357	173	249	422	268

1991-92 statistics:

GP	G	A	TP	+/-	PIM	PP	SH	GW	GT	S	PCT
80	32	54	86	+26	72	7	2	5	0	249	12.9

1992-93 statistics:

GP	G	A	TP	+/-	PIM	PP	SH	GW	GT	S	PCT
73	34	53	87	+33	72	13	4	3	0	217	15.7

1993-94 statistics:

GP	G	A	TP	+/-	PIM	PP	SH	GW	GT	S	PCT
82	56	64	120	+48	34	13	4	10	0	337	16.6

1994-95 statistics:

GP	G	A	TP	+/-	PIM	PP	SH	GW	GT	S	PCT
45	20	30	50	+6	24	7	3	5	0	147	13.6

LAST SEASON

Led team in shorthanded goals and game-winning goals. Second on team in goals, assists and points. Unsuccessful on penalty shot attempt versus Kelly Hrudey. Missed one game with the flu. Missed two games with a hamstring injury. Served three-game suspension from 1994 playoff incident.

THE FINESSE GAME

Fedorov is a tremendous package of offensive and defensive skills. He can go from checking the opponent's top centre to powering the power play from shift to shift. His skating is nothing short of phenomenal, and he can handle the puck while he is dazzling everyone with his blades.

He likes to gear up from his own defensive zone on the rush, using his acceleration and balance to drive wide to his right, carrying the puck on his backhand and protecting it with his body. If the defenseman lets up at all, then Fedorov is by him, pulling the puck quickly to his forehand. Nor is he by any means selfish. He has 360-degree vision of the ice and makes solid, confident passes right under opponents' sticks and smack onto the tape of his teammates. Fedorov will swing behind the opposing net from left to right, fooling the defense into thinking he is going to continue to curl around, but he can quickly reverse with the puck on his backhand, shake his shadow and wheel around for a shot or goalmouth pass. He does it all in a flash.

Fedorov also has the strength and acceleration to drive right between two defenders, keep control of the puck and wrist a strong shot on goal. He does all of these scary things while playing some of the best defense in the league.

THE PHYSICAL GAME

Fedorov is wiry, and though he would prefer to stay in open ice, he will go to the trenches when he has to. Much of his power is generated from his strong skating. For the most part, his defense is dominated by his reads, anticipation and quickness in knocking down passes and breaking up plays. He is not much of a bodychecker and he gets most of his penalties from stick and restraining fouls. He gets exasperated by some of the tactics used against him and will retaliate with his stick.

Fedorov has a great work ethic and can skate all night, which is usually what Detroit asks him to do.

THE INTANGIBLES

Fedorov is another one of the Red Wings who feels the frustration of last year's playoff failure. He was slowed by a shoulder separation (an ill-disguised injury that the Red Wings tried to hide), and was so sore he couldn't take face-offs. Fedorov feels he has a lot to prove and could have a monster year.

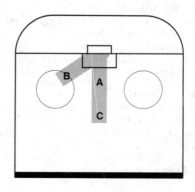

STU GRIMSON

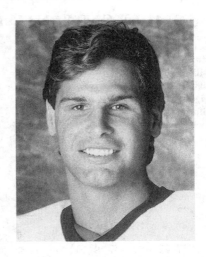

Yrs. of NHL service: 5
Born: Kamloops, B.C.; May 20, 1965
Position: left wing
Height: 6-5
Weight: 220
Uniform no.: 32
Shoots: left

Career statistics:

GP	G	A	TP	PIM
290	4	10	14	978

1991-92 statistics:

GP	G	A	TP	+/-	PIM	PP	SH	GW	GT	S	PCT
54	2	2	4	-2	234	0	0	0	0	23	8.7

1992-93 statistics:

GP	G	A	TP	+/-	PIM	PP	SH	GW	GT	S	PCT
78	1	1	2	+2	193	1	0	0	0	14	7.1

1993-94 statistics:

GP	G	A	TP	+/-	PIM	PP	SH	GW	GT	S	PCT
77	1	5	6	-6	199	0	0	0	0	34	2.9

1994-95 statistics:

GP	G	A	TP	+/-	PIM	PP	SH	GW	GT	S	PCT
42	0	1	1	-11	147	0	0	0	0	18	0.0

good for his one goal a year (except for those darn lockout years).

LAST SEASON

Led team in PIM. Acquired from Anaheim with Mark Ferner and a sixth-round draft pick in 1996 for Mike Sillinger and Jason York.

THE FINESSE GAME

Grimson is a limited role player. He is smart enough to know that this kind of player is starting to vanish from the NHL scene, and he has been working at improving his skills. Right now the catch is that Grimson can't get much ice because he's not good enough, and he doesn't have any chance of getting better until he gets more ice.

With only two or three shifts a game, it is hard to judge much of Grimson's skills. He has little confidence to do much more than what is expected of him, which, for the moment, is to fight.

Grimson has a hard shot but it's not accurate. Probably every one of his NHL goals (all four of 'em) has come from no more than 20 feet out.

THE PHYSICAL GAME

Grimson doesn't have much of a physical presence for someone who has the reputation of being a good fighter. The problem is obvious: he can't be a factor unless he is on the ice more often. Detroit acquired him for some health insurance for their smaller skilled players, but Grimson seldom dressed and didn't pose much of a threat from the press box.

THE INTANGIBLES

Grimson is a limited role player, but he is a catalyst when he does swing into action. He loves the game and knows exactly why he's here. And he's always

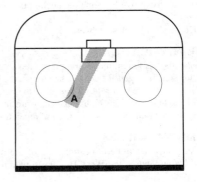

VLADIMIR KONSTANTINOV

Yrs. of NHL service: 4
Born: Murmansk, Russia; Mar. 19, 1967
Position: right defense
Height: 5-11
Weight: 176
Uniform no.: 16
Shoots: right

Career statistics:

GP	G	A	TP	PIM
288	28	74	102	548

1991-92 statistics:

GP	G	A	TP	+/-	PIM	PP	SH	GW	GT	S	PCT
79	8	25	33	+25	172	1	0	2	0	102	7.4

1992-93 statistics:

GP	G	A	TP	+/-	PIM	PP	SH	GW	GT	S	PCT
82	5	17	22	+22	137	0	0	0	0	85	5.9

1993-94 statistics:

GP	G	A	TP	+/-	PIM	PP	SH	GW	GT	S	PCT
80	12	21	33	+30	138	1	3	3	0	97	12.4

1994-95 statistics:

GP	G	A	TP	+/-	PIM	PP	SH	GW	GT	S	PCT
47	3	11	14	+10	101	0	0	0	0	57	5.3

defensive-minded partners last season, but could use a more gifted offensive player as a complement, so that he can concentrate on defense.

LAST SEASON

Second on team in PIM. Only game missed due to coaches' decision.

THE FINESSE GAME

Dynamic skating buoys Konstantinov's game. He is all over the ice, to the extent that he has to be calmed down or else he is too aggressive in the neutral zone and gets caught. He does not get overly involved in the attack, but when he does he'll make a good passing play rather than waste a shot when he is in deep, because he doesn't want to risk the shot being blocked before he has a chance to turn back up ice. In fact, he probably is too reluctant to fire. Konstantinov prefers to break out of the zone with a smart pass, but he can wheel the puck out of danger if under pressure.

Konstantinov is a fine skater with speed, agility, lateral movement, balance and strength. He is used on the first penalty-killing unit and will be on the ice to protect a lead late. He has good hand skills but sometimes is guilty of overhandling the puck in the defensive zone.

He does not block shots well.

THE PHYSICAL GAME

Konstantinov is tough, mean, and plays much bigger than his size. If he gets the chance, he will put the hurt on an attacker. He will ride a skater into the boards, and he might use his stick high, too. People are always trying to swat him, but he's not afraid of retaliation.

THE INTANGIBLES

Konstantinov has quickly become one of the most hated defensemen in the West. He played with more

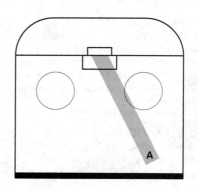

VYACHESLAV KOZLOV

Yrs. of NHL service: 2
Born: Voskresensk, Soviet Union; Feb. 14, 1975
Position: centre/left wing
Height: 5-10
Weight: 172
Uniform no.: 13
Shoots: left

Career statistics:

GP	G	A	TP	PIM
147	51	62	113	111

1991-92 statistics:

GP	G	A	TP	+/-	PIM	PP	SH	GW	GT	S	PCT
7	0	2	2	-2	2	0	0	0	0	9	0.0

1992-93 statistics:

GP	G	A	TP	+/-	PIM	PP	SH	GW	GT	S	PCT
17	4	1	5	-1	14	0	0	0	0	26	15.4

1993-94 statistics:

GP	G	A	TP	+/-	PIM	PP	SH	GW	GT	S	PCT
77	34	39	73	+27	50	8	2	6	0	202	16.8

1994-95 statistics:

GP	G	A	TP	+/-	PIM	PP	SH	GW	GT	S	PCT
46	13	20	33	+12	45	5	0	3	0	97	13.4

THE INTANGIBLES

Kozlov played most of the season with Sergei Fedorov and Doug Brown, and fit in comfortably. He has to take that next step to be a star. Given his talent level and ice time, 60 points is insufficient. Kozlov should be in the 80-point range.

LAST SEASON

Second full NHL season. Missed two games with a foot injury.

THE FINESSE GAME

At age 15, Kozlov was considered to be the most skilled player in his age group in the world. Detroit drafted him 45th overall in 1990, the highest selection of a Russian player to that point, and Kozlov has done nothing to indicate the early reports won't be borne out in the mature player.

He came up through the ranks as a centre, and even though the Red Wings have slotted him on the left wing, Kozlov uses all of the ice and fits in with the team's freewheeling offensive style. He doesn't just skate up and down his wing, but cuts and wheels and bursts into openings on the ice. He can split the defense if it plays him too close or drive the defense back with his speed and use the open ice to find a teammate. He has great control of the puck at high speed and plays an excellent transition game.

Kozlov needs to find consistency. He has been brilliant for a stretch, then quiet for another, but stardom awaits.

THE PHYSICAL GAME

Kozlov is highly competitive and will fight his way through checks. He exceeded a lot of expectations in Detroit, but he is a stranger to the league no longer and draws considerable checking attention. The Russian earned respect points for returning to one playoff game after being clobbered by one of the game's biggest hitters, New Jersey's Scott Stevens.

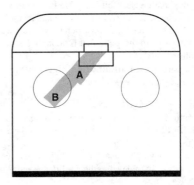

MARTIN LAPOINTE

Yrs. of NHL service: 2
Born: Lachine, Que.; Sept. 12, 1973
Position: right wing
Height: 5-11
Weight: 185
Uniform no.: 20
Shoots: right

Career statistics:

GP	G	A	TP	PIM
96	12	15	27	133

1991-92 statistics:

GP	G	A	TP	+/-	PIM	PP	SH	GW	GT	S	PCT
4	0	1	1	+2	5	0	0	0	0	2	0.0

1992-93 statistics:

GP	G	A	TP	+/-	PIM	PP	SH	GW	GT	S	PCT
3	0	0	0	-2	0	0	0	0	0	2	0.0

1993-94 statistics:

GP	G	A	TP	+/-	PIM	PP	SH	GW	GT	S	PCT
50	8	8	16	+7	55	2	0	0	0	45	17.8

1994-95 statistics:

GP	G	A	TP	+/-	PIM	PP	SH	GW	GT	S	PCT
39	4	6	10	+1	73	0	0	1	0	46	8.7

that will come with more ice time.

LAST SEASON
Second NHL season.

THE FINESSE GAME
Lapointe is as much a finisher as a playmaker. He has a good short game, working passes low between the face-off dots. He doesn't have breakaway speed, but his acceleration helps him create odd-man situations deep in the zone, and he is adept at getting open for the return pass on a give-and-go. He likes to drive to the net and isn't shy about clearing a path for himself.

Yet another sparkler from the blueblooded 1991 draft (taken 10th overall by Detroit), Lapointe is a strong, powerful, quick skater, with a work ethic that enhances all of his natural skills.

THE PHYSICAL GAME
Lapointe is an opportunist around the net, jumping on loose pucks like a miner pouncing on gold nuggets. He finishes his checks and, with his sturdy build and dynamic skating, can hit hard. He has improved his upper body strength and cardiovascular conditioning over the past three seasons, which may indicate a mature approach to the game that is about to become his livelihood.

Lapointe isn't afraid to hit bigger players. He plays like a much bigger man.

THE INTANGIBLES
Lapointe is aggressive and fiery, and was probably Detroit's best forward in the finals. He will be a regular this season.

Lapointe won't cheat a team. He plays every shift, and needs only to develop the confidence in his game

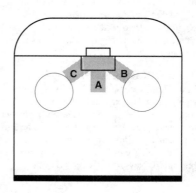

NICKLAS LIDSTROM

Yrs. of NHL service: 4
Born: Västerås, Sweden; Apr. 28, 1970
Position: left defense
Height: 6-1
Weight: 176
Uniform no.: 5
Shoots: left

Career statistics:

GP	G	A	TP	PIM
291	38	145	183	82

1991-92 statistics:

GP	G	A	TP	+/-	PIM	PP	SH	GW	GT	S	PCT
80	11	49	60	+36	22	5	0	1	1	168	6.5

1992-93 statistics:

GP	G	A	TP	+/-	PIM	PP	SH	GW	GT	S	PCT
84	7	34	41	+7	28	3	0	2	0	156	4.5

1993-94 statistics:

GP	G	A	TP	+/-	PIM	PP	SH	GW	GT	S	PCT
84	10	46	56	+43	26	4	0	3	0	200	5.0

1994-95 statistics:

GP	G	A	TP	+/-	PIM	PP	SH	GW	GT	S	PCT
43	10	16	26	+15	6	7	0	0	0	90	11.1

LAST SEASON

Missed first games (five due to a back injury) since NHL career began; ends consecutive games-played streak at 284. Second among team defensemen in scoring. Tied for second on team in power play goals.

THE FINESSE GAME

Lidstrom is an excellent skater and has good vision of the ice. He prefers to look for the breakout pass, rather than carry the puck, and he has an excellent point shot. He is not as effective moving the puck in the attacking zone, though he sees point duty on the second power play unit. Playing with Paul Coffey has given him the confidence to pick his spots when moving in deep into the offensive zone. Now Lidstrom will carry in deep with the puck and look for a play, or just shoot on net to see what happens. Good things usually develop.

He seems to have a little trouble handling the puck in his feet, which is unusual for European skaters, who traditionally have some soccer training.

THE PHYSICAL GAME

Lidstrom does not take the body well, but he does take great pains to protect the puck with his body. He won't cough up the puck out of fear of getting hit. He is a very solid skater, though playing with Coffey and being more aggressive himself usually means Lidstrom has to scramble back on defense.

THE INTANGIBLES

Coffey has had a beneficial effect on Lidstrom, who still has his best hockey ahead of him. Lidstrom may never dictate the tempo of a game the way Coffey could, but he is just a cut below the NHL's elite offensive defensemen at this stage.

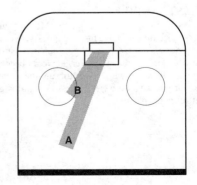

DARREN MCCARTY

Yrs. of NHL service: 2
Born: Burnaby, B.C.; April, 1972
Position: right wing
Height: 6-1
Weight: 214
Uniform no.: 25
Shoots: right

Career statistics:

GP	G	A	TP	PIM
98	14	25	39	269

1993-94 statistics:

GP	G	A	TP	+/-	PIM	PP	SH	GW	GT	S	PCT
67	9	17	26	+12	181	0	0	2	0	81	11.1

1994-95 statistics:

GP	G	A	TP	+/-	PIM	PP	SH	GW	GT	S	PCT
31	5	8	13	+5	88	1	0	2	0	27	18.5

LAST SEASON

Second NHL season. Missed eight games with a separated right shoulder. Missed two games with a hand
injury. Missed five games with a left knee injury.

THE FINESSE GAME

McCarty has decent offensive skills to go along with
his physical game. He led the OHL with 55 goals in
1991-92 while playing for Belleville. Although his totals at the minor league and NHL levels have not been
as impressive, the potential is there to be a reliable
power forward.

Skating is McCarty's major drawback and the
probable reason why he has not been productive as a
scorer. He has an awkward stride and a slow first few
steps. He has good hands, though, and will score the
majority of his goals in tight. He is not terribly creative but plays a basic power game.

THE PHYSICAL GAME

Mean, big, strong, tough and fearless. All the components are there, along with the desire to throw his body
around and get involved. If a game is off to a quiet
start, look for McCarty to wake everyone up. He is not
a great fighter because his balance is only so-so, but
he is willing.

THE INTANGIBLES

Big guys take longer to develop, and McCarty may
not get the ice time to move forward quickly. We said
in last year's *HSR* that we would give him two seasons
to see what kind of impact player he would become.
Due to the lockout, we'll give him another year's
grace, but will add we were impressed with his grit
and effort in the playoffs.

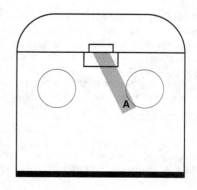

KEITH PRIMEAU

Yrs. of NHL service: 5
Born: Toronto, Ont.; Nov. 24, 1971
Position: left wing/centre
Height: 6-4
Weight: 220
Uniform no.: 55
Shoots: left

Career statistics:

GP	G	A	TP	PIM
289	70	108	178	613

1991-92 statistics:

GP	G	A	TP	+/-	PIM	PP	SH	GW	GT	S	PCT
35	6	10	16	+9	83	0	0	0	0	27	22.2

1992-93 statistics:

GP	G	A	TP	+/-	PIM	PP	SH	GW	GT	S	PCT
73	15	17	32	-6	152	4	1	2	1	75	20.0

1993-94 statistics:

GP	G	A	TP	+/-	PIM	PP	SH	GW	GT	S	PCT
78	31	42	73	+34	173	7	3	4	2	155	20.0

1994-95 statistics:

GP	G	A	TP	+/-	PIM	PP	SH	GW	GT	S	PCT
45	15	27	42	+17	99	1	0	3	0	96	15.6

LAST SEASON

Led team forwards in plus-minus. Fourth on team in points. Missed two games with a right thumb injury. Missed one game with the flu.

THE FINESSE GAME

Primeau's greatest improvement continues to be in his skating. With better skating has come more ice time, more confidence, more responsibility, and a role as a powerhouse centre for a powerful squad.

Primeau naturally invites comparisons to Eric Lindros, though Primeau is less bulky and more agile. He has a huge stride with a long reach. A left-hand shot, he will steam down the right side, slide the puck to his backhand, get his feet wide apart for balance, shield the puck with his body and use his left arm to fend off the defenseman before shovelling the puck to the front of the net for a linemate.

Primeau is clever enough to accept the puck at top speed and make a move instead of wondering what to do with the puck. In tight, his backhand is as likely to be used as his forehand, and he will wade into traffic for loose pucks.

Primeau plays on both special teams and in four-on-four situations. He's improved his face-offs, and is on the verge of becoming the kind of player the opposition will have to worry about stopping as much as they fret about Sergei Fedorov and Steve Yzerman — making a powerful trio of centres for Detroit.

THE PHYSICAL GAME

It used to be that if Primeau had contact with someone, he would be the one to fall. Now, he has improved posture and balance, and can knock some pretty big men on their cans. He would rather go through you than around you.

Primeau has a fiery temper and can lose control. Emotion is a desirable quality, but he has become too valuable a player to spend too much time in the penalty box.

THE INTANGIBLES

Primeau has gone from being the object of trade rumours to the object of desire. A stud centre is at the top of every GM's wish list, and the Red Wings atoned for the mistake they made years ago (when they gave up prematurely on Adam Graves) by allowing Primeau time to develop. What a payoff.

He will continue to be an impact player and should set his sights on 40 goals as he continues to develop into a complete player.

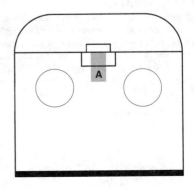

JAMIE PUSHOR

Yrs. of NHL service: 0
Born: Lethbridge, Alta.; Feb. 11, 1973
Position: defense
Height: 6-3
Weight: 205
Uniform no.: n.a.
Shoots: right

1994-95 AHL statistics:

GP	G	A	TP	PIM
58	2	11	13	129

LAST SEASON
Will be entering first NHL season.

THE FINESSE GAME
Pushor is a steady, stay-at-home type of defenseman with a mature game. He is a good skater with decent speed and accleration. He won't rush the puck up-ice, but he will move it sharply and smartly out of his zone with a pass.

Pushor reads plays well defensively. He uses his range to take away the passing lanes and force attackers to the boards. He also does the dirty work along the walls and in the corners. He is aware that his size is what will get him to the NHL and it will be his willingness to use his strength that will keep him there.

Pushor is a solid penalty killer. He doesn't get involved much offensively, but if the right spot opens up he will jump into the attack. Don't expect to see him stray in much beyond the blueline, however.

THE PHYSICAL GAME
Pushor takes the body well and finishes his checks. He isn't a big open-ice hitter because he lacks mobility, but he has good lower body strength for battles along the boards. He has a mean streak and will nail someone if the check is there.

THE INTANGIBLES
Detroit gave an edge to older players last year in its push to a Stanley Cup, but it may be tough to overlook Pushor again this season. After two years in the minors, he is ready to step ahead of some of the creaky defensemen the Red Wings employed last season.

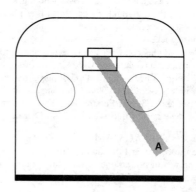

RAY SHEPPARD

Yrs. of NHL service: 8
Born: Pembroke, Ont.; May 27, 1966
Position: right wing
Height: 6-1
Weight: 182
Uniform no.: 26
Shoots: right

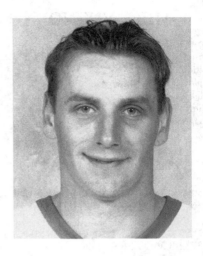

Career statistics:

GP	G	A	TP	PIM
487	238	184	422	149

1991-92 statistics:

GP	G	A	TP	+/-	PIM	PP	SH	GW	GT	S	PCT
74	36	26	62	+7	27	11	1	4	1	178	20.2

1992-93 statistics:

GP	G	A	TP	+/-	PIM	PP	SH	GW	GT	S	PCT
70	32	34	66	+7	29	10	0	1	0	183	17.5

1993-94 statistics:

GP	G	A	TP	+/-	PIM	PP	SH	GW	GT	S	PCT
82	52	41	93	+13	26	19	0	5	0	260	20.0

1994-95 statistics:

GP	G	A	TP	+/-	PIM	PP	SH	GW	GT	S	PCT
43	30	10	40	+11	17	11	0	5	1	125	24.0

LAST SEASON

Led team in goals. One of only five players in NHL with 30 or more goals. Led team and second in league in shooting percentage. Led team in power play goals. Mised two games with back injuries.

THE FINESSE GAME

Sheppard is a finisher. He is not a great skater. He looks excruciatingly slow, but this is deceptive because he is almost always in a good scoring position. He doesn't turn quickly and doesn't have great balance, but he can curl out of the right circle on his backhand and get off a wrist or snap shot. He is also strong enough to ward off a defender with one hand and shovel a pass or push a shot towards the net with his other hand. He must play with a centre who will get him the puck.

There are times when Sheppard looks like a puck magnet. He is always eager to move to the puck and has good hockey sense and vision. Although he is a winger, he has a centre's view of the ice. He is also not selfish; he loves to shoot but will dish off if he spies a teammate with a better percentage shot. He has good hands with a quick release and doesn't waste time with a big backswing. He prefers efficiency and accuracy.

Because of his sluggish skating, Sheppard is a defensive liability. He is usually the last player back when play breaks back out of the offensive zone.

THE PHYSICAL GAME

Sheppard does not play a big game. He's an average-sized forward who plays below his size. He won't work along the boards but will go to the front of the net, so he has to play with one grinder to get him the puck and one quick forward to serve as the safety valve defensively. Sheppard has improved his lower body strength.

THE INTANGIBLES

Count Detroit as the third organization about to give up on Sheppard. Despite his scoring touch, he was scratched in some playoff games and saw only a minor role. He should be in a new outfit this year. We predicted 40 goals for Sheppard last season, and were a bit short of the mark if his goals were prorated. He could net 40 again in the right slot, but it would be his last year at that level.

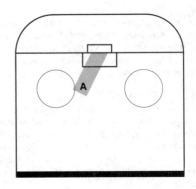

MIKE VERNON

Yrs. of NHL service: 10
Born: Calgary, Alta.; Feb. 24, 1963
Position: goaltender
Height: 5-9
Weight: 170
Uniform no.: 30
Catches: left

Career statistics:

GP	MINS	GA	SO	GAA	A	PIM
497	28385	1530	10	3.23	30	184

1991-92 statistics:

GP	MINS	GAA	W	L	T	SO	GA	S	SAPCT	PIM
63	3640	3.58	24	30	9	0	217	1853	.883	8

1992-93 statistics:

GP	MINS	GAA	W	L	T	SO	GA	S	SAPCT	PIM
64	3732	3.26	29	26	9	2	203	1804	.887	42

1993-94 statistics:

GP	MINS	GAA	W	L	T	SO	GA	S	SAPCT	PIM
48	2798	2.81	26	17	5	3	131	1209	.892	14

1994-95 statistics:

GP	MINS	GAA	W	L	T	SO	GA	S	SAPCT	PIM
30	1807	2.52	19	6	4	1	76	710	.893	8

LAST SEASON

Lowest GAA of career.

THE PHYSICAL GAME

As Vernon gets older, he relies more on his angle play than his reflexes, and technique was never the best part of his game. He has a quick glove hand, and he does a good job of setting himself to tempt the shooter to try for the top right corner. Now they are beating him there more often than they did in the past.

Vernon is aggressive, and at the top of his game he is on the top of his crease, trying to make his small body look bigger. He forces the shooter to make a quick decision. He is a good skater from post to post. He stops the puck well behind the net, but does not try to move it often. When he does, it's with a one-handed swing.

Vernon does use his stick well to break up plays around the net, cutting off low passes and sweeping his stick at a forward trying to come out from behind the net.

He recovers fairly well for a second shot. His reflexes just seem a tad slower, probably the result of a knee injury two years ago. Vernon needs to be rested, and with Chris Osgood in Detroit, he has a solid young partner who can handle his share of starts.

THE MENTAL GAME

Vernon had a fine regular season, but the reason he was acquired wasn't to help Detroit win the Presidents' Trophy. He was supposed to help the Red Wings win the Stanley Cup. Of all the players who have to be faulted for the team's failure to do so last season, Vernon will be saddled with more than his share of the blame.

THE INTANGIBLES

Vernon was involved in a contract flap over the summer and there were numerous rumours of the team looking elsewhere for another number one goalie.

STEVE YZERMAN

Yrs. of NHL service: 12
Born: Cranbrook, B.C.; May 9, 1965
Position: centre
Height: 5-11
Weight: 183
Uniform no.: 19
Shoots: right

Career statistics:

GP	G	A	TP	PIM
862	487	679	1160	552

1991-92 statistics:

GP	G	A	TP	+/-	PIM	PP	SH	GW	GT	S	PCT
79	45	58	103	+26	64	9	8	9	0	295	15.3

1992-93 statistics:

GP	G	A	TP	+/-	PIM	PP	SH	GW	GT	S	PCT
84	58	79	137	+33	44	13	7	6	0	307	18.9

1993-94 statistics:

GP	G	A	TP	+/-	PIM	PP	SH	GW	GT	S	PCT
58	24	58	82	+11	36	7	3	3	1	217	11.1

1994-95 statistics:

GP	G	A	TP	+/-	PIM	PP	SH	GW	GT	S	PCT
47	12	26	38	+6	40	4	0	1	0	134	9.0

LAST SEASON

Only game missed was coaches' decision.

THE FINESSE GAME

Yzerman is a model of consistency. His lapses during the season are few, and he seldom goes through a prolonged scoring slump. Considering how much ice time he gets and how active a skater he is, this is a great tribute to his devotion to conditioning and preparing himself for a game. Yzerman has always seemed mature beyond his years, even when he broke into the league at age 18.

He is a sensational skater. He zigs and zags all over the ice, spending very little time in the centre. He can turn on a dime and give a nickel change. He has great balance and quick feet, and is adroit at kicking the puck up onto his blade for a shot, in seamless motion. Yzerman is also strong for an average-sized forward. He protects the puck well with his body and has the arm strength for wraparound shots and off-balance shots through traffic.

Yzerman prefers to stickhandle down the right side of the ice. In addition to using his body to shield the puck, he uses the boards to protect it, and if a defender starts reaching in with his stick he usually ends up pulling Yzerman down for a penalty.

He uses his stop-and-start skating to great effect on the power play. He works down low from the left wing, creating havoc as he lures defenders into chasing him while Keith Primeau is camped in front of the net, Sergei Fedorov is wheeling and Paul Coffey is loading up his shot from the point.

One of Yzerman's weaknesses is on face-offs. He is only average for a centre of his overall skill and reputation. Defensively, he still has a few flaws, but he is an outstanding penalty killer because of his speed and anticipation.

THE PHYSICAL GAME

Yzerman sacrifices his body willingly in the right circumstances. Detroit certainly doesn't want to see him going haywire and checking bigger players all over the ice. He will pay the price along the boards and around the net, and he's deceptively strong and durable. Yzerman returned to good health during the regular season and plays hurt (as he did in the playoffs).

THE INTANGIBLES

The only knock on Yzerman is his failure to achieve any playoff success in Detroit. Reaching the finals last season wasn't good enough. Yzerman struggled through the last round on a bad knee and was a nonfactor. He will undoubtedly be the target of trade rumours again.

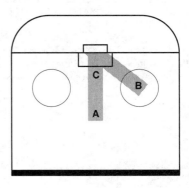

EDMONTON OILERS

Players' Statistics 1994-95

POS	NO.	PLAYER	GP	G	A	PTS	+/-	PIM	PP	SH	GW	GT	S	PCTG
C	39	DOUG WEIGHT	48	7	33	40	-17	69	1		1		104	6.7
C	7	JASON ARNOTT	42	15	22	37	-14	128	7		1		156	9.6
L	9	SHAYNE CORSON	48	12	24	36	-17	86	2		1		131	9.2
R	20	*DAVID OLIVER	44	16	14	30	-11	20	10			1	79	20.3
C	26	*TODD MARCHANT	45	13	14	27	-3	32	3	2	2		95	13.7
L	16	KELLY BUCHBERGER	48	7	17	24		82	2	1	5		73	9.6
C	17	SCOTT THORNTON	47	10	12	22	-4	89		1	1		69	14.5
D	21	IGOR KRAVCHUK	36	7	11	18	-15	29	3	1			93	7.5
C	25	MIKE STAPLETON	46	6	11	17	-12	21	3		2		59	10.2
D	22	LUKE RICHARDSON	46	3	10	13	-6	40	1	1	1		51	5.9
D	28	JIRI SLEGR	31	2	10	12	-5	46	1		1		69	2.9
R	18	KIRK MALTBY	47	8	3	11	-11	49		2	1	1	73	11.0
D	32	DEAN KENNEDY	40	2	8	10	2	25			1		45	4.4
D	15	FREDRIK OLAUSSON	33		10	10	-4	20					52	
D	2	BORIS MIRONOV	29	1	7	8	-9	40					48	2.1
D	6	KEN SUTTON	24	4	3	7	-3	42			1		40	10.0
C	27	*PETER WHITE	9	2	4	6	1		2				13	15.4
D	24	BRYAN MARCHMENT	40	1	5	6	-11	184					57	1.8
L	8	ZDENO CIGER	5	2	2	4	-1		1		1		10	20.0
C	38	IAIN FRASER	13	3		3							7	42.9
L	29	LOUIE DEBRUSK	34	2		2	-4	93					14	14.3
D	6	GORDON MARK	18		2	2	-9	35					21	
G	30	BILL RANFORD	40		2	2		2						
C	23	*JASON BONSIGNORE	1	1		1	-1						3	33.3
C	14	KENT NILSSON	6	1		1	-5		1				2	50.0
C	19	TYLER WRIGHT	6	1		1	1	14					6	16.7
C	36	*RALPH INTRANUOVO	1		1	1	1						1	
G	1	*JOAQUIN GAGE	2		1	1								
C	12	MICAH AIVAZOFF	21		1	1	-2	2					6	
D	43	*DENNIS BONVIE	2											
L	10	*RYAN SMYTH	3				-1						2	
R	33	*MARKO TUOMAINEN	4										5	
L	37	DEAN MCAMMOND	6				-1						3	
G	31	*FRED BRATHWAITE	14											
D	34	RYAN MCGILL	20				-4	21					8	

GP = games played; G = goals; A = assists; PTS = points; +/- = goals-for minus goals-against while player is on ice; PIM = penalties in minutes; PP = power play goals; SH = shorthanded goals; GW = game-winning goals; GT = game-tying goals; S = no. of shots; PCTG = percentage of goals to shots; * = rookie

JASON ARNOTT

Yrs. of NHL service: 2
Born: Collingwood, Ont.; Oct. 11, 1974
Position: centre
Height: 6-3
Weight: 193
Uniform no.: 7
Shoots: right

Career statistics:

GP	G	A	TP	PIM
120	48	57	105	175

1993-94 statistics:

GP	G	A	TP	+/-	PIM	PP	SH	GW	GT	S	PCT
78	33	35	68	+1	104	10	0	4	1	194	17.0

1994-95 statistics:

GP	G	A	TP	+/-	PIM	PP	SH	GW	GT	S	PCT
42	15	22	37	-14	128	7	0	1	0	156	9.6

LAST SEASON

Second on team in goals, points and PIM. Led team in shots. Missed games with a concussion.

THE FINESSE GAME

For a player of his size, Arnott has tremendous skills. As a skater, he has speed, balance, a long stride and agility in turning to either side. And he has added muscle to his frame without losing any edge in his skating.

Arnott's biggest asset, though, is his hockey sense. As gifted as he is offensively, he doesn't overstay his welcome and is diligent in playing defensively.

Arnott is just as good a scorer as a passer, which makes it difficult for defenders who can't overplay him. His timing with his passes is fine, as he holds onto the puck until a teammate is in the open. If the shot is his, he will use an assortment — snap, slap or wrist — and is accurate with a quick release. He is fair on draws but will have to improve. Arnott is well on his way to becoming a dominant power centre.

Arnott works down low on the power plays and is on the Oilers' first unit. He also kills penalties.

THE PHYSICAL GAME

Arnott has serious grit. He found out as a sophomore that people are going to be gunning for him — he's no longer the surprise freshman of 1994 — and he's had to adjust his game. Instead of the hunter, he was the hunted. That learning experience made for an erratic season, but Arnott will probably learn and grow with the experience. Because of the lockout-shortened season, he is basically a year-and-a-half player instead of having two full seasons under his belt. He is big and plays to his size. He has a mean streak, and he's honest as well. He loves to hit and gets involved, especially in the attacking zone. He was less consistent last year than in his first season, and has to learn to pay the price every night.

A well-conditioned athlete, he gets a lot of ice time and can handle it.

THE INTANGIBLES

Arnott could wilt under the kind of pressure that a lot of highly touted young players have experienced earlier in their careers, or he could continue to improve. We suspect the latter, especially as the younger (and cheaper) Oilers continue to grow around him. This kid is tough and honest. Stability on the coaching side (the Oilers had the youngest coach in the NHL last season, but George Burnett didn't last the year) would help.

Arnott is proud of his abilities but has to maintain the balance between pride and arrogance, between a solid work ethic and big paychecks. Arnott is mature and if he continues on the right path, he will emerge as a leader on the Oilers. His problem is the lack of a veteran role model. Craig MacTavish was there to help him through the first half of his rookie season. But with the exception of Shayne Corson (with whom Arnott reportedly did not get along), he's on his own in Edmonton.

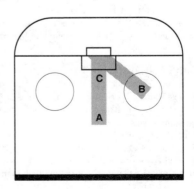

JASON BONSIGNORE

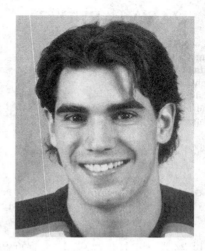

Yrs. of NHL service: 0
Born: Rochester, N.Y.; Apr. 15, 1976
Position: centre
Height: 6-4
Weight: 208
Uniform no.: 23
Shoots: right

Career statistics:

GP	G	A	TP	PIM
1	1	0	1	0

1994-95 statistics:

GP	G	A	TP	+/-	PIM	PP	SH	GW	GT	S	PCT
1	1	0	1	-1	0	0	0	0	0	3	33.3

LAST SEASON

Will be entering first full NHL season. Fourth in goals for Sudbury (OHL) with 27. Scored 62 points in 49 games.

THE FINESSE GAME

The first American player drafted in 1994, Bonsignore had scouts thinking of Mario Lemieux. The size and the scoring touch are there, but Bonsignore has not yet shown Lemieux's ability to dominate a game and help raise his teammates to a higher level.

Bonsignore is highly skilled. He is a terrific skater for his size, with straightaway speed that he can kick into a number of gears. A better playmaker than scorer, he uses his speed to drive back the defense, then finds a trailing teammate coming into open ice and hits him with a flat pass. Bonsignore headmans the puck well and has good vision.

His hockey sense has been questioned, and, like many junior players, he needs to develop a more well-rounded game.

THE PHYSICAL GAME

Bonsignore is not aggressive and needs to add more assertiveness if he is going to carve out a successful NHL career. Finesse is a grand thing, but either he learns to stand up for himself or he'll have to keep picking himself up off the ice. He is a well-conditioned athlete who can handle a lot of ice time, but he has not shown much consistency in his intensity level.

THE INTANGIBLES

Bonsignore has not performed well on the international stage in top junior competitions. He is a highly skilled player whose only question mark is his desire.

Bonsignore was ticketed to start last season with the Oilers, but because of the lockout was sent back to junior. He got off to such a dismal start there that the team brought him up for only one game. The Oilers will give him every chance to make the squad in train-ing camp, but odds are he is not yet ready to take the step, at least not at the start of the season. He has played on three different junior teams in three years, and may need an attitude adjustment.

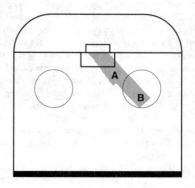

KELLY BUCHBERGER

Yrs. of NHL service: 7
Born: Langenburg, Sask.; Dec. 2, 1966
Position: left wing
Height: 6-2
Weight: 210
Uniform no.: 16
Shoots: right

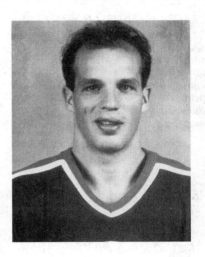

Career statistics:

GP	G	A	TP	PIM
498	53	93	136	1214

1991-92 statistics:

GP	G	A	TP	+/-	PIM	PP	SH	GW	GT	S	PCT
79	20	24	44	+9	157	0	4	3	1	90	7.3

1992-93 statistics:

GP	G	A	TP	+/-	PIM	PP	SH	GW	GT	S	PCT
83	12	18	30	-27	133	1	2	3	0	92	13.0

1993-94 statistics:

GP	G	A	TP	+/-	PIM	PP	SH	GW	GT	S	PCT
84	3	18	21	-20	199	0	0	0	0	93	3.2

1994-95 statistics:

GP	G	A	TP	+/-	PIM	PP	SH	GW	GT	S	PCT
48	7	17	24	0	82	2	1	5	0	73	9.6

LAST SEASON
One of three Oilers to appear in all 48 games. Led team in game-winning goals.

THE FINESSE GAME
Buchberger is an ideal third-line player. Night in and night out, he faces other teams' top forwards and does a terrific shadow job, harassing without taking bad penalties.

He works hard and provides a consistent effort. He will grind, go to the net, kill penalties — all of the grunt work. He can finish off some plays now and then, but that is not his objective. The biggest change in Buchberger is that he has developed some degree of confidence in his finesse moves and is now willing to try something that looks too difficult for a "defensive" player. Sometimes it works, sometimes it doesn't.

Buchberger has some straight-ahead speed and will go to the net and muck, but this kind of player needs some luck to get goals. He has earned a great deal of respect for his work ethic.

THE PHYSICAL GAME
Buchberger is a legitimately tough customer. Honest and gritty, he won't get knocked around and is a solid hitter who likes the physical part of the game. He is a very disciplined player. He's also very determined. He keeps his legs moving constantly, and a player who lets up on this winger will be sorry, because Buchberger will keep plugging with the puck or to the net.

THE INTANGIBLES
Buchberger's job is to be aggressive and kill penalties, and any points are a bonus. His 20 goals (four seasons ago) look more than ever like a misprint in the media guide. He is definitely on the downside of his career, but remains a tenacious checker whose offensive role is more and more limited.

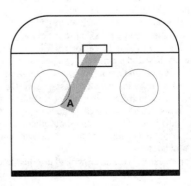

SHAYNE CORSON

Yrs. of NHL service: 9
Born: Barrie, Ont.; Aug. 13, 1966
Position: centre
Height: 6-0
Weight: 175
Uniform no.: 9
Shoots: left

Career statistics:

GP	G	A	TP	PIM
612	174	250	424	1304

1991-92 statistics:

GP	G	A	TP	+/-	PIM	PP	SH	GW	GT	S	PCT
64	17	36	53	+15	118	3	0	2	0	165	10.3

1992-93 statistics:

GP	G	A	TP	+/-	PIM	PP	SH	GW	GT	S	PCT
80	16	31	47	-19	209	9	2	1	0	164	9.8

1993-94 statistics:

GP	G	A	TP	+/-	PIM	PP	SH	GW	GT	S	PCT
64	25	29	54	-8	118	11	0	3	1	171	14.6

1994-95 statistics:

GP	G	A	TP	+/-	PIM	PP	SH	GW	GT	S	PCT
48	12	24	36	-17	86	2	0	1	0	131	9.2

LAST SEASON

Third on team in points. One of three Oilers to appear in all 48 games.

THE FINESSE GAME

Corson makes a lot of things happen by overpowering people around the net. Like Bob Probert in his prime, he has surprising scoring ability for a player who is considered a mucker. People give Corson an extra foot or two because of his muscle, which allows him extra time to pick up loose pucks out of scrums and jam his shots in tight, or lift shots over a goalie's stick.

He played more wing than centre last season, a continuing trend and one that makes the best use of his size and willingness to fight for the puck.

Corson gets a lot of rebound goals if he plays on a line with people who throw the puck to the net, because he will go barrelling in for it. He's free to play that style more on the left wing than at centre, but he also has some nice playmaking abilities when put in the middle. He won't do anything too fancy but is intelligent enough to play a basic short game.

Corson is a powerful skater but not very fast or agile. He has good balance for his work along the boards. He has all the attributes of a power forward.

He can work both special teams, though he was not often used killing penalties last season. He does his dirty work in front of the net for screens and deflections and has the hands to guide hard point shots. He is wildly inaccurate with any shots other than close range, so on the off nights when he is not winning his duels around the net, he is a non-factor.

Corson can be used on draws and uses his strength to neutralize opposing forwards.

THE PHYSICAL GAME

Corson is tremendous along the wall. He has grit, and plays tough and hard every shift. He is dangerous because of his short fuse. Opponents never known when he will go off, and since he's strong and can throw punches, few people want to be around when he does. He inspires fear. He hits to hurt, and because he is so unpredictable he earns himself a lot of room on the ice. Corson has become more consistently smart and aggressive.

THE INTANGIBLES

Corson could be the number one subject of every trade rumour heard. He is a valuable player, but the Oilers have shown a tendency to dish off veterans with big price tags to acquire two or three prospects with low six-digit salaries. Corson is a highly productive winger with size, and Glen Sather will have a lot of suitors. Corson could easily hit the 35-40 goal mark.

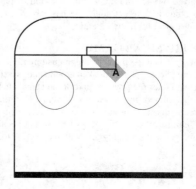

IGOR KRAVCHUK

Yrs. of NHL service: 3
Born: Ufa, Russia; Sept. 13, 1966
Position: right defense
Height: 6-1
Weight: 200
Uniform no.: 21
Shoots: left

Career statistics:

GP	G	A	TP	PIM
190	30	74	104	81

1991-92 statistics:

GP	G	A	TP	+/-	PIM	PP	SH	GW	GT	S	PCT
18	1	8	9	-3	4	0	0	1	0	40	2.5

1992-93 statistics:

GP	G	A	TP	+/-	PIM	PP	SH	GW	GT	S	PCT
55	10	17	27	+3	32	4	0	0	0	143	7.0

1993-94 statistics:

GP	G	A	TP	+/-	PIM	PP	SH	GW	GT	S	PCT
81	12	38	50	-12	16	5	0	2	0	197	6.1

1994-95 statistics:

GP	G	A	TP	+/-	PIM	PP	SH	GW	GT	S	PCT
36	7	11	18	-15	29	3	1	0	0	93	7.5

LAST SEASON

Led team defensemen in scoring. Missed 12 games with a knee injury.

THE FINESSE GAME

Kravchuk is a big defenseman who does a lot of little things well. There is no one facet of his game that stands out from the rest, but there are no serious flaws, either. Kravchuk's skills are subtle. He has very good offensive instincts, but his sound defensive game is the basis for his world-class skills.

An exceptionally mobile skater, he can pivot like a figure skater with the puck and accelerate quickly. He likes to jump into the play and keeps the puck moving. Kravchuk sees the ice well. He is able to carry the puck out of the defensive zone to alleviate pressure on his goalie, something no other Oilers defensemen do well. But he will sometimes make a mistake in joining the rush too soon, and he often gets caught when there's a turnover. He is a little over-aggressive offensively.

Kravchuk plays the point on the first power play unit and will freeze a defenseman with a fake slap shot before sliding a pass down low. He can also fire, and he has the moves to beat a defender in open ice.

Kravchuk is an intelligent penalty killer and utilizes his skating well. He is strong in four-on-four team play.

THE PHYSICAL GAME

Kravchuk has some strength but he is a pusher, not a hitter. He will tie up his man in front of the net, or lean with his stick on top of an opponent's to keep that player from doing something with the puck, but

Kravchuk won't wipe anyone out. It won't hurt to keep him paired with a more physical partner.

THE INTANGIBLES

Kravchuk is a two-way defenseman who will produce 15-20 goals a season when healthy. He would be a superb number three defenseman on a deeper team, but with the Oilers has to carry to the role of a number one. He's in a bit over his head, though he tries to shoulder the burden.

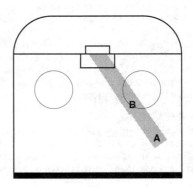

KIRK MALTBY

Yrs. of NHL service: 2
Born: Guelph, Ont.; Dec. 22, 1972
Position: right wing
Height: 6-0
Weight: 180
Uniform no.: 18
Shoots: right

Career statistics:

GP	G	A	TP	PIM
115	19	11	30	123

1993-94 statistics:

GP	G	A	TP	+/-	PIM	PP	SH	GW	GT	S	PCT
68	11	8	19	-2	74	0	1	1	0	89	12.4

1994-95 statistics:

GP	G	A	TP	+/-	PIM	PP	SH	GW	GT	S	PCT
47	8	3	11	-11	49	0	2	1	1	73	11.0

LAST SEASON

Second NHL season. Missed one game with a laceration above his right eye that required 17 stitches.

THE FINESSE GAME

Possessing very good hockey sense, which has stamped him as a strong two-way winger, Maltby has good speed and just loves to flatten people with clean checks. There are few nights when you watch an Oilers game and don't notice Maltby.

Maltby's size and drive are similar to Kirk Muller's. He isn't overly creative, but he will work tirelessly along the boards and in the corners to keep the puck alive, as Muller does. He has a good wrist and slap shot, though he works more at setting up his linemates.

Defensively, Maltby's skating helps keep him in position. He is seldom caught up-ice and plays well without the puck. He understands the game well and is highly coachable. He is also turning into a good penalty killer and is a willing shot-blocker. Maltby is valuable in his ability to stabilize a game. He wants to win the race for the loose puck, and won't settle for being second.

THE PHYSICAL GAME

Maltby loves to bash, and he is fearless. He is not huge, but he is very solid, and he won't back down from a challenge.

Maltby's power is derived from his lower-body drive. He is strong and balanced on his feet, and will punish with his hits. He finishes every check. His work ethic and conditioning are strong and he eats up as much ice time as the coaches give him.

THE INTANGIBLES

Maltby can bring the crowd and his teammates to their feet with an intense shift. He is evolving into a smart hitter, not a wild and wanton one, and is going to be one of the people in the dressing room other players look up to. He lacks offensive skills and won't be a big point producer, but he is at the nucleus of a young Edmonton team that may be a contender in a season or two. Maltby could produce 10-15 goals a season, and may turn out to be as valuable a player for the Oilers as Randy McKay is for the New Jersey Devils, though he lacks McKay's fighting ability.

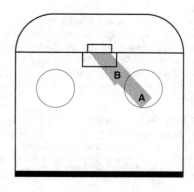

TODD MARCHANT

Yrs. of NHL service: 1
Born: Buffalo, N.Y.; Aug. 12, 1973
Position: centre
Height: 6-0
Weight: 190
Uniform no.: 26
Shoots: left

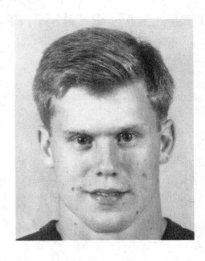

Career statistics:

GP	G	A	TP	PIM
49	13	15	28	34

1993-94 statistics:

GP	G	A	TP	+/-	PIM	PP	SH	GW	GT	S	PCT
4	0	1	1	-2	2	0	0	0	0	6	0.0

1994-95 statistics:

GP	G	A	TP	+/-	PIM	PP	SH	GW	GT	S	PCT
45	13	14	27	-3	32	3	2	2	0	95	13.7

LAST SEASON

First NHL season. Fifth among NHL rookies in points. Tied for third among NHL rookies in assists. Tied for NHL rookie lead and team lead in short-handed goals. Third among NHL rookies in shots. Fifth on team in scoring.

THE FINESSE GAME

Marchant is a strong one-on-one player with zippy outside speed. His quick hand skills keep pace with his feet, and he is particularly adept at tempting the defender with the puck then dragging it through the victim's legs. He then continues to the net for his scoring chances, and he is a strong finisher. Marchant is a product of the U.S. national program, which despite producing lousy results at the Olympics has been highly successful as a breeding ground for high-flying NHL stars. The experience on the bigger European ice surfaces has contributed to Marchant's skating.

Marchant is opportunistic, and with his pace reminds scouts of a young Theo Fleury. Whether he will ever develop the gift for scoring Fleury has will mark his next NHL step.

Marchant is smart, sees the ice well and is a solid playmaker as well as shooter. He is no puck hog. He is an excellent penalty killer.

THE PHYSICAL GAME

Marchant is average size but grit makes him look bigger. He sacrifices his body, but, as with scrappy Jeremy Roenick, you have to wonder how long his body will last under the stress he puts it through. He is well conditioned and can handle a lot of ice time. The mental toughness is there, too. He will take a hit to make a play, but has to get smarter about picking his spots in order to survive. Edmonton has turned into a very mobile team, which kept a lot of teams on the defensive with their puck movement. So Marchant's lack of size might not be as much of a detriment as it could be on other teams.

THE INTANGIBLES

The problem for Marchant is finding a role on the Oilers. He spent most of last season as a third-line checking centre, but he doesn't have the physical ability to match up with the league's better power centres. He has drive and a professional attitude towards his job.

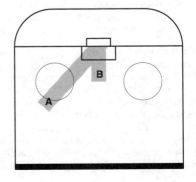

BRYAN MARCHMENT

Yrs. of NHL service: 5
Born: Toronto, Ont.; May 1, 1969
Position: left defense
Height: 6-1
Weight: 200
Uniform no.: 24
Shoots: left

Career statistics:

GP	G	A	TP	PIM
268	17	45	62	952

1991-92 statistics:

GP	G	A	TP	+/-	PIM	PP	SH	GW	GT	S	PCT
58	5	10	15	-4	168	2	0	0	0	55	9.1

1992-93 statistics:

GP	G	A	TP	+/-	PIM	PP	SH	GW	GT	S	PCT
78	5	15	20	+15	313	1	0	1	0	75	6.7

1993-94 statistics:

GP	G	A	TP	+/-	PIM	PP	SH	GW	GT	S	PCT
55	4	11	15	-14	166	0	1	1	0	92	4.3

1994-95 statistics:

GP	G	A	TP	+/-	PIM	PP	SH	GW	GT	S	PCT
40	1	5	6	-11	184	0	0	0	0	57	1.8

LAST SEASON

Led team and third in NHL in PIM. Missed two games with suspension. Awarded as compensation for Hartford signing of free agent Steve Rice.

THE FINESSE GAME

Because of Marchment's reputation as a ferocious hitter, his skills are often overlooked, but they are impressive for a big man.

He loves to play, and he loves to get involved from the very first shift. He's never happier than when there's some blood on his jersey, even if it's his own.

Marchment has to make better decisions without the puck, and to always be aware that pinching in a tight game can get his team in trouble. He lacks the skating ability to cover up for some of his mental errors, though he is competent enough to join in on rushes.

Marchment has an underrated shot and can drill a one-timer or snap a quick shot on net. He is not much of a passer, since he doesn't sense when to feather or fire a puck to a receiver. His mental game is something he needs to improve on.

THE PHYSICAL GAME

One scout described Marchment as "the ultimate leg-breaker." Marchment put the big hurt on some big names last season, Pavel Bure, Mike Gartner and Teemu Selanne among them.

He is a throwback to the days of the big open-ice hitters. This dying art is being revived by the likes of Scott Stevens, and it requires great strength along with good lateral mobility, or else the checker can be left spinning around at centre ice and watching the back of the puck carrier tearing up-ice on a breakaway. Marchment will make mistakes, but they are usually errors of aggression. Where he won't make mistakes is in his down-low coverage. He makes the transition game for the opposition a little slower when he's on the ice.

In keeping with the old-fashioned theme, Marchment is a good fighter. He also finishes every check, blocks shots and uses his upper body well. In one-on-one battles, however, he lacks drive from his legs, and he is not a balanced skater.

THE INTANGIBLES

Marchment's life skills have improved, possibly due to the stability of marriage and children, and he may be settling down to the real business of hockey. He is paying better attention to his conditioning and appears to be overcoming the injury problems that have plagued him over past seasons.

Marchment had to break in with another new team (his third in three years), but made a swift adjustment. Coaches love him because he constantly works hard at trying to improve his game and is a good team man.

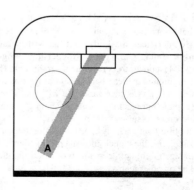

BORIS MIRONOV

Yrs. of NHL service: 2
Born: Moscow, Russia; March 21, 1972
Position: defense
Height: 6-3
Weight: 196
Uniform no.: 2
Shoots: right

Career statistics:

GP	G	A	TP	PIM
108	8	31	39	150

1993-94 statistics:

GP	G	A	TP	+/-	PIM	PP	SH	GW	GT	S	PCT
79	7	24	31	-33	110	5	0	0	1	145	4.8

1994-95 statistics:

GP	G	A	TP	+/-	PIM	PP	SH	GW	GT	S	PCT
29	1	7	8	-9	40	0	0	0	0	48	2.1

LAST SEASON

Second NHL season.

THE FINESSE GAME

Mironov could prove to be a steal of a deal for the Oilers, who obtained him along with Mats Lindgren from the Winnipeg Jets for Dave Manson in 1993-94. Mironov has an instinctive understanding of the game, which, coupled with his skills, means a great upside potential for his development.

Mironov is basically a stay-at-home defenseman, but he has the talent to get involved offensively when he wants to. He has a huge slap shot and is a good puckhandler as well, so he can start a rush out of his own zone and finish things up at the other end.

He uses his size well to protect the puck, but getting it away from an attacker is another matter. Mironov tends to give up on his checks, and he doesn't always read plays coming at him well, so he gets beaten wide by lesser skaters. He doesn't see much time on the penalty-killing unit because of some of his defensive deficiencies.

Mironov plays well on the point on the power play, getting his heavy low shot through or working a pass in deep. He seldom ventures in below the tops of the circles.

THE PHYSICAL GAME

Mironov is big and mobile. He isn't a thumper, but he's strong and he eliminates people. He has been compared to Viacheslav Fetisov, and although he will probably never be a checker who puts victims into the mezzanine, we would like to see him play more to his size.

THE INTANGIBLES

Mironov will be entering his third NHL season. His adjustment to North America, and what appears to be an improvement in his life skills, bode well. He could really step up and surprise people this season and we wouldn't be a bit shocked if he leads the team defensemen in scoring and becomes more of an on-ice leader. Mironov is a world-class talent who was the defense partner of Sandis Ozolinsh for the Soviet Junior National Team a few seasons ago.

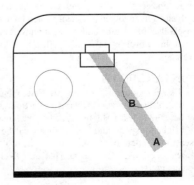

DAVID OLIVER

Yrs. of NHL service: 1
Born: Sechelt, B.C.; April 17, 1971
Position: right wing
Height: 5-11
Weight: 185
Uniform no.: 20
Shoots: right

Career statistics:

GP	G	A	TP	PIM
44	16	14	30	20

1994-95 statistics:

GP	G	A	TP	+/-	PIM	PP	SH	GW	GT	S	PCT
44	16	14	30	-11	20	10	0	0	1	79	20.3

LAST SEASON

First NHL season. Led team and NHL rookies in power play goals. Led NHL rookies in power play points (16). Third among NHL rookies and fourth on team in points. Led team and tied for second among NHL rookies in goals. Led team and third among NHL rookies in shooting percentage. One of only three NHL rookies to record a hat trick.

THE FINESSE GAME

Oliver is one-dimensional. He's a sniper, pure and simple, and exceptionally good at what he does. Goal scoring can't be taught, and teams will often live with other deficiencies if a guy can bury the puck. Oliver has a lightning release and is close to unstoppable on the power play, where he was a major force for the Oilers (he produced 10 of the team's 42 goals, and assisted on six others).

Oliver plays a very mature game offensively. He's strong on the puck, but is decidedly more shooter than playmaker.

He has problems in his own zone. The defense is so much more active in the NHL than in college that Oliver struggled defensively, losing his man. He is too focused on the puck.

THE PHYSICAL GAME

Oliver reminds scouts of Joey Mullen. He has a wiry strength and gets involved physically when he has to, but wisely uses his skating ability to get himself in the open. He has poise in traffic and will take a hit to make a play.

THE INTANGIBLES

Even Mike Bossy learned to play defense. Coming from the college ranks (University of Michigan), Oliver has a lot to learn. But his goal-den touch makes him a bright prospect, and it doesn't appear he's a one-season wonder. In a season of bright rookies, Oliver was overlooked last season. That's not likely to happen again.

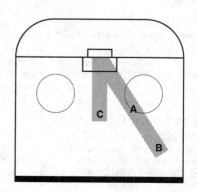

BILL RANFORD

Yrs. of NHL service: 9
Born: Brandon, Man.; Dec. 14, 1966
Position: goaltender
Height: 5-10
Weight: 170
Uniform no.: 30
Catches: left

Career statistics:

GP	MINS	GA	SO	GAA	A	PIM
401	24678	1422	10	3.46	19	52

1991-92 statistics:

GP	MINS	GAA	W	L	T	SO	GA	S	SAPCT	PIM
67	3822	3.58	27	26	10	1	228	1971	.884	4

1992-93 statistics:

GP	MINS	GAA	W	L	T	SO	GA	S	SAPCT	PIM
67	3753	3.84	17	38	6	1	240	2065	.885	10

1993-94 statistics:

GP	MINS	GAA	W	L	T	SO	GA	S	SAPCT	PIM
71	4070	3.48	22	34	11	1	236	2325	.898	2

1994-95 statistics:

GP	MINS	GAA	W	L	T	SO	GA	S	SAPCT	PIM
40	2203	3.62	15	20	3	2	133	1134	.883	2

LAST SEASON

GAA over 3.00 for seventh consecutive year.

THE PHYSICAL GAME

The athletic Ranford is notable for his great first-save capability. He is probably among the top five goalies in the league in that regard, but Edmonton was such a poor team defensively last season (again) that he was frequently called upon to make the third, fourth and fifth saves. That would be too much for even Georges Vezina.

Ranford is a shining example of a goalie who made it to the NHL on his reflexes and continues there because he added elements of angle play and focus. He comes out of his net and, when he is on his game, he doesn't leave a lot of rebounds.

Very patient, Ranford hardly ever commits before the shooter does. He has good lateral movement and great confidence in his skating. He moves with the shooter well, keeping the five-hole closed. He doesn't drop down unless he has to; when he does, he bounces back up quickly. He uses his stick aggressively around the net to break up passes. He also stops hard-arounds and whips passes out to his teammates.

THE MENTAL GAME

A tremendous competitor, Ranford is mature and experienced, and his concentration is unwavering. He is confident without being cocky, and doesn't gripe and moan (at least publicly) about his GM not getting enough talent to help him out. Ranford is starting to fall into the trap of doing too much, and he sees a lot of high-quality shots, which can be draining.

THE INTANGIBLES

Despite the unimpressive numbers, Ranford is still among the five best goaltenders in the NHL. But if the Oilers don't improve soon (or let Ranford go to a better team), the constant losing and inflated goals-against may take their toll on him mentally. He always keeps his team in contention, and seldom, if ever, loses a game with a subpar effort. Ranford is easily the most underrated goalie in the NHL.

LUKE RICHARDSON

Yrs. of NHL service: 8
Born: Ottawa, Ont.; Mar. 26, 1969
Position: left defense
Height: 6-3
Weight: 215
Uniform no.: 22
Shoots: left

Career statistics:

GP	G	A	TP	PIM
550	21	81	102	987

1991-92 statistics:

GP	G	A	TP	+/-	PIM	PP	SH	GW	GT	S	PCT
75	2	19	21	-9	118	0	0	0	0	85	2.4

1992-93 statistics:

GP	G	A	TP	+/-	PIM	PP	SH	GW	GT	S	PCT
82	3	10	13	-18	142	0	2	0	0	78	3.8

1993-94 statistics:

GP	G	A	TP	+/-	PIM	PP	SH	GW	GT	S	PCT
69	2	6	8	-13	131	0	0	0	0	92	2.2

1994-95 statistics:

GP	G	A	TP	+/-	PIM	PP	SH	GW	GT	S	PCT
46	3	10	13	-6	40	1	1	1	0	51	5.9

LAST SEASON

Second among team defensemen in scoring.

THE FINESSE GAME

Someone as big and mobile as Richardson should be far more of an impact player than he is, but he has yet to take the next step to become a smart, take-charge defenseman.

Richardson can sometimes play solid defense, but he is more often indecisive. He makes poor reads — which may be a result of fatigue from playing more minutes than he should.

He is a good skater with lateral mobility and balance, but not much speed. He can't carry the puck and doesn't jump up into the rush well. He seldom uses his point shot, which is merely adequate.

Defensively, Richardson doesn't know when to stay in front of his net and when to challenge in the corners. It's now his seventh year in the league and the necessary improvement hasn't shown. He always seems to be trying hard, but on replays of an opposing team's goal, he is often seen skating in with a late hit.

THE PHYSICAL GAME

Richardson is the kind of player you hate to play against but love to have on your side. He hits to hurt and is an imposing presence on the ice. He scares people. Richardson separates the puck carrier from the puck down low, which is especially important on a fast transition team like Edmonton's.

He will take that too far, though, and start running around getting caught out of position. He needs to improve his patience and reads. He overcame a serious cheekbone injury two seasons ago without losing any of his lust for physical play, which underlines his genuine toughness. When he checks, he separates the puck carrier from the puck and doesn't let the man get back into the play. When Richardson is on the ice, his teammates play a bit bigger and braver.

THE INTANGIBLES

Hockey sense is slow in coming to Richardson. He has good size and strength, but his lack of effectiveness on special teams limits his usefulness. Pairing him with a gifted offensive defenseman would help. If he played the right side, we would suggest Rangers' GM Neil Smith reopen the Edmonton-New York pipeline to obtain Richardson as a new defense partner for Brian Leetch.

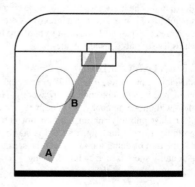

JIRI SLEGR

Yrs. of NHL service: 3
Born: Litvinov, Czechoslovakia; May 30, 1971
Position: left defense
Height: 5-11
Weight: 190
Uniform no.: 24
Shoots: left

Career statistics:

GP	G	A	TP	PIM
150	11	65	76	241

1992-93 statistics:

GP	G	A	TP	+/-	PIM	PP	SH	GW	GT	S	PCT
41	4	22	26	+16	109	2	0	0	0	89	4.5

1993-94 statistics:

GP	G	A	TP	+/-	PIM	PP	SH	GW	GT	S	PCT
78	5	33	38	0	86	1	0	0	0	160	3.1

1994-95 statistics:

GP	G	A	TP	+/-	PIM	PP	SH	GW	GT	S	PCT
31	2	10	12	-5	46	1	0	1	0	69	2.9

present, he is strictly a one-way offensive defenseman. If someone in Edmonton can find the key to unlocking his game, Slegr could have a breakout season.

LAST SEASON

Acquired from Vancouver for Roman Oksiuta.

THE FINESSE GAME

Slegr is a one-dimensional defenseman, with his outstanding skills applied almost exclusively to the offensive part of his game. He is a power play specialist, moving to the right point.

Some nights, Slegr looks preoccupied or nervous and, despite his fine skating, leaves huge gaps in the coverage.

An excellent skater, he is fluid and mobile, with good balance. His forte is puck control, and he rushes the puck well. From the offensive part of the redline in, Slegr looks fine. It's the other half of the ice where he is still a student of the game. He does not read defensive plays well and needs a great deal of improvement in handling the rush until he can emerge as an everyday player.

Slegr especially has trouble handling a strong fore-check. He doesn't move the puck quickly enough under pressure. On offense, he doesn't like to play dump and chase and will hold on to the puck too long or make bad plays at the blueline.

THE PHYSICAL GAME

Slegr is very strong, and when so inclined, he can tie up opponents in front of the net. He isn't big enough to bulldoze people out of the slot, so he usually resorts to his finesse skills, trying to pick off passes or playing the attacker's stick. He tends to carry his stick high. He doesn't like to get hit.

THE INTANGIBLES

More intense coaching will be the key to any improvement by Slegr — along with his willingness to listen to his teachers. His overall game needs work. At

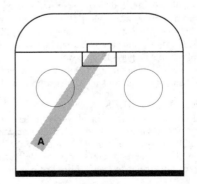

MIKE STAPLETON

Yrs. of NHL service: 5
Born: Sarnia, Ont.; May 5, 1966
Position: centre/right wing
Height: 5-10
Weight: 183
Uniform no.: 25
Shoots:

Career statistics:

GP	G	A	TP	PIM
330	68	54	85	159

1991-92 statistics:

GP	G	A	TP	+/-	PIM	PP	SH	GW	GT	S	PCT
19	4	4	8	0	8	1	0	0	0	32	12.5

1992-93 statistics:

GP	G	A	TP	+/-	PIM	PP	SH	GW	GT	S	PCT
78	4	9	13	-8	10	0	1	1	0	78	5.1

1993-94 statistics:

GP	G	A	TP	+/-	PIM	PP	SH	GW	GT	S	PCT
81	12	13	25	-5	46	4	0	0	1	102	11.8

1994-95 statistics:

GP	G	A	TP	+/-	PIM	PP	SH	GW	GT	S	PCT
46	6	11	17	-12	21	3	0	2	0	59	10.2

LAST SEASON

Half of his six goals came on the power play.

THE FINESSE GAME

Stapleton is a gritty forward, and a good skater and role player who gives everything he's got. There is nothing hard to decipher about his style. He plays an up and down role at centre or wing, is alert defensively and can make a pest of himself merely by getting in the way.

He has decent enough finishing skills to see some time on the power play. The Oilers like to use a big forward down low, which allows smaller players such as Stapleton to dart in and out and find the holes. He doesn't have much of a shot, but finds his range from the hash marks in. Stapleton's second and third efforts when other players might give up on the play are what results in his scoring chances.

THE PHYSICAL GAME

Too small to do much damage, Stapleton is compact and has decent leg drive; most of all he's willing to stick his nose in and at least try to nudge people off the puck. He won't dominate anyone and he is not an impact player, but he plays his role well.

Stapleton at least tries to body check, which is more than can be said for a lot of bigger players.

THE INTANGIBLES

Stapleton is a journeyman player who has been through waivers and is in his third NHL organization. He will likely spend the rest of his career on the bubble no matter where he plays, and will deliver his brand of honest hustle every shift. There won't be many big goals from Stapleton, but there will always be a big effort.

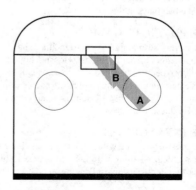

SCOTT THORNTON

Yrs. of NHL service: 3
Born: London, Ont.; Jan. 9, 1971
Position: centre
Height: 6-2
Weight: 200
Uniform no.: 17
Shoots: left

Career statistics:

GP	G	A	TP	PIM
165	15	24	39	266

1991-92 statistics:

GP	G	A	TP	+/-	PIM	PP	SH	GW	GT	S	PCT
15	0	1	1	-6	43	0	0	0	0	11	0.0

1992-93 statistics:

GP	G	A	TP	+/-	PIM	PP	SH	GW	GT	S	PCT
9	0	1	1	-4	0	0	0	0	0	7	0.0

1993-94 statistics:

GP	G	A	TP	+/-	PIM	PP	SH	GW	GT	S	PCT
61	4	7	11	-15	104	0	0	0	0	65	6.2

1994-95 statistics:

GP	G	A	TP	+/-	PIM	PP	SH	GW	GT	S	PCT
47	10	12	22	-4	89	0	1	1	0	69	14.5

LAST SEASON

Career highs in goals, assists and points.

THE FINESSE GAME

Thornton's best asset is his face-off ability. He is outstanding on draws, especially in the defensive zone, and matches up against just about any centre in the league when it comes to winning puck battles. If Thornton doesn't win a draw outright, he will use his muscle to tie up the opponent and work the puck to a teammate.

He uses his toughness to get rid of a defender, then has good hands when he works in tight to get his scoring chances. Thornton is by no means a sniper, and even though he has concentrated more and more on the defensive aspects of the game, he is able to convert a scoring chance when the opportunity presents itself. He was a scorer at the junior level, and knows what to do with the puck around the cage.

Thornton is a good skater, not overly fast but no plodder. He is very strong and balanced on his feet and is hard to knock off the puck. He is alert positionally. If one of his defensemen goes in deep on the attack, Thornton will be the forward back covering for him.

THE PHYSICAL GAME

Thornton is a big, solid defensive center, a young Joel Otto but with better mobility. He has serious toughness without being chippy or taking bad penalties. He can play against just about any big number one centre in the league.

THE INTANGIBLES

The Oilers matched a contract offer from L.A. to keep Thornton in 1994 — and keeping in mind the frugality of the organization, that should prove just how valuable he is to the Oilers. He will never be a big point producer, but he will fill a steady checking role for the team in many seasons to come. Expect a lot of trade rumours surrounding him every playoff year if Edmonton isn't in contention, because he's the kind of reliable, defensive forward any team could use for a serious Cup run. Because Thornton never fulfilled his offensive promise as a high draft pick (third overall in 1989 by Toronto), he might have been viewed as a failure, but he delivers in other areas.

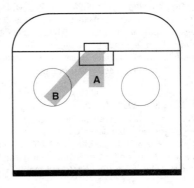

DOUG WEIGHT

Yrs. of NHL service: 4
Born: Mt. Clemens, Mich.; Jan. 21, 1971
Position: centre
Height: 5-11
Weight: 195
Uniform no.: 39
Shoots: left

Career statistics:

GP	G	A	TP	PIM
263	56	136	192	204

1991-92 statistics:

GP	G	A	TP	+/-	PIM	PP	SH	GW	GT	S	PCT
53	8	22	30	-3	23	0	0	2	0	72	11.1

1992-93 statistics:

GP	G	A	TP	+/-	PIM	PP	SH	GW	GT	S	PCT
78	17	31	48	+2	65	3	0	1	0	125	13.6

1993-94 statistics:

GP	G	A	TP	+/-	PIM	PP	SH	GW	GT	S	PCT
84	24	50	74	-22	47	4	1	1	0	188	12.8

1994-95 statistics:

GP	G	A	TP	+/-	PIM	PP	SH	GW	GT	S	PCT
48	7	33	40	-17	69	1	0	1	0	104	6.7

LAST SEASON

Led team in assists and points, both for second consecutive season. One of three Oilers to appear in all 48 games.

THE FINESSE GAME

The emergence of Jason Arnott has allowed Weight to settle neatly into the perfect role for him. He's a number two centre — and a nice number two with some two-way ability, though his game is more heavily weighted (pun intended) to the offensive side. To become a better two-way centre, à la Ron Francis, Weight has to work to improve his down low coverage.

Playmaking is Weight's strong suit. He has very good vision and passes well to either side. His hands are good. When he utilizes his shot, he has quick and accurate wrist and snap shots. He handles the puck well in traffic, is strong on the puck and creates a lot of scoring chances. If the Oilers ever get a finishing winger to team with him, Weight's numbers will soar.

Weight won't win many foot races, but he keeps his legs pumping and he often surprises people on the rush who think they had him contained, only to see him push his way past. He frequently draws penalties. He has decent quickness, good balance and a fair change of direction.

THE PHYSICAL GAME

Weight is inconsistent in his physical play. He shows flashes of grittiness, but doesn't bring it to the ice every night. He is built like a little fire hydrant, and on the night when he's on, he hits with enthusiasm, finishing every check. He will initiate and annoy.

He's also a bit of a trash talker, yapping and playing with a great deal of spirit. He can be counted on to provide a spark to the darkest of nights.

Weight has worked on his strength and conditioning and can handle a lot of ice time. He is very strong on his skates and hard to push off the puck.

THE INTANGIBLES

Weight lost an arbitration settlement — he was seeking $1.3, but was awarded Cdn.$750,000. That can affect a player mentally, but Weight has indicated he is happy playing in Edmonton and is likely to take the "loss" (still a raise from the $550,000 the Oilers wanted to give him) in return for the ice time. He's in an ideal spot, getting a lot of ice time for a young team. Weight relishes the responsibility of producing points. A legitimate top six forward on almost any team.

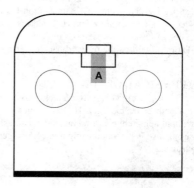

PETER WHITE

Yrs. of NHL service: 1
Born: Montreal, Que.; March 15, 1969
Position: left wing
Height: 5-11
Weight: 200
Uniform no.: 27
Shoots: left

Career statistics:

GP	G	A	TP	PIM
35	5	9	14	2

1993-94 statistics:

GP	G	A	TP	+/-	PIM	PP	SH	GW	GT	S	PCT
26	3	5	8	+1	2	0	0	0	0	17	17.6

1994-95 statistics:

GP	G	A	TP	+/-	PIM	PP	SH	GW	GT	S	PCT
9	2	4	6	+1	0	2	0	0	0	13	15.4

LAST SEASON

Led AHL in scoring with 36-69 — 105 in 65 games for Cape Breton.

THE FINESSE GAME

White has improved his skating, but unless he is able to make even greater strides (pun intended) he is doomed to be one of those high-scoring minor league players that fans are always puzzling about. Hey, look at those numbers! Boy, the Oilers (who averaged 2.83 goals-for last season) sure could use him!

White has an excellent release, but he is one-dimensional. A shooter, but not a playmaker. He is also older than many NHL novices, since he has four full years at Michigan State and three seasons played mostly in the minor leagues on his résumé.

Like many players from the college ranks, White has had to work at his defensive game and he has shown good awareness and a sense for positional play. His forte, though, will always be scoring.

THE PHYSICAL GAME

White's slowness hurts him because he can't get the momentum he needs to be much of a checker. In the trenches, though, he is sturdy and balanced, and he will fight for the puck around the net. If he picks up a loose puck he can get it away quickly and on net.

THE INTANGIBLES

This could be the make-or-break season for White. He has played big in some big games, and at 26 should be ready to bring a well-rounded game into the NHL. He has potential, and his numbers will always encourage a team to give him a second chance.

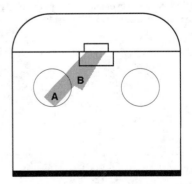

FLORIDA PANTHERS

Players' Statistics 1994-95

POS	NO.	PLAYER	GP	G	A	PTS	+/-	PIM	PP	SH	GW	GT	S	PCTG
C	26	JESSE BELANGER	47	15	14	29	-5	18	6		3	1	89	16.9
C	14	STU BARNES	41	10	19	29	7	8	1		2		93	10.8
R	27	SCOTT MELLANBY	48	13	12	25	-16	90	4		5		130	10.0
D	5	GORD MURPHY	46	6	16	22	-14	24	5				94	6.4
L	10	DAVE LOWRY	45	10	10	20	-3	25	2		3		70	14.3
R	12	JODY HULL	46	11	8	19	-1	8			4		63	17.5
L	11	BILL LINDSAY	48	10	9	19	1	46		1			63	15.9
R	21	TOM FITZGERALD	48	3	13	16	-3	31					78	3.8
C	20	BRIAN SKRUDLAND	47	5	9	14		88	1				44	11.4
L	29	JOHAN GARPENLOV	40	4	10	14	1	2					44	9.1
L	18	MIKE HOUGH	48	6	7	13	1	38			2		58	10.3
D	6	JASON WOOLLEY	34	4	9	13	-1	18	1			1	76	5.3
L	15	GAETAN DUCHESNE	46	3	9	12	-3	16					62	4.8
C	44	ROB NIEDERMAYER	48	4	6	10	-13	36	1				58	6.9
R	22	BOB KUDELSKI	26	6	3	9	2	2	3		1		29	20.7
D	7	BRIAN BENNING	24	1	7	8	-6	18	1				26	3.8
D	28	MAGNUS SVENSSON	19	2	5	7	5	10	1				41	4.9
L	19	ANDREI LOMAKIN	31	1	6	7	-5	6	1				25	4.0
D	3	PAUL LAUS	37		7	7	12	138					18	
D	25	GEOFF SMITH	47	2	4	6	-5	22					40	5.0
D	16	RANDY MOLLER	17		3	3	-5	16					12	
D	24	*ROBERT SVEHLA	5	1	1	2	3		1				6	16.7
D	8	DALLAS EAKINS	17		1	1	2	35					3	
D	2	JOE CIRELLA	20		1	1	-7	21					13	
G	34	J. VANBIESBROUCK	37		1	1		6						
D	38	STEPHANE RICHER	1					2						
L	23	JEFF DANIELS	3											
R	42	*JAMIE LINDEN	4				-1	17						
C	17	DAVE TOMLINSON	5				-2							
D	4	KEITH BROWN	13				1	2					10	
G	30	MARK FITZPATRICK	15											

GP = games played; G = goals; A = assists; PTS = points; +/- = goals-for minus goals-against while player is on ice; PIM = penalties in minutes; PP = power play goals; SH = shorthanded goals; GW = game-winning goals; GT = game-tying goals; S = no. of shots; PCTG = percentage of goals to shots; * = rookie

STU BARNES

Yrs. of NHL service: 4
Born: Edmonton, Alta.; Dec. 25, 1970
Position: centre
Height: 5-11
Weight: 180
Uniform no.: 14
Shoots: right

Career statistics:

GP	G	A	TP	PIM
202	53	62	115	82

1991-92 statistics:

GP	G	A	TP	+/-	PIM	PP	SH	GW	GT	S	PCT
46	8	9	17	-2	26	4	0	0	0	75	10.7

1992-93 statistics:

GP	G	A	TP	+/-	PIM	PP	SH	GW	GT	S	PCT
38	12	10	22	-3	10	3	0	3	0	73	16.4

1993-94 statistics:

GP	G	A	TP	+/-	PIM	PP	SH	GW	GT	S	PCT
77	23	24	47	+4	38	8	1	3	0	172	13.4

1994-95 statistics:

GP	G	A	TP	+/-	PIM	PP	SH	GW	GT	S	PCT
41	10	19	29	+7	8	1	0	2	0	93	10.8

LAST SEASON

Led team in assists. Tied for team lead in points. Missed seven games with an eye injury.

THE FINESSE GAME

Seeing the enthusiasm with which Barnes killed penalties, it was hard to believe he had never been asked to perform in that role before coming to Florida. He showed good puck pursuit and finished his checks.

Barnes has sharply honed puck skills and offensive instincts, which he puts to especially effective use on the power play. He has good quickness and can control the puck in traffic. He uses a slap shot or a wrist shot in tight.

Barnes has a good work ethic, and his effort overcomes his deficiency in size. He's clever and plays a smart small man's game.

THE PHYSICAL GAME

Barnes is not big, but he gets in the way. Sometimes a trade is a wake-up call for a young player, and Barnes played with a lot more spirit, which he has to continue to do.

THE INTANGIBLES

We thought Barnes might be a candidate for 40 goals, but it looks at though 30 is a more reliable ceiling for him. He is a plucky competitor.

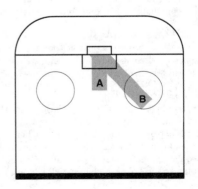

JESSE BELANGER

Yrs. of NHL service: 2
Born: St-Georges-de-Beauce, Que.; June 15, 1969
Position: centre
Height: 6-0
Weight: 170
Uniform no.: 29
Shoots: right

Career statistics:

GP	G	A	TP	PIM
140	36	49	115	38

1991-92 statistics:

GP	G	A	TP	+/-	PIM	PP	SH	GW	GT	S	PCT
4	0	0	0	-1	0	0	0	0	0	4	0.0

1992-93 statistics:

GP	G	A	TP	+/-	PIM	PP	SH	GW	GT	S	PCT
19	4	2	6	+1	4	0	0	0	0	24	16.7

1993-94 statistics:

GP	G	A	TP	+/-	PIM	PP	SH	GW	GT	S	PCT
70	17	33	50	-4	16	11	0	3	1	104	16.3

1994-95 statistics:

GP	G	A	TP	+/-	PIM	PP	SH	GW	GT	S	PCT
47	15	14	29	-5	18	6	0	3	1	89	16.9

depth player as the team improves.

LAST SEASON

Second NHL season. Led team in goals and power play goals. Tied for team lead in points. Missed one game with illness.

THE FINESSE GAME

Belanger was a flashy scorer at the junior and minor league levels, apprenticed as an heir to Guy Carbonneau while in the Montreal system, and has emerged in Florida as the best of both worlds. He is developing into a solid two-way centre.

He has decent speed and anticipation, and all the makings of a successful two-way forward who works hard at both ends of the ice. He is a smart playmaker who is always looking to work off his teammates.

He has a quality short game. He sees his options well and uses a wrist shot from close range. He also uses a one-timer to great effect. He often sees duty against other teams' better checking lines and has the instincts and finesse skills to take advantage of the scoring opportunities that come from turnovers.

THE PHYSICAL GAME

Belanger does not have a physical presence, but he uses his wiry strength and good balance well around the net. He gets involved.

THE INTANGIBLES

Belanger brings confidence and enthusiasm to whatever role the defensive-minded Panthers ask of him. He needs to play with some gritty partners, but he can make clunkly players better. He brings a winning attitude to the ice and is a reliable all-around centre. He lacks the size to dominate, but he will be a valuable

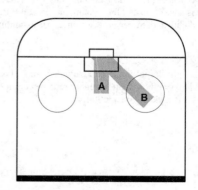

TOM FITZGERALD

Yrs. of NHL service: 5
Born: Melrose, Mass.; Aug. 28, 1968
Position: right wing/centre
Height: 6-1
Weight: 195
Uniform no.: 21
Shoots: right

Career statistics:

GP	G	A	TP	PIM
336	46	71	117	185

1991-92 statistics:

GP	G	A	TP	+/-	PIM	PP	SH	GW	GT	S	PCT
45	6	11	17	-3	28	0	2	2	0	71	8.5

1992-93 statistics:

GP	G	A	TP	+/-	PIM	PP	SH	GW	GT	S	PCT
77	9	18	27	-2	34	0	3	1	0	83	10.8

1993-94 statistics:

GP	G	A	TP	+/-	PIM	PP	SH	GW	GT	S	PCT
83	18	14	32	-3	54	0	3	1	0	144	12.5

1994-95 statistics:

GP	G	A	TP	+/-	PIM	PP	SH	GW	GT	S	PCT
48	3	13	16	-3	31	0	0	0	0	78	3.8

LAST SEASON

One of four Panthers to appear in all 48 games.

THE FINESSE GAME

Fitzgerald is a good penalty killer but has moved his game ahead another step by becoming a reliable crunch-time player.

He is very quick and uses his outside speed to take the puck to the net. He is also less shy about using his shot, perhaps because he is working to get himself into better shooting situations.

Fitzgerald played both centre and right wing last season and the constant shifting didn't faze him. There is a logjam at centre in Florida, so his versatility will help him get his ice time.

THE PHYSICAL GAME

Fitzgerald is gritty and strong. He has fairly good size and uses it along the boards and in front of the net, and he's a pesky checker who gets people teed off, though his own discipline keeps him from taking many cheap penalties. He gives his team some bang and pop and finishes his checks. Although he isn't huge, he is among the best open-ice hitters in the league.

THE INTANGIBLES

Fitzgerald has never lived up to the role expected from first-round draft choices (he was 17th overall in 1986), but he is a solid checking forward who can contribute 10-15 goals a season. His spunk always adds something extra to his shifts.

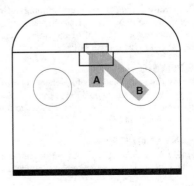

JOHAN GARPENLOV

Yrs. of NHL service: 5
Born: Stockholm, Sweden; Mar. 21, 1968
Position: left wing
Height: 5-11
Weight: 183
Uniform no.: 29
Shoots: left

Career statistics:

GP	G	A	TP	PIM
298	68	118	186	112

1991-92 statistics:

GP	G	A	TP	+/-	PIM	PP	SH	GW	GT	S	PCT
28	6	7	13	+13	8	1	0	1	0	34	17.6

1992-93 statistics:

GP	G	A	TP	+/-	PIM	PP	SH	GW	GT	S	PCT
79	22	44	66	-26	56	14	0	1	0	171	12.9

1993-94 statistics:

GP	G	A	TP	+/-	PIM	PP	SH	GW	GT	S	PCT
80	18	35	53	+9	28	7	0	3	0	125	14.4

1994-95 statistics:

GP	G	A	TP	+/-	PIM	PP	SH	GW	GT	S	PCT
40	4	10	14	+1	2	0	0	0	0	44	9.1

LAST SEASON
Acquired from San Jose for a conditional draft pick in 1998.

THE FINESSE GAME
A strong skater with good balance, Garpenlov will carry the puck through checks. He has a hard wrist shot from the off-wing and shoots well in stride, but he doesn't shoot often enough. His quickness gets him into high-quality scoring areas, but he then looks to make a pass.

Garpenlov is a better playmaker than finisher. A solid fore-checker, he will create turnovers and then look to do something intelligent with the puck.

The story is different on the power play, perhaps because the open ice gives him more time and confidence. He likes to work low and use his one-timer from the left circle. If he were as eager to shoot in five-on-five situations, he could elevate his game another level.

Garpenlov played for general manager Bryan Murray while the two were in Detroit, and Garpenlov can be expected to get a lot of ice time, thanks to Murray's faith in his finesse skills.

THE PHYSICAL GAME
Garpenlov is not physical. His fore-checking pressure comes not from physical contact, but from his skating ability, which gets him in on top of a player to force a pass he can intercept.

THE INTANGIBLES
Garpenlov remains shot-shy, and we doubt he'll net more than 25 goals in a season unless he gets a little more selfish, but he can help the Panthers if teamed with a sniper.

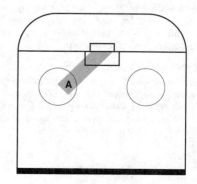

JODY HULL

Yrs. of NHL service: 6
Born: Cambridge, Ont.; Feb. 2, 1969
Position: right wing
Height: 6-2
Weight: 200
Uniform no.: 12
Shoots: right

Career statistics:

GP	G	A	TP	PIM
286	54	70	124	65

1991-92 statistics:

GP	G	A	TP	+/-	PIM	PP	SH	GW	GT	S	PCT
3	0	0	0	-4	2	0	0	0	0	4	0.0

1992-93 statistics:

GP	G	A	TP	+/-	PIM	PP	SH	GW	GT	S	PCT
69	13	21	34	-24	14	5	1	0	1	134	9.7

1993-94 statistics:

GP	G	A	TP	+/-	PIM	PP	SH	GW	GT	S	PCT
69	13	13	26	+6	8	0	1	5	1	100	13.0

1994-95 statistics:

GP	G	A	TP	+/-	PIM	PP	SH	GW	GT	S	PCT
46	11	8	19	-1	8	0	0	4	0	63	17.5

LAST SEASON

Led team in shooting percentage. Missed two games with a viral infection.

THE FINESSE GAME

Hull has some fine natural skills. His powerful skating stride is almost syrupy smooth. He has some range and can skate with people, slowing them down and picking off passes.

His snap shot is heavy and effective, though he takes a while on the release. There are times when it seems you can hear him thinking. He will cut into the middle at the blueline, then outguess himself on the proper play. Even if he has skating room and could take the puck closer to the net, he does not penetrate, drive the defense and pull the goalie out to him.

Hull kills penalties well and will play positionally in a checking role. He has been given a lot more responsibility with Florida and has responded.

THE PHYSICAL GAME

Hull is a polite player. There is no mean streak to speak of. He can be goaded into an occasional slash, just to prove there is a pulse.

THE INTANGIBLES

Hull has a lot of ability he appears not to use. He does not show much expression on the ice and tends to fade into the background. He does more defensive than offensive things, but there are too many players of his ilk to make him anything more than a marginal player. He could probably last for another dozen NHL seasons doing what he does without any particular distinction, since he doesn't hurt a team.

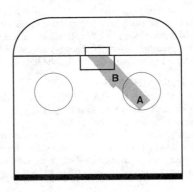

ED JOVANOVSKI

Yrs. of NHL service: 0
Born: Windsor, Ont.; June 26, 1976
Position: left defense
Height: 6-2
Weight: 205
Uniform no.: na
Shoots: left

1993-94 junior statistics:

GP	G	A	TP	PIM
62	15	35	50	221

1994-95 junior statistics:

GP	G	A	TP	PIM
50	23	42	65	198

LAST SEASON

Will be entering first NHL season. Fourth in scoring for Windsor (OHL).

THE FINESSE GAME

It wouldn't do Jovanovski any good to be as big as he is if he were just a huge lummox cemented in one spot on the ice all night. Good news for the Panthers, and bad news for the rest of the league: Jovanovski has other skills to go along with the massive frame.

He is strong on his feet with a powerful, quick stride. He has more quickness than most big men, perhaps because of early soccer training, and he can use his feet to move the puck if his stick is tied up. His powerful hitting is made more wicked by the fact that he gets so much speed and leg drive.

Jovanovski can also score. He has an excellent point shot and good vision of the ice for passing. He may develop along Scott Stevens/Ray Bourque lines and be a defenseman who can dominate in all zones.

THE PHYSICAL GAME

Call him Jovan-ouch-ski. This massive defenseman — who may still be growing — doesn't just hit to hurt. He hits to kill. His intensity is no question mark; he thrives on the physical part of the game. It's what set him apart from the rest of the junior crop of '94. Instead of worrying whether he is up for a game, coaches will probably have to curb some of his natural aggressiveness to keep him from headhunting and taking bad penalties. Every NHL heavyweight will be testing this kid his first time through the league.

THE INTANGIBLES

Jovanovski is ready to make the jump to the NHL, but while he has been tossing kids around in junior, he will have a harder time when he faces people such as Eric Lindros and Brendan Shanahan for the first time. Jovanovski also has to deal with a serious off-ice matter, a charge of sexual misconduct (to be handled in the courts).

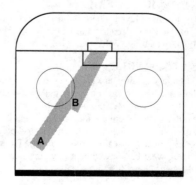

PAUL LAUS

Yrs. of NHL service: 2
Born: Beamsville, Ont.; Sept. 26, 1970
Position: right defense
Height: 6-1
Weight: 212
Uniform no.: 3
Shoots: right

Career statistics:

GP	G	A	TP	PIM
76	2	7	9	247

1993-94 statistics:

GP	G	A	TP	+/-	PIM	PP	SH	GW	GT	S	PCT
39	2	0	2	+9	109	0	0	1	9	15	13.3

1994-95 statistics:

GP	G	A	TP	+/-	PIM	PP	SH	GW	GT	S	PCT
37	0	7	7	+12	138	0	0	0	0	18	0.0

LAST SEASON

Led team in plus-minus and PIM. Missed six games with a groin injury. Missed one game with a shoulder injury.

THE FINESSE GAME

People don't like to play against a club that has Laus on it. He is a legitimate tough guy, but one who has worked at the other aspects of his game to become a more useful player.

Laus has borderline NHL skating speed. He is powerful and well balanced for battles along the boards and in the corners. He seems to know his limitations and doesn't try to overextend himself. He needs to be paired with a mobile partner, since he doesn't cover a lot of ice.

Laus uses his size and strength effectively at all times. He has to control both his temper and his playing style. His success in the NHL will come from him playing his position and not running around head-hunting.

Laus doesn't have much offensive instinct, but gets a little room to take shots from the point because no one wants to come near him.

THE PHYSICAL GAME

Laus hits. Anyone. At any opportunity. Since his skating isn't great, he can't catch people in open ice, but he's murder along the boards, in the corners and in front of the net. He hits to hurt. He's big, but not scary-sized like a lot of today's NHL defensemen. He is, however, powerful and mean.

THE INTANGIBLES

Mark Tinordi is the perfect blueprint for Laus. He may not be be the leader that Tinordi has become, but he is aware of his value to the team. He will make his teammates braver, and if his skills keep improving, that will keep him on the ice.

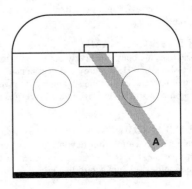

BILL LINDSAY

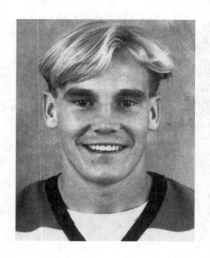

Yrs. of NHL service: 3
Born: Big Fork, Mont.; May 17, 1971
Position: left wing
Height: 5-11
Weight: 185
Uniform no.: 11
Shoots: left

Career statistics:

GP	G	A	TP	PIM
199	22	28	50	173

1991-92 statistics:

GP	G	A	TP	+/-	PIM	PP	SH	GW	GT	S	PCT
23	2	4	6	-6	14	0	0	1	0	35	5.7

1992-93 statistics:

GP	G	A	TP	+/-	PIM	PP	SH	GW	GT	S	PCT
44	4	9	13	0	16	0	0	0	0	58	6.9

1993-94 statistics:

GP	G	A	TP	+/-	PIM	PP	SH	GW	GT	S	PCT
84	6	6	12	-2	97	0	0	0	0	90	6.7

1994-95 statistics:

GP	G	A	TP	+/-	PIM	PP	SH	GW	GT	S	PCT
48	10	9	19	+1	46	0	1	0	0	63	15.9

LAST SEASON

One of four Panthers to appear in all 48 games. Career high in goals despite short season. Scored team's only shorthanded goal.

THE FINESSE GAME

Probably the biggest surprise on the Panthers last season, Lindsay developed confidence in his offensive skills. He has always been a player who relied on his defense first, even though he has a huge shot. He has a long reach and scores many of his goals from his effort in front of the net. He has decent hands, but it's his second and third effort that make the difference.

Lindsay is a support player who, teamed with more offensive linemates, acts as a safety valve. He is not very creative, but he will follow the play to the net.

His skating speed and agility are average, but he is balanced and strong on his skates. He has good size, which he uses in a checking role. He sometimes gets a bit lazy and doesn't keep his feet moving. When he doesn't take that extra step, he will take a bad hooking or tripping penalty.

THE PHYSICAL GAME

Lindsay uses his body effectively but doesn't go out and thrash people. He is sturdy and occasionally will get it into his head to stir things up and try to give his team a bit of a spark. He plays much bigger than his size.

THE INTANGIBLES

Lindsay's efforts took him beyond his designated fourth-line role, but as the team gets deeper, he will probably settle back into a third-line role.

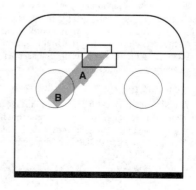

DAVE LOWRY

Yrs. of NHL service: 10
Born: Sudbury, Ont.; Feb. 14, 1965
Position: left wing
Height: 6-1
Weight: 195
Uniform no.: 10
Shoots: left

Career statistics:

GP	G	A	TP	PIM
601	97	104	201	878

1991-92 statistics:

GP	G	A	TP	+/-	PIM	PP	SH	GW	GT	S	PCT
75	7	13	20	-11	77	0	0	1	0	85	8.2

1992-93 statistics:

GP	G	A	TP	+/-	PIM	PP	SH	GW	GT	S	PCT
58	5	8	13	-18	101	0	0	0	0	59	8.5

1993-94 statistics:

GP	G	A	TP	+/-	PIM	PP	SH	GW	GT	S	PCT
80	15	22	37	-4	64	3	0	3	1	122	12.3

1994-95 statistics:

GP	G	A	TP	+/-	PIM	PP	SH	GW	GT	S	PCT
45	10	10	20	-3	25	2	0	3	0	70	14.3

LAST SEASON

Scored 100th career assist.

THE FINESSE GAME

Skating stands out among Lowry's skills. He is fast and powerful, though he lacks subtlety. All Lowry knows is straight ahead, whether it's to smack into an opponent or to crash the net for a scoring chance. He does little in the way of shooting from anywhere other than dead in front of the net.

Not a creative playmaker, Lowry is most content in the role of an up-and-down winger. He can handle some power play duty because he has a good scoring touch. He is a strong fore-checker and defensive forward. He showed a good scoring touch in junior and the minors, but he has never been able to bring his offensive game up to NHL tempo.

THE PHYSICAL GAME

Lowry has decent size, and when he combines it with his speed he becomes an effective hitter. He will harry the puck carrier on a fore-checking mission and will use his stick and body to slow down a skater. He plays on the second penalty-killing unit.

THE INTANGIBLES

Lowry played a prominent role last season, though ideally he is a third- or fourth-line role player who gives his team 15 to 20 goals a season. He will always be fighting for ice time, especially if the Panthers proceed with their youth movement.

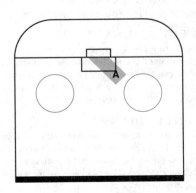

SCOTT MELLANBY

Yrs. of NHL service: 9
Born: Montreal, Que,; June 11, 1966
Position: right wing
Height: 6-1
Weight: 205
Uniform no.: 27
Shoots: right

Career statistics:

GP	G	A	TP	PIM
632	164	200	364	1277

1991-92 statistics:

GP	G	A	TP	+/-	PIM	PP	SH	GW	GT	S	PCT
80	23	27	50	+5	197	7	0	5	0	159	14.5

1992-93 statistics:

GP	G	A	TP	+/-	PIM	PP	SH	GW	GT	S	PCT
69	15	17	32	-4	147	6	0	3	1	114	13.2

1993-94 statistics:

GP	G	A	TP	+/-	PIM	PP	SH	GW	GT	S	PCT
80	30	30	60	0	149	17	0	4	1	204	14.7

1994-95 statistics:

GP	G	A	TP	+/-	PIM	PP	SH	GW	GT	S	PCT
48	13	12	25	-16	90	4	0	5	0	130	10.0

will get the ice time and power play time and should flirt with 30 goals.

LAST SEASON

Led team in game-winning goals and shots. Third on team in points. Worst plus-minus on team. One of four Panthers to appear in all 48 games.

THE FINESSE GAME

Not having great deal of speed or agility, Mellanby generates most of his effectiveness in tight spaces where he can use his size. He is good on the power play, working down low for screens and tips. He doesn't have many moves, but he can capitalize on a loose puck.

Mellanby seems to score goals that count. Twenty-three out of his 101 goals over the past five seasons have been game-winners (22.7 per cent). Goals don't come naturally to him, but he is determined and pays the price in front of the net.

He has become very responsible defensively and can kill penalties, though he is never a shorthanded threat. He lacks the speed bursts or scoring instincts to convert turnovers into dangerous scoring chances.

THE PHYSICAL GAME

Mellanby fore-checks aggressively, using his body well to hit and force mistakes in the attacking zone. He participates in one-on-one battles in tight areas and tries to win his share. He is also willing to mix it up and takes penalties for aggression.

THE INTANGIBLES

Mellanby has to maintain his work ethic to keep an NHL job. He came to the Panthers as a career third- or fourth-line player but has become a number one or number two winger. If he can keep up his energy, he

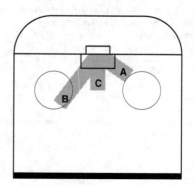

GORD MURPHY

Yrs. of NHL service: 7
Born: Willowdale, Ont.; Mar. 23, 1967
Position: right defense
Height: 6-2
Weight: 195
Uniform no.: 5
Shoots: right

Career statistics:

GP	G	A	TP	PIM
482	59	160	219	462

1991-92 statistics:

GP	G	A	TP	+/-	PIM	PP	SH	GW	GT	S	PCT
73	5	14	19	-2	84	0	0	0	0	132	3.8

1992-93 statistics:

GP	G	A	TP	+/-	PIM	PP	SH	GW	GT	S	PCT
49	5	12	17	-13	62	3	0	2	0	68	7.4

1993-94 statistics:

GP	G	A	TP	+/-	PIM	PP	SH	GW	GT	S	PCT
84	14	29	43	-11	71	9	0	2	3	172	8.1

1994-95 statistics:

GP	G	A	TP	+/-	PIM	PP	SH	GW	GT	S	PCT
46	6	16	22	-14	24	5	0	0	0	94	6.4

LAST SEASON

Led team defensemen in scoring for second consecutive season. Missed one game with a sprained ankle.

THE FINESSE GAME

Murphy has emerged as the team's top offensive defenseman. He is a strong and agile skater, and he executes tight turns and accelerates in a stride or two, which makes him an ideal player in smaller buildings. He moves the puck well and then joins the play eagerly.

He also carries the puck well, although he gets into trouble when he overhandles in his own zone. He usually makes a safe pass, holding on until he is just about decked and then making a nice play. Murphy plays the point on the power play, and uses a pull and drag shot, rather than a big slap shot, giving him a very quick release.

THE PHYSICAL GAME

Murphy uses his finesse skills to defend. His long reach makes him an effective poke-checker, and he would rather wrap his arms around an attacker than move him out of the crease with a solid hit. He's more of a pusher than a hitter. He is responsible defensively and is used to kill penalties. He logged a lot of ice time and held up well under the grind.

THE INTANGIBLES

Murphy is not, and will never be, a tough customer, but he has improved his positional play and can step up and provide some offensive spark. He is most effective with a physical, stay-at-home partner.

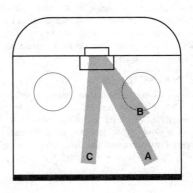

ROB NIEDERMAYER

Yrs. of NHL service: 2
Born: Cassiar, B.C.; Dec. 28, 1974
Position: centre
Height: 6-2
Weight: 200
Uniform no.: 44
Shoots: left

Career statistics:

GP	G	A	TP	PIM
113	13	23	36	87

1993-94 statistics:

GP	G	A	TP	+/-	PIM	PP	SH	GW	GT	S	PCT
65	9	17	26	-11	51	3	0	2	0	67	13.4

1994-95 statistics:

GP	G	A	TP	+/-	PIM	PP	SH	GW	GT	S	PCT
48	4	6	10	-13	36	1	0	0	0	58	6.9

LAST SEASON

Second NHL season. One of four Panthers to appear in all 48 games.

THE FINESSE GAME

Niedermayer has the makings of a power forward. He is big and strong and he has the speed to stay with some of the league's best power centres. He drives to the net and uses his strong skating — he just has to develop the confidence to play that way on a nightly basis.

He has good speed but needs better jump. He is a strong passer and an unselfish player, probably too unselfish. The only knock against him is that he might not be able to produce goals at the NHL level. He controls the puck well at tempo and can beat a defender one-on-one. Because he has so many duties as a centre, the Panthers gave him some time on the wing. Right now he is in-between. His playmaking isn't topnotch, but he's not finishing the way he should, either.

Niedermayer gets his shot away too slowly, a common problem for players in their first season out of junior.

THE PHYSICAL GAME

While not overly physical, Niedermayer has good size and is still growing. He has a bit of a temper, but he is an intelligent player and doesn't hurt his team by taking bad penalties. His attitude is outstanding. A coachable kid and good team man. He works hard along the boards and in the corners.

THE INTANGIBLES

Niedermayer has hit physical and mental speed bumps in his first two seasons, and it may take another two or three seasons before he really hits his stride. His progress is slow, but will be helped if the team gets stronger. Florida is not yet discouraged with his progress, sluggish though it may be.

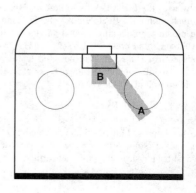

172

BRIAN SKRUDLAND

Yrs. of NHL service: 10
Born: Peace River, Alta.; July 31, 1963
Position: centre
Height: 6-0
Weight: 185
Uniform no.: 20
Shoots: left

Career statistics:

GP	G	A	TP	PIM
617	100	177	277	826

1991-92 statistics:

GP	G	A	TP	+/-	PIM	PP	SH	GW	GT	S	PCT
42	3	3	6	-4	36	0	0	1	0	51	5.9

1992-93 statistics:

GP	G	A	TP	+/-	PIM	PP	SH	GW	GT	S	PCT
39	7	7	14	+4	65	0	2	1	0	51	13.7

1993-94 statistics:

GP	G	A	TP	+/-	PIM	PP	SH	GW	GT	S	PCT
79	15	25	40	+13	136	0	2	1	0	110	13.6

1994-95 statistics:

GP	G	A	TP	+/-	PIM	PP	SH	GW	GT	S	PCT
47	5	9	14	0	88	1	0	0	0	44	11.4

younger players. He can be a valuable asset to a deep team, maybe a player who will make a difference in a playoff run (as Neal Broten did for New Jersey last season).

LAST SEASON
Missed one game with a hip injury.

THE FINESSE GAME
Skrudland is among the top face-off men in the league, and that, along with his strong skating and tenacious fore-checking, helps make him a reliable defensive forward who can chip in 15 or so goals as well.

His primary job is to keep the other team's top lines off the board, and he will get his scoring chances from forcing turnovers. He has a good short game and will look to make a creative play with the puck once he gains control. If he ever stays healthy through a full season, he could score 20 goals — but that's a mighty big "if" given the way the past few seasons have gone for him.

He is an outstanding penalty killer and short-handed threat.

THE PHYSICAL GAME
Skrudland is tough to knock off balance. He has a wide skating stance, which also gives him a strong power base for checking. He seldom fails to get a piece of his opponent. He has a compact build and makes his presence felt.

If anything, Skrudland takes too much emotion into a game and will take a bad penalty at what always seems to be the worst time. It's a small price to pay for someone who never takes a night off.

THE INTANGIBLES
Skrudland will probably be on the move this season as the Panthers bite the bullet and bring in some of their

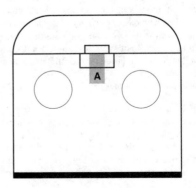

JOHN VANBIESBROUCK

Yrs. of NHL service: 11
Born: Detroit, Mich.; Sept. 4, 1963
Position: goaltender
Height: 5-9
Weight: 175
Uniform no.: 34
Catches: left

Career statistics:

GP	MINS	GA	SO	GAA	A	PIM
543	30907	1689	21	3.29	26	256

1991-92 statistics:

GP	MINS	GAA	W	L	T	SO	GA	S	SAPCT	PIM
45	2526	2.85	27	13	3	2	120	1331	.910	23

1992-93 statistics:

GP	MINS	GAA	W	L	T	SO	GA	S	SAPCT	PIM
48	2757	3.31	20	18	7	4	152	1525	.900	18

1993-94 statistics:

GP	MINS	GAA	W	L	T	SO	GA	S	SAPCT	PIM
57	3440	2.53	21	25	11	1	145	1912	.924	38

1994-95 statistics:

GP	MINS	GAA	W	L	T	SO	GA	S	SAPCT	PIM
37	2087	2.47	14	15	4	4	86	1000	.914	6

LAST SEASON

Tied for third in NHL in shutouts.

THE PHYSICAL GAME

Vanbiesbrouck blends a strong technical game with good reflexes, anticipation and confidence. He isn't very big, so he plays his angles and squares himself to the shooter to take away as much of the net as possible. He is very aggressive, forcing the shooter to make the first move. He plays breakaways well and is patient against even such one-on-one stars as Pavel Bure. (Vanbiesbrouck stopped the only penalty shot he faced last season.)

He plays an inverted-V style but does not put too much pressure on his inside edges, so he is able to move quickly to either side. He takes away much of the low net and has a good glove hand as well, so most shooters hope to take advantage of him on the stick side.

This is possible because Vanbiesbrouck is very active with his stick, using it to poke-check, guide rebounds, break up passes or whack at any ankles camping out too close to his crease. Billy Smith had a reputation as a stick man. Vanbiesbrouck's not quite as mean, but he won't surrender a centimetre of his ice, either. Vanbiesbrouck is also confident out of his net with the puck, sometimes overly so.

THE MENTAL GAME

The one-time Vezina Trophy winner is tops in his approach to the game. Vanbiesbrouck is a fighter. If a game starts off badly, he digs in, and bad goals don't seem to bother him. He also says what he thinks, so some of his teammates had better brace themselves.

The important thing is that his teammates believe in him.

Vanbiesbrouck steals games, and with an expansion team, that's about all you can ask of a goalie.

THE INTANGIBLES

The veteran gave the Panthers instant credibility and made them into playoff contenders, but he has ruffled the fur of management with a big win in salary arbitration. Odds are Vanbiesbrouck will be moving on this season, despite his value as a marquee player for the team, since there are a number of teams looking for a number one goalie and his trade value is high.

Vanbiesbrouck clearly has a season or two of top level performance left in him, and wants to finish his career with a contender.

HARTFORD WHALERS

Players' Statistics 1994-95

POS	NO.	PLAYER	GP	G	A	PTS	+/-	PIM	PP	SH	GW	GT	S	PCTG
C	21	ANDREW CASSELS	46	7	30	37	-3	18	1		1		74	9.5
C	89	DARREN TURCOTTE	47	17	18	35	1	22	3	1	3		121	14.0
C	8	GEOFF SANDERSON	46	18	14	32	-10	24	4		4		170	10.6
R	12	STEVEN RICE	40	11	10	21	2	61	4		1	1	57	19.3
L	28	PAUL RANHEIM	47	6	14	20	-3	10			1		73	8.2
D	4	FRANTISEK KUCERA	48	3	17	20	3	30			1		73	4.1
C	33	JIMMY CARSON	38	9	10	19	5	29	4		3		58	15.5
C	18	ROBERT KRON	37	10	8	18	-3	10	3	1	1		88	11.4
R	11	*ANDREI NIKOLISHIN	39	8	10	18	7	10	1	1			57	14.0
D	6	ADAM BURT	46	7	11	18		65	3		1		73	9.6
D	20	GLEN WESLEY	48	2	14	16	-6	50	1		1		125	1.6
D	44	CHRIS PRONGER	43	5	9	14	-12	54	3		1		94	5.3
L	26	JOCELYN LEMIEUX	41	6	5	11	-7	32			1		78	7.7
C	13	TED DRURY	34	3	6	9	-3	21					31	9.7
C	22	MARK JANSSENS	46	2	5	7	-8	93					33	6.1
D	7	BRIAN GLYNN	43	1	6	7	-2	32					35	2.9
L	14	*KEVIN SMYTH	16	1	5	6	-3	13					20	5.0
C	32	IGOR CHIBIREV	8	3	1	4	1						9	33.3
R	27	KELLY CHASE	28		4	4	1	141					15	
D	36	GLEN FEATHERSTONE	19	2	1	3	-7	50					22	9.1
L	24	JIM STORM	6		3	3	2						3	
L	17	*SCOTT DANIELS	12		2	2	1	55					7	
D	23	*MAREK MALIK	1		1	1	1							
D	10	BRAD MCCRIMMON	33		1	1	7	42					13	
G	1	SEAN BURKE	42		1	1		8						
C	39	ROBERT PETROVICKY	2										1	
G	35	JEFF REESE	11											
R	52	JIM SANDLAK	13				-10						13	
D	5	ALEXANDER GODYNYUK	14				1	8					16	

GP = games played; G = goals; A = assists; PTS = points; +/- = goals-for minus goals-against while player is on ice; PIM = penalties in minutes; PP = power play goals; SH = shorthanded goals; GW = game-winning goals; GT = game-tying goals; S = no. of shots; PCTG = percentage of goals to shots; * = rookie

SEAN BURKE

Yrs. of NHL service: 6
Born: Windsor, Ont.; Jan. 29, 1967
Position: goaltender
Height: 6-4
Weight: 210
Uniform no.: 1
Catches: left

Career statistics:

GP	MINS	GA	SO	GAA	A	PIM
301	16887	981	6	3.49	7	165

1991-92 statistics:
Did not play in NHL

1992-93 statistics:

GP	MINS	GAA	W	L	T	SO	GA	S	SAPCT	PIM
50	2656	4.16	16	27	3	0	184	1485	.876	25

1993-94 statistics:

GP	MINS	GAA	W	L	T	SO	GA	S	SAPCT	PIM
47	2750	2.99	17	24	5	2	137	1458	.906	16

1994-95 statistics:

GP	MINS	GAA	W	L	T	SO	GA	S	SAPCT	PIM
42	2418	2.68	17	19	4	0	108	1233	.912	8

LAST SEASON

Lowest GAA of career. Fourth in NHL in minutes played. Missed two games with a groin injury.

THE PHYSICAL GAME

Burke has improved most in his consistency. Over the past several seasons, he had been plagued by nights when he would beat himself, giving up long, soft goals and taking his team out of the game early. That hasn't happened as frequently in the past two years. Burke challenges the shooter well and comes out to the top of his crease, instead of sitting back, an old habit he appears to have shed.

Burke handles the puck well. He is confident and active on the dump-ins, and with the type of neutral-zone defense Hartford plays, his work out of the net is crucial. He gives his defensemen a chance to handle the puck more easily and break out of the zone with less effort.

Burke fills up the net and is very quick for a goalie of his size. He may be one of the best big goalies in the league on shots in tight because of his superior reflexes. He has improved his angle play and control of rebounds, though the latter is one area where he could still improve.

Burke has a quick glove hand, but he will often drop it and give the shooter the top corner over his left shoulder. He also holds his blocker hand too low on his stick, which makes him lean over too far and throws him off balance.

THE MENTAL GAME

Burke needs to feel he is a team's number one goalie. Competition for the starting role does not bring out the best in him. Fortunately for Burke, there doesn't appear to be any crowd in the crease in the Whalers' immediate future.

THE INTANGIBLES

Burke is hitting goalie prime, but needs an improved team in front of him. He became one of the highest paid goalies in the NHL with a four-year, $9-million contract last season, but the money didn't affect him. He wants to give a team its money's worth. He did so last season, and should repeat the feat this year.

ADAM BURT

Yrs. of NHL service: 6
Born: Detroit, Mich.; Jan. 15, 1969
Position: left defense
Height: 6-0
Weight: 195
Uniform no.: 6
Shoots: left

Career statistics:

GP	G	A	TP	PIM
350	29	72	101	523

1991-92 statistics:

GP	G	A	TP	+/-	PIM	PP	SH	GW	GT	S	PCT
66	9	15	24	-16	93	4	0	1	0	89	10.1

1992-93 statistics:

GP	G	A	TP	+/-	PIM	PP	SH	GW	GT	S	PCT
65	6	14	20	-11	116	0	0	0	0	81	7.4

1993-94 statistics:

GP	G	A	TP	+/-	PIM	PP	SH	GW	GT	S	PCT
63	1	17	18	-4	75	0	0	0	0	91	1.1

1994-95 statistics:

GP	G	A	TP	+/-	PIM	PP	SH	GW	GT	S	PCT
46	7	11	18	0	65	3	0	1	0	73	9.6

LAST SEASON
Missed two games with a knee injury.

THE FINESSE GAME
Burt is reliable night in and night out. He plays a strong physical game, and brings the puck out of the zone with authority, if not great speed.

Burt gets involved in the attack, but not to an overwhelming extent. He gets time on the second power play unit, but is not a top-flight point man.

An excellent one-on-one defender on a transition defense, Burt will strip the puck from a player using a poke-check and stand up to skaters at the blueline.

Burt has evolved into a pretty smart defenseman. He makes much better decisions with the puck and has limited his mental mistakes. He moves the puck smartly without creating opportunities for the opposing team — once one of his greatest weaknesses — and has cut down on his turnovers.

THE PHYSICAL GAME
Big but not strong, Burt works hard off the ice to gain more upper body and leg strength. He does not consistently control his man along the wall, nor does he drive people off the puck as well as a player of his size should. He is aware that his team needs him to establish a more physical presence, and he combines a willingness to hit with the desire to build himself up so he can be a legitimate thrasher. A more uptempo physical game will give him more room to move and more time to make better plays — an asset, since his hand and foot speed is only average.

Fighting does not come naturally to Burt, but he will do it and hold his own in order to make a point or aid a teammate.

THE INTANGIBLES
Burt is a coach's favourite, since no one ever has to worry about whether or not he will show up every night. He is never going to accumulate showy point totals — 40 points in a healthy, full season should be his max — but he will be a steady defenseman who can contribute in all zones. His attitude is upbeat and he is quick to learn and improve.

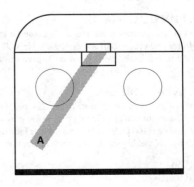

JIMMY CARSON

Yrs. of NHL service: 9
Born: Southfield, Mich.; July 20, 1968
Position: centre/right wing
Height: 6-1
Weight: 200
Uniform no.: 33
Shoots: right

Career statistics:

GP	G	A	TP	PIM
615	274	286	560	254

1991-92 statistics:

GP	G	A	TP	+/-	PIM	PP	SH	GW	GT	S	PCT
80	34	35	69	+17	30	11	0	3	0	150	22.7

1992-93 statistics:

GP	G	A	TP	+/-	PIM	PP	SH	GW	GT	S	PCT
86	37	36	73	-2	32	17	0	5	0	189	19.6

1993-94 statistics:

GP	G	A	TP	+/-	PIM	PP	SH	GW	GT	S	PCT
59	11	17	28	-15	24	3	0	1	0	129	8.5

1994-95 statistics:

GP	G	A	TP	+/-	PIM	PP	SH	GW	GT	S	PCT
38	9	10	19	+5	29	4	0	3	0	58	15.5

LAST SEASON

Signed as free agent. Tied for team lead in power play goals. Missed 10 games with a shoulder injury.

THE FINESSE GAME

Carson is a nifty skater with good acceleration and direction changes, all with firm control of the puck. He can make a lot of dekes and moves in a short space, and excels from between the circles in. He's more of a finisher than a playmaker.

Carson is a short-game player, all nine irons and pitching wedges. He is not a well-balanced skater and gets tipped over on some hits by smaller skaters, but he can maintain his edges fairly well when he dances through traffic.

He won't pay the price in other areas of the ice, which is one of the reasons why Carson changes addresses so often. On face-offs, for example, he does not tie up the opposing centre. He also tends to overhandle the puck at the blueline.

THE PHYSICAL GAME

Carson is fairly durable, but mostly because he stays out of areas where he will get crunched. He will use his body to shield the puck but won't drive through checks. He's a pretty soft player.

THE INTANGIBLES

Carson will never be much more than a 20-goal scorer again. Few teams can afford to carry a power play specialist, and he is too unreliable to earn a lot of ice time, though he will get his shifts by default in Hartford.

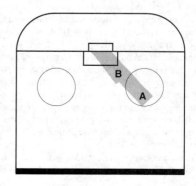

ANDREW CASSELS

Yrs. of NHL service: 5
Born: Bramalea, Ont.; July 23, 1969
Position: centre
Height: 6-0
Weight: 192
Uniform no.: 21
Shoots: left

Career statistics:

GP	G	A	TP	PIM
336	63	185	248	157

1991-92 statistics:

GP	G	A	TP	+/-	PIM	PP	SH	GW	GT	S	PCT
67	11	30	41	+3	18	2	2	3	0	99	11.1

1992-93 statistics:

GP	G	A	TP	+/-	PIM	PP	SH	GW	GT	S	PCT
84	21	64	85	-11	62	8	3	6	2	235	16.6

1993-94 statistics:

GP	G	A	TP	+/-	PIM	PP	SH	GW	GT	S	PCT
79	16	42	58	-21	37	8	1	3	0	126	12.7

1994-95 statistics:

GP	G	A	TP	+/-	PIM	PP	SH	GW	GT	S	PCT
46	7	30	37	-3	18	1	0	1	0	74	9.5

LAST SEASON

Led team in assists for third consecutive season. Led team in points.

THE FINESSE GAME

The first word most people associate with Cassels is smart. He is a very intelligent player with terrific hockey instinct, who knows when to recognize passing situations, when to move the puck and who to move it to. He has a good backhand pass in traffic and is almost as good on his backhand as his forehand. He is a creative passer who is aware of his teammates.

Cassels was never a great shooter, but he's worked to improve that. He spends a lot of time after practice working on his shot and release. He has quick hands and can swipe a shot off a bouncing puck in mid-air. He doesn't always fight through checks to get the kind of shots he should.

A mainstay on both specialty teams, Cassels has improved on draws to the point where he was Hartford's best defensive centre on many nights. He back-checks and blocks shots. Cassels has good speed but lacks one-step quickness. He has improved his puckhandling at a high tempo.

THE PHYSICAL GAME

To complement his brains, Cassels needs brawn. He is facing a lot of defensive pressure now and has to force his way through strong fore-checks and traffic around the net. He tends to get run down late in the season or during a tough stretch in the schedule, and when he gets fatigued, he is not nearly as effective.

THE INTANGIBLES

Cassels is capable of returning to 85-90 point form — his talent level is there, and he's being paid to do it. Hartford traded away Pat Verbeek and doesn't have a strong finisher to play on his right side, unless Steven Rice steps up to fill that role this season. Cassels needs a complementary player or his numbers will sag back down around 50-60 points, and that's not good enough.

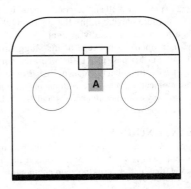

MARK JANSSENS

Yrs. of NHL service: 5
Born: Surrey, B.C.; May 19, 1968
Position: centre
Height: 6-3
Weight: 216
Uniform no.: 22
Shoots: left

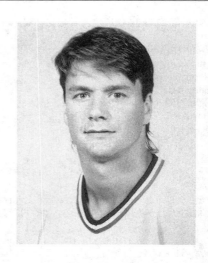

Career statistics:

GP	G	A	TP	PIM
366	30	47	67	265

1991-92 statistics:

GP	G	A	TP	+/-	PIM	PP	SH	GW	GT	S	PCT
7	0	0	0	-2	5	0	0	0	0	1	0.0

1992-93 statistics:

GP	G	A	TP	+/-	PIM	PP	SH	GW	GT	S	PCT
76	12	17	29	-15	237	0	0	1	0	63	19.0

1993-94 statistics:

GP	G	A	TP	+/-	PIM	PP	SH	GW	GT	S	PCT
84	2	10	12	-13	137	0	0	0	0	52	3.8

1994-95 statistics:

GP	G	A	TP	+/-	PIM	PP	SH	GW	GT	S	PCT
46	2	5	7	-8	93	0	0	0	0	33	6.1

LAST SEASON

Missed two games with a concussion.

THE FINESSE GAME

Janssens does a lot of little things well and he is the prototypical team player. He is very slow afoot — the major reason why he spent a great deal of time in the minors in the early part of his career — but compensates for his flawed skating with smarts and hustle. He seldom looks out of place on the ice because he's so solid positionally.

Janssens is excellent on face-offs and takes the key defensive draws. He is part of the number one penalty-killing unit and is a tenacious hitter and forechecker. He never loses his zeal for the game, even on nights when he gets only a handful of shifts.

THE PHYSICAL GAME

Janssens will fight if he has to, and his courage in these situations is remarkable given the fact that he suffered a fractured skull and cerebral concussion during a fight while playing in the IHL in 1988-89. His size is a big asset, especially in tight. While he can flounder in open ice because of his sluggish foot speed, he is at his best in the slot or in the corners because of his strength and balance. He has the ability to sway momentum in a game with his physical play. Janssens always finishes his checks and will rub his glove in an opponent's face.

THE INTANGIBLES

Janssens is a talkative, upbeat player on the bench and in the room and is very popular with his teammates, who know that he fights for the team and not himself.

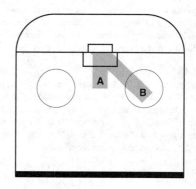

ROBERT KRON

Yrs. of NHL service: 5
Born: Brno, Czechoslovakia; Feb. 27, 1967
Position: centre
Height: 5-10
Weight: 174
Uniform no.: 18
Shoots: left

Career statistics:

GP	G	A	TP	PIM
271	62	69	131	59

1991-92 statistics:

GP	G	A	TP	+/-	PIM	PP	SH	GW	GT	S	PCT
36	2	2	4	-9	2	0	0	0	0	49	4.1

1992-93 statistics:

GP	G	A	TP	+/-	PIM	PP	SH	GW	GT	S	PCT
45	14	13	27	+5	18	4	2	2	1	97	14.4

1993-94 statistics:

GP	G	A	TP	+/-	PIM	PP	SH	GW	GT	S	PCT
77	24	26	50	0	8	2	1	3	0	194	12.4

1994-95 statistics:

GP	G	A	TP	+/-	PIM	PP	SH	GW	GT	S	PCT
37	10	8	18	-3	10	3	1	1	0	88	11.4

LAST SEASON

One of three Whalers tied with one shorthanded goal. Missed games with a hand injury.

THE FINESSE GAME

Kron has great speed and can control the puck at high tempo, which gives him the ability to intimidate and drive opposing defensemen back off the blueline. He has moved into a second-line role and continues to improve as he gets more ice time.

One of the best things to happen to his career was the reinstatement of four-on-four play in the case of coincidental minor penalties. Kron thrives on the extra open ice. There are many game situations where four-on-four comes into play, and it fits in well with some of the more skilled forwards the Whalers are quietly accumulating.

Kron is aware in all three zones. He can kill penalties and work on the power play as well. Defensively reliable, he can be used on the ice at any time in the game. He is a very creative player, more of a playmaker than a shooter, but he needs to shoot more because of his good hands. He tries to be too fine with his shot and misses the net frequently when he is in a prime scoring area. He likes to use a snap shot more than a slapper and will get a quick release away from 15 to 20 feet out.

THE PHYSICAL GAME

Kron is very fit but has just had a second season interrupted by injury. He is a small player and doesn't play a physical style, but he's not afraid and doesn't bail out of tough situations. He will need to be shored up by big forwards, but linemates with hands, since Kron will create good scoring chances that shouldn't go to waste.

THE INTANGIBLES

Kron has improved slightly over the past two seasons, but now needs to take a big stride forward and produce 25-30 goals and contribute consistent play.

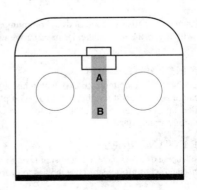

FRANTISEK KUCERA

Yrs. of NHL service: 5
Born: Prague, Czechoslovakia; Feb. 3, 1968
Position: left defense
Height: 6-2
Weight: 205
Uniform no.: 4
Shoots: left

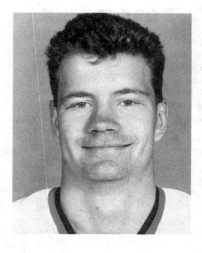

Career statistics:

GP	G	A	TP	PIM
296	18	69	83	205

1991-92 statistics:

GP	G	A	TP	+/-	PIM	PP	SH	GW	GT	S	PCT
61	3	10	13	+3	36	1	0	1	0	82	3.7

1992-93 statistics:

GP	G	A	TP	+/-	PIM	PP	SH	GW	GT	S	PCT
71	5	14	19	+7	59	1	0	1	0	117	4.3

1993-94 statistics:

GP	G	A	TP	+/-	PIM	PP	SH	GW	GT	S	PCT
76	5	16	21	-3	48	3	0	0	0	122	4.1

1994-95 statistics:

GP	G	A	TP	+/-	PIM	PP	SH	GW	GT	S	PCT
48	3	17	20	+3	30	0	0	1	0	73	4.1

LAST SEASON

One of two Whalers to appear in all 48 games. Led team defensemen in scoring.

THE FINESSE GAME

Kucera is a solid, reliable third or fourth defenseman who gives the Whalers some depth on defense that has been lacking the past few seasons. If Kucera gets too much ice time, he tends to wear down and make careless plays. He is far more effective when getting about 18 minutes a night.

Kucera plays the point on the power play and is a good penalty killer because he reads plays well. Defensively, his skating makes it very difficult for the opposition to outmanoeuvre him one-on-one or anywhere in open ice. He sends a nice breakout pass out of the defensive zone, which he prefers to trying to carry the puck out. Offensively, he will sometimes try to make a play at the opposition's blueline, resulting in a turnover, as he is reluctant to just throw the puck in deep.

Kucera's English is good and he communicates well with his partner and goalie. He has a strong work ethic.

THE PHYSICAL GAME

Kucera has to develop more consistency in his physical game. He is a good-sized defenseman who plays smaller, and he loses many of the one-on-one confrontations around the net.

THE INTANGIBLES

Since Kucera does not have the high skill level to be a defenseman whose forte is offense, he has to become stronger and cement his game in the defensive zone. He is worth watching, since he could become a reliable two-way defenseman as long as he does not have to work on the team's top defense pair. Last season, the Whalers had him in their fourth or fifth slot, which is ideal.

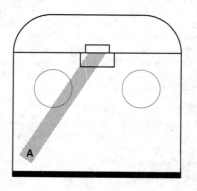

JOCELYN LEMIEUX

Yrs. of NHL service: 8
Born: Mont-Laurier, Que.; Nov. 18, 1967
Position: right wing
Height: 5-10
Weight: 200
Uniform no.: 26
Shoots: left

Career statistics:

GP	G	A	TP	PIM
499	71	74	145	668

1991-92 statistics:

GP	G	A	TP	+/-	PIM	PP	SH	GW	GT	S	PCT
78	6	10	16	-2	80	0	0	1	0	103	5.8

1992-93 statistics:

GP	G	A	TP	+/-	PIM	PP	SH	GW	GT	S	PCT
81	10	21	31	+5	111	1	0	2	1	117	8.5

1993-94 statistics:

GP	G	A	TP	+/-	PIM	PP	SH	GW	GT	S	PCT
82	18	9	27	-3	82	0	0	2	1	151	11.9

1994-95 statistics:

GP	G	A	TP	+/-	PIM	PP	SH	GW	GT	S	PCT
41	6	5	11	-7	32	0	0	1	0	78	7.7

LAST SEASON

Missed seven games with a rotator cuff injury.

THE FINESSE GAME

Lemieux is not likely to join the ranks of the great productive power forwards like Cam Neely and Brendan Shanahan, but he has the ability to create havoc off his fore-checks. He just lacks the deft scoring touch and instincts in tight that could boost him into the 40-goal range. Lemieux may not score often, but his goals tend to be big ones in key pressure situations.

Lemieux skates with short, powerful strides. He is very well balanced and does not get knocked off the puck easily. He has good end-to-end speed, but is not real fancy and doesn't have a clever head. Lemieux is not creative enough to get much power play time, but his puck pursuit makes him a strong penalty killer.

His quick little strides serve him well along the boards and in the corners, and he keeps driving through traffic. He has a good wrist and snap shot.

THE PHYSICAL GAME

Lemieux is not coy. His theory is that the shortest distance between two points means eliminating one of the points, which he usually does with a flattening check. He loves to play through his checks and he makes opposing defensemen hesitant with his persistent pressure.

A bulldog with the puck or without it, Lemieux has little regard for his physical safety or, it seems, his lifespan, as he fearlessly throws himself in the face of bigger players with even meaner reputations than his. He leads by example and is unselfish. Lemieux knows that physical play is the biggest part of his game and he brings it to the ice almost every night. He keeps himself in phenomenal shape and can take increased ice time. He played through a very painful shoulder injury.

THE INTANGIBLES

Lemieux is consistently feisty and physical and will be an attractive free agent during the off-season. If he comes back healthy and in the right slot, he might net a team 25 goals and will be a headache to play against and a handful to contain.

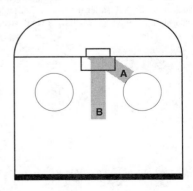

MAREK MALIK

Yrs. of NHL service: 0
Born: Ostrava, Czechoslovkia; June 24, 1975
Position: defense
Height: 6-5
Weight: 185
Uniform no.: 23
Shoots: left

Career statistics:

GP	G	A	TP	PIM
1	0	1	1	0

1994-95 statistics:

GP	G	A	TP	+/-	PIM	PP	SH	GW	GT	S	PCT
1	0	1	1	+1	0	0	0	0	0	0	0.0

LAST SEASON

Will be entering first NHL season. Played for Springfield (AHL), with 11-30 — 41 in 58 games and 91 PIM.

THE FINESSE GAME

Malik is an excellent skater for his size. His uses his range mostly as a defensive tool, and isn't much involved in the attack.

Malik is poised with the puck. He is a good passer and playmaker and moves the puck out of his own end quickly. He won't try to do too much himself but will use his teammates well. He's big, but does a lot of the little things, which makes him a solid defensive player. He limits his offensive contribution to a shot from the point.

THE PHYSICAL GAME

Tall but weedy, Malik needs to fill out more to be able to handle some of the NHL's big boys. Like Kjell Samuelsson, he takes up a lot of space with his arms and stick, and is more of an octopus-type defenseman than a solid hitter. He is strong in front of his net. He doesn't have much of a mean streak.

THE INTANGIBLES

Malik made the Whalers' roster during training camp, but was sent to the AHL after the lockout started and suffered a shoulder injury. He will figure in the team's plans this season.

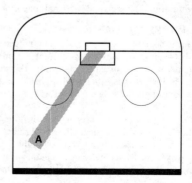

ANDREI NIKOLISHIN

Yrs. of NHL service: 1
Born: Vorkuta, USSR; March 25, 1973
Position: left wing/centre
Height: 5-11
Weight: 180
Uniform no.: 11
Shoots: left

Career statistics:

GP	G	A	TP	PIM
39	8	10	18	10

1994-95 statistics:

GP	G	A	TP	+/-	PIM	PP	SH	GW	GT	S	PCT
39	8	10	18	+7	10	1	1	0	0	57	14.0

LAST SEASON

First NHL season. Led team in plus-minus.

THE FINESSE GAME

Nikolishin is a very good skater with a powerful stride. His great talent is puckhandling, but like many Europeans he tends to hold onto the puck too long and leaves himself open for hits.

Nikolishin sees the ice well and is a gifted play-maker. He needs to shoot more so that his game will be less predictable. Hartford went through a lot of changes last season, which didn't help his adjustment. He needs to play with a power winger who can finish off plays and stand up for him a bit. He is eager to learn the game. Nikolishin saw time on the second power play unit and killed some penalties. Toward the end of the season he took draws in the offensive and defensive zone. He is defensively aware, back-checks, and blocks shots.

THE PHYSICAL GAME

Nikolishin is extremely strong on his skates. He is tough to knock off balance and has a low centre of gravity. He has adapted smoothly to the more physical style of play in the NHL, and while he isn't very big, he will plow into heavy going for the puck.

THE INTANGIBLES

Nikolishin was a captain of Moscow Dynamo at age 21, and it wouldn't be a surprise to see him wearing a letter someday for the Hartford Whalers. Although he is still polishing his English, he has become very popular with his teammates.

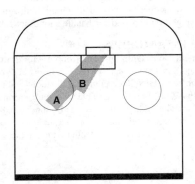

JEFF O'NEILL

Yrs. of NHL service: 0
Born: King City, Ont.; Feb. 23, 1976
Position: centre
Height: 6-0
Weight: 176
Uniform no.: n.a.
Shoots: right

1993-94 junior statistics:

GP	G	A	TP	PIM
66	45	81	126	95

1994-95 junior statistics:

GP	G	A	TP	PIM
57	43	81	124	56

LAST SEASON

Drafted by Hartford in the first round of the 1994 Entry Draft, fifth overall. Led junior team (Guelph, OHL) in assists and points for second consecutive season. Fourth in league in scoring.

THE FINESSE GAME

O'Neill is a youngster who has already shown signs of a solid two-way game. Offensively, he is an excellent skater with balance, speed, acceleration and quickness.

An outstanding playmaker, O'Neill has a good sense of timing and is patient with his passes. He's a scorer as well, with good wrist and slap shots. He uses all of the ice. He works the point on the power play.

Puck control and defense are a big part of O'Neill's game, and he is smart enough to know that playing good defense doesn't detract from offense. When the game is on the line, whether his team needs to score a goal or protect a lead, O'Neill wants the puck.

THE PHYSICAL GAME

O'Neill doesn't have the size to tangle with NHL heavyweights, but one of his idols is Jeremy Roenick, and a smaller frame never stopped Roenick from going full-tilt. O'Neill is feisty and will get involved.

He works hard on his conditioning, both aerobic and weight training, and can handle a lot of ice time.

THE INTANGIBLES

The next Doug Gilmour? The trouble with drafting kids at 18 is that you can see the size of the body, but not the heart. O'Neill certainly has the tools, and if he and the Whalers had been able to come to terms in time last season, he would have had a shot at making the team. Now safely under contract, he may be able to step in and give the team depth up the middle.

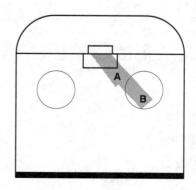

PAUL RANHEIM

Yrs. of NHL service: 5
Born: St. Louis, Mo.; Jan. 25, 1966
Position: left wing
Height: 6-0
Weight: 195
Uniform no.: 28
Shoots: right

Career statistics:

GP	G	A	TP	PIM
416	100	117	217	117

1991-92 statistics:

GP	G	A	TP	+/-	PIM	PP	SH	GW	GT	S	PCT
80	23	20	43	+16	32	1	3	3	0	159	14.5

1992-93 statistics:

GP	G	A	TP	+/-	PIM	PP	SH	GW	GT	S	PCT
83	21	22	43	-4	26	3	4	1	0	179	11.7

1993-94 statistics:

GP	G	A	TP	+/-	PIM	PP	SH	GW	GT	S	PCT
82	10	17	27	-18	22	0	2	2	0	131	7.6

1994-95 statistics:

GP	G	A	TP	+/-	PIM	PP	SH	GW	GT	S	PCT
47	6	14	20	-3	10	0	0	1	0	73	8.2

THE INTANGIBLES

Don't expect any new spots on this leopard. He is a role player with a top potential of 20 goals a season.

LAST SEASON

Has missed only four games in last four seasons.

THE FINESSE GAME

Does Ranheim play a checking role because he has speed but no finishing skills, or are his point totals low because he usually plays such a defensive role? Ranheim had one huge year in the minors (68 goals with Salt Lake of the IHL in 1988-89), but the sides of the North American highways are littered with the bus-weary bones of minor leaguers whose skills stalled at the NHL level.

Ranheim is a right-handed shot who plays the left wing, meaning he takes most of his passes on the backhand and needs more time to handle the pass. He is an excellent skater, one of the fastest in the NHL, and gets a huge number of chances just off his speed. His chief flaw is his utter lack of creativity with his shot. He is also astoundingly inaccurate, which may be a result of looking too much at the puck and not enough at his target. He merits little power play time. Ranheim is a strong penalty killer, using his break-away speed to create shorthanded chances.

Defensively, Ranheim is top drawer. He has worked hard to improve in this area after coming out of the college ranks (University of Wisconsin) as a scorer.

THE PHYSICAL GAME

Ranheim plays a solid physical game, though with his leg drive and power he could deliver more impressive hits. He does not initiate hits as well as he should.

STEVEN RICE

Yrs. of NHL service: 3
Born: Kitchener, Ont.; May 26, 1971
Position: right wing
Height: 6-0
Weight: 215
Uniform no.: 12
Shoots: right

Career statistics:

GP	G	A	TP	PIM
145	31	31	62	131

1991-92 statistics:

GP	G	A	TP	+/-	PIM	PP	SH	GW	GT	S	PCT
3	0	0	0	-2	0	0	0	0	0	2	0.0

1992-93 statistics:

GP	G	A	TP	+/-	PIM	PP	SH	GW	GT	S	PCT
28	2	5	7	-4	28	0	0	0	0	29	6.9

1993-94 statistics:

GP	G	A	TP	+/-	PIM	PP	SH	GW	GT	S	PCT
63	17	15	32	-10	36	6	0	1	1	129	13.2

1994-95 statistics:

GP	G	A	TP	+/-	PIM	PP	SH	GW	GT	S	PCT
40	11	10	21	+2	61	4	0	1	1	57	19.3

LAST SEASON

Led team in shooting percentage. Tied for team lead in power play goals. Signed as free agent from Edmonton. Missed games with a concussion.

THE FINESSE GAME

Rice has solid skating ability and balance. He has a good slap shot with a quick release, and is strong and determined around the net.

He can make a play but is more effective when he doesn't overhandle the puck.

Rice is a dependable defensive player, although his main role is to put points on the board. He is very good on the power play, using his big frame to screen the goalie.

THE PHYSICAL GAME

Rice has begun to use his size effectively, at last. He will take a hit to make a play and protects the puck. He needs to consistently drive to the net, which is where he generates his best scoring chances. He came into last year's camp a bit overweight — not out of shape, but probably carrying about 10 to 15 pounds too much to be as mobile as he can be.

THE INTANGIBLES

Rice is projected as a number one winger for Hartford, moving up into Pat Verbeek's old spot on the top line. He will get his share of ice time and has to produce.

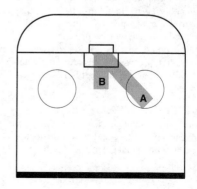

GEOFF SANDERSON

Yrs. of NHL service: 4
Born: Hay River, Northwest Territories; Feb. 1, 1972
Position: left wing
Height: 6-0
Weight: 185
Uniform no.: 8
Shoots: left

Career statistics:

GP	G	A	TP	PIM
276	119	101	220	112

1991-92 statistics:

GP	G	A	TP	+/-	PIM	PP	SH	GW	GT	S	PCT
64	13	18	31	+5	18	2	0	1	0	98	13.3

1992-93 statistics:

GP	G	A	TP	+/-	PIM	PP	SH	GW	GT	S	PCT
82	46	43	89	-21	28	21	2	4	0	271	17.0

1993-94 statistics:

GP	G	A	TP	+/-	PIM	PP	SH	GW	GT	S	PCT
82	41	26	67	-13	42	15	1	6	2	266	15.4

1994-95 statistics:

GP	G	A	TP	+/-	PIM	PP	SH	GW	GT	S	PCT
46	18	14	32	-10	24	4	0	4	0	170	10.6

LAST SEASON

Led team in goals for third consecutive season. Tied for team lead in power play goals. Third on team in points. Led team in shots for second consecutive season. Led team in game-winning goals for second consecutive season.

THE FINESSE GAME

Sanderson is a southpaw version of Mike Gartner in the making. His speed gives him a tremendous edge over the majority of NHL players, and he combines it with good puckhandling ability, vision and instincts. Unlike a lot of players who are simply fast, Sanderson knows how to make use of the opportunities his vapour trails create. Yet, he can do even more.

He drives wide and utilizes his speed and shot while in motion. By intimidating with his speed, he pushes the defensemen back and gets plenty of room to unleash his shot.

He has an excellent release and a superb one-timer on the power play. He also uses his skating to beat defenders wide and bear down on the goalie from the right circle on his off-wing. Sanderson sees his share of feeds from centre Andrew Cassels, who is a left-handed shooter but is just as good a backhand passer as a forehand playmaker. Sanderson loves to shoot. When he gets a chance, it's on goal, and he always has his head up looking for the holes.

Sanderson can also kill penalties. His speed makes him a shorthanded threat.

THE PHYSICAL GAME

Sanderson has to learn and desire to fight his way through checkers. He is wiry but gets outmuscled, and while his speed keeps him clear of a lot of traffic, he has to battle when the room isn't there.

THE INTANGIBLES

Sanderson has the speed and the trigger to be a 50-goal scorer. The step to that elite class will take some help from his teammates, but a lot more has to come from Sanderson's mental toughness and commitment. The question is whether Sanderson wants to work harder to become an elite player, or if he is content being a very good one.

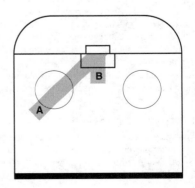

BRENDAN SHANAHAN

Yrs. of NHL service: 8
Born: Mimico, Ont.; Jan. 23, 1969
Position: left wing
Height: 6-3
Weight: 210
Uniform no.: 19
Shoots: right

Career statistics:

GP	G	A	TP	PIM
558	244	276	520	1216

1991-92 statistics:

GP	G	A	TP	+/-	PIM	PP	SH	GW	GT	S	PCT
80	33	36	69	-3	171	13	0	2	2	215	15.3

1992-93 statistics:

GP	G	A	TP	+/-	PIM	PP	SH	GW	GT	S	PCT
71	51	43	94	+10	174	18	0	8	8	232	22.0

1993-94 statistics:

GP	G	A	TP	+/-	PIM	PP	SH	GW	GT	S	PCT
81	52	50	102	-9	211	15	7	8	1	397	13.1

1994-95 statistics:

GP	G	A	TP	+/-	PIM	PP	SH	GW	GT	S	PCT
45	20	21	41	+7	136	6	2	6	0	153	13.1

LAST SEASON

Tied for team lead in game-winning goals. Led team in PIM. Second on team in points and power play goals. Missed three games with a virus. Acquired by Hartford for Chris Pronger.

THE FINESSE GAME

Shanahan is a wonderful package of grit, skills and smarts. He will battle in front of the net for a puck, but he is also savvy enough to avoid an unnecessary thrashing. On the power play, he is one of the best in the league at staying just off the crease, waiting for a shot to come from the point, then timing his entry to the front of the net for the moving screen, the tip or the rebound.

He has wonderfully soft hands for nifty goal-mouth passes, and he has a hard, accurate snap and slap shot with a quick release. He will take some face-offs, especially in the offensive zone, and succeeds by tying up the opposing centre and using his feet to control the puck. He has become one of the Blues' top go-to guys. Even though he plays on the "off" wing, his backhand is good enough to take passes and create some offense. Shanahan can fill in at centre (his position in junior) in a pinch.

One of Shanahan's few flaws is his skating. He lacks quickness but does have great strength and balance.

THE PHYSICAL GAME

The Shanahan dilemma for rival teams: if you play Shanahan aggressively, it brings out the best in him. If you lay off and give him room, he will kill you with his skills. Shanahan spent his formative NHL years establishing his reputation by dropping his gloves with anybody who challenged him, but he has gotten smarter without losing his tough edge. He will still lose it once in awhile, which only makes rivals a little more wary.

He will take or make a hit to create a play. He is willing to eat glass to make a pass.

THE INTANGIBLES

Another victim of the Mike Keenan housecleaning, Shanahan will get his chance to help the floundering Whalers' franchise.

The *HSR* jumped on the Shanahan bandwagon many editions ago, and all he does is make us look smarter and smarter. Shanahan is among the top power forwards in the league, and should return to the 100-point mark this season. He is a leader, a gamer.

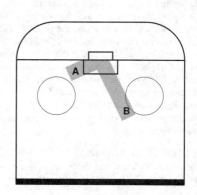

DARREN TURCOTTE

Yrs. of NHL service: 6
Born: Boston, Mass.; Mar. 2, 1968
Position: centre
Height: 6-0
Weight: 180
Uniform no.: 89
Shoots: right

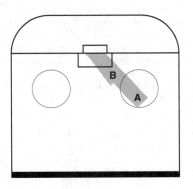

Career statistics:

GP	G	A	TP	PIM
391	141	162	303	209

1991-92 statistics:

GP	G	A	TP	+/-	PIM	PP	SH	GW	GT	S	PCT
71	30	23	53	+11	57	13	1	4	1	216	13.9

1992-93 statistics:

GP	G	A	TP	+/-	PIM	PP	SH	GW	GT	S	PCT
71	25	28	53	-3	40	7	3	3	1	213	11.7

1993-94 statistics:

GP	G	A	TP	+/-	PIM	PP	SH	GW	GT	S	PCT
32	4	15	19	-13	17	0	0	0	0	60	6.7

1994-95 statistics:

GP	G	A	TP	+/-	PIM	PP	SH	GW	GT	S	PCT
47	17	18	35	+1	22	3	1	3	0	121	14.0

LAST SEASON

Second on team in points, goals and assists.

THE FINESSE GAME

Turcotte is much better on special teams than at even strength, though he is a capable five-on-five player. With the extra open ice — even when his team is shorthanded — he makes things happen. A fine skater, Turcotte seems to have recovered completely from his knee surgery of a season ago. He appears to hover over the ice. He takes long, fluid strides that cover a lot of territory and creates space with his speed, driving the defenders back and daring them to come up to challenge him.

Turcotte kills penalties aggressively. He forces the point men and when he gets a turnover he springs down-ice on a break. He makes the point men nervous, and teams who use forwards at the point are especially vulnerable to his pressure.

On the power play, Turcotte works down low but can drop back to handle the point if the defenseman comes in deep. He has a fine snap shot, as well as a good wrist and one-timer. He has sharp hand-eye coordination and is skilled on draws.

THE PHYSICAL GAME

Turcotte will take a hit to make a play, but he is not a physical player. He will go into traffic with the puck and has the hand skills to control the puck in a crowd.

THE INTANGIBLES

Turcotte gets a lot of ice time with the Whalers (although trade rumours had him heading to Ottawa) and he quietly makes linemates better through his subtle play. Nothing he does is eye-opening, but he will net 70 points and is a solid number two centre.

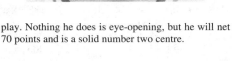

GLEN WESLEY

Yrs. of NHL service: 8
Born: Red Deer, Alta.; Oct. 2, 1968
Position: defense
Height: 6-1
Weight: 195
Uniform no.: 20
Shoots: left

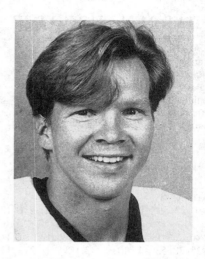

Career statistics:

GP	G	A	TP	PIM
585	79	244	323	471

1991-92 statistics:

GP	G	A	TP	+/-	PIM	PP	SH	GW	GT	S	PCT
78	9	37	46	-9	54	4	0	1	0	211	4.3

1992-93 statistics:

GP	G	A	TP	+/-	PIM	PP	SH	GW	GT	S	PCT
64	8	25	33	-2	47	4	1	0	0	183	4.4

1993-94 statistics:

GP	G	A	TP	+/-	PIM	PP	SH	GW	GT	S	PCT
81	14	44	58	+1	64	6	1	1	1	265	5.3

1994-95 statistics:

GP	G	A	TP	+/-	PIM	PP	SH	GW	GT	S	PCT
48	2	14	16	-6	50	1	0	1	0	125	1.6

LAST SEASON

One of two Whalers to appear in all 48 games. Signed as free agent from Boston (Hartford gave up two first-round draft picks as compensation).

THE FINESSE GAME

Much was expected of Wesley in Boston, where he was often compared to Ray Bourque. His acquisition by Hartford put even more pressure on him, and the results weren't always pretty.

Wesley simply isn't an offensive force, and he played much of the season with the inexperienced Chris Pronger. Wesley deserves credit for his solid play.

He is very good with the puck. He works well on the power play because he knows when to jump into the holes. He has good but not great offensive instincts, gauging when to pinch, when to rush, when to pass the puck and when to back off. He is a good skater who is not afraid to veer into the play deep; he seldom gets trapped there. He has a good slap shot from the point and snap shot from the circle. You could count on two hands the number of times Wesley has been beaten one-on-one throughout his career, and there are very few defensemen you can say that about. He makes defensive plays with confidence and is poised even when outnumbered in the rush. He has to keep his feet moving.

THE PHYSICAL GAME

Wesley is not a bone-crunching defenseman, but neither was Jacques Laperriere, and he's in the Hall of Fame. We're not suggesting that Wesley is in that class, but just that you don't have to shatter glass to be

a solid checker, which he is. He's not a mean hitter, but he will execute a take-out check and not let his man get back into the play.

He is also very sly about running interference for his defense partner, allowing him time to move the puck and giving him confidence that he won't get hammered by a fore-checker.

THE INTANGIBLES

Wesley's numbers were a disappointment to Hartford, who were probably planning on 20 goals and 60 points. But Wesley isn't that kind of number one defenseman. He needs support, and he doesn't have it with the Whalers.

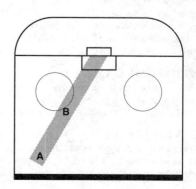

LOS ANGELES KINGS

Players' Statistics 1994-95

POS	NO.	PLAYER	GP	G	A	PTS	+/-	PIM	PP	SH	GW	GT	S	PCTG
C	99	WAYNE GRETZKY	48	11	37	48	-20	6	3		1		142	7.7
R	22	RICK TOCCHET	36	18	17	35	-8	70	7	1	3		95	18.9
C	7	DAN QUINN	44	14	17	31	-3	32	2		4	3	78	17.9
L	17	JARI KURRI	38	10	19	29	-17	24	2			1	84	11.9
L	21	TONY GRANATO	33	13	11	24	9	68	2		3		106	12.3
D	25	DARRYL SYDOR	48	4	19	23	-2	36	3			1	96	4.2
D	33	MARTY MCSORLEY	41	3	18	21	-14	83	1			1	75	4.0
R	19	JOHN DRUCE	43	15	5	20	-3	20	3		1		75	20.0
L	44	RANDY BURRIDGE	40	4	15	19	-4	10	2				52	7.7
D	24	MICHEL PETIT	40	5	12	17	4	84	2				70	7.1
L	28	*ERIC LACROIX	45	9	7	16	2	54	2	1	1		64	14.1
L	15	PAT CONACHER	48	7	9	16	-9	12		1			64	10.9
C	13	ROBERT LANG	36	4	8	12	-7	4					38	10.5
D	4	ROB BLAKE	24	4	7	11	-16	38	4		1		76	5.3
C	12	KEVIN TODD	33	3	8	11	-5	12			1		34	8.8
C	14	GARY SHUCHUK	22	3	6	9	-2	6					16	18.8
D	29	*CHRIS SNELL	32	2	7	9	-7	22	2				45	4.4
D	77	ROB COWIE	32	2	7	9	-6	20					39	5.1
C	39	*YANIC PERREAULT	26	2	5	7	3	20			1		43	4.7
D	26	PHILIPPE BOUCHER	15	2	4	6	3	4					30	6.7
R	8	*KEVIN BROWN	23	2	3	5	-7	18					25	8.0
R	55	TROY CROWDER	29	1	2	3		99					4	25.0
D	6	*SEAN O'DONNELL	15		2	2	-2	49					12	
L	10	*JEFF SHEVALIER	1	1		1	1						1	00.0
L	34	*MATT JOHNSON	14	1		1		102					4	25.0
D	35	ARTO BLOMSTEN	5		1	1	2	2					1	
L	27	DAVE THOMLINSON	1				-1							
D	5	TIM WATTERS	1				1						1	
D	38	*ERIC LAVIGNE	1				-1							
G	36	*PAULI JAKS	1											
R	9	ROB BROWN	2				-2						1	
G	31	*JAMIE STORR	5											
G	31	GRANT FUHR	17					2						
D	3	*DENIS TSYGUROV	25				-3	15					20	
G	32	KELLY HRUDEY	35											

GP = games played; G = goals; A = assists; PTS = points; +/- = goals-for minus goals-against while player is on ice; PIM = penalties in minutes; PP = power play goals; SH = shorthanded goals; GW = game-winning goals; GT = game-tying goals; S = no. of shots; PCTG = percentage of goals to shots; * = rookie

AKI-PETTERI BERG

Yrs. of NHL service: 0
Born: Raisio, Finland; July 28, 1977
Position: defense
Height: 6-3
Weight: 196
Uniform no.: n.a.
Shoots: left

1994-95 statistics (Finland):

GP	G	A	TP	PIM
20	3	9	12	34

LAST SEASON
Will be entering first NHL season.

THE FINESSE GAME
Berg is a pleasing combination of offensive and defensive skills. His skating is top-notch. He has a powerful stride with great mobility and balance. And he gets terrific drive from perfect leg extension and deep knee bends.

He sees the ice well and has excellent passing skills. He can also rush with the puck, but he prefers to make a pass and then join the play. He should be able to quarterback anyone's NHL power play.

While his offensive skills grab the attention, the young Finn is also conscientious defensively. He is a solid prospect as a two-way defenseman.

THE PHYSICAL GAME
Berg loves to hit. He's big and strong, and has the mobility to lay down some serious open-ice checks. His punishing checks have had some scouts comparing him to Scott Stevens. Berg seems to possess Stevens' intensity as well. He is very fit and should be able to handle a full 84-game grind.

THE INTANGIBLES
Some onlookers believed Berg was the best player available in the 1995 draft, but he was slowed by mononucleosis last season. If he had been 100 per cent, he would have been ranked higher than number three by the Central Scouting Bureau. Berg will probably not join his team until late in the season.

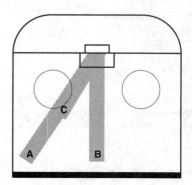

ROB BLAKE

Yrs. of NHL service: 5
Born: Simcoe, Ont.; Dec. 10, 1969
Position: right defense
Height: 6-3
Weight: 215
Uniform no.: 4
Shoots: right

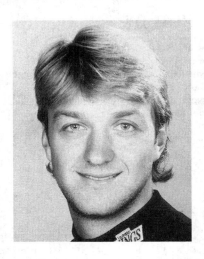

Career statistics:

GP	G	A	TP	PIM
320	59	145	204	558

1991-92 statistics:

GP	G	A	TP	+/-	PIM	PP	SH	GW	GT	S	PCT
57	7	13	20	-5	102	5	0	0	0	131	5.3

1992-93 statistics:

GP	G	A	TP	+/-	PIM	PP	SH	GW	GT	S	PCT
76	16	43	59	+18	152	10	0	4	1	243	6.6

1993-94 statistics:

GP	G	A	TP	+/-	PIM	PP	SH	GW	GT	S	PCT
84	20	48	68	-7	137	7	0	6	0	304	6.6

1994-95 statistics:

GP	G	A	TP	+/-	PIM	PP	SH	GW	GT	S	PCT
24	4	7	11	-16	38	4	0	1	0	76	5.3

LAST SEASON

Missed 24 games with groin injuries.

THE FINESSE GAME

Blake is a prototype for the '90s defenseman. He hits, he plays defense, and he possesses enough finesse skills to make an impact in any zone of the ice.

He is a powerful skater, quick and agile, with good balance, and he skates well backwards. He likes to step up and challenge at the blueline. He has great anticipation and is quite bold, forcing turnovers at the blueline with his body positioning and quick stickwork. On occasion, he will rely too much on his poke-checks and will get caught flatfooted. He has to play a physical game to be at his best.

Blake works the point on the power play, though he doesn't have the vision to be as creative as he could be. (Note that 11 of his 24 goals over the past two seasons came on the power play.) He does have a good, low shot, and he can rifle it off the pass. He has quality hand skills and is not afraid to skip in deep and try to make something happen low. He has become more confident about attempting to force the play deep in the offensive zone, and has good enough passing skills to use a backhand pass across the goalmouth.

THE PHYSICAL GAME

When healthy, Blake is among the hardest hitters in the league, along with Scott Stevens, a defenseman whose style his closely resembles. Blake has a nasty streak and will bring up his gloves and stick them into the face of an opponent when he thinks the referee isn't watching. He can dominate with his physical play; when he does he opens up a lot of ice for himself and his teammates.

THE INTANGIBLES

Blake's nagging groin problem (he was sidelined on two separate occasions) is a concern, since it may be one of those injuries that affect a player for the rest of his career, or requires surgery. Since so much of Blake's game comes from his power, he had a lost season last year due to the injury.

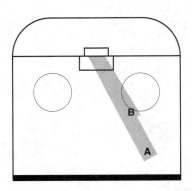

PHILIPPE BOUCHER

Yrs. of NHL service: 2
Born: St. Apollinaire, Que.; March 24, 1973
Position: right defense
Height: 6-2
Weight: 189
Uniform no.: 26
Shoots: right

Career statistics:

GP	G	A	TP	PIM
71	8	16	24	47

1992-93 statistics:

GP	G	A	TP	+/-	PIM	PP	SH	GW	GT	S	PCT
18	0	4	4	+1	14	0	0	0	0	8	0.0

1993-94 statistics:

GP	G	A	TP	+/-	PIM	PP	SH	GW	GT	S	PCT
38	6	8	14	-1	29	4	0	1	0	67	9.0

1994-95 statistics:

GP	G	A	TP	+/-	PIM	PP	SH	GW	GT	S	PCT
15	2	4	6	+3	4	0	0	0	0	30	6.7

LAST SEASON

Acquired from Buffalo with Denis Tsygurov and Grant Fuhr for Alexei Zhitnik, Charlie Huddy and Robb Stauber. Suffered season-ending torn ligaments in his wrist.

THE FINESSE GAME

Boucher has a booming slap shot that draws most of the attention, but he also has more subtle finesse skills, such as deft puckhandling. He sees the ice and moves the puck well. He has slow feet, though, and it takes him a few strides to get up to speed. Attackers can get a step on him.

He moves the puck well and likes to jump up into the play. He is often too anxious to get into the attack and will leave a partner exposed when he forces a play in the neutral zone and turns over the puck. He was a one-way defenseman in junior and still prefers that part of the game, but needs to improve defensively.

THE PHYSICAL GAME

Boucher is a fair size but doesn't play to it. He needs to develop more upper-body strength to become an assertive checker. He doesn't have the temperament to be a mean hitter, but he has the leg drive to be more effective with his take-outs. He doesn't cover well, doesn't close quickly, and doesn't have impact.

THE INTANGIBLES

Boucher is likely to be among the Kings' top six defensemen by default, thanks to his offensive ability, but he is not a complete player.

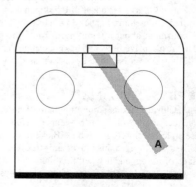

KEVIN BROWN

Yrs. of NHL service: 1
Born: Birmingham, England; May 11, 1974
Position: right wing
Height: 6-1
Weight: 212
Uniform no.: 8
Shoots: right

Career statistics:

GP	G	A	TP	PIM
23	2	3	5	18

1994-95 statistics:

GP	G	A	TP	+/-	PIM	PP	SH	GW	GT	S	PCT
23	2	3	5	-7	18	0	0	0	0	25	8.0

LAST SEASON
First NHL season. Missed games with a shoulder injury.

THE FINESSE GAME
Brown is a big, ugly skater, but he's good around the net. And although his speed is always going to be a question mark, he can put the numbers up. It is no surprise that one of the players Brown admires most is Cam Neely, because Brown has the potential to be a power forward. He can play and be effective from the blueline in. In a half-ice game, coming off the wall, he is at his best. He uses a big reach to keep the puck away from defenders and he's strong on his stick.

In addition to his good shot, Brown is also a quality playmaker with hockey sense. He gives a well-timed pass to the open man, and always seems to find the breaking teammate and lead with the proper feed. He can also stickhandle through traffic.

He is an unselfish player.

THE PHYSICAL GAME
Brown is very physical, especially around the net. He may develop into one of those power play specialists who is impossible to budge. Brown is very strong on his skates and will take punishment to create a scoring chance. He seldom takes bad penalties. It wouldn't hurt him to go nuts once in awhile, just to get people leery of him.

THE INTANGIBLES
The Kings might just have to bite the bullet on Brown with regard to his slow feet, since he brings so many other elements to a game, including the attributes the Kings lack the most: youth, enthusiasm and size. He has a good shot at winning a regular job this season, and with power play time he could net 20 goals.

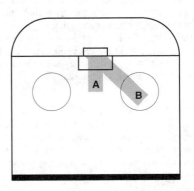

TONY GRANATO

Yrs. of NHL service: 7
Born: Downers Grove, Ill.; July 25, 1964
Position: right wing
Height: 5-10
Weight: 185
Uniform no.: 21
Shoots: right

Career statistics:

GP	G	A	TP	PIM
446	174	184	358	992

1991-92 statistics:

GP	G	A	TP	+/-	PIM	PP	SH	GW	GT	S	PCT
80	39	29	68	+4	187	7	2	8	1	223	17.5

1992-93 statistics:

GP	G	A	TP	+/-	PIM	PP	SH	GW	GT	S	PCT
81	37	45	82	-1	171	14	2	6	0	247	15.0

1993-94 statistics:

GP	G	A	TP	+/-	PIM	PP	SH	GW	GT	S	PCT
50	7	14	21	-2	150	2	0	0	0	117	6.0

1994-95 statistics:

GP	G	A	TP	+/-	PIM	PP	SH	GW	GT	S	PCT
33	13	11	24	+9	68	2	0	3	0	106	12.3

LAST SEASON

Led team in plus-minus. Missed 15 games with a broken foot.

THE FINESSE GAME

Granato has a wide scoring stance, which makes it tough to knock him off balance, and he's fast and quick, which makes it hard for anyone to catch him or even try.

He can play any forward position and with any other forwards. This versatility has probably hurt him in the long run, because a coach doesn't hesitate to move him around, knowing he will fit in anywhere and complement the players he is teamed with. Other skaters might complain that all the shifting around hurts their game because they don't become familiar with their linemates, but if that's what the coach wants, it's good enough for Tony.

Granato uses his quickness to good effect down low. He will jump in and out of holes and drive defensemen batty. They think they have him contained, yet he manages to slip free for a shot.

He has very strong wrists, a quick release and an accurate shot. Most of his goals come from within 10 feet of the net. With his quick hands, he has an infuriating knack for lifting an opponent's stick to steal the puck.

THE PHYSICAL GAME

Few small players loom larger than this buzz saw. He is fierce and intense — sometimes overly so, in that he gets frustrated and will take bad penalties. But he knocks down, eludes or outwits bigger players on a consistent basis, and is fearless.

Granato also draws calls. He has the quickness to get his body between the puck and the defender, and he keeps his legs pumping to attract holding and hooking fouls. He still lacks defensive awareness but is always outworking his rivals, so it doesn't hurt him too much. He will also use his stick as a weapon when he's fed up.

THE INTANGIBLES

Granato's kamikaze style of play is finally catching up with him. He had a tough season production-wise and seems to be increasingly fragile. The seasons of 35 goals are a thing of the past, but teams will still want to keep him around for his character and inspirational play.

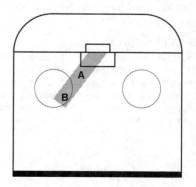

WAYNE GRETZKY

Yrs. of NHL service: 16
Born: Brantford, Ont.; Jan. 26, 1961
Position: centre
Height: 6-0
Weight: 170
Uniform no.: 99
Shoots: left

Career statistics:

GP	G	A	TP	PIM
1173	814	1692	2506	473

1991-92 statistics:

GP	G	A	TP	+/-	PIM	PP	SH	GW	GT	S	PCT
74	31	90	121	-12	34	12	2	2	1	215	14.4

1992-93 statistics:

GP	G	A	TP	+/-	PIM	PP	SH	GW	GT	S	PCT
45	16	49	65	+6	6	0	2	1	0	141	11.3

1993-94 statistics:

GP	G	A	TP	+/-	PIM	PP	SH	GW	GT	S	PCT
81	38	92	130	-25	20	14	4	0	1	233	16.3

1994-95 statistics:

GP	G	A	TP	+/-	PIM	PP	SH	GW	GT	S	PCT
48	11	37	48	-20	6	3	0	1	0	142	7.7

LAST SEASON

Led team in assists, points and shots. One of three Kings to appear in all 48 games. Worst plus-minus on team for second consecutive season. Scored 2,500th career point. Failed to appear among top three NHL scorers for only second time in career.

THE FINESSE GAME

There are some things about Gretzky that remain constant. One is the "Gretzky curl," the little circle he makes just inside the blueline as he wheels around looking for his best options. Few checkers dare to challenge him.

But Gretzky's game has changed. If anything, he has perhaps become an even better all-around forward. He tried to do too much last season, however, taking long shifts and overextending himself. He would be a little weary at the end of his turn, and that's where the mistakes seep in. With the Kings on their way to a second playoff miss, Gretzky's desire was understandable, but he ended up hurting instead of helping the club.

Gretzky is more eager to shoot than in the past, when he was known primarily as a passer. Playmaking is still his forte, but defenders can no longer just look to shut off his passing lanes, because Gretzky will rifle one of his deceptive shots if they play off him. He doesn't overpower goalies, but he masks his shot well and gets it off quickly.

Gretzky has lost half a step in his skating, but he has such great anticipation that this is barely noticeable. As ever, he is patient, patient, patient with the puck, waiting until the last split-second to dish off.

THE PHYSICAL GAME

Anyone seeing Gretzky in civilian clothes for the first time is shocked at how slightly built the Great One is. His image and aura are so imposing that you expect him to be built more along the lines of Mario Lemieux, or the Statue of Liberty, but he remains whippet lean — and that makes his career all the more remarkable. He has back problems and tends to stay away from areas where he could be creamed along the boards.

THE INTANGIBLES

Another season, another Gretzky retirement rumour. We have the feeling this will be the last, though Gretzky hasn't said.

Like his good friend Mark Messier, Gretzky was obtained from Edmonton to bring a Cup to his new city. Messier did it for New York and you can bet it rankles Gretzky that he hasn't done the same for L.A.

And we'll repeat one warning: If you haven't had a chance to see Gretzky in person, get a ticket the next time he's in town. It could be your last chance. He's still pretty Wayne-derful.

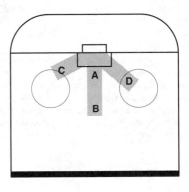

KELLY HRUDEY

Yrs. of NHL service: 12
Born: Edmonton, Alta.; Jan. 13, 1961
Position: goaltender
Height: 5-10
Weight: 180
Uniform no.: 32
Catches: left

Career statistics:

GP	MINS	G	SO	AVG	A	PIM
565	32015	1859	16	3.58	16	167

1991-92 statistics:

GP	MINS	GAA	W	L	T	SO	GA	S	SAPCT	PIM
60	3509	3.37	26	17	13	1	197	1916	.897	12

1992-93 statistics:

GP	MINS	GAA	W	L	T	SO	GA	S	SAPCT	PIM
50	2718	3.86	18	21	6	2	175	1552	.887	10

1993-94 statistics:

GP	MINS	GAA	W	L	T	SO	GA	S	SAPCT	PIM
64	3712	3.68	22	31	7	1	228	2219	.897	6

1994-95 statistics:

GP	MINS	GAA	W	L	T	SO	GA	S	SAPCT	PIM
35	1894	3.14	14	13	5	0	99	1099	.910	0

LAST SEASON

Stopped two penalty shot attempts. GAA four-season best. Missed four games with a bruised right kneecap.

THE PHYSICAL GAME

Despite the "Hollywood" design on his mask, Hrudey is very much a working class goalie. He has a lot of stamina and can handle long stretches of duty and games with a lot of shots without losing much of his edge.

Like many of today's goalies, Hrudey puts the paddle of his stick low across the front of the net on wraparounds. The key for the attacker is to take the extra step and get the shot up, but few shooters have that kind of patience. Hrudey plays with short leg pads (one of the reasons why he suffered his knee injury last season was the lack of protection). The short pads give him added mobility. He drops down to one knee on screen shots.

Hrudey's technique has improved, but he is still prone to lapses in discipline. He lives by his reflexes, and on his worst nights he's a lunging, sprawling mess. On wide drives, he will lie down, leaving the short side high open for a shot.

Hrudey loves to challenge the shooter, and one of his biggest flaws is that he is overly aggressive. He also likes to handle the puck and has worked hard to improve in this important area over the past few seasons. He is a good skater and moves confidently in and out of his net. Hrudey's aggressiveness is one of the reasons why he is so adept at stopping penalty shots.

THE MENTAL GAME

Hrudey has developed a big save capacity. He plays on emotion and he gained a tremendous amount of respect from his teammates. Teams may try to take Hrudey off his game with goalie-running tactics, but he doesn't get rattled and often strikes the first blow himself with his blocker or stick.

THE INTANGIBLES

Hrudey kept his game intact despite playing behind a brutal Kings team. It's going to be another tough season in L.A. and Hrudey isn't getting any younger, but if he doesn't get moved he will be effective again.

JARI KURRI

Yrs. of NHL service: 13
Born: Helsinki, Finland; May 18, 1960
Position: right wing
Height: 6-1
Weight: 195
Uniform no.: 17
Shoots: right

Career statistics:

GP	G	A	TP	PIM
1028	565	731	1296	482

1991-92 statistics:

GP	G	A	TP	+/-	PIM	PP	SH	GW	GT	S	PCT
73	23	37	60	-24	24	10	1	3	0	167	13.8

1992-93 statistics:

GP	G	A	TP	+/-	PIM	PP	SH	GW	GT	S	PCT
82	27	60	87	+19	38	12	2	3	0	210	12.9

1993-94 statistics:

GP	G	A	TP	+/-	PIM	PP	SH	GW	GT	S	PCT
81	31	46	77	-24	48	14	4	3	1	198	15.7

1994-95 statistics:

GP	G	A	TP	+/-	PIM	PP	SH	GW	GT	S	PCT
38	10	19	29	-17	24	2	0	0	1	84	11.9

LAST SEASON

Played in 1,000th NHL game. Second on team in goals and third in points. Missed 10 games with a groin injury.

THE FINESSE GAME

Kurri has become more of a defensive presence than an offensive force. He has lost his spot alongside Wayne Gretzky, his one-timers no longer terrorize goalies and he has lost a half-step on the outside move that used to burn defenders.

Kurri's quickness and anticipation make him a great shorthanded threat when killing penalties. The spark is still there, but the 50-goal days are gone. He is a very intelligent player who can still help a team, but he is no longer a presence.

THE PHYSICAL GAME

Kurri has become more and more of a perimeter player. Maybe he has soured on the physical part of the game, because he used to be willing to pay the price along the wall to fight for the puck. Although he never used to be a physical force, he wasn't intimidated, but now it appears he is.

THE INTANGIBLES

If next season is Gretzky's last in the NHL, it might be Kurri's as well. No doubt he wants one last hurrah, but his days as a big-time scorer are over. His contributions have changed dramatically.

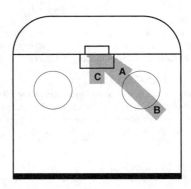

ERIC LACROIX

Yrs. of NHL service: 1
Born: Montreal, Que.; July 15, 1971
Position: left wing
Height: 6-1
Weight: 200
Uniform no.: 28
Shoots: left

Career statistics:

GP	G	A	TP	PIM
48	9	7	16	56

1993-94 statistics:

GP	G	A	TP	+/-	PIM	PP	SH	GW	GT	S	PCT
3	0	0	0	0	2	0	0	0	0	3	0.0

1994-95 statistics:

GP	G	A	TP	+/-	PIM	PP	SH	GW	GT	S	PCT
45	9	7	16	+2	54	2	1	1	0	64	14.1

LAST SEASON

Acquired from Toronto with Chris Snell for Dixon Ward, Guy Leveque, Shayne Toporowski and Kelly Fairchild. Missed 16 games in the minors (Phoenix, IHL) with a broken knuckle. Missed three NHL games with a sprained knee. First NHL season.

THE FINESSE GAME

Lacroix brings such zest and inspiration to every shift that it didn't take long for Wayne Gretzky to demand that the young rookie be put on his line. Lacroix is a bigger, more skilled version of Edmonton's Kirk Maltby.

If Lacroix has the proper work ethic, he will become more than a big banger. Hitters and fighters like L.A. teammate Rick Tocchet turned themselves into productive scorers first by earning room on the ice, then by practising shooting drills to make use of that extra space. He doesn't have great hands or a quick release, so any improvement will not come easy. He appears willing to work.

He is a good skater with balance and speed.

THE PHYSICAL GAME

Lacroix hits to hurt but has to learn to be more selective. He makes such thunderous contact that he gets penalized too often, because he leaves his feet and sometimes brings his elbows up.

With just a tad more control Lacroix could turn himself into a serious, clean checker who will scare puck carriers into coughing up the rubber.

THE INTANGIBLES

Lacroix has a lot of upside. Improving to the 20-goal range would be a big step forward, and he can probably achieve that in the next season or two. There is a lot to like about him, starting with his heart.

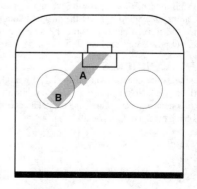

ROBERT LANG

Yrs. of NHL service: 2
Born: Most, Czechoslovakia; Dec. 19, 1970
Position: centre
Height: 6-2
Weight: 189
Uniform no.: 13
Shoots: right

Career statistics:

GP	G	A	TP	PIM
79	13	23	36	16

1992-93 statistics:

GP	G	A	TP	+/-	PIM	PP	SH	GW	GT	S	PCT
11	0	5	5	-3	2	0	0	0	0	3	0.0

1993-94 statistics:

GP	G	A	TP	+/-	PIM	PP	SH	GW	GT	S	PCT
32	9	10	19	+7	10	0	0	0	0	41	22.0

1994-95 statistics:

GP	G	A	TP	+/-	PIM	PP	SH	GW	GT	S	PCT
36	4	8	12	-7	4	0	0	0	0	38	10.5

LAST SEASON
Second NHL season.

THE FINESSE GAME
Coaches have a love-hate relationship with players like Lang. He has so much talent that he is able to turn a game around with several moves. But he is inconsistent, and has nights where he is invisible.

Lang has excellent skating ability with quickness and balance. He has great hockey sense to go along with his skills and the potential to develop into a crafty playmaker. He is a very good backhand passer, so players on both sides of him have to be prepared for feeds. He is patient with the puck, often holding on too long; he will always opt for a pass instead of a shot. He draws defenders to him to open up ice, but he will not take a hit to make a play around the net. He will sometimes dish off early if he thinks he's going to get hit.

Lang covers a lot of ice with his long, strong stride and is conscientious about getting back into position for back-checking, though he doesn't do much more than look to intercept passes.

THE PHYSICAL GAME
Lang has to show more of a willingness to use his body. He will never trounce anyone, but he has to be willing to fight for the puck and battle through checks. His intensity level is not yet consistent enough for the NHL.

THE INTANGIBLES
Lang will be battling for a job again in training camp. He has to be good enough to be a number two centre, because he can't fill a third-line role and he wouldn't be of much use on a fourth line — but that's where he'll be if he doesn't show enough.

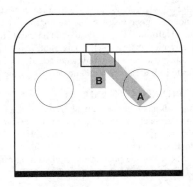

MARTY MCSORLEY

Yrs. of NHL service: 12
Born: Hamilton, Ont.; May 18, 1963
Position: right defense
Height: 6-1
Weight: 235
Uniform no.: 33
Shoots: right

Career statistics:

GP	G	A	TP	PIM
707	88	200	288	2725

1991-92 statistics:

GP	G	A	TP	+/-	PIM	PP	SH	GW	GT	S	PCT
71	7	22	29	-13	268	2	1	0	0	119	5.9

1992-93 statistics:

GP	G	A	TP	+/-	PIM	PP	SH	GW	GT	S	PCT
81	15	26	41	+1	401	3	3	0	0	197	7.6

1993-94 statistics:

GP	G	A	TP	+/-	PIM	PP	SH	GW	GT	S	PCT
65	7	24	31	-12	194	1	0	1	1	160	4.4

1994-95 statistics:

GP	G	A	TP	+/-	PIM	PP	SH	GW	GT	S	PCT
41	3	18	21	-14	83	1	0	0	1	75	4.0

LAST SEASON

Missed four games with a groin injury.

THE FINESSE GAME

One of the first things you notice about McSorley is his feet. His skates are big and heavy (he has custom-made skates that are more cumbersome than the average player's). Add to that his sluggish skating and you get a player whose rushes can be timed with a calendar.

To compensate for his lack of speed, McSorley works hard and plays a pretty smart game. He has been used almost exclusively on the backline by the Kings (and Penguins) over the past two seasons, although he can go up front on the power play at times. (The Kings did that often while Rick Tocchet was out of the lineup.) If he is back on the point, McSorley is smart enough to use a wrist shot or otherwise snake the puck through rather than just blasting a senseless shot.

McSorley's finesse skills are average at best. He does not have good vision of the ice for creative play-making. Unfortunately, every so often he tries to make the fancy play instead of the safe shot, and he gets burned because he can't recover quickly defensively. He has to be paired with a mobile defense partner.

THE PHYSICAL GAME

McSorley is a conditioned athlete who can take all the ice time a coach wants to give him. He also ranks among the top five fighters in the league. He does annoying things after the whistle — well after the whistle — like shoot the puck at the goalie on an offside call or give an attacker a shove after a save.

McSorley has a "V" cut out of the back of his jersey to enable him to get it up and over his helmet in case of a scrap. He is intense and does start running around sometimes, but this is a sin of commission, since he is always trying so hard. It's no wonder Wayne Gretzky wanted him back.

THE INTANGIBLES

In addition to being a Gretzky favourite, McSorley is a pretty complete player for a tough guy, as long as he doesn't try to do too much.

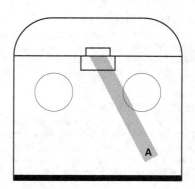

YANIC PERREAULT

Yrs. of NHL service: 1
Born: Sherbrooke, Que.; Apr. 4, 1971
Position: centre
Height: 5-11
Weight: 182
Uniform no.: 39
Shoots: left

Career statistics:

GP	G	A	TP	PIM
39	5	8	13	20

LAST SEASON
Acquired from Toronto for a conditional draft pick in 1996. First NHL season.

THE FINESSE GAME
Perreault has been a success at the junior and minor league levels, but appears to lack NHL speed. He has all of the gears except top speed.

He has very good hands and always has his head up, looking at the goal for openings. While he doesn't have open ice speed, he has short bursts of quickness that he uses to good effect in the attacking zone to elude checkers. He waits for the goalie to commit.

Tricky and solid on his feet, Perreault works the power play well on the half boards.

THE PHYSICAL GAME
Perreault lacks the size to do the work in traffic areas and lacks the speed to be a strictly open ice player. He is an in-betweener, and if forced to play hard in all zones the flaws in his game are apparent.

THE INTANGIBLES
What may separate Perreault from other minor league stars who can't quite make the jump is his desire. He wants the NHL badly, and he's in the ideal spot to earn a job, given the thin talent up front on the Kings. At the very least, he'll be able to get an honest shot in training camp.

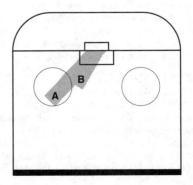

CHRIS SNELL

Yrs. of NHL service: 1
Born: Regina, Sask.; May 12, 1971
Position: left defense
Height: 5-11
Weight: 200
Uniform no.: 29
Shoots: left

Career statistics:

GP	G	A	TP	PIM
34	2	7	9	24

LAST SEASON

Acquired from Toronto with Eric Lacroix and Toronto's fourth round pick in 1996 for Dixon Ward, Guy Leveque, Kelly Fairchild and Shayne Toporowski. Led team in shorthanded goals.

THE FINESSE GAME

Snell has very good offensive instincts. He spies openings, and hits teammates with slick, well-timed passes. He has a good first stride to the puck, and seems instantly aware of his options.

Snell can rush the puck, but he is much more effective when making the pass and following the play. He saw significant time on the point on the power play, and he has a good slap shot. He is also slick enough to lead a rush and split the opponent's defense.

Now, can we talk about defense? All of that description sounds like a forward, and Snell is an offensive defenseman. He uses his finesse skills to play a positional game, but his defensive reads aren't sound and he is often running around on the ice.

Snell has a lot of learning to do.

THE PHYSICAL GAME

Snell is listed at a generous 200 pounds, but he looks about 10 pounds lighter. He plays as big as he is able, working the boards and corners. It helped that he was often paired with the more physical Marty McSorley, because Snell is not a very aggressive player. He is sneaky at holding an opponent's stick and throwing himself to the ice as though hooked. It worked a few times, but the act will wear thin fast.

THE INTANGIBLES

Snell looked like a throw-in in an exchange of minor league players, but ended up with a regular role on the decimated Kings squad. He can do some nice things offensively, but he will have to improve his defense to merit a regular role when the team is healthy. He deserves credit for stepping in as well as he did last season, but he will have to earn a job in training camp.

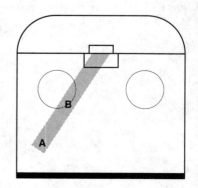

DARRYL SYDOR

Yrs. of NHL service: 3
Born: Edmonton, Alta.; May 13, 1972
Position: right defense
Height: 6-0
Weight: 205
Uniform no.: 25
Shoots: left

Career statistics:

GP	G	A	TP	PIM
230	19	74	90	215

1991-92 statistics:

GP	G	A	TP	+/-	PIM	PP	SH	GW	GT	S	PCT
18	1	5	6	-3	22	0	0	0	0	18	5.6

1992-93 statistics:

GP	G	A	TP	+/-	PIM	PP	SH	GW	GT	S	PCT
80	6	23	29	-2	63	0	0	1	0	112	5.4

1993-94 statistics:

GP	G	A	TP	+/-	PIM	PP	SH	GW	GT	S	PCT
84	8	27	35	-9	94	1	0	0	0	146	5.5

1994-95 statistics:

GP	G	A	TP	+/-	PIM	PP	SH	GW	GT	S	PCT
48	4	19	23	-2	36	3	0	0	1	96	4.2

LAST SEASON

One of three Kings to appear in all 48 games; has not missed a game in two seasons. Led team defensemen in scoring.

THE FINESSE GAME

Sydor is a very good skater with balance and agility and excellent lateral movement. He can accelerate well for a big skater and changes directions easily.

He has a fine shot from the point and can handle power play time. He has good sense for jumping into the attack, and controls the puck ably when carrying it, though he doesn't always protect it well with his body. He makes nice outlet passes and has good vision of the ice. He can rush with the puck or play dump and chase.

Sydor will develop into a reliable player on both special teams. He is clever and shows a great deal of poise. He handled a lot of ice time due to Rob Blake's injury and was probably overextended, but he never stopped trying.

THE PHYSICAL GAME

Sydor needs to establish more of a physical presence. He sometimes gives up on his man in front of the net and seems confused about his defensive assignments, but he's still young and needs to learn he can't always take the easy road. He uses his stick well defensively to break up plays. He is a willing shot blocker.

THE INTANGIBLES

Sydor has leader written all over him. He loves the game and is a fast learner. He struggled along with many of his teammates last season. He has to concern himself less with his offense — that part of the game will come naturally — and work on his defense to become a better all-around player.

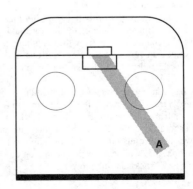

RICK TOCCHET

Yrs. of NHL service: 11
Born: Scarborough, Ont.; Apr. 9, 1964
Position: right wing
Height: 6-0
Weight: 205
Uniform no.: 22
Shoots: right

Career statistics:

GP	G	A	TP	PIM
717	309	567	676	2190

1991-92 statistics:

GP	G	A	TP	+/-	PIM	PP	SH	GW	GT	S	PCT
61	27	32	59	+15	151	8	1	2	1	166	16.3

1992-93 statistics:

GP	G	A	TP	+/-	PIM	PP	SH	GW	GT	S	PCT
80	48	61	109	+28	252	20	4	5	0	240	20.0

1993-94 statistics:

GP	G	A	TP	+/-	PIM	PP	SH	GW	GT	S	PCT
51	14	26	40	-15	134	5	1	2	1	150	9.3

1994-95 statistics:

GP	G	A	TP	+/-	PIM	PP	SH	GW	GT	S	PCT
36	18	17	35	-8	70	7	1	3	0	95	18.9

LAST SEASON

Acquired from Los Angeles with a second-round draft pick in 1995 for Luc Robitaille. Led team in goals and power play goals. Second on team in points. Missed 12 games with back injuries.

THE FINESSE GAME

A player with Tocchet's physical style can't have a back injury and play effectively, but it has plagued him for two years now. Every hard check is like a jolt of electric pain. His conditioning is affected. His career hinges on his ability to recover.

Tocchet has worked hard to make the most of the finesse skills he possesses and that makes everything loom larger. His skating is powerful, though he does not have great mobility. He is explosive in short bursts and is most effective in small areas. He works extremely well down low and in traffic. Tocchet exceeded all expectations on his power play work last season. He drives to the front of the net and into the corners for the puck.

His shooting skills are better than his passing skills. He has limited vision of the ice for making a creative play, but he is a master at the bang-bang play. He'll smack in rebounds and deflections and set screens as defenders try to budge him or knock him down.

He has a strong, accurate wrist shot and gets most of his goals from close range, though he can also fire a one-timer from the tops of the circles. He'll rarely waste a shot from the blueline. He is a good give-and-go player because his quickness allows him to jump into the holes. He will beat few people one-on-one because he lacks stickhandling prowess.

THE PHYSICAL GAME

Figure Tocchet gets 20 shifts a game. That's like going 20 rounds with Joe Frazier, a heavyweight who comes at you again and again with everything he's got. There is no hiding from Tocchet. He is a tough hitter and frequently gets his stick and elbows up. He has long had a history of letting his emotions get the better of him, and while he has matured somewhat, he is acutely aware of his position as one of the few tough, physical forwards on a team of finesse players. Tocchet knows he has to play rugged to be effective and he can do that cleanly, but he will also get everyone's attention by bending the rules.

THE INTANGIBLES

Who was the most valuable player on the Kings last season? Put it this way, if Tocchet had been healthy down the stretch, the Kings would have been in the playoffs. There's a reason why Wayne Gretzky wanted this hardrock on his team.

Tocchet's work ethic is inspiring. He is always one of the last players off the ice, usually working on puckhandling drills. Before games, he's one of the first to the rink and is riding the bike; after games, he's lifting weights. He started his career as a goon, but has remade himself into a solid NHL player. Tocchet will need a clean bill of health to be his old self, and that remains a huge question mark.

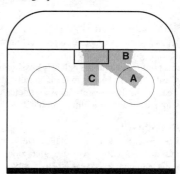

KEVIN TODD

Yrs. of NHL service: 4
Born: Winnipeg, Man.; May 4, 1968
Position: centre
Height: 5-10
Weight: 180
Uniform no.: 12
Shoots: left

Career statistics:

GP	G	A	TP	PIM
217	41	78	119	131

1991-92 statistics:

GP	G	A	TP	+/-	PIM	PP	SH	GW	GT	S	PCT
80	21	42	63	+8	69	2	0	2	1	131	16.0

1992-93 statistics:

GP	G	A	TP	+/-	PIM	PP	SH	GW	GT	S	PCT
55	9	14	23	-9	26	0	0	3	0	87	10.3

1993-94 statistics:

GP	G	A	TP	+/-	PIM	PP	SH	GW	GT	S	PCT
47	8	14	22	-3	24	4	0	1	0	65	12.3

1994-95 statistics:

GP	G	A	TP	+/-	PIM	PP	SH	GW	GT	S	PCT
33	3	8	11	-5	12	0	0	1	0	34	8.8

LAST SEASON
Missed 15 games with a torn knee cartilage.

THE FINESSE GAME
Not an impressive skater, Todd gets his goals in tight because his wide-based stance allows him to dig in despite his small stature. He is wiry and tough, and he digs for rebounds. He isn't overly creative, but he keeps goalies guessing because he is just as likely to shoot as pass.

Todd is the best face-off man on the Kings. He can win on his forehand or backhand. He is built so low to the ice that it gives him an edge, but he is also very intense and competitive. He had to fight to get his shot at the NHL and he wants to pay the price to stay there.

THE PHYSICAL GAME
Todd is small, but works tirelessly along the boards and the corners, often squirting free because biggers defenders tend to aim high with their checks and Todd is able to duck under and maintain his balance. He is not intimidated and will take abuse in pursuit of the puck. He'll strike back, too.

THE INTANGIBLES
Todd can be a number three checking centre, or even a number two if he is teamed with the right players. On a stronger team, he might get lost in the shuffle, but on the Kings he gets a lot of ice time.

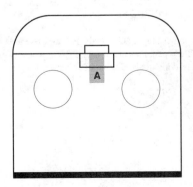

MONTREAL CANADIENS

Players' Statistics 1994-95

POS	NO.	PLAYER	GP	G	A	PTS	+/-	PIM	PP	SH	GW	GT	S	PCTG
R	8	MARK RECCHI	49	16	32	48	-9	28	9		3		121	13.2
C	77	PIERRE TURGEON	49	24	23	47		14	5	2	4		160	15.0
L	25	VINCENT DAMPHOUSSE	48	10	30	40	15	42	4		4		123	8.1
L	22	BENOIT BRUNET	45	7	18	25	7	16	1	1	2	1	80	8.8
D	38	VLADIMIR MALAKHOV	40	4	17	21	-3	46	1				91	4.4
R	12	MIKE KEANE	48	10	10	20	5	15	1				75	13.3
C	49	*BRIAN SAVAGE	37	12	7	19	5	27					64	18.8
L	23	BRIAN BELLOWS	41	8	8	16	-7	8	1		1		110	7.3
D	43	PATRICE BRISEBOIS	35	4	8	12	-2	26			2		67	6.0
D	29	YVES RACINE	47	4	7	11	-1	42	2		1		63	6.3
D	24	LYLE ODELEIN	48	3	7	10	-13	152					74	4.1
D	48	J.J. DAIGNEAULT	45	3	5	8	2	40					36	8.3
R	30	*TURNER STEVENSON	41	6	1	7		86			1		35	17.1
D	44	BRYAN FOGARTY	21	5	2	7	-3	34	3				41	12.2
R	6	OLEG PETROV	12	2	3	5	-7	4					26	7.7
R	31	ED RONAN	30	1	4	5	-7	12					14	7.1
D	34	PETER POPOVIC	33		5	5	-10	8					23	
R	18	*VALERI BURE	24	3	1	4	-1	6			1		39	7.7
C	17	MARK LAMB	47	1	2	3	-12	20					30	3.3
L	35	*DONALD BRASHEAR	20	1	1	2	-5	63			1		10	10.0
C	28	*CRAIG CONROY	6	1		1	-1						4	25.0
D	52	*CRAIG RIVET	5		1	1	2	5					2	
L	26	*YVES SARAULT	8		1	1	-1						9	
G	33	PATRICK ROY	43		1	1		20						
C	46	*CRAIG FERGUSON	1										3	
D	56	*DAVID WILKIE	1											
R	57	CHRIS MURRAY	3					4						
L	36	GERRY FLEMING	6				-1	17					1	
G	1	RON TUGNUTT	7											
L	32	MARIO ROBERGE	9				-2	34						
L	20	PIERRE SEVIGNY	19				-5	15					6	

GP = games played; G = goals; A = assists; PTS = points; +/- = goals-for minus goals-against while player is on ice; PIM = penalties in minutes; PP = power play goals; SH = shorthanded goals; GW = game-winning goals; GT = game-tying goals; S = no. of shots; PCTG = percentage of goals to shots; * = rookie

PATRICE BRISEBOIS

Yrs. of NHL service: 4
Born: Montreal, Que.; Jan. 27, 1971
Position: right defense
Height: 6-2
Weight: 175
Uniform no.: 43
Shoots: right

Career statistics:

GP	G	A	TP	PIM
194	18	60	78	192

1991-92 statistics:

GP	G	A	TP	+/-	PIM	PP	SH	GW	GT	S	PCT
26	2	8	10	+9	20	0	0	1	0	37	5.4

1992-93 statistics:

GP	G	A	TP	+/-	PIM	PP	SH	GW	GT	S	PCT
70	10	21	31	+6	79	4	0	2	0	123	8.1

1993-94 statistics:

GP	G	A	TP	+/-	PIM	PP	SH	GW	GT	S	PCT
53	2	21	23	+5	63	1	0	0	0	71	2.8

1994-95 statistics:

GP	G	A	TP	+/-	PIM	PP	SH	GW	GT	S	PCT
35	4	8	12	-2	26	0	0	2	0	67	6.0

LAST SEASON

Second among team defensemen in scoring. Missed 12 games with a herniated disk in his back.

THE FINESSE GAME

Brisebois has a nice first step to the puck. He has a good stride with some quickness, although he won't rush end-to-end. He carries the puck with authority, but will usually take one or two strides and look for a pass, or else make the safe dump out of the zone. He steps up in the neutral zone to slow a rush.

He has some finesse skills he can use on the attack. He plays the point well enough to merit more power play time in the future, but he doesn't have the rink vision that marks truly successful point men. Brisebois has a great point shot, with a sharp release, and he keeps it low and on target. He doesn't often venture to the circles on offense, but when he does he has the passing skills and the shot to make something happen.

Brisebois improved on his positional play but often starts running around as if he is looking for someone to belt. He winds up hitting no one, while his partner is left outnumbered in the front of the net. He is a good outlet passer but will get flustered and throw the puck away.

THE PHYSICAL GAME

Brisebois earned the nickname "breeze-by" when he let Petr Klima get past him for an overtime goal in a key late-season game, highlighting some of his defensive weaknesses.

He does not take the body much and will play the puck instead of the man. He'll have to work on his conditioning since he does not appear to be a very strong player — at least, he doesn't use his body well. He's tough only when he has a stick in his hands.

THE INTANGIBLES

Brisebois is developing slowly, but thus far hasn't shown the will to become a take-charge defenseman. His likely future is as a solid number three or four, more of a support player than a leader.

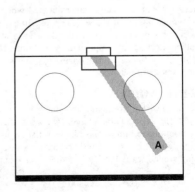

BENOIT BRUNET

Yrs. of NHL service: 3
Born: Pointe-Claire, Que.; Aug. 24, 1968
Position: left wing
Height: 5-11
Weight: 184
Uniform no.: 22
Shoots: left

Career statistics:

GP	G	A	TP	PIM
200	32	63	95	69

1991-92 statistics:

GP	G	A	TP	+/-	PIM	PP	SH	GW	GT	S	PCT
18	4	6	10	+4	14	0	0	0	0	37	10.8

1992-93 statistics:

GP	G	A	TP	+/-	PIM	PP	SH	GW	GT	S	PCT
47	10	15	25	+13	19	0	0	1	1	71	14.1

1993-94 statistics:

GP	G	A	TP	+/-	PIM	PP	SH	GW	GT	S	PCT
71	10	20	30	+14	20	0	3	1	0	92	10.9

1994-95 statistics:

GP	G	A	TP	+/-	PIM	PP	SH	GW	GT	S	PCT
45	7	18	25	+7	16	1	1	2	1	80	8.8

LAST SEASON

Fourth on team in points. Missed two games with a hamstring injury.

THE FINESSE GAME

Brunet is one of the most anonymous Montreal forwards because of his quiet, efficient role as a checking winger on the third line. Developing into a top penalty killer, he is strong on his skates and fore-checks tenaciously.

When Brunet does choose to do anything offensively, he cuts to the net and uses a confident, strong touch in deep. He is always hustling back on defense, though, and seldom makes any high-risk plays deep in his own zone. He takes few chances, and seems to come up with big points.

Brunet's hands aren't great, or he would be able to create more scoring off his fore-check.

THE PHYSICAL GAME

Brunet isn't very big and is overmatched when he plays against many of the league's top lines. His strength is his positional play. He takes fewer steps than other players to accomplish the same chore. He's not a big hitter, but he will tie up an opponent's stick and play smothering defense.

THE INTANGIBLES

Brunet has a strong work ethic and comes to play every night. He is like a good referee. On his best nights, you seldom notice him because he won't show up in the highlight films — he's either scoring a goal or standing around while Patrick Roy digs a puck out of the net.

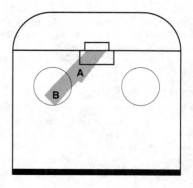

VALERI BURE

Yrs. of NHL service: 1
Born: Moscow, Russia; June 13, 1974
Position: right wing
Height: 5-11
Weight: 164
Uniform no.: 18
Shoots: right

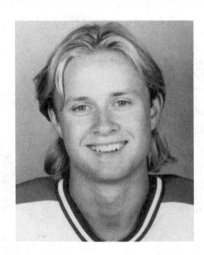

Career statistics:

GP	G	A	TP	PIM
24	3	1	4	6

1994-95 statistics:

GP	G	A	TP	+/-	PIM	PP	SH	GW	GT	S	PCT
24	3	1	4	-1	6	0	0	1	0	39	7.7

LAST SEASON

First NHL season. Missed two games with a bruised forearm.

THE FINESSE GAME

Valeri Bure isn't as fast as his famous older brother, Pavel, but he has his own distinct qualities. He has a great sense of anticipation, and wants the puck every time he's on the ice. And he can make things happen, though he sometimes tries to force the action rather than let the game flow as naturally as it should. He will get carried away in his pursuit of the puck and get caught out of position, whereas if he just showed patience the puck would come to him.

Bure has great hands to go along with his speed and seems to get a shot on goal or a scoring chance on every shift. He is smart and creative, and can make plays as well as finish. He needs to get used to the pace of the NHL.

THE PHYSICAL GAME

Bure still has to learn how to cope with the physical aspect of the game. Montreal had a dismal road record last season, and needs its scorers (like Bure) to develop more confidence and more of a presence. Teams still get fired up to play Montreal. Bure has to help the Canadiens respond in kind.

THE INTANGIBLES

Bure missed part of last season in the minors with a shoulder separation, which slowed his development and perhaps made him leery of physical contact. A lot of questions, but a lot of promise, and he'll get a shot on Montreal's second line.

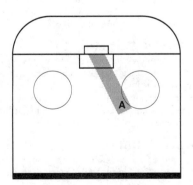

MARC BUREAU

Yrs. of NHL service: 4
Born: Trois-Riviers, Que.; May 19, 1966
Position: centre
Height: 6-1
Weight: 198
Uniform no.: 28
Shoots: right

Career statistics:

GP	G	A	TP	PIM
251	26	50	76	231

1991-92 statistics:

GP	G	A	TP	+/-	PIM	PP	SH	GW	GT	S	PCT
46	6	4	10	-5	50	0	0	0	0	53	11.3

1992-93 statistics:

GP	G	A	TP	+/-	PIM	PP	SH	GW	GT	S	PCT
63	10	21	31	-12	111	1	2	1	0	132	7.6

1993-94 statistics:

GP	G	A	TP	+/-	PIM	PP	SH	GW	GT	S	PCT
75	8	7	15	-9	30	0	1	1	0	110	7.3

1994-95 statistics:

GP	G	A	TP	+/-	PIM	PP	SH	GW	GT	S	PCT
48	2	12	14	-8	30	0	1	0	1	72	2.8

hard-working specialist.

LAST SEASON

One of two Lightning players to appear in all 48 games. Acquired from Tampa Bay for Brian Bellows.

THE FINESSE GAME

Bureau plays with concentration and intensity, and is terrier-like in his pursuit of the puck. His tenacity makes penalty killing his greatest asset. He is also dogged on face-offs and takes nearly all of Tampa Bay's defensive-zone draws. He constantly works hard on fore-checking and forces turnovers.

Bureau has overcome a skating deficiency. He is a chopper when he moves and his skating is laboured, but he gets to where he has to be with vigour and effort. He has no end-to-end speed, but in the throes of a game he is highly effective. Bureau knows he must work hard to get his ice time. He will get to the puck as fast as he can and is able to do something useful with it when he arrives.

Bureau's offensive contribution is virtually nil, although he has decent hands and an average shot. He just can't afford to gamble offensively.

THE PHYSICAL GAME

Bureau is a blue-collar player and an agitator. He's very feisty and skilled and gets opponents ticked off enough to take runs or swats at him. He could be a stronger hitter, but he doesn't have good balance; when he hits people he is usually the one to fall. To his credit, he pops right back up and rejoins the fray.

THE INTANGIBLES

Bureau will be on the bubble, but a team in need of defensive help can always find room on its roster for a

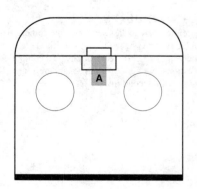

J.J. DAIGNEAULT

Yrs. of NHL service: 10
Born: Montreal, Que.; Oct. 12, 1965
Position: left defense
Height: 5-11
Weight: 185
Uniform no.: 48
Shoots: left

Career statistics:

GP	G	A	TP	PIM
581	39	139	170	433

1991-92 statistics:

GP	G	A	TP	+/-	PIM	PP	SH	GW	GT	S	PCT
79	4	14	18	+16	36	2	0	0	1	108	3.7

1992-93 statistics:

GP	G	A	TP	+/-	PIM	PP	SH	GW	GT	S	PCT
66	8	10	18	+25	57	0	0	1	0	68	11.8

1993-94 statistics:

GP	G	A	TP	+/-	PIM	PP	SH	GW	GT	S	PCT
68	2	12	14	+16	73	0	0	1	0	61	3.3

1994-95 statistics:

GP	G	A	TP	+/-	PIM	PP	SH	GW	GT	S	PCT
45	3	5	8	+2	40	0	0	0	0	36	8.3

LAST SEASON
Only regular Montreal defenseman with a plus rating.

THE FINESSE GAME
Daigneault uses his considerable finesse skills on defense. While he can join in a rush, he's concerned with defense first. He will move the puck out of the zone to get the forwards moving with a pass. He is a very good skater, but does not handle the puck well at top speed and won't stickhandle his way through the neutral zone.

He has a good slap shot from the point, but he is also smart enough to use his long wrist shot for more accuracy.

Daigneault angles his attackers to the wall. He does not read plays well defensively and can sometimes be duped by crisscrossing forwards, getting caught flat-footed. Overall his positional play has improved.

THE PHYSICAL GAME
Daigneault does not use his body well. He lacks the size and strength to be a powerful force in front of the net, so he must concentrate on his angles and on taking away the passing lane. He will do what he can to keep his man tied up. He is limited by his size. He gets hit a lot but stays in the trenches.

THE INTANGIBLES
A solid NHL defenseman with two-way skills, Daigneault is starting the downside of his career and shouldn't be counted on as one of the top two defensemen on the team. If given less ice time, he would be able to respond with a healthier effort, but at the moment there is little help on the horizon for Montreal's depleted defense corps.

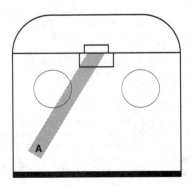

VINCENT DAMPHOUSSE

Yrs. of NHL service: 9
Born: Montreal, Que.; Dec. 17, 1967
Position: left wing
Height: 6-1
Weight: 185
Uniform no.: 25
Shoots: left

Career statistics:

GP	G	A	TP	PIM
690	245	401	646	530

1991-92 statistics:

GP	G	A	TP	+/-	PIM	PP	SH	GW	GT	S	PCT
80	38	51	89	+10	53	12	1	8	1	247	15.4

1992-93 statistics:

GP	G	A	TP	+/-	PIM	PP	SH	GW	GT	S	PCT
84	39	58	97	+5	98	9	3	8	1	287	13.6

1993-94 statistics:

GP	G	A	TP	+/-	PIM	PP	SH	GW	GT	S	PCT
84	40	51	91	0	75	13	0	10	1	274	14.6

1994-95 statistics:

GP	G	A	TP	+/-	PIM	PP	SH	GW	GT	S	PCT
48	10	30	40	+15	42	4	0	4	0	123	8.1

LAST SEASON

One of five Canadiens to appear in all 48 games. Led team in plus-minus. Tied for team lead in game-winning goals. Second on team in assists. Third on team in points. Has played in 690 of 696 games in his nine NHL seasons.

THE FINESSE GAME

Cool in tight, Damphousse has a marvellous backhand shot that he can roof, and he will create opportunites low by shaking and faking checkers with his skating. Like his new linemate Pierre Turgeon, Damphousse likes to set up from beind the net to make plays.

Damphousse, who can also play centre, shows poise with the puck. While he is primarily a finisher, he will also dish off to a teammate if that is a better option. He's superb player in the four-on-four situations. He has good offensive instincts, though his defensive game is woefully lacking.

Damphousse won't leave any vapour trails with his skating, but he is quick around the net, especially with the puck. He has exceptional balance to hop through sticks and checks. In open ice, he will use his weight to shift and change direction, making it appear as if he's going faster than he is — and he can juke without losing the puck and while looking for his passing and shooting options.

THE PHYSICAL GAME

Damphousse will use his body to protect the puck, but he is not much of a grinder and loses most of his one-on-one battles. He has to be supported with physical linemates who will get him the puck. He will expend a great deal of energy in the attacking zone, but little in his own end of the ice. He is a well-conditioned athlete who can handle long shifts and lots of ice time. He is not shy about getting his stick up, but he does not take dumb penalties.

THE INTANGIBLES

Damphousse's production dropped off sharply (he scored a pro-rated 69 points after two seasons with 75 or more). His chemistry with Pierre Turgeon bodes well, since Turgeon's left wings benefit from his play-making, but Montreal's number one trio will face a lot of checking pressure until/if the team can create a strong second line. Damphousse should reach the 100-point mark for the first time. He gets top power play time.

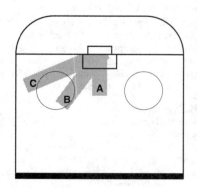

MIKE KEANE

Yrs. of NHL service: 7
Born: Winnipeg, Man.; May 28, 1967
Position: right wing
Height: 5-11
Weight: 175
Uniform no.: 12
Shoots: right

Career statistics:

GP	G	A	TP	PIM
488	80	172	262	490

1991-92 statistics:

GP	G	A	TP	+/-	PIM	PP	SH	GW	GT	S	PCT
67	11	30	41	+16	64	2	0	2	1	116	9.5

1992-93 statistics:

GP	G	A	TP	+/-	PIM	PP	SH	GW	GT	S	PCT
77	15	45	60	+29	95	0	0	1	0	120	12.5

1993-94 statistics:

GP	G	A	TP	+/-	PIM	PP	SH	GW	GT	S	PCT
80	16	30	46	+6	119	6	2	2	1	129	12.4

1994-95 statistics:

GP	G	A	TP	+/-	PIM	PP	SH	GW	GT	S	PCT
48	10	10	20	+5	15	1	0	0	0	75	13.3

LAST SEASON

One of five Canadiens to appear in all 48 games, despite suffering a broken jaw.

THE FINESSE GAME

Keane is one of the NHL's most underrated forwards. There are few better on the boards and in the corners, and he's the perfect linemate for a finisher. If you want the puck, he'll get it. Not only will he win the battle for it, he'll make a pass and then set a pick or screen. He can be used on the power play and does a decent job.

He is a good skater and will use his speed to forecheck or create shorthanded threats when killing penalties. He is not much of a finisher, though he will contribute the odd goal from his work in front of the net.

Keane can play all three forward positions, but is most effective on the right side. He is a smart player who can be thrust into almost any playing situation. Last season, the Canadiens used him extensively on the checking line, and Keane still produced 46 points.

THE PHYSICAL GAME

Keane is a physical catalyst. He is constantly getting in someone's way. He always finishes his checks in all three zones. He is aggressive and will stand up for his teammates, though he is not a fighter.

Anyone who questioned Keane's hockey courage had only to watch him play when a broken jaw forced him to take his meals through a straw.

THE INTANGIBLES

Keane has taken over as the team's top checking forward, with the bonus of being able to score 15 to 20 goals a season. He is a team leader, and was named the Canadiens' captain — not an honor to be taken lightly — after Kirk Muller was traded.

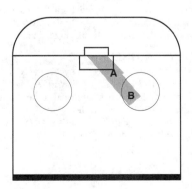

SAKU KOIVU

Yrs. of NHL service: 0
Born: Turku, Finland; Nov. 23, 1974
Position: centre
Height: 5-9
Weight: 165
Uniform no.: n.a.
Shoots: left

Career statistics (Finland):

GP	G	A	TP	PIM
149	53	84	137	143

1992-93 statistics (Finland):

GP	G	A	TP	PIM
46	3	7	10	28

1993-94 statistics (Finland):

GP	G	A	TP	PIM
47	23	30	53	42

1994-95 statistics (Finland):

GP	G	A	TP	PIM
56	27	47	74	73

LAST SEASON

Will be entering first full NHL season.

THE FINESSE GAME

Koivu brings brilliance and excitement to every shift. Considered one of the world's best playmakers, he makes things happen with his speed and intimidates by driving the defense back, then using the room to create scoring chances.

Koivu has great hands and can handle the puck at a fast pace. He stickhandles through traffic and reads plays well. He is intelligent and involved.

He has a variety of shots. Like many Europeans, he has an effective backhand for shooting or passing. He also has a strong wrist shot and is deadly accurate.

THE PHYSICAL GAME

The lone knock on Koivu is his lack of size. He gets involved in a scrappy way, but hasn't yet been tested on smaller North American ice surfaces. Montreal was a meek team last season and Koivu could get shoved around. He will have to pay a physical price to stick. He has demonstrated grit and feistiness at the international level, and is aware of the need to get stronger. Just don't expect him to get any bigger. He will use his stick to level the playing field a bit.

THE INTANGIBLES

The 1995 title for best player not yet in the NHL went to Koivu (the 1994 unofficial winner was Peter Forsberg, and look what happened to him). Koivu won't accept a part-time role, however. If it looks like he isn't among the top six forwards in training camp, he will likely play another year in Europe.

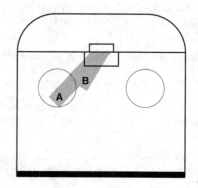

MARK LAMB

Yrs. of NHL service: 6
Born: Ponteix, Sask.; Aug. 3, 1964
Position: centre
Height: 5-9
Weight: 180
Uniform no.: 17
Shoots: left

Career statistics:

GP	G	A	TP	PIM
402	46	100	146	291

1991-92 statistics:

GP	G	A	TP	+/-	PIM	PP	SH	GW	GT	S	PCT
59	6	22	28	+4	46	2	0	1	0	61	9.8

1992-93 statistics:

GP	G	A	TP	+/-	PIM	PP	SH	GW	GT	S	PCT
71	7	19	26	-40	64	1	0	0	0	123	5.7

1993-94 statistics:

GP	G	A	TP	+/-	PIM	PP	SH	GW	GT	S	PCT
85	12	24	36	-44	72	4	1	2	0	124	9.7

1994-95 statistics:

GP	G	A	TP	+/-	PIM	PP	SH	GW	GT	S	PCT
47	1	2	3	-12	20	0	0	0	0	30	3.3

LAST SEASON

Acquired from Philadelphia on waivers.

THE FINESSE GAME

Lamb has decent skating skills, with hands and instincts better suited to defense than the attack. He uses his quickness on the fore-check to harry a puck carrier and force the opponent to make a play quicker than he wants to. It isn't that Lamb is going to blast anybody with a check, more that he is going to swarm the opponent and force a turnover if the puck is not moved quickly.

Should that occur, Lamb tends to look for an open man rather than try to carry the mail in front. He will use the element of surprise to come in front occasionally, but prefers to make use of a nice passing touch.

Lamb is a smart player who can work on the power play and killing penalties. Except against big power forwards, Lamb can hold his own shadowing and checking.

THE PHYSICAL GAME

Lamb plays way bigger than his size, using anticipation and hockey sense to make up for an absence of stature. He is not at all afraid of being hit, and he is persistent. He refuses to take a larger player's "No" for an answer.

Lamb will wear down, however, and needs to have his ice time monitored.

THE INTANGIBLES

Lamb is the quintessential team player, and while he is always on the bubble, he's a reliable defensive player. Only his size prevents him from being a trusted regular, since he doesn't match up against the league's top power centres.

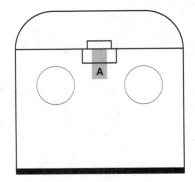

VLADIMIR MALAKHOV

Yrs. of NHL service: 3
Born: Sverdlovsk, Russia; Aug. 30, 1968
Position: right defense
Height: 6-2
Weight: 207
Uniform no.: 38
Shoots: left

Career statistics:

GP	G	A	TP	PIM
180	28	102	130	185

1992-93 statistics:

GP	G	A	TP	+/-	PIM	PP	SH	GW	GT	S	PCT
64	14	38	52	+14	59	7	0	0	0	178	7.9

1993-94 statistics:

GP	G	A	TP	+/-	PIM	PP	SH	GW	GT	S	PCT
76	10	47	57	+29	80	4	0	2	0	235	4.3

1994-95 statistics:

GP	G	A	TP	+/-	PIM	PP	SH	GW	GT	S	PCT
40	4	17	21	-3	46	1	0	0	0	91	4.4

LAST SEASON

Acquired from the New York Islanders with Pierre Turgeon for Kirk Muller, Matt Schneider and Craig Darby. Led team defensemen in scoring. Missed games with a hip injury.

THE FINESSE GAME

Malakhov has an absolute bullet shot, which he rifles off the one-timer or on the fly. He has outstanding offensive instincts for both shooting and playmaking. He is a lot like Brian Leetch in his ability to move the puck and jump into the play, but he has a better shot than Leetch does. What he lacks is Leetch's vision and lateral movement — and confidence.

Malakhov is so talented he never looks like he's trying hard. Most nights he's not. The 84-game grind is still something he is getting used to. He has learned on the job, and as he doesn't speak English well, he struggled through some of the learning process. He seemed discouraged at times when things weren't going smoothly, but on the nights he delivers the goods he is awesome.

Malakhov is also very strong defensively and can be used on both special teams. He is a mobile skater, with good agility and balance. He has huge strides, which he developed playing bandy — a Russian game similar to hockey, but played on ice the size of a soccer field.

THE PHYSICAL GAME

Malakhov relies on his positioning and anticipation for his defensive plays more than his hitting. He could be a major physical force because of his size and strength, but injuries may have made him leery of getting hurt.

THE INTANGIBLES

Malakhov can do things other defensemen can't. Some nights he is in his own class, playing with authority, but he does not yet deliver consistently. He needs to feel he is special, but to get respect, you have to earn it. While teammates and coaches are in awe of Malakhov's skills, they aren't thrilled by his lack of intensity. This season should determine whether he is indeed destined to become a star, or whether he'll go into the books as an overrated flop.

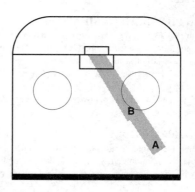

LYLE ODELEIN

Yrs. of NHL service: 5
Born: Quill Lake, Sask.; July 21, 1968
Position: right defense
Height: 5-10
Weight: 205
Uniform no.: 24
Shoots: left

Career statistics:

GP	G	A	TP	PIM
341	17	61	78	1137

1991-92 statistics:

GP	G	A	TP	+/-	PIM	PP	SH	GW	GT	S	PCT
71	1	7	8	+15	212	0	0	0	0	43	2.3

1992-93 statistics:

GP	G	A	TP	+/-	PIM	PP	SH	GW	GT	S	PCT
83	2	14	16	+35	205	0	0	0	0	79	2.5

1993-94 statistics:

GP	G	A	TP	+/-	PIM	PP	SH	GW	GT	S	PCT
79	11	29	40	+8	276	6	0	2	0	116	9.5

1994-95 statistics:

GP	G	A	TP	+/-	PIM	PP	SH	GW	GT	S	PCT
48	3	7	10	-13	152	0	0	0	0	74	4.1

LAST SEASON

One of five Canadiens to play in all 48 games. Led team in PIM for third consecutive season. Worst plus-minus on team.

THE FINESSE GAME

Odelein deserves great credit for having molded himself into more than an overachieving goon. He is Montreal's most reliable defenseman, a physical presence despite being smaller than most NHL defensemen — and smaller than many NHL forwards.

Defense is his forte. Odelein is very calm with the puck. He can hold on until a player is on top of him and then carry the puck or find an open man. His skating is average at best, but he keeps himself out of trouble by playing a conservative game and not getting caught out of position. An attacker who comes into Odelein's piece of the ice will have to pay the price by getting through him.

Odelein's finesse skills are modest at best, but he has developed sufficient confidence to get involved in the attack if needed. He prefers to limit his contribution to shots from the point. He needs to be paired with a puck-carrying partner.

THE PHYSICAL GAME

Odelein is a banger, a limited player who knows what those limits are, stays within them and plays effectively as a result. He's rugged and doesn't take chances, he takes the man at all times in front of the net and he plays tough. Heavy but not tall, he gives the impression of being a much bigger man. He will fight, but not very well. He is forced to engage in fisticuffs as the biggest, toughest Canadien — often the only big, tough Canadien.

He has become more disciplined and willing to take a shot in the chops to get a power play (sure, now that he gets to play the point), although the transgressor will usually pay later in the game. Odelein doesn't forget.

THE INTANGIBLES

Reliable and physical, Odelein is a solid defenseman who continues to improve season by season. He is one of the team's quiet leaders, and will be more effective if the team can add some toughness up front so that he doesn't have to do it all.

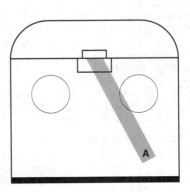

STEPHANE QUINTAL

Yrs. of NHL service: 7
Born: Boucherville, Que.; Oct. 22, 1968
Position: right defense
Height: 6-3
Weight: 215
Uniform no.: 4
Shoots: right

Career statistics:

GP	G	A	TP	PIM
583	23	70	93	546

1991-92 statistics:

GP	G	A	TP	+/-	PIM	PP	SH	GW	GT	S	PCT
75	4	16	20	-11	109	0	0	0	0	71	5.6

1992-93 statistics:

GP	G	A	TP	+/-	PIM	PP	SH	GW	GT	S	PCT
75	1	10	11	-6	100	0	1	0	0	81	1.2

1993-94 statistics:

GP	G	A	TP	+/-	PIM	PP	SH	GW	GT	S	PCT
81	8	18	26	-25	119	1	1	1	0	154	5.2

1994-95 statistics:

GP	G	A	TP	+/-	PIM	PP	SH	GW	GT	S	PCT
43	6	17	23	0	78	3	0	2	0	107	5.6

LAST SEASON

Led team defensemen in scoring for second consecutive season. Acquired by Montreal for second-round pick in 1995. Missed five games with a sprained ankle.

THE FINESSE GAME

Quintal's game is limited by his lumbering skating. He has some nice touches, like a decent point shot and a good head and hands for passing, but his best moves have to be executed at a virtual standstill. He needs to be paired with a quick skater or his shifts will be spent solely in the defensive zone.

Fortunately, Quintal is as aware as anyone else of his flaws. He plays a smart positional game and doesn't get involved in low-percentage plays in the offensive zone. He won't step up in the neutral zone to risk an interception, but will fall back into a defensive mode. He takes up a lot of ice with his body and stick, and when he doesn't overcommit, he reduces the space available to a puck carrier.

While he can exist as an NHL regular in the five-on-five mode, Quintal is a risky proposition for any specialty teams play. When he was in Winnipeg, the Jets used him on the point on power plays out of necessity, but it isn't his specialty.

Quintal does not like to carry the puck, and under pressure in the right corner he will simply slam it out along the left corner boards behind the net.

THE PHYSICAL GAME

Quintal is slow but very strong on his skates. He thrives on contact and works hard along the boards and in front of the net. He hits hard without taking penalties and is a tough and willing fighter.

THE INTANGIBLES

Quintal will never be better than a number five or six defenseman, and when a coach shortens his bench in a game, Quintal will be sitting on it. Still, he tries hard and that gets him a second chance. How he handles the pressures of playing in Montreal will affect his season. It could spur him to his best season or be a great weight.

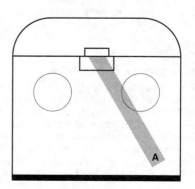

YVES RACINE

Yrs. of NHL service: 6
Born: Matane, Que.; Feb. 7, 1969
Position: right defense
Height: 6-0
Weight: 185
Uniform no.: 29
Shoots: left

Career statistics:

GP	G	A	TP	PIM
345	38	156	194	320

1991-92 statistics:

GP	G	A	TP	+/-	PIM	PP	SH	GW	GT	S	PCT
61	2	22	24	-6	94	1	0	0	0	103	1.9

1992-93 statistics:

GP	G	A	TP	+/-	PIM	PP	SH	GW	GT	S	PCT
80	9	31	40	+10	80	5	0	0	0	163	5.5

1993-94 statistics:

GP	G	A	TP	+/-	PIM	PP	SH	GW	GT	S	PCT
67	9	43	52	-11	48	5	1	1	1	142	6.3

1994-95 statistics:

GP	G	A	TP	+/-	PIM	PP	SH	GW	GT	S	PCT
47	7	11	18	-1	42	2	0	1	0	63	6.3

LAST SEASON
Acquired from Philadelphia for Kevin Haller. Missed one game with the flu.

THE FINESSE GAME
Racine is a good skater with agility and quickness. He can carry the puck on a rush, but he is also capable of finding the open man for a long up-ice pass.

He likes to get involved in the attack and will make the occasional foray deep into the offensive zone. He controls the puck well and protects it with his body. Racine has a second gear that he shifts into only sporadically, which makes it frustrating for coaches who want him to play at his high level every night. He tends to go through shaky periods when is afraid to handle the puck.

When he steps up his physical play, Racine is more confident and more involved in the attack. He has a decent point shot, but doesn't have a quick release.

THE PHYSICAL GAME
Racine tends to play soft. He is not a big defenseman, but since he lacks overwhelming finesse skills, he has to play a more physical style to earn an NHL job on a nightly basis.

He is susceptible to a strong fore-check, and he tends to hurry his passes or overhandle the puck under pressure.

THE INTANGIBLES
Racine has never shown the consistency to make him anything more than a number four defenseman. He deserves a full season in Montreal before the move is assessed, but his major contribution would appear to be limited to power play work.

MARK RECCHI

Yrs. of NHL service: 6
Born: Kamloops, B.C.; Feb. 1, 1968
Position: right wing/centre
Height: 5-9
Weight: 185
Uniform no.: 8
Shoots: left

Career statistics:

GP	G	A	TP	PIM
464	223	334	557	357

1991-92 statistics:

GP	G	A	TP	+/-	PIM	PP	SH	GW	GT	S	PCT
80	43	54	97	-21	96	20	1	5	1	210	20.5

1992-93 statistics:

GP	G	A	TP	+/-	PIM	PP	SH	GW	GT	S	PCT
84	53	70	123	+1	95	15	4	6	0	274	19.3

1993-94 statistics:

GP	G	A	TP	+/-	PIM	PP	SH	GW	GT	S	PCT
84	40	67	107	-2	46	11	0	5	0	217	18.4

1994-95 statistics:

GP	G	A	TP	+/-	PIM	PP	SH	GW	GT	S	PCT
49	16	32	48	-9	28	9	0	3	0	121	13.2

LAST SEASON

Acquired from Philadelphia with a third round pick for Eric Desjardins, John LeClair and Gilbert Dionne. One of three players to appear in more than 48 games. Led team in assists, points and power play goals.

THE FINESSE GAME

Recchi is a small package with a lot of firepower. He may be the best small player in the game (we can think of only Theo Fleury and Ray Ferraro as challengers). Recchi is feisty and is a relentless worker in the offensive zone. He busts into open ice, finding the holes almost before they open. He excels at the give-and-go, and is versatile enough to play wing or centre, though he is better on the wing.

Recchi has a dangerous shot from the off wing. While he is not as dynamic as Maurice Richard, he likes to use the Richard cut-back while rifling a wrist shot back across. It's heavy, it's on net and it requires no backswing. He will follow his shot to the net for a rebound. He can make a play as well. He has excellent hands, vision and anticipation for any scoring opportunity.

Recchi has worked hard to improve his defense and is getting better, though it is still the weakest part of his game. He kills penalties well because he hounds the point men aggressively and knocks the puck out of the zone. Then he heads off on a breakaway or forces the defender to pull him down.

He isn't a pretty skater but he always keeps his feet moving. While other players are coasting, Recchi's blades are in motion. He is ready to spring into any play. He resembles a puck magnet because he is always going where the puck is.

THE PHYSICAL GAME

Recchi gets chopped at because he doesn't hang around the perimeter. He accepts the punishment to get the job done. He is a solid player with a low centre of gravity, and is tough to knock off the puck. He is remarkably durable for the style of game he plays.

THE INTANGIBLES

Recchi has a fat contract (six years at $15 million) and is the fall guy for the trade that is credited with putting Philadelphia into the playoffs — and knocking the Canadiens out. As if playing in Montreal wasn't pressure enough.

Recchi clicked well with Pierre Turgeon and Vincent Damphousse on the line that was assembled late in the season after another big trade. Still, that is the only line the Canadiens have to provide scoring and they can expected to be checked into the ground.

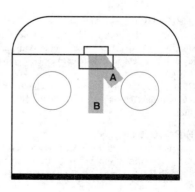

PATRICK ROY

Yrs. of NHL service: 10
Born: Quebec City, Que.; Oct. 5, 1965
Position: goaltender
Height: 6-0
Weight: 175
Uniform no.: 33
Catches: left

Career statistics:

GP	MINS	GA	SO	GAA	A	PIM
529	30658	1414	28	2.77	28	104

1991-92 statistics:

GP	MINS	GAA	W	L	T	SO	GA	S	SAPCT	PIM
67	3935	2.36	36	22	8	5	155	1806	.914	4

1992-93 statistics:

GP	MINS	GAA	W	L	T	SO	GA	S	SAPCT	PIM
62	3595	3.20	31	25	5	2	192	1814	.894	16

1993-94 statistics:

GP	MINS	GAA	W	L	T	SO	GA	S	SAPCT	PIM
68	3867	2.50	35	17	11	7	161	1956	.918	30

1994-95 statistics:

GP	MINS	GAA	W	L	T	SO	GA	S	SAPCT	PIM
43	2566	2.97	17	20	6	1	127	1357	.906	20

LAST SEASON
Led NHL goalies in minutes played and PIM. First losing season since joining NHL.

THE PHYSICAL GAME
Roy's technique might not be textbook perfect — he flops too much for purists — but he has perfected what he does. He is tall but not broad, yet he uses his body well. He plays his angles, stays at the top of his crease and squares his body to the shooter. He is able to absorb the shot and deaden it, so there are few juicy rebounds left on his doorstep.

A butterfly goalie, he goes down much sooner than he did earlier in his career. The book on Roy is to try to beat him high. Usually there isn't much net there and it's a small spot for a shooter to hit. He is most vulnerable five-hole, and when he is in a slump that is where he gives up the goals. He also has trouble with wide-angle shots taken from the blueline to the top of the circle.

Roy comes back to the rest of the pack in his puck-handling, where he is merely average. As for his skating, he seldoms moves out of his net. When he gets in trouble, he will move back and forth on his knees rather than try to regain his feet. His glove hand isn't great, either. It's good, but he prefers to use his body.

THE MENTAL GAME
Roy is aggressive but doesn't always force the action. He's a very patient goalie, holding his ground and making the shooter commit first.

Roy battled fatigue and the puck at times last season, often allowing goals in the closing minutes of a period. His defense slumped in front of him, which didn't help.

THE INTANGIBLES
The key to beating Roy is to get to him early. The longer he goes in a game without allowing a goal, the bigger he gets in the nets. Coming off a subpar season, Roy will be looking to bounce back big time this year, but he can't do it alone.

BRIAN SAVAGE

Yrs. of NHL service: 1
Born: Sudbury, Ontario; Feb. 24, 1971
Position: centre
Height: 6-2
Weight: 191
Uniform no.: 49
Shoots: centre

Career statistics:

GP	G	A	TP	PIM
40	13	7	20	27

1993-94 statistics:

GP	G	A	TP	+/-	PIM	PP	SH	GW	GT	S	PCT
3	1	0	1	0	0	0	0	0	0	3	33.3

1994-95 statistics:

GP	G	A	TP	+/-	PIM	PP	SH	GW	GT	S	PCT
37	12	7	19	+5	27	0	0	0	0	64	18.8

LAST SEASON

First NHL season. Led team and tied for third among rookies in shooting percentage. Missed 10 games with a knee injury.

THE FINESSE GAME

Savage's stock has risen sharply since he was a 171st pick overall in 1991. A scorer at the collegiate level (Miami-Ohio), he spent two years in the Canadian national program, winning a silver medal in 1994 and improving his skating with his work on the larger international-size rinks.

Savage is skilled as a playmaker and shooter. He isn't shy about firing the puck, which is something the Canadiens need.

He has quick hands for picking up the puck and for working on face-offs. He is an intelligent player who reads plays well and has great potential.

THE PHYSICAL GAME

Savage doesn't use his body well yet, but playing with tough linemate Turner Stevenson last season gave him heart and inspiration. Savage is strong on his skates and has decent size. He may not initiate, but he won't be intimidated.

THE INTANGIBLES

A knee injury early in the season slowed Savage's progress. A job is waiting for him in training camp and he could develop into a number two centre, the perfect spot for him behind Pierre Turgeon. Savage can produce, and 20-25 goals should be within easy reach.

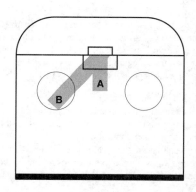

TURNER STEVENSON

Yrs. of NHL service: 1
Born: Prince George, B.C.; May 18, 1972
Position: right wing
Height: 6-3
Weight: 200
Uniform no.: 30
Shoots: right

Career statistics:

GP	G	A	TP	PIM
44	6	1	7	88

1992-93 statistics:

GP	G	A	TP	+/-	PIM	PP	SH	GW	GT	S	PCT
1	0	0	0	-1	0	0	0	0	0	0	0.0

1993-94 statistics:

GP	G	A	TP	+/-	PIM	PP	SH	GW	GT	S	PCT
2	0	0	0	-2	2	0	0	0	0	0	0.0

1994-95 statistics:

GP	G	A	TP	+/-	PIM	PP	SH	GW	GT	S	PCT
41	6	1	7	0	86	0	0	1	0	35	17.1

LAST SEASON
First NHL season.

THE FINESSE GAME
A big, strong two-way winger, Stevenson is the type of forward desperately needed by Montreal.

A good skater for a player of his size, he has a good long stride and is balanced and agile.

Stevenson is a finisher. He has a variety of shots and uses all of them with power and accuracy. He will follow the puck to the net and not give up on shots. Stevenson is also a decent passer and possesses some vision and creativity.

THE PHYSICAL GAME
Stevenson has an impressive mean streak. The problem for the coaching staff will be lighting a fire under him on a regular basis, because he doesn't bring the same intensity to the ice every night. He seems to have no idea what kind of physical presence he can add to the team.

THE INTANGIBLES
Stevenson has been slow to develop, like a lot of big forwards, but Montreal believes he will be worth the wait. He scored his six goals over the last 12 games of the season while Montreal was in the playoff hunt, a good sign.

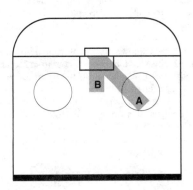

PIERRE TURGEON

Yrs. of NHL service: 8
Born: Rouyn, Que.; Aug. 29, 1969
Position: centre
Height: 6-1
Weight: 203
Uniform no.: 77
Shoots: left

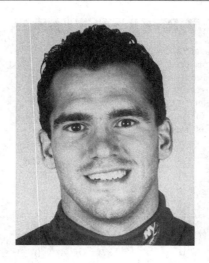

Career statistics:

GP	G	A	TP	PIM
592	280	403	683	193

1991-92 statistics:

GP	G	A	TP	+/-	PIM	PP	SH	GW	GT	S	PCT
77	40	55	95	+7	20	13	0	6	0	207	19.3

1992-93 statistics:

GP	G	A	TP	+/-	PIM	PP	SH	GW	GT	S	PCT
83	58	74	132	-1	26	24	0	10	2	301	19.3

1993-94 statistics:

GP	G	A	TP	+/-	PIM	PP	SH	GW	GT	S	PCT
69	38	56	94	+14	18	10	4	6	0	254	15.0

1994-95 statistics:

GP	G	A	TP	+/-	PIM	PP	SH	GW	GT	S	PCT
49	24	23	47	0	14	5	2	4	0	160	15.0

LAST SEASON

Acquired from New York Islanders with Vladimir Malakhov for Kirk Muller, Matt Schneider and Craig Darby. Led team in goals, shorthanded goals and shots. Tied for team lead in game-winning goals. Second on team in points. One of three players to appear in 49 games last season.

THE FINESSE GAME

Turgeon's skills are amazing. He never seems to be looking at the puck, yet he is always in perfect control of it. He has a style unlike just about anyone else in the NHL. He's not a fast skater, but he can deke a defender or make a sneaky surprise pass. He is tough to defend against, because if you aren't aware of where he is on the ice and don't deny him the pass, he can kill a team with several moves.

Turgeon can slow or speed up the tempo of a game. He lacks the breakout speed of a Pat LaFontaine, but because he is slippery and can change speeds so smoothly, he's deceptive. His control with the puck down low is remarkable. He protects the puck well with the body.

While best known for his playmaking, Turgeon has an excellent shot. He will curl out from behind the net with a wrist shot, shoot off the fly from the right wing (his preferred side of the ice) or stand just off to the side of the net on a power play and reach for a tip or redirection of a point shot. He doesn't have a bazooka shot, but he uses quick, accurate wrist and snap shots. He has to create odd-man rushes. This is when he is at his finest.

THE PHYSICAL GAME

Turgeon has to decide if he wants to be a good statistical player or a winner, and to be the latter he will have to add a more physical element to his game. He is strong, but clearly does not like the contact part of the game, and he can be taken out of a game by a team that hounds him. Turgeon must play through it. He will be the number one centre in Montreal without a true number two to back him up, and will face tough checking without relief this season.

THE INTANGIBLES

Turgeon isn't Wayne Gretzky or Doug Gilmour. He isn't a leader. He will create a certain amount of brilliance — and it is considerable — but never take his game to the next level, and he won't bring the team along with him. Turgeon has shied from publicity in cities where only one or two reporters routinely travel with the team. How will he handle the swell of media attention in Montreal? So far, he swears he loves it and that playing for Montreal is a dream come true. A full season in a Canadiens sweater will prove just how comfortable a fit that dream jersey is.

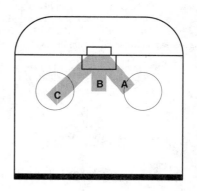

NEW JERSEY DEVILS

Players' Statistics 1994-95

POS	NO.	PLAYER	GP	G	A	PTS	+/-	PIM	PP	SH	GW	GT	S	PCTG
R	44	STEPHANE RICHER	45	23	16	39	8	10	1	2	5	1	133	17.3
C	9	NEAL BROTEN	47	8	24	32	1	24	2		3		72	11.1
R	15	JOHN MACLEAN	46	17	12	29	13	32	2	1			139	12.2
R	12	BILL GUERIN	48	12	13	25	6	72	4		3		96	12.5
D	4	SCOTT STEVENS	48	2	20	22	4	56	1		1		111	1.8
D	29	SHAWN CHAMBERS	45	4	17	21	2	12	2				67	6.0
L	16	BOBBY HOLIK	48	10	10	20	9	18			2		84	11.9
R	22	CLAUDE LEMIEUX	45	6	13	19	2	86	1		1		117	5.1
D	27	SCOTT NIEDERMAYER	48	4	15	19	19	18	4				52	7.7
L	17	TOM CHORSKE	42	10	8	18	-4	16			2		59	16.9
C	14	*BRIAN ROLSTON	40	7	11	18	5	17	2		3		92	7.6
L	19	BOB CARPENTER	41	5	11	16	-1	19				2	69	7.2
D	23	BRUCE DRIVER	41	4	12	16	-1	18	1		1	1	62	6.5
D	6	TOMMY ALBELIN	48	5	10	15	9	20	2				60	8.3
C	18	*SERGEI BRYLIN	26	6	8	14	12	8					41	14.6
R	21	RANDY MCKAY	33	5	7	12	10	44					44	11.4
L	8	MIKE PELUSO	46	2	9	11	5	167			1		27	7.4
R	20	DANTON COLE	38	4	5	9	-1	14	1				76	5.3
C	11	JIM DOWD	10	1	4	5	-5		1				14	7.1
L	25	VALERI ZELEPUKIN	4	1	2	3	3	6					6	16.7
D	3	KEN DANEYKO	25	1	2	3	4	54					27	3.7
D	7	*CHRIS MCALPINE	24		3	3	4	17					19	
G	30	MARTIN BRODEUR	40		2	2		2						
R	24	*DAVID EMMA	6		1	1	-2						4	
D	28	*KEVIN DEAN	17		1	1	6	4					11	
D	26	JASON SMITH	2				-3						5	
L	33	*REID SIMPSON	9				-1	27					5	
D	5	JAROSLAV MODRY	11				-1						10	
G	31	CHRIS TERRERI	15											

GP = games played; G = goals; A = assists; PTS = points; +/- = goals-for minus goals-against while player is on ice; PIM = penalties in minutes; PP = power play goals; SH = shorthanded goals; GW = game-winning goals; GT = game-tying goals; S = no. of shots; PCTG = percentage of goals to shots; * = rookie

MARTIN BRODEUR

Yrs. of NHL service: 2
Born: Montreal, Que.; May 6, 1972
Position: goaltender
Height: 6-1
Weight: 205
Uniform no.: 30
Catches: left

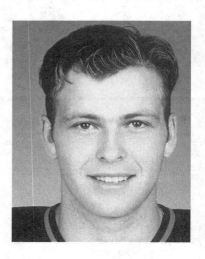

Career statistics:

GP	MINS	GA	SO	GAA	A	PIM
91	4983	204	6	2.46	2	4

1991-92 statistics:

GP	MINS	GAA	W	L	T	SO	GA	SA	SAPCT	PIM
4	179	3.35	2	1	0	0	10	85	.882	0

1992-93 statistics:

P	MINS	GAA	W	L	T	SO	GA	SA	SAPCT	PI
				Did not play in NHL						

1993-94 statistics:

GP	MINS	GAA	W	L	T	SO	GA	SA	SAPCT	PIM
47	2625	2.40	27	11	8	3	105	1238	.915	2

1994-95 statistics:

GP	MINS	GAA	W	L	T	SO	GA	SA	SAPCT	PIM
40	2184	2.45	19	11	6	3	89	908	.902	2

LAST SEASON

Second NHL season. Tied for fourth in NHL in wins.

THE PHYSICAL GAME

Technically, Brodeur is almost flawless. He stands so upright in the net and squares himself so well to the shooter that he looks enormous. Add his ability to use his stick around the net to break up plays (an ever-improving technique), and he takes away the close game as well.

Opponents want to get Brodeur's feet moving — wraparound plays, rebounds, anything involving his skates plays on his weaknesses. Yet because of his puck control, Brodeur prevents a lot of scrambles and minimizes his flaws.

Brodeur has improved his play out of the net but has to guard against cockiness. He has visions of becoming the next goalie to score a goal, and will get carried away in his shots through the middle of the ice. He is still working on improving his play with the puck behind the net.

Brodeur's physique is an advantage against crease-crashers. He also guards against poachers with the occasional ankle whack or jab to the back.

THE MENTAL GAME

Bad games and bad goals don't rattle Brodeur for long. While he has a tendency to show his frustration on-ice, he also bounces back quickly with strong efforts. He concentrates and doesn't lose his intensity throughout a game. Teammates love playing in front of him for the confidence he exudes — even through the layers of padding and the mask. When Brodeur is on, his glove saves are snappy and he bounces on his feet with a flair.

In his freshman year, Brodeur had trouble winning in certain buildings (like the gone-but-not-forgotten Boston Garden and Madison Square Garden), but he had outstanding performances in both of those arenas last season and shut out the Bruins three times in only five games in the first round of the playoffs, with two of those whitewashes coming on the road.

THE INTANGIBLES

Success did not spoil Brodeur, but dollars might. He has toiled near the top of his profession for two seasons at the NHL's minimum salary ($140,000 U.S.). He stands to get a raise upwards of $2 million per year — a pretty heady sum, even for a young goalie who seems to have a good head on his shoulders. Brodeur has proven himself a workhorse in the regular season and a game stealer in the playoffs. If his work ethic remains strong, he could be on his way to becoming one of the game's greats. He's proven himself a money goalie; now how will he react as a moneyed one?

NEAL BROTEN

Yrs. of NHL service: 14
Born: Roseau, Minn.; Nov. 29, 1959
Position: centre
Height: 5-9
Weight: 170
Uniform no.: 7
Shoots: left

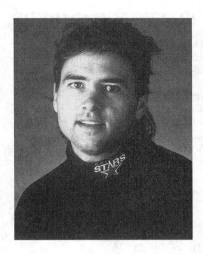

Career statistics:

GP	G	A	TP	PIM
1002	274	606	880	543

1991-92 statistics:

GP	G	A	TP	+/-	PIM	PP	SH	GW	GT	S	PCT
76	8	26	34	-15	16	4	1	1	0	119	6.7

1992-93 statistics:

GP	G	A	TP	+/-	PIM	PP	SH	GW	GT	S	PCT
82	12	21	33	+7	22	0	3	3	0	123	9.8

1993-94 statistics:

GP	G	A	TP	+/-	PIM	PP	SH	GW	GT	S	PCT
79	17	35	52	+10	62	2	1	0	0	153	11.1

1994-95 statistics:

GP	G	A	TP	+/-	PIM	PP	SH	GW	GT	S	PCT
47	8	24	32	+1	24	2	0	3	0	72	11.1

LAST SEASON

Played 1,000th career NHL game (third U.S.-born player to reach milestone). Second among U.S.-born players in career scoring. Scored 600th career assist. Led team in assists and second on team in points. Acquired from Dallas for Corey Millen on February 27, 1995.

THE FINESSE GAME

Two moves in two seasons might have been a shock to Broten's system. He left his native Minnesota with the Stars in 1993-94, then seemed dazed by a trade from the organization where he began his career to New Jersey.

Both changes were positive ones for Broten. While he thrived in the team's first season in Dallas, he was off to a slow start (four assists in 17 games, and a minus -8 ranking) and was relegated to a third-line role before he career was revived by the move to the Devils. Under New Jersey's defensive system, the veteran centre played either a number one or number two role, and responded by scoring 8-20-28 in 30 games with the Devils, and posted a plus-9 ranking. Broten was especially valuable in the playoffs, where he could either check a centre such as Adam Oates or be counted on for offensive punch.

Broten was able to fit in very quickly with his new linemates (usually veterans Claude Lemieux and John MacLean) because of his vision. Broten is not a speedy skater anymore, but his good hands and quick thinking leave teammates in the clear, and give the impression that he's faster than he looks. Broten also sees the ice surface like a chessboard, back-checks diligently and doesn't gamble, so he is seldom caught scrambling to get back into the play defensively.

Broten isn't great on draws, but wins his share. He is capable enough to be used as a point man on a power play, but New Jersey coach Jacques Lemaire does not use his forwards on the point.

THE PHYSICAL GAME

Broten has never been a physical presence, but he will lean on an opponent to slow his progress. Broten keeps his stick down, plays it clean, and while he will be overmatched physically he won't often be out-smarted.

THE INTANGIBLES

The unassuming Broten seemed taken aback by the only modest hoopla that marked his 1,000th NHL game, but there is no doubt he has made his mark as one of the pioneer American skaters. One of two players left in the NHL last season from the 1980 U.S. gold medal-winning hockey team (Detroit's Mike Ramsey was the other), Broten can still contribute as a defensive-minded centre who can put the occasional assist (maybe 40 or so over the course of a full season) on the board.

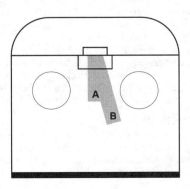

SHAWN CHAMBERS

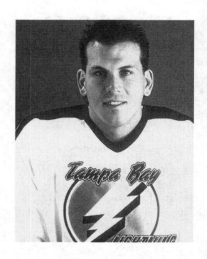

Yrs. of NHL service: 8
Born: Royal Oaks, Mich.; Oct. 11, 1966
Position: left defense
Height: 6-2
Weight: 200
Uniform no.: 29
Shoots: left

Career statistics:

GP	G	A	TP	PIM
366	40	116	156	279

1991-92 statistics:

GP	G	A	TP	+/-	PIM	PP	SH	GW	GT	S	PCT
2	0	0	0	-3	2	0	0	0	0	1	0.0

1992-93 statistics:

GP	G	A	TP	+/-	PIM	PP	SH	GW	GT	S	PCT
55	10	29	39	-21	36	5	0	1	0	152	6.6

1993-94 statistics:

GP	G	A	TP	+/-	PIM	PP	SH	GW	GT	S	PCT
66	11	23	34	-6	23	6	1	1	0	142	7.7

1994-95 statistics:

GP	G	A	TP	+/-	PIM	PP	SH	GW	GT	S	PCT
45	4	17	21	+2	12	2	0	0	0	67	6.0

LAST SEASON

Acquired from Tampa Bay with Danton Cole for Alexander Semak and Ben Hankinson. Second among team defensemen in scoring.

THE FINESSE GAME

Chambers has developed into a fairly reliable two-way defenseman. He still has enough of an offensive instinct that a coach has to worry when Chambers might take an ill-advised risk, but he played well within his abilities last season.

Often working on the Devils' first power play unit, he has an awkward-looking shot, but he manages to get it away quickly, low and on net. He has the poise and the hand skills to be able to fake out a checker with a faux slapper, move to the top of the circle and drill it. Chambers has a nice touch for keeping the puck in along the blueline.

His smarts put him a cut above the rest. Although his finesse skills may be average, he has great anticipation. He understands the game well and knows where the puck is going before the play is made. He does the little things well — little wrist shots, little dump-ins, nothing that shouts out.

Chambers prefers to move the puck out of the zone with a quick pass rather than lug it. His skating isn't dazzling, but he's got a little bit of wheels and is more efficient than his style indicates.

THE PHYSICAL GAME

A big defenseman, Chambers was not much of a hitter until he joined the Devils, where the sacrifice was demanded. Confidence in his knee (he underwent arthroscopic surgery in 1993-94) showed with his willingness to play the body. Although he won't put people into the third row of the stands, he will hit often enough and hard enough that later in a game the puck carrier will move the puck a little faster and maybe get hurried into a mistake.

He plays with a lot of enthusiasm and is a workhorse. He thrives on ice time and seems to have fun playing the game.

THE INTANGIBLES

A salary dispute in Tampa Bay led to Chambers's exit, but he seems to have found a comfortable home with the Devils for at least another season among their top six, as their younger defensemen continue to develop.

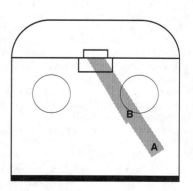

TOM CHORSKE

Yrs. of NHL service: 5
Born: Minneapolis, Minn.; Sept. 18, 1966
Position: left wing
Height: 6-1
Weight: 204
Uniform no.: 17
Shoots: right

Career statistics:

GP	G	A	TP	PIM
315	69	69	138	139

1991-92 statistics:

GP	G	A	TP	+/-	PIM	PP	SH	GW	GT	S	PCT
76	19	17	36	+8	32	0	3	2	0	143	13.3

1992-93 statistics:

GP	G	A	TP	+/-	PIM	PP	SH	GW	GT	S	PCT
50	7	12	19	-1	25	0	0	1	0	63	11.1

1993-94 statistics:

GP	G	A	TP	+/-	PIM	PP	SH	GW	GT	S	PCT
76	21	20	41	+14	32	1	1	4	0	131	16.0

1994-95 statistics:

GP	G	A	TP	+/-	PIM	PP	SH	GW	GT	S	PCT
42	10	8	18	-4	16	0	0	2	0	59	16.9

LAST SEASON

Worst plus-minus on team.

THE FINESSE GAME

Chorske has outstanding breakaway speed and considerable size — which make him one of the most perplexing players on the Devils. On any given night, he will use his body along the boards and take headman passes to key a quick attack. But those nights are rare.

True, he works a largely defensive role as the left winger on New Jersey's checking line, but he has too many skills to be a mere grinder. Chorske does not play heads-up when he has the puck. He is always looking down at it, instead of at the goalie to find an opening or to a teammate for a pass. Breakaways or two-on-ones that involve him tend to get everyone excited until they realize, "Oh, it's Chorske." As one scout constantly mutters after his missed scoring opportunities, "American hands."

While that is an unfair slap (Pat LaFontaine, Joe Mullen and Jeremy Roenick might argue the assets of the American scoring touch), Chorske does lack the hand skills to make more of his speed.

He works diligently in his checking role. With his quickness he gets many shorthanded scoring opportunities, but he doesn't bury as many as he should.

In addition to just being straight-line fast, Chorske is balanced and strong on his skates, getting great leg-drive for board and corner work. He is agile, but not when carrying the puck — then, his moves are pretty limited.

THE PHYSICAL GAME

Chorske came out of the college ranks and doesn't play a vicious game, but he is a solid hitter and won't back down. He will take the body in all zones and hits cleanly. He takes very few bad penalties.

THE INTANGIBLES

With his speed and size, Chorske will always go into the books as a disappointment for barely netting more than 20 goals in a season, but that appears to be his limit. He is one of those players who will always be on the bubble.

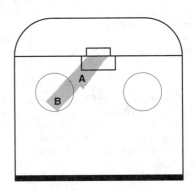

KEN DANEYKO

Yrs. of NHL service: 11
Born: Windsor, Ont.; Apr. 17, 1964
Position: right defense
Height: 6-0
Weight: 210
Uniform no.: 3
Shoots: left

Career statistics:

GP	G	A	TP	PIM
716	28	98	126	1933

1991-92 statistics:

GP	G	A	TP	+/-	PIM	PP	SH	GW	GT	S	PCT
80	1	7	8	+7	170	0	0	0	0	57	1.8

1992-93 statistics:

GP	G	A	TP	+/-	PIM	PP	SH	GW	GT	S	PCT
84	2	11	13	+4	236	0	0	0	0	71	2.8

1993-94 statistics:

GP	G	A	TP	+/-	PIM	PP	SH	GW	GT	S	PCT
78	1	9	10	+27	176	0	0	1	0	60	1.7

1994-95 statistics:

GP	G	A	TP	+/-	PIM	PP	SH	GW	GT	S	PCT
25	1	2	3	+4	54	0	0	0	0	19	3.7

LAST SEASON

Missed 23 games with a knee injury.

THE FINESSE GAME

Break down Daneyko's game — average skater, average passer, below-average shooter — and he looks like someone who would have trouble getting ice time. The edge is Daneyko's competitive drive. This is a player who will do anything to win a hockey game. Add to that Daneyko's strength and sound hockey sense, and the result is a powerful defensive defenseman who has been coveted by other teams for many years.

Despite his lack of footwork, Daneyko has evolved into one of the team's top penalty killers. He is a good shot-blocker, though he could still use some improvement. When he goes down and fails to block a shot, he does little more than screen his goalie with his burly body.

A Daneyko rush is a rare thing. He's smart enough to recognize his limitations and he seldom joins the play or gets involved deep in the attacking zone. His offensive involvement is usually limited to a smart, safe breakout pass.

Although not a fast skater, Daneyko is fairly agile for his size in tight quarters.

THE PHYSICAL GAME

Daneyko is very powerful, with great upper and lower body strength. His legs give him drive when he's moving opposing forwards out from around the net. He is a punishing hitter, and when he makes a take-out hit, the opponent stays out of the play. He is smart enough not to get beaten by superior skaters and will

force an attacker to the perimeter. He has cut down on his bad penalties; emotions still sometimes get the better of him, but he will usually get his two or five minutes' worth.

Daneyko is a very good fighter, a player few are willing to tangle with, and he has to prove himself less frequently these days. If somebody wants a scrap, though, he's willing and extremely able, and he stands up for his teammates. It helps that players such as Randy McKay and Mike Peluso are on hand, and Daneyko can spend more time on the ice than in the box.

THE INTANGIBLES

Last year's injury, which forced him to miss half of the lockout-shortened season, was an aberration for the remarkably durable Daneyko, and there is still a slight chance his injured knee may require off-season surgery.

He is one of the Devils' most consistent defensemen; his leadership on and off the ice has become even more apparent. He will speak up in the dressing room to quell teammates' arguments, and a coach never has to worry about Daneyko being "up" for a game. Off nights are rare, because he knows his limitations and plays well within the boundaries.

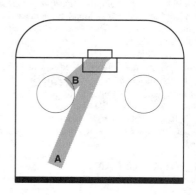

BRUCE DRIVER

Yrs. of NHL service: 11
Born: Toronto, Ont.; Apr. 29, 1962
Position: left defense
Height: 6-0
Weight: 185
Uniform no.: 23
Shoots: left

Career statistics:

GP	G	A	TP	PIM
702	26	316	399	534

1991-92 statistics:

GP	G	A	TP	+/-	PIM	PP	SH	GW	GT	S	PCT
78	7	35	42	+5	66	3	1	1	0	205	3.4

1992-93 statistics:

GP	G	A	TP	+/-	PIM	PP	SH	GW	GT	S	PCT
83	14	40	54	-10	66	6	0	0	0	177	7.9

1993-94 statistics:

GP	G	A	TP	+/-	PIM	PP	SH	GW	GT	S	PCT
66	8	24	32	+29	63	3	1	0	1	109	7.3

1994-95 statistics:

GP	G	A	TP	+/-	PIM	PP	SH	GW	GT	S	PCT
41	4	12	16	-1	18	1	0	1	0	62	6.5

LAST SEASON

Missed three games with a shoulder injury. Missed one game with a stiff neck.

THE FINESSE GAME

Driver's game is based in his feet and in his helmet. He's a fluid skater, with secure strides and quick acceleration. He is hardly greased lightning, but he can get the jump on faster skaters with his mobility, and he's very good moving laterally and backwards.

Driver sees the ice well offensively and defensively and can kill penalties or work on the power play. He has a nice wrist shot, which he uses when he cheats into the right circle, but his point shot is a waste. Despite his skills, Driver is a poor choice to use high on the power play. He would be much better posted low, using his one-timer, but the Devils play a static, stand-around style on their power play. If they ever got into moving and weaving, Driver would excel. He knows when to time a rush or pinch and seldom makes poor choices on the attack.

He has very good hand skills for passing, receiving a pass or carrying the puck, and he is an above-average playmaker.

THE PHYSICAL GAME

Driver does not play a hitting game. He lacks the size, strength and temperament for it. He plays defense by body position and containment, trying to occupy as much good ice space as possible by his positioning against the rush, and then using his poke-check to try to knock the puck free. With his good finesse kills, he can easily mount a countering rush.

He fails in the one-on-one battles in the trenches, simply outmuscled along the boards and in front of the net. With the NHL trend towards power forwards like Eric Lindros and Trevor Linden, this makes the weak link in Driver's game more of a detriment, since he does not have the high-scoring numbers to offset it.

THE INTANGIBLES

Driver had to use an even more restrictive shoulder harness following his return from injury, and underwent off-season shoulder surgery. He is a smart player, but at 33 is starting on the downside and will become less and less of a factor in the team's top six, especially since there are a number of young defensemen (notably Kevin Dean, who plays a similar game) who will be looking to graduate this season. Driver was a free agent without compensation, and lots of other teams will be interested in his expertise if the Devils are not.

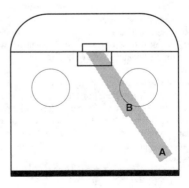

BILL GUERIN

Yrs. of NHL service: 3
Born: Wilbraham, Mass.; Nov. 9, 1970
Position: right wing
Height: 6-2
Weight: 190
Uniform no.: 12
Shoots: right

Career statistics:

GP	G	A	TP	PIM
199	51	53	104	245

1991-92 statistics:

GP	G	A	TP	+/-	PIM	PP	SH	GW	GT	S	PCT
5	0	1	1	0	9	0	0	0	0	8	0.00

1992-93 statistics:

GP	G	A	TP	+/-	PIM	PP	SH	GW	GT	S	PCT
65	14	20	34	+14	63	0	0	2	0	123	11.4

1993-94 statistics:

GP	G	A	TP	+/-	PIM	PP	SH	GW	GT	S	PCT
81	25	19	44	+14	101	2	0	3	0	195	12.8

1994-95 statistics:

GP	G	A	TP	+/-	PIM	PP	SH	GW	GT	S	PCT
48	12	13	25	+6	72	4	0	3	0	96	12.5

LAST SEASON

Tied for team lead in game-winning goals. One of five Devils to appear in all 48 games. Fourth on team in points.

THE FINESSE GAME

Guerin may be on the verge of becoming one of the league's top power forwards, but he has to add a few elements to his game first. He has a terrifying slap shot, a wicked screamer that he unleashes off the wing in full flight. But like a young pitcher who lives off his fastball, Guerin must master the change-up. There are times when a snap or wrist shot is the better choice, especially when he is set up for a one-timer.

Combined with Guerin's powerful skating, his shot becomes even more of a potent weapon. He puts on a strong burst of speed and has good balance and agility. He is an excellent passer who leads the man well. He does not telegraph his passes, but frankly, with his shot, he should be more selfish and skip the passes. There are times when Guerin hesitates, holds up and waits for help, instead of trying to drive wide on the defender. For some reason, Guerin tended to drive wide left instead of right often last season, which put him on his backhand and rendered him essentially useless.

Hockey sense and creativity are lagging a tad behind his other attributes, but Guerin is a smart and conscientious player, and those qualities will develop. He is aware defensively and has worked hard at learning that part of the game, although he will still lose his checking assignments and start running around in the defensive zone.

THE PHYSICAL GAME

The more physical the game is, the more Guerin gets involved. He is big, strong and tough in every sense of the word. He can play it clean or mean, with big body checks or the drop of a glove. He will move to the puck carrier and battle for control until he gets it, and he's hard to knock off his skates.

In front of the net, Guerin is at his best. He works to establish position and has the hand skills to make something happen with the puck when it gets to his stick.

THE INTANGIBLES

Guerin was a mystery last season, and his erratic play was tied to his insecurity. Guerin played out his option, and isn't the kind of player with enough confidence to produce under that kind of pressure. After a strong playoffs for the Stanley Cup champions, Guerin should be amply rewarded and content, and we expect a 30-goal season.

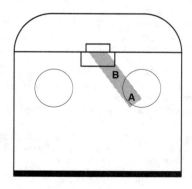

BOBBY HOLIK

Yrs. of NHL service: 5
Born: Jihlava, Czechoslovakia; Jan. 1, 1971
Position: centre
Height: 6-3
Weight: 210
Uniform no.: 16
Shoots: right

Career statistics:

GP	G	A	TP	PIM
333	85	95	180	323

1991-92 statistics:

GP	G	A	TP	+/-	PIM	PP	SH	GW	GT	S	PCT
76	21	24	45	+4	44	1	0	2	1	207	10.1

1992-93 statistics:

GP	G	A	TP	+/-	PIM	PP	SH	GW	GT	S	PCT
61	20	19	39	-6	76	7	0	4	0	180	11.1

1993-94 statistics:

GP	G	A	TP	+/-	PIM	PP	SH	GW	GT	S	PCT
70	13	20	33	+28	72	2	0	3	0	130	10.0

1994-95 statistics:

GP	G	A	TP	+/-	PIM	PP	SH	GW	GT	S	PCT
48	10	10	20	+9	18	0	0	2	0	84	11.9

LAST SEASON

One of five Devils to appear in all 48 games.

THE FINESSE GAME

Holik centred the most effective fourth line in the NHL last season, the "Crash Line," and the trio helped the Devils win the Stanley Cup. They were a classic example of the total being greater than the sum of its parts, because taken individually, Holik, Randy McKay and Mike Peluso are players of modest, even below-average ability. Together, they held their own against the top lines in the East.

Holik is a far more effective player with his two usual mates. Put him with anyone else on the team and his power and usefulness are diminished. While he is a strong skater with some passing skills and a hard, if often inaccurate, shot, he suffers from severe tunnel vision.

Holik has a terrific shot, a bullet drive that he gets away quickly from a rush down the left side. He also has the great hands to work in tight, in traffic and off the backhand. On the backhand (at which Europeans are so much more adept than North Americans), Holik uses his great bulk to obscure the vision of his defenders, protecting the puck and masking his intentions. He has a fair wrist shot.

Playing centre (Holik played the position almost exclusively last season after spins on the wing the previous few years) gets Holik more consistently involved. While he lacks the creativity to be a truly effective centre, he brings other assets to the table. He crashes the net, and while the Devils are known as the leading practitioners of the neutral zone trap, their Crash Line was actually a powerful fore-checking force.

Although he's a powerful skater with good balance, Holik lacks jump and agility. Once he starts churning, he can get up a good head of steam, but he can be caught out of position if his team loses the puck and the opposition breaks back the other way. He often loses his man defensively and he leaves the defensive zone too quickly, although he paid more attention defensively last season.

THE PHYSICAL GAME

Holik is just plain big, and his linemates have helped light a fire in him that brings out his best on a nightly basis. Never given much credit for being an intelligent player, he has adapted to the defensive style of the Devils and is reliable to the point that Jacques Lemaire is never afraid to throw his fourth line out on the ice in the most crucial situations.

Holik is a serious hitter and applies his bone-jarring body checks at the appropriate times. He takes few bad penalties.

THE INTANGIBLES

Holik will never develop into the kind of power forward the Hartford Whalers envisioned when they made him a first-round pick in 1989, but by earning his Cup ring as a key member of the Devils, he has reached the pinnacle of his style. He now takes great pride in what he can accomplish. He was one of the most consistent players on the team all season.

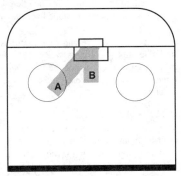

CLAUDE LEMIEUX

Yrs. of NHL service: 9
Born: Buckingham, Que.; July 16, 1965
Position: right wing
Height: 6-1
Weight: 215
Uniform no.: 22
Shoots: right

Career statistics:

GP	G	A	TP	PIM
636	222	226	448	1117

1991-92 statistics:

GP	G	A	TP	+/-	PIM	PP	SH	GW	GT	S	PCT
74	41	27	68	+9	109	13	1	8	3	296	13.9

1992-93 statistics:

GP	G	A	TP	+/-	PIM	PP	SH	GW	GT	S	PCT
77	30	51	81	+2	155	13	0	3	2	311	9.6

1993-94 statistics:

GP	G	A	TP	+/-	PIM	PP	SH	GW	GT	S	PCT
79	18	26	44	+13	86	5	0	5	0	181	9.9

1994-95 statistics:

GP	G	A	TP	+/-	PIM	PP	SH	GW	GT	S	PCT
45	6	13	19	+2	86	1	0	1	0	117	5.1

LAST SEASON

Missed three games with suspension. Won 1995 Conn Smythe Trophy.

THE FINESSE GAME

So selfish that his teammates have called him Claude "Le Me," Lemieux sacrificed egotistical style in the playoffs to become the ultimate team man — and was rewarded with the ultimate personal triumph.

Lemieux was asked to shadow Cam Neely at the start of the playoffs, but ended up emerging from the shadow into the spotlight. Increased ice time, plus the awareness that a defensive role can be parlayed into offensive opportunities, turned Lemieux into an unstoppable force in the post-season, where he scored more than twice as many goals as he did during the regular season.

Lemieux is a shooter, a disturber, a force. He loves the puck, wants the puck, needs the puck and is sometimes obsessed with the puck. When he is struggling, that selfishness hurts the team. But when he gets into his groove everyone is happy to stand back and let him fly.

When Lemieux is on, he can rock the house. He has a hard slap shot and shoots well off the fly. He isn't afraid to go to the front of the net for tips and screens and will battle for loose pucks. He has great hands for close-in shots.

THE PHYSICAL GAME

Lemieux is strong, with good skating balance and great upper body and arm strength. He is very tough along the boards and in traffic in front of the net, outduelling many bigger opponents because of his fierce desire. Because he is always whining and yapping, the abuse Lemieux takes is often ignored, but it's not unusual to find him with welts across his arms and cuts on his face. The satisfaction comes from knowing that his opponent usually looks even worse, but he still takes dumb penalties by jawing at the referees, who have little patience with him after all these years.

THE INTANGIBLES

Opponents hate Lemieux. Sometimes, his teammates do, too, but not last season. He was able to put an acrimonious divorce, a dressing room battle with team captain Scott Stevens, a public trade request and a poor regular season behind him to emerge as one of the team's key performers.

Lemieux was a different player in the playoffs for two reasons: One, Lemieux is "Monsieur Printemps," and Mr. Spring knows that the playoffs are more important that the regular season. Two, he was rewarded with a new $1.3-million, four-year contract just prior to the start of the playoffs, and with Lemieux, you get what you pay for.

You might not take this Jersey winger in your regular-season hockey pool, but don't skip over him in the playoffs.

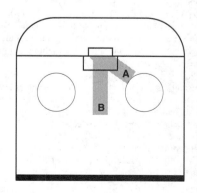

JOHN MACLEAN

Yrs. of NHL service: 11
Born: Oshawa, Ont.; Nov. 20, 1964
Position: right wing
Height: 6-0
Weight: 200
Uniform no.: 15
Shoots: right

Career statistics

GP	G	A	TP	PIM
706	278	281	559	982

1991-92 statistics

Did not play in NHL

1992-93 statistics:

GP	G	A	TP	+/-	PIM	PP	SH	GW	GT	S	PCT
80	24	24	48	-6	102	7	1	3	0	195	12.3

1993-94 statistics:

GP	G	A	TP	+/-	PIM	PP	SH	GW	GT	S	PCT
80	37	33	70	+30	95	8	0	4	0	277	13.4

1994-95 statistics:

GP	G	A	TP	+/-	PIM	PP	SH	GW	GT	S	PCT
46	17	12	29	+13	32	2	1	0	0	139	12.2

LAST SEASON

Led team in shots. Second on team in goals and third on points. Led forwards and second on team in plus-minus. Missed one game with a bruised foot.

THE FINESSE GAME

There is no such thing as an impossible angle for MacLean. He will shoot anytime, from anywhere on the ice, and will usually put the puck on net or out into traffic in front of the crease where there is always a chance the puck will hit someone or something and go skittering into the net. So what if all of his scoring chances are no longer the briliiant highlight shots that characterized his pre-surgery (1991) career? His pure goal-scoring instincts still make MacLean a threat.

The reconstructive knee surgery, however, has forced MacLean to become another kind of player from the 50-goal scorer he was once targeted to be. Former Devils coach Herb Brooks used penalty-killing stints to help MacLean rehabilitate his knee, and darned if MacLean didn't turn into one of the team's most determined penalty-killers. He attacks the points fearlessly and anticipates passes well.

Last season, MacLean put even more emphasis on his defensive play. If he weren't such a slow skater, he would get checking assignments against top NHL wingers, but MacLean can't keep up with the league's better wheels. Somehow, though, he churns and manages to get where he has to go.

Slow in open ice but strong along the boards and in the corners, he chugs and churns, and by keeping his feet in motion he draws restraining fouls.

THE PHYSICAL GAME

Careful attention to his knee has forced MacLean to stick to a strict training regimen. He tends to wear down late in a season, however, and in future yars may have to be given the occasional night off just to recharge his batteries.

MacLean uses a wide-based skating stance and is tough to budge from the front of the net. He will take a lot of abuse to get the job done in traffic, and will not be intimidated. He has cut down on his retaliatory penalties. He is extremely competitive.

THE INTANGIBLES

MacLean's was one of the more remarkable come-backs from major knee surgery. Many athletes are never the same, not because of the physical changes, but because they are fearful of another injury to the same area. MacLean's mental toughness overcame that obstacle. His big-number days are over as he has become more of a two-way forward, but he can still kick in 25 goals a season and is a strong presence in the dressing room.

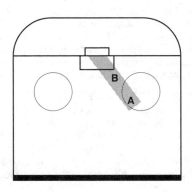

RANDY MCKAY

Yrs. of NHL service: 6
Born: Montreal, Que.; Jan. 25, 1967
Position: right wing
Height: 6-1
Weight: 185
Uniform no.: 21
Shoots: right

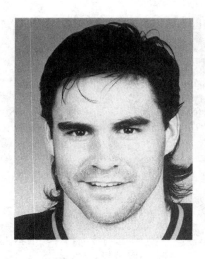

Career statistics:

GP	G	A	TP	PIM
347	49	62	111	974

1991-92 statistics:

GP	G	A	TP	+/-	PIM	PP	SH	GW	GT	S	PCT
80	17	16	33	+6	246	2	0	1	0	111	15.3

1992-93 statistics:

GP	G	A	TP	+/-	PIM	PP	SH	GW	GT	S	PCT
73	11	11	22	0	206	1	0	2	0	94	11.7

1993-94 statistics:

GP	G	A	TP	+/-	PIM	PP	SH	GW	GT	S	PCT
78	12	15	27	+24	244	0	0	1	1	77	15.6

1994-95 statistics:

GP	G	A	TP	+/-	PIM	PP	SH	GW	GT	S	PCT
33	5	7	12	+10	44	0	0	0	0	44	11.4

LAST SEASON
Missed 15 games with groin injuries.

THE FINESSE GAME
Calling McKay the best fourth-line right wing in the NHL might be considered a backhanded compliment, but not when a player has a backhand shot like McKay's. More than once last season McKay beat a defender one-on-one by setting his skates wide, dangling the puck, then drawing it through the defenseman's legs and blowing past him for a shot — and often a goal.

So much for the old goon reputation. That vanished with a key overtime goal against Boston in the first round of the playoffs, and continued as McKay was given time up front on the Devils' power play, which was almost twice as effective in the post-season as the regular season, thanks largely to McKay's screening work.

As part of the Devils' popular and hugely effective "Crash Line," (with Mike Peluso and Bobby Holik), McKay helped wake up the Devils on some of their doleful regular-season nights. McKay never cruises through a game. His reputation earns him extra ice and extra time, and he makes use of both. He has worked hard to improve his shooting and passing skills.

THE PHYSICAL GAME
McKay is an absolutely ferocious fighter. He is a legitimate heavyweight who is among the first to step in to protect a teammate, yet he won't initiate with cheap nonsense. He does everything with intensity, whether it's a body check or bulling his way to the front of the net. He is astoundingly strong on his skates, tough to knock down and nearly impossible to knock out.

THE INTANGIBLES
McKay makes everyone around him braver. He will leap to the defense of a teammate, yet he seldom gets involved in histrionics. He picks his spots and doesn't hurt his team by being selfish. Throw in 10-15 goals and he is invaluable. Coaches never have to worry about McKay being up for a game.

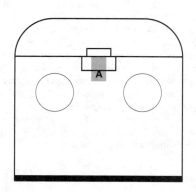

SCOTT NIEDERMAYER

Yrs. of NHL service: 3
Born: Edmonton, Alta.; Aug. 31, 1973
Position: right defense
Height: 6-0
Weight: 200
Uniform no.: 27
Shoots: left

Career statistics:

GP	G	A	TP	PIM
213	25	81	106	109

1991-92 statistics:

GP	G	A	TP	+/-	PIM	PP	SH	GW	GT	S	PCT
4	0	1	1	+1	2	0	0	0	0	4	0.0

1992-93 statistics:

GP	G	A	TP	+/-	PIM	PP	SH	GW	GT	S	PCT
80	11	29	40	+8	47	5	0	0	1	131	8.4

1993-94 statistics:

GP	G	A	TP	+/-	PIM	PP	SH	GW	GT	S	PCT
81	10	36	46	+34	42	5	0	2	1	135	7.4

1994-95 statistics:

GP	G	A	TP	+/-	PIM	PP	SH	GW	GT	S	PCT
48	4	15	19	+19	18	4	0	0	0	52	7.7

LAST SEASON

Led team in plus-minus. Tied for team lead in power play goals. One of five Devils to appear in all 48 games.

THE FINESSE GAME

Niedermayer has often been compared to Paul Coffey because of his phenomenal skating, but the comparison is not really apt. Niedermayer will never be the offensive force that Coffey is (even though he outplayed Coffey one-on-one for a memorable goal in the 1995 Stanley Cup Final). But Niedermayer is a better defensive player than Coffey is, or ever was.

Niedermayer carries the puck well on the rush, but is still learning to create great offensive chances by using his speed in the attacking zone. No doubt much of his caution stems from the Devils' conservative style, but the common cry coming from the ice now is "Go Nieds, go!" as his teammates exhort him to motor. He needs little urging.

There are few defensemen who are able to control the flow of a game with puck control. Brian Leetch is tops in the game right now, but Niedermayer may be his successor.

The 22-year-old is an exceptional skater, one of the best-skating defensemen in the NHL. Niedermayer has it all: speed, balance, agility, mobility, lateral movement and strength. He has unbelievable edge for turns and eluding pursuers. Even when he makes a commitment mistake in the offensive zone, he can get back so quickly his defense partner is seldom outnumbered.

Niedermayer has great confidence in his puck-carrying ability and can lead a rush or join the attack and come in for a late one-timer. He can make a soft lead pass or a firm, crisp one, and he always sees his options well. He has a good, low point shot that he gets away quickly, and he will develop into a first-rate point man.

THE PHYSICAL GAME

An underrated body checker because of the focus on the glitzier parts of his game, Niedermayer has continued to improve his strength and is a willing if not vicious hitter. His skating ability helps him tremendously, giving more impetus to his open-ice checks. He will sacrifice his body to block shots.

THE INTANGIBLES

Niedermayer had a coming out party in the Stanley Cup playoffs. His play seemed to improve once he was paired with a less experienced defenseman (Kevin Dean) after Bruce Driver was injured. Niedermayer became the leader, and continued that role even after Driver's return.

On a less defensive-minded team, Niedermayer would probably net 70 points, but whether he likes it or not, his two-year tutelage under Jacques Lemaire will end up making him a superior all-around defenseman than if he had just been allowed to roam at will in his first few NHL seasons.

Niedermayer earned $275,000 last season. As a Group Two free agent, his price tag will be driven higher by off-season offers, which the Devils retain the right to match.

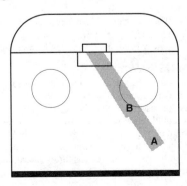

MIKE PELUSO

Yrs. of NHL service: 5
Born: Pengilly, Minn.; Nov. 8, 1965
Position: left wing
Height: 6-4
Weight: 200
Uniform no.: 8
Shoots: left

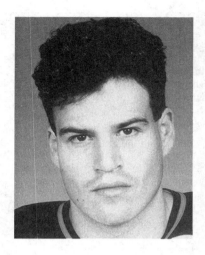

Career statistics:

GP	G	A	TP	PIM
314	33	39	72	1451

1991-92 statistics:

GP	G	A	TP	+/-	PIM	PP	SH	GW	GT	S	PCT
63	6	3	9	+1	408	2	0	0	0	32	18.8

1992-93 statistics:

GP	G	A	TP	+/-	PIM	PP	SH	GW	GT	S	PCT
81	15	10	25	-35	318	2	0	1	0	93	16.1

1993-94 statistics:

GP	G	A	TP	+/-	PIM	PP	SH	GW	GT	S	PCT
69	4	16	20	+19	238	0	0	0	0	44	9.1

1994-95 statistics:

GP	G	A	TP	+/-	PIM	PP	SH	GW	GT	S	PCT
46	2	9	11	+5	167	0	0	1	0	27	7.4

LAST SEASON
Led team in PIM.

THE FINESSE GAME
Peluso has enough straightaway speed to get in on top of a defenseman, and seeing a player of his size rocketing in can force many a panicky pass. He can't do much with the puck, however, so any scoring chances result off a fore-check and a scramble around the net. He gets so much room in front that he will get two or three swats at the puck when most forwards would get only one.

His balance isn't very good, though, and this prevents him from standing in front of the goal as well as he should. He can be tipped over by smaller players. If he learns better technique, he could add five to 10 goals a season just by screening in front and letting pucks plunk in off his massive body, especially on the power play. However, the Devils show no inclination to use him in this role, probably because his skating is a detriment.

His offensive skills are below average. He doesn't have good hands for shooting or passing, and he doesn't know when to move the puck hard or soft.

THE PHYSICAL GAME
Peluso is a mean son-of-a-gun, but showed in the playoffs that he can back off if it means avoiding a penalty for his team. Who would have thought that Peluso could show such restraint? Peluso and his "Crash Line" mates, Bobby Holik and Randy McKay, create a stir with their tenacious fore-checking. No need to throw fists when you can throw checks and get the opponents to cough up loose pucks.

THE INTANGIBLES
Peluso is an intense player who makes opponents leery because they never know when he'll go off. Frankly, he's scary. He is usually the first player at the rink — sometimes three or four hours before face-off — and is fanatical in his approach to conditioning. He will never be more than a fourth-line player, but he is health insurance for a team's skilled players.

But even tough guys have their soft side. The most indelible image from the Devils' Stanley Cup win was the sight of a weeping Peluso on the bench, too overcome with emotion to complete his last shift in the game. But we wouldn't tease him about it.

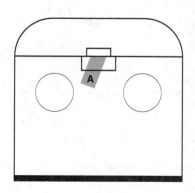

STEPHANE RICHER

Yrs. of NHL service: 10
Born: Ripon, Que.; June 7, 1966
Position: right wing
Height: 6-2
Weight: 200
Uniform no.: 44
Shoots: right

Career statistics:

GP	G	A	TP	PIM
690	324	290	614	457

1991-92 statistics

GP	G	A	TP	+/-	PIM	PP	SH	GW	GT	S	PCT
74	29	35	64	-1	25	5	1	6	1	240	12.1

1992-93 statistics:

GP	G	A	TP	+/-	PIM	PP	SH	GW	GT	S	PCT
78	38	35	73	-1	44	7	1	7	1	286	13.3

1993-94 statistics:

GP	G	A	TP	+/-	PIM	PP	SH	GW	GT	S	PCT
80	36	36	72	+31	16	7	3	9	3	217	16.6

1994-95 statistics:

GP	G	A	TP	+/-	PIM	PP	SH	GW	GT	S	PCT
45	23	16	39	+8	10	1	2	5	1	133	17.3

LAST SEASON

Led team in goals, points, shorthanded goals, game-winning goals, and shooting percentage. Missed three games with a groin injury.

THE FINESSE GAME

Richer remains one of the league's more intriguing, enigmatic performers. His days as a 50-goal scorer are behind him, but the combination of size, speed and shot make him the most dangerous player on the ice on any given night. Coaches simply don't know what night that will be.

Richer gets great drive from his legs. He has powerful acceleration and true rink-length speed. He can intimidate with his rush, opening up the ice for himself and his linemates. He can also be crafty, slipping in and out of the open ice. He has very good vision offensively and keen hockey sense.

He possesses a true goal-scorer's slap shot, a wicked blur that he loves to fire from the tops of the circles. He has even improved on it. Teeing up a shot used to be a laborious process for Richer, but now he has a hair-trigger release. When the shot isn't there, he will wisely opt for a pass.

A player with Richer's abilities should be more successful on the power play, but he has not hit double figures in four seasons, and that is a genuine puzzle. Richer saw extensive time killing penalties, an indication that he is becoming a better all-around player, and he saw duty in the playoffs as a right wing on the checking line. Because he is so strong on his stick and has a long reach, he can strip an opponent of the puck when his body isn't even close, and the puck carrier is always surprised.

Richer complained publicly about his lack of playing time on the power play (for a team that had one of the worst power plays in the league), but it wasn't until late in the season that he saw any time with the man advantage.

Evidence of Richer's ability to score big goals is his total of five game-winners. Of those, three were scored in the third period and one in overtime. He is one of the great clutch scorers in playoff history.

THE PHYSICAL GAME

Richer is much better in open ice than in traffic. Although he has the size, strength and balance for trench warfare, he doesn't always show the inclination. He will go to the net with the puck, though, and has a wonderful long reach that allows him to be checked and still whip off a strong shot on net. When Richer is determined, it is just about impossible to peel him off the puck. He is slow to rile and seldom takes bad penalties.

THE INTANGIBLES

Even before the season opened, Richer was making headlines. As the three-month hockey lockout dragged on, Richer spoke out and said his union brethren would vote to start playing again. This did not sit well with the leaders of the rank and file, and once NHL play did resume, there was speculation Richer would be the victim of player backlash. However, there was no retribution, and he enjoyed a fine regular season.

Prior to the playoffs, Richer became embroiled in controversy again when a dispute with two coaches made headlines on the eve of the playoffs; Richer was quoted as saying that he was not enthusiastic about the post-season. He responded with an excellent playoffs, despite a slight back injury. He has always been a player who speaks before he thinks, and controvsery will continue to follow him. As long as he maintains his standard of play, who cares? Richer is developing into a solid two-way forward and is the closest thing the Devils have to a game-breaker.

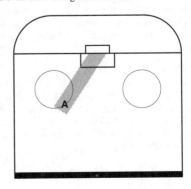

BRIAN ROLSTON

Yrs. of NHL service: 1
Born: Flint, Mich.; Feb. 21, 1973
Position: centre/left wing
Height: 6-2
Weight: 185
Uniform no.: 14
Shoots: left

Career statistics:

GP	G	A	TP	PIM
40	7	11	18	17

1994-95 statistics:

GP	G	A	TP	+/-	PIM	PP	SH	GW	GT	S	PCT
40	7	11	18	+5	17	2	0	3	0	92	7.6

LAST SEASON

First NHL season. Tied for first among rookies in game-winning goals.

THE FINESSE GAME

Rolston's game is speed. He is a fast, powerful skater who drives to the net and loves to shoot. He played centre most of his collegiate career, but the Devils broke him in at left wing at the NHL level so he wouldn't have to concern himself with the additional duties of a pivotman. The tactic worked as Rolston relaxed into his role.

Rolston passes well forehand and backhand, and reads breakout plays by leading his man smartly. He's better as a shooter, though. He has a cannon shot from the top of the circles in with a quick release. He tends to hurry his shots, even when he has time to wait, but that may improve as he becomes more comfortable. His anticipation is excellent, and so is his attitude. No one has to worry about Rolston being up for a game.

Consistency was the big question mark about Rolston as he made the jump from college to the pros last season; he answered by being at his best in the big games. He has a history of clutch moments. He scored the NCAA championship goal for Lake Superior State as a freshman, and was one of the top U.S. performers at the 1994 Olympics.

Defensively, Rolston has worked hard to play under the team's defensive system. He will still make mistakes, but his skating helps compensate for some of them.

THE PHYSICAL GAME

Rolston will take a hit to make a play, and he has taken the next step to start initiating to fight for pucks. His lack of toughness and tenacity was a concern, but he has indicated he can't be kicked around. He needs to add more strength for work along the boards if he is going to remain at wing.

THE INTANGIBLES

Rolston stepped in for the injured Valeri Zelepukin and performed well above expectations. Finding a role for him next season will be difficult, but Rolston may just force his way into the lineup. If he gets sufficient ice time, he could start flirting with the 25-goal mark.

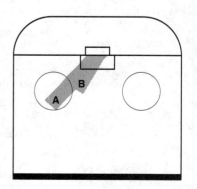

SCOTT STEVENS

Yrs. of NHL service: 13
Born: Kitchener, Ont.; Apr. 11, 1964
Position: left defense
Height: 6-2
Weight: 215
Uniform no.: 4
Shoots: left

Career statistics:

GP	G	A	TP	PIM
959	152	542	694	2190

1991-92 statistics:

GP	G	A	TP	+/-	PIM	PP	SH	GW	GT	S	PCT
68	17	42	59	+24	124	7	1	2	0	156	10.9

1992-93 statistics:

GP	G	A	TP	+/-	PIM	PP	SH	GW	GT	S	PCT
81	12	45	57	+14	120	8	0	1	0	146	8.2

1993-94 statistics:

GP	G	A	TP	+/-	PIM	PP	SH	GW	GT	S	PCT
83	18	60	78	+53	112	5	1	4	0	215	8.4

1994-95 statistics:

GP	G	A	TP	+/-	PIM	PP	SH	GW	GT	S	PCT
48	2	20	22	+4	56	1	0	1	0	111	1.8

LAST SEASON

Led team defensemen in scoring for second consecutive season. Second on team in assists. One of five Devils to appear in all 48 games.

THE FINESSE GAME

A career year in 1993-94 made Stevens the most attractive free agent in the off-season, and it came as no surprise that the St. Louis Blues tried to get him back in their lineup with a four-year, $17.1-million offer. The Devils matched it to keep him in New Jersey, and that was both a blessing and a curse.

The regular season was a near-disaster for Stevens. He struggled with his game on the ice and battled the media and a teammate or two off the ice. But under the ultimate pressure of the playoffs, he emerged as possibly the club's best player as he led the Devils to the Stanley Cup.

On a nightly basis through the post-season, Stevens was brilliant. He dominated players such as Eric Lindros physically, he terrorized the Red Wings with a jarring hit on Vyachelsav Kozlov, he scored big goals, he made passes under pressure and he refused to be goaded into bad penalties. It was one of the best playoff performances ever by a defensive defenseman.

Stevens has a nice pair of hands for work in close to the net. He usually stays out at the point, and does a fine job by taking something off his drive instead of spraying wild, untippable slap shots.

A very good skater, secure and strong, he is capable both forwards and backwards and has good lateral mobility. He no longer overhandles the puck in the defensive zone, a probable influence of assistant coach Larry Robinson.

Stevens has a tremendous work ethic that more than makes up for some of his shortcomings (and most of those are sins of commission rather than omission). He is a bear on penalty killing because he just won't quit, but sometimes he is unable to make a simple bank off the boards for a clearance and keeps his team pinned in. Stevens is a very good shot blocker.

THE PHYSICAL GAME

The most punishing open-ice hitter in the NHL, Stevens has the skating ability to line up the puck-carrier, and the size and strength to explode on impact. He simply shovels most opponents out from in front of the net and crunches them along the boards.

Stevens fights well when provoked and other teams make a point of trying to lure him into bad penalties. He has matured and is now able to keep a better lid on his temper.

THE INTANGIBLES

Money brings pressure, and Stevens dealt poorly with it at the start of last season. But he rebounded in the playoffs and has earned his Stanley Cup ring. It is a mark of his leadership and character that the Devils had barely finished celebrating their victory when Stevens started talking about a repeat bid. He is a winner.

Although the Devils have the right to match any contract offer Stevens receives, his salary is likely to triple ($3.5 million would be a conservative estimate), and he might be moved to relieve the team's payroll.

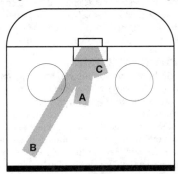

VALERI ZELEPUKIN

Yrs. of NHL service: 4
Born: Voskresensk, Russia; Sept. 17, 1968
Position: left wing
Height: 5-11
Weight: 180
Uniform no.: 25
Shoots: left

Career statistics:

GP	G	A	TP	PIM
208	63	92	155	174

1991-92 statistics:

GP	G	A	TP	+/-	PIM	PP	SH	GW	GT	S	PCT
44	13	18	31	+11	28	3	0	3	0	94	13.8

1992-93 statistics:

GP	G	A	TP	+/-	PIM	PP	SH	GW	GT	S	PCT
78	23	41	64	+19	70	5	1	2	0	174	13.2

1993-94 statistics:

GP	G	A	TP	+/-	PIM	PP	SH	GW	GT	S	PCT
82	26	31	57	+36	70	8	0	0	0	155	16.8

1994-95 statistics:

GP	G	A	TP	+/-	PIM	PP	SH	GW	GT	S	PCT
4	1	2	3	+3	6	0	0	0	0	6	16.7

LAST SEASON

Missed 42 games with an eye injury.

THE FINESSE GAME

Zelepukin was hit in the eye with a teammate's stick just days into the NHL season. His depth perception was affected, and he had to wear a visor that further impaired his vision, especially when the puck was in his feet. But the injury didn't stop Zelepukin from playing his hard-charging game.

He gets his accurate shots from prime scoring areas by working to get into those zones. He is still a bit too unselfish, and on odd-man rushes the defenders can always guess pass. Zelepukin has a shot worth using. He has very strong wrists and with his constant motion is almost always in a high percentage position. He has a good one-timer. He also has great hands for finding the puck in skates along the boards or in the crease.

Zelepukin is not straightaway fast, but he has good one-step quickness. He is strong and balanced on his skates and he thinks creatively in getting involved in the rush. He reads plays well and is a sound defensive player, but he is not used to killing penalties.

THE PHYSICAL GAME

Zelepukin heads into high-traffic areas, jumping in and out of holes and getting worked over fiercely by opponents. Some Russian players claim that North American referees have a bias against them and do not call penalties with the same consistency as when an American or Canadian player is fouled. Regardless of the reason, Zelepukin seems to always take high sticks and slashes, with rarely a power play to show for it.

THE INTANGIBLES

Zelepukin has to prove he is all the way back from his injury. His conditioning was obviously affected by the time he had to spend off the ice, but he missed few playoff games. He complements Bill Guerin well, and that line (with Jim Dowd or Sergei Brylin at centre) made key contributions during the Devils' Stanley Cup run.

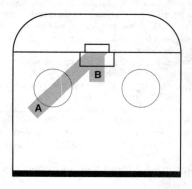

NEW YORK ISLANDERS

Players' Statistics 1994-95

POS	NO.	PLAYER	GP	G	A	PTS	+/-	PIM	PP	SH	GW	GT	S	PCTG
C	20	RAY FERRARO	47	22	21	43	1	30	2		1	2	94	23.4
D	72	MATHIEU SCHNEIDER	43	8	21	29	-8	79	3		2		118	6.8
L	9	KIRK MULLER	45	11	16	27	-18	47	4	1	2	1	97	11.3
R	26	PATRICK FLATLEY	45	7	20	27	9	12	1		1		81	8.6
L	32	STEVE THOMAS	47	11	15	26	-14	60	3		2		133	8.3
L	27	DEREK KING	43	10	16	26	-5	41	7				118	8.5
L	68	*ZIGMUND PALFFY	33	10	7	17	3	6	1		1		75	13.3
C	18	MARTY MCINNIS	41	9	7	16	-1	8			1		68	13.2
D	7	SCOTT LACHANCE	26	6	7	13	2	26	3				56	10.7
C	39	TRAVIS GREEN	42	5	7	12	-10	25					59	8.5
D	37	DENNIS VASKE	41	1	11	12	3	53					48	2.1
D	2	BOB BEERS	22	2	7	9	-8	6	1				38	5.3
D	24	BRENT SEVERYN	28	2	4	6	-2	71	1				32	6.3
R	15	BRAD DALGARNO	22	3	2	5	-8	14	1	1		1	18	16.7
C	17	*CHRIS MARINUCCI	12	1	4	5	-1	2					11	9.1
C	14	RON SUTTER	27	1	4	5	-8	21			1		29	3.4
R	75	*BRETT LINDROS	33	1	3	4	-8	100			1		35	2.9
D	6	CHRIS LUONGO	47	1	3	4	-2	36					44	2.3
D	25	PAUL STANTON	18		4	4	-6	9					28	
C	28	*CHRIS TAYLOR	10		3	3	1	2					13	
L	34	*YAN KAMINSKY	2	1	1	2	2						4	25.0
D	47	RICHARD PILON	20	1	1	2	-3	40					11	9.1
C	10	*CRAIG DARBY	13		2	2	-6						5	
D	3	DEAN CHYNOWETH	32		2	2	9	77					22	
R	12	MICK VUKOTA	40		2	2	1	109					11	
G	35	*TOMMY SALO	6		1	1								
C	10	KIP MILLER	8		1	1	1						11	
D	11	DARIUS KASPARAITIS	13		1	1	-11	22					8	
D	36	*JASON WIDMER	1				-1							
D	34	*MILAN TICHY	2				-1	2					1	
L	38	*ANDREI VASILIEV	2					2					2	
D	8	GORD DINEEN	9				-5	2					4	
L	9	DAVE CHYZOWSKI	13				-2	11					11	
G	29	*JAMIE MCLENNAN	21					2						
G	30	TOMMY SODERSTROM	26					2						

GP = games played; G = goals; A = assists; PTS = points; +/- = goals-for minus goals-against while player is on ice; PIM = penalties in minutes; PP = power play goals; SH = shorthanded goals; GW = game-winning goals; GT = game-tying goals; S = no. of shots; PCTG = percentage of goals to shots; * = rookie

TODD BERTUZZI

Yrs. of NHL service: 0
Born: Sudbury, Ont.; Feb. 2, 1975
Position: centre
Height: 6-3
Weight: 227
Uniform no.: n.a.
Shoots: left

1994-95 junior statistics:

GP	G	A	TP	PIM
62	54	65	119	58

LAST SEASON

Will be entering first NHL season. Second in scoring for Guelph (OHL).

THE FINESSE GAME

Bertuzzi has good size and uses it to get to the net. He is quick for his size and mobile, and he's got a good, soft pair of hands to complement his skating.

He is effective in the slot area, but he is also creative with the puck and can make some plays. He can find people down low and make things happen on the power play. He is not used to killing penalties.

Bertuzzi can play the off wing as well as centre. He is a smart player and does not take stupid penalties.

THE PHYSICAL GAME

Bertuzzi made a gigantic leap in his last year of junior, but now he will be a boy among men. In junior he was able to pick up the puck in his own end and bull his way down the ice. He won't be able to do that against the league's big defensemen.

Bertuzzi is strong but not mean. He will battle for space, but he's not going to be a tough, aggressive player. He is chippy and retaliatory, but does not establish his space.

THE INTANGIBLES

Bertuzzi is a leader, though he didn't wear a letter on his jersey in junior. That doesn't mean he won't in the NHL.

He is a gifted, elite player for his age. He may be ready to step into NHL right away. Some believe he could become a Mikael Renberg within a year or two.

Bertuzzi had a reputation as "not being committed to winning," but when the game was on the line in junior, he was the one who stepped up and did something. He had a tough year personally: his father was involved in a serious auto accident, from which he recovered.

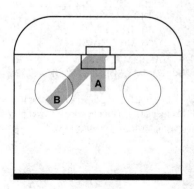

PATRICK FLATLEY

Yrs. of NHL service: 12
Born: Toronto, Ont.; Oct. 3, 1963
Position: right wing
Height: 6-2
Weight: 195
Uniform no.: 26
Shoots: right

Career statistics:

GP	G	A	TP	PIM
665	152	319	471	639

1991-92 statistics:

GP	G	A	TP	+/-	PIM	PP	SH	GW	GT	S	PCT
38	8	28	36	+14	31	4	1	0	0	76	10.5

1992-93 statistics:

GP	G	A	TP	+/-	PIM	PP	SH	GW	GT	S	PCT
80	13	47	60	+4	63	1	2	1	0	139	9.4

1993-94 statistics:

GP	G	A	TP	+/-	PIM	PP	SH	GW	GT	S	PCT
64	12	30	42	+12	40	2	1	2	0	112	10.7

1994-95 statistics:

GP	G	A	TP	+/-	PIM	PP	SH	GW	GT	S	PCT
45	7	20	27	+9	12	1	0	1	0	81	8.6

LAST SEASON

Led team in plus-minus. Third on team in assists. Fourth on team in points. Missed two games with a hip injury.

THE FINESSE GAME

The sum of Flatley's game is much greater than its parts. Broken down into components, we have a slow skater with average hand skills and a tendency to get damaged. But all assembled, the package is a solid, two-way forward with tremendous heart. Flatley's desire to get the job done helps him find a way from Point A to Point B, even if that means going through a bigger player. He isn't fast in open ice, but he's sneaky-quick in tight.

Flatley is superb along the boards and in the corners. He fights for the puck; when he gets it he protects it with his body until a teammate is in position for a pass. That is one of the reasons why Flatley has been seriously hurt in the past. He will leave himself physically vulnerable in order to make the right play. He will also hurl his body in front of shots. He goes all-out — even in exhibition games.

His scoring touch is minimal. He does seem to score timely goals, and he works with great poise in front of the net whether the game is in the first minute or sudden-death overtime.

THE PHYSICAL GAME

Flatley will bang on every shift. He is gritty and determined. His work ethic dictates that, whatever he has to do to win, he will attempt it, and he's fearless.

THE INTANGIBLES

Flatley is a leader in every sense of the word. He is the team's heart and soul, but injury-free seasons are rare. When he is in the lineup he's the team's stabilizer.

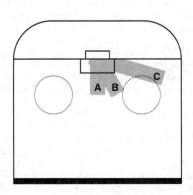

TRAVIS GREEN

Yrs. of NHL service: 3
Born: Creston, B.C.; Dec. 20, 1970
Position: centre
Height: 6-0
Weight: 195
Uniform no.: 39
Shoots: right

Career statistics:

GP	G	A	TP	PIM
186	30	47	77	112

1992-93 statistics:

GP	G	A	TP	+/-	PIM	PP	SH	GW	GT	S	PCT
61	7	18	25	+4	43	1	0	0	0	115	6.1

1993-94 statistics:

GP	G	A	TP	+/-	PIM	PP	SH	GW	GT	S	PCT
83	18	22	40	+16	44	1	0	2	0	164	11.0

1994-95 statistics:

GP	G	A	TP	+/-	PIM	PP	SH	GW	GT	S	PCT
42	5	7	12	-10	25	0	0	0	0	59	8.5

LAST SEASON

Missed six games due to coach's decision.

THE FINESSE GAME

Green has taken some time to develop. A scorer at the minor league and junior level, with a seemingly terminal weakness in his defensive game, he was tutored by an excellent defensive centre in Butch Goring in the AHL and obviously paid attention in class.

Green is now on the ice in the waning seconds of the period or the game to protect a lead. He has worked hard to improve his skating and has better balance and agility, with some quickness, although he lacks straight-ahead speed.

He controls the puck well. He plays more of a finesse game than a power game, and he has to learn to charge the net with more authority. He is an unselfish player and passes equally well to either side. He sees the ice well, but he takes too long to get his shot off and will never score in gobs at the NHL level. When he has room to get a shot away, he has a hard, booming slapper.

Green is the Islanders' top man on draws. He uses his body to tie up an opponent and allow his linemates to skate in for the puck.

THE PHYSICAL GAME

Green has learned to be involved in the play. He's not a huge guy, but he will use his body to get in the way. He is not by nature an intense competitor, but now that he has had his taste of NHL life, it looks as if he wants to work to stay there.

THE INTANGIBLES

We said in last year's HSR that he could score 20 to 25 goals as a two-way forward, and we'll stick to it as long as Green sticks to his game.

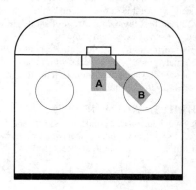

DARIUS KASPARAITIS

Yrs. of NHL service: 3
Born: Elektrenai, Lithuania; Oct. 16, 1972
Position: right defense
Height: 5-11
Weight: 187
Uniform no.: 11
Shoots: left

Career statistics:

GP	G	A	TP	PIM
168	5	28	33	330

1992-93 statistics:

GP	G	A	TP	+/-	PIM	PP	SH	GW	GT	S	PCT
79	4	17	21	+15	166	0	0	0	0	92	4.3

1993-94 statistics:

GP	G	A	TP	+/-	PIM	PP	SH	GW	GT	S	PCT
76	1	10	11	-6	142	0	0	0	0	81	1.2

1994-95 statistics:

GP	G	A	TP	+/-	PIM	PP	SH	GW	GT	S	PCT
13	0	1	1	-11	22	0	0	0	0	8	0.0

LAST SEASON

Missed 35 games with torn anterior cruciate ligament in his right knee and subsequent surgery.

THE FINESSE GAME

Kasparaitis is a strong, powerful skater who can accelerate in all directions. You can run, but you can't hide from this defenseman, who accepts all challenges. He is aggressive in the neutral zone, sometimes overly so, stepping up to break up a team's attack.

He concentrates mainly on his defensive role, but Kasparaitis has the skills to get more involved in the offense. He will make a sharp outlet pass and then follow up into the play. He also has good offensive instincts, moves the puck well and, if he plays on his off side, will open up his forehand for the one-timer.

Kasparaitis has infectious enthusiasm that is an inspiration to the rest of his team. There is a purpose to whatever he does, and he's highly competitive. When he develops more consistency, he may become the team's number one defenseman. His skills are world class. Much will depend on his recovery from the knee injury.

THE PHYSICAL GAME

Kasparaitis is well on his way to succeeding Ulf Samuelsson as the player most of the NHL would like to see run over by a bus. It's always borderline interference with Kasparaitis, who uses his stick liberally, waiting three or four seconds after a victim has gotten rid of the puck to apply the lumber. Cross-check, butt-end, high stick — through the course of a season Kasparaitis will illustrate all of the stick infractions.

His timing isn't always the best, and he has to think about the good of the team rather than indulging his own vendettas.

But Kasparaitis is legitimately tough. It doesn't matter whose name is on back of the jersey — Lemieux, Tocchet, McKay, Messier — he will goad the stars and the heavyweights equally. He yaps, too, and is as irritating as a car alarm at 3 a.m.

THE INTANGIBLES

It was a lost season for Kasparaitis, who went into alcohol rehab prior to last season, then saw his year end prematurely with the knee surgery. Reportedly, new coach Mike Milbury was down on Kasparaitis before the defenseman had played a single game for him, so Kasparaitis may be on the move. There are plenty of teams who would love his toughness and skill. Wherever he starts the season, expect a slow first half until he is back in shape from his knee problem.

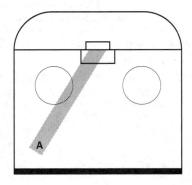

DEREK KING

Yrs. of NHL service: 8
Born: Hamilton, Ont.; Feb. 11, 1967
Position: left wing
Height: 6-1
Weight: 200
Uniform no.: 27
Shoots: left

Career statistics:

GP	G	A	TP	PIM
507	176	238	414	301

1991-92 statistics:

GP	G	A	TP	+/-	PIM	PP	SH	GW	GT	S	PCT
80	40	38	78	-10	46	21	0	6	2	189	21.2

1992-93 statistics:

GP	G	A	TP	+/-	PIM	PP	SH	GW	GT	S	PCT
77	38	38	76	-3	47	21	0	7	0	201	18.9

1993-94 statistics:

GP	G	A	TP	+/-	PIM	PP	SH	GW	GT	S	PCT
78	30	40	70	+18	59	10	0	7	1	171	17.5

1994-95 statistics:

GP	G	A	TP	+/-	PIM	PP	SH	GW	GT	S	PCT
43	10	16	26	-5	41	7	0	0	0	118	8.5

LAST SEASON

Led team in power play goals.

THE FINESSE GAME

King is at his best from the face-off dot of the left circle to the front of the net. He has great concentration through traffic and soft, soft hands for cradling passes and then snapping off the shot the instant the puck hits his blade. He has to play with someone who will get him the puck.

Among the best in the league on the power play, King has good anticipation and reads the offensive plays well. He is not a great skater but has improved his defensive awareness.

THE PHYSICAL GAME

King is a solid and durable player who takes a pounding in front of the net. He doesn't use his body well in other areas of the ice, though, which is one of the reasons for his defensive problems.

He has improved his off-ice habits and his conditioning, a problem in the past. Sometimes it takes time for a young player to realize that playing in the NHL is a job, not just a game.

THE INTANGIBLES

We thought last year that King could bounce back with a 40-goal season, but his prorated total was half that. He is a player who can go either way this season. He needs a playmaking centre to team up with, but the Islanders may not have the ideal mate for him.

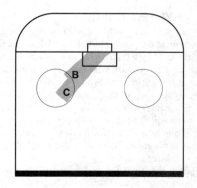

SCOTT LACHANCE

Yrs. of NHL service: 3
Born: Charlottesville, Va.; Oct. 22, 1972
Position: left defense
Height: 6-1
Weight: 197
Uniform no.: 7
Shoots: left

Career statistics:

GP	G	A	TP	PIM
192	17	39	56	172

1991-92 statistics:

GP	G	A	TP	+/-	PIM	PP	SH	GW	GT	S	PCT
17	1	4	5	+13	9	0	0	0	1	20	5.0

1992-93 statistics:

GP	G	A	TP	+/-	PIM	PP	SH	GW	GT	S	PCT
75	7	17	24	-1	67	0	1	2	0	62	11.3

1993-94 statistics:

GP	G	A	TP	+/-	PIM	PP	SH	GW	GT	S	PCT
74	3	11	14	-5	70	0	0	1	0	59	5.1

1994-95 statistics:

GP	G	A	TP	+/-	PIM	PP	SH	GW	GT	S	PCT
26	6	7	13	+2	26	3	0	0	0	56	10.7

LAST SEASON

Second among team defensemen in scoring. Missed 22 games with a broken left ankle.

THE FINESSE GAME

Young, and still learning, Lachance has terrific hockey sense. He is very clever with the puck, and it wouldn't be a surprise to see him get more power play time this season. He moves the puck smartly and is poised under pressure. He doesn't take many chances down low but uses a strong shot from the point.

Lachance is not an exceptional skater. He has to work on his quickness (his feet look a little heavy at times), but he is balanced and strong on his skates.

He might make a good pairing with the gritty Darius Kasparaitis, if the two can stay healthy.

THE PHYSICAL GAME

This is the area where Lachance has to apply himself most. Though not a very big defenseman, he is built solidly enough to be an effective if not devastating checker, but there were nights when he just let his attacker skate through without paying the price. Lachance kills penalties well and blocks shots. His mental toughness has to improve.

THE INTANGIBLES

Lachance has been bothered by injuries over the past two seasons. We would like to see him healthy for a full year, because there is a chance he could be something special.

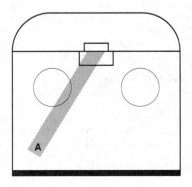

BRETT LINDROS

Yrs. of NHL service: 1
Born: London, Ont.; Dec. 2, 1975
Position: right wing
Height: 6-4
Weight: 215
Uniform no.: 75
Shoots: right

Career statistics:

GP	G	A	TP	PIM
33	1	3	4	100

1994-95 statistics:

GP	G	A	TP	+/-	PIM	PP	SH	GW	GT	S	PCT
33	1	3	4	-8	100	0	0	1	0	35	2.9

LAST SEASON

First NHL season. Second on team in PIM. Missed eight games with a concussion. Missed one game with a bruised wrist. Missed two games with a sprained knee. Missed four games with back spasms.

THE FINESSE GAME

Lindros's skating is somewhat laboured, but he has a big, strong stride. He can cover a lot of ice with one stroke. He is quite agile, very balanced for solid hits. He is a big open-ice checker, and works along the boards and corners as well as in front of the net.

Lindros has a couple of surprising finesse moves. He will use the boards intelligently as a "linemate" to pass the puck to himself. He isn't a very good play-maker overall, however, nor does he have a real finishing touch with the puck. His goals will be generated from his play in tight, overpowering defensemen to battle for loose pucks. He may be used up front on the power play on the second unit. Certainly new coach Mike Milbury (who coached in Boston) may try to use him in the Cam Neely role, but don't expect Neely numbers. That's not what Lindros is about.

THE PHYSICAL GAME

Checks bounce off Lindros, but he is not invincible, as his frequent trips to the trainer's room attest. He is still a young man, and growing. He has to stay away from bad penalties because everyone in the league will be gunning for him, thanks to his famous sibling. He has a bit of a chip on his shoulder, but there's nothing wrong with that as long as he can handle himself.

THE INTANGIBLES

Because of the financial stake the Islanders had in him, and because of the state of the team, Lindros was rushed into the NHL before he was ready last season. He should be better prepared this year, but his laundry list of injuries is a concern, especially the concussion. No one wants a player this big and tough wearing a shield.

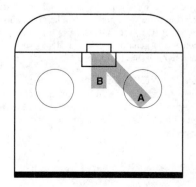

CHRIS MARINUCCI

Yrs. of NHL service: 0
Born: Grand Rapids, Minn.; Dec. 29, 1971
Position: centre
Height: 6-0
Weight: 175
Uniform no.: 17
Shoots: left

Career statistics:

GP	G	A	TP	PIM
12	1	4	5	2

1994-95 statistics:

GP	G	A	TP	+/-	PIM	PP	SH	GW	GT	S	PCT
12	1	4	5	-1	2	0	0	0	0	11	9.1

LAST SEASON
Will be entering first NHL season. Won 1994 Hobey Baker Award.

THE FINESSE GAME
Marinucci has been a scorer at the college (Minnesota-Duluth) and minor league levels, and has gotten most of his points on the power play. He was third in scoring for Denver (IHL) last season with 29-40 — 69 in 74 games before joining the Islanders late in the season.

Marinucci has very good offensive instincts, but his skating isn't good enough to get him a lot of prime ice time. He is going to have to work on that aspect, to merit the power play minutes where he can really make things happen. Marinucci has excellent hockey intelligence. He has a good shot with a quick release, but the key lies in knowing when to shoot and when to pass, when to jump in the holes and when to back off, and Marinucci has that knack.

THE PHYSICAL GAME
Marinucci doesn't avoid contact, but he doesn't initiate. He will fight for the puck, bot doesn't have much of a mean streak. He needs to improve his upper-body strength.

THE INTANGIBLES
The Islanders liken Marinucci to Pat Flatley because of his good work ethic and effort along the boards. Flatley has been a strong role player for the team since 1984, so Marinucci has quite a model to emulate. A strong rookie season could mean 50 points for Marinucci.

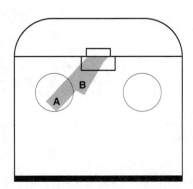

BRYAN MCCABE

Yrs. of NHL service: 0
Born: St. Catharines, Ont.; June 8, 1975
Position: defense
Height: 6-2
Weight: 205
Uniform no.: n.a.
Shoots: left

Career junior statistics:				
GP	G	A	TP	PIM
254	51	241	292	745

1994-95 junior statistics:				
GP	G	A	TP	PIM
62	20	49	69	153

LAST SEASON

Will be entering first NHL season. Led Brandon Wheat Kings (WHL) in defense scoring.

THE FINESSE GAME

McCabe is a defenseman with great size whose offensive game is ahead of his defensive game. McCabe has tremendous offensive instincts. He jumps up into the attacking zone and reads plays well. He has a major league slap shot.

McCabe's skating style is unorthodox. It's not fluid, and there appears to be a hitch in his stride.

Defensively, McCabe is hesitant about his reads, but in the NHL, he who hesitates get burned. He needs to improve the game in his own end before he becomes an NHL regular.

THE PHYSICAL GAME

McCabe is not afraid to drop his gloves, as his career WHL PIM total indicates. He is big and strong and shows leadership.

THE INTANGIBLES

The word used around McCabe is potential. He has an excellent chance to make the squad this fall, since he is just the type of player new coach Mike Milbury loves.

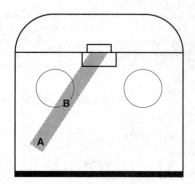

MARTY McINNIS

Yrs. of NHL service: 3
Born: Hingham, Mass.; June 2, 1970
Position: centre
Height: 6-0
Weight: 185
Uniform no.: 18
Shoots: right

Career statistics:

GP	G	A	TP	PIM
193	47	63	110	56

1991-92 statistics:

GP	G	A	TP	+/-	PIM	PP	SH	GW	GT	S	PCT
15	3	5	8	+6	0	0	0	0	0	24	12.5

1992-93 statistics:

GP	G	A	TP	+/-	PIM	PP	SH	GW	GT	S	PCT
56	10	20	30	+7	24	0	1	0	0	60	16.7

1993-94 statistics:

GP	G	A	TP	+/-	PIM	PP	SH	GW	GT	S	PCT
81	25	31	56	+31	24	3	5	3	1	136	18.4

1994-95 statistics:

GP	G	A	TP	+/-	PIM	PP	SH	GW	GT	S	PCT
41	9	7	16	-1	8	0	0	1	0	68	13.2

LAST SEASON

Missed one game with a wrist injury.

THE FINESSE GAME

McInnis does a lot of the little things well. He plays positionally, is smart and reliable defensively, and turns his checking work into scoring opportunities with quick passes and his work down low.

He isn't fast, but he is deceptive with a quick first few strides to the puck. He seems to be more aware of where the puck is than his opponents, so while they're looking for the puck, he's already heading towards it.

McInnis is a good penalty killer because of his tenacity and anticipation. He reads plays well on offense and defense. Playing the off wing opens up his shot for a quick release. He is always a shorthanded threat.

THE PHYSICAL GAME

McInnis is not very big, but he is sturdy and will use his body to bump and scrap for the puck. He always tries to get in the way.

THE INTANGIBLES

McInnis was inconsistent last season and got shuffled around. He never seemed to settle into the consistent play he showed in 1993-94, but is too determined not to bounce back. He can handle a third-line checking role and still score 20-25 goals.

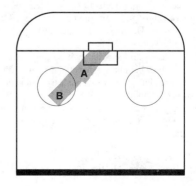

KIRK MULLER

Yrs. of NHL service: 11
Born: Kingston, Ont.; Feb. 8, 1966
Position: centre
Height: 6-0
Weight: 200
Uniform no.: 9
Shoots: left

Career statistics:

GP	G	A	TP	PIM
835	292	483	775	878

1991-92 statistics:

GP	G	A	TP	+/-	PIM	PP	SH	GW	GT	S	PCT
78	36	41	77	+15	86	15	1	7	1	191	18.8

1992-93 statistics:

GP	G	A	TP	+/-	PIM	PP	SH	GW	GT	S	PCT
80	37	57	94	+8	77	12	0	4	0	231	16.0

1993-94 statistics:

GP	G	A	TP	+/-	PIM	PP	SH	GW	GT	S	PCT
76	23	34	57	-1	96	9	2	3	0	168	13.7

1994-95 statistics:

GP	G	A	TP	+/-	PIM	PP	SH	GW	GT	S	PCT
45	11	16	27	-18	47	4	1	2	1	97	11.3

LAST SEASON

Acquired from Montreal with Mathieu Schneider and Craig Darby for Pierre Turgeon and Vladimir Malakhov. Worst plus-minus on team. Tied for team lead in game-winning goals. Tied for second on team in goals. Tied for third on team in points. Has missed only 18 games due to injury out of 853 in NHL career. Missed three games failing to report after trade.

THE FINESSE GAME

Muller's leadership comes from example. He is a gritty player who makes the most of his skills — which are above average, but shy of world class — by exerting himself to the utmost. He has become a more heady and intelligent player; where he once ran around making noisy but ineffective plays, it now looks as though there is a purpose to everything he does.

Muller plays at his best with linemates who have keen enough hockey sense to pounce on the pucks he works free with his efforts along the wall. He is a sturdy player through traffic and has some speed, but he won't dazzle. He doesn't give up until the buzzer sounds, and he takes nothing for granted.

Muller is not an especially gifted playmaker or shooter. None of his plays will make highlight films. Their ooh and ahh factor is low, but the result is in the net one way or another.

Muller is defensively strong and can shut down the opposing team's top centres. He can work both special teams.

THE PHYSICAL GAME

Muller blocks shots. He ties up players along the boards and uses his feet to kick the puck to a teammate. Ditto for his work on face-offs. Strong on his skates, he uses his skate blades almost as well as his stick blade.

THE INTANGIBLES

We're not sure where Muller's head is. He was unhappy with the trade to the Islanders and was talking trade even before he arrived, but maybe new coach Mike Milbury will change his mind and give him a more positive outlook. On the other hand, when he gets his first look at those new uniforms, he might be calling his agent again.

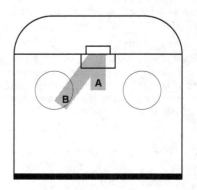

ZIGMUND PALFFY

Yrs. of NHL service: 1
Born: Skalica, Slovakia; May 5, 1972
Position: left wing
Height: 5-10
Weight: 169
Uniform no.: 68
Shoots: left

Career statistics:

GP	G	A	TP	PIM
38	10	7	17	6

1993-94 statistics:

GP	G	A	TP	+/-	PIM	PP	SH	GW	GT	S	PCT
5	0	0	0	-6	0	0	0	0	0	5	0.0

1994-95 statistics:

GP	G	A	TP	+/-	PIM	PP	SH	GW	GT	S	PCT
33	10	7	17	+3	6	1	0	1	0	75	13.3

LAST SEASON
First NHL season.

THE FINESSE GAME
When it comes to offensive instincts, Pallfy is among the league's elite. But the rest of the pieces haven't fallen into place yet, and there are nights when you're not sure they will. Other nights, Palffy looks brilliant.

Palffy has deceptive quickness. He has a quick first step and is very shifty, and he can handle the puck while he's dancing across the ice. The effort isn't constant, night in and night out, and because of that inconsistency he couldn't find a regular role. He can run a power play, but few teams can afford a pure power play specialist.

Palffy has excellent hands for passing or shooting. His size is his biggest drawback. He is more of a playmkaer than a finisher, but he has to learn to shoot more to make his game less predictable.

THE PHYSICAL GAME
Palffy is decidedly on the small side. He can't afford to get into any battles in tight areas where he'll get crunched. He can jump in and out of holes and pick his spots, and he often plays with great spirit.

THE INTANGIBLES
Over the last 10 games of the Islanders' dismal season, Palffy was probably the best player on the club. If he can sustain that over 82 games, he could score 40 goals. He's that good, but it's a mighty big "if."

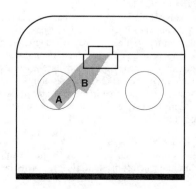

WADE REDDEN

Yrs. of NHL service: 0
Born: Lloydminster, Sask.; June 12, 1977
Position: left defense
Height: 6-1 1/2
Weight: 193
Uniform no.: n.a.
Shoots: left

Career junior statistics:

GP	G	A	TP	PIM
127	18	81	99	181

1993-94 junior statistics:

GP	G	A	TP	PIM
63	4	35	39	98

1994-95 junior statistics:

GP	G	A	TP	PIM
64	14	46	60	83

LAST SEASON

Will be entering first NHL season. Member of 1995 Canadian World Junior Championship team. Named to WHL East Division Second All-Star Team. Seventh among WHL defensemen in scoring. Named WHL Top Draft Prospect.

THE FINESSE GAME

Redden has tried to pattern his game after Ray Bourque, and the young defenseman has a few things in common with the Boston great. He is a good skater who can change gears swiftly and smoothly, and his superb rink vision enables him to get involved in his team's attack. He has a high skill level. His shot is hard and accurate and he is a patient and precise passer. He worked both the power play and penalty killing units for Brandon.

Scouts have been most impressed with Redden's poise. He plays older than his years and has a good grasp of the game. As he has been tested at higher and higher levels of competition he has elevated his game.

Redden has been given enthusiastic reviews for his work habits and attitude. He seems to be a player who is willing to learn in order to improve his game at the NHL level, and is a blue-chip prospect.

THE PHYSICAL GAME

Redden is not a big hitter, but he finishes his checks and stands up well. What he lacks in aggressiveness he makes up for with his competitive nature. He can handle a lot of ice time. He plays an economical game without a lot of wasted effort, is durable, and can skate all night long. Any questions about his ability to take punishment were answered in the WHL playoffs, but he would move up a step if he dished it out instead of just taking it.

THE INTANGIBLES

Redden was ranked number two by Central Scouting in the last rating before the draft. He is the "safe" bet, a reliable defenseman who won't be a superstar but is projected as a number two or three defenseman for a team, if not this year then the next — and then for the next decade.

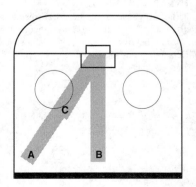

MATT SCHNEIDER

Yrs. of NHL service: 6
Born: New York, N.Y.; June 12, 1969
Position: left defense
Height: 5-11
Weight: 180
Uniform no.: 72
Shoots: left

Career statistics:

GP	G	A	TP	PIM
373	66	142	208	344

1991-92 statistics:

GP	G	A	TP	+/-	PIM	PP	SH	GW	GT	S	PCT
78	8	24	32	+10	72	2	0	1	0	194	4.1

1992-93 statistics:

GP	G	A	TP	+/-	PIM	PP	SH	GW	GT	S	PCT
60	13	31	44	+8	91	3	0	2	0	169	7.7

1993-94 statistics:

GP	G	A	TP	+/-	PIM	PP	SH	GW	GT	S	PCT
75	20	32	52	+15	62	11	0	4	0	193	10.4

1994-95 statistics:

GP	G	A	TP	+/-	PIM	PP	SH	GW	GT	S	PCT
43	8	21	29	-8	79	3	0	2	0	118	6.8

LAST SEASON

Acquired from Montreal with Kirk Muller and Craig Darby for Pierre Turgeon and Vladimir Malakhov. Led team defensemen in points. Tied for team lead in assists. Tied for team lead in game-winning goals. Second on team in scoring.

THE FINESSE GAME

Schneider has developed into a good two-way defenseman. He has the offensive skills to get involved in the attack and work the point on the power play; his major concern is his solid positional play. He makes fewer high-risk plays as he has gained more experience.

A talented skater, strong, balanced and agile, he lacks breakaway speed but is quick with his first step and changes directions smoothly. He can carry the puck but does not lead many rushes.

Schneider has improved his point play, doing more with the puck than just drilling shots. He handles the puck well and looks for the passes down low. Given the green light, he is likely to get involved down low more often. He has the skating ability to recover quickly when he takes the chance.

THE PHYSICAL GAME

Schneider plays with determination, but he lacks the size and strength to be an impact defenseman physically. His goal is to play a containment game and move the puck quickly and intelligently out of the zone, which he does well. He is matched against other teams' top scoring lines and always tries to do the job. He is best when paired with a physical defenseman.

THE INTANGIBLES

Schneider was happy to get out of Montreal, and he will be expected to be a leader on an Islanders team that will have a lot of young players this season. Patience will be a virtue. But if the Isles' defense stays healthy, it could be the foundation for a much improved team and Schneider could post career numbers.

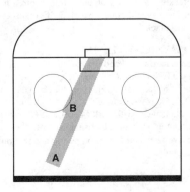

STEVE THOMAS

Yrs. of NHL service: 11
Born: Stockport, England; July 15, 1963
Position: left wing
Height: 5-11
Weight: 185
Uniform no.: 32
Shoots: left

Career statistics:

GP	G	A	TP	PIM
667	269	308	577	888

1991-92 statistics:

GP	G	A	TP	+/-	PIM	PP	SH	GW	GT	S	PCT
82	30	48	78	+8	97	3	0	3	1	245	12.2

1992-93 statistics:

GP	G	A	TP	+/-	PIM	PP	SH	GW	GT	S	PCT
79	37	50	87	+3	111	12	0	7	0	264	14.0

1993-94 statistics:

GP	G	A	TP	+/-	PIM	PP	SH	GW	GT	S	PCT
78	42	33	75	-9	139	17	0	5	2	249	16.9

1994-95 statistics:

GP	G	A	TP	+/-	PIM	PP	SH	GW	GT	S	PCT
47	11	15	26	-14	60	3	0	2	0	133	8.3

LAST SEASON

Led team in shots. Tied for team lead in game-winning goals. Tied for second on team in goals. Missed one game with a sore back and sore thumb.

THE FINESSE GAME

Thomas has a great shot and he loves to fire away. He will look to shoot first instead of pass, sometimes to his detriment, but subtlety is not his forte. His game is speed and power.

He has a strong wrist shot and an excellent one-timer. He likes to win the battle for the puck in deep, feed his centre, then head for the right circle for the return pass.

Thomas is a wildly intense player. His speed is straight ahead, without much deking or trying to put a move on a defender. He works along the boards and in the corners, willing to do the dirty work. He works hard and has the knack for scoring big goals.

Defense remains a problem. Thomas often has a tendency to leave the zone too early in his eagerness to get on the attack.

THE PHYSICAL GAME

Thomas is hard-nosed and finishes his checks. He is a very good fore-checker because he comes at the puck carrier like a human train. He is not big, but he is wide, and tough. He is great along the boards and among the best in the league (with Kirk Muller and Peter Zezel) at keeping the puck alive by using his feet.

He is a feisty and fierce competitor and will throw the odd punch.

THE INTANGIBLES

Thomas is a finisher, and he remains a streaky scorer. Mentally, he gets down on himself, and it shows in his game when things aren't going well. He will try to get too cute and make the perfect play instead of relying on his instincts. Thomas was a free agent after last season and will be courted by a number of teams.

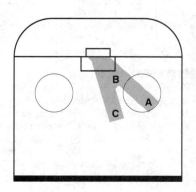

DENNIS VASKE

Yrs. of NHL service: 4
Born: Rockford, Ill.; Oct. 11, 1967
Position: left defense
Height: 6-2
Weight: 210
Uniform no.: 37
Shoots: left

Career statistics:

GP	G	A	TP	PIM
177	4	28	32	168

1991-92 statistics:

GP	G	A	TP	+/-	PIM	PP	SH	GW	GT	S	PCT
39	0	1	1	+5	39	0	0	0	0	26	0.0

1992-93 statistics:

GP	G	A	TP	+/-	PIM	PP	SH	GW	GT	S	PCT
27	1	5	6	+9	32	0	0	0	0	15	6.7

1993-94 statistics:

GP	G	A	TP	+/-	PIM	PP	SH	GW	GT	S	PCT
65	2	11	13	+21	76	0	0	0	0	71	2.8

1994-95 statistics:

GP	G	A	TP	+/-	PIM	PP	SH	GW	GT	S	PCT
41	1	11	12	+3	53	0	0	0	0	48	2.1

LAST SEASON

Matched career high in assists. Missed seven games game with a broken ankle.

THE FINESSE GAME

Vaske has made progress over the past few seasons and is establishing himself as a steady, stay-at-home defenseman.

He has what is a common flaw among young defensemen: he ocassionally get mesmerized and starts playing the puck instead of the body. Overall, however, he plays a sound positional game and forces attackers to try to get through him.

Although strong on his skates, Vaske doesn't have great speed or quickness, so when he stands his ground and forces the play to come to him he is the most effective.

THE PHYSICAL GAME

Vaske is a solid hitter. Because he doesn't skate well and lacks the first few steps to drive into an opponent, he doesn't bowl people over, but he is incredibly strong in the tough, close, one-on-one battles. He likes the physical play, too, but doesn't fight much.

THE INTANGIBLES

Vaske has been developing slowly, but oh so steadily, and was among the team's top four rotation at the time of injury. He has become a quiet team leader. A lot of long-time Islander observers have compared Vaske in size, style and demeanour to Dave Langevin.

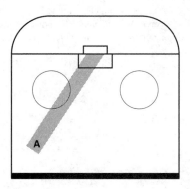

263

NEW YORK RANGERS

Players' Statistics 1994-95

POS	NO.	PLAYER	GP	G	A	PTS	+/-	PIM	PP	SH	GW	GT	S	PCTG
C	11	MARK MESSIER	46	14	39	53	8	40	3	3	2		126	11.1
D	2	BRIAN LEETCH	48	9	32	41		18	3		2		182	4.9
D	21	SERGEI ZUBOV	38	10	26	36	-2	18	6				116	8.6
R	17	PAT VERBEEK	48	17	16	33	-2	71	7		2	1	131	13.0
C	9	ADAM GRAVES	47	17	14	31	9	51	9		3		185	9.2
R	28	STEVE LARMER	47	14	15	29	8	16	3	1	4		116	12.1
R	27	ALEXEI KOVALEV	48	13	15	28	-6	30	1	1	1		103	12.6
R	16	BRIAN NOONAN	45	14	13	27	-3	26	7		1		95	14.7
C	10	PETR NEDVED	46	11	12	23	-1	26	1		3		123	8.9
C	13	SERGEI NEMCHINOV	47	7	6	13	-6	16			3		67	10.4
D	25	A. KARPOVTSEV	47	4	8	12	-4	30	1		1		82	4.9
L	14	TROY LONEY	30	5	4	9	-2	23	2		1		47	10.6
D	24	JAY WELLS	43	2	7	9		36					38	5.3
C	22	NATHAN LAFAYETTE	39	4	4	8	3	2		1			35	11.4
L	32	STEPHANE MATTEAU	41	3	5	8	-8	25					37	8.1
D	4	KEVIN LOWE	44	1	7	8	-2	58	1				35	2.9
L	20	MARK OSBORNE	37	1	3	4	-2	19					32	3.1
L	19	NICK KYPREOS	40	1	3	4		93					16	6.3
D	23	JEFF BEUKEBOOM	44	1	3	4	3	70					29	3.4
R	26	JOEY KOCUR	48	1	2	3	-4	71					25	4.0
D	5	*MATTIAS NORSTROM	9		3	3	2	2					4	
L	15	*DARREN LANGDON	18	1	1	2		62					6	16.7
D	29	JOBY MESSIER	10		2	2	2	18					4	
G	30	GLENN HEALY	17		2	2		2						
R	8	*JEAN-YVES ROY	3	1		1	-1	2					8	12.5
C	39	*SHAWN MCCOSH	5	1		1	1	2					2	50.0
L	37	*DAN LACROIX	24	1		1	-2	38					14	7.1
L	18	MIKE HARTMAN	1					4						
G	35	MIKE RICHTER	35					2						

GP = games played; G = goals; A = assists; PTS = points; +/- = goals-for minus goals-against while player is on ice; PIM = penalties in minutes; PP = power play goals; SH = shorthanded goals; GW = game-winning goals; GT = game-tying goals; S = no. of shots; PCTG = percentage of goals to shots; * = rookie

JEFF BEUKEBOOM

Yrs. of NHL service: 9
Born: Ajax, Ont.; Mar. 28, 1965
Position: right defense
Height: 6-4
Weight: 215
Uniform no.: 23
Shoots: right

Career statistics:

GP	G	A	TP	PIM
534	24	95	119	1248

1991-92 statistics:

GP	G	A	TP	+/-	PIM	PP	SH	GW	GT	S	PCT
74	1	15	16	+23	200	0	0	0	0	48	2.1

1992-93 statistics:

GP	G	A	TP	+/-	PIM	PP	SH	GW	GT	S	PCT
82	2	17	19	+9	153	0	0	0	0	54	3.7

1993-94 statistics:

GP	G	A	TP	+/-	PIM	PP	SH	GW	GT	S	PCT
68	8	8	16	+18	170	1	0	0	0	58	13.8

1994-95 statistics:

GP	G	A	TP	+/-	PIM	PP	SH	GW	GT	S	PCT
44	1	3	4	+3	70	0	0	0	0	29	3.4

LAST SEASON

Missed one game with neck spasms. Missed three games with a bruised chest.

THE FINESSE GAME

Beukeboom is not an agile skater, but he takes up a lot of room on the ice, especially when he uses his long reach. He has a quick stick. On penalty-killing shifts, he is able to get the stick down on the left or right side of his body into the passing lanes. He will also use his stick to reach around a puck carrier and knock the puck loose, or for a sweep-check at the blueline.

Beukeboom needs a mobile partner so he can play a simple defensive game. He is most effective when he angles the attacker to the corners, then uses his superior size and strength to eliminate the player physically. Attackers think they can burn Beukeboom to the outside because of his lumbering style, but they find themselves running out of real estate fast. But Beukeboom can get burned himself on ill-timed pinches, which happened at some key moments in last year's playoffs.

Beukeboom moves the puck fairly well. He certainly has no fear of anyone bearing down on him, but he needs support because he can't carry the puck out himself. That's what Brian Leetch is there for.

THE PHYSICAL GAME

Beukeboom almost swaggers about his size, as though he dares you to come hit him. He makes you worry about him; he's not going to worry about you. He commands room. He takes his time getting to the puck because not many people want to throw themselves at him. He worries about the man first, the puck second

at all times.

He is most effective crunching along the boards, and he clears the front of his net efficiently. The bigger the game, the more thunderous his hits. Beukeboom blocks shots fearlessly and often limps to the bench, only to return on his next shift.

THE INTANGIBLES

There simply aren't that many big players who know their limits but play to their maximum. Beukeboom keeps it simple. The Fancy Dan accolades can go to more polished partners like Leetch, while Beukeboom stays back and does the dirty work. He knows what his role is and he performs it well. He rarely lets himself get distracted from the task at hand. He is consistent.

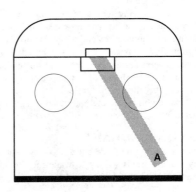

RAY FERRARO

Yrs. of NHL service: 11
Born: Trail, B.C.; Aug. 23, 1964
Position: centre
Height: 5-10
Weight: 185
Uniform no.: 20
Shoots: left

Career statistics:

GP	G	A	TP	PIM
758	273	312	589	730

1991-92 statistics:

GP	G	A	TP	+/-	PIM	PP	SH	GW	GT	S	PCT
80	40	40	80	+25	92	7	0	4	2	154	26.0

1992-93 statistics:

GP	G	A	TP	+/-	PIM	PP	SH	GW	GT	S	PCT
46	14	13	27	0	40	3	0	1	0	72	19.4

1993-94 statistics:

GP	G	A	TP	+/-	PIM	PP	SH	GW	GT	S	PCT
82	21	32	53	+1	83	5	0	3	3	136	15.4

1994-95 statistics:

GP	G	A	TP	+/-	PIM	PP	SH	GW	GT	S	PCT
47	22	21	43	+1	30	2	0	1	2	94	23.4

LAST SEASON

Led team in goals and points. Tied for team lead in assists. Led team and fourth in NHL in shooting percentage. Scored 20 or more goals for ninth time in career. Missed one game with a bruised left knee. Signed as a free agent by the Rangers.

THE FINESSE GAME

Ferraro excels at the short game. From the bottoms of the circles in, he uses his quickness and hand skills to work little give-and-go plays through traffic.

A streaky player, when he is in the groove he plays with great concentration and hunger around the net. He is alert to not only his first, but also his second and third options, and he makes a rapid play selection. His best shot is his wrist shot from just off to the side of the net, which is where he likes to work on the power play. He has good coordination and timing for deflections. When his confidence is down, however, Ferraro gets into serious funks.

Ferraro's skating won't win medals. He has a choppy stride and lacks rink-long speed, but he shakes loose in a few quick steps and maintains his balance well. Handling the puck does not slow him down.

Defensively, Ferraro has improved tremendously and is no longer a liability. In fact, he's a pretty decent two-way centre, though the scales still tip in favour of his offensive ability. He has particularly improved in his defensive work down low. He's good on face-offs.

THE PHYSICAL GAME

Ferraro is on the small side but is deceptively strong. Many players aren't willing to wade into the areas where they will get crunched, and Ferraro will try to avoid those situations when he can. But if it's the right play, he will take the abuse and whack a few ankles himself.

THE INTANGIBLES

Ferraro dedicated this season to his father, who passed away in December. It was a tough year mentally for Ferraro, and he responded like a pro. He was a free agent after last season and may be on the move as new coach Mike Milbury establishes "his" kind of players.

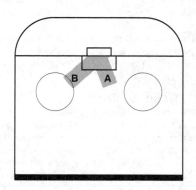

ADAM GRAVES

Yrs. of NHL service: 7
Born: Toronto, Ont.; Apr. 12, 1968
Position: left wing
Height: 6-0
Weight: 185
Uniform no.: 9
Shoots: left

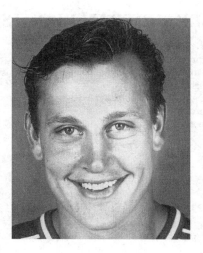

Career statistics:

GP	G	A	TP	PIM
512	154	140	294	1107

1991-92 statistics:

GP	G	A	TP	+/-	PIM	PP	SH	GW	GT	S	PCT
80	26	33	59	+19	139	4	4	4	0	228	11.4

1992-93 statistics:

GP	G	A	TP	+/-	PIM	PP	SH	GW	GT	S	PCT
84	36	29	65	-4	148	12	1	6	1	275	13.1

1993-94 statistics:

GP	G	A	TP	+/-	PIM	PP	SH	GW	GT	S	PCT
84	52	27	79	+27	127	20	4	4	1	291	17.9

1994-95 statistics:

GP	G	A	TP	+/-	PIM	PP	SH	GW	GT	S	PCT
47	17	14	31	+9	51	9	0	3	0	185	9.2

LAST SEASON

Tied for team lead in goals. Streak of 311 consecutive games ended with an elbow injury; was second-longest active streak in NHL. Led team in power play goals for second consecutive season. Led team in shots. Led team in plus-minus.

THE FINESSE GAME

Graves underwent back surgery prior to the lockout and came back about four months early — and that's about all you need to know about what went wrong for him last season. It was a horror show and he accomplished virtually nothing, but he was so seriously injured that it was a great testament to what kind of competitor Graves is that he played at all.

When healthy, Graves is a short-game player who scores a whopping percentage of his goals off deflections, rebounds and slam-dunks. A shot from the top of the circle is a long-distance effort for him. He favours the wrist shot, and his slap shot barely exists, so seldom does he use it. He is much better when working on instinct, because when he has time to make plays, he will out-think himself. Although a somewhat awkward skater, his balance and strength are good and he can get a few quick steps on a rival, although he isn't very fast in open ice. He is smart with the puck. He protects it with his body and is strong enough to fend off a checker with one arm and shovel the puck to a linemate with the other.

Graves is excellent on draws.

THE PHYSICAL GAME

Because of his back surgery, Graves couldn't do the things that make him Adam Graves. He couldn't generate any scoring, couldn't check, couldn't take the punishment around the net and lacked stamina.

Assuming he comes back full throttle, Graves is a physical player who plays (or at least tries to play) Eric Lindros-size. He grinds and plays against other teams' top defensemen without fear. He blocks shots and is a force on the ice. Other teams are always aware when Graves is around, because he doesn't play a quiet game. He finishes every check.

He stands up for his teammates and fights when necessary. He's so valuable to his team that the Rangers hate to see him in the box, and he's gotten much better at controlling his temper and not getting goaded into bad trade-off penalties. A tenacious forechecker, he plows into the corners and plunges into his work along the boards with intelligence, but no fear. Graves is one of the best goalie-screeners in the league.

THE INTANGIBLES

Graves is not a 50-goal scorer, and the 1993-94 goal figure is an aberration and an indication of just how well everything can fall for a team in a Stanley Cup season. He could be a 70-80 point man again, and should be counted on for a huge rebound season after the injury that made him a virtual nonentity last year.

Graves is a natural leader, and on those nights when the rest of his teammates fail to show up, he does. On nights when the points aren't coming, he never hurts his team but contributes in other ways. He is absurdly modest. Off the ice, Graves is one of the genuine good guys.

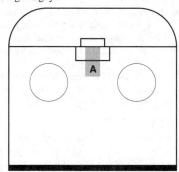

ALEXANDER KARPOVTSEV

Yrs. of NHL service: 2
Born: Moscow, Russia; Feb. 25, 1974
Position: left defense
Height: 6-2
Weight: 211
Uniform no.: 25
Shoots: left

Career statistics:

GP	G	A	TP	PIM
114	7	23	30	88

1993-94 statistics:

GP	G	A	TP	+/-	PIM	PP	SH	GW	GT	S	PCT
67	3	15	18	+12	58	1	0	1	0	78	3.8

1994-95 statistics:

GP	G	A	TP	+/-	PIM	PP	SH	GW	GT	S	PCT
47	4	8	12	-4	30	1	0	1	0	82	4.9

LAST SEASON

Missed one game with an ankle injury.

THE FINESSE GAME

Karpovtsev is a strong skater with some quickness and agility. He turns nicely in both directions.

He has decent puck-carrying skills but has no interest whatsoever in doing anything beyond getting to the redline and dumping the puck into the corner or making a short outlet pass. He does, at times, show a good instinct for seeing a better passing option than the obvious in the attacking zone. He has an effective shot from the point, low and reasonably accurate and very hard.

Karpovtsev is a bang-it-off-the-boards guy from behind his own net, and looked quicker on his feet last season.

THE PHYSICAL GAME

Karpovtsev is an extremely strong skater who is not shy about using that strength in front of the net or in the corners. He does not hesitate to get involved if things turn nasty, and while hardly a polished fighter, he is a willing one. He likes the big hit, but doesn't mind the smaller ones.

He is a crease-clearer and shot-blocker who is far more comfortable and poised in front of his net than when he chases to the corners or sideboards to challenge the puck. Once he gets away from the slot, with or without the puck, he loses either confidence or focus or both, which can lead to unforced errors or turnovers that result in scoring chances.

Still, he is an effective weapon against a power forward. He can tie up the guy in front, lean on him, hit and skate with a Cam Neely or Eric Lindros.

THE INTANGIBLES

Karpovtsev has lots of raw talent and rough edges, most of which seem to stem from an unfamiliarity with the North American game. This is a stay-at-home defender whose game right now is better suited for a complementary role in a number four or number five slot on the depth chart.

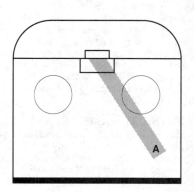

ALEXEI KOVALEV

Yrs. of NHL service: 3
Born: Togliatti, Russia; Feb. 24, 1973
Position: right wing/centre
Height: 6-1
Weight: 189
Uniform no.: 27
Shoots: left

Career statistics:

GP	G	A	TP	PIM
189	56	64	122	263

1992-93 statistics:

GP	G	A	TP	+/-	PIM	PP	SH	GW	GT	S	PCT
65	20	18	38	-10	79	3	0	3	1	134	14.9

1993-94 statistics:

GP	G	A	TP	+/-	PIM	PP	SH	GW	GT	S	PCT
76	23	33	56	+18	154	7	0	3	0	184	12.5

1994-95 statistics:

GP	G	A	TP	+/-	PIM	PP	SH	GW	GT	S	PCT
48	13	15	28	-6	30	1	1	1	0	103	12.6

LAST SEASON

One of four Rangers to appear in all 48 games.

THE FINESSE GAME

You don't often see hands as quick as Kovalev's on a player of his size. He has the dexterity, puck control skills, strength, balance and speed to beat the first fore-checker coming out of the zone or the first line of defense once he crosses the attacking blueline. He gets into trouble, though, when it comes down to what should be done after those men are beaten. Half of that problem is not his fault. If his linemates don't move to open ice while he is drawing the attention of two or three defenders, Kovalev's options are reduced.

However, there are too many occasions when the slithery moves don't do enough offensive damage. Sometimes he overhandles, then turns the puck over. Other times, too many times, he fails to get the puck deep. This is confounding, because Kovalev is a terrific passer and has a keen mind for sending passes to open ice that his wings can skate into with speed.

He is one of the few players in the NHL agile and balanced enough to duck under a check at the sideboards and maintain possession of the puck. Exceptional hands allow him to make remarkable moves, but he doesn't always finish them off well.

THE PHYSICAL GAME

Kovalev is sneaky dirty. He will run goalies and try to make it look as if he was pushed in by a defender. He's so strong and balanced on his skates that when he goes down odds are it's a dive. He aggravates opponents, who feel Kovalev is an Oscar-winner for feigning injuries. The chippier the game, the happier Kovalev is; he'll bring his stick up and wade into the fray.

Kovalev has very good size and is a willing hitter.

He likes to make highlight reel hits that splatter people. Because he is such a strong hitter, he is very hard to knock down, unless he's leaning. Kovalev makes extensive use of his edges, because he combines balance and a long reach to keep the puck well away from his body, and from a defender's. But there are moments when he seems at a 45-degree angle and then he can be nudged over.

He thrives on extra ice time and has to be dragged off the ice to make a line change.

THE INTANGIBLES

It's time for Kovalev to step up. He has shown enough to convince us he's extremely strong on his skates, strong in his will, tough, quick, agile, and marvellously skilled. Now it's time for him to live up to the predictions he makes for himself. He needs more focus, more consistency amd more maturity, but he is very near. Kovalev has to learn that you don't get style points to go along with goals and assists. He likes to show off his skill, but simpler is often better.

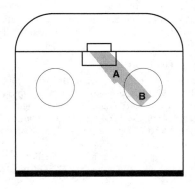

NICK KYPREOS

Yrs. of NHL service: 6
Born: Toronto, Ont.; June 4, 1966
Position: left wing
Height: 6-0
Weight: 195
Uniform no.: 19
Shoots: left

Career statistics:

GP	G	A	TP	PIM
346	39	37	76	1041

1991-92 statistics:

GP	G	A	TP	+/-	PIM	PP	SH	GW	GT	S	PCT
65	4	6	10	-3	206	0	0	0	0	28	14.3

1992-93 statistics:

GP	G	A	TP	+/-	PIM	PP	SH	GW	GT	S	PCT
75	17	10	27	-5	325	0	0	2	0	81	21.0

1993-94 statistics:

GP	G	A	TP	+/-	PIM	PP	SH	GW	GT	S	PCT
56	3	5	8	-16	139	0	0	1	0	34	8.8

1994-95 statistics:

GP	G	A	TP	+/-	PIM	PP	SH	GW	GT	S	PCT
40	1	3	4	0	93	0	0	0	0	16	6.3

LAST SEASON
Led team in PIM.

THE FINESSE GAME
Kypreos probably had the team's worst Stanley Cup hangover. He went through training camp without touching a soul, thinking he was king of the hill, and accordingly got off to a slow start. But in the last few weeks of the season, he came up very big and in the playoffs was a responsible player who delivered the hard hits when they were needed.

If Kypreos isn't going to come out decking people, there is little point in giving him a sweater. His offensive contributions are going to be limited to slam-ins from five feet away on the third rebound. He won't carry the puck, but he will go into the corner and try to win it. Even if he just keeps the puck alive for someone to come along and pick up, he has done his job.

Kypreos may handle some checking roles, but he is not fast enough to keep up with a quick offensive line and that kind of thinking doesn't come naturally to him. He's a up-and-down wing who wants to fore-check.

THE PHYSICAL GAME
Kypreos is a hard, even vicious hitter. He couldn't care less if his hit is dirty or not, and he can throw the kind of checks that can intimidate a team right out of the game during the regular season. It's a little different in the playoffs, but that alone is enough of a commodity to keep him in the lineup. Kypreos has a physical presence and makes his teammates a little braver.

THE INTANGIBLES
Kypreos is a third- or fourth-line contributor. His offense is minimal, but at least he can keep a defenseman occupied in a corner and get a team running around defensively. He has to do that more consistently to merit serious ice time, and he's not always in the proper mental groove to be helpful.

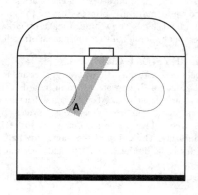

STEVE LARMER

Yrs. of NHL service: 14
Born: Peterborough, Ont.; June 16, 1961
Position: right wing
Height: 5-11
Weight: 189
Uniform no.: 28
Shoots: left

Career statistics:

GP	G	A	TP	PIM
1006	441	571	1012	532

1991-92 statistics:

GP	G	A	TP	+/-	PIM	PP	SH	GW	GT	S	PCT
80	29	45	74	+10	65	11	2	3	0	292	9.9

1992-93 statistics:

GP	G	A	TP	+/-	PIM	PP	SH	GW	GT	S	PCT
84	35	35	70	+23	48	14	4	6	1	228	15.4

1993-94 statistics:

GP	G	A	TP	+/-	PIM	PP	SH	GW	GT	S	PCT
68	21	39	60	+14	41	6	4	7	0	146	14.4

1994-95 statistics:

GP	G	A	TP	+/-	PIM	PP	SH	GW	GT	S	PCT
47	14	15	29	+8	16	3	1	4	0	116	12.1

LAST SEASON

Played 1,000th NHL game and scored 1000th NHL point. Tied for second on team in plus-minus. Led team in game-winning goals for second consecutive season. Missed one game with a back injury.

THE FINESSE GAME

Larmer may be getting on in years and he's certainly played a lot of hockey, but he still comes up with the big goals and still has some zip on his slap shot. He is very solid on the fundamentals, down to the small details of keeping his stick on the ice with the blade open to accept a pass. He is always around the front of the net, poaching, lurking, looking for a rebound to convert or a shot to tip.

Honest offensively and reliable defensively, he is an intelligent player in all zones. His hand-eye coordination is excellent. His slap and snap shots are threatening. He will look low and fire high to deceive the goalie. Larmer's skating, never great to begin with, has started to tail off dramatically.

THE PHYSICAL GAME

Larmer is an extremely physical player — out and out fearless. He never hesitates to throw a check or take a hit. If he's the first man in the zone, he'll go to the boards against two opponents and scrap for the puck. If he's the puck carrier, he has the hands for playmaking. If he's the third man, a superior hockey intellect always puts him in the perfect position to back-check. He is one of the best in the game at cutting the rink in half lengthwise and blocking the cross-ice passes that most other players let go through.

He does an outstanding job of using his body to shield the puck. If you tie up his arms, he'll kick the puck. If you pin him on the boards, he'll wriggle his arms loose and get something done. He is relentless. He does not stop on offense or defense. If his second effort doesn't get the job done, he'll make a third try.

THE INTANGIBLES

Larmer is not getting any bigger, younger, or faster. He remains utterly devoted to the game and his intelligence will help him compensate as his game continues to ebb, but that 884 consecutive games played streak took a lot out of Larmer. He now has to take games off. While he remains a creditable performer, he could find himself reduced to more of a part-time role than he would prefer.

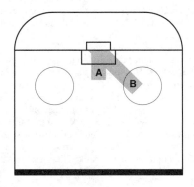

BRIAN LEETCH

Yrs. of NHL service: 8
Born: Corpus Christi, Tex.; Mar. 3, 1968
Position: left defense
Height: 5-11
Weight: 192
Uniform no.: 2
Shoots: left

Career statistics:

GP	G	A	TP	PIM
485	122	375	487	255

1991-92 statistics:

GP	G	A	TP	+/-	PIM	PP	SH	GW	GT	S	PCT
80	22	80	102	+25	26	10	1	3	1	245	9.0

1992-93 statistics:

GP	G	A	TP	+/-	PIM	PP	SH	GW	GT	S	PCT
36	6	30	36	+2	26	2	1	1	0	150	4.0

1993-94 statistics:

GP	G	A	TP	+/-	PIM	PP	SH	GW	GT	S	PCT
84	23	56	79	+28	67	17	1	4	0	328	7.0

1994-95 statistics:

GP	G	A	TP	+/-	PIM	PP	SH	GW	GT	S	PCT
48	9	32	41	0	18	3	0	2	0	182	4.9

LAST SEASON

One of four Rangers to appear in all 48 games. Led team defensemen and fourth among NHL defensemen in scoring. Second on team in assists and points.

THE FINESSE GAME

Such quick hands, feet and thoughts. Leetch is a premier passer who sees the ice so clearly, identifies the optimum passing option on the move and hits his target with a forehand or backhand pass. He is terrific at picking passes out of the air and keeping attempted clearing passes from getting by him at the point.

Leetch has a fine first step that sends him towards top speed almost instantly. He can be posted at the point, then see an opportunity to jump into the play down low and fairly bolt into action. Watch him move and then recall that his ankle is held together by screws and plates. It's only amazing.

His anticipation is superb. He knows what he's going to do with the puck before he has it. He seems to be thinking about five minutes ahead of everyone else on the ice. He instantly starts a transition from defense to offense, and always seems to make the correct decision to pass or skate with the puck.

Leetch has a remarkable knack for getting his point shot through traffic and to the net. He even uses his eyes to fake. He is adept as looking and/or moving in one direction, then passing the opposite way.

Leetch smartly jumps into holes to make the most of a odd-man rush, and he is more than quick enough to hop back on defense if the puck turns the other way. He has astounding lateral movement, the best in the league among defensemen, leaving forwards completely out of room when it looked like there was open

ice to get by him. He uses this as a weapon on offense to open up space for his teammates.

Leetch has a range of shots. He'll use a clever shot from the point — usually through a screen because it won't overpower any NHL goalie — but he'll also use a wrist shot from the circle. He also is gifted with the one-on-one moves that help him wriggle in front for 10-footers on the forehand or backhand.

THE PHYSICAL GAME

Not a punishing hitter, Leetch does initiate contact and doesn't hesitate to make plays in the face of being hit. He is more dependable in front of his net than he once was, and much more responsible in his defensive zone. He simply does not have the strength to manhandle people, but he gets involved. Because taking the body is not his first option, he does more stickhandling than he should. Still, he competes on the puck and has significantly improved on defense. He has developed into a first-rate penalty killer.

Leetch cuts off the ice, gives the skater nowhere to go, strips the puck or steals a pass, then starts the transition game. He'll then follow the rush and may finish off the play with a goal.

THE INTANGIBLES

Leetch can utterly take over a game when the Rangers need him to. While his game will always involve more offense than defense, he is a complete player.

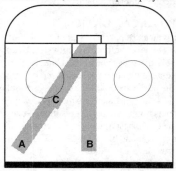

KEVIN LOWE

Yrs. of NHL service: 16
Born: Lachute, Que.; Apr. 15, 1959
Position: left defense
Height: 6-2
Weight: 195
Uniform no.: 4
Shoots: left

Career statistics:

GP	G	A	TP	PIM
1130	82	329	411	1350

1991-92 statistics:

GP	G	A	TP	+/-	PIM	PP	SH	GW	GT	S	PCT
55	2	7	9	-4	107	0	0	0	0	33	6.1

1992-93 statistics:

GP	G	A	TP	+/-	PIM	PP	SH	GW	GT	S	PCT
49	3	12	15	-2	58	0	0	0	0	52	5.8

1993-94 statistics:

GP	G	A	TP	+/-	PIM	PP	SH	GW	GT	S	PCT
71	5	14	19	+4	70	0	0	1	0	50	10.0

1994-95 statistics:

GP	G	A	TP	+/-	PIM	PP	SH	GW	GT	S	PCT
44	1	7	8	-2	58	1	0	0	0	35	2.9

LAST SEASON

Missed one game with the flu. Missed two games with a pinched nerve in his neck.

THE FINESSE GAME

Lowe gets by on his head now, not his talent. He is slow to manoeuvre. He pinches down, probably more than he should. He is still terrific at angling a player off the play, giving the skater with the puck no room to go. He always screens for his partner.

Lowe's contributions are subtle. He is not a big playmaker, but he makes the big defensive plays. He has mastered the quick clutch and grabs, just enough to slow down a rival without getting the attention of the referee. He was the perfect complement for the roving Sergei Zubov, who could always rely on Lowe to be back where he belonged.

Lowe also has a calming influence on a younger, inexperienced partner like Zubov. He communicates with his partner on the ice and continues the lesson on the bench or in the dressing room. He doesn't get involved in the attack. He simply moves the puck. When Lowe is asked to do too much, he gets in trouble.

THE PHYSICAL GAME

Lowe absorbs the hit but keeps his stick free, so the contact nullifies the man and gives him room to move the puck. Not a towering specimen, he makes the effective take-outs and keeps the front of his net tidy. He blocks shots well. He keeps his cool and is a crunch time player.

THE INTANGIBLES

Lowe survived a job challenge last season to remain the team's number four defenseman, but if any of the younger players are ready to step up, Lowe will be a living example for them to watch. He will show them how the game should be played. A class act, he's near the end of his distinguished career but is a quiet leader, well respected around the league and still valuable for his modest capabilities. His ice time will be reduced, but he is an invaluable role player.

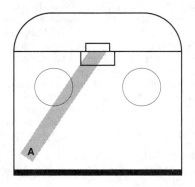

STEPHANE MATTEAU

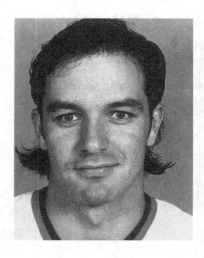

Yrs. of NHL service: 4
Born: Rouyn-Noranda, Que.; Sept. 2, 1969
Position: left wing
Height: 6-3
Weight: 195
Uniform no.: 32
Shoots: left

Career statistics:

GP	G	A	TP	PIM
299	58	69	127	337

1991-92 statistics:

GP	G	A	TP	+/-	PIM	PP	SH	GW	GT	S	PCT
24	6	8	14	+5	64	1	0	0	0	38	15.8

1992-93 statistics:

GP	G	A	TP	+/-	PIM	PP	SH	GW	GT	S	PCT
79	15	18	33	+6	98	2	0	4	0	95	15.8

1993-94 statistics:

GP	G	A	TP	+/-	PIM	PP	SH	GW	GT	S	PCT
77	19	19	38	+15	57	3	0	2	1	135	14.1

1994-95 statistics:

GP	G	A	TP	+/-	PIM	PP	SH	GW	GT	S	PCT
41	3	5	8	-8	25	0	0	0	0	37	8.1

LAST SEASON

Missed one game with the flu. Missed two games with back spasms.

THE FINESSE GAME

Matteau's most dangerous asset is his ability to get to the boards, hurry a defenseman into a turnover, then get to the front of the net for a deflection or to set a screen. The problem is, you might see that play out of him once in a game, then maybe not again for a week or more. He is mentally fragile. He gets down on himself, which leads to catastrophic slumps, and this just a year after his self-esteem had to be at an all-time high. Some players need a pat on the back, some need a kick in the pants. Matteau needs both at differing times.

Matteau is not going to overpower goalies with many shots. His goals come from short range — rebounds, deflections, backhands, wraparounds. More often, though, he's the player causing a distraction and getting cross-checked while a teammate converts the garbage. He shows good hustle and works hard to get into scoring position in front of the net, but he doesn't have the touch to finish off the play. When he wants to, he will skate through a check. Too often, it takes too little to stop his legs. He's got a big reach and a reasonably quick wit with the puck.

Matteau plays more without the puck than with it. He plays best when he gets the puck, moves it, then moves himself. Coaches keep looking at Matteau and thinking Kevin Stevens, but all they get is . . . Matteau. He's not a very threatening offensive force.

THE PHYSICAL GAME

Matteau is big enough to make himself useful, strong enough to make himself a force, fast enough to be intimidating, but he's also inconsistent enough to make you understand why so many teams have given up on him.

He finishes his checks, hard at times, but tends to use his size in more subtle ways. He makes the defenseman tie him up in front of the net, which leaves openings down low for teammates. He does a decent job along the boards, shielding the puck and kicking it to his stick.

THE INTANGIBLES

Matteau's size and effort make him valuable, but he has to play consistently all season. Get him stirred up and you've got yourself a player. If he doesn't play ticked-off, he doesn't play at all. Despite their disappointment with Matteau, the Rangers re-signed their 1994 playoff hero for two seasons.

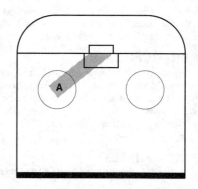

MARK MESSIER

Yrs. of NHL service: 16
Born: Edmonton, Alta.; Jan. 18, 1961
Position: centre
Height: 6-1
Weight: 210
Uniform no.: 11
Shoots: left

Career statistics:

GP	G	A	TP	PIM
1127	492	877	1369	1386

1991-92 statistics:

GP	G	A	TP	+/-	PIM	PP	SH	GW	GT	S	PCT
79	35	72	107	+31	76	12	4	6	0	212	16.5

1992-93 statistics:

GP	G	A	TP	+/-	PIM	PP	SH	GW	GT	S	PCT
75	25	66	91	-6	72	7	2	2	0	215	11.6

1993-94 statistics:

GP	G	A	TP	+/-	PIM	PP	SH	GW	GT	S	PCT
76	26	58	84	+25	76	6	2	5	0	216	12.0

1994-95 statistics:

GP	G	A	TP	+/-	PIM	PP	SH	GW	GT	S	PCT
46	14	39	53	+8	40	3	3	2	0	126	11.1

LAST SEASON

Led team in assists, points and shorthanded goals. Missed two games with a back injury. Tied for 10th in NHL in scoring. Fifth in NHL in assists.

THE FINESSE GAME

The surprising thing about Messier last year was how much the Rangers relied on him for his defensive attributes, particularly face-offs. He is experienced enough to know you can win a draw by not losing it; he ties his man up long enough to see how much his opponent wants to fight to get untangled. The puck sits there, meanwhile, and often a teammate can come in and sweep it away. On defensive zone draws, he will send the puck behind the net, hold up his man, then release the player just as his defenseman is making the breakout pass — leaving the fore-checker caught in between.

He loves the wrist shot off the back foot from the right wing circle, which is where he always seems to gravitate. He makes more use of passing and shooting to score, than any other North American player in the league. Messier will weave to the right wing circle, fake a centering pass, get the goalie to cheat away from the post, then flip a backhand under the crossbar. He shoots from almost anywhere and is becoming even more unpredictable in his shot selection. Sometimes he will not bother with the pretty play, but just throw it to the net through a screen to make things happen.

Messier is smart when he is being shadowed. In the offensive zone he will go into an area where there is another defensive player, drawing his checker with him. That puts two defenders in a small zone and opens up ice for his teammates.

He is so gifted with the puck that he will try anything. He can lift the puck from behind the net over the netting to the front corner for a teammate (a move he says he learned from Wayne Gretzky). He will use his speed to drive the defenders back, then stop and quickly check his options, making the most of the time and space he has earned. Messier is unlikely to try many one-on-one moves, but he makes the utmost use of his teammates.

Messier still has tremendous acceleration and a powerful burst of straightaway speed, which is tailor-made for killing penalties and scoring shorthanded goals. He is strong on his skates, changes directions, pivots, bursts into open ice and does it all with or without the puck.

THE PHYSICAL GAME

Messier plays so much that he can't be expected to throw the big hits often, but he waits for the chance when one big hit, especially early in a game, will set the tone, wake up his team, and scare the living daylights out of a rival. Messier knows when to keep his cool, or when to jaw away, or hit an opponent after a whistle. He has a mean streak a mile wide and will hit late and blindside people. Teammates play bigger and braver alongside Messier.

THE INTANGIBLES

Messier was overtaxed last year. His shoulders are broad, but not broad enough to carry 20 players for six months. The smartest thing to do would be to give him 12 or 15 minutes a game until the All-Star break, then crank up the engines.

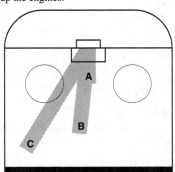

PETR NEDVED

Yrs. of NHL service: 5
Born: Liberec, Czechoslovakia; Dec. 9, 1971
Position: centre
Height: 6-3
Weight: 178
Uniform no.: 10
Shoots: left

Career statistics:

GP	G	A	TP	PIM
287	80	87	167	186

1991-92 statistics:

GP	G	A	TP	+/-	PIM	PP	SH	GW	GT	S	PCT
77	15	22	37	-3	36	5	0	1	1	99	15.2

1992-93 statistics:

GP	G	A	TP	+/-	PIM	PP	SH	GW	GT	S	PCT
84	38	33	71	+20	96	2	1	3	0	149	25.5

1993-94 statistics:

GP	G	A	TP	+/-	PIM	PP	SH	GW	GT	S	PCT
19	6	14	20	+2	8	2	0	0	1	63	9.5

1994-95 statistics:

GP	G	A	TP	+/-	PIM	PP	SH	GW	GT	S	PCT
46	11	12	23	-1	26	1	0	3	0	123	8.9

LAST SEASON

Acquired from St. Louis for Esa Tikkanen and Doug Lidster. Missed two games with an abdominal strain.

THE FINESSE GAME

Nedved's biggest improvement over the past few years has been in his skating, and it was sharpened by playing in the bigger rinks in international hockey. He's traded his choppiness for a more fluid stride with better balance and power. Tall but slightly built, he can handle the puck well in traffic or in open ice at tempo. He uses his forehand and backhand equally well for a pass or a shot. He sees the ice very well and has a creative mind. Nedved has a sense of where his teammates are.

He is shooting more. Nedved gets his best chances down low, using a wrist shot in tight, and is an incredibly accurate shooter when he does pull the trigger. He needs to drive to the net more and take advantage of the space that that will get him.

Although he lacks a big slap shot, Nedved can run a power play from the point. He does none of that with the Rangers due to their gifted point duo of Brian Leetch and Sergei Zubov.

Nedved will pay the price occasionally along the boards if he's not the inside man, the guy who will get hit. If there's a chance of contact, he generally won't be the first to the puck.

THE PHYSICAL GAME

Good on attacking-zone draws, he knows his way around a face-off. He has good hand quickness and cheats well. On offensive-zone draws, he turns his body so he is almost facing the boards. He's not as gutsy in defensive-zone draws.

Nedved protects the puck well with his body. He doesn't initiate much. It would help to see more competitive fire.

THE INTANGIBLES

Nedved remains enigmatic. He wants to be a number one centre, but isn't in New York behind Mark Messier. Unless his defensive game improves, he will not be a real front-line centre. Dashes of brilliance aren't enough to sustain him.

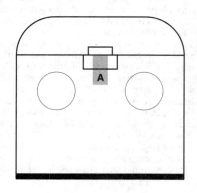

SERGEI NEMCHINOV

Yrs. of NHL service: 4
Born: Moscow, Russia; Jan. 14, 1964
Position: centre
Height: 6-0
Weight: 205
Uniform no.: 13
Shoots: left

Career statistics:

GP	G	A	TP	PIM
277	82	92	174	101

1991-92 statistics:

GP	G	A	TP	+/-	PIM	PP	SH	GW	GT	S	PCT
73	30	28	58	+19	15	2	0	5	0	124	24.2

1992-93 statistics:

GP	G	A	TP	+/-	PIM	PP	SH	GW	GT	S	PCT
81	23	31	54	+15	34	0	1	3	0	144	16.0

1993-94 statistics:

GP	G	A	TP	+/-	PIM	PP	SH	GW	GT	S	PCT
76	22	27	49	+13	36	4	0	6	0	144	15.3

1994-95 statistics:

GP	G	A	TP	+/-	PIM	PP	SH	GW	GT	S	PCT
47	7	6	13	-6	16	0	0	3	0	67	10.4

LAST SEASON

Missed one game with a bruised Achilles tendon.

THE FINESSE GAME

Defensively, Nemchinov is probably the Rangers' best forward. If there is a five-on-three against, this is the forward who is sent out for the draw. He backchecks well, coming back on his man, throwing him off-stride with a shoulder-check, collecting the puck and trying to do something with it. He is a very willing soldier in the battle along the boards.

He has the hand skills to play with almost any finesse player. Nemchinov is very fond of the backhand shot but isn't as accurate as he wants to be most of the time. Just as his strength powers his defensive game, it is critical to his offensive game as well. Nemchinov will win a puck along the boards, muscle it into the scoring zone and create a chance. He is strong enough, also, to get away a shot when his stick is being held or when he is fending off a checker. He lacks only a finishing touch.

Nemchinov carries the puck in a classic fashion, well to the side, which makes him much more difficult to fore-check. He is unpredictable in whether he will shoot or pass, because the puck is always ready for either option and he does not telegraph his moves.

He is not a pretty skater and lacks acceleration. He doesn't have the skating ability usually associated with players out of the old Soviet system, but he is strong and balanced and is a dedicated chopper. Nemchinov's leg strength makes him sneaky-fast.

THE PHYSICAL GAME

Powerfully built, he fore-checks with zest and drives through the boards and the corners. Linemates have to be alert, because Nemchinov will churn up loose pucks. He is very sneaky at holding an opponent's stick when the two players are tied up in a corner and his body shields the infraction from the officials. He takes every hit and keeps coming. Nemchinov is as mentally tough as any player in the league. He is enormously strong, and never stops competing.

Nemchinov gets checking assignments against behemoths like Mario Lemieux, Eric Lindros and Joel Otto, and he more than holds his own. He always seems to pin an opponent's stick to the ice at the last second when a pass is arriving in a quality scoring area.

He blocks shots, hits and takes hits to make plays, and ties up his opposing centre on draws.

THE INTANGIBLES

Don't mistake his stoicism for a lack of emotion or intensity. Nemchinov is a quiet leader, a player of character who is committed to winning. Of his 15-20 goals per season, about half turn out to be scored in pressure situations. He is becoming more and more a defensive specialist.

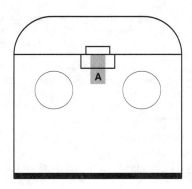

MATTIAS NORSTROM

Yrs. of NHL service: 0
Born: Mora, Sweden; Jan. 2, 1972
Position: defense
Height: 6-1
Weight: 200
Uniform no.: 5
Shoots: left

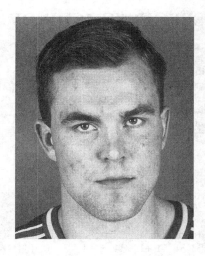

Career statistics

GP	G	A	TP	PIM
18	0	4	4	8

1993-94 statistics:

GP	G	A	TP	+/-	PIM	PP	SH	GW	GT	S	PCT
9	0	1	1	0	6	0	0	0	0	3	0.0

1994-95 statistics:

GP	G	A	TP	+/-	PIM	PP	SH	GW	GT	S	PCT
9	0	3	3	+2	2	0	0	0	0	4	0

LAST SEASON

Will be entering first NHL season. Spent most of last season with Binghamton (AHL), where he was 9-10 — 19 in 63 games.

THE FINESSE GAME

Norstrom is an above-average skater who is still working on his pivots and turns. He does have straight ahead speed, to a degree, thanks to a long stride. Along the boards, he delivers strong hits.

His foot skills outdistance his hand skills, however. Norstrom can make a decent pass, but mostly he'll keep things simple with the puck — smack it around the boards if he gets into trouble, rather than try to make a play.

For so large a player, Norstrom uses a surprisingly short stick that cuts down on his reach defensively and limits some of his offensive options. But he feels his responsibility is to break down the play, rather than create it. He will pinch down the boards occasionally, but only to drive the puck deeper, not to grab the puck and make a play. And he won't jump into the play on offense until he has more confidence with his puck skills.

THE PHYSICAL GAME

The things that stand out about Norstrom are his willingness to do what it takes to help his team and his willingness to hit. He is solidly built and likes to throw big, loud hits. If he doesn't hit, he's not going to be around long, because his talent is not going to carry him and his hockey sense needs a lot of improvement. He knows what he's good at. Norstrom has tremendously powerful legs and is strong on his skates. He has confidence in his power game and has developed a great enthusiasm for physical play.

THE INTANGIBLES

Norstrom is a hard-working athlete who loves to practice, a player drafted more for his character than for his abilities, which are limited. He will be a defensive-style defenseman who will give his coach what's asked for, but won't try to do things that will put the puck, or the team, in trouble. Norstrom could easily handle 10 minutes a game and be a responsible guy in his own end.

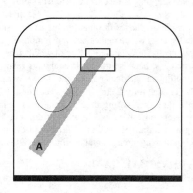

MIKE RICHTER

Yrs. of NHL service: 6
Born: Abingdon, Pa.; Sept. 22, 1966
Position: goaltender
Height: 5-10
Weight: 185
Uniform no.: 35
Catches: left

Career statistics:

GP	MINS	GA	SO	GAA	A	PIM
250	14023	710	11	3.04	6	16

1991-92 statistics:

GP	MINS	GAA	W	L	T	SO	GA	S	SAPCT	PIM
41	2298	3.11	23	12	2	3	119	1205	.901	6

1992-93 statistics:

GP	MINS	GAA	W	L	T	SO	GA	S	SAPCT	PIM
38	2105	3.82	13	19	3	1	134	2105	.886	2

1993-94 statistics:

GP	MINS	GAA	W	L	T	SO	GA	S	SAPCT	PIM
68	3710	2.57	42	12	6	5	159	1758	.910	2

1994-95 statistics:

GP	MINS	GAA	W	L	T	SO	GA	S	SAPCT	PIM
35	1993	2.92	14	17	2	2	97	884	.890	2

LAST SEASON
Stopped sixth career penalty shot.

THE PHYSICAL GAME
Richter has thighs the size of redwood trunks, which give him the explosive lateral movement that is the key to his success. He is agile, flexible and athletic, and he depends on his reflexes to reach second-chance shots off rebounds or slam-dunk one-timers off odd-man rushes. His motion isn't always all of one piece, however, and he will leave openings with a jerky, choppy movement.

He stays on his angle without charging out. He has worked hard at making his feet quicker, and as a result is much better down low, where he frustrates shooters by taking away the corners. Richter could play entire periods without productive use of his stick or gloves. He rarely catches shots, and hardly ever catches them cleanly.

Richter is starting to use his stick to play the puck more, but that is still not a natural part of his game, and while he is at last starting to use his stick for poke-checks, he still doesn't use it nearly enough as a defensive tool. Rather than use the poke-check, he concedes the pass across the crease and relies on his lateral movement to make the save.

He stands up well but leaves a lot of rebounds. His defense helps him out by scooping up the junk. Richter is getting better on shots through traffic but still has trouble with wraparounds and the occasional long shot.

THE MENTAL GAME
Richter is such a marvellous athlete that it appears more than half his battle is mental. When he plays on autopilot and when he lets his athletic skill run the show, he can win a game by himself. When he thinks too much, it all falls apart. He absolutely must feel he is the team's number one goalie.

He has learned how to survive. When he gives up a bad goal, which used to devastate him, he hangs tough now. He can improve. There are nights when he will make a great save, then blow a shot that seems routine.

THE INTANGIBLES
Richter has to be the main man, but various flaws induce doubt season after season, and it's usually something new each year. He started getting beat on the high glove side with regularity last season, a danger sign to be watched this year.

The lack of completeness in his stick work prevents Richter from moving up from "very good" to "great," but he is a winner.

NIKLAS SUNDSTROM

Yrs. of NHL service: 0
Born: Ornskoldsvik, Sweden; June 6, 1975
Position: left wing
Height: 6-0
Weight: 190
Uniform no.: n.a.
Shoots: left

Career statistics (Sweden):

GP	G	A	TP	PIM
119	23	39	62	76

1994-95 statistics:

GP	G	A	TP	PIM
33	8	13	21	30

LAST SEASON

Fourth in scoring for MoDo (Swedish Elite League).
Will be entering first full NHL season.

THE FINESSE GAME

Nagging injuries and illnesses slowed Sundstrom's
progress last season, and he played for a mediocre
MoDo team. Despite that, the Rangers' hopes remain
high for their first-round pick (eighth overall) of 1993.

Sundstrom is expected to become a very strong
two-way player. Some onlookers in Sweden think he
is more advanced than Peter Forsberg was at the same
stage, but the two players are different. Sundstrom is a
passer more than a scorer. He has to learn to shoot the
puck and drive to the net to add another facet to his
game and make him less predictable. He reads plays
very well. Defensively, he is aware and always makes
the safe decision. He could become a more creative
version of Sergei Nemchinov.

Sundstrom plays a smart game, and does a lot of
little, subtle things well.

THE PHYSICAL GAME

Sundstrom will not get much bigger, but after a brief
visit and look at NHL action last season, he knows he
has to get stronger. He is a deceptively fast skater with
good balance and a strong stride.

THE INTANGIBLES

Sundstrom will need to adjust to North America and
the NHL, and the odds are the Rangers will bring him
along slowly. But they didn't make it a priority to sign
him just to play him in the minors. Sundstrom will be
a Ranger this season, but may not see significant ice
time until the second half of the year. He played in
three World Junior tournaments, so he is used to per-
forming under pressure.

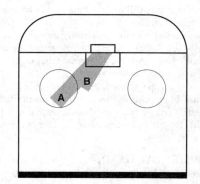

PAT VERBEEK

Yrs. of NHL service: 12
Born: Sarnia, Ont.; May 24, 1964
Position: right wing
Height: 5-9
Weight: 195
Uniform no.: 17
Shoots: right

Career statistics:

GP	G	A	TP	PIM
915	372	367	739	2105

1991-92 statistics:

GP	G	A	TP	+/-	PIM	PP	SH	GW	GT	S	PCT
76	22	35	57	-16	243	10	0	3	0	163	13.5

1992-93 statistics:

GP	G	A	TP	+/-	PIM	PP	SH	GW	GT	S	PCT
84	39	43	82	-7	197	16	0	6	2	235	16.6

1993-94 statistics:

GP	G	A	TP	+/-	PIM	PP	SH	GW	GT	S	PCT
84	37	38	75	-15	177	15	1	3	1	226	16.4

1994-95 statistics:

GP	G	A	TP	+/-	PIM	PP	SH	GW	GT	S	PCT
48	17	16	33	-2	71	7	0	2	1	131	13.0

LAST SEASON

Acquired from Hartford for Glen Featherstone, Michael Stewart, a 1995 first-round draft choice and a 1996 fourth-round draft choice. One of four Rangers to appear in all 48 games. Has missed only four games over past six seasons and has played in 237 consecutive games. Tied for team lead in goals. Tied for second on team in power play goals.

THE FINESSE GAME

Verbeek has a choppy stride, so much of his best work is done in small spaces rather than open ice. He is very strong on his skates and likes to go into traffic zones. Larger players think they can hit him, but Verbeek is so chunky and has a low centre of gravity that he is nearly impossible to bowl over. He is very good at carrying the puck along the boards, but is no stickhandler in open ice. He has no better than fair speed.

For a player who takes as many shots as Verbeek does, he is remarkably accurate, and wastes few quality scoring chances. Most of his shots come from in tight. Nothing brings out his competitive edge more than some serious crashing around the crease, most of which he initiates.

Verbeek's hands are soft and quick enough to surprise with a backhand shot. He feels the puck on his stick and looks for openings in the net, instead of scrapping with his head down and taking poor shots. Verbeek is also effective coming in late and drilling the shot.

THE PHYSICAL GAME

Verbeek is among the best in the league at drawing penalties. He can cleverly hold the opponent's stick and fling himself to the ice as if he were the injured party, and it is an effective tactic. He also draws calls honestly with his hard work by driving to the net and forcing the defender to slow him down by any means possible.

Verbeek is tough, rugged and strong, with a nasty disposition that he is learning to tame without losing his ferocious edge.

THE INTANGIBLES

Verbeek is a leader by example on the ice. He comes to play every night, plays hard through every shift and is reliable and consistent. He should produce near the 80-point range again this season. Verbeek played out his option last year, and while the Rangers said at season's end they would re-sign him, he was the focus of many trade rumours.

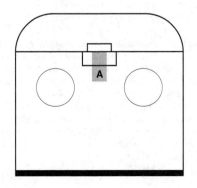

SERGEI ZUBOV

Yrs. of NHL service: 3
Born: Moscow, Russia; July 22, 1970
Position: left defense
Height: 6-0
Weight: 187
Uniform no.: 21
Shoots: right

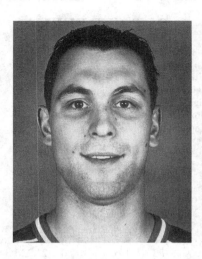

Career statistics:

GP	G	A	TP	PIM
165	30	126	156	61

1992-93 statistics:

GP	G	A	TP	+/-	PIM	PP	SH	GW	GT	S	PCT
49	8	23	31	-1	4	3	0	0	0	93	8.6

1993-94 statistics:

GP	G	A	TP	+/-	PIM	PP	SH	GW	GT	S	PCT
78	12	77	89	+20	39	9	0	1	0	222	5.4

1994-95 statistics:

GP	G	A	TP	+/-	PIM	PP	SH	GW	GT	S	PCT
38	10	26	36	-2	18	6	0	0	0	116	8.6

LAST SEASON

Second among team defensemen in scoring. Third on team in points. Missed nine games with surgery on his right wrist.

THE FINESSE GAME

Zubov plays the left side on defense, yet generates most of his scoring from the right side. He plays the right point on the power play with Brian Leetch, perhaps the best point combination in the league.

Zubov's defensive game is defined by his defiance at the blueline. He will use his reach, superior body positioning or his agility to force the play and compel the puck carrier to make a decision. He is a powerful skater who can accelerate on the glide and is capable of dropping to one knee on the glide to break up two-on-one passes.

He is still a high-risk defenseman, but his brutal plays are fewer and his brilliant plays more common-place. He loves to roam all over the ice — he has steady Kevin Lowe as his anchor — and has the puck most of the time when he's on. Some nights he will still make a nightmarish diagonal breakout pass in his own zone, a guaranteed turnover.

He has some world-class skills. He is an elite skater, with good balance and power from his leg drive. He is agile in his stops and starts, even backwards. Zubov had a good slap shot and one-times the puck with accuracy. He's not afraid to come in deep, either. Heck, sometimes he fore-checks behind the goal line on a power play. He has very strong lateral acceleration, but he also is well educated enough to keep skating stride for stride with the wing who is trying to beat him to the outside. So many other defensemen speed up a couple of strides then try to slow their men with stick checks.

THE PHYSICAL GAME

Zubov is not physical, but he is solidly built and will take a hit to make a play. His boyhood idol was Viacheslav Fetisov, and that role model should give you some idea of Zubov's style. He gets his body in the way with his great skating, then often strips the puck when the attacker finds no path to the net. He doesn't initiate much, but he doesn't mind getting hit to make a play.

THE INTANGIBLES

Trade rumours have surrounded Zubov for the past year, and it is likely he will be in a new uniform this season.

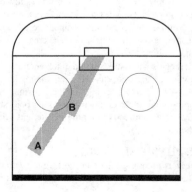

OTTAWA SENATORS

Players' Statistics 1994-95

POS	NO.	PLAYER	GP	G	A	PTS	+/-	PIM	PP	SH	GW	GT	S	PCTG
C	19	ALEXEI YASHIN	47	21	23	44	-20	20	11		1		154	13.6
C	91	ALEXANDRE DAIGLE	47	16	21	37	-22	14	4	1	2		105	15.2
L	61	SYLVAIN TURGEON	33	11	8	19	-1	29	2		1		83	13.3
R	82	MARTIN STRAKA	37	5	13	18	-1	16					49	10.2
C	74	*STEVE LAROUCHE	18	8	7	15	-5	6	2		2		38	21.1
D	3	SEAN HILL	45	1	14	15	-11	30					107	.9
C	10	ROB GAUDREAU	36	5	9	14	-16	8					65	7.7
L	49	MICHEL PICARD	24	5	8	13	-1	14	1				33	15.2
R	26	SCOTT LEVINS	24	5	6	11	4	51					34	14.7
C	17	DAVE MCLLWAIN	43	5	6	11	-26	22	1				48	10.4
C	76	*RADEK BONK	42	3	8	11	-5	28	1				40	7.5
L	7	RANDY CUNNEYWORTH	48	5	5	10	-19	68	2				71	7.0
R	25	PAT ELYNUIK	41	3	7	10	-11	51					58	5.2
L	18	TROY MALLETTE	23	3	5	8	6	35			1		21	14.3
D	6	CHRIS DAHLQUIST	46	1	7	8	-30	36	1				45	2.2
R	78	*PAVOL DEMITRA	16	4	3	7	-4		1				21	19.0
L	29	PHIL BOURQUE	38	4	3	7	-17	20					34	11.8
D	5	KERRY HUFFMAN	37	2	4	6	-17	46	2				68	2.9
C	15	DAVID ARCHIBALD	14	2	2	4	-7	19			1		27	7.4
D	94	*STANISLAV NECKAR	48	1	3	4	-20	37					34	2.9
D	21	DENNIS VIAL	27		4	4		65					9	
R	11	EVGENY DAVYDOV	3	1	2	3	2						2	50.0
D	24	*DANIEL LAPERRIERE	17	1	1	2	-3	15	1				18	5.6
D	2	JIM PAEK	29		2	2	-5	28					16	
L	23	CLAUDE BOIVIN	3		1	1	-1	6						
D	56	LANCE PITLICK	15		1	1	-5	6					11	
G	35	*MIKE BALES	1											
D	4	BRAD SHAW	2				3						3	
R	46	*DANIEL GUERARD	2											
G	30	DARRIN MADELEY	6											
D	44	*RADIM BICANEK	6				3						6	
G	33	DON BEAUPRE	37					10						

GP = games played; G = goals; A = assists; PTS = points; +/- = goals-for minus goals-against while player is on ice; PIM = penalties in minutes; PP = power play goals; SH = shorthanded goals; GW = game-winning goals; GT = game-tying goals; S = no. of shots; PCTG = percentage of goals to shots; * = rookie

DON BEAUPRE

Yrs. of NHL service: 15
Born: Kitchener, Ont.; Sept. 19, 1961
Position: goaltender
Height: 5-9
Weight: 165
Uniform no.: 33
Catches: left

Career statistics:

GP	MINS	G	SO	AVG	A	PIM
622	35120	2002	15	3.42	6	252

1991-92 statistics:

GP	MINS	GAA	W	L	T	SO	GA	S	SAPCT	PIM
54	3108	3.20	29	17	6	1	166	1435	.884	30

1992-93 statistics:

GP	MINS	GAA	W	L	T	SO	GA	S	SAPCT	PIM
58	3282	3.31	27	23	5	1	181	1530	.882	20

1993-94 statistics:

GP	MINS	GAA	W	L	T	SO	GA	S	SAPCT	PIM
53	2853	2.84	24	16	8	2	135	1122	.880	16

1994-95 statistics:

GP	MINS	GAA	W	L	T	SO	GA	S	SAPCT	PIM
37	2101	3.37	7	25	3	1	118	1143	.897	10

LAST SEASON
Acquired from Washington for a fifth-round draft pick in 1995. Missed one game with the flu.

THE PHYSICAL GAME
Beaupre is a butterfly-style goalie, but also a bit of a flopper. When he "overflops," which happens frequently with the Senators because he (like every other netminder there) tries to do so much to help the team, it becomes counterproductive.

Beaupre is extremely athletic and acrobatic, and he makes the routine saves look a bit more spectacular. It's a technique that proved popular with the Ottawa fans last season. Beaupre's style suits the east-west game most teams employ.

He is a good skater and stays with the shooter well. He is especially adept moving to his right with the attacker while remaining limber and ready to kick in that direction if a shot heads to the lower corner. Beaupre is among the older school of goalies who don't use their sticks much. He knows enough to not even try to make a long cross-ice pass. He likes to stop the puck behind the net and let the defense move it.

He has a quick glove and a good sense of anticipation, which allows him to get a piece of bang-bang plays. Last season he showed a very strong work ethic, beyond what is expected of a veteran goalie.

THE MENTAL GAME
Beaupre keeps his team in games. He can come up with the big stop on a consistent basis and will keep the score close, at least giving the Senators a chance to win or tie one. Playing behind this team will be mentally gruelling over the course of a full season, but for the time being Beaupre appears to be up to the task.

THE INTANGIBLES
Beaupre added veteran leadership to a team in desperate need of that quality. Buried in the Capitals' goaltending depth, and perhaps eager to leave some of his playoff failures behind, Beaupre came to Ottawa with a bright attitude, which was a factor in Ottawa's re-signing him.

Throughout most of his career, he has had to battle for the number one role and hasn't usually handled the challenge well. He likes knowing he's the man. He's also been saddled with the tag of being a goalie who can't win the big one. There won't be many big ones in Ottawa.

BRYAN BERARD

Yrs. of NHL service: 0
Born: Woonsocket, R.I.; March 5, 1977
Position: left defense
Height: 6-1
Weight: 190
Uniform no.: n.a.
Shoots: left

Career junior statistics:

GP	G	A	TP	PIM
58	20	54	74	97

1994-95 statistics:

GP	G	A	TP	PIM
58	20	54	74	97

LAST SEASON

Will be entering first NHL season. Won Max Kaminsky Trophy as the OHL's top defenseman. Won Emms Family Trophy as OHL's Rookie of the Year. Named to OHL First All-Star Team. Named CHL Top Draft Prospect.

THE FINESSE GAME

Berard is a sleek, swift attacking defenseman, a joy to watch because of his speedy yet effortless skating style. He loves to rush with the puck, but like New Jersey's Scott Niedermayer he is so quick to recover from any counterattack that he's usually back in a defensive posture in no time. He is seldom caught out of position.

Berard carries the puck with confidence and does not panic under pressure. His show is low and accurate, and in an OHL coaches' poll, his was voted the hardest shot in the league's Western Division. He is also a fine passer. With his combination of skills and intelligence he can control the tempo of a game.

Berard is an excellent two-way defenseman. He does not neglect his duties in his own zone. He takes pride in his complete game.

THE PHYSICAL GAME

While not overly physical, Berard has shown a willingness to use his body to slow people down. He is also very good using his stick to poke-check or break up passes, and opponents would be wise not to make cross-ice passes high in the attacking zone or he will easily step up and pick them off. He tends to run around and try to do too much sometimes, but coaches prefer sins of commission to sins of omission.

THE INTANGIBLES

With only a year of junior hockey under his belt, it's unlikely Berard is ready to take that big step and start this season in the NHL. He was ranked number one by Central Scouting prior to the 1995 draft, not just because of his ability, but because of his enormous potential. He was the first player ever to win top rookie and top defenseman in the same year in the OHL. Anyone who picks him and is willing to be patient may have the next Brian Leetch.

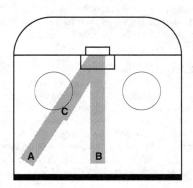

RADEK BONK

Yrs. of NHL service: 1
Born: Koprivnice, Czech Republic; Jan. 9, 1976
Position: centre
Height: 6-3
Weight: 215
Uniform no.: 76
Shoots: left

Career statistics:

GP	G	A	TP	PIM
42	3	8	11	28

1994-95 statistics:

GP	G	A	TP	+/-	PIM	PP	SH	GW	GT	S	PCT
42	3	8	11	-5	28	1	0	0	0	40	7.5

LAST SEASON
First NHL season. Missed four games with an ankle injury.

THE FINESSE GAME
Bonk doesn't skate extremely well, but he is a puck magnet; the puck always seems to end up on his stick in the slot. Bonk scores the majority of his goals from work in tight, getting his stick free and using a quick, accurate release. He is a smart and creative passer and plays well in advance of his years, with a great deal of poise.

Defensively, Bonk was not used much and needs to improve in this area. He is decent on face-offs and can be used to kill penalties because of his anticipation. He seemed enthused by the addition of Martin Straka. Not only is Straka a countryman, but his skill will help Bonk on the ice. He can also tell Bonk a thing or two about the pressure Jaromir Jagr faced (and handled well) in Pittsburgh.

THE PHYSICAL GAME
Bonk has a mean streak, and chippy play doesn't faze him a bit. Although he has good size, he does not show signs of becoming a power forward, but he is aggressive in his pursuit of the puck. He goes into the corners and wins many one-on-one battles because of his strength and hand skills. He is also getting smarter about when to hit, rather than just wasting energy. Other people will be gunning for him, and he will have to be mature enough to handle it.

THE INTANGIBLES
Bonk entered the NHL with a lucrative contract (five years, $6.125 million) and a lot of expectations. He didn't live up to either. He was simply not ready to play in the NHL, and was overmatched and overwhelmed by the level of competition. But Bonk had better get used to playing wing or he will be a fourth-line centre in Ottawa. He's young, and there's a big upside, but he has a lot of work ahead of him.

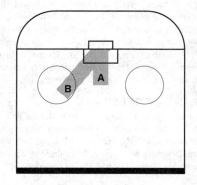

PHIL BOURQUE

Yrs. of NHL service: 7
Born: Chelmsford, Mass.; June 8, 1962
Position: left wing
Height: 6-1
Weight: 196
Uniform no.: 29
Shoots: done

Career statistics:

GP	G	A	TP	PIM
464	87	110	197	502

1991-92 statistics:

GP	G	A	TP	+/-	PIM	PP	SH	GW	GT	S	PCT
58	10	16	26	-6	58	0	1	3	0	51	19.6

1992-93 statistics:

GP	G	A	TP	+/-	PIM	PP	SH	GW	GT	S	PCT
55	6	14	20	-9	39	0	0	2	0	71	8.5

1993-94 statistics:

GP	G	A	TP	+/-	PIM	PP	SH	GW	GT	S	PCT
27	2	4	6	-4	8	0	2	0	0	21	9.5

1994-95 statistics:

GP	G	A	TP	+/-	PIM	PP	SH	GW	GT	S	PCT
38	4	3	7	-17	20	0	0	0	0	34	11.8

LAST SEASON

Missed five games with a knee injury. Missed one game with the flu. Underwent knee surgery in off-season.

THE FINESSE GAME

Bourque's top skill is his speed; he can do a lot of little things with it to help a club in subtle ways. If used on the power play, he will bring the puck up-ice intelligently, though he is not overly creative. He kills penalties with intense effort.

The drawback is that Bourque can't do much with the puck at tempo. He will drive a defender back, but won't make it pay off by using the space that opens up for him. He has a basic dump-and-chase style. He can sometimes surprise the defense by racing out from behind the net with a stuff shot.

His other valuable asset is his leadership. He is versatile enough to do whatever a team asks, include playing defense in an emergency.

THE PHYSICAL GAME

Bourque is an effort guy who has no second thoughts about diving for loose pucks. He will crash, bang and battle along the boards, in the corners and in front of the net. Bourque's on-ice courage has not faltered despite serious injury.

THE INTANGIBLES

It was typical of the kind of year Bourque had that on the day he found out he was Ottawa's nominee for the 1995 Masterton Trophy, he suffered a season-ending knee injury. Bourque's comeback last season from a life-threatening injury (suffered off-ice in a rock-climbing accident) underscores this player's grit. He is a character player who would be welcome on any team. Injuries and age are catching up, but he is still competitive, and confident enough to think he merits playing time alongside Alexei Yashin.

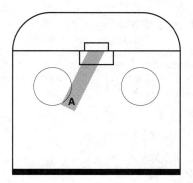

RANDY CUNNEYWORTH

Yrs. of NHL service: 10
Born: Etobicoke, Ont.; May 10, 1961
Position: left wing
Height: 6-0
Weight: 180
Uniform no.: 7
Shoots: left

Career statistics:

GP	G	A	TP	PIM
624	156	169	325	988

1991-92 statistics:

GP	G	A	TP	+/-	PIM	PP	SH	GW	GT	S	PCT
39	7	10	17	-5	71	0	0	1	0	63	11.1

1992-93 statistics:

GP	G	A	TP	+/-	PIM	PP	SH	GW	GT	S	PCT
39	5	4	9	-1	63	0	0	1	0	47	10.6

1993-94 statistics:

GP	G	A	TP	+/-	PIM	PP	SH	GW	GT	S	PCT
79	13	11	24	-1	100	0	1	2	0	154	8.4

1994-95 statistics:

GP	G	A	TP	+/-	PIM	PP	SH	GW	GT	S	PCT
48	5	5	10	-19	68	2	0	0	0	71	7.0

LAST SEASON

Signed as free agent. One of two Senators to appear in all 48 games. Led team in PIM.

THE FINESSE GAME

Cunneyworth has good straight-ahead speed with a decent shot. He sprints. He hustles. He has had two injury-free seasons after a lot of physical woes, and he competes hard every night.

He has above-average hand skills and scores most of his goals from in tight around the net. He is a good passer and likes to work give-and-go plays, although at this stage of his career he is not a great finisher.

Cunneyworth is also an effective penalty killer and does everything asked of him. He is consistent in his effort.

THE PHYSICAL GAME

Cunneyworth will hit and agitate. He isn't big but he will check and use his body in any zone. He is very annoying to play against.

THE INTANGIBLES

Cunneyworth played his junior hockey for the Ottawas 67s, and is a huge fan favourite. He was named team captain, and the Senators need his veteran savvy and leadership. He can contribute effectively for another season.

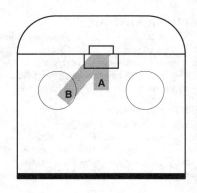

CHRIS DAHLQUIST

Yrs. of NHL service: 8
Born: Fridley, Minn.; Dec. 14, 1962
Position: right defense
Height: 6-1
Weight: 195
Uniform no.: 6
Shoots: left

Career statistics:

GP	G	A	TP	PIM
508	18	70	88	474

1991-92 statistics:

GP	G	A	TP	+/-	PIM	PP	SH	GW	GT	S	PCT
74	1	3	4	-10	68	0	0	0	0	63	1.6

1992-93 statistics:

GP	G	A	TP	+/-	PIM	PP	SH	GW	GT	S	PCT
74	3	7	10	0	66	0	0	1	0	64	4.7

1993-94 statistics:

GP	G	A	TP	+/-	PIM	PP	SH	GW	GT	S	PCT
77	1	11	12	+5	52	0	0	0	0	57	1.8

1994-95 statistics:

GP	G	A	TP	+/-	PIM	PP	SH	GW	GT	S	PCT
46	1	7	8	-30	36	1	0	0	0	45	2.2

LAST SEASON

Signed as free agent.

THE FINESSE GAME

Dahlquist uses all of his skills in the defensive zone. He was a steadying influence on the young Stanislav Neckar, who was his regular partner most of last season. Dahlquist is a little slow with his passes, but is always conscious of protecting the puck with his body. He is a good skater who is better at taking a stride or two and just guiding the puck to centre ice rather than trying to make a play.

Dahlquist is very much stay-at-home and seldom gets involved at the other end of the ice. He has a decent shot off the one-timer, but does not venture down deep. He is not a scoring threat. He kills penalties and is a great shot blocker.

THE PHYSICAL GAME

Dahlquist is not very big by today's standards, but he battles in front of the net and will move larger guys once in awhile by sheer effort. He will also get a bit chippy with his stick or elbow. He pays the toll in the corners and along the boards.

THE INTANGIBLES

Dahlquist is not getting any younger, but he wore the "A" for Ottawa last season in a quiet but key role. He started to wear down late in the season and may need to be spotted more this year.

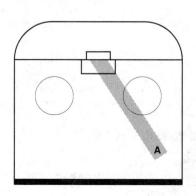

ALEXANDRE DAIGLE

Yrs. of NHL service: 2
Born: Laval, Que.; Feb. 7, 1975
Position: centre
Height: 6-0
Weight: 170
Uniform no.: 91
Shoots: left

Career statistics:

GP	G	A	TP	PIM
131	36	52	88	54

1993-94 statistics:

GP	G	A	TP	+/-	PIM	PP	SH	GW	GT	S	PCT
84	20	31	51	-45	40	4	0	2	0	168	11.9

1994-95 statistics:

GP	G	A	TP	+/-	PIM	PP	SH	GW	GT	S	PCT
47	16	21	37	-22	14	4	1	2	0	105	15.2

LAST SEASON

Missed first game of NHL career with benching on Feb. 17. Second on team in points, goals and assists, all for second consecutive season. Led team in shooting percentage. Scored team's only shorthanded goal. Tied for team lead in game-winning goals.

THE FINESSE GAME

Daigle was such a brilliant player in certain areas at the junior level that he's never had to work at many parts of his game, and he hasn't yet indicated he is willing to change. He has fine, soft hands, but in junior he could just swat the puck past somebody and say "Let's race for it," and would win most of those races. But the same move in the NHL doesn't pay off. He wins maybe half. The other chances go to waste. Daigle would be much more effective learning to work a give-and-go play.

He demonstrates a great enthusiasm for the game, but is impatient and stubborn. He has problems with teams that play a neutral zone trap. He has straight-on speed, but when the ice is closed off he looks bewildered, because he is not seeking the best options.

Like teammate Alexei Yashin, Daigle suffered from a lack of complementary linemates. He saw some ice time on the wing with Yashin simply because the Senators wanted to have their best talent on the ice at the same time, but he will be used more at centre.

Daigle has a smooth stride with one-step quickness. He handles the puck well at tempo. A strong fore-checker, he's effective as a penalty killer not because of his defensive awareness, but because he wants the puck so desperately. He has worked hard to improve his play in the defensive zone.

THE PHYSICAL GAME

Daigle is feisty and will get involved in the offensive zone, but has learned to stay away from taking dumb penalties. He could use his body better without getting creamed, but since he's not very big it's a wise idea to stay out of the corners.

THE INTANGIBLES

Daigle has not shown himself to be a superstar, and it will be a long wait if that's what's expected of him. He's just a shade below that elite level, but he will improve and become a good player — just not a great one.

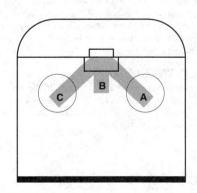

PAVOL DEMITRA

Yrs. of NHL service: 0
Born: Dubnica, Czechoslovkia; Nov. 29, 1974
Position: left wing
Height: 6-0
Weight: 189
Uniform no.: 78
Shoots: left

Career statistics:

GP	G	A	TP	PIM
28	5	4	9	4

1993-94 statistics:

GP	G	A	TP	+/-	PIM	PP	SH	GW	GT	S	PCT
12	1	1	2	-7	4	1	0	0	0	10	10.0

1994-95 statistics:

GP	G	A	TP	+/-	PIM	PP	SH	GW	GT	S	PCT
16	4	3	7	-4	0	1	0	0	0	21	19.0

LAST SEASON
Will be entering first full NHL season.

THE FINESSE GAME
Demitra is a one-dimensional offensive player. He broke an ankle in his first month of the 1993-94 season, and his skating — which was always outstanding — deteriorated to merely good. Even a year later, he no longer has the outside burst of speed he once did.

Demitra is an exceptional puckhandler, and has a quick, deceptive shot. He likes to drag the puck into his skates and then shoot it through a defenseman's legs. The move gets the rearguard to move up a little bit, and Demitra gets it by him on net.

He plays the off-wing, and will move to the middle on his forehand and throw the puck back against the grain.

THE PHYSICAL GAME
Demitra is not very big, which will probably hurt his long-term chances of being a regular in the NHL. He needs to use his speed to stay out of situations where he will get crunched.

THE INTANGIBLES
Demitra is an offensive spark, but his overall game lacks too much to earn him a full-time role. He will get another chance in training camp. If his conditioning and speed improve, he will get his share of ice time. He could be a sleeper.

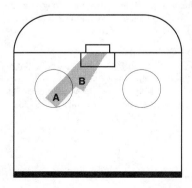

ROB GAUDREAU

Yrs. of NHL service: 3
Born: Lincoln, R.I.; Jan. 20, 1970
Position: right wing
Height: 5-11
Weight: 185
Uniform no.: 10
Shoots: right

Career statistics:

GP	G	A	TP	PIM
179	43	49	92	54

1992-93 statistics:

GP	G	A	TP	+/-	PIM	PP	SH	GW	GT	S	PCT
59	23	20	43	-18	18	5	2	1	0	191	12.0

1993-94 statistics:

GP	G	A	TP	+/-	PIM	PP	SH	GW	GT	S	PCT
84	15	20	35	-10	28	6	0	4	0	151	9.9

1994-95 statistics:

GP	G	A	TP	+/-	PIM	PP	SH	GW	GT	S	PCT
36	5	9	14	-16	8	0	0	0	0	65	7.7

LAST SEASON

Acquired on waivers from San Jose.

THE FINESSE GAME

Gaudreau is a very sleek, quick, up-and-down winger. He has nice scoring instincts and a good shot. He doesn't have a scary slapper; most of his goals come from going to the net and getting the shot away quickly. He is stocky and can keep his balance with the puck through traffic.

Gaudreau works both special teams. He handles the point on the power play on the second unit or will swing down low. He is a pure finisher. Defensively, his quickness enables him to step up and pick off passes or tip shots wide.

He takes pride in his defensive play and works hard at it. He played defense in his last year of college, so in a pinch can help out on the blueline. In five-on-five situations, he can be used as a checking winger against fast opponents (like Vyacheslav Kozlov) but not big ones like Cam Neely.

THE PHYSICAL GAME

Gaudreau is small and gritty like Tony Granato, but lacks Granato's emotion. Gaudreau will give up his body to make a play or score a goal.

THE INTANGIBLES

Gaudreau is a smart finesse player who will rate considerable time on Ottawa's special teams. Since he will be a third-line winger, he won't get the kind of numbers he had when he was one of San Jose's top forwards for two seasons.

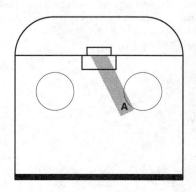

SEAN HILL

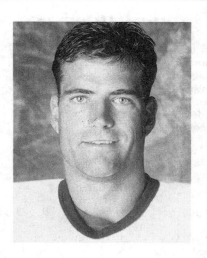

Yrs. of NHL service: 3
Born: Duluth, Minn.; Feb. 14, 1970
Position: right defense
Height: 6-0
Weight: 195
Uniform no.: 3
Shoots: right

Career statistics:

GP	G	A	TP	PIM
144	10	40	50	162

1992-93 statistics:

GP	G	A	TP	+/-	PIM	PP	SH	GW	GT	S	PCT
31	2	6	8	-5	54	1	0	1	0	37	5.4

1993-94 statistics:

GP	G	A	TP	+/-	PIM	PP	SH	GW	GT	S	PCT
68	7	20	27	-12	78	2	1	1	0	165	4.2

1994-95 statistics:

GP	G	A	TP	+/-	PIM	PP	SH	GW	GT	S	PCT
45	1	14	15	-11	30	0	0	0	0	107	0.9

LAST SEASON

Acquired from Anaheim along with 1994 ninth-round pick for Ottawa's 1994 third-round pick. Led team defensemen in scoring.

THE FINESSE GAME

A good skater, Hill is agile, strong and balanced, if not overly fast. He can skate the puck out of danger or make a smart first pass. He learned defense in the Montreal system but has since evolved into more of a specialty team player.

Hill has a good point shot and good offensive sense. He likes to carry the puck and start things off a rush, or he will jump into the play. His development allowed Ottawa to deal off Norm Maciver. Hill assumed most of Maciver's ice time on the power play.

Hill's best quality is his competitiveness. He will hack and whack and badger puck carriers like an annoying terrier ripping and nipping your socks and ankles.

THE PHYSICAL GAME

For a smallish player, Hill gets his share of points, and he gets them by playing bigger than his size. He has a bit of a mean streak, and while he certainly can't overpower people, he is a solidly built player who doesn't get pushed around easily.

THE INTANGIBLES

A poor man's Al MacInnis, Hill stepped up with the added ice time he got in Ottawa last season. He has extensive college experience and played on a Cup winner in Montreal, so Hill brings a veteran composure to the Senators. He is also a product of the U.S. Olympic program, which despite achieving no recent success at the Olympic Games, has turned out excellent pro players.

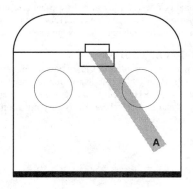

KERRY HUFFMAN

Yrs. of NHL service: 7
Born: Peterborough, Ont.; Jan. 3, 1968
Position: left defense
Height: 6-2
Weight: 200
Uniform no.: 5
Shoots: left

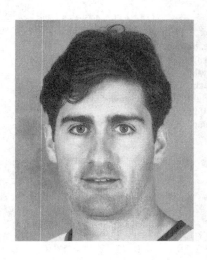

Career statistics:

GP	G	A	TP	PIM
354	32	96	128	292

1991-92 statistics:

GP	G	A	TP	+/-	PIM	PP	SH	GW	GT	S	PCT
60	14	18	32	+1	41	4	0	2	0	123	11.4

1992-93 statistics:

GP	G	A	TP	+/-	PIM	PP	SH	GW	GT	S	PCT
52	4	18	22	0	54	3	0	0	0	86	4.7

1993-94 statistics:

GP	G	A	TP	+/-	PIM	PP	SH	GW	GT	S	PCT
62	4	14	18	-28	40	2	1	0	1	112	3.6

1994-95 statistics:

GP	G	A	TP	+/-	PIM	PP	SH	GW	GT	S	PCT
37	2	4	6	-17	46	2	0	0	0	68	2.9

LAST SEASON

Missed two games with a groin injury. Missed five games with a shoulder injury.

THE FINESSE GAME

Huffman's offensive skills far outstrip his defensive ability, yet they aren't sufficient to regard him as a gifted one-way defenseman.

He is a good skater, with smooth turns to either side. He gains the blueline with enough speed that the opposing defense has to back off. He is agile and mobile enough to get the puck out of his zone and brings the puck up like a point guard on the power play. His decision-making process is much too slow, though, especially in his own zone. He takes some startling risks and sometimes makes passes dangerously close to his own goalie.

THE PHYSICAL GAME

Huffman's physical game is limited. He's big, but his personality doesn't allow him to use his size effectively. He isn't the least bit mean. He will bump some along the boards, but not with any authority.

THE INTANGIBLES

Huffman is the prototypical journeyman defenseman who will be on the bubble if a young defenseman is ready to step up. He is very good some nights, average on most and bad on others. He is very much on the down side.

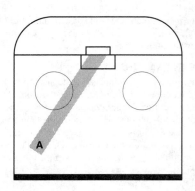

SCOTT LEVINS

Yrs. of NHL service: 2
Born: Spokane, Wash.; Jan. 30, 1970
Position: centre/right wing
Height: 6-4
Weight: 210
Uniform no.: 26
Shoots: right

Career statistics:

GP	G	A	TP	PIM
95	13	18	31	231

1992-93 statistics:

GP	G	A	TP	+/-	PIM	PP	SH	GW	GT	S	PCT
9	0	1	1	-2	18	0	0	0	0	8	0.0

1993-94 statistics:

GP	G	A	TP	+/-	PIM	PP	SH	GW	GT	S	PCT
62	8	11	19	-26	162	4	0	1	0	77	10.4

1994-95 statistics:

GP	G	A	TP	+/-	PIM	PP	SH	GW	GT	S	PCT
24	5	6	11	+4	51	0	0	0	0	34	14.7

LAST SEASON

Missed one game with an ear infection.

THE FINESSE GAME

Far too awkward to be considered a playmaker, by rights, this guy should be banging and finishing in front of the net, and that's why he spent three seasons in the minors before 1993-94 and saw another stint there last year.

Levins is big and lumbering as he moves up and down the wing (it's hard to believe he started out as a centre). He has a reputation as an unselfish team player. His skating is borderline NHL level for quickness and agility, but he is strong on his feet. He is responsible defensively and works well along the boards.

He will stand in front of the net and gets some power play time there, but pucks will have to bounce in off him since he lacks the hands and stick skills to make things happen.

THE PHYSICAL GAME

Levins is genuinely tough but not mean. He has a very long fuse and is slow to fire. He throws his weight around and works along the boards and in the corners. He's been in some heavy-duty fights, although he doesn't have the inclination to get involved.

THE INTANGIBLES

Levins is valuable just to use as a screen and to set picks, kind of like a human traffic cone. He was a decent scorer in junior, so maybe there is a scoring touch lurking under the rough exterior. Otherwise, he is destined to be a fourth-line banger.

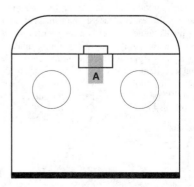

STANISLAV NECKAR

Yrs. of NHL service: 1
Born: Ceske Budejovice, Czechoslovakia; Dec. 22, 1975
Position: left defense
Height: 6-1
Weight: 196
Uniform no.: 94
Shoots: left

Career statistics:

GP	G	A	TP	PIM
48	1	3	4	37

1994-95 statistics:

GP	G	A	TP	+/-	PIM	PP	SH	GW	GT	S	PCT
48	1	3	4	-20	37	0	0	0	0	34	2.9

LAST SEASON

One of two Senators to appear in all 48 games. First NHL season.

THE FINESSE GAME

Neckar has an almost inexhaustible supply of energy, which is a good thing because the Senators gave him a ton of ice time last season and plan to do it again this year.

In addition to his physical play, which is his best asset, Necker is a polished skater, especially backwards. He is not often beaten wide. Tricky guys can get through him but he learns fast and seldom gets beaten twice.

He has decent offensive instincts, good enough to earn him time on the second power play unit, but his forte is defensive play. He doesn't have a devastating shot.

THE PHYSICAL GAME

Neckar is not a good open-ice hitter, but is very strong along the boards and in the corners. He will fight if provoked, but he isn't very good at it.

THE INTANGIBLES

Neckar's abominable plus-minus can be chalked up to his on-the-job learning against other team's top players. He is a much better all-around player than that statistic indicates. He made a lot of mistakes and will make plenty more, but he is a long-term project and the investment should play off. Gaining more familiarity with the language will help this season. Neckar has an excellent attitude and is a pleasure to coach. Although it is not common for European players to wear a "C" or an "A," Neckar might one day sport a letter on his jersey.

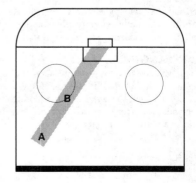

JIM PAEK

Yrs. of NHL service: 4
Born: Seoul, South Korea; Apr. 7, 1967
Position: left defense
Height: 6-1
Weight: 195
Uniform no.: 2
Shoots: left

Career statistics:

GP	G	A	TP	PIM
217	5	29	31	155

1991-92 statistics:

GP	G	A	TP	+/-	PIM	PP	SH	GW	GT	S	PCT
49	1	7	8	0	36	0	0	0	0	33	3.0

1992-93 statistics:

GP	G	A	TP	+/-	PIM	PP	SH	GW	GT	S	PCT
77	3	15	18	+13	64	0	0	0	0	57	5.3

1993-94 statistics:

GP	G	A	TP	+/-	PIM	PP	SH	GW	GT	S	PCT
59	1	5	6	-8	18	0	0	0	0	35	2.9

1994-95 statistics:

GP	G	A	TP	+/-	PIM	PP	SH	GW	GT	S	PCT
29	0	2	2	-5	28	0	0	0	0	16	0.0

LAST SEASON

Acquired from Los Angeles for future considerations.

THE FINESSE GAME

Paek is a stay-at-home defenseman. He's not flashy or skilled with the puck, nor is he fast on his feet. But things like his shot-blocking, and little safe plays like chipping the puck off the glass, make him a sensible player to have on the ice in critical defensive situations.

Paek is a leader and earned a Stanley Cup ring with the Penguins. His role and his ice time will diminish as the team's younger defensemen progress, but if they backslide, he will be ready to step in with steady play. His offensive contributions are almost nonexistent, although he can spring a player on a breakaway with a sharp pass up the middle, but it will have to be a high-percentage move for him to try it.

THE PHYSICAL GAME

Paek gets in the way but isn't a big hitter. He is determined in his protection of the net, and attackers will have to go through him to get there, but he doesn't initiate a lot of hitting. He is very strong on his stick and can pin an opponent's stick on the ice. He can pick off and control the strongest passes, and uses his reach well to deflect pucks.

THE INTANGIBLES

Paek overcame long odds to make it to the NHL (his Pittsburgh jersey is in the Hockey Hall of Fame, as he is the first NHLer from South Korea). Having made it, he battles to stay here.

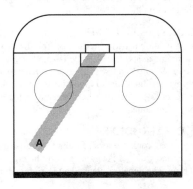

MARTIN STRAKA

Yrs. of NHL service: 3
Born: Pilsen, Czechoslovakia; Sept. 3, 1972
Position: centre
Height: 5-10
Weight: 178
Uniform no.: 82
Shoots: left

Career statistics:

GP	G	A	TP	PIM
163	38	60	98	69

1992-93 statistics:

GP	G	A	TP	+/-	PIM	PP	SH	GW	GT	S	PCT
42	3	13	16	+2	29	0	0	1	0	28	10.7

1993-94 statistics:

GP	G	A	TP	+/-	PIM	PP	SH	GW	GT	S	PCT
84	30	34	64	+24	24	2	0	6	1	130	23.1

1994-95 statistics:

GP	G	A	TP	+/-	PIM	PP	SH	GW	GT	S	PCT
37	5	13	18	-1	16	0	0	0	0	49	10.2

the end of the season and he could get a great deal of ice time as a number two centre behind Alexei Yashin if Ottawa keeps Alexandre Daigle on the wing.

LAST SEASON

Acquired from Pittsburgh for Troy Murray and Norm Maciver. Missed eight games with a season-ending knee injury.

THE FINESSE GAME

Straka is a speedy little centre — a water bug with imagination. He makes clever passes that always land on the tape and give the recipient time to do something with the puck. He's more of a playmaker than a shooter and will have to learn to go to the net more to make his game less predictable. He draws people to him and creates open ice for his linemates.

Straka was able to adjust to smaller North American ice surfaces because of his ability to stop and start. He doesn't have the outside speed to burn defenders, but creates space for himself with his wheeling in tight spaces. He has good balance and is tough to knock off his feet even though he's not big. He complemented countryman Radek Bonk well, and may help Bonk's development this season.

Not a great defensive player, Straka is effective in five-on-five situations. He is an offensive threat every time he steps on the ice.

THE PHYSICAL GAME

Straka has shown little inclination for the typical North American style of play. He is small and avoids corners and walls, and will have to be teamed with more physical linemates to give him some room. He has to learn to protect the puck better with his body and buy some time.

THE INTANGIBLES

After a strong rookie season, Straka saw surprisingly little ice time with the Penguins prior to his trade late last season. The Senators planned on re-signing him at

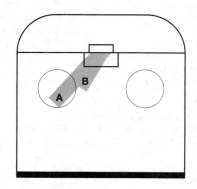

SYLVAIN TURGEON

Yrs. of NHL service: 12
Born: Noranda, Que.; Jan. 17, 1965
Position: left wing
Height: 6-0
Weight: 200
Uniform no.: 61
Shoots: left

Career statistics:

GP	G	A	TP	PIM
669	269	226	495	691

1991-92 statistics:

GP	G	A	TP	+/-	PIM	PP	SH	GW	GT	S	PCT
56	9	11	20	-4	39	6	0	1	0	99	9.1

1992-93 statistics:

GP	G	A	TP	+/-	PIM	PP	SH	GW	GT	S	PCT
72	25	18	43	-29	104	8	0	2	1	249	10.0

1993-94 statistics:

GP	G	A	TP	+/-	PIM	PP	SH	GW	GT	S	PCT
47	11	15	26	-25	52	7	0	2	2	116	9.5

1994-95 statistics:

GP	G	A	TP	+/-	PIM	PP	SH	GW	GT	S	PCT
33	11	8	19	-1	29	2	0	1	0	83	13.3

LAST SEASON

Missed one game with a bruised foot. Third on team in points.

THE FINESSE GAME

Turgeon still has some speed and quickness to go along with his scoring instincts. He can do one thing well, and that's pull the trigger. He has sound instincts around the net and a wicked release. He doesn't give up on a shot, but will follow to the net for a rebound. He is not a creative playmaker. He gets his assists from teammates scoring off his shots.

On the power play, Turgeon will stand off to the side and sneak in for a tip or redirect. He has sharp hand-eye co-ordination and he still has the moves to beat a defender one-on-one. He would be much more effective if he looked to use his linemates, but that is never an option for him. He is hopeless on defense.

THE PHYSICAL GAME

Turgeon is in better shape and has shown improved willingness to mix it up. He battles for the puck and shields the puck well. He turns his back and absorbs a hit to protect the puck and keep it alive along the boards. He keeps his stick high.

THE INTANGIBLES

A work ethic has come late to Turgeon. If he worked as hard early in his career as he does now, he would still be a Hartford Whaler. Because of Ottawa's lack of scoring depth on the wings, he gets one more last chance. Turgeon was assigned to the minor league squad when training camp broke prior the lockout last season, and the message sunk in.

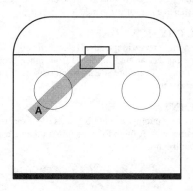

DENNIS VIAL

Yrs. of NHL service: 3
Born: Sault Ste. Marie, Ont.; Apr. 10, 1969
Position: left defense
Height: 6-2
Weight: 218
Uniform no.: 21
Shoots: left

Career statistics:

GP	G	A	TP	PIM
148	3	10	13	448

1991-92 statistics:

GP	G	A	TP	+/-	PIM	PP	SH	GW	GT	S	PCT
27	1	0	1	+1	72	0	0	0	0	6	16.7

1992-93 statistics:

GP	G	A	TP	+/-	PIM	PP	SH	GW	GT	S	PCT
9	0	1	1	+1	20	0	0	0	0	5	0.0

1993-94 statistics:

GP	G	A	TP	+/-	PIM	PP	SH	GW	GT	S	PCT
55	2	5	7	-9	214	0	0	0	0	37	5.4

1994-95 statistics:

GP	G	A	TP	+/-	PIM	PP	SH	GW	GT	S	PCT
27	0	4	4	0	65	0	0	0	0	9	0.0

LAST SEASON

Missed one game with an ankle injury.

THE FINESSE GAME

Vial's best asset is his strength. When his team faces players with big power forwards, it is Vial who usually gets the chore of trying to move them out from in front of the net.

Vial is prone to bad giveaways. Often his mistakes end up in the net. He will gamble with a cross-ice breakout pass and has to learn to make the safe plays, such as banking the puck off the boards. By doing more of the little things right, he could move up on Ottawa's depth chart from sixth or seventh to as high as fourth. But the glaring mistakes dog him.

Vial is a strong skater and well-balanced. He's not quick, however, and that's what has kept him in the minors or on the bubble throughout his career. He likes to play a containment game, forcing the skaters to come to him. He has no involvement whatsoever in the offensive part of the game.

THE PHYSICAL GAME

Vial is a legitimate tough guy. He's mean, too, and has earned respect around the NHL from other genuine tough guys. There are nights when it is best not to wake Vial up.

THE INTANGIBLES

Vial is very intelligent, but his smarts don't sneak into his game often enough to make him a reliable every-day contributor.

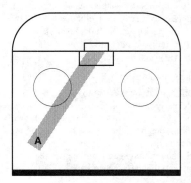

ALEXEI YASHIN

Yrs. of NHL service: 2
Born: Sverdlovsk, Russia; Nov. 5, 1973
Position: centre
Height: 6-2
Weight: 196
Uniform no.: 19
Shoots: right

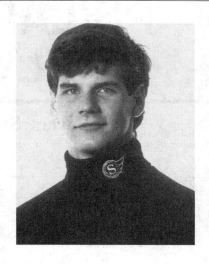

Career statistics:

GP	G	A	TP	PIM
130	51	72	123	42

1993-94 statistics:

GP	G	A	TP	+/-	PIM	PP	SH	GW	GT	S	PCT
83	30	49	79	-49	22	11	2	3	0	232	12.9

1994-95 statistics:

GP	G	A	TP	+/-	PIM	PP	SH	GW	GT	S	PCT
47	21	23	44	-20	20	11	0	1	0	154	13.6

LAST SEASON

Led team in goals, assists, points, power play goals and shots, for second consecutive season.

THE FINESSE GAME

Yashin isn't a flashy skater, but he has drawn comparisons to Ron Francis in his quiet effectiveness. He is spectacular at times, but he gets up to 30 minutes of ice time a night (a compliment to his skill and an indictment of the team's lack of depth).

Understandably, Yashin didn't go all-out every shift, and there were times when he looked like he was either pacing himself or was genuinely fatigued. Yashin can be the best player on the ice one night, and the next you have to go back and check the videotape to see if he was dressed. He is a good friend of Alexei Kovalev, a player who has heard similar criticism in New York.

Yashin's skills rank with any of the new guard of players who have entered the league in the past two seasons. He has great hands and size. He is deliberate. As he stickhandles in on the rush, he can put the puck through the legs of two or three defenders en route to the net. He has to learn, though, that he can go directly to the net and not wait for the defense to come to him, so that he can dazzle by using their legs as croquet wickets. Basically, Yashin has to simply go to the net more and shed the notion that he gets style points for dangling the puck.

He doesn't have breakaway speed, but he is powerful and balanced. He has good sense with the puck and will drive to the net or dish it off. His biggest problem in Ottawa is the lack of a finisher to play with, and that problem will persist this season.

Yashin routinely plays the full two minutes on the power play, handling the first portion down low, then dropping back to the point on the second unit. He also killed a lot of penalties, not because of any particular defensive brilliance (he's actually rather weak) but because of his overall skills.

THE PHYSICAL GAME

Yashin uses his size and strength well to control and protect the puck. He takes a pounding but doesn't have anyone on the team to step in for him, so he has to fight his own battles.

THE INTANGIBLES

Yashin was a very popular player in the room in his first season with the Senators, but his constant squabbles over contracts and trade demands are starting to wear thin. He is an exceptional talent and a player to build a franchise around. The Senators would be loath to move him, but if they do they could get the same kind of talent infusion Quebec did when they were forced to deal Eric Lindros. Odds are, though, Yashin won't be dealt.

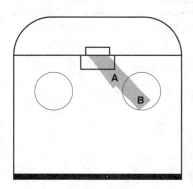

PHILADELPHIA FLYERS

Players' Statistics 1994-95

POS	NO.	PLAYER	GP	G	A	PTS	+/-	PIM	PP	SH	GW	GT	S	PCTG
C	88	ERIC LINDROS	46	29	41	70	27	60	7		4	1	144	20.1
L	19	MIKAEL RENBERG	47	26	31	57	20	20	8		4		143	18.2
C	10	JOHN LECLAIR	46	26	28	54	20	30	6		7		131	19.8
C	17	ROD BRIND'AMOUR	48	12	27	39	-4	33	4	1	2		86	14.0
D	37	ERIC DESJARDINS	43	5	24	29	12	14	1		1		93	5.4
D	2	DIMITRI YUSHKEVICH	40	5	9	14	-4	47	3	1	1		80	6.3
R	11	KEVIN DINEEN	40	8	5	13	-1	39	4		2		55	14.5
D	6	*CHRIS THERIEN	48	3	10	13	8	38	1				53	5.7
R	18	BRENT FEDYK	30	8	4	12	-2	14	3		2		41	19.5
C	14	CRAIG MACTAVISH	45	3	9	12	2	23					38	7.9
C	44	ANATOLI SEMENOV	41	4	6	10	-12	10	2				69	5.8
C	25	SHJON PODEIN	44	3	7	10	-2	33			1		48	6.3
D	5	KEVIN HALLER	36	2	7	9	16	48					26	7.7
L	45	GILBERT DIONNE	26		9	9	-4	4					33	
D	24	KARL DYKHUIS	33	2	6	8	7	37	1		1		46	4.3
D	23	PETR SVOBODA	37		8	8	-5	70					39	
L	12	*PATRIK JUHLIN	42	4	3	7	-13	6			1		44	9.1
C	9	ROB DIMAIO	36	3	1	4	8	53				1	34	8.8
R	21	DAVE BROWN	28	1	2	3	-1	53					8	12.5
C	22	JIM MONTGOMERY	13	1	1	2	-4	8					13	7.7
G	27	RON HEXTALL	31		1	1		13						
D	20	ROB ZETTLER	32		1	1	-3	34					17	
D	37	SHAWN ANDERSON	1											
D	23	STEWART MALGUNAS	4				-1	4					1	
D	28	JASON BOWEN	4				-2						2	
G	33	DOMINIC ROUSSEL	19					6						
L	15	*YANICK DUPRE	22				-7	8					21	
L	8	SHAWN ANTOSKI	32				-4	107					16	

GP = games played; G = goals; A = assists; PTS = points; +/- = goals-for minus goals-against while player is on ice; PIM = penalties in minutes; PP = power play goals; SH = shorthanded goals; GW = game-winning goals; GT = game-tying goals; S = no. of shots; PCTG = percentage of goals to shots; * = rookie

JASON BOWEN

Yrs. of NHL service: 2
Born: Port Alice, B.C.; Nov. 11, 1973
Position: left defense
Height: 6-4
Weight: 210
Uniform no.: 28
Shoots: left

Career statistics:

GP	G	A	TP	PIM
67	2	5	7	89

1992-93 statistics:

GP	G	A	TP	+/-	PIM	PP	SH	GW	GT	S	PCT
7	1	0	1	+1	2	0	0	0	0	3	33.3

1993-94 statistics:

GP	G	A	TP	+/-	PIM	PP	SH	GW	GT	S	PCT
56	1	5	6	+12	87	0	0	1	0	50	2.0

1994-95 statistics:

GP	G	A	TP	+/-	PIM	PP	SH	GW	GT	S	PCT
4	0	0	0	-2	0	0	0	0	0	2	0.0

LAST SEASON

Played most of season with Hershey (AHL), recording
5-5 — 10 and 116 PIM in 55 games.

THE FINESSE GAME

Bowen uses his size well and is not afraid to move up
into the attack and get involved in the offensive play.
He doesn't have a lot of clever moves. But since he
has played some left wing through his career he has
confidence in his offensive abilities. That versatility
marks him as a valuable commodity.

Bowen continues to adjust to the NHL pace. His
decision-making process is slow — you can almost
watch him thinking on the ice — and he gets caught as
a result, particularly in the neutral zone. He tends to
run around and lose his assignment in the defensive
zone, and he has to learn to trust his partner and play
better positionally.

Bowen's skating is solid. He has excellent
straightaway speed and surprising quickness for such
a big skater. He is very strong on his skates.

THE PHYSICAL GAME

Bowen is big and tough, and he appears to have the
hunger and eagerness to pay the price in the NHL.
Once he establishes himself, he will merit a lot of
room. He has an imposing physical presence.

THE INTANGIBLES

Bowen was slowed by injuries at the start of the season while he was in the minors, but his progress was
steady and he can be expected to join the Flyers' improving defense corps this season. He could get a lot
of power play time.

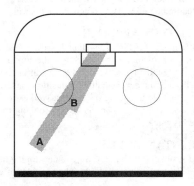

ROD BRIND'AMOUR

Yrs. of NHL service: 6
Born: Ottawa, Ont.; Aug. 9, 1970
Position: centre/left wing
Height: 6-1
Weight: 202
Uniform no.: 17
Shoots: left

Career statistics:

GP	G	A	TP	PIM
450	160	249	409	446

1991-92 statistics:

GP	G	A	TP	+/-	PIM	PP	SH	GW	GT	S	PCT
80	33	44	77	-3	100	8	4	5	0	202	16.3

1992-93 statistics:

GP	G	A	TP	+/-	PIM	PP	SH	GW	GT	S	PCT
81	37	49	86	-8	89	13	4	4	1	206	18.0

1993-94 statistics:

GP	G	A	TP	+/-	PIM	PP	SH	GW	GT	S	PCT
84	35	62	97	-9	85	14	1	4	0	230	15.2

1994-95 statistics:

GP	G	A	TP	+/-	PIM	PP	SH	GW	GT	S	PCT
48	12	27	39	-4	33	4	1	2	0	86	14.0

and defense along with strength and grinding. The next step for him will be to develop Muller's intense focus and concentration. Brind'amour stepped up big time when Eric Lindros missed the start of the playoffs with an eye injury.

LAST SEASON

One of two Flyers to appear in all 48 games and has not missed a game in two seasons. Fourth on team in points.

THE FINESSE GAME

Brind'amour's biggest asset is that he is a complete player. He is not fancy and won't beat many players one-on-one in open ice, but he will outwork defenders along the boards and use a quick burst of speed to drive to the net. He's a playmaker in the mucking sense, with scoring chances emerging from his hard work and checking.

Brind'amour has a long, powerful stride with a quick first step to leave a defender behind. He has the hand skills to go along with the hard work. He drives well into a shot on the fly, and he also has a quick-release snap shot and a strong backhand. His passes are crisp to either side.

Brind'Amour is as good without the puck as with it, because he will work ferociously for control.

THE PHYSICAL GAME

Brind'Amour uses his size well and is a strong skater. He can muck with the best of them in the corners and along the boards. He will carry the puck through traffic in front of the net and battle for position for screens and tip-ins. He is among the hardest workers on the team, even in practice, and is always looking to improve his game.

THE INTANGIBLES

Brind'amour could be very close to developing into a solid Kirk Muller-style forward who provides offense

ERIC DESJARDINS

Yrs. of NHL service: 7
Born: Rouyn, Que.; June 14, 1969
Position: right defense
Height: 6-1
Weight: 200
Uniform no.: 37
Shoots: right

Career statistics:

GP	G	A	TP	PIM
439	48	155	203	363

1991-92 statistics:

GP	G	A	TP	+/-	PIM	PP	SH	GW	GT	S	PCT
77	6	32	38	+17	50	4	0	2	0	141	4.3

1992-93 statistics:

GP	G	A	TP	+/-	PIM	PP	SH	GW	GT	S	PCT
82	13	32	45	+20	98	7	0	1	0	163	8.0

1993-94 statistics:

GP	G	A	TP	+/-	PIM	PP	SH	GW	GT	S	PCT
84	12	23	35	-1	97	6	1	3	0	193	6.2

1994-95 statistics:

GP	G	A	TP	+/-	PIM	PP	SH	GW	GT	S	PCT
43	5	24	29	+12	14	1	0	1	0	93	5.4

LAST SEASON

Acquired from Montreal with John LeClair and Gilbert Dionne for Mark Recchi and a 1995 third-round draft pick. Led team defensemen in scoring. Missed four games with a groin injury.

THE FINESSE GAME

Desjardins is an all-around defenseman who is solid in all areas without being exceptional in any single facet of the game.

Defensively, he's stalwart. He has good defensive instincts and plays well positionally. He seldom loses his cool and doesn't run around getting caught up-ice.

Offensively, his game has improved but it's likely this is the top end. He is a very good skater with speed, balance and agility, and he is willing to join the attack. He can work the point on the power play and has an excellent one-timer, probably his best shot. He also moves the puck well, either breaking out of his own zone or sliding along the blueline and looking to move the puck in deep.

Desjardins is also an excellent penalty killer because of his skating and his anticipation. He seldom drops down to the ice to block shots, but uses his stick or skate and stays on his feet to control the puck.

THE PHYSICAL GAME

Desjardins has worked hard to become stronger. He is very strong and patrols the front of his net like a doberman. He makes take-out checks, and if his team needs a booming hit as a wake-up call, he will deliver the collision. He has a long fuse and does not fight. Desjardins plays hurt.

THE INTANGIBLES

While most people called Bob Clarke's big trade the "John LeClair deal," many hockey insiders referred to it as the "Eric Desjardins deal," since it was the acquisition of this defenseman that allowed a lot of the pieces of Philadelphia's defensive puzzle to fall into place. He is a quiet leader, and while he isn't a true number one defenseman, he is a great player in the dressing room and improves any player he is paired with. He is ultrareliable.

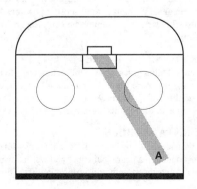

KEVIN DINEEN

Yrs. of NHL service: 11
Born: Quebec City, Que.; Oct. 28, 1963
Position: right wing
Height: 5-11
Weight: 195
Uniform no.: 11
Shoots: right

Career statistics:

GP	G	A	TP	PIM
747	302	318	620	1504

1991-92 statistics:

GP	G	A	TP	+/-	PIM	PP	SH	GW	GT	S	PCT
80	30	32	62	-5	143	6	3	5	0	225	13.3

1992-93 statistics:

GP	G	A	TP	+/-	PIM	PP	SH	GW	GT	S	PCT
83	35	28	63	+14	201	6	3	7	1	241	14.5

1993-94 statistics:

GP	G	A	TP	+/-	PIM	PP	SH	GW	GT	S	PCT
71	19	23	42	-9	113	5	1	2	1	156	12.2

1994-95 statistics:

GP	G	A	TP	+/-	PIM	PP	SH	GW	GT	S	PCT
40	8	5	13	-1	39	4	0	2	0	55	14.5

LAST SEASON

Runner-up for 1995 Masterton Trophy. Missed six games with a shoulder injury.

THE FINESSE GAME

A streaky scorer, Dineen's veteran experience shows through even when he's not seeing the results on the scoresheet. He never fails to contribute in other ways when he is in a drought, by hitting, killing penalties and keeping up the grinding part of his game.

Dineen never seems to be still. His feet keep moving and pumping and he does a good job drawing penalties. He is very scrappy in battles for the loose puck. Confident and determined, he has the skating and hand quickness to make things happen when he gains control.

During his slumps, Dineen appears to double-clutch his stick and just about grind it into sawdust. When he's connecting, the game looks easy, but it's all a result of his hard effort. He doesn't waste his shots. He gets into high-quality scoring positions low and uses his wrist shot, though he can also fire from the wing.

THE PHYSICAL GAME

Dineen's skating gives him the momentum to pile into traffic for the loose puck. He has a hard edge to him most nights and, while he is not a very big player, he doles out every last ounce of himself.

THE INTANGIBLES

Dineen had some run-ins with coach Terry Murray, but responded in a positive manner and was a key performer down the stretch and in the playoffs. Dineen was a free agent after last season, and, while he might be tempted to find a change of scenery, the nearing image of a Stanley Cup in Philadelphia probably looks appealing to this veteran. His future is as a checking winger who can also step up in the occasional offensive role for the team. Wear and tear is catching up with him physically, but he has a big heart.

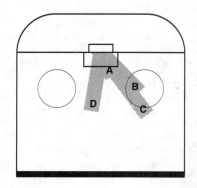

KARL DYKHUIS

Yrs. of NHL service: 1
Born: Sept-Iles, Que.,; July 8, 1972
Position: right defense
Height: 6-3
Weight: 195
Uniform no.: 24
Shoots: left

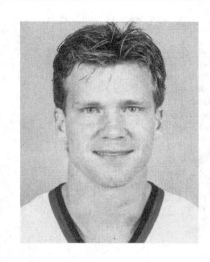

Career statistics:

GP	G	A	TP	PIM
51	3	14	17	41

1991-92 statistics:

GP	G	A	TP	+/-	PIM	PP	SH	GW	GT	S	PCT
6	1	3	4	-1	4	1	0	0	0	12	8.3

1992-93 statistics:

GP	G	A	TP	+/-	PIM	PP	SH	GW	GT	S	PCT
12	0	5	5	+2	0	0	0	0	0	10	0.0

1993-94 statistics:

P	G	A	TP	+/-	PIM	PP	SH	GW	GT	S	PC

Did not play in NHL

1994-95 statistics:

GP	G	A	TP	+/-	PIM	PP	SH	GW	GT	S	PCT
33	2	6	8	+7	37	1	0	1	0	46	4.3

LAST SEASON

Acquired from Chicago for Bob Wilkie.

THE FINESSE GAME

Dykhuis has excellent mobility and quickness, with a quick shift of gears that allows him to get up the ice in a hurry. He was a former first-round pick of Chicago (16th overall in 1990). While he was slow to develop, he didn't get shuffled around and was able to stay in one organization and learn to play the game. He has acquired a lot of experience, and it shows in his poise.

Dykhuis's game has an edge on the offensive side, but he also uses his finesse skills well in his own end of the ice. One of the reasons why the Flyers were an improved team defensively last year is that they were able to move the puck out of the zone efficiently. Dykhuis was one of the best defensemen in that category.

Smart, with good hands for passing or drilling shots from the point, Dykhuis won't venture down low unless the decision to pinch is a sound one. He can kill penalties and play four-on-four.

THE PHYSICAL GAME

Although tall and rangy, Dykhuis isn't a heavyweight. He is strong and makes solid contact. He is such a good skater that he can break up a play, dig out the loose puck, and be off in just a stride or two to start an odd-man rush.

Dykhuis has a mean streak and can handle himself in a fight. He will stand up for his teammates.

THE INTANGIBLES

Dykhuis loves to play the game, and after three sea-sons in the minors has paid the price and wants to stay in the NHL. The adrenaline rush of his quick rise last year should not subside.

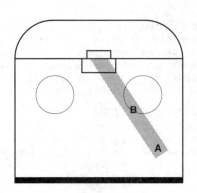

KEVIN HALLER

Yrs. of NHL service: 4
Born: Trocho, Alta.; Dec. 5, 1970
Position: left defense
Height: 6-3
Weight: 182
Uniform no.: 5
Shoots: left

Career statistics:

GP	G	A	TP	PIM
266	26	55	81	395

1991-92 statistics:

GP	G	A	TP	+/-	PIM	PP	SH	GW	GT	S	PCT
66	8	17	25	-9	92	3	0	1	0	85	9.4

1992-93 statistics:

GP	G	A	TP	+/-	PIM	PP	SH	GW	GT	S	PCT
73	11	14	25	+7	117	6	0	1	0	126	8.7

1993-94 statistics:

GP	G	A	TP	+/-	PIM	PP	SH	GW	GT	S	PCT
68	4	9	13	+3	118	0	0	1	0	72	5.6

1994-95 statistics:

GP	G	A	TP	+/-	PIM	PP	SH	GW	GT	S	PCT
36	2	7	9	+16	48	0	0	0	0	26	7.7

of the team's top defense pairing.

LAST SEASON

Led team defensemen in plus-minus. Missed six games with a groin strain.

THE FINESSE GAME

Haller has good finesse skills, but over the past two seasons has paid a great deal of attention to his defensive play. While he still has trouble reading the rush, he is developing into a reliable two-way defenseman.

Haller still shines brightly on offense. An excellent skater with an easy stride, he makes skating look effortless, and he likes to carry the puck. He will join the attack or even lead a rush. Haller can make a play. He is a good passer who spots the open receiver and can find a second option quickly.

He has a hard, low shot from the point that seems to get through traffic. He probably won't ever be among the NHL leaders in scoring by defensemen, but he can improve over the numbers he's put up the past few seasons.

THE PHYSICAL GAME

Haller is still a little light and needs to add more muscle, but he is playing tougher and mentally is more prepared to handle the rigors of a full season. He competes every night, and wants the responsibility of being on the ice in key situations.

THE INTANGIBLES

Haller is on the third team of his young career, but seems to have found a home in Philadelphia. He has a good coach (Terry Murray) and a good veteran defense partner (Eric Desjardins) to work with, and he's still only 25. He will get a lot of prime ice time as half

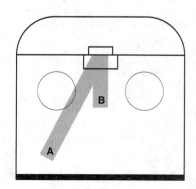

RON HEXTALL

Yrs. of NHL service: 8
Born: Brandon, Man.; May 3, 1964
Position: goaltender
Height: 6-3
Weight: 192
Uniform no.: 27
Catches: left

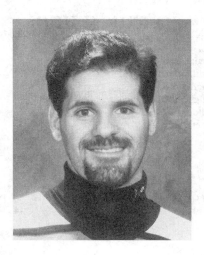

Career statistics:

GP	MINS	G	SO	AVG	A	PIM
431	24631	1330	10	3.24	21	501

1991-92 statistics:

GP	MINS	GAA	W	L	T	SO	GA	S	SAPCT	PIM
45	2668	3.40	16	21	6	3	151	1294	.883	35

1992-93 statistics:

GP	MINS	GAA	W	L	T	SO	GA	S	SAPCT	PIM
54	2988	3.45	29	16	5	0	172	1529	.888	56

1993-94 statistics:

GP	MINS	GAA	W	L	T	SO	GA	S	SAPCT	PIM
65	3581	3.08	27	26	6	5	184	1801	.898	52

1994-95 statistics:

GP	MINS	GAA	W	L	T	SO	GA	S	SAPCT	PIM
31	1824	2.89	17	9	1	1	88	801	.890	13

THE INTANGIBLES
Hextall still figures to be Philadelphia's number one goalie next season. The team has improved so much defensively in front of him that the work load should be easy for him to handle, and the high-quality scoring opportunities will be fewer.

LAST SEASON
Acquired from the New York Islanders with sixth-round draft pick in 1995 for Tommy Soderstrom. Best GAA of career.

THE PHYSICAL GAME
Hextall's puckhandling ability is still among the best in the league, and he's like a third defenseman. He can get overconfident and make the occasional bad pass, but he never loses his faith in his ability to whip the puck off the glass or find an open teammate with a pass. Hextall is a penalty-killing goalie, and his defense takes its cue from him when to get the puck and when to wheel off for a feed.

Hextall is not a great skater laterally. In the playoffs, the Devils were able to exploit the fact that Hextall didn't move from post to post well when the puck was being moved out from behind the net. He is one of the most aggressive goalies in the NHL at challenging shooters. He comes well out to the top of his crease; some teams try to tempt him to come too far out so they can get him to overcommit. Hextall is quick down low, but has trouble on the glove side.

THE MENTAL GAME
Hextall is extremely competitive. He has matured and is a lot less hotheaded than he was in the past, but he will still whack ankles and jump on somebody's head if opponents are trespassing. Teams like to try to get Hextall off his game. They still think he's vulnerable mentally, but last season he resulted in a big infusion of confidence.

PATRIK JUHLIN

Yrs. of NHL service: 1
Born: Huddinge, Sweden; April 24, 1970
Position: right wing
Height: 6-0
Weight: 187
Uniform no.: 12
Shoots: left

Career statistics:

GP	G	A	TP	PIM
42	4	3	7	6

1994-95 statistics:

GP	G	A	TP	+/-	PIM	PP	SH	GW	GT	S	PCT
42	4	3	7	-13	6	0	0	1	0	44	9.1

LAST SEASON

First NHL season. Missed three games with a sprained knee. Worst plus-minus on team.

THE FINESSE GAME

Juhlin was a big scorer in big games — he scored seven goals for gold medalist Sweden in the 1994 Olympics — but he had to make the adjustment to smaller ice surfaces, more physical NHL play and North American life all at once. The transition was not smooth and it is far from complete.

Juhlin has a lot of jump, good hands and good skills, but the scoring chances didn't materialize for him because of some of the shortcomings in his game. He was not good in traffic. He has to learn when to go in deep offensively and when to drop back and support his team defensively. Too often he gets trapped in deep and doesn't make the commitment to his team defensively. As a result, Juhlin's ice time was cut and he didn't get a chance to improve.

THE PHYSICAL GAME

Juhlin needs to get stronger. He's not a big man, but he plays a wispy game even for his size and doesn't have the kind of overwhelming skills that might allow him to play a less involved game.

THE INTANGIBLES

Juhlin has a great deal of upside, but right know he's raw talent that hasn't been honed. The decision will be up to Juhlin. He has the potential to be a strong, second-line winger to give the Flyers needed scoring depth, but he has to become mentally tougher.

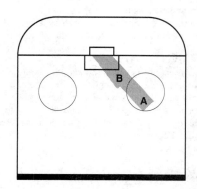

JOHN LECLAIR

Yrs. of NHL service: 4
Born: St. Albans, Vt.; July 5, 1969
Position: left wing
Height: 6-2
Weight: 215
Uniform no.: 10
Shoots: left

Career statistics:

GP	G	A	TP	PIM
261	74	93	167	101

1991-92 statistics:

GP	G	A	TP	+/-	PIM	PP	SH	GW	GT	S	PCT
59	8	11	19	+5	14	3	0	0	0	73	11.0

1992-93 statistics:

GP	G	A	TP	+/-	PIM	PP	SH	GW	GT	S	PCT
72	19	25	44	+11	33	2	0	2	0	139	13.7

1993-94 statistics:

GP	G	A	TP	+/-	PIM	PP	SH	GW	GT	S	PCT
74	19	24	43	+17	32	1	0	1	0	153	12.4

1994-95 statistics:

GP	G	A	TP	+/-	PIM	PP	SH	GW	GT	S	PCT
46	26	28	54	+20	30	6	0	7	0	131	19.8

LAST SEASON

Acquired from Montreal with Eris Desjardins and Gilbert Dionne, for Mark Recchi and a 1995 third round draft pick. Tied for second on team in goals with career high. Led team and tied for second in NHL in game-winning goals. Tied for second on team in plus-minus. Third on team in assists and points. Missed one game with a hip injury.

THE FINESSE GAME

LeClair has a hard shot and can dominate with speed, size and hands. He is a strong skater who can drive the defense back when they see this big dude with the puck barrelling at them in overdrive. LeClair sees the ice well and makes creative plays. He is not an instinctive scorer and has to work hard for what he achieves.

LeClair can pass to either side and makes good use of the extra ice he gets, getting the puck free to a linemate if he attracts too much defensive attention.

He had a reluctance to shoot, but since going to the Flyers has become the kind of sniper the Canadiens were waiting (in vain) for him to develop into. He gets into a zone now where he just shoots, even if he doesn't known where the puck is going, and it's usually on target.

The knock on LeClair was his inconsistency, but the move to Philadelphia and playing on the team's top line there seems to have been the alarm clock LeClair needs.

THE PHYSICAL GAME

LeClair wins the one-on-one battles and beats everyone to the loose pucks. The fact that he is no longer the only big forward (as he was in Montreal) but now gets to play with big, strong linemates has given him more confidence. LeClair can be a dominant forward. He doesn't have much of a mean streak, though.

THE INTANGIBLES

The knock on LeClair was his inconsistency, but the move to Philadelphia and playing on the top line with Eric Lindros and Mikael Renberg seems to be the nightly alarm clock LeClair needs. There are a few scouts who are holding out and saying LeClair won't do it over the course of a full season, but the majority believe LeClair has finally become the 40-goal power scorer his size had promised. One caveat: LeClair's disappointing performance against New Jersey in the playoffs.

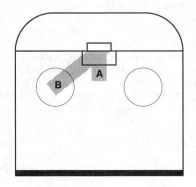

ERIC LINDROS

Yrs. of NHL service: 3
Born: London, Ont.; Feb. 28, 1973
Position: centre
Height: 6-5
Weight: 227
Uniform no.: 88
Shoots: right

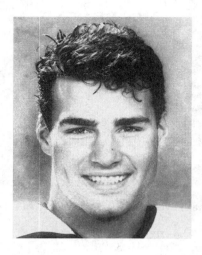

Career statistics:

GP	G	A	TP	PIM
172	114	128	242	310

1992-93 statistics:

GP	G	A	TP	+/-	PIM	PP	SH	GW	GT	S	PCT
61	41	34	75	+28	147	8	1	5	1	180	22.8

1993-94 statistics:

GP	G	A	TP	+/-	PIM	PP	SH	GW	GT	S	PCT
65	44	53	97	+16	103	13	2	9	1	197	22.3

1994-95 statistics:

GP	G	A	TP	+/-	PIM	PP	SH	GW	GT	S	PCT
46	29	41	70	+27	60	7	0	4	1	144	20.1

LAST SEASON

Led team in points and tied for NHL scoring lead, but lost Art Ross Trophy due to scoring three fewer goals than Jaromir Jagr. Won 1995 Hart Trophy. Named to 1995 NHL First All-Star Team. Led team in goals for second consecutive season. Led team and fourth in NHL in plus/minus. Led team in shooting percentage. Second on team in power play goals. Led team and tied for fourth in NHL in assists. Had 14-game point streak, tied for longest in NHL last season. Missed one game with the flu.

THE FINESSE GAME

Lindros may be the best big skater the game has ever seen. He isn't the least bit clumsy, gets up to speed in just a few strides and can hurdle a defenseman to avoid a check, keeping his balance and the puck.

Lindros works for his goals. He is not a natural goal-scorer rifling shots from the top of the circles, but drives down low and intimidates the defense and the goalie. He can take a pass with his soft hands and whistle a wrist or snap shot. He has strong arms and can roof the puck as well as anyone in the league. None of this comes easily — Lindros has worked hard on his shots and the results show. He uses a stick with a very stiff shaft and can get a lot of power on a one-handed shot.

He is a better finisher than playmaker, but he can make accurate passes off his forehand or backhand. He does just about everything well except kill penalties, but there are enough teammates to handle that.

Lindros is good on face-offs because he simply overpowers his opposite number.

THE PHYSICAL GAME

Lindros doesn't need to score to be effective, which is something he is still learning. He can dominate a game without getting on the scoreboard. There are still nights when he will float and not do much with or without the puck.

When there is a race to the puck in the corner, the opponent doesn't want to get there ahead of Lindros, because he knows he'll get smashed. So he slows to arrive at the same time, and Lindros has the hand skills and the muscle to win the battle for the puck. There are very few defensemen and no opposing centres able to match up to Lindros physically. His body slams make other players tentative. Instead of concerning themselves first with what to do with the puck, they are bracing themselves for the Lindros hit, and the puck goes bye-bye.

THE INTANGIBLES

The lessons learned from Philadelphia's loss in the 1995 Eastern Conference Finals were studied by Lindros during the off-season. He's got the money, he's got an MVP award, but now he needs to become a winner. His "Legion of Doom" line will face the same intense pressure it did last season, and Lindros will have to deal with it better than he did against the Devils. Fortunately for him, few teams match up as well against the Flyers as New Jersey does, and he should be among the NHL's scoring leaders again.

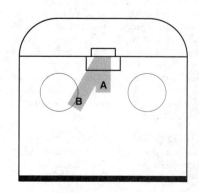

CRAIG MACTAVISH

Yrs. of NHL service: 13
Born: London, Ont.; Aug. 15, 1958
Position: centre
Height: 6-1
Weight: 195
Uniform no.: 14
Shoots: left

Career statistics:

GP	G	A	TP	PIM
975	206	254	460	788

1991-92 statistics:

GP	G	A	TP	+/-	PIM	PP	SH	GW	GT	S	PCT
80	12	18	30	-1	98	0	2	1	0	86	14.0

1992-93 statistics:

GP	G	A	TP	+/-	PIM	PP	SH	GW	GT	S	PCT
82	10	20	30	-16	110	0	3	3	0	101	9.9

1993-94 statistics:

GP	G	A	TP	+/-	PIM	PP	SH	GW	GT	S	PCT
78	20	13	33	-14	91	1	0	2	1	122	16.4

1994-95 statistics:

GP	G	A	TP	+/-	PIM	PP	SH	GW	GT	S	PCT
45	3	9	12	+2	23	0	0	0	0	38	7.9

LAST SEASON

Missed three games with foot injuries.

THE FINESSE GAME

MacTavish plays the whole ice well, but is exceptional in the 25 feet from the attacking slot to the lane behind the net. He is relentless, smart, strong, tough and quick. He can create a turnover or he can finish a scoring chance. He also matches up defensively against all but the fastest centres in the league.

MacTavish is among the best in the league at face-offs. That is, he is among the best in the league at cheating on face-offs. MacTavish always seems to have his body turned a little more than he should, or doesn't have his stick on the ice the way he is supposed to. Subtle enough to not get caught, effective enough to give him an edge.

MacTavish plays a basic offensive game, just getting the puck and moving it quickly. He can hang on and rag the puck when he's killing penalties, but he seldom overhandles.

He keeps himself fit and his effort is nonstop.

THE PHYSICAL GAME

MacTavish's competitive fire still burns. He gives his all and his durability is amazing given the way he sacrifices every night. He enjoyed the challenge of helping to bring New York its first Stanley Cup in 54 years, then helped bully the Flyers into making the playoffs for the first time since 1988-89.

He fore-checks tenaciously, and he will drive to the net dragging a defender with him.

THE INTANGIBLES

Although he is very near the end of his career, MacTavish remains a terrific penalty killer and clutch player. He was a captain in Edmonton and has been a member of four Cup-winning teams. He'll probably have one more NHL season, and wants to help Eric Lindros and the young Flyers rebound from last season's playoff disappointment. He's a third-line centre, but a most effective one.

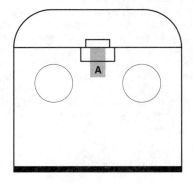

MIKAEL RENBERG

Yrs. of NHL service: 2
Born: Pitea, Sweden; May 5, 1972
Position: right wing
Height: 6-1
Weight: 218
Uniform no.: 19
Shoots: left

Career statistics:

GP	G	A	TP	PIM
130	64	75	139	56

1993-94 statistics:

GP	G	A	TP	+/-	PIM	PP	SH	GW	GT	S	PCT
83	38	44	82	+8	36	9	0	1	0	195	19.5

1994-95 statistics:

GP	G	A	TP	+/-	PIM	PP	SH	GW	GT	S	PCT
47	26	31	57	+20	20	8	0	4	0	143	18.2

LAST SEASON

Led team in power play goals. Second on team in points and assists. Tied for second on team in goals and plus-minus. Missed one game with a shoulder injury.

THE FINESSE GAME

Renberg isn't overwhelming in any single facet of his game. He is an average skater in terms of speed, but he has a long, strong stride with excellent balance and appears to be building along the lines of a power forward.

He drives to the net. He is strong enough to shrug off a lot of checks or even shovel a one-handed shot or pass if one arm is tied up. He likes to come in on the off-wing, especially on the power play, and snap a strong shot off his back foot. He sees the ice well and is always looking for a teammate whom he can hit with a forehand or backhand pass, but Renberg has to think "shoot" more often.

He can score in a lot of ways, but Renberg's best shots are his quick release wrists or snaps with little backswing. He is defensively aware and will be a solid two-way forward who can be on the ice in almost any situation.

THE PHYSICAL GAME

Renberg adapted quickly to the North American style of hockey. He doesn't fight, but he has a bit of a nasty streak and he likes to hit hard. He won't be intimidated. Since he isn't a great skater, his adjustment to the smaller ice surfaces actually helped his game. Playing with John LeClair and Eric Lindros on the "Legion of Doom" line has made him even braver.

Renberg just kept growing after his draft year and might actually play better a few pounds lighter, but he is very strong.

THE INTANGIBLES

What sophomore slump? Renberg barely missed a

beat after a strong rookie season and is among the league's top right wings. He is going to get even better, and may have a shot at a 50-goal season.

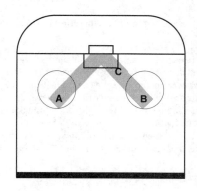

KJELL SAMUELSSON

Yrs. of NHL service: 9
Born: Tyngsryd, Sweden; Oct. 18, 1958
Position: right defense
Height: 6-6
Weight: 235
Uniform no.: 28
Shoots: right

Career statistics:

GP	G	A	TP	PIM
609	40	117	157	1031

1991-92 statistics:

GP	G	A	TP	+/-	PIM	PP	SH	GW	GT	S	PCT
74	5	11	16	+1	110	0	0	1	0	91	5.5

1992-93 statistics:

GP	G	A	TP	+/-	PIM	PP	SH	GW	GT	S	PCT
63	3	6	9	+25	106	0	0	1	0	63	4.8

1993-94 statistics:

GP	G	A	TP	+/-	PIM	PP	SH	GW	GT	S	PCT
59	5	8	13	+18	118	1	0	0	0	57	8.8

1994-95 statistics:

GP	G	A	TP	+/-	PIM	PP	SH	GW	GT	S	PCT
41	1	6	7	+8	54	0	0	0	0	37	2.7

LAST SEASON

Missed six games with the flu. Missed one game with a groin injury. Signed as a free agent by Philadelphia.

THE FINESSE GAME

One NHL opponent said playing against Samuelsson is like playing in seaweed. He has the wingspan of a condor and is strong with his long stick, so that he can control the puck dangling miles away from his body after he has knocked it off the puck carrier's blade.

Samuelsson's enormous stride just eats up the ice. It doesn't look like he's moving fast, because he doesn't have to. He isn't very quick and doesn't get involved in the rush, but instead concentrates on his own zone. He makes the simple play, forcing the attacking player to the boards and taking him out of the play with a solid hit. He doesn't do much with the puck, just banking it off the boards or driving it deep. He won't be caught looking for the perfect play. He doesn't amass many points, or many minuses, with his ultraconservative style. Samuelsson has a strong point shot but does not get it away very quickly. He won't be found deep, either, so don't expect to see him scrambling to get back into defensive position. He's already there.

THE PHYSICAL GAME

Samuelsson is a strong and nasty hitter for someone who looks so benign. In addition to using his body and powerful leg drive, he will rub his glove or elbow against an opponent's jaw or offer his stick for use as a dental device. He also clutches and grabs, but does it in a smart veteran way, hanging on just long enough to provoke irritation but not long enough to merit a penalty. He will also yap to distraction.

He will pay the physical price to block shots and clear his crease.

THE INTANGIBLES

Samuelsson has great poise for pressure situations. He has started looking slower than ever, however, and needs to be paired with a more mobile defense partner so he can continue to be effective in his plodding way. The revamped Flyers have a number of young players who could develop as perfect partners for him.

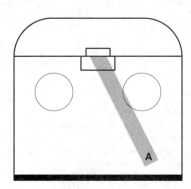

PETR SVOBODA

Yrs. of NHL service: 11
Born: Most, Czechoslovakia; Feb. 14, 1966
Position: left defense
Height: 6-1
Weight: 170
Uniform no.: 23
Shoots: left

Career statistics:

GP	G	A	TP	PIM
684	44	242	286	1031

1991-92 statistics:

GP	G	A	TP	+/-	PIM	PP	SH	GW	GT	S	PCT
71	6	22	28	+1	146	1	0	3	0	111	5.4

1992-93 statistics:

GP	G	A	TP	+/-	PIM	PP	SH	GW	GT	S	PCT
40	2	24	26	+3	59	1	0	1	0	61	3.3

1993-94 statistics:

GP	G	A	TP	+/-	PIM	PP	SH	GW	GT	S	PCT
60	2	14	16	+11	89	1	0	0	0	80	2.5

1994-95 statistics:

GP	G	A	TP	+/-	PIM	PP	SH	GW	GT	S	PCT
37	0	8	8	-5	70	0	0	0	0	39	0.0

LAST SEASON

Acquired from Buffalo for Garry Galley. Missed one game with a neck injury.

THE FINESSE GAME

Svoboda was robbed of some of his skating power by knee surgery and injury over the previous two seasons. He was never strong on his skates, but he had great quickness, balance and agility — and you can't hit what you can't catch.

Svoboda has a long stride. Not a very solid player, he is lean and wiry, and his skating is economical.

He has excellent instincts. He can carry the puck well and join the rush. He has a quick release on his wrist and snap shots, and also a good one-timer that he uses on the power play. He reads plays well offensively and defensively.

THE PHYSICAL GAME

Not one for physical play, he is still a feisty foe who will take the body and then use his stick to rap a player in the choppers or pull his skates out from under him. He ticks off a lot of people.

Svoboda is very lean and can't do much one-on-one in a close battle. He will ride an opponent out of the play well when he can use his skating to generate some power.

THE INTANGIBLES

Svoboda's neck injury lingered into the playoffs, and the Flyers missed him. He is part of a deep and improving defense corps, but his continuing health problems make him a long-haul risk.

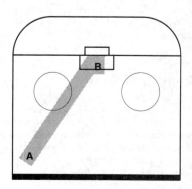

CHRIS THERIEN

Yrs. of NHL service: 1
Born: Ottawa, Ont.; Dec. 14, 1971
Position: left defense
Height: 6-3
Weight: 240
Uniform no.: 6
Shoots: left

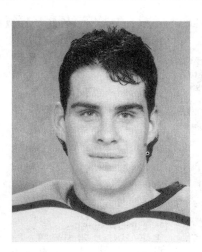

Career statistics:

GP	G	A	TP	PIM
48	3	10	13	38

1994-95 statistics:

GP	G	A	TP	+/-	PIM	PP	SH	GW	GT	S	PCT
48	3	10	13	+8	38	1	0	0	0	53	5.7

LAST SEASON
First NHL season. One of two Flyers to appear in all 48 games.

THE FINESSE GAME
Therien was one of the surprises of training camp. No, make that a shock. Few expected this product of the 1994 Canadian Olympic team to have an impact on the Flyers' lineup, and he turned out to be a key member of a defensive-minded team that saw its team goals-against average drop from 3.74 (in 1993-94) to 2.75.

Therien's improvement started in the summer of 1994, when he took up the invitation offered by the team to come in for fitness testing. Therien then made the commitment to work on his conditioning, and it paid off with an NHL job. He is one of the team's hardest checkers.

Therien also likes to skate with the puck, and he has very good mobility for a big man. He concentrated on his own end of the ice last season, but he will become more involved in the attack. He can get up the ice in a hurry and has a good sense of offensive plays. Therien can play the point on the power play.

THE PHYSICAL GAME
Therien is the strongest defenseman on the Flyers — so strong that he's the one teammate Eric Lindros can't mow down in practice. As he gains more experience and confidence, Therien will become a more physically dominating defenseman. He doesn't have that presence now, but he has that potential. He has to get more aggressive.

THE INTANGIBLES
Therien's commitment to improving his game indicates a mature approach to the sport. He needs to improve his defensive reads, so he will know when to step up for a hit or when to back off, and he will develop into a solid two-way defenseman. He figures to be among the Flyers' top four defensemen next season. He will make more mistakes, but he will learn from them.

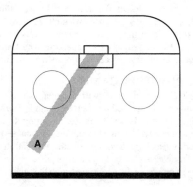

DIMITRI YUSHKEVICH

Yrs. of NHL service: 3
Born: Cherepovets, Russia; Nov. 19, 1971
Position: right defense
Height: 5-11
Weight: 187
Uniform no.: 2
Shoots: left

Career statistics:

GP	G	A	TP	PIM
197	15	61	76	204

1992-93 statistics:

GP	G	A	TP	+/-	PIM	PP	SH	GW	GT	S	PCT
82	5	27	32	+12	71	1	0	1	0	155	3.2

1993-94 statistics:

GP	G	A	TP	+/-	PIM	PP	SH	GW	GT	S	PCT
75	5	25	30	-8	86	1	0	2	0	136	3.7

1994-95 statistics:

GP	G	A	TP	+/-	PIM	PP	SH	GW	GT	S	PCT
40	5	9	14	-4	47	3	1	1	0	80	6.3

LAST SEASON

Second among team defensemen in scoring. Missed five games with a knee injury. Scored first career shorthanded goal.

THE FINESSE GAME

Yushkevich is a terrific skater in all facets. He is strong and well balanced; he can move laterally, pivot and put on a burst of short speed or sustain a rush the length of the rink; he has the stamina to play all night long. Occasionally, he can be beaten with outside speed, but it takes a pretty fast and powerful skater to do it.

Positionally, Yushkevich plays a smart game. He is intelligent and poised, and he gets the crunch-time exposure because he is capable of making the big plays, offensively and defensively. He gets into trouble because he does not always read plays coming at him well. He also tends to make some nonchalant plays, and was benched during the season for indifferent defensive play.

He can work the point on the power play, using his hard, low shot or moving the puck around.

Yushkevich has all the skills but is also willing to play a grinding game. He follows up the play well and gets involved in the attack. He puts so much on his shots that defensemen have been known to limp off the ice after blocking his (wrist) shots from the point.

THE PHYSICAL GAME

The Flyers were unhappy with the shape Yushkevich was in when he arrived for training camp in 1994. He dropped 15 pounds playing in Russia during the lockout and reported back in possibly the best shape of his career. Yushkevich has to maintain his commitment. He can be expected to handle a lot of ice time, and needs to recapture the aggressive edge that marked his rookie season. He can be an enthusistic hitter, and likes to wade in and use his body to win puck battles. He can hit to hurt, and is annoying to play against.

THE INTANGIBLES

Yushkevich can't afford another in-and-out start to his season. It may make a difference that for the first time in three years there will be a real battle for jobs on defense in the Flyer camp, so Yushkevich can't come in with a complacent feeling. Terry Murray won't hesitate to bench him.

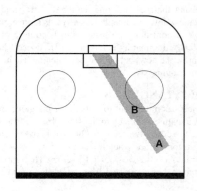

PITTSBURGH PENGUINS

Players' Statistics 1994-95

POS	NO.	PLAYER	GP	G	A	PTS	+/-	PIM	PP	SH	GW	GT	S	PCTG
R	68	JAROMIR JAGR	48	32	38	70	23	37	8	3	7		192	16.7
C	10	RON FRANCIS	44	11	48	59	30	18	3		1		94	11.7
R	17	TOMAS SANDSTROM	47	21	23	44	1	42	4	1	3	1	116	18.1
L	20	LUC ROBITAILLE	46	23	19	42	10	37	5		3	1	109	21.1
D	55	LARRY MURPHY	48	13	25	38	12	18	4		3		124	10.5
R	7	JOE MULLEN	45	16	21	37	15	6	5	2	3		78	20.5
C	11	JOHN CULLEN	46	13	24	37	-4	66	2		1		88	14.8
L	25	KEVIN STEVENS	27	15	12	27		51	6		4		80	18.8
C	15	SHAWN MCEACHERN	44	13	13	26	4	22	1	2	1		97	13.4
D	22	NORM MACIVER	41	4	16	20	-2	16	2				50	8.0
C	12	TROY MURRAY	46	4	12	16	-2	39			1		45	8.9
D	5	ULF SAMUELSSON	44	1	15	16	11	113					47	2.1
D	23	CHRIS JOSEPH	33	5	10	15	3	46	3				73	6.8
C	9	*LEN BARRIE	48	3	11	14	-4	66			1		37	8.1
C	16	MIKE HUDSON	40	2	9	11	-1	34			1		33	6.1
D	28	KJELL SAMUELSSON	41	1	6	7	8	54					37	2.7
D	4	GREG HAWGOOD	21	1	4	5	2	25	1				17	5.9
R	29	MARKUS NASLUND	14	2	2	4		2					13	15.4
D	37	*GREG ANDRUSAK	7		4	4	-1	6					7	
L	33	JIM MCKENZIE	39	2	1	3	-7	63			1		16	12.5
D	2	*CHRIS TAMER	36	2		2		82					26	7.7
D	44	DRAKE BEREHOWSKY	29		2	2	-9	28					14	
D	18	FRANCOIS LEROUX	40		2	2	7	114					19	
C	34	*RUSTY FITZGERALD	4	1		1	2						5	20.0
C	26	*RICHARD PARK	1		1	1	1	2					4	
D	32	PETER TAGLIANETTI	13		1	1	1	12					5	
L	34	*JEFF CHRISTIAN	1										2	
G	30	*PHILIPPE DE ROUVILLE	1											
G	35	TOM BARRASSO	2											
G	1	WENDELL YOUNG	10					2						
G	31	KEN WREGGET	38					14						

GP = games played; G = goals; A = assists; PTS = points; +/- = goals-for minus goals-against while player is on ice; PIM = penalties in minutes; PP = power play goals; SH = shorthanded goals; GW = game-winning goals; GT = game-tying goals; S = no. of shots; PCTG = percentage of goals to shots; * = rookie

TOM BARRASSO

Yrs. of NHL service: 12
Born: Boston, Mass.; Mar. 31, 1965
Position: goaltender
Height: 6-3
Weight: 211
Uniform no.: 35
Catches: right

Career statistics:

GP	MINS	GA	SO	GAA	A	PIM
548	31555	1802	21	3.43	40	377

1991-92 statistics:

GP	MINS	GAA	W	L	T	SO	GA	S	SAPCT	PIM
57	3329	3.53	25	22	9	2	196	1702	.885	30

1992-93 statistics:

GP	MINS	GAA	W	L	T	SO	GA	S	SAPCT	PIM
63	3702	3.01	43	14	5	4	186	1885	.901	24

1993-94 statistics:

GP	MINS	GAA	W	L	T	SO	GA	S	SAPCT	PIM
44	2482	3.36	22	15	5	2	139	1304	.893	42

1994-95 statistics:

GP	MINS	GAA	W	L	T	SO	GA	S	SAPCT	PIM
2	125	3.84	0	1	1	0	8	75	.893	0

LAST SEASON
Missed 44 games with surgery on his right wrist to repair tendon and cartilage damage.

THE PHYSICAL GAME
Barrasso is ideally suited to his team's style of play. The Penguins tend to give up a lot of odd-man rushes and Barrasso makes the save, handling the puck quickly to get his team going on a counterattack. It's doubtful if he would have played as well in recent years if he had been with a more conservative team.

One of the most impressive things about Barrasso is that although he is often on his knees, he is almost never on his side. He might be the best in the league at recovering from going down and will be back on his skates with his glove in position for the next shot. He leaves a lot of long rebounds but plays with veteran defensemen who help him out when things gets scrambly. And if Barrasso has to freeze the puck for a draw, who better than Ron Francis to hop over the boards and help the Penguins control it.

Barrasso loves to handle the puck; he's like a third defenseman in both his willingness to leave the crease and his ability to pass. He is a good skater who is able to get to and control a lot of pucks that most goalies wouldn't dare try to reach. Staying on his feet more (a fundamental he has improved with experience) allows him to make the most of his skating skills. Most of the time he will use the boards for his passes, rather than make a risky play up the middle, but every so often he is vulnerable to the interception.

Because of Barrasso's range, teams have to adapt their attack. Hard dump-ins won't work, because he will stop them behind the net and zip the puck right back out for an alert counterattack by his teammates. Since he comes out around the post to his right better than his left, teams have to aim soft dumps to his left, making him more hesitant about making the play and giving the fore-checkers time to get in on him. Barrasso's lone weakness appears to be shots low on the glove side.

THE MENTAL GAME
Barrasso's confidence borders on arrogance, and it's visible from the way he carries himself on the ice. The flip side of this is that he doesn't think he gets the credit he deserves, and he gets whiny and petulant if, for example, he thinks he should have been one of the three stars of the game and isn't. This is petty for a goaltender of his stature.

Barrasso has good anticipation and concentration, almost a sixth sense of what the shooter is going to do. He has to be beaten because he seldom beats himself.

THE INTANGIBLES
The Penguins face a dilemma in the nets if Barrasso — who took a back seat to Ken Wregget in the playoffs — is back to 100 per cent. He is the goalie who led the Penguins to two Stanley Cups, but Wregget is popular with his teammates and held down the fort last season. Barrasso would be tough to move because of his age, contract and recent injuries. He and Wregget may have to share the load.

RON FRANCIS

Yrs. of NHL service: 14
Born: Sault Ste. Marie, Ont.; Mar. 1, 1963
Position: centre
Height: 6-2
Weight: 200
Uniform no.: 10
Shoots: left

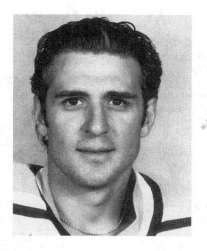

Career statistics:

GP	G	A	TP	PIM
1008	349	789	1138	737

1991-92 statistics:

GP	G	A	TP	+/-	PIM	PP	SH	GW	GT	S	PCT
70	21	33	54	-7	30	5	1	2	1	121	17.4

1992-93 statistics:

GP	G	A	TP	+/-	PIM	PP	SH	GW	GT	S	PCT
84	24	76	100	+6	68	9	2	4	0	215	11.2

1993-94 statistics:

GP	G	A	TP	+/-	PIM	PP	SH	GW	GT	S	PCT
82	27	66	93	-3	62	8	0	2	1	216	12.5

1994-95 statistics:

GP	G	A	TP	+/-	PIM	PP	SH	GW	GT	S	PCT
44	11	48	59	+30	18	3	0	1	0	94	11.7

LAST SEASON

Won 1995 Lady Byng Trophy. Led NHL in assists and plus-minus. Second on team and fifth in NHL in points. Reached 1,000-game and 1,100-point milestones. Missed three games with the flu and one game with a back injury.

THE FINESSE GAME

Francis may be the Einstein of face-offs. Call him Dr. Draw. On rare nights when he is struggling with an opposing centre, he'll tinker with his changes in the neutral zone, then save what he has learned for a key draw deep in either zone. Just as a great scorer never shows a goalie the same move twice in a row, he never uses the same technique in succession. He has good hand-eye coordination and uses his body well at the dot. Pittsburgh goalies have no fear about freezing the puck because of Francis' superiority on face-offs. Few players win their draws as outright as Francis does on a consistent basis.

One of the best two-way centres in the league, he is the ultimate number two centre who has filled the role of number one for the past two seasons due to the absence of Mario Lemieux. Francis can still put points on the board. Technically, he is a choppy skater who gets where he has to be with a minimum amount of style. His understanding of the game is key because he has great awareness of his positioning. He gets a lot of ice time (far too much), so he has learned to pace himself to conserve his energy. There are few useless bursts of speed.

While he focuses on a defensive role, Francis has the hands and the vision to come out of a defensive scramble into an attacking rush. He anticipates passes, blocks shots, then springs an odd-man breakout with a smart play. He plays with Jaromir Jagr, who is always hanging and circling and looking for the opportunity, and Francis often finds him.

Francis doesn't have a screamingly hard shot, nor is he a flashy player. He works from the centre of the ice, between the circles, and has a quick release on a one-timer. He can kill penalties or work the point on the power play with equal effectiveness. He complements any kind of player.

THE PHYSICAL GAME

Not a big, imposing hitter, Francis will use his body to get the job done. He will bump and grind and go into the trenches. Back on defense, he can function as a third defenseman; on offense, you will find him going into the corners or heading for the front of the net for tips and rebounds. He is a strong and balanced skater with quickness, though he doesn't have a pretty stride.

Francis gets a lot of ice time but keeps himself in great shape. Still, despite the lockout-shortened season, he was a worn and weary player in the playoffs, and the Penguins desperately need to shore up their middle to give their 32-year-old centre a break.

THE INTANGIBLES

Poise and professionalism have always marked Francis's career, and he has only enhanced that reputation with the way he has conducted himself in his four seasons in Pittsburgh. He has never gotten the credit he deserves because he lacks the charisma of so many other Penguins stars, but without his acquisition from the Whalers in 1991, the Penguins probably wouldn't have won a single Cup, let alone two. Despite the grey hair showing in his locks, Francis was on a pace for another 100-point season last year, and should be at that range again, but he is getting perilously near the point where his defense will outweigh his point production.

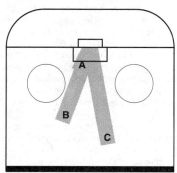

JAROMIR JAGR

Yrs. of NHL service: 5
Born: Kladno, Czechoslovakia; Feb. 15, 1972
Position: right wing
Height: 6-2
Weight: 208
Uniform no.: 68
Shoots: left

Career statistics:

GP	G	A	TP	PIM
359	157	232	389	235

1991-92 statistics:

GP	G	A	TP	+/-	PIM	PP	SH	GW	GT	S	PCT
70	32	37	69	+12	34	4	0	4	0	194	16.5

1992-93 statistics:

GP	G	A	TP	+/-	PIM	PP	SH	GW	GT	S	PCT
81	34	60	94	+30	61	10	1	9	0	242	14.0

1993-94 statistics:

GP	G	A	TP	+/-	PIM	PP	SH	GW	GT	S	PCT
80	32	67	99	+15	61	9	0	6	2	298	10.7

1994-95 statistics:

GP	G	A	TP	+/-	PIM	PP	SH	GW	GT	S	PCT
48	32	38	70	+23	37	8	3	7	0	192	16.7

LAST SEASON

Won Art Ross Scoring Trophy. Finalist for 1995 Hart Trophy. Led team and second in NHL in goals. Led team in points for second consecutive season. Second on team in assists and plus-minus. Led team and fourth in NHL in shots. Led team and tied for second in NHL in game-winning goals. Led team in power play goals and shorthanded goals. One of three Penguins to appear in all 48 games.

THE FINESSE GAME

Jagr is as close to a perfect skater as there is in the NHL. He keeps his body centred over his skates, giving him a low centre of gravity and making it very tough for anyone to knock him off the puck. He has a deep knee bend, for quickness and power. His strokes are long and sure, he has control over his body, and his lateral mobility helps him beat almost any defender in the league one-on-one. Add to that his ability to handle the puck while he's dazzling everyone with his footwork, and the sum is perhaps the best offensive player in the NHL.

He is certainly the most dynamic. Jagr lives and loves to play the game and he brings that joy to the ice. His long hair flowing out from beneath his helmet, Jagr is poetry is motion with his beautifully effortless skating style. With Mario Lemieux out of the lineup again last season, Jagr responded well to the extra responsibility. Playing with the more defensive-minded Ron Francis as his safety valve gives the flashy Czech even more freedom to freewheel, and no one does it like Jagr.

With his Lemieux-like reach, he can dangle the puck while he's gliding and swooping. Jagr will fake the backhand and go to his forehand in a flash. He is powerful enough to drag a defender with him to the net and push off a strong one-handed shot. He has a big slap shot and can drive it on the fly or with a one-timer off a pass.

Jagr uses his teammates slightly better than in the past, but the key to his game is getting him isolated in a one-on-one situation.

One of the reasons for Jagr's wicked shots are his barely legal sticks. He gets them illegally curved on order from the factory, and sharp-eyed opposing coaches (or their equipment managers) should keep a lookout for those he hasn't doctored to NHL specifications. The more severe the curve, though, the less control Jagr has of a backhand shot that could be a more effective weapon with a straighter blade.

THE PHYSICAL GAME

Jagr can be intimidated, and that is one of the worst-kept secrets in the NHL. He will draw penalties with his speed and forces people to back off, but he can be taken out of a game if hit early.

He is in excellent physical condition and is often double-shifted.

THE INTANGIBLES

Jagr hasn't hit the ceiling yet. At only 23, he has a season or two to hit his best stride. He has continued to improve, which is a positive sign, and if it hadn't been for the lockout, Jagr probably would have hit the 50-goal mark for the first time. But he should be a 60- or even 70-goal scorer with his skill level.

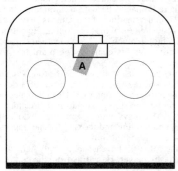

CHRIS JOSEPH

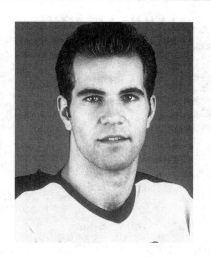

Yrs. of NHL service: 4
Born: Burnaby, B.C.; Sept. 10, 1969
Position: right defense
Height: 6-2
Weight: 210
Uniform no.: 23
Shoots: right

Career statistics:

GP	G	A	TP	PIM
270	27	72	99	371

1991-92 statistics:

GP	G	A	TP	+/-	PIM	PP	SH	GW	GT	S	PCT
7	0	0	0	-1	8	0	0	0	0	5	0.0

1992-93 statistics:

GP	G	A	TP	+/-	PIM	PP	SH	GW	GT	S	PCT
33	2	10	12	-9	48	1	0	0	0	49	4.1

1993-94 statistics:

GP	G	A	TP	+/-	PIM	PP	SH	GW	GT	S	PCT
76	11	20	31	-21	136	8	0	0	0	179	6.1

1994-95 statistics:

GP	G	A	TP	+/-	PIM	PP	SH	GW	GT	S	PCT
33	5	10	15	+3	46	0	0	0	0	73	6.8

LAST SEASON

Acquired from Tampa Bay in waiver draft. Missed 14 games with ligament damage in his right knee.

THE FINESSE GAME

Joseph has good skating skills forward and backward. He can skate and stickhandle with the puck or pass it out of the defensive zone. He joins the rush effectively because of his speed. It sounds like all of the ingredients for a top offensive defenseman, but several key components are lacking.

Joseph's offensive reads and sense of pace are off. Injuries to Pittsburgh defensemen late in the playoffs resulted in more ice time, and while he played capably, he did not make the big step up and it's unlikely at this stage of his career that he will.

He has the hand skills to beat players one-on-one, but he doesn't choose his spots for pinching or rushing wisely. He has a decent point shot, but isn't a great power play quarterback. Joseph doesn't see the ice well and often tries to force plays that result in turnovers.

THE PHYSICAL GAME

Joseph plays much smaller than his size. Strength and aggressiveness would help him clear out his crease.

THE INTANGIBLES

There is no doubt Joseph was rushed into the NHL, and now at 26 he is at one of those crossroads — working to become a top three defenseman on a team or remain on the bubble. He doesn't appear to be a self-starter, and may need the right coach to push him if he hopes to stick in the bigs.

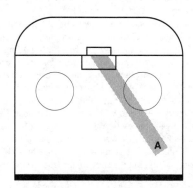

MARIO LEMIEUX

Yrs. of NHL service: 10
Born: Montreal, Que.; Oct. 5, 1965
Position: centre
Height: 6-4
Weight: 210
Uniform no.: 66
Shoots: right

Career statistics:

GP	G	A	TP	PIM
599	494	717	1211	618

1991-92 statistics:

GP	G	A	TP	+/-	PIM	PP	SH	GW	GT	S	PCT
64	44	87	131	+27	94	12	4	5	1	249	17.7

1992-93 statistics:

GP	G	A	TP	+/-	PIM	PP	SH	GW	GT	S	PCT
60	69	91	160	+55	38	16	6	10	0	286	24.1

1993-94 statistics:

GP	G	A	TP	+/-	PIM	PP	SH	GW	GT	S	PCT
22	17	20	37	-2	32	7	0	4	0	92	18.5

1994-95 statistics:

P	G	A	TP	+/-	PIM	PP	SH	GW	GT	S	PC
				Did not play in NHL							

LAST SEASON

Took off entire season to recuperate from a back injury and the effects of treatment for Hodgkins disease. Announced he will return on a limited basis.

THE FINESSE GAME

Lemieux is the foundation of Pittsburgh's franchise, but there are more than a few cracks in the foundation due to his continuing battle with various illnesses and injuries. These aren't nagging little muscle pulls and fractured fingers, but major things such as Hodgkin's disease and a near-crippling back ailment.

At his peak, Lemieux always seems to have some new move ready to dazzle and amaze, as if he spends his idle hours reinventing the game. He is one of those rare athletes who can seize a game by the throat, as if to say, "Enough fooling around. I want to win this thing." He then goes out and does what has to be done, whether it is breaking a goalie's heart with a shorthanded breakaway or calmly sneaking into the slot to bury a power play rebound.

Lemieux has such tremendous presence on the ice that the defense has to back off him. Step up to challenge Lemieux and he is by you in a flash, pulling the puck through a defender's legs with his huge reach. Back off him, and he will use the open ice to wheel and send a perfect pass to a breaking teammate.

His shots are accurate, and he never telegraphs where they are going, which makes him nearly unbeatable on a breakaway. With his long, strong reach, he can flick off a shot when he looks out of position and off balance. The goalie will position himself for Lemieux's body, but the shot comes from so far away that the netminder is at his mercy.

Lemieux can do everything at high tempo. He is an excellent skater, and his vision of the ice is so acute he seems to be watching from one of those overhead cameras hanging from the centre ice scoreboard. He knows where everyone is and where they're going. This makes him as dangerous killing penalties as he is on the power play.

THE PHYSICAL GAME

When healthy, Lemieux is the single most dominant player in the NHL. Lindros may catch him one day, but he isn't at Mario's elite level yet.

THE INTANGIBLES

Lemieux will probably play about 60 games this season. Expect him to rest a game when the Pens play back-to-back contests, for example, and to sit out any lengthy road trips. It will be a cautious season for him, and it may have a disruptive effect on the team. There is serious doubt about what level of play Lemieux will be able to attain.

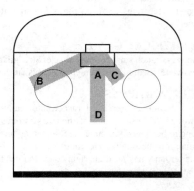

SHAWN MCEACHERN

Yrs. of NHL service: 3
Born: Waltham, Mass.; Feb. 28, 1969
Position: centre/left wing
Height: 6-1
Weight: 180
Uniform no.: 15
Shoots: left

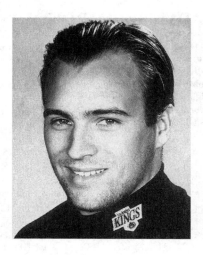

Career statistics:

GP	G	A	TP	PIM
219	61	72	133	102

1991-92 statistics:

GP	G	A	TP	+/-	PIM	PP	SH	GW	GT	S	PCT
15	0	4	4	0	0	0	0	0	0	14	0.0

1992-93 statistics:

GP	G	A	TP	+/-	PIM	PP	SH	GW	GT	S	PCT
84	28	33	61	+21	46	7	0	6	0	196	14.3

1993-94 statistics:

GP	G	A	TP	+/-	PIM	PP	SH	GW	GT	S	PCT
76	20	22	42	+14	34	0	5	1	0	159	12.6

1994-95 statistics:

GP	G	A	TP	+/-	PIM	PP	SH	GW	GT	S	PCT
44	13	13	26	+4	22	1	2	1	0	97	13.4

LAST SEASON

Served two-game suspension for stick incident in 1994 playoffs.

THE FINESSE GAME

McEachern suffers from serious tunnel vision, which negates much of the advantage his speed brings to the lineup. He skates with his head down, looking at the ice instead of the play around him. He is strong and fast, with straightaway speed, but he tends to expend his energy almost carelessly and has to take short shifts.

He was bit of a long shot to make the NHL (selected 110th overall in 1987 out of Boston University), and even after joining the Penguins for his first stint after the 1992 Olympics there was some doubt whether he would be able to crack the lineup. He simply forced his way in. But now that we know McEachern works hard, he has to work smart.

He can shift speeds and direction smoothly without losing control of the puck. He can play both left wing and centre but is better on the wing. A very accurate shooter with a hard wrist shot, he has a quick release on his slap shot that he likes to drive after using his outside speed. He is strong on face-offs and is a smart penalty killer.

THE PHYSICAL GAME

Generally an open-ice player, McEachern will also pursue the puck with some diligence in the attacking zone. But he is light, and, although he can sometimes build up momentum with his speed for a solid bump, he loses most of the close-in battles for the puck.

THE INTANGIBLES

McEachern is a worker who has overcome long odds to get to the NHL. Because of the Penguins' depth at centre, he will probably play another season on the wing, which will guarantee him more ice time, although it is not his preferred position. He is more effective as a wing, however, since his playmaking skills are limited due to his lack of vision.

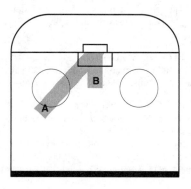

DMITRI MIRONOV

Yrs. of NHL service: 3
Born: Moscow, Russia; Dec. 25, 1965
Position: left defense
Height: 6-2
Weight: 217
Uniform no.: 15
Shoots: right

Career statistics:

GP	G	A	TP	PIM
175	22	63	85	146

1991-92 statistics:

GP	G	A	TP	+/-	PIM	PP	SH	GW	GT	S	PCT
7	1	0	1	-4	0	0	0	1	0	7	14.3

1992-93 statistics:

GP	G	A	TP	+/-	PIM	PP	SH	GW	GT	S	PCT
59	7	24	31	-1	40	4	0	1	1	105	6.7

1993-94 statistics:

GP	G	A	TP	+/-	PIM	PP	SH	GW	GT	S	PCT
76	9	27	36	+5	78	3	0	0	2	147	6.1

1994-95 statistics:

GP	G	A	TP	+/-	PIM	PP	SH	GW	GT	S	PCT
33	5	12	17	+6	28	2	0	0	0	68	7.4

LAST SEASON

Led team defensemen in plus-minus. Missed 15 games with separated shoulder. Acquired from Toronto with a second round pick in 1996 for Larry Murphy.

THE FINESSE GAME

In skills alone, Mironov was probably among the top six players on the Leafs last season. He can do phenomenal things with the puck, but the problem is getting it out of him every night. Right now, he is teasing with glimpses of the kind of player he can be. Maybe Mironov doesn't even know. Certainly his teammates have been stunned by some of his passes that snake their way through defenders.

Mironov understands the game well. He can shoot bullets, but is often reluctant to shoot. He can work the puck up the ice, handle the point on the power play, sees the ice well and is a good passer, but he does none of those things with authority. He is a good skater, but doesn't jump into the holes or force back defenders the way he should. On many nights, he is only an average player.

THE PHYSICAL GAME

Mironov has a long reach and is big, but he plays very soft and doesn't use either to his best advantage.

THE INTANGIBLES

Mironov is a shy person and is uncomfortable with a leadership role. With more confidence and consistency, he could easily produce in the 50-60 point range, but if his inconsistent play continues he will only be a sixth defenseman — and that's frustrating,

given his talent. His injury is another question mark. He didn't come back until the final game of the season and he was leery of being reinjured. This could be a critical season for him, since his period of adjustment to the NHL and North America should be complete. He's not young and has to step up. He may be happier in a more offensive role with the Penguins, having escaped the Leafs' conservative defensive system.

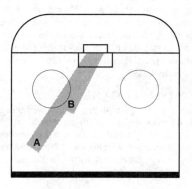

JOE MULLEN

Yrs. of NHL service: 14
Born: New York, N.Y.; Feb. 26, 1957
Position: right wing
Height: 5-9
Weight: 180
Uniform no.: 7
Shoots: right

Career statistics:

GP	G	A	TP	PIM
971	487	539	1026	237

1991-92 statistics:

GP	G	A	TP	+/-	PIM	PP	SH	GW	GT	S	PCT
77	42	45	87	+12	30	14	0	4	1	226	18.6

1992-93 statistics:

GP	G	A	TP	+/-	PIM	PP	SH	GW	GT	S	PCT
72	33	37	70	+19	70	9	3	3	2	175	18.9

1993-94 statistics:

GP	G	A	TP	+/-	PIM	PP	SH	GW	GT	S	PCT
84	38	32	70	+9	41	6	2	9	0	231	16.5

1994-95 statistics:

GP	G	A	TP	+/-	PIM	PP	SH	GW	GT	S	PCT
45	16	21	37	+15	6	5	2	3	0	78	20.5

LAST SEASON

Became first American-born player to reach 1,000-point milestone and is the all-time leading scorer among U.S. players. Missed three games with a back injury.

THE FINESSE GAME

Players who last a long time in the NHL usually do so because of their skating ability, and Mullen has lost little of his edge (or his edges) in this department through the seasons and despite knee problems. He doesn't have straightaway speed and is an unlikely candidate to win a one-on-one rush in open ice. He doesn't have a long reach, but he will get the jump on defenders with his deceptive quickness and lateral movement.

Mullen's shot is sneaky, too. He hides the puck with his body and uses his patience with the puck to create space for his linemates. He is a terrific give-and-go player. He will hit a teammate with a smart pass, giving that player sufficient time to manoeuvre, then head to open ice for a return pass. He has a great head for the power play. He'll dart in and out of openings around the net, and he's tough to knock off his feet because of his balance. Mullen has quick feet and can kick pucks up onto his stick and get the shot away in an instant. He has great hands in traffic for a shot or pass.

THE PHYSICAL GAME

Mullen is not a physical player, due to his small size, but he plays with a grit and determination that should embarrass a lot of bigger fellas. He will sacrifice his body to make a defensive play or to pursue the puck in the attacking zone. He is smart about it, though, and won't try to make noise when the more intelligent choice is to back off. He is a very quick skater who keeps himself in good defensive position.

Mullen didn't pay too much attention to conditioning early in his career, but now he keeps himself in top shape with good diet and exercise. It looks like he could play forever.

THE INTANGIBLES

An unrestricted free agent, Mullen will be mulling offers from several teams, and will likely pick the team that would give him the best shot at another Stanley Cup, something he desperately wants to finish his outstanding career on the highest of notes. He may be good for another season of 25 goals in the right spot, and should join the exclusive 500-goal club this season. A quality player and person, he'll be a productive addition to whatever team he plays for.

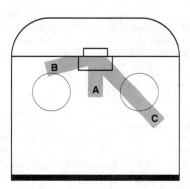

LUC ROBITAILLE

Yrs. of NHL service: 9
Born: Montreal, Que.; Feb. 17, 1966
Position: left wing
Height: 6-1
Weight: 190
Uniform no.: 20
Shoots: left

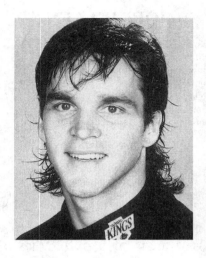

Career statistics:

GP	G	A	TP	PIM
686	415	430	845	599

1991-92 statistics:

GP	G	A	TP	+/-	PIM	PP	SH	GW	GT	S	PCT
80	44	63	107	-4	95	26	0	6	1	240	18.3

1992-93 statistics:

GP	G	A	TP	+/-	PIM	PP	SH	GW	GT	S	PCT
84	63	62	125	+18	100	24	2	8	1	265	23.8

1993-94 statistics:

GP	G	A	TP	+/-	PIM	PP	SH	GW	GT	S	PCT
83	44	42	86	-20	86	24	0	3	0	267	16.5

1994-95 statistics:

GP	G	A	TP	+/-	PIM	PP	SH	GW	GT	S	PCT
46	23	19	42	+10	37	5	0	3	1	109	21.1

LAST SEASON

Led team in shooting percentage. Second on team in goals. Fourth on team in points. Served two-game suspension for high-sticking incident. Scored 400th career goal.

THE FINESSE GAME

A pure shooter, Robitaille is one of the best in the league at roofing a shot. Most of his goals come from in tight. He is so strong with his arms and stick that a defender will think he has him wrapped up, only to see the puck end up in the net after Robitaille has somehow gotten his hands free for a shot on net.

Robitaille is often among the NHL leaders in shooting percentage (he led the Penguins). He works to get himself in the high percentage areas, and he doesn't waste any time with his shots. He unloads quickly, before a goalie has time to move, and his shots are not easily blocked because of his short release. He simply buries his passes.

He will fake goalies when he has time, looking high and shooting low, or vice versa. He has great hands for work in front of the net on the power play, tipping shots. His skating is only average, but he has improved and it doesn't hurt his game.

THE PHYSICAL GAME

Robitaille wins a lot of one-on-one battles in the attacking zone through determination and will. He loves to score so much that he will pay almost any price to do it. He is a frequent target of other teams' hitters yet is not easily intimidated. He doesn't do nearly as good a job away from the puck, although his defensive awareness has improved.

THE INTANGIBLES

Robitaille played half of the season on the first line when Kevin Stevens was injured, but didn't tail off a bit when put on the second line. In fact, his first-half stats (12-8 — 20) nearly mirrored his second half (11-11 — 22), illustrating his consistency and adaptability. The change from L.A. to Pittsburgh was positive, but we don't project him to hit the 100-point range unless Mario Lemieux returns and Robitaille gets to play with him or Ron Francis.

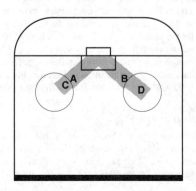

ULF SAMUELSSON

Yrs. of NHL service: 11
Born: Fagersta, Sweden; Mar. 26, 1964
Position: left defense
Height: 6-1
Weight: 195
Uniform no.: 5
Shoots: left

Career statistics:

GP	G	A	TP	PIM
740	42	227	269	1914

1991-92 statistics:

GP	G	A	TP	+/-	PIM	PP	SH	GW	GT	S	PCT
62	1	14	15	+2	206	1	0	1	0	75	1.3

1992-93 statistics:

GP	G	A	TP	+/-	PIM	PP	SH	GW	GT	S	PCT
77	3	26	29	+36	249	0	0	1	0	96	3.1

1993-94 statistics:

GP	G	A	TP	+/-	PIM	PP	SH	GW	GT	S	PCT
80	5	24	29	+23	199	1	0	0	1	106	4.7

1994-95 statistics:

GP	G	A	TP	+/-	PIM	PP	SH	GW	GT	S	PCT
44	1	15	16	+11	113	0	0	0	0	47	2.1

LAST SEASON

Second on team in PIM. Missed four games with surgery to remove bone chips from his right elbow. Missed one game with a knee injury.

THE FINESSE GAME

Samuelsson has wonderful skills that are often overshadowed by the more irritating aspects of his nature. He is a very good skater for his size, with flat-out speed and one-step quickness, agility, mobility and balance. He skates very well backwards. He reads plays well defensively and is always well positioned. He is tough to beat one-on-one and sometimes even two-on-one because of his anticipation.

He is not as effective offensively. He can't carry the puck at high tempo and is better off making the escape pass than trying to rush it up-ice himself. Although he likes trying to handle the puck himself, this is a mistake. He just doesn't read offensive plays well. He does have a nice shot but lacks poise and confidence in the attacking zone.

Samuelsson is an excellent penalty killer. He blocks shots and challenges aggressively. His biggest drawback remains his lack of mental sharpness. While he has improved over the seasons, Samuelsson is still prone to vapour lock at odd times.

THE PHYSICAL GAME

Samuelsson plays with so much extra padding that you wonder how he can even move. He should look like a kid whose overprotective parent has stuffed him into a snowsuit, with his arms sticking out at right angles and his skate a mere waddle. But all of that body armour, including a flak jacket, couldn't protect him

from a playoff injury that forced him to miss the Eastern Conference semi-finals last season.

The protection does permit him to be absolutely fearless in shot-blocking, and as high as the opponent's shot totals are against Pittsburgh goalies, just think how much worse it would be without him gobbling up shots.

Samuelsson is a big hitter, sometimes too big. He will try to put someone through the wall when a simple take-out would do. He also needs to hit cleaner, but bringing his stick up on a hit is the most natural move, and he takes many unnecessary penalties because of this tendency. Some of the physical wear and tear appears to be taking a toll on him.

THE INTANGIBLES

One of the most aggravating players in the NHL, Samuelsson can distract another player — sometimes, an entire opposing team — from the task at hand. Instead of focussing on the game, they cry "Get Ulf!" Samuelsson can just chuckle behind his high sticks. He has more than enough talent to go with the goonery, but sometimes gets so carried away that he forgets that the game is more important than his antics. He still lacks the mental edge that might place him among the league's top defensemen, and his game might be starting on its downward slide.

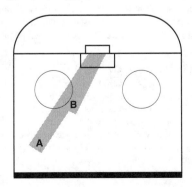

TOMAS SANDSTROM

Yrs. of NHL service: 11
Born: Jakobstad, Finland; Sept. 4, 1964
Position: right wing
Height: 6-2
Weight: 200
Uniform no.: 17
Shoots: left

Career statistics:

GP	G	A	TP	PIM
716	317	378	695	949

1991-92 statistics:

GP	G	A	TP	+/-	PIM	PP	SH	GW	GT	S	PCT
49	17	22	39	-2	70	5	0	4	0	147	11.6

1992-93 statistics:

GP	G	A	TP	+/-	PIM	PP	SH	GW	GT	S	PCT
39	25	27	52	+12	57	8	0	3	1	134	18.7

1993-94 statistics:

GP	G	A	TP	+/-	PIM	PP	SH	GW	GT	S	PCT
78	23	35	58	-7	83	4	0	3	1	193	11.9

1994-95 statistics:

GP	G	A	TP	+/-	PIM	PP	SH	GW	GT	S	PCT
47	21	23	44	+1	42	4	1	3	1	116	18.1

LAST SEASON

Third on team in goals and points. Missed one game with a foot injury.

THE FINESSE GAME

Sandstrom is one of the few players in the league who can release a shot when the puck is in his feet. He uses a short backswing and surprises goalies with the shot's velocity and accuracy. He can beat a goalie in a number of ways, but this shot is unique.

Sandstrom combines size, speed, strength and skill. He doesn't react well to change. He wants a regular role and lots of ice time, but injuries (his own and his team's) have made a set lineup almost impossible in recent seasons. One thing is certain: Sandstrom needs to play to keep his legs going. He had trouble fitting in once he moved to Pittsburgh and was ineffective.

His skating is impressive for a skater of his dimensions. Quick and agile, he intimidates with his speed. He has a superb passing touch and shoots well on the fly or off the one-timer. He has all the weapons to be a 100-point scorer, but has never been able to attain that mark.

THE PHYSICAL GAME

Wildly abrasive, Sandstrom will give facials with his gloves, make late hits, get his stick up and take the body. Usually he hits and runs, resulting in angry opponents chasing him around the ice.

Sandstrom will also pay an honest physical price along the boards and in front of the net. He wants the puck and will scrap to control it.

THE INTANGIBLES

Sandstrom's move up to a second-line winger with the Penguins has revitalized his career. He was close to a 40-goal pace last season. If he is able to hold on to the number two role, Sandstrom may enjoy another season at a good scoring clip. He seems to have shaken the injuries that plagued him for several season in L.A.

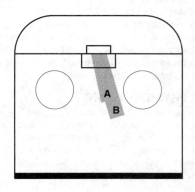

KEVIN STEVENS

Yrs. of NHL service: 8
Born: Brockton, Mass.; Apr. 15, 1965
Position: left wing
Height: 6-3
Weight: 217
Uniform no.: 25
Shoots: left

Career statistics:

GP	G	A	TP	PIM
457	251	276	527	968

1991-92 statistics:

GP	G	A	TP	+/-	PIM	PP	SH	GW	GT	S	PCT
80	54	69	123	+8	252	19	0	4	0	325	16.6

1992-93 statistics:

GP	G	A	TP	+/-	PIM	PP	SH	GW	GT	S	PCT
72	55	56	111	+17	177	26	9	5	1	325	16.9

1993-94 statistics:

GP	G	A	TP	+/-	PIM	PP	SH	GW	GT	S	PCT
83	41	47	88	-24	155	21	0	4	0	284	14.4

1994-95 statistics:

GP	G	A	TP	+/-	PIM	PP	SH	GW	GT	S	PCT
27	15	12	27	0	51	6	0	4	0	80	18.8

LAST SEASON

Second on team in power play goals and game-winning goals. Missed 21 games with a fractured left ankle.

THE FINESSE GAME

Stevens is starting to become an injury magnet, a bad trend for a power forward. After making a remarkable recovery from a career-threatening face injury in the 1993 playoffs, Stevens eagerly anticipated last season's start, only to be thwarted first by the lockout and then by a hairline ankle fracture just a few games in.

He has the size and strength to battle for and win position in front of the net. He has an astonishingly quick release on his shot. His objective is to get rid of the puck as fast as he can, even if he doesn't know where it's going, and he always follows up on his shot for a first and second rebound.

Stevens simply drops anchor in the slot on the power play. His huge frame blocks the goalie's view and he has good hand-eye coordination for tips and deflections. Those moves aren't instinctive, but came from hours of practice. He also has a devastating one-timer. He does not have to be overly clever with the puck, since he can overpower goalies with his shot. Stevens is a power play specialist. His work on the give-and-go is pure instinct.

His play at even strength is not as strong, as he still needs to improve his defensive awareness. He is an average skater at best, and he often seems overanxious to get started on the attacking rush to keep up with his fleeter linemates. His reach and range make him appear faster than he is.

THE PHYSICAL GAME

Stevens has always been a player who pays great attention to working out, and after two disappointing seasons probably spent most of the 1995 off-season in a gym.

Stevens has to initiate. He doesn't react well to being knocked down. (It's surprising, given his size and strength, that he all too often is.) He isn't one of the meanest guys around, although he can throw 'em (punches and devastating hits both). He needs to be more consistent with his physical play, and look as hungry as he did when he was breaking in.

THE INTANGIBLES

Stevens has a lot to prove, and no one knows it better than the man himself. His post-season play came under fire (for the second consecutive season) and he wants more than anything to prove he is the Stevens of old. He has great pride in the work he's done to be ranked among the premier left wings in the NHL. Now he has to work to stay there.

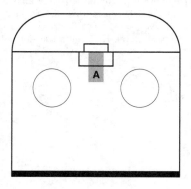

CHRIS TAMER

Yrs. of NHL service: 1
Born: Dearborn, Mich.; Nov. 17, 1970
Position: left defense
Height: 6-2
Weight: 185
Uniform no.: 2
Shoots: left

Career statistics:

GP	G	A	TP	PIM
48	2	0	2	91

1993-94 statistics:

GP	G	A	TP	+/-	PIM	PP	SH	GW	GT	S	PCT
12	0	0	0	+3	9	0	0	0	0	10	0.0

1994-95 statistics:

GP	G	A	TP	+/-	PIM	PP	SH	GW	GT	S	PCT
36	2	0	2	0	82	0	0	0	0	26	7.7

LAST SEASON

First NHL season. Led Cleveland (IHL) in PIM with 204 in 48 games at time of recall.

THE FINESSE GAME

Tamer plays a conservative, stay-at-home style. He has limited skating and stick skills but is smart enough to stay within his limitations and play a positional game.

He was a rookie last season, but he was an experienced one after four years at Michigan, a stint with the U.S. national team and a season-and-a-half in the minors. He makes mistakes, but they are less glaring and less frequent than most rookies commit.

Tamer does the little things well, chipping a puck off the boards or angling an attacker to the wall.

THE PHYSICAL GAME

Tamer doesn't nail people, but he has some strength and will use it to push people out of the crease and battle in the corners. He doesn't have a good skating base to be a big open-ice hitter. He will defend himself or stick up for a teammate, but he doesn't have a serious nasty side.

THE INTANGIBLES

Tamer is close to becoming a fixture among the team's top four defensemen. He will never be a star, but he will give solid support and can complement a more offensive player. His point production will be low.

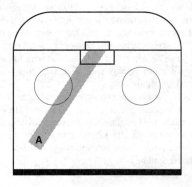

KEN WREGGET

Yrs. of NHL service: 10
Born: Brandon, Man.; March 25, 1964
Position: goaltender
Height: 6-1
Weight: 180
Uniform no.: 31
Catches: left

Career statistics:

GP	MINS	G	SO	AVG	A	PIM
421	23237	1501	3	3.86	19	154

1991-92 statistics:

GP	MINS	GAA	W	L	T	SO	GA	S	SAPCT	PIM
32	1707	3.74	14	11	3	0	106	759	.860	2

1992-93 statistics:

GP	MINS	GAA	W	L	T	SO	GA	S	SAPCT	PIM
25	1368	3.42	13	7	2	0	78	692	.887	6

1993-94 statistics:

GP	MINS	GAA	W	L	T	SO	GA	S	SAPCT	PIM
42	2456	3.37	21	12	7	1	138	1291	.893	8

1994-95 statistics:

GP	MINS	GAA	W	L	T	SO	GA	S	SAPCT	PIM
38	2208	3.21	25	9	2	0	118	1219	.903	14

goalie. But there are concerns about his being able to handle a 60-game load, especially considering the number of shots the Penguins typically give up on a nightly basis. Wregget may assume the number one job in Pittsburgh again this season if the Penguins feel they can't handle Tom Barrasso's salary and are able to move him.

LAST SEASON

Led NHL goalies in wins. Missed seven games with knee injury. Goals-against average was career-best.

THE PHYSICAL GAME

Wregget doesn't do anything great, but does everything well. He maximizes his size by squaring himself to the shooter, coming out to the top of his crease and staying on his feet to play the angle. He uses his size to advantage on screen shots and other play around the net by moving to the shooter.

Wregget is not a great skater. He doesn't regain his stance well and gets in trouble if he starts flopping. His lateral movement is fine. He has a good glove hand but has not made much improvement in his use of the stick. He prefers to simply stop the puck and let his defense come back to move it. He is not very active with his stick, breaking up plays around the net. He sees a lot of shots, but tends to steer away rebounds so he doesn't have to see a lot of second shots.

THE MENTAL GAME

Wregget has always had quiet pride in his ability, and is a hard worker even when he is the obvious backup goalie. His teammates enjoyed his success last season almost as much as he did. Wregget was a former number one goalie in Toronto and Philadelphia, but oddly, wherever he has been the management was always looking for someone else, perhaps because Wregget has only taken a team so far in the playoffs.

THE INTANGIBLES

Wregget pulled the Penguins through a shortened regular season, and proved himself as the number one

SAN JOSE SHARKS

Players' Statistics 1994-95

POS	NO.	PLAYER	GP	G	A	PTS	+/-	PIM	PP	SH	GW	GT	S	PCTG
R	22	ULF DAHLEN	46	11	23	34	-2	11	4	1	4		85	12.9
C	15	CRAIG JANNEY	35	7	20	27	-1	10	3		1		40	17.5
L	39	*JEFF FRIESEN	48	15	10	25	-8	14	5	1	2		86	17.4
C	14	RAY WHITNEY	39	13	12	25	-7	14	4		1		67	19.4
D	6	SANDIS OZOLINSH	48	9	16	25	-6	30	3	1	2		83	10.8
R	24	SERGEI MAKAROV	43	10	14	24	-4	40	1		1	1	56	17.9
C	7	IGOR LARIONOV	33	4	20	24	-3	14			1		69	5.8
R	8	KEVIN MILLER	36	8	12	20	4	13	1	1	2		60	13.3
R	17	PAT FALLOON	46	12	7	19	-4	25			3		91	13.2
D	41	TOM PEDERSON	47	5	11	16	-14	31				2	59	8.5
C	18	CHRIS TANCILL	26	3	11	14	1	10	1				39	7.7
C	13	JAMIE BAKER	43	7	4	11	-7	22	1				60	11.7
D	40	MIKE RATHJE	42	2	7	9	-1	29					38	5.3
R	23	*ANDREI NAZAROV	26	3	5	8	-1	94					19	15.8
R	36	JEFF ODGERS	48	4	3	7	-8	117			1		47	8.5
D	2	JIM KYTE	18	2	5	7	-7	33			1		14	14.3
D	4	JAY MORE	45		6	6	7	71					25	
D	3	ILYA BYAKIN	13		5	5	-9	14					19	
D	38	*MICHAL SYKORA	16		4	4	6	10					6	
C	09	V. BUTSAYEV	6	2		2	-2						6	33.3
R	47	*VIKTOR KOZLOV	16	2		2	-5	2					23	8.7
C	16	*DODY WOOD	9	1	1	2		29					5	20.0
D	26	VLASTIMIL KROUPA	14		2	2	-7	16					4	
D	44	SHAWN CRONIN	29		2	2		61					12	
G	31	WADE FLAHERTY	18		1	1								
R	42	*SHEAN DONOVAN	14				-6	6					13	
G	32	ARTURS IRBE	38					4						

GP = games played; G = goals; A = assists; PTS = points; +/- = goals-for minus goals-against while player is on ice; PIM = penalties in minutes; PP = power play goals; SH = shorthanded goals; GW = game-winning goals; GT = game-tying goals; S = no. of shots; PCTG = percentage of goals to shots; * = rookie

JAMIE BAKER

Yrs. of NHL service: 4
Born: Ottawa, Ont.; Aug. 31, 1966
Position: centre
Height: 6-0
Weight: 190
Uniform no.: 13
Shoots: left

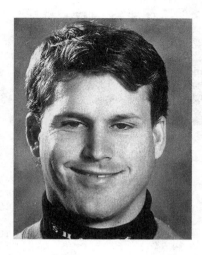

Career statistics:

GP	G	A	TP	PIM
255	47	48	95	154

1991-92 statistics:

GP	G	A	TP	+/-	PIM	PP	SH	GW	GT	S	PCT
52	7	10	17	-5	32	3	0	1	0	77	9.1

1992-93 statistics:

GP	G	A	TP	+/-	PIM	PP	SH	GW	GT	S	PCT
76	19	29	48	-20	54	10	0	2	0	160	11.9

1993-94 statistics:

GP	G	A	TP	+/-	PIM	PP	SH	GW	GT	S	PCT
65	12	5	17	+2	38	0	0	2	0	68	17.6

1994-95 statistics:

GP	G	A	TP	+/-	PIM	PP	SH	GW	GT	S	PCT
43	7	4	11	-7	22	0	1	0	0	60	11.7

LAST SEASON

Scored one of the Sharks' four shorthanded goals. Missed five games with a shoulder injury.

THE FINESSE GAME

Baker plays a largely defensive role, but he also has the skills to pop in some points even when he is working as a checker. In fact, that's what makes Baker a "tweener" — between defense and offense — because he always looks like he has the ability to deliver more than he shows on the stat sheet.

Baker does his best work in the corners. He hustles and is always quickly onto the puck carrier on the fore-check. He reads offensive plays nicely, so if he is able to force a turnover, he knows where to make the pass and whether or not to head to the net. He protects the puck well along the boards and while skating. This is his biggest asset.

Baker will keep the puck alive with his stick even when he's been knocked flat to the ice. He won't just cough it up. He's a better playmaker than scorer, but he can finish around the net when given the chance. He passes off his forehand or backhand, and is effective down low. He has a choppy stride but can move quickly for the first step or two. On the power play, Baker is a set-up man, and he likes to lurk behind the goal line.

Baker is average on draws. He is a determined and aggressive penalty killer and is a reliable man to have on the ice at crunch time.

THE PHYSICAL GAME

Baker has good size and has added some strength to make himself a more effective hitter, but continued work in the muscle department would help his career. The effort is always there with Baker: he goes full out, regardless of the score.

THE INTANGIBLES

Baker will probably find himself on the bubble if San Jose continues its youth movement this season, but he is the kind of reliable defensive centre who can always find a job somewhere.

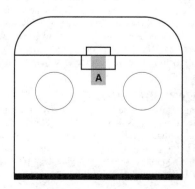

ULF DAHLEN

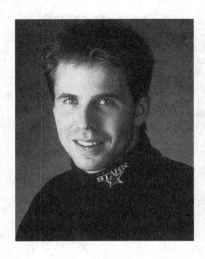

Yrs. of NHL service: 8
Born: Östersund, Sweden; Jan. 12, 1967
Position: centre/right wing
Height: 6-2
Weight: 195
Uniform no.: 22
Shoots: left

Career statistics:

GP	G	A	TP	PIM
554	201	218	419	149

1991-92 statistics:

GP	G	A	TP	+/-	PIM	PP	SH	GW	GT	S	PCT
79	36	30	66	-5	10	16	1	5	0	216	16.7

1992-93 statistics:

GP	G	A	TP	+/-	PIM	PP	SH	GW	GT	S	PCT
83	35	39	74	-20	6	13	0	6	0	223	15.7

1993-94 statistics:

GP	G	A	TP	+/-	PIM	PP	SH	GW	GT	S	PCT
78	25	44	69	-1	10	15	0	5	1	190	13.2

1994-95 statistics:

GP	G	A	TP	+/-	PIM	PP	SH	GW	GT	S	PCT
46	11	23	34	-2	11	4	1	4	0	85	12.9

LAST SEASON

Led Sharks in assists and points, both for second consecutive season. Led team in game-winning goals. Scored one of team's three shorthanded goals.

THE FINESSE GAME

Dahlen is an intelligent hockey player who sees the ice well. He has great puck skill, although he does not move the puck quickly. He is extremely effective down low on the power play and is a good possession player. He lures defenders to him and opens up ice for his teammates. Dahlen scores goals that are tough to defend against — wraparounds and jam-ins — and those are goals that frustrate a goaltender.

Dahlen is an unusual skater, slow but with some deceptive moves. He has good balance and strength and always protects the puck with his body. Along the boards, it's almost impossible to beat him to the puck. It doesn't matter what the size or speed of the opponent is, Dahlen won't surrender the puck. He is one of the best board and corner men in the league as long as the puck is on his blade. Dahlen has good hands and scores all of his goals from 10 inches to 10 feet away from the net. He slides out once in a while, but he is usually willing to pay the price to stay in the heavy traffic zone.

THE PHYSICAL GAME

Hitting Dahlen is like hitting a fire hydrant. It takes two or three checks to knock him down. Dahlen doesn't initiate. While he is willing to do just about anything to protect the puck when he has control, he will not win many one-on-one fights to strip the puck away from an opponent. He lacks the aggressiveness to bump his game up a notch.

THE INTANGIBLES

While San Jose jettisoned much of its veteran lineup last season, Dahlen stayed and was an integral part of the team. Used a great deal with the rookie Jeff Friesen, Dahlen saw a lot of prime ice time last season and can be expected to again as the team matures around him.

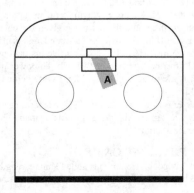

SHEAN DONOVAN

Yrs. of NHL service: 0
Born: Timmins, Ont.; Jan. 22, 1975
Position: right wing
Height: 6-2
Weight: 190
Uniform no.: 42
Shoots: right

Career statistics:

GP	G	A	TP	PIM
14	0	0	0	6

1994-95 statistics:

GP	G	A	TP	+/-	PIM	PP	SH	GW	GT	S	PCT
14	0	0	0	-6	6	0	0	0	0	13	0.0

LAST SEASON
Will be entering first full NHL season.

THE FINESSE GAME
Donovan has big-league speed. His quickness and powerful stride allow him to shift directions with agility. And he doesn't waste energy. He knows where he is supposed to be positioned and reads plays well. He has good anticipation, which stamps him as a strong penalty-killer.

Donovan doesn't finish well. He may never be a great point-getter because of his lack of scoring or playmaking touch, but it will not be for lack of effort. He is a diligent worker, and may develop into one of the top defensive forwards in the NHL. He isn't fazed by facing some of the league's better forwards, either.

THE PHYSICAL GAME
Donovan has added about 15 pounds since his draft year (1993) but needs to get stronger. He doesn't have much of a mean streak, nor will he agitate. He takes the body, but doesn't punish people. He is well-conditioned and has good stamina.

THE INTANGIBLES
Because of his outstanding speed, teams will always expect more production out of Donovan, but at this stage it seems he lacks the instinct for big-time scoring. He has a great attitude and should step into a full-time checking role with the Sharks this season.

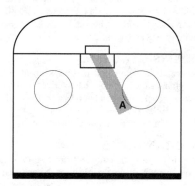

PAT FALLOON

Yrs. of NHL service: 4
Born: Foxwarren, Man.; Sept. 22, 1972
Position: centre/right wing
Height: 5-11
Weight: 192
Uniform no.: 17
Shoots: right

Career statistics:

GP	G	A	TP	PIM
222	73	86	159	71

1991-92 statistics:

GP	G	A	TP	+/-	PIM	PP	SH	GW	GT	S	PCT
79	25	34	59	-32	16	5	0	1	2	181	13.8

1992-93 statistics:

GP	G	A	TP	+/-	PIM	PP	SH	GW	GT	S	PCT
41	14	14	28	-25	12	5	1	1	0	131	10.7

1993-94 statistics:

GP	G	A	TP	+/-	PIM	PP	SH	GW	GT	S	PCT
83	22	31	53	-3	18	6	0	1	0	193	11.4

1994-95 statistics:

GP	G	A	TP	+/-	PIM	PP	SH	GW	GT	S	PCT
46	12	7	19	-4	25	0	0	3	0	91	13.2

season. He is not a franchise player but could step up his production to the 75-80 point range, especially if he gets to play with Janney this season.

LAST SEASON
Led team in shots for second consecutive season.

THE FINESSE GAME
Although Falloon came up through the junior ranks as a centre, he has been used a lot by the Sharks as a right wing. Puck control is his forte. He has great patience with the puck and can dish off to either side.

Not a natural goal-scorer, Falloon is opportunistic around the net, following up a shot and pouncing on a loose rebound. He works to get open and always has his stick ready. He has soft hands and good instincts for the right play. He played alongside a gifted passer in Craig Janney last year after Janney was picked up from St. Louis. Falloon had only three goals before Janney came on board, and nine the rest of the season.

Falloon employs a smart array of shots, using a wrist or slap with confidence. His major drawback is that he is a shade slow when carrying the puck; teammates who build up some speed for a charge across the blueline either have to put on the brakes or go offside.

He needs to work on his defensive game. He has shown progress and a willingness to improve.

THE PHYSICAL GAME
Falloon gets a great deal of checking attention. Although his game can't be characterized as physical, he uses his stocky build and good skating to work free of those checks. He goes willingly into the traffic areas in front of the net and along the boards.

THE INTANGIBLES
Falloon is just a year removed from a serious injury and like many NHLers wasn't in peak condition last

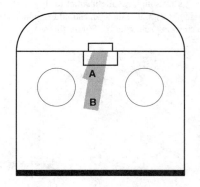

JEFF FRIESEN

Yrs. of NHL service: 1
Born: Meadow Lake, Sask.; Aug. 5, 1976
Position: left wing/centre
Height: 6-0
Weight: 185
Uniform no.: 39
Shoots: left

Career statistics:

GP	G	A	TP	PIM
48	15	10	25	14

1994-95 statistics:

GP	G	A	TP	+/-	PIM	PP	SH	GW	GT	S	PCT
48	15	10	25	-8	14	5	1	2	0	86	17.4

LAST SEASON

Led team and tied for fourth among NHL rookies in goals. Led team and fifth among NHL rookies in power play goals. Third on team in points. One of three Sharks to appear in all 48 games. Scored one of team's three shorthanded goals.

THE FINESSE GAME

Friesen is fast enough to shadow Sergei Fedorov and skilled enough to lead his team in goals in his first year in the NHL. He simply doesn't play like he's only 18. Known as an all-offense player in junior, he has exceptional skills. He is a fast, strong skater, handles the puck well and has the size to go with those qualities.

In junior hockey, Friesen was seldom asked to do anything defensively, but the Sharks put him to work as a penalty killer and he spent most of the season as part of the teams's top shorthanded forward pair. Fittingly, his first NHL goal was scored shorthanded.

He is a better finisher than playmaker. He has a quick, strong release on his snap or wrist shot, and played well with Ulf Dahlen, whose game is puck protection and getting the pass to the front of the net. Friesen is shifty with a smooth change of speed.

He never seems to get rattled or forced into making bad plays. In fact, he's the one who forces opponents into panic moves with his pressure. He will draw penalties by keeping his feet moving as he drives to the net or digs for the puck along the boards. He is strong on face-offs.

THE PHYSICAL GAME

Friesen has worked on his conditioning and at getting stronger. He needs to maintain that edge and not quit, since the Sharks will be giving him a lot of ice time this season, and in a full 84-game schedule. He could still improve his upper-body strength.

THE INTANGIBLES

The youngest player in the NHL last season, Friesen was used in crucial situations by the Sharks, and responded with big efforts. He was mature and consistent for such a young player, and is an unlikely candidate for a sophomore slump because of his work ethic. Surprisingly, the rap on Friesen as a junior was that he was lazy.

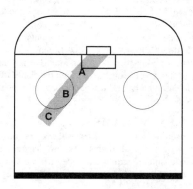

ARTURS IRBE

Yrs. of NHL service: 4
Born: Riga, Latvia; Feb. 2, 1967
Position: goaltender
Height: 5-8
Weight: 180
Uniform no.: 32
Catches: left

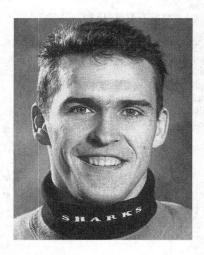

Career statistics:

GP	MINS	GA	SO	GAA	A	PIM
161	9174	510	8	3.33	3	30

1991-92 statistics:

GP	MINS	GAA	W	L	T	SO	GA	SA	SAPCT	PIM
13	645	4.47	2	6	3	0	48	365	.868	0

1992-93 statistics:

GP	MINS	GAA	W	L	T	SO	GA	SA	SAPCT	PIM
36	2074	4.11	7	26	0	1	142	1250	.886	10

1993-94 statistics:

GP	MINS	GAA	W	L	T	SO	GA	SA	SAPCT	PIM
74	4412	2.84	30	28	16	3	209	2064	.899	16

1994-95 statistics:

GP	MINS	GAA	W	L	T	SO	GA	SA	SAPCT	PIM
38	2043	3.25	14	19	3	4	111	1056	.895	4

LAST SEASON

Tied for third in NHL in shutouts with career high. Missed one game with a foot injury. Underwent off-season surgery on middle finger of right (stick) hand.

THE PHYSICAL GAME

If you didn't know Irbe was a goalie, you might guess he was a gymnast. He has that kind of slender, muscular build, and if Mary Lou Retton played goal, she would probably play it as Irbe does: diving, rolling, scrambling and coming up a "10." Irbe is so astoundingly flexible that when he does a split, he doesn't have to use his stick to cover up what little five-hole opening is left. His, er, cup is right on the ice. Teams have to try to beat him high.

Irbe is unbelievably quick. He has great confidence in his abilities and will challenge shooters by coming out at them well beyond the crease. He is so effective that two seasons ago teams complained his pads were too wide; last season they challenged him on the width of his stick blade (which was found to be illegal once).

Irbe needs to improve on his work outside of the net. He doesn't move the puck well and gets caught while he's trying to make decisions. He is just as likely to shoot a clearing attempt into the skates of his own defenseman behind the net as he is to move the puck smartly.

THE MENTAL GAME

Last season wasn't easy on Irbe, as the Sharks began a youth movement and the less reliable players led to more defensive breakdowns. Added to Irbe's erratic style, that led to some disastrous streaks for the goalie

and the team, and the little Latvian did not handle the challenge by Wade Flaherty well.

THE INTANGIBLES

Irbe actually lost the number one role in the playoffs to Flaherty, who started five of the team's last six playoff games. Irbe played out his option, and since he is no youngster (he will turn 29 during the season), he may have trouble getting the lucrative, long-term contract he wants, either with San Jose or another team.

Irbe will have to improve technically, because he can't thrive in the NHL for long on reflexes alone. He has a great work ethic — they can't get him off the ice, even in warmups — but his attitude is now a question mark. He said his problems were not connected to his hand injury, which was caused by a dog bite and required off-season surgery.

CRAIG JANNEY

Yrs. of NHL service: 8
Born: Hartford, Conn.; Sept. 26, 1967
Position: centre
Height: 6-1
Weight: 190
Uniform no.: 15
Shoots: left

Career statistics:

GP	G	A	TP	PIM
475	138	398	636	92

1991-92 statistics:

GP	G	A	TP	+/-	PIM	PP	SH	GW	GT	S	PCT
78	18	69	87	+6	22	6	0	2	0	127	14.2

1992-93 statistics:

GP	G	A	TP	+/-	PIM	PP	SH	GW	GT	S	PCT
84	24	82	106	-4	12	8	0	6	0	137	17.5

1993-94 statistics:

GP	G	A	TP	+/-	PIM	PP	SH	GW	GT	S	PCT
69	16	68	84	-14	24	8	0	7	0	95	16.8

1994-95 statistics:

GP	G	A	TP	+/-	PIM	PP	SH	GW	GT	S	PCT
35	7	20	27	-1	10	3	0	1	0	40	17.5

LAST SEASON

Acquired from St. Louis for Jeff Norton, a fourth-round draft pick and future considerations. Second on team in points. Tied for second on team in assists.

THE FINESSE GAME

Probably one of the top five passers in the NHL, Janney finds his target, and finds him in time to allow the shooter enough room to do something with the puck. He will draw the defender to him to open up ice, but by keeping the puck close to his body (he uses a very short stick) he makes it difficult for anyone fishing for the puck to knock it away. He then makes the pretty pass.

Janney is very creative and sees the ice and all of his options well. Get into the open and Janney will get the puck to you. He will usually disguise his intentions well enough so that the defense is caught napping. Linemates have to stay alert because Janney will turn what seems to be a dead play into a sudden scoring chance.

Janney has few flaws, but one of them is his unselfishness. He should be worth at least 30 goals with his quick release, but he would rather pass than shoot. He is patient with the puck and will wait for the goalie to commit, and he has pinpoint accuracy, but he usually has to be wide open before he will take a shot.

Not a speed demon, Janney possesses slick moves that he puts on in a burst just when it appears he is about to come to a standstill. Defensively, he remains suspect.

THE PHYSICAL GAME

Janney isn't more of a scoring threat because he isn't strong enough to win the one-on-one battles in traffic. His conditioning has improved to handle all the ice time he usually gets.

The opponent's book is to hit Janney early and often. He will keep himself out of the trenches. He has fairly good size, but doesn't have the upper body strength to knock anyone off the puck or prevent the puck being stripped from him. He is not a coward, though, and will take a hit to make a play since he controls the puck until the last moment, waiting for the perfect play.

THE INTANGIBLES

Janney ran afoul of St. Louis coach Mike Keenan, who benched him. He then went AWOL and ended up being dealt to San Jose, where he played the role of the good soldier and produced 20 points in 25 games for the Sharks. The team is developing some big, solid finishers on the wing. That could help Janney's production.

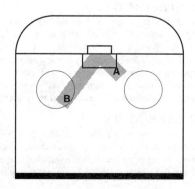

VIKTOR KOZLOV

Yrs. of NHL service: 0
Born: Togliatti, Russia; Feb. 14, 1975
Position: right wing
Height: 6-5
Weight: 235
Uniform no.: 16
Shoots: right

Career statistics:

GP	G	A	TP	PIM
16	2	0	2	2

1994-95 statistics:

GP	G	A	TP	+/-	PIM	PP	SH	GW	GT	S	PCT
16	2	0	2	-5	2	0	0	0	0	23	8.7

LAST SEASON

Will be entering first full NHL season. Missed 13 games with an ankle injury.

THE FINESSE GAME

Unlike many European players who have to adjust from the wide open spaces of their larger ice surfaces to the smaller North American rinks, Kozlov is an even better player on the 200 by 85 sheet of ice than he is in a larger rink. He overpowered people at the minor league level (he played 18 games with the Kansas City Blades of the IHL), and now has to do the same in the majors.

He is a beautiful skater for his size. He has the moves of a 150-pounder, with quickness and agility. Kozlov has learned to come off the boards much quicker, and is shooting with more authority.

Kozlov has superb hockey sense and is a good passer possessing timing and accuracy. He can score in a variety of ways and has an accurate shot with a quick trigger.

What's missing? Intensity. On the nights when Kozlov is on, he dominates the ice. But when he's not — and this has occurred too many times in too many key situations — his perimeter play leads to a glaringly dull effort.

THE PHYSICAL GAME

Kozlov's new physique has enabled him to be a lot sturdier in contact. He will still have to prove he has a taste for the North American style.

Kozlov has a long reach but doesn't care to play the body defensively, although offensively he will work with the puck to get in front of the net into scoring position. He needs to develop lower body strength.

THE INTANGIBLES

Kozlov is still making the adjustment to North American hockey, and didn't get much chance to truly flex his muscles given the short season and the serious ankle injury (which included ligament damage) he suffered while playing in Russia during the lockout. There were many positive signs in the brief glimpses we did see, and this will be his true rookie season. He will have an impact.

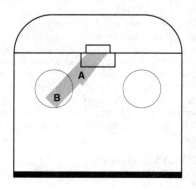

IGOR LARIONOV

Yrs. of NHL service: 5
Born: Voskresensk, Russia; Dec. 3, 1960
Position: centre
Height: 5-9
Weight: 160
Uniform no.: 7
Shoots: left

Career statistics:

GP	G	A	TP	PIM
303	73	150	223	142

1991-92 statistics:

GP	G	A	TP	+/-	PIM	PP	SH	GW	GT	S	PCT
72	21	44	65	+7	54	10	3	4	0	97	21.6

1992-93 statistics:

Did not play in NHL

1993-94 statistics:

GP	G	A	TP	+/-	PIM	PP	SH	GW	GT	S	PCT
60	18	38	56	+20	40	3	2	2	1	72	25.0

1994-95 statistics:

GP	G	A	TP	+/-	PIM	PP	SH	GW	GT	S	PCT
33	4	20	24	-3	14	0	0	0	1	69	5.8

LAST SEASON

Tied for second on team in assists. Missed 15 games with a broken foot.

THE FINESSE GAME

Larionov is one of the game's intellectuals. He can discuss strategies with coaches and teammates, then go out on the ice and execute with great precision. At 34, he was San Jose's number one centre, and they suffered woefully in his absence. Unquestionably, he was the team's MVP.

Among the best playmakers ever to come out of the old Soviet system, Larionov is an agile, elusive skater with marvellous hand skills and a creative mind. He waits for his wingers to get open, and he has an exceptional passing touch for finding the breaking man. He is tough to defend against. He looks so wispy and easy to take out of the play, but if challenged around the net, he dishes off the puck to someone for an easy tap-in or a one-timer.

Larionov does not shoot much. He cannot overpower a goalie with his shot but prefers to work in tight, deking a defender, getting a step and using an accurate wrist shot. He works the point on the power play because of his superb passing skills and vision, not because of his shot.

Larionov is smart and plays well positionally. He can be used on both special teams and is a shorthanded scoring threat because of his crafty play.

THE PHYSICAL GAME

Small and slightly built, Larionov will sometimes take a hit to make a play, but it doesn't make much sense to ask him to get into one-on-one confrontations. He is tough to knock off the puck, and he tested among the highest on the team for fitness. He has the type of muscles that give him explosive one-step quickness.

THE INTANGIBLES

Injuries cost Larionov production-wise last season, and he is not likely to visit the 70-point neighbourhood again. He has played a lot of hockey at the international and NHL levels, and the well may be drying up. But there is so much this classy individual can teach the young Sharks forwards that he figures to be a factor for another year.

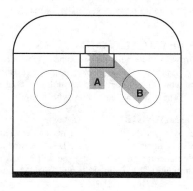

SERGEI MAKAROV

Yrs. of NHL service: 6
Born: Chelyabinsk, Russia; June 19, 1958
Position: right wing
Height: 5-11
Weight: 185
Uniform no.: 24
Shoots: left

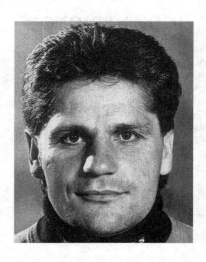

Career statistics:

GP	G	A	TP	PIM
420	134	250	384	317

1991-92 statistics:

GP	G	A	TP	+/-	PIM	PP	SH	GW	GT	S	PCT
68	22	48	70	+14	60	6	0	2	0	83	26.5

1992-93 statistics:

GP	G	A	TP	+/-	PIM	PP	SH	GW	GT	S	PCT
71	18	39	57	0	40	5	0	3	0	105	17.1

1993-94 statistics:

GP	G	A	TP	+/-	PIM	PP	SH	GW	GT	S	PCT
80	30	38	68	+11	78	10	0	5	0	155	19.4

1994-95 statistics:

GP	G	A	TP	+/-	PIM	PP	SH	GW	GT	S	PCT
43	10	14	24	-4	40	1	0	1	1	56	17.9

contributions are limited to offense, he is nearing the end of his NHL days.

LAST SEASON

Second on team in shooting percentage.

THE FINESSE GAME

Makarov never looks too involved or concerned, which has led many observers to think he's cruising, but he simply has the arrogance that goes with being one of the game's most skilled players. He has poise and a special presence that rubs off on his younger teammates. He is seldom flustered.

Makarov has superb hand skills and rink vision. He has lost some speed but is still very strong and balanced, especially with the puck. He has little energy for the defensive part of the game, and because he has absolutely no interest, he must always play with line-mates who do, or he will be buried in minuses. However, on the attack he will make brilliant little passes through traffic.

Like most players from the old Soviet system, Makarov doesn't shoot often enough. When he does, it will be a high-quality shot, usually a wrist shot, from the face-off dots in.

THE PHYSICAL GAME

Makarov is solidly built, and when he has the puck it's almost impossible for a checker to part him from it. But he won't fight to get the puck along the boards or in the corners, and he has to play with a grinder.

THE INTANGIBLES

Makarov is on the downside of his career. This is likely to be his last productive NHL season, and if his ice time is curtailed in San Jose, he will have a hard time hitting the 20-goal mark again. Since Makarov's

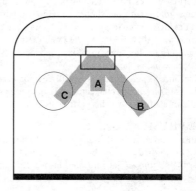

KEVIN MILLER

Yrs. of NHL service: 5
Born: Lansing, Mich.; Sept. 9, 1965
Position: right wing
Height: 5-11
Weight: 190
Uniform no.: 8
Shoots: right

Career statistics:

GP	G	A	TP	PIM
387	100	127	227	320

1991-92 statistics:

GP	G	A	TP	+/-	PIM	PP	SH	GW	GT	S	PCT
80	20	26	46	+6	53	3	1	4	0	130	15.4

1992-93 statistics:

GP	G	A	TP	+/-	PIM	PP	SH	GW	GT	S	PCT
82	24	25	49	+2	100	8	3	4	2	163	14.7

1993-94 statistics:

GP	G	A	TP	+/-	PIM	PP	SH	GW	GT	S	PCT
75	23	25	48	+6	83	6	3	5	0	154	14.9

1994-95 statistics:

GP	G	A	TP	+/-	PIM	PP	SH	GW	GT	S	PCT
36	8	12	20	+4	13	1	1	2	0	60	13.3

used to shadow some of the best scorers in the NHL. His work ethic is unquestioned.

LAST SEASON

Acquired from St. Louis for Todd Elik.

THE FINESSE GAME

Like his older brother, Kelly, in Washington, Kevin Miller is a two-way forward with a tremendous work ethic. The role of checker was once limited to players who didn't have scoring skills, but players like the Miller brothers, who can create turnovers with their smart, persistent fore-checking, and have the finesse skills to produce points as well, have redefined the role.

Miller is an energetic skater who is all over the ice. He is a better playmaker than finisher. He's not overly clever and most of his scoring chances come from opportunities from the fore-check. He has fairly quick hands but lacks a soft goal-scorer's touch.

He has succeeded at every level he has played — college, Olympic and minor league — and now has stamped himself as an NHL regular. The knock is that he's small, but he plays much larger.

THE PHYSICAL GAME

The spunky Miller takes the body well, although he doesn't have great size. He is very strong and has a low centre of gravity, which makes it tough to knock him off the puck. He will get overpowered in heavy traffic areas, but that doesn't keep him from trying. Miller will frustrate opponents into taking swings at him and draws penalties.

THE INTANGIBLES

Miller has the unique ability to fill a checking or scoring role. He will produce 20 goals a season and can be

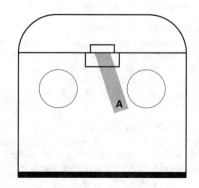

ANDREI NAZAROV

Yrs. of NHL service: 1
Born: Chelyabinsk, Soviet Union; May 22, 1974
Position: right wing
Height: 6-5
Weight: 230
Uniform no.: 23
Shoots: right

Career statistics:

GP	G	A	TP	PIM
27	3	5	8	94

1993-94 statistics:

GP	G	A	TP	+/-	PIM	PP	SH	GW	GT	S	PCT
1	0	0	0	0	0	0	0	0	0	0	0.0

1994-95 statistics:

GP	G	A	TP	+/-	PIM	PP	SH	GW	GT	S	PCT
26	3	5	8	-1	94	0	0	0	0	19	15.8

once he starts flexing his muscles.

LAST SEASON
First NHL season.

THE FINESSE GAME
Nazarov has been optimistically compared to Dave Andryechuk, and certainly some of the comparisons are apt. Nazarov is big and rangy, almost gawky — as if he's still growing into his body — and he uses his long reach effectively around the net. As yet, however, he doesn't seem to be as strong on his stick as Andreychuk, nor does he have the same commanding presence around the net of the three-time 40-goal scorer.

Still, Andreychuk didn't get 40 goals in his first NHL season. Odds are Nazarov just doesn't know how strong he can be yet. He has a powerful wrist shot, his best weapon.

Although he doesn't have great quickness, Nazarov has a powerful, ground-eating stride. He gets good drive from his legs, and when he plants himself around the net, he is tough to budge. In addition to his offensive prowess, he has a well-developed all-around game and won't hurt his team defensively. Sometimes he looks more like a left defenseman than a left wing, since the Sharks have a lot of rushing defensemen and Nazarov is alert enough to drop back to cover their position when they go in deep.

THE PHYSICAL GAME
Nazarov protects the puck well in both zones and has a streak of mean in him. He won the hearts of San Jose management when he fought Rick Tocchet in a preseason game against the L.A. Kings. But he has a tendency to get mesmerized by the puck and abandon his physical game.

THE INTANGIBLES
While San Jose is a defense-minded team, Nazarov has the skills and should get the ice time to develop into a 30-goal scorer. He will earn plenty of room

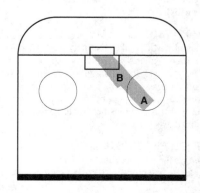

JEFF ODGERS

Yrs. of NHL service: 4
Born: Spy Hill, Sask.; May 31, 1969
Position: right wing
Height: 6-0
Weight: 195
Uniform no.: 36
Shoots: right

Career statistics:

GP	G	A	TP	PIM
256	36	30	66	809

1991-92 statistics:

GP	G	A	TP	+/-	PIM	PP	SH	GW	GT	S	PCT
61	7	4	11	-21	217	0	0	0	0	64	10.9

1992-93 statistics:

GP	G	A	TP	+/-	PIM	PP	SH	GW	GT	S	PCT
66	12	15	27	-26	253	6	0	0	0	100	12.0

1993-94 statistics:

GP	G	A	TP	+/-	PIM	PP	SH	GW	GT	S	PCT
81	13	8	21	-13	222	7	0	0	1	73	17.8

1994-95 statistics:

GP	G	A	TP	+/-	PIM	PP	SH	GW	GT	S	PCT
48	4	3	7	-8	117	0	0	1	0	47	8.5

LAST SEASON

One of three Sharks to appear in all 48 games. Led team in PIM.

THE FINESSE GAME

Odgers is a meat and potatoes skater. He patrols up and down his wing with diligence, if not much style or creativity. Any scoring opportunities he generates come from his hard work off the fore-check.

He lacks the hands skills and the vision to be much of a playmaker, but anyone playing with him is smart to follow in his wake because he churns up a lot of loose pucks. And he's smart enough to play as a safety valve on a line with better offensive talent. He will drop back to cover high if his winger and/or defenseman move deep into the attacking zone.

Odgers has some good speed and balance, but only if he's travelling in a straight line without the puck. He lacks mobility and agility, but effort can compensate for a lot of finesse shortcomings.

THE PHYSICAL GAME

Odgers takes the body and plays tough. He loves to fore-check and finds it a special challenge to outwit goalies who are strong stickhandlers, getting in on top of them quickly to try to force a bad pass. He takes a lot of aggressive penalties, though he has cut down on the bad penalties that hurt his team. He used to see some power play time as a big guy willing to plant himself in front of the net, but with the improvement in the Sharks' skill level he did little of that last season.

THE INTANGIBLES

After Bob Errey was traded, Odgers was voted team captain by his teammates, a good indicator of how well regarded he is in the Sharks' dressing room.

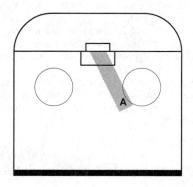

SANDIS OZOLINSH

Yrs. of NHL service: 3
Born: Riga, Latvia; Aug. 3, 1972
Position: left defense
Height: 6-1
Weight: 189
Uniform no.: 6
Shoots: left

Career statistics:

GP	G	A	TP	PIM
166	42	70	112	94

1992-93 statistics:

GP	G	A	TP	+/-	PIM	PP	SH	GW	GT	S	PCT
37	7	16	23	-9	40	2	0	0	0	83	8.4

1993-94 statistics:

GP	G	A	TP	+/-	PIM	PP	SH	GW	GT	S	PCT
81	26	38	64	+16	24	4	0	3	0	157	16.6

1994-95 statistics:

GP	G	A	TP	+/-	PIM	PP	SH	GW	GT	S	PCT
48	9	16	25	-6	30	3	1	2	0	83	10.8

LAST SEASON

Led team defensemen in points. One of three Sharks to appear in all 48 games despite suffering a slight concussion. Tied for third on team in scoring.

THE FINESSE GAME

Ozolinsh settled down to play a wee bit more defense last season, but his play still tended heavily towards jumping into the offense. Ozolinsh likes to start things by pressing in the neutral zone, where he will gamble and try to pick off cross-ice passes.

When he does deign to visit his own zone, Ozolinsh will start the breakout play with his smooth skating, then spring a teammate with a crisp pass. He can pass on his forehand or backhand, which is a good thing because he is all over the ice. He will follow up the play to create an odd-man rush, trail in for a drop pass, or drive to the net for a rebound. He is a true offenseman.

Ozolinsh has good straightaway speed, but he can't make a lot of agile, pretty moves the way Paul Coffey can. Because he can't weave his way through a number of defenders, he has to power his way into open ice with the puck and drive the defenders back through intimidation.

He sometimes hangs on to the puck too long. He has a variety of shots, with his best a one-timer from the off side on the power play. He is not as effective when he works down low.

Ozolinsh does not stop and start well, especially when moving backwards, and he tends to get mixed up on checking assignments when the attacking team crisscrosses.

THE PHYSICAL GAME

Ozolinsh goes into areas of the ice where he gets hit a lot, and he is stronger than he looks. He is all business on the ice and pays the price to get the puck, but he needs to develop more strength to clear out his crease.

THE INTANGIBLES

Ozolinsh has overcome knee surgery and appears to be over the mental as well as the physical hurdles. He is a sure bet for 50 points if he stays healthy, and a yearly improvement on those numbers should be expected. He should be among the top ten defensemen in scoring in the next season or two.

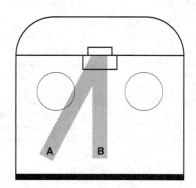

MIKE RATHJE

Yrs. of NHL service: 2
Born: Mannville, Alta.; May 11, 1974
Position: left defense
Height: 6-5
Weight: 203
Uniform no.: 40
Shoots: left

Career statistics:

GP	G	A	TP	PIM
89	3	16	19	88

1993-94 statistics:

GP	G	A	TP	+/-	PIM	PP	SH	GW	GT	S	PCT
47	1	9	10	-9	59	1	0	0	0	30	3.3

1994-95 statistics:

GP	G	A	TP	+/-	PIM	PP	SH	GW	GT	S	PCT
42	2	7	9	-1	29	0	0	0	0	38	5.3

LAST SEASON

Tied for team lead in playoff goals with five, all scored on the power play. Missed five games with a knee injury and a hip flexor.

THE FINESSE GAME

Rathje is a quick skater for his size — just ask anyone who's been smashed like a bug against the glass by the Sharks' young defenseman.

A stay-at-home defenseman whose skills may at first seem too subtle to help the Sharks improve right away, Rathje is a cornerstone for a new and improved defense. He will become even more effective once he learns to use his reach and eliminate more of the ice.

He has the ability to get involved in the attack but is prized primarily for his defense. He helps get the puck out of the zone quickly. He can either carry the puck out and make a smart headman pass, then follow the play, or make the safe move and chip the puck out along the wall.

He has great poise for a young player. He will probably have to be paired with a more offensive defenseman, though he does a nice job on the right point on the power play. He combines his lateral mobility with a good low shot to get the puck on the net without being blocked.

He has to improve his defensive reads, but that should come with experience.

THE PHYSICAL GAME

Rathje has good size and he is adding more muscle — remember, he's just 21, and we're sure he's not finished growing. He has a little bit of mean in him, and he likes to hit, but he doesn't eliminate as well as he should. Smaller guys that he should just smush against the boards are able to wriggle free.

THE INTANGIBLES

Rathje is a blue-chip prospect, one of the most promising young defensemen in the NHL. He showed progress last season and is coming off a very strong playoff performance. Most good defenseman don't start hitting their peak until 24 or 25. Rathje is ahead of schedule.

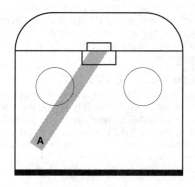

RAY WHITNEY

Yrs. of NHL service: 3
Born: Fort Saskatchewan, Alta.; May 8, 1972
Position: left wing/centre
Height: 5-9
Weight: 170
Uniform no.: 14
Shoots: right

Career statistics:

GP	G	A	TP	PIM
128	31	47	78	32

1991-92 statistics:

GP	G	A	TP	+/-	PIM	PP	SH	GW	GT	S	PCT
2	0	3	3	-1	0	0	0	0	0	4	0.0

1992-93 statistics:

GP	G	A	TP	+/-	PIM	PP	SH	GW	GT	S	PCT
26	4	6	10	-14	4	1	0	0	0	24	16.7

1993-94 statistics:

GP	G	A	TP	+/-	PIM	PP	SH	GW	GT	S	PCT
61	14	26	40	+2	14	1	0	0	1	82	17.1

1994-95 statistics:

GP	G	A	TP	+/-	PIM	PP	SH	GW	GT	S	PCT
39	13	12	25	-7	14	4	0	1	0	67	19.4

LAST SEASON

Led team in shooting percentage. Second on team in goals. Fourth on team in points. Missed nine games with an eye infection and a knee injury.

THE FINESSE GAME

Whitney is small but determined. Nifty and crafty, he compensates for a lack of quickness with his keen anticipation. He jumps into the right spot simply by knowing it's the right place to be before the defender is aware, and that makes him appear quicker than he really is. In traffic, he is steady on his skates, and handles the puck well through a crowd. He has exceptionally good hands and can lift a backhand shot when he is practically on top of the goalie.

While things came very easy to him in junior (where he was a linemate of Pat Falloon), Whitney has learned the hard way that NHL players are bigger, faster and stronger than they were in the WHL.

He does a lot of nice things just inside the blueline, carrying in and wheeling to hit a trailing teammate or throwing the puck in deep if that is the better play. He would rather pass than shoot, but he has a deceptive shot. He saw some time on San Jose's second power play unit.

THE PHYSICAL GAME

Whitney has started to work out for the first time in his life; he added about 15 pounds of muscle last season. He can now shed a defender's hook and drive to the net, something he wouldn't have done a season ago. While he won't outmuscle the league's big defenders, he'll outwork them now and again. He plays a smart, small man's game. He doesn't head into too many ar-

eas where he'll get crunched, but darts in and out of holes.

THE INTANGIBLES

Instead of taking his skills for granted as he did for the past few seasons, Whitney has turned into a dogged practice player who is trying to improve all aspects of his shot. He could turn into a consistent 25-goal scorer if he continues working.

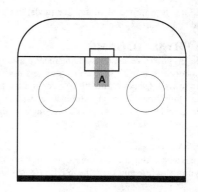

ST. LOUIS BLUES

Players' Statistics 1994-95

POS	NO.	PLAYER	GP	G	A	PTS	+/-	PIM	PP	SH	GW	GT	S	PCTG
R	16	BRETT HULL	48	29	21	50	13	10	9	3	6		200	14.5
L	19	BRENDAN SHANAHAN	45	20	21	41	7	136	6	2	6		153	13.1
D	28	STEVE DUCHESNE	47	12	26	38	29	36	1		1		116	10.3
L	10	ESA TIKKANEN	43	12	23	35	13	22	5	2	1	1	107	11.2
C	20	ADAM CREIGHTON	48	14	20	34	17	74	3		1		81	17.3
D	5	JEFF NORTON	48	3	27	30	22	72			1		48	6.3
D	2	AL MACINNIS	32	8	20	28	19	43	2				110	7.3
C	22	*IAN LAPERRIERE	37	13	14	27	12	85	1		1		53	24.5
R	9	GLENN ANDERSON	36	12	14	26	9	37			3		54	22.2
L	7	GREG GILBERT	46	11	14	25	22	11			3		57	19.3
C	14	TODD ELIK	35	9	14	23	8	22	4			2	76	11.8
D	33	BILL HOULDER	41	5	13	18	16	20	1				59	8.5
R	27	*DENIS CHASSE	47	7	9	16	12	133	1				48	14.6
C	21	GUY CARBONNEAU	42	5	11	16	11	16	1		1		33	15.2
C	25	*PATRICE TARDIF	27	3	10	13	4	29	1				46	6.5
L	15	*DAVID ROBERTS	19	6	5	11	2	10	3		2	1	41	14.6
L	12	VITALI KARAMNOV	26	3	7	10	7	14					22	13.6
D	6	DOUG LIDSTER	37	2	7	9	9	12	1				37	5.4
L	23	*CRAIG JOHNSON	15	3	3	6	4	6					19	15.8
D	4	RICK ZOMBO	23	1	4	5	7	24			1		18	5.6
L	17	BASIL MCRAE	21		5	5	4	72					14	
D	34	MURRAY BARON	39		5	5	9	93					28	
L	18	TONY TWIST	28	3		3		89			1		8	37.5
D	32	DONALD DUFRESNE	22		3	3	2	10					11	
C	26	PETER STASTNY	6	1	1	2	1						9	11.1
G	29	*GEOFF SARJEANT	4		1	1		2						
G	31	CURTIS JOSEPH	36		1	1								
L	36	PHILIPPE BOZON	1											
L	25	VITALI PROKHOROV	2				1							
L	9	DENNY FELSNER	3				-1	2					2	
D	44	*TERRY HOLLINGER	5				-1	2					1	
D	37	*JEFF BATTERS	10				-5	21					3	
G	30	JON CASEY	19											

GP = games played; G = goals; A = assists; PTS = points; +/- = goals-for minus goals-against while player is on ice; PIM = penalties in minutes; PP = power play goals; SH = shorthanded goals; GW = game-winning goals; GT = game-tying goals; S = no. of shots; PCTG = percentage of goals to shots; * = rookie

MURRAY BARON

Yrs. of NHL service: 6
Born: Prince George, B.C., June 1, 1967
Position: left defense
Height: 6-3
Weight: 210
Uniform no.: 34
Shoots: left

Career statistics:

GP	G	A	TP	PIM
319	20	34	54	455

1991-92 statistics:

GP	G	A	TP	+/-	PIM	PP	SH	GW	GT	S	PCT
67	3	8	11	-3	94	0	0	0	0	55	5.5

1992-93 statistics:

GP	G	A	TP	+/-	PIM	PP	SH	GW	GT	S	PCT
53	2	2	4	-5	59	0	0	1	0	42	4.8

1993-94 statistics:

GP	G	A	TP	+/-	PIM	PP	SH	GW	GT	S	PCT
77	5	9	14	-14	123	0	0	0	0	73	6.8

1994-95 statistics:

GP	G	A	TP	+/-	PIM	PP	SH	GW	GT	S	PCT
39	0	5	5	+9	93	0	0	0	0	28	0.0

LAST SEASON
Missed eight games with a knee injury.

THE FINESSE GAME
Baron possesses good hockey skills, but little hockey sense. A strong skater with some agility, he jumps into the play rather than leading a rush, but he doesn't do anything the least bit creative. He doesn't seem to know when a hard or a soft lead pass is required. He can lug the puck at a pretty good clip, but does little more than stop inside the blueline and fire a shot from the point. His shot is merely average. You will rarely find Baron gambling in deep. He seldom works on specialty teams.

Baron has developed more poise defensively and is now less likely to get rid of the puck in a panic. Instead, he will make a safe, if unspectacular, play.

THE PHYSICAL GAME
Baron has stepped up his physical play. Once noted for being a rather timid player for his size, he is doing a better job of clearing out the front of his crease. He even got into a couple of fights and stood up for his teammates, which endeared him to coach Mike Keenan and resulted in more ice time.

THE INTANGIBLES
Baron is 28, and may be developing just a season or two late into the kind of player the Blues long thought (hoped) he could be. He progressed beyond being a mere role player last year, and may continue to improve this season. The points will be negligible.

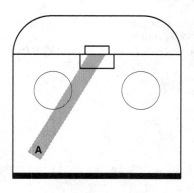

DENIS CHASSE

Yrs. of NHL service: 1
Born: Montreal, Que.; Feb. 7, 1970
Position: right wing
Height: 6-2
Weight: 190
Uniform no.: 27
Shoots: right

Career statistics:

GP	G	A	TP	PIM
50	7	10	17	148

1993-94 statistics:

GP	G	A	TP	+/-	PIM	PP	SH	GW	GT	S	PCT
3	0	1	1	+1	15	0	0	0	0	5	0.0

1994-95 statistics:

GP	G	A	TP	+/-	PIM	PP	SH	GW	GT	S	PCT
47	7	9	16	+12	133	1	0	0	0	48	14.6

LAST SEASON

First NHL season. Second on team in PIM. Tied for third among NHL rookies in plus-minus.

THE FINESSE GAME

Chasse is a basic blue-collar winger. His skating is a bit of a question mark, but he patrols the right side of the ice well and is strong along the boards and in the corners.

He has decent hands and some scoring touch, but he hasn't yet evolved into the Randy McKay type of winger who can make plays and get his team big goals. Most of Chasse's scoring will come from crashing and banging rather than any slick moves. He saw a lot of ice time with the fleet Ian Laperriere, which helped cover up some of Chasse's skating deficiencies.

THE PHYSICAL GAME

Chasse is strong and tough and fights when he has to. His reputation gets him a little extra room, which is important because he needs a little extra time to make plays. Once in awhile, he can explode, and that makes him a scary opponent.

THE INTANGIBLES

Chasse is an older rookie who knocked around in the minors before getting a full-time role with the Blues last season. The question is, can he carry his enthuiasm of the lockout-shortened year over a full season? He reminded one scout of Troy Mallette in his first two seasons with the Rangers.

Chasse was a throw-in in the Steve Duchesne deal. Will he be a throw-out in a season or two? Mike Keenan likes him, and that means he'll get a chance to make his major league stand.

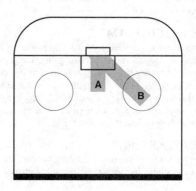

GEOFF COURTNALL

Yrs. of NHL service: 11
Born: Victoria, B.C.; Aug. 18, 1962
Position: left wing
Height: 6-1
Weight: 190
Uniform no.: 14
Shoots: left

Career statistics:

GP	G	A	TP	PIM
788	288	336	624	1152

1991-92 statistics:

GP	G	A	TP	+/-	PIM	PP	SH	GW	GT	S	PCT
70	23	34	57	-6	118	12	0	3	0	281	8.2

1992-93 statistics:

GP	G	A	TP	+/-	PIM	PP	SH	GW	GT	S	PCT
84	31	46	77	+27	167	9	0	11	0	214	14.5

1993-94 statistics:

GP	G	A	TP	+/-	PIM	PP	SH	GW	GT	S	PCT
82	26	44	70	+15	123	12	1	2	0	264	9.8

1994-95 statistics:

GP	G	A	TP	+/-	PIM	PP	SH	GW	GT	S	PCT
45	16	18	34	+2	81	7	0	1	0	144	11.1

LAST SEASON

Second on Canucks in power play goals. Third on team in goals. Fourth on team in points. Signed as a free agent by St. Louis.

THE FINESSE GAME

Throughout his NHL career, Courtnall has been a streaky scorer. When he's hot he uses a variety of shots to pepper the net. He can score off the backhand, muscle a close-range shot to the top shelf, use a snap shot off the wing on the fly, or wrist in a rebound.

He finds the holes and is a textbook give-and-go player. He makes the first pass, burns for the opening, then rips a one-timer from the circle to complete the play.

Courtnall has good hands for passing, making especially nice touch passes to breaking teammates. He has sharp hand-eye coordination to play up front on the power play. He doesn't stand in front of the net to take punishment, but instead times his moves in for deflections with his stick.

THE PHYSICAL GAME

Courtnall is a good-sized forward who has never had much of a physical element to his game. He goes to his stick first when he is trying to intimidate an opponent or battle along the boards for the puck. He will sometimes use his body, but not consistently. If opponents come at him hard enough early in the game, Courtnall will mail in the rest of the game.

THE INTANGIBLES

Given his skills, with prime ice time Courtnall should be a consistent 30-goal scorer, but that consistency continues to elude him. A change of scene might help — and Courtnall has voluntarily chosen to play for Mike Keenan in St. Louis, so perhaps he knows he needs someone on his case.

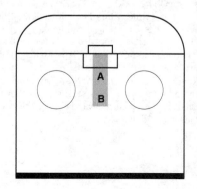

STEVE DUCHESNE

Yrs. of NHL service: 9
Born: Sept-Iles, Que.; June 30, 1965
Position: right defense
Height: 5-11
Weight: 195
Uniform no.: 28
Shoots: left

Career statistics:

GP	G	A	TP	PIM
625	157	342	499	590

1991-92 statistics:

GP	G	A	TP	+/-	PIM	PP	SH	GW	GT	S	PCT
78	18	38	56	-7	86	7	2	3	0	229	7.9

1992-93 statistics:

GP	G	A	TP	+/-	PIM	PP	SH	GW	GT	S	PCT
82	20	62	82	+15	57	8	0	2	1	227	8.8

1993-94 statistics:

GP	G	A	TP	+/-	PIM	PP	SH	GW	GT	S	PCT
36	12	19	31	+1	14	8	0	1	0	115	10.4

1994-95 statistics:

GP	G	A	TP	+/-	PIM	PP	SH	GW	GT	S	PCT
47	12	26	38	+29	36	1	0	1	0	116	10.3

LAST SEASON

Led team defensemen in scoring for second consecutive season. Tied for fifth among NHL defensemen in points. Led team and tied for second in NHL in plus-minus. Second on team in assists and third in points.

THE FINESSE GAME

The potentially deadly power play point pairing of Duchesne on the left and Al MacInnis on the right never became fully realized last season due to the injuries suffered by the latter. Duchesne is a fluid, quick, smart skater who loves to join the attack. He often plays like a fourth forward. He is unfraid to gamble down deep, but he is such a good skater that he recovers quickly and is back in position in a flash. He does not waste time with the puck. He has sharp offensive sense; when the play is over he's out of there.

Duchesne has good poise and patience, and he can either drill a puck or take a little edge off it for his teammates to handle in front.

In the defensive zone, Duchesne uses his lateral mobility and quickness to maintain position. He is almost impossible to beat one-on-one in open ice. He helps his team out tremendously by being able to skate the puck out of danger or make a brisk headman pass. He is more interested in the puck than the man.

THE PHYSICAL GAME

Not only does Duchesne fail to knock anyone down in front of the net, most of the time he doesn't even tie them up effectively. He is not big or strong, and he doesn't play tough. Positioning is the key to Duchesne's defense, and he needs to play with a physical partner.

THE INTANGIBLES

At 30, Duchesne is at the peak of his game, but he should be able to maintain it for several seasons. The Blues have made a serious commitment to acquiring big-ticket talent, and their first unit, at least, will create some great offense. Without a healthy MacInnis, the power play was a so-so 16.4 per cent last year, but that should improve.

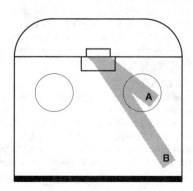

TODD ELIK

Yrs. of NHL service: 6
Born: Brampton, Ont.; Apr. 15, 1966
Position: centre
Height: 6-2
Weight: 190
Uniform no.: 14
Shoots: left

Career statistics:

GP	G	A	TP	PIM
358	94	173	267	360

1991-92 statistics:

GP	G	A	TP	+/-	PIM	PP	SH	GW	GT	S	PCT
62	15	31	46	0	125	4	3	1	0	118	12.7

1992-93 statistics:

GP	G	A	TP	+/-	PIM	PP	SH	GW	GT	S	PCT
60	14	27	41	-4	56	4	0	1	1	104	13.5

1993-94 statistics:

GP	G	A	TP	+/-	PIM	PP	SH	GW	GT	S	PCT
79	25	41	66	-3	95	9	0	4	1	185	13.5

1994-95 statistics:

GP	G	A	TP	+/-	PIM	PP	SH	GW	GT	S	PCT
35	9	14	23	+8	22	4	0	0	2	76	11.8

LAST SEASON

Acquired from San Jose for Kevin Miller.

THE FINESSE GAME

Elik's hand skills aren't up to his high speed, so he can't carry the puck or make many moves at high tempo. He often looks off-balance when he starts a rush because he is having trouble moving the puck.

He has to work hard for his goals by going to the net. He doesn't shoot well in stride because he has to slow down to get the shot off. He has a decent wrist shot, which he uses at close range.

Elik will have an occasional night when everything is going his way offensively, and he can dazzle, but when his offensive contributions aren't forthcoming, he gets down mentally and does little to help his team in any other way. He makes high-risk plays, which can either pay off or kill a team.

THE PHYSICAL GAME

Elik has the size and speed to be more of an impact player physically. He will use his body fairly consistently in the offensive zone, and he has the agility to be a good fore-checker. But he isn't very strong and he loses many of the one-on-one battles in traffic.

THE INTANGIBLES

Elik never seems to find a comfortable role anywhere for the long-term. He will be on the bubble in St. Louis again. If Dale Hawerchuk is healthy, and with the emergence of young Ian Laperriere and the resurrection of Mike Keenan favourite Adam Creighton, ice time will be scarce for Elik unless he is moved again.

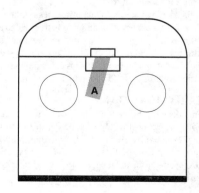

DALE HAWERCHUK

Yrs. of NHL service: 14
Born: Toronto, Ont.; Apr. 4, 1963
Position: centre
Height: 5-11
Weight: 185
Uniform no.: 10
Shoots: left

Career statistics:

GP	G	A	TP	PIM
1055	489	823	1314	672

1991-92 statistics:

GP	G	A	TP	+/-	PIM	PP	SH	GW	GT	S	PCT
77	23	75	98	-22	27	13	0	4	0	242	9.5

1992-93 statistics:

GP	G	A	TP	+/-	PIM	PP	SH	GW	GT	S	PCT
81	16	80	96	-17	52	8	0	2	0	259	6.2

1993-94 statistics:

GP	G	A	TP	+/-	PIM	PP	SH	GW	GT	S	PCT
81	35	51	86	+10	91	13	1	7	0	227	15.4

1994-95 statistics:

GP	G	A	TP	+/-	PIM	PP	SH	GW	GT	S	PCT
23	5	11	16	-2	2	2	0	2	0	56	8.9

LAST SEASON

Missed 25 games with groin and hip injuries. Signed as a free agent by St. Louis.

THE FINESSE GAME

An arthritic hip condition endangers the career of this fine skater. The durable Hawerchuk had missed only 19 games over 13 seasons until last year, when injuries caught up to him and put his future in doubt.

When he is healthy and at his full power, Hawerchuk needs less space to turn than just about any NHL player, and he can do it quickly and with control of the puck. Shifty and smart, he lacks the breakaway speed to be a dynamic skater who can intimidate through power skating, but he can outwit most defenders because he's downright sneaky.

He is a terrific passer. He sees all of his passing options, and if the lanes are closed down he'll dance down the ice with the puck himself. He has such a fine touch and is so confident that he will make bold feeds through a defender's legs and stick or feather a fine backhander. Anyone playing with Hawerchuk has to be alert, because he will make a creative play out of what looks like a closed-off situation. He is excellent on draws, using his hand-eye coordination and quick stick to win most face-offs outright.

Hawerchuk can run a power play from the point, keeping things in motion and avoiding chaos with his timing and control. He can also work down low, drawing defenders to him and slipping a pass to the open man.

He is an intelligent player who hardly ever makes a mistake in a crucial situation.

THE PHYSICAL GAME

Hawerchuk doesn't go around slamming people or wasting his energy on futile battles in the corners. He doles himself out like a parent does an allowance, making the big hit when he's sure his team will control the puck, or else using his stick to whack at ankles for possession. However, he fails to use his body well on draws. If he does not win it cleanly, he will not always tie up the opposing centre as well as he should.

THE INTANGIBLES

Despite Hawerchuk's age and potential injury problems, the Blues needed a centre badly enough to take a shot at signing him. If Hawerchuk stays healthy, his presence will help Brett Hull and the Blues' power play.

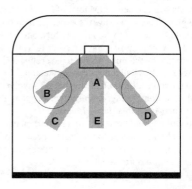

BILL HOULDER

Yrs. of NHL service: 5
Born: Thunder Bay, Ont.; Mar. 11, 1967
Position: left defense
Height: 6-3
Weight: 218
Uniform no.: 23
Shoots: left

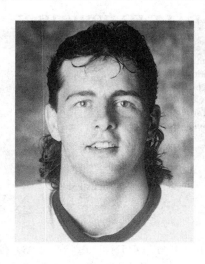

Career statistics:

GP	G	A	TP	PIM
232	25	61	81	118

1991-92 statistics:

GP	G	A	TP	+/-	PIM	PP	SH	GW	GT	S	PCT
10	1	0	1	-2	8	0	0	0	0	18	5.6

1992-93 statistics:

GP	G	A	TP	+/-	PIM	PP	SH	GW	GT	S	PCT
15	3	5	8	+5	6	0	0	0	1	29	10.3

1993-94 statistics:

GP	G	A	TP	+/-	PIM	PP	SH	GW	GT	S	PCT
80	14	25	39	-18	40	3	0	3	0	187	7.5

1994-95 statistics:

GP	G	A	TP	+/-	PIM	PP	SH	GW	GT	S	PCT
41	5	13	18	+16	20	1	0	0	0	59	8.5

LAST SEASON

Acquired from Anaheim for Jason Marshall.

THE FINESSE GAME

Houlder has a big shot, but otherwise his overall skills are pretty average. Although he struggles as a skater, especially in his turns, he has a decent first step to the puck and is strong on his skates.

He makes smart options with his passes. He does not like to carry the puck but is a stay-at-home type who is aware he is limited by his range; he will make a pass to a teammate or chip the puck out along the wall rather than try to carry it past a checker.

Houlder's offensive input is minimal and mostly limited to point shots, though he will get brave once in a while and gamble to the top of the circle. Most of his goals come from 60 feet out.

THE PHYSICAL GAME

How frustrating for coaches to look at a player of Houlder's size and see a PIM total of 20. Houlder is a gentle giant. There is always the expectation of bigger players that they will make monster hits, but we have the feeling that a lot of them were big as youngsters and were told by their parents not to go around picking on smaller kids. Houlder is definitely among the big guys who don't hit to hurt. If he did get involved he would be a dominating defenseman, but that's not about to happen at this stage of his career.

He will take out his man with quiet efficiency. He has to angle the attacker to the boards because of his lack of agility. He is vulnerable to outside speed when he doesn't close off the lane.

THE INTANGIBLES

Expansion gave Houlder his last chance to become a regular in the NHL, and he made the most of the situation with the playing time he got in Anaheim. The move to St. Louis put him among a group of good offensive defenseman, where he is not required to carry the mail, and he can concentrate on his defensive duties. Houlder can get 10 goals a season, but his biggest concern is his team's GAA. He is a reliable fifth or sixth defenseman.

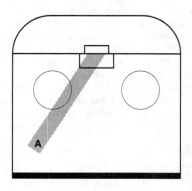

BRETT HULL

Yrs. of NHL service: 8
Born: Belleville, Ont.; Aug. 9, 1964
Position: right wing
Height: 5-10
Weight: 201
Uniform no.: 16
Shoots: right

Career statistics:

GP	G	A	TP	PIM
588	442	308	750	232

1991-92 statistics:

GP	G	A	TP	+/-	PIM	PP	SH	GW	GT	S	PCT
73	70	39	109	-2	48	20	5	9	1	408	17.2

1992-93 statistics:

GP	G	A	TP	+/-	PIM	PP	SH	GW	GT	S	PCT
80	54	47	101	-27	41	29	0	2	1	390	13.8

1993-94 statistics:

GP	G	A	TP	+/-	PIM	PP	SH	GW	GT	S	PCT
81	57	40	97	-3	38	25	3	6	1	392	14.5

1994-95 statistics:

GP	G	A	TP	+/-	PIM	PP	SH	GW	GT	S	PCT
48	29	21	50	+13	10	9	3	6	0	200	14.5

LAST SEASON

Led team in goals and power play goals for second consecutive season. Led team in points and shorthanded goals. Tied for team lead in game-winning goals. Led team and second in NHL in shots. One of three Blues to appear in all 48 games.

THE FINESSE GAME

The sight of Hull taking face-offs, killing penalties and blocking shots probably required more than one scout to seek medical attention — but no, they were not delusional.

Hull's game is evolving, and while he is no longer the 86-goal threat he was three seasons ago, he has become a better all-around player. Hull plays harder now and in all three zones. He'll never be mistaken for Doug Gilmour, but he performed well enough to earn a great deal of playing time from the very demanding Mike Keenan.

Hull still shoots the puck a thousand miles an hour, but not with the same accuracy that made his one-timers so deadly. His confidence, once supreme, has been obviously lacking. The Blues have never found a centre to replace Adam Oates as Hull's running mate. Dale Hawerchuk, signed as a free agent, may restore Hull's touch.

Hull is always working to get himself in position for a pass. On the power play, he will be in open ice, constantly moving, and he can fire off any kind of shot, accurately. His release may be the quickest in the NHL. Hull usually moves to his off-wing on the power play.

Hull is also an underrated playmaker who can thread a pass through traffic right onto the tape of a teammate. He has become a serviceable penalty killer as well and is a shorthanded threat.

THE PHYSICAL GAME

Hull is compact and when he wants to hit, it's a solid check. He is not as physically involved as he was when he was scoring goals at an absurd rate, but he will bump people.

THE INTANGIBLES

Hull's prorated total would have brought him close to the 50-goal mark again. He is healthy and with the proper centre and an improved offensive contribution from the defense, he should continue to be one of the league's best power play threats.

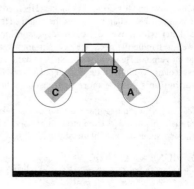

CURTIS JOSEPH

Yrs. of NHL service: 6
Born: Keswick, Ont.; Apr. 29, 1967
Position: goaltender
Height: 5-10
Weight: 182
Uniform no.: 31
Catches: left

Career statistics:

GP	MINS	GA	SO	GAA	A	PIM
280	15987	810	5	3.04	16	24

1991-92 statistics:

GP	MINS	AVG	W	L	T	SO	GA	S	SAPCT	PIM
60	3494	3.01	27	20	10	2	175	1953	.910	12

1992-93 statistics:

GP	MINS	AVG	W	L	T	SO	GA	S	SAPCT	PIM
68	3890	3.02	29	28	9	1	196	2202	.911	8

1993-94 statistics:

GP	MINS	AVG	W	L	T	SO	GA	S	SAPCT	PIM
71	4127	3.10	36	23	0	1	213	2382	.911	4

1994-95 statistics:

GP	MINS	AVG	W	L	T	SO	GA	S	SAPCT	PIM
36	1914	2.79	20	10	1	1	89	904	.902	0

LAST SEASON

Fourth in NHL in wins. GAA career best. Missed four games with a hamstring injury. Missed two games with a groin injury.

THE PHYSICAL GAME

Nothing Joseph does is by the book. He always looks unorthodox and off-balance, but he is one of those hybrid goalies — like Ed Belfour and Felix Potvin — whose success can't be argued with.

Joseph positions himself well, angling out to challenge the shooter, and is one of the best goalies against the breakaway in the NHL. He has stopped all four penalty shot attempts he has faced over the past four seasons. Joseph goes to his knees quickly, but bounces back to his skates fast for the rebound. He tends to keep rebounds in front of him. His glove hand is outstanding.

A strong, if bizarre, stickhandler, he has to move his hands on the stick, putting the butt-end into his catching glove and lowering his blocker. His favourite move is a weird backhand whip off the boards. He is a good skater who moves out of his cage confidently and well to handle the puck. He needs to improve his lateral movement. He also uses his stick to harass anyone who dares to camp on his doorstep. He's not Billy Smith, but he's getting more aggressive with his whacks.

Joseph had some nagging leg injuries last season, which make his numbers even more impressive, since he relies so much on his athletic ability.

THE MENTAL GAME

Joseph loves to play as often as a team will let him, and mentally he usually remains sharp no matter what kind of wild flurries go on in front of him. But he often battled the puck last season, and his mental state was unsettled because of his feuding with the coach (see below). He was a long way from his mental peak last year.

THE INTANGIBLES

Joseph told acquaintances there was no way he would play another minute for Mike Keenan. At press time, he had not been moved, but we would be shocked to find Cujo back in the Blues nets this year.

IAN LAPERRIERE

Yrs. of NHL service: 1
Born: Montreal, Que.; Jan. 19, 1974
Position: centre
Height: 6-0
Weight: 191
Uniform no.: 22
Shoots: right

Career statistics:

GP	G	A	TP	PIM
38	13	14	27	85

1993-94 statistics:

GP	G	A	TP	+/-	PIM	PP	SH	GW	GT	S	PCT
1	0	0	0	0	0	0	0	0	0	1	0.0

1994-95 statistics:

GP	G	A	TP	+/-	PIM	PP	SH	GW	GT	S	PCT
37	13	14	27	+12	85	1	0	1	0	53	24.5

LAST SEASON

Led NHL in shooting percentage. First NHL season. Tied for fourth among NHL rookies in points. Tied for third among NHL rookies in assists and plus-minus. Missed games with a concussion.

THE FINESSE GAME

The knock on Laperriere earlier in his career was his skating ability, but he has improved tremendously in that department. Although he'll never be a speed demon, Laperriere doesn't look out of place at the NHL level. He will always try to take the extra stride when he is back-checking so he can make a clean check, instead of taking the easy way out and committing a lazy hooking foul. Laperriere wins his share of races for the loose puck.

Laperriere grew up watching Guy Carbonneau (now his St. Louis teammate) in Montreal, and he learned well. Laperriere knows how to win a draw between his feet. He uses his stick and his body to make sure the opposing centre doesn't get the puck. He gets his right (bottom) hand way down on the stick and tries to win draws on his backhand.

Laperriere is ever willing to use the backhand, either for shots or to get the puck deep. He is very reliable defensively and shows signs of becoming a two-way centre.

THE PHYSICAL GAME

Laperriere is an obnoxious player in the Bob Bassen mold. He really battles for the puck. Though smallish, he has absolutely no fear of playing in the "circle" that extends from the lower inside of the face-off circles to behind the net. He will pay any price. He finishes every check and gives the extra effort. But he will have to learn to apportion his resources better over the course of a full 84-game season, or he will be worn out before the playoffs.

THE INTANGIBLES

A late-round surprise, Laperriere adds true grit to the lineup despite his small size. His nightly effort puts a lot of bigger guys to shame. He lost any bad habits the hard way by playing for a hard-nosed coach (Mike Keenan), who dispatched him to the minors early in the season. Laperriere took it well and came back a more determined player. He was probably the Blues' best centre last season, but didn't see any time on the big line. He is best suited as a number two centre who may produce 60-70 points.

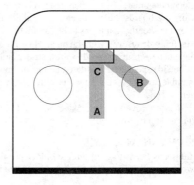

AL MACINNIS

Yrs. of NHL service: 11
Born: Inverness, N.S.; July 11, 1963
Position: right defense
Height: 6-2
Weight: 195
Uniform no.: 2
Shoots: right

Career statistics:

GP	G	A	TP	PIM
835	221	629	850	993

1991-92 statistics:

GP	G	A	TP	+/-	PIM	PP	SH	GW	GT	S	PCT
72	20	57	77	+13	83	11	0	0	1	304	6.6

1992-93 statistics:

GP	G	A	TP	+/-	PIM	PP	SH	GW	GT	S	PCT
50	11	43	54	+15	61	7	0	4	0	201	5.5

1993-94 statistics:

GP	G	A	TP	+/-	PIM	PP	SH	GW	GT	S	PCT
75	28	54	82	+35	95	12	1	5	0	324	8.6

1994-95 statistics:

GP	G	A	TP	+/-	PIM	PP	SH	GW	GT	S	PCT
32	8	20	28	+19	43	2	0	0	0	110	7.3

LAST SEASON

Acquired from Calgary with fourth round draft pick in 1997 for Phil Housley. Missed 16 games with shoulder injuries.

THE FINESSE GAME

What makes his shot so good is that MacInnis knows the value of a change-up, and he won't always fire with the same velocity. If there is traffic in front, MacInnis will take a little off his shot to make it more tippable (and so he doesn't break too many teammates' ankles). One-on-one, of course, MacInnis will fire the laser and can just about knock a goalie into the net.

MacInnis knows when to jump into the play and when to back off. He can start a rush with a rink-wide pass, then be quick enough to burst up-ice and be in position for a return pass. Because his shot is such a formidable weapon, he can freeze the opposition by faking a big wind-up, then quickly dish a pass in low to an open teammate. Even when he merely rings the puck off the boards, he's a threat, since there is so much on the shot the goalie has to be careful to stop it.

MacInnis skates well with the puck. He is not very mobile, but he gets up to speed in a few strides and can hit his outside speed to beat a defender one on one. He will gamble and is best paired with a defensively alert partner.

He has improved his defensive play and is very smart against a two-on-one.

THE PHYSICAL GAME

MacInnis has been plagued with shoulder problems for two seasons, and has been even less physical than in the past. He reads defenses well, and positions himself to tie up attackers rather than try to knock them down. He gets caught fishing for the puck instead of taking the body, and this is an especially dangerous bad habit at his own blue line. In his own way, he is a tough competitor who will pay the price to win.

THE INTANGIBLES

The *HSR* told you of MacInnis' imminent departure from Calgary last season, but didn't foresee that his shoulder injury would still be such a factor. MacInnis should return to his rightful position among the NHL defense scoring leaders, but only if healthy.

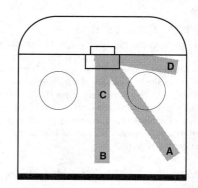

BASIL MCRAE

Yrs. of NHL service: 10
Born: Beaverton, Ont.; Jan. 5, 1961
Position: left wing
Height: 6-2
Weight: 205
Uniform no.: 17
Shoots: left

Career statistics:

GP	G	A	TP	PIM
550	52	82	134	2405

1991-92 statistics:

GP	G	A	TP	+/-	PIM	PP	SH	GW	GT	S	PCT
59	5	8	13	-14	245	0	0	0	0	64	7.8

1992-93 statistics:

GP	G	A	TP	+/-	PIM	PP	SH	GW	GT	S	PCT
47	3	6	9	-16	169	2	0	0	0	45	6.7

1993-94 statistics:

GP	G	A	TP	+/-	PIM	PP	SH	GW	GT	S	PCT
40	1	2	3	-7	103	0	0	0	0	23	4.3

1994-95 statistics:

GP	G	A	TP	+/-	PIM	PP	SH	GW	GT	S	PCT
21	0	5	5	+4	72	0	0	0	0	14	0.0

LAST SEASON
Missed 10 games with a back injury.

THE FINESSE GAME
McRae's already limited finesse skills have continued to deteriorate. Age (he will turn 35 this season) and injuries have slowed him, but he is such a smart and heady player that he merits a jersey ahead of some more talented players.

He has pretty good hands for someone who has staked his reputation on being a tough dude. He can handle the puck and make a play — not at top speed, true, but he is usually given some extra skating room and makes good use of it. McRae will score his precious few goals from around the crease.

McRae is a strong fore-checker but becomes more and more of a defensive liability as he slows down.

THE PHYSICAL GAME
McRae wants to play and will do whatever it takes to stay on the ice — even if it means having to go off the ice to serve yet another penalty. He will protect his team's finesse players. Anyone who wants to mess with a teammate will have to answer to McRae.

THE INTANGIBLES
McRae's value is not always readily apparent on the ice. But every coach he has ever played for speaks glowingly of his value in the dressing room and on the bench. He is a character player, and when he is able to keep himself in the lineup he allows his teammates to play a little bigger. We said in last year's *HSR* that McRae had one more useful season left in him, but he is coming off a pretty good effort in the playoffs and the short season didn't take much out of him. He will be back for another year as a role player.

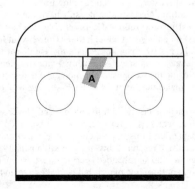

BRIAN NOONAN

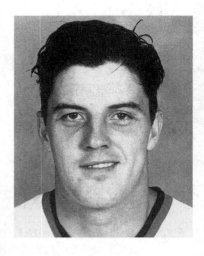

Yrs. of NHL service: 6
Born: Boston, Mass.; May 29, 1965
Position: right wing
Height: 6-1
Weight: 192
Uniform no.: 16
Shoots: right

Career statistics:

GP	G	A	TP	PIM
386	81	100	181	338

1991-92 statistics:

GP	G	A	TP	+/-	PIM	PP	SH	GW	GT	S	PCT
65	19	12	31	+9	81	4	0	0	2	154	12.3

1992-93 statistics:

GP	G	A	TP	+/-	PIM	PP	SH	GW	GT	S	PCT
63	16	14	30	+3	82	5	0	3	0	129	12.4

1993-94 statistics:

GP	G	A	TP	+/-	PIM	PP	SH	GW	GT	S	PCT
76	18	23	41	+7	69	10	0	6	1	160	11.3

1994-95 statistics:

GP	G	A	TP	+/-	PIM	PP	SH	GW	GT	S	PCT
45	14	13	27	-3	26	7	0	1	0	95	14.7

LAST SEASON

Missed three games with a sprained right knee. Tied for second on Rangers in power play goals. Led team in shooting percentage. Signed as a free agent by St. Louis.

THE FINESSE GAME

Noonan's strongest attribute is his willingness to go into the corners for the puck, win a battle for it, and come out and do something with it by either finding a man at the point with a pass or taking it to the net himself. He might also draw a penalty.

Noonan has good-enough hands and moves to win the blue line almost every time he attacks it with the puck. Defensemen seem to have a difficult time reading him, so they retreat, which buys him an extra 10 feet of ice in which to make a decision. He also varies his attacks to the blueline, which adds an unpredictable element, but he doesn't always identify the best passing option when he gains the line.

No speedster, and often seeming to be moving in slow motion, Noonan also doesn't have the world's smallest turning radius. He is reliable defensively, however, and is smart enough to maximize what little speed he has by changing gears a lot. He doesn't always skate at top speed, but can get an extra step by cranking up the pace just at the moment a defenseman has to make the pivot from back-skating to front-skating.

Noonan is crafty with his hands, and clever with his shot, which is never overpowering but often unstoppable due to its unpredictability. He also knows his defensive responsibility and can kill a penalty, although he's no shorthanded scoring threat. Noonan is a second or third line player, but he makes a team better because of his honest effort. He never cheats on his shifts.

THE PHYSICAL GAME

Noonan is a cruiserweight who uses his skating strength and balance and is difficult to knock down. He favours what might be called a flying hip check, where he throws himself into an onrushing opponent at the sideboards.

He has become more consistent at finishing his checks. He pins his target to the wall, and keeps him out of the play. He also plays the gut-check areas on offense. Noonan goes to the front of the net and gives up his body on tips and screens. He is a short-game player who pays the price to be in the right spot. He makes good use of his weight with a quiet strength.

THE INTANGIBLES

Noonan is a poker-faced guy who doesn't show much emotion and who doesn't really draw a lot of attention to himself. He keeps the game basic, nothing really fancy, but he has a nice amount of smarts and savvy. Noonan is a humble kid from a large family who made it to the NHL on hard work, and he will have to keep at it to have a regular job. He is willing to get involved physically. He will always be found along the walls and in the corners. In short, Noonan is the perfect Mike Keenan player, and now Keenan will be coaching him for the third time on three teams.

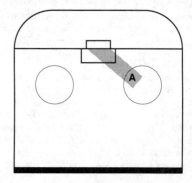

JEFF NORTON

Yrs. of NHL service: 7
Born: Acton, Mass.; Nov. 25, 1965
Position: right defense
Height: 6-2
Weight: 195
Uniform no.: 5
Shoots: left

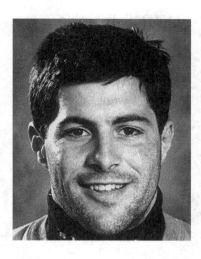

Career statistics:

GP	G	A	TP	PIM
394	32	226	258	340

1991-92 statistics:

GP	G	A	TP	+/-	PIM	PP	SH	GW	GT	S	PCT
28	1	18	19	+2	18	0	1	0	0	34	2.9

1992-93 statistics:

GP	G	A	TP	+/-	PIM	PP	SH	GW	GT	S	PCT
66	12	38	50	-3	45	5	0	0	0	127	9.4

1993-94 statistics:

GP	G	A	TP	+/-	PIM	PP	SH	GW	GT	S	PCT
64	7	33	40	+16	36	1	0	0	0	92	7.6

1994-95 statistics:

GP	G	A	TP	+/-	PIM	PP	SH	GW	GT	S	PCT
48	3	27	30	+22	72	0	0	1	0	48	6.3

LAST SEASON

Acquired with a conditional pick in 1997 from San Jose for Craig Janney and cash. Led team in assists. Second among team defensemen in scoring. Tied for second on team in plus/minus. One of three Sharks to appear in all 48 games.

THE FINESSE GAME

An offensive defenseman, Norton's game is based on his exceptional skating. Among NHL defensemen, perhaps only Paul Coffey is better (Brian Leetch and Scott Niedermayer are in similar company).

Norton has deep edges and seems to make his turns and cuts with his body at a 45-degree angle to the ice. His skating ability allows him to cover up for some of his more erratic defensive play. Norton gets too excited about going on the attack and forgets gap control or makes ill-timed pinches. Many times, he is able to gallop back into position, but he still makes a risky defensive proposition.

His hockey sense is good, especially offensively, but he has never been able to combine his skating with the kind of scoring impact he should. He doesn't have a great shot. He will generate a play with his skating and puckhandling and get the puck into the attacking zone, but he never seems to have the finishing touch, either with a shot or the good pass down low. In St. Louis, he is playing with some gifted offensive defensemen, which takes the pressure off Norton to be the man. He is a very intelligent player.

THE PHYSICAL GAME

Norton is not strong in his own end of the ice. On many nights, he will drift up as if he is ready to leave the zone prematurely and leave his teammates scrambling behind. His mental toughness is a question mark, and his focus and concentration waver, but he may improve defensively under taskmaster Mike Keenan. Norton was healthy last year for the first time in a long time, and that made him a more confident player.

THE INTANGIBLES

Norton is among the top three or four defensemen in St. Louis and enjoys that role, He has great pride in his ability and wants the responsibility. While his mental toughness has come into question in the past, he survived a year under Keenan, which is more than can be said for others. His offensive numbers should improve, possibly to the 60-point range.

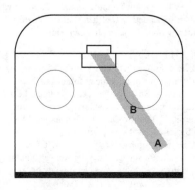

CHRIS PRONGER

Yrs. of NHL service: 2
Born: Dryden, Ont.; Oct. 10, 1974
Position: left defense
Height: 6-6
Weight: 190
Uniform no.: 44
Shoots: left

Career statistics:

GP	G	A	TP	PIM
124	10	34	44	167

1993-94 statistics:

GP	G	A	TP	+/-	PIM	PP	SH	GW	GT	S	PCT.
81	5	25	30	-3	113	2	0	0	0	174	2.9

1994-95 statistics:

GP	G	A	TP	+/-	PIM	PP	SH	GW	GT	S	PCT.
43	5	9	14	-12	54	3	0	1	0	94	5.3

LAST SEASON

Second NHL season. Missed four games with a shoulder injury. Acquired by St. Louis for Brendan Shanahan.

THE FINESSE GAME

Pronger has been touted as a young Larry Robinson, and while he has a long way and a handful of Stanley Cup rings to go before he can touch that comparison, there are similarities. Pronger is lanky, almost weedy at this youthful stage, with a powerful skating stride for angling his man to the boards for a take-out. He blends his physical play with good offensive instincts and skills.

He also handles the puck well when skating and is always heads-up for passing opportunities. His vision shows in his work on the power play. He patrols the point smartly, using a low, tippable shot. Like a lot of tall defensemen, Pronger doesn't get his slap shot away quickly, but he compensates with a snap shot that he uses liberally. He makes unique plays that make him stand out, great breakout passes and clever plays through the neutral zone. He is also wise enough to dump and chase rather than hold onto the puck and force a low percentage pass.

Disciplined away from the puck and alert defensively, Pronger shows good anticipation, going where the puck is headed before it's shot there. He is very confident with the puck in his own end.

THE PHYSICAL GAME

Pronger, who has difficulty keeping weight on, sees up to 30 minutes of ice time at times, but gets drained when he does. Since he has yet to indicate he knows how to take care of his body through conditioning, rest and nutrition, this problem will persist until he wakes up to the notion that this is his job.

A healthy, energetic Pronger will finish every check with enthusiasm, and even shows something of a nasty streak with his stick. He makes his stand between the blueline and the top of the circle, forcing the forward to react. His long reach has a lot to do with making that style effective. He also uses his stick and reach killing penalties.

THE INTANGIBLES

Pronger was supposed to be a franchise player for the Whalers, but Hartford got tired of waiting — in just two seasons — for him to demonstrate his commitment to the job. Pronger may yet become a franchise player, but it will have to be somewhere else. That role carries with it a great deal of responsibility and maturity, and not every promising youngster grows into the job. He can be a dominating defenseman and a force to build a team around.

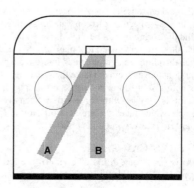

DAVID ROBERTS

Yrs. of NHL service: 0
Born: Alameda, Calif.; May 28, 1970
Position: left wing
Height: 6-0
Weight: 185
Uniform no.: 15
Shoots: left

Career statistics:

GP	G	A	TP	PIM
20	6	5	11	12

1993-94 statistics:

GP	G	A	TP	+/-	PIM	PP	SH	GW	GT	S	PCT
1	0	0	0	0	2	0	0	0	0	1	0.0

1994-95 statistics:

GP	G	A	TP	+/-	PIM	PP	SH	GW	GT	S	PCT
19	6	5	11	+2	10	3	0	2	1	41	14.6

LAST SEASON

Will be entering first full NHL season.

THE FINESSE GAME

Roberts has great skills and skating ability. He is another graduate of the U.S. Olympic program, which has produced some excellent pro players despite having little success in the Games.

Because he has also played defense, and can drop back in a pinch to play that position, Roberts is highly aware defensively and is a complete player. He could probably be asked to do more than the Blues asked of him last season. He saw little power play time, for example, but he has good vision and a fine shot from the point. Understandably, he ranks behind Steve Duchesne and Al MacInnis in that department, but give him time and he will be a very capable power play quarterback. He is very creative.

Roberts handles the puck at high speed and doesn't get cornered with it. He has the sense to escape and use other players to open up ice.

THE PHYSICAL GAME

Roberts is finesse oriented but has great heart. He will finish his checks. He won't dominate physically and he's not mean, but he's not afraid, either.

THE INTANGIBLES

Roberts has a lot of upside, and if he gets enough playing time he could start piling up some points. Shanahan's departure has opened up some room on the left wing and Roberts could possibly join the Blues' top line, but he can also be used in a checking role. Roberts started the season in the minors after suffering a broken nose in training camp, but played well after his recall.

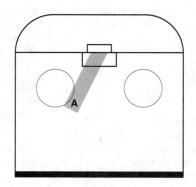

ESA TIKKANEN

Yrs. of NHL service: 10
Born: Helsinki, Finland; Jan. 25, 1965
Position: left wing
Height: 6-1
Weight: 200
Uniform no.: 10
Shoots: left

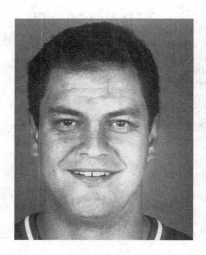

Career statistics:

GP	G	A	TP	PIM
663	204	318	502	913

1991-92 statistics:

GP	G	A	TP	+/-	PIM	PP	SH	GW	GT	S	PCT
40	12	16	28	-8	44	6	2	1	0	117	10.3

1992-93 statistics:

GP	G	A	TP	+/-	PIM	PP	SH	GW	GT	S	PCT
81	16	24	40	-24	94	2	4	3	0	202	7.9

1993-94 statistics:

GP	G	A	TP	+/-	PIM	PP	SH	GW	GT	S	PCT
83	22	32	54	+5	114	5	3	4	0	257	8.6

1994-95 statistics:

GP	G	A	TP	+/-	PIM	PP	SH	GW	GT	S	PCT
43	12	23	35	+13	22	5	2	1	1	107	11.2

LAST SEASON

Acquired from the New York Rangers with Doug Lidster for Petr Nedved. Fourth on team in points. Finalist for 1995 Selke Trophy.

THE FINESSE GAME

Tikkanen can play all three forward positions and applies all his considerable finesse skills to the defensive aspects of the game. Once a consistent 30-goal scorer, he's unlikely to hit that mark again, though he can provide 20 and some solid two-way play.

He has good speed, which he uses most effectively killing penalties, and he is an aggressive fore-checker, creating offensive chances off his work in the offensive zone. He blocks shots, hooks, holds and bumps, and if assigned to shadow a specific player will hound that mark relentlessly.

Tikkanen has accomplished enough offensive skills to work on the power play as well, from either the point or by working the puck down low. He has confidence in his puckhandling ability and sees the ice well. Despite taking chances low, he will be the first forward back to help out on defense. He likes to work out from behind the net, curl in front and shoot. Tikkanen also has a laser blast that he likes to go high with on the goalie's left side.

He is a choppy skater but chugs hard and gets to where he has to go.

THE PHYSICAL GAME

Tikkanen plays a grinding game. He cycles and works the boards and corners eagerly. The size of the opponent is of no concern: he will hurl his body at the biggest guy on the ice. Tikkanen is in your face — and also in your armpit or crawling up your back. He is as annoying as a mosquito and almost impossible to swat, since he is a master at the hit and run. One of the funniest sights in hockey is Tikkanen's wounded-victim look after he has goaded an opponent into taking a bad penalty. He often starts a war that one of his teammates ends up fighting.

THE INTANGIBLES

One of the items Mike Keenan wanted packed in his luggage when he moved from New York to St. Louis last season was the feisty Tikkanen. He is obnoxious, but he has the Stanley Cup rings to prove he's more than a mere brat.

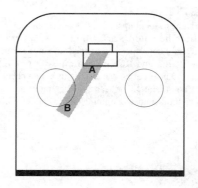

TAMPA BAY LIGHTNING

Players' Statistics 1994-95

POS	NO.	PLAYER	GP	G	A	PTS	+/-	PIM	PP	SH	GW	GT	S	PCTG
C	19	BRIAN BRADLEY	46	13	27	40	-6	42	3		2		111	11.7
L	15	PAUL YSEBAERT	44	12	16	28	3	18			1		93	12.9
C	77	CHRIS GRATTON	46	7	20	27	-2	89	2				91	7.7
R	85	PETR KLIMA	47	13	13	26	-13	26	4		3		75	17.3
R	14	JOHN TUCKER	46	12	13	25	-10	14	2		1		81	14.8
D	44	ROMAN HAMRLIK	48	12	11	23	-18	86	7	1	2		134	9.0
C	27	ALEXANDER SEMAK	41	7	11	18	-7	25			1		71	9.9
R	29	*ALEXANDER SELIVANOV	43	10	6	16	-2	14	4		3		94	10.6
L	7	ROB ZAMUNER	43	9	6	15	-3	24		3	1		74	12.2
C	28	MARC BUREAU	48	2	12	14	-8	30		1		1	72	2.8
L	34	MIKAEL ANDERSSON	36	4	7	11	-3	4					36	11.1
D	39	ENRICO CICCONE	41	2	4	6	3	225					43	4.7
D	25	MARC BERGEVIN	44	2	4	6	-6	51		1			32	6.3
D	4	*CORY CROSS	43	1	5	6	-6	41			1		35	2.9
D	21	BOB HALKIDIS	31	1	4	5	-10	46					25	4.0
L	9	*JASON WIEMER	36	1	4	5	-2	44					10	10.0
D	3	*ERIC CHARRON	45	1	4	5	1	26					33	3.0
D	6	ADRIEN PLAVSIC	18	2	2	4	8	8					35	5.7
R	33	*BRANTT MYHRES	15	2		2	-2	81			1		4	50.0
D	20	RUDY POESCHEK	25	1	1	2		92					14	7.1
R	16	*BEN HANKINSON	26		2	2	-5	13					26	
C	49	*BRENT GRETZKY	3		1	1	-2						1	
G	93	DAREN PUPPA	36		1	1		2						
L	17	GERARD GALLANT	1										1	
D	26	CHRIS LIPUMA	1				2						1	
G	30	J.C. BERGERON	17					2						

GP = games played; G = goals; A = assists; PTS = points; +/- = goals-for minus goals-against while player is on ice; PIM = penalties in minutes; PP = power play goals; SH = shorthanded goals; GW = game-winning goals; GT = game-tying goals; S = no. of shots; PCTG = percentage of goals to shots; * = rookie

BRIAN BELLOWS

Yrs. of NHL service: 13
Born: St. Catharines, Ont.; Sept. 1, 1964
Position: left wing
Height: 5-11
Weight: 195
Uniform no.: 23
Shoots: left

Career statistics:

GP	G	A	TP	PIM
953	423	474	897	625

1991-92 statistics:

GP	G	A	TP	+/-	PIM	PP	SH	GW	GT	S	PCT
80	30	45	75	-20	41	12	1	4	0	255	11.8

1992-93 statistics:

GP	G	A	TP	+/-	PIM	PP	SH	GW	GT	S	PCT
82	40	48	88	+4	44	16	0	5	0	260	15.5

1993-94 statistics:

GP	G	A	TP	+/-	PIM	PP	SH	GW	GT	S	PCT
77	33	38	71	+9	36	13	0	2	1	251	13.1

1994-95 statistics:

GP	G	A	TP	+/-	PIM	PP	SH	GW	GT	S	PCT
41	8	8	16	-7	8	1	0	1	0	110	7.3

LAST SEASON
Missed five games a with shoulder separation. Acquired from Montreal for Marc Bureau.

THE FINESSE GAME
Last season was a major disappointment for Bellows. A goal-scorer all his hockey life, his touch and confidence deserted him and he was relegated to a checking role, which he did not embrace with great enthusiasm.

While you won't notice him much in open ice, Bellows is scary around the net. A power play specialist, he has great hands and instincts in deep. He is not as big as the prototypical power forward, but he plays that style in driving to the crease. He is nimble in traffic and can handle the puck in a scrum. He has good balance for scrapping in front. He works down low on the first power play unit.

Bellows moves and shoots the puck quickly — he doesn't like to fool around with it. He has a strong one-timer and powerful wrist shot. Once in a while he'll score from a drive off the wing, but most of his goals come from in close.

Bellows's five-on-five play improves when he is teamed with the kind of centre who will get the puck to him and is defensively alert.

THE PHYSICAL GAME
Bellows plays bigger than his size. He will bump and crash and work the boards in the offensive zone, but he is better as a finisher in front of the net. When he has the right linemate, he can concentrate on scoring.

THE INTANGIBLES
After trailing off so badly last season, Bellows desperately needed a change in scenery. The Florida sun may help restore his scoring touch.

Last year was also a difficult season for Bellows personally, as his father died before the start of the season, a day before the birth of Bellows's daughter.

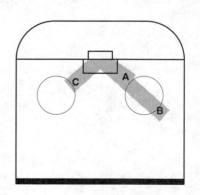

BRIAN BRADLEY

Yrs. of NHL service: 8
Born: Kitchener, Ont.; Jan. 21, 1965
Position: centre
Height: 5-10
Weight: 177
Uniform no.: 19
Shoots: right

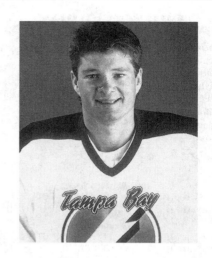

Career statistics:

GP	G	A	TP	PIM
527	150	243	393	429

1991-92 statistics:

GP	G	A	TP	+/-	PIM	PP	SH	GW	GT	S	PCT
59	10	21	31	-3	48	4	0	3	0	78	12.8

1992-93 statistics:

GP	G	A	TP	+/-	PIM	PP	SH	GW	GT	S	PCT
80	42	44	86	-24	92	16	0	6	1	205	20.5

1993-94 statistics:

GP	G	A	TP	+/-	PIM	PP	SH	GW	GT	S	PCT
78	24	40	64	-8	56	6	0	2	0	180	13.3

1994-95 statistics:

GP	G	A	TP	+/-	PIM	PP	SH	GW	GT	S	PCT
46	13	27	40	-6	42	3	0	2	0	111	11.7

LAST SEASON

Led team in assists and points for third consecutive season. Tied for team lead in goals. Missed two games with a charley horse.

THE FINESSE GAME

Bradley makes the most of his ice-time. He is an above-average skater with good speed, a nice shot and passing skills. He prefers shooting to passing. He has a neat move where he drives wide to the right wing, then uses a little delay and a half-snap to handcuff the goalie.

Bradley will work low around the net and likes to use his backhand in tight. He has always had a nose for the net, but he doesn't have a big cannon. He has the quickness to jump into holes and the good hockey sense to work give-and-gos. He opens up some room for his linemates with his stickhandling, and he will also drive to the net himself with the puck.

Bradley is used on the point on the power play, more for his common sense with the puck than his shot. He puts low, tippable shots towards the goal.

THE PHYSICAL GAME

Bradley is a small centre and doesn't play a physical game. He uses fairly good leg drive and will force people to drag him down and take penalties. His deceptive change of speed has defenders thinking they've got him covered, until he squirts out of their grasp.

THE INTANGIBLES

Bradley reestablished his role as the team's number one centre last season, as sophomore Chris Gratton slumped, and he continued to be the team's go-to guy. The only original member from the 1992 Expansion Draft left on Tampa Bay, the old reliable scored at a pro-rated 73-point pace, which was more than the 50-60 point range we predicted for him last year. He should net 60 points again this season.

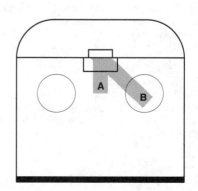

ERIC CHARRON

Yrs. of NHL service: 1
Born: Verdun, Que.; Jan. 14, 1970
Position: defense
Height: 6-3
Weight: 192
Uniform no.: 3
Shoots: left

Career statistics:

GP	G	A	TP	PIM
52	1	4	5	32

1992-93 statistics:

GP	G	A	TP	+/-	PIM	PP	SH	GW	GT	S	PCT
3	0	0	0	0	2	0	0	0	0	0	0.0

1993-94 statistics:

GP	G	A	TP	+/-	PIM	PP	SH	GW	GT	S	PCT
4	0	0	0	-3	4	0	0	0	0	5	0.0

1994-95 statistics:

GP	G	A	TP	+/-	PIM	PP	SH	GW	GT	S	PCT
45	1	4	5	+1	26	0	0	0	0	33	3.0

LAST SEASON

First NHL season. Missed one game with a bruised knee.

THE FINESSE GAME

Charron is one of those players for whom a defensive defenseman trophy may one day be required in the NHL. He patrols his own zone and clears the front of his net. He needs to improve his defensive reads and puck movement, but he has shown signs of being willing to work on those areas. He was paired for much of the season with Roman Hamrlik, an offensively minded sort, and the chemistry worked. But Charron is also a decent skater who will get involved in the attack once he gains more confidence in his abilities.

He shoots the puck well from the point but seldom takes any chances beyond the blueline. His objective is keeping the puck out of his own end.

THE PHYSICAL GAME

Charron is big and strong on his skates. He takes the body well, hits hard, but isn't overly aggressive or mean. He would benefit from becoming a more dominating hitter, and that could come. He made great strides in his rookie season, getting a lot of ice time and being allowed to make mistakes without fear of being benched. He is very steady and doesn't take bad penalties.

THE INTANGIBLES

You can't go wrong with a defenseman out of the Montreal system, as the Philadelphia Flyers learned last season. Charron is a building block for a very young Lightning defense, and could anchor them for seasons to come.

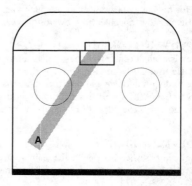

ENRICO CICCONE

Yrs. of NHL service: 3
Born: Montreal, Que.; Apr. 10, 1970
Position: left defense
Height: 6-4
Weight: 200
Uniform no.: 39
Shoots: left

Career statistics:

GP	G	A	TP	PIM
140	3	7	10	614

1991-92 statistics:

GP	G	A	TP	+/-	PIM	PP	SH	GW	GT	S	PCT
11	0	0	0	-2	48	0	0	0	0	2	0.0

1992-93 statistics:

GP	G	A	TP	+/-	PIM	PP	SH	GW	GT	S	PCT
31	0	1	1	2	115	0	0	0	0	13	0.0

1993-94 statistics:

GP	G	A	TP	+/-	PIM	PP	SH	GW	GT	S	PCT
57	1	2	3	-4	226	0	0	0	0	33	3.0

1994-95 statistics:

GP	G	A	TP	+/-	PIM	PP	SH	GW	GT	S	PCT
41	2	4	6	+3	225	0	0	0	0	43	4.7

LAST SEASON

Led NHL in PIM with team record. Led team in PIM for second consecutive season. Tied for team lead in plus-minus. Served two-game suspension for a head butt. Missed one game with a back injury. Missed one game with a neck injury.

THE FINESSE GAME

To improve Ciccone's overall play, coaches keep whispering two words: "Mark Tinordi." Tinordi is the classic example of a former goon who developed into a respected two-way defenseman without losing an iota of his toughness. Now Ciccone is trying to tread the same path.

Ciccone's overall play is limited because of his skating. He has slow feet, and while he is well balanced in tight quarters, he is at a disadvantage where any quick turn of foot is needed, even in corners or around the net. Since being told a regular job among Tampa Bay's top six defensemen is his if he wants it badly enough, Ciccone has worked to improve his puck movement and positioning — two skills that can minimize his slow turn of foot.

He tends to overhandle the puck, especially in the defensive zone. He does block shots well, but he would be better off using bigger gloves (small ones come off more easily for fights) for defensive purposes.

THE PHYSICAL GAME

Ciccone doesn't back down from any challenge and often goes around issuing them himself. He can fight, and he is a punishing checker. Coaches have tried to rein in his enthusiasm a bit, but they don't want to take away his physical presence. You can be tough without being dumb, and Ciccone is starting to learn the difference.

THE INTANGIBLES

The Lightning showed faith in Ciccone by putting him out in key situations, and he is responding. He is only 25. Another season or two of intensive tutelage could turn him into a valuable asset.

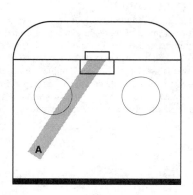

CORY CROSS

Yrs. of NHL service: 1
Born: Lloydminster, Alta.; Jan. 3, 1971
Position: left defense
Height: 6-5
Weight: 212
Uniform no.: 4
Shoots: left

Career statistics:

GP	G	A	TP	PIM
48	1	5	6	47

1993-94 statistics:

GP	G	A	TP	+/-	PIM	PP	SH	GW	GT	S	PCT
5	0	0	0	-3	6	0	0	0	0	5	0.0

1994-95 statistics:

GP	G	A	TP	+/-	PIM	PP	SH	GW	GT	S	PCT
43	1	5	6	-6	41	0	0	1	0	35	2.9

LAST SEASON
First NHL season.

THE FINESSE GAME
Cross's most impressive asset may be his intelligence. He is smart enough to recognize the mistakes he makes and learn from them. He is highly skilled, a fine skater who can either lug the puck out of his zone or start things with a pass and then jump up into the play. He has a good shot and will make wise pinches to keep the puck in the zone.

Cross was the first player taken in the 1992 Supplemental Draft and shot his way up the Lightning depth chart in two seasons. He may be good enough with the puck to merit more power play time on the point. (Last season, Tampa Bay used Brian Bradley, a forward, on the point on the first unit with Roman Hamrlik.) Cross needs more adjusting to the speed of the NHL.

THE PHYSICAL GAME
Cross did not play in a physical environment at the collegiate level, but he has taken a real shine to NHL play. He is a solid skater with good size, and is just learning how truly big and powerful he is.

THE INTANGIBLES
Cross played Canadian collegiate hockey, which hasn't been much of a breeding ground for NHLers. But after just one season in the minors he's made the jump to the NHL. His game is flawed, and he may be two seasons away from being a complete, competent defenseman, but he could prove to be a sleeper. Cross concentrated on learning defense last season, but the Lightning could turn him loose more this year.

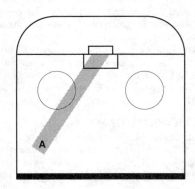

AARON GAVEY

Yrs. of NHL service: 0
Born: Gloucester, Mass.; Feb. 22, 1974
Position: centre
Height: 6-1
Weight: 170
Uniform no.: n.a.
Shoots: left

Career IHL statistics:

GP	G	A	TP	PIM
66	18	17	35	85

1994-95 IHL statistics:

GP	G	A	TP	PIM
66	18	17	35	85

LAST SEASON
Will be entering first full NHL season.

THE FINESSE GAME
Gavey could prove to be the steal of the 1992 draft. He wasn't ranked among the top 100 draft prospects of that year, but taken 74th by the Lightning, he is probably the top young player heading into this year's training camp.

Gavey will not stun people with his numbers, but there is every chance he could develop into a Mike Ridley type of centre. He will get points, make plays and kill penalties, and he will never hurt your team. The Lightning coaches won't be afraid to put Gavey into the lineup in any situation, and for a team desperate for calm and stability on the ice, he could prove to be a gem.

Gavey has a very good shot, a strong wrist or snap. He is also very good on face-offs, and may enter camp as the team's best man on draws. He reads plays with exceptional intelligence for a young player. His defensive game is advanced for his age.

THE PHYSICAL GAME
Gavey needs to get stronger. He is a weedy 6-1 and needs to bulk up a little — not much, or it will throw his overall game off. But he won't succeed at the NHL level without more strength. He is very competitive and plays to the last second of a period.

THE INTANGIBLES
Gavey was a key member of the 1994 Canadian World Junior team that won a gold medal and has continued to exhibit leadership skills at every level he has competed at. While Tampa Bay has never rushed its young players, the organization feels that Gavey is ready to play an important role next season.

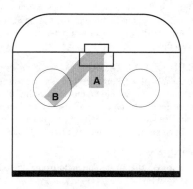

CHRIS GRATTON

Yrs. of NHL service: 2
Born: Brantford, Ont.; July 5, 1975
Position: centre
Height: 6-3
Weight: 202
Uniform no.: 77
Shoots: left

Career statistics:

GP	G	A	TP	PIM
130	20	49	69	212

1993-94 statistics:

GP	G	A	TP	+/-	PIM	PP	SH	GW	GT	S	PCT
84	13	29	42	-25	123	5	1	2	1	161	8.1

1994-95 statistics:

GP	G	A	TP	+/-	PIM	PP	SH	GW	GT	S	PCT
46	7	20	27	-2	89	2	0	0	0	91	7.7

LAST SEASON

Plus-minus improved by +23. Second on team in assists. Third on team in points. Missed two games with a bruised shoulder.

THE FINESSE GAME

Gratton's game is meat and potatoes. He's a grinder and not a very good skater, who needs to work hard every shift, every night, to make an impact.

He has a hard shot, which he needs to use more. He gets his goals from digging around the net, but there's some Cam Neely in him, too. He has to improve his skating and develop a longer, stronger and more efficient stride to become Neely-deadly around the net. He has good hand-eye coordination and can pick passes out of midair for a shot.

Gratton is an unselfish playmaker. He's not the prettiest of passers, but he has some poise with the puck and knows when to pass and when to shoot.

He worked on the power play — a unit that ranked 24th in the league last season — where he battles and screens in front. Because of his skating, he was not used to killing penalties (which he did in junior) or to four-on-four situations. He is becoming better at draws.

The Lightning shifted Gratton to left wing for a stretch late in the season to help him gain some confidence in his play, but he finished the season at centre and is projected as the team's number one player at that position.

THE PHYSICAL GAME

Gratton is a hard-working sort who doesn't shy from contact, but he has to initiate more. Once his skating improves, he will be able to establish a more physical presence. He won't be an NHL impact player until he does, but he has the skill and character to do so.

THE INTANGIBLES

It's time for Gratton to step up and assume one of the leadership roles on his young team. Lack of confidence affected him in his first two seasons in the NHL, but with his solid work ethic and his touch around the net, he is ready to take the next step. This is a big season for him.

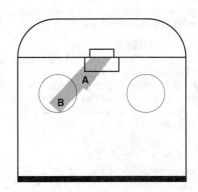

ROMAN HAMRLIK

Yrs. of NHL service: 3
Born: Gottwaldov, Czechoslovakia; Apr. 12, 1974
Position: left defense
Height: 6-2
Weight: 189
Uniform no.: 44
Shoots: left

Career statistics:

GP	G	A	TP	PIM
179	21	44	65	292

1992-93 statistics:

GP	G	A	TP	+/-	PIM	PP	SH	GW	GT	S	PCT
67	6	15	21	-21	71	1	0	1	0	113	5.3

1993-94 statistics:

GP	G	A	TP	+/-	PIM	PP	SH	GW	GT	S	PCT
64	3	18	21	-14	135	0	0	0	0	158	1.9

1994-95 statistics:

GP	G	A	TP	+/-	PIM	PP	SH	GW	GT	S	PCT
48	12	11	23	-18	86	7	1	2	0	134	9.0

LAST SEASON

Led team defensemen in scoring. Led team in power play goals and shots. Worst plus-minus on team. One of two Lightning players to appear in all 48 games.

THE FINESSE GAME

Hamrlik is very close to becoming the NHL's next star defenseman. He has all of the tools. He is a fast, strong skater forwards and backwards. Although he needs to improve his reads a bit, he's getting better. Tampa Bay coaches told him at the start of the season that he would be their number one defenseman, and that it was time for him to step up and shoulder the responsibility. Hamrlik responded.

He is a mobile defenseman with a solid shot and good passing skills, but he is not very creative. Right now, the young Czech thinks he can just overpower people, and he frequently can, but he could also learn to outsmart them and not make the game so difficult. Hamrlik loves to get involved offensively. He plays nearly the full two minutes of a power play on the point, but he won't hesitate to jump into the play low. He has an excellent shot with a quick release.

He has adjusted to the NHL pace because of his strong skating. He makes fewer high-risk plays and saw more ice time as a result.

Hamrlik is paired with the stay-at-home Eric Charron, which gives Hamrlik the confidence to take some chances. The pair was inexperienced and made their mistakes, but faced other teams' top lines game after game and improved accordingly. Defensively, Hamrlik runs into problems when he is trying to move the puck out of his zone and when forced to handle the puck on his backhand.

THE PHYSICAL GAME

Hamrlik answered questions about his toughness with his successful return from knee surgery. He was nearly a year ahead of the recovery schedule doctors had predicted for him, so there is a chance he will be even stronger, faster and more confident this season. Hamrlik is aggressive and likes physical play, although he is not a huge, splashy hitter. He is in great shape, and routinely plays 27-30 minutes a night. He could wear down over the course of a full season (and playoffs, if the team gets that far). But until Tampa Bay develops more faith in its other defensemen, Hamrlik will be the man.

THE INTANGIBLES

Ask anyone in the Tampa Bay organization about Hamrlik and the response is unrestrained enthusiasm.

Now that he has adjusted to North America, how will he react to a big new contract? Tampa Bay gave him a five-year, $8.5-million deal, and not all players handle that kind of money (and the pressure that goes with it) well. Hamrlik could start reaching the 20-goal, 50-point range this season, and improve from there as the team gets better.

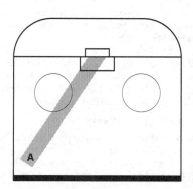

PETR KLIMA

Yrs. of NHL service: 10
Born: Choamutov, Czechoslovakia; Dec. 23, 1964
Position: left wing
Height: 6-0
Weight: 190
Uniform no.: 85
Shoots: right

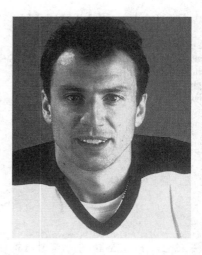

Career statistics:

GP	G	A	TP	PIM
671	288	268	506	587

1991-92 statistics:

GP	G	A	TP	+/-	PIM	PP	SH	GW	GT	S	PCT
57	21	13	34	-18	52	5	0	0	0	107	19.6

1992-93 statistics:

GP	G	A	TP	+/-	PIM	PP	SH	GW	GT	S	PCT
68	32	16	48	-15	100	13	0	2	0	175	18.3

1993-94 statistics:

GP	G	A	TP	+/-	PIM	PP	SH	GW	GT	S	PCT
75	28	77	55	-15	76	10	0	2	0	167	16.8

1994-95 statistics:

GP	G	A	TP	+/-	PIM	PP	SH	GW	GT	S	PCT
47	13	13	26	-13	26	4	0	3	0	75	17.3

LAST SEASON

Tied for team lead in goals and game-winning goals. Led team in shooting percentage for second consecutive season. Fourth on team in points.

THE FINESSE GAME

During a game against the Montreal Canadiens last season, Klima sidled up to an opponent and admitted, "I play this game one way — wide open." Later in the same game, as the teams went into overtime, he told a Montreal player, "Why don't we just settle for a tie?" Then Klima went and fired home the game-winner.

Talented and exasperating, Klima on one night will make a careless play and be indifferent to defense. On another, he will be dazzling. Few of his goals, however, are crunch-time tallies.

There are a lot of things he can do. He can score in a variety of ways and in a variety of areas on the ice. He has elite speed with the puck and without it. He is flashy and blessed with great offensive instinct.

Klima is an expert at drawing penalties. He keeps his legs pumping, grasps an opponent's stick and jumps into the air before falling to the ice. Is it a dive? Sure, but a penalty for diving has been so infrequently called over the past two seasons it might just as well be eliminated from the rule book. He will also take cheap shots with his stick or an elbow and tends to take these penalties at inopportune moments.

THE PHYSICAL GAME

Klima is inconsistent in the application of his body. Some nights he will check, and hard, or sneak up from behind a player and hound him until he strips the puck away. He uses his feet well and keeps the puck alive along the boards. But on even more nights, he'll do none of those things.

THE INTANGIBLES

The Lightning need a 40-goal season from this sniper, but it's a mystery as to whether they will ever get it. While Klima seems to have cleaned up his act, he remains one of the most erratic performers in the NHL, just as capable of a brilliant streak as he is of a month-long goal drought. There are too many young, hungry players on this Tampa Bay team for Klima to float. If his position is seriously challenged (which it hasn't been for two seasons), he may elevate his game.

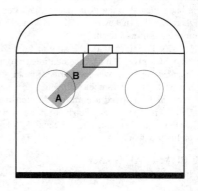

BRANTT MYHRES

Yrs. of NHL service: 0
Born: Edmonton, Alta.; March 18, 1974
Position: right wing
Height: 6-3
Weight: 200
Uniform no.: 33
Shoots: right

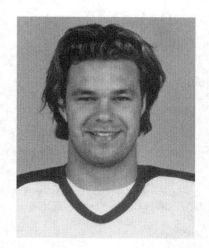

Career statistics:

GP	G	A	TP	PIM
15	2	0	2	81

1994-95 statistics:

GP	G	A	TP	+/-	PIM	PP	SH	GW	GT	S	PCT
15	2	0	2	-2	81	0	0	0	0	14	7.1

LAST SEASON

Will be entering first full NHL season. Played 40 games with Atlanta (IHL), scoring 5-5 — 10 with 213 PIM. Missed one game with a shoulder injury.

THE FINESSE GAME

Until last season, Myhres didn't have much of a skills package to speak of. It's still minimal, but Myhres is a willing worker who knows it takes more than an attitude to earn a regular shift in the NHL.

While his penalty minutes will always outstrip his point totals, he shows promise of developing into a solid third-line player. He drives to the net well for loose pucks or to distract the goalie. His skating is average, but he is strong and has good balance. He also has fairly good hands, and his reputation will give him space to make plays.

Myhres needs to improve his overall hockey sense and positioning. Defensive awareness will be key for him to earn more ice time and to improve.

THE PHYSICAL GAME

Myhres can throw 'em. He's a left-handed puncher, which gives him an edge in almost any scrap. With the gloves on, he's a legitimate tough guy, a serious body checker. His mean streak always has opponents guessing and earns him extra room.

THE INTANGIBLES

The Lightning harbour hopes that Myhres can develop along Randy McKay lines, and be a player who brings toughness and intensity to the ice every night along with a scoring touch. It may take awhile for him to develop to that level; it took McKay a good four seasons or so.

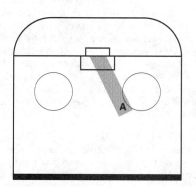

DAREN PUPPA

Yrs. of NHL service: 8
Born: Kirkland Lake, Ont.; Mar. 23, 1965
Position: goaltender
Height: 6-3
Weight: 205
Uniform no.: 93
Catches: right

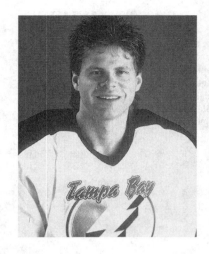

Career statistics:

GP	MINS	GA	SO	GAA	A	PIM
322	17909	941	12	3.15	16	30

1991-92 statistics:

GP	MINS	GAA	W	L	T	SO	G	S	SAPCT	PIM
33	1757	3.89	11	14	4	0	114	932	.878	2

1992-93 statistics:

GP	MINS	GAA	W	L	T	SO	G	S	SAPCT	PIM
32	1785	3.23	17	7	4	1	96	938	.898	0

1993-94 statistics:

GP	MINS	GAA	W	L	T	SO	G	S	SAPCT	PIM
63	3653	2.71	22	33	6	4	165	1637	.899	2

1994-95 statistics:

GP	MINS	GAA	W	L	T	SO	G	S	SAPCT	PIM
36	2013	2.68	14	19	2	1	90	946	.905	2

LAST SEASON

Career best GAA. Missed four games with a right wrist injury.

THE PHYSICAL GAME

A big player, with big pads, Puppa stands up well to make himself look even bigger in the nets. He tries to stay on his feet and play his angles, and he challenges shooters. He plays a butterfly style, and even when he drops to his knees there is still a lot of torso blocking the net.

Puppa has a good glove. He catches right-handed, which is an advantage (much like left-handed tennis players and pitchers have) because shooters are used to looking at left-gloved goalies. His weakness is high stick-side (as with most goalies), but shooters who think they are going stick-side on him are shooting to his glove side.

He is very good on low shots, though he gets in trouble when he drops down too early, and flounders.

Puppa moves in and out of his net well. He will set picks or interfere with the opposition trying to get in, and he helps his defensemen by holding up forwards (illegal, but he gets away with it). He does not handle the puck well, however, and since he isn't playing behind a mobile defense corps, it would really help his cause if he could improve in this area. He uses his stick well around the net to knock away loose pucks and cut off passes near the crease.

THE MENTAL GAME

Puppa laboured long in the Buffalo and Toronto systems as a backup goalie. Expansion gave him his shot to be number one, and he has handled the role well for Tampa Bay for the past two seasons. He will be challenged this season by the youngster Derek Wilkinson, and will have to maintain confidence in himself to be effective.

THE INTANGIBLES

Puppa is under great pressure every night, since a team that scores as few goals as Tampa Bay cannot afford to have its goalie allow any soft ones. It's not what Puppa stops, but what he lets in, that count. The Lightning's netminder basically has to be one of the game's three stars for the team to have any chance to win. Puppa was voted the team's MVP last season.

Two factors may affect Puppa's mental state this season. The first is the result of his salary arbitration. The second is the well-publicized game late in the season when a TV camera at Madison Square Garden caught coach Terry Crisp's note to himself reading, "Kicked in net himself...All Puppa...They were dead and buried." That kind of public criticism, although it was meant to stay private, can sting a long time. Puppa was pulled from that game and the next, and did not start the last two games for Tampa Bay.

ALEXANDER SELIVANOV

Yrs. of NHL service: 1
Born: Moscow, Russia; March 23, 1971
Position: right wing
Height: 6-1
Weight: 187
Uniform no.: 29
Shoots: left

Career statistics:

GP	G	A	TP	PIM
43	10	6	16	14

1994-95 statistics:

GP	G	A	TP	+/-	PIM	PP	SH	GW	GT	S	PCT
43	10	6	16	-2	14	4	0	3	0	94	10.6

LAST SEASON

First NHL season. Tied for team lead and tied for lead among NHL rookies in game-winning goals.

THE FINESSE GAME

Selivanov is very clever with the puck. He can beat people one-on-one with his speed and puckhandling, but needs to learn to use his teammates better. Once he does, he will be much more productive. Selivanov loves to score, and he works to get himself in position for a quality shot. He needs to play with someone who will get the puck to him, because he can finish.

Selivanov tends to take very long shifts, which drives his coaches crazy, but that is a common tendency with Russian players. Communication was also a problem.

The Lightning had trouble finding a regular slot for Selivanov during the lockout-shortened season, but he is in their plans for next season as one of their top forwards.

THE PHYSICAL GAME

Selivanov is wiry but he is not terribly strong or aggressive. If Tampa Bay plans to play him with a small, crafty centre (he did his best work with Denis Savard last season), the line will need a big winger for protection.

THE INTANGIBLES

Selivanov faced a difficult adjustment to North America. A bout of homesickness while he was playing in the minors prompted the team to send him home to Russia for a visit. The arrival of fellow Russian Alexander Semak late in the year made Selivanov more comfortable, and there is a big upside to his game. He could easily score in the 20-25 goal range.

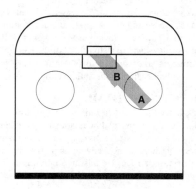

ALEXANDER SEMAK

Yrs. of NHL service: 4
Born: Ufa, Russia; Feb. 11, 1966
Position: centre
Height: 5-10
Weight: 180
Uniform no.: 27
Shoots: right

Career statistics:

GP	G	A	TP	PIM
202	61	76	137	117

1991-92 statistics:

GP	G	A	TP	+/-	PIM	PP	SH	GW	GT	S	PCT
25	5	6	11	+5	0	0	0	1	0	45	11.1

1992-93 statistics:

GP	G	A	TP	+/-	PIM	PP	SH	GW	GT	S	PCT
82	37	42	79	+24	70	4	1	6	1	217	17.1

1993-94 statistics:

GP	G	A	TP	+/-	PIM	PP	SH	GW	GT	S	PCT
54	12	17	29	+6	22	2	2	2	0	88	13.6

1994-95 statistics:

GP	G	A	TP	+/-	PIM	PP	SH	GW	GT	S	PCT
41	7	11	18	-7	25	0	0	1	0	71	9.9

LAST SEASON

Acquired from New Jersey with Ben Hankinson for Danton Cole and Shawn Chambers.

THE FINESSE GAME

Semak is a master of deception. Will he shoot or pass? Forehand or backhand? The guessing game foils defensemen and goalies, but it can also baffle linemates who don't know how to read him, and he needs to play with someone who is truly simpatico. Tampa Bay may have that ideal linemate in Alexander Selivanov.

Semak has a nice variety of moves and runs through his options very quickly, in just a few strides from the blueline to the hash marks. He will open, close and re-open his stickface, and has a strong wrist shot off either foot.

He is not a fast skater in the breakaway sense, but Semak is shifty with deceptive speed and one-step quickness that can leave a checker in the embarrassing position of slamming himself into the boards while Semak continues on his merry way to the net. He is very creative, seeing or sensing teammates coming in late behind him for a drop pass. He works well on crisscross plays, and likes to use all of the ice.

Semak is so-so on face-offs. He is a very good penalty killer because of his anticipation.

THE PHYSICAL GAME

Semak lacks the speed to intimidate and drive back opponents on the rush and he is not strong enough to win one-on-one battles in tight quarters, so he must always work hard at the weaving game with his partners to find open ice. He has an annoying habit of staying down on the ice when he is fouled and getting left out of the play when the referee doesn't call anything.

THE INTANGIBLES

The Lightning hope a change of scene will bring back the Semak of 1992-93. He seemed a bit bewildered by the trade and needed time to adjust. If he doesn't come through this season, you can just about write him off.

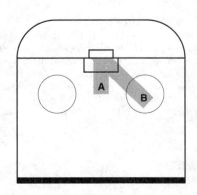

JOHN TUCKER

Yrs. of NHL service: 10
Born: Windsor, Ont.; Sept. 29, 1964
Position: right wing/centre
Height: 6-0
Weight: 200
Uniform no.: 14
Shoots: right

Career statistics:

GP	G	A	TP	PIM
593	174	252	426	267

1991-92 statistics:

Did not play in the NHL

1992-93 statistics:

GP	G	A	TP	+/-	PIM	PP	SH	GW	GT	S	PCT
78	17	39	56	-12	69	5	1	1	0	179	9.5

1993-94 statistics:

GP	G	A	TP	+/-	PIM	PP	SH	GW	GT	S	PCT
66	17	23	40	+9	28	2	0	6	1	126	13.5

1994-95 statistics:

GP	G	A	TP	+/-	PIM	PP	SH	GW	GT	S	PCT
46	12	13	25	-10	14	2	0	1	0	81	14.8

ing the most of his ice time with the Lightning. His goal production fell off in relation to the quality of his ice time, and if some of the team's younger forwards come through, they will be pushing the veteran for a job. But if they don't, expect Tucker to provide his reliable play and another 15-20 goals.

LAST SEASON

Fourth on team in points. Second on team in shooting percentage.

THE FINESSE GAME

Tucker is an honest, up-and-down winger who fits nicely into coach Terry Crisp's style. Nothing about him is flashy, but he has the anticipation to get himself into the right situations, plus the nifty hand skills to make things happen.

A finisher who also worked the corners for centre Brian Bradley, he took advantage of being put into a responsible situation, an opportunity he didn't have with other teams (Tampa Bay is his fourth NHL organization). Tucker's hands, quick release and his good hockey sense blend well for a dangerous threat down low. He won't stand in front of the net and take needless punishment, but instead will dart in and out of holes. He even played some left wing late in the season, despite being a right-handed shot.

Tucker tends to score goals that count, and he plays a sound two-way game. He has a wide-based skating stance and can put on a burst of quickness to go through or beat a defender one-on-one. He can play alongside almost any kind of linemates. He will stay third man high if that's what the coach asks for, or he will throw himself in deep as a fore-checker.

THE PHYSICAL GAME

Tucker makes good use of his size along the boards and is not afraid to work through traffic in the offensive zone.

THE INTANGIBLES

Tucker is an average journeyman player who is mak-

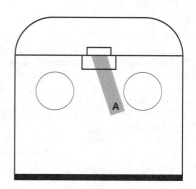

JASON WIEMER

Yrs. of NHL service: 1
Born: Kimberley, B.C.; Apr. 14, 1976
Position: left wing
Height: 6-1
Weight: 215
Uniform no.: 9
Shoots: left

Career statistics:

GP	G	A	TP	PIM
36	1	4	5	44

1994-95 statistics:

GP	G	A	TP	+/-	PIM	PP	SH	GW	GT	S	PCT
36	1	4	5	-2	44	0	0	0	0	10	10.0

LAST SEASON

First NHL season. Missed one game with the flu.

THE FINESSE GAME

Breaking into the league at age 18 is daunting for any prospect, but especially so for Wiemer, who needed time to adjust to the speed of the league and never really got the opportunity.

Wiemer is a budding power forward in the Cam Neely mode — the power forward by whom all others are measured — but, of course, he has a long way to go to catch up to his role model.

Wiemer has the build and the touch for standing in the traffic areas and picking pucks out of scrambles. He also has a touch of mean that merits him some room and time to execute. And he shares the same junior team as Neely (Portland of the WHL).

Wiemer's major shortcoming at this stage is his skating. While Neely is no Pavel Bure, he has a long, strong first stride to the puck and is so balanced on his skates that you need a backhoe to move him out from in front of the goalie. Wiemer has worked hard to strengthen his skating, but he will need to continue improving in order to achieve NHL speed. He does have power in his legs.

He doesn't play a creative game, but relies on his strength and reach. He has a good shot with a quick release.

THE PHYSICAL GAME

Wiemer relishes body contact and will usually initiate checks to intimidate. He drives to the net and pushes defenders back, and isn't shy about dropping his gloves or raising his elbows. He's a young gun who will get tested when he gets to the NHL, but he appears to have the desire to take on all challengers. While he works best as a finisher, he can also function as the grinder on a line since he will scrap along the boards and in the corners for the puck. He can complement almost any linemate.

THE INTANGIBLES

The lockout-shortened season hurt Wiemer, since the Lightning had a shot at making the playoffs until the last few weeks and the youngster wasn't given much of a chance to win a regular role. Considering Tampa Bay's desperate need for scoring, the team will probably give Wiemer a better chance to make an impact this season.

PAUL YSEBAERT

Yrs. of NHL service: 5
Born: Sarnia, Ont.; May 15, 1966
Position: left wing
Height: 6-1
Weight: 190
Uniform no.: 15
Shoots: left

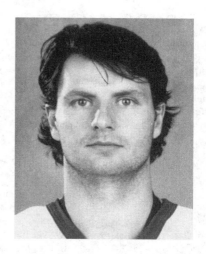

Career statistics:

GP	G	A	TP	PIM
346	115	132	247	163

1991-92 statistics:

GP	G	A	TP	+/-	PIM	PP	SH	GW	GT	S	PCT
79	35	40	75	+44	55	3	4	3	1	211	16.6

1992-93 statistics:

GP	G	A	TP	+/-	PIM	PP	SH	GW	GT	S	PCT
80	34	28	62	+19	42	3	3	8	1	186	18.3

1993-94 statistics:

GP	G	A	TP	+/-	PIM	PP	SH	GW	GT	S	PCT
71	14	21	35	-7	26	3	0	1	0	151	9.3

1994-95 statistics:

GP	G	A	TP	+/-	PIM	PP	SH	GW	GT	S	PCT
44	12	16	28	+3	18	0	0	1	0	93	12.9

players who need good examples to follow; Ysebaert can show the way. Nothing he does is spectacular, but he will seldom cost a team a game and his point production will be in the 50-point range as he has become more defense-minded.

LAST SEASON

Acquired from Chicago with Rich Sutter for Jim Cummins, Jeff Buchanan and Tom Tilley. Tied for team lead in plus-minus. Second on team in points. Missed two games with a groin injury.

THE FINESSE GAME

Ysebaert thrives on his skating. He accelerates in a heartbeat and has the speed and balance to beat defenders wide. He has a wide scoring stance, which makes him tough to knock off the puck even though he's not overly strong.

He has a good array of shots and will work diligently for his scoring opportunities around the net. He goes to the net hard with the puck, but last season he showed more of a tendency to hurry his shots and to not work to get into the high-percentage scoring areas. He has a quick release, and his shot is heavy.

Ysebaert needs someone to open up a bit of ice so he can use his skating to jump into the holes. He can kill penalties and contribute shorthanded.

THE PHYSICAL GAME

Ysebaert has worked on his upper body strength and has increased confidence in his ability to win battles along the wall. He might still get outmuscled by bigger defenders, but he'll scrap for the puck with great enthusiasm. He isn't much of a fighter, but he won't be intimidated, either.

THE INTANGIBLES

Ysebaert has made himself into a solid all-around player. His attitude and consistent effort will be a bonus for Tampa Bay, which has a load of young

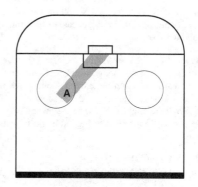

ROB ZAMUNER

Yrs. of NHL service: 3
Born: Oakville, Ont.; Sept. 17, 1969
Position: left wing
Height: 6-2
Weight: 202
Uniform no.: 7
Shoots: left

Career statistics:

GP	G	A	TP	PIM
195	31	42	73	142

1991-92 statistics:

GP	G	A	TP	+/-	PIM	PP	SH	GW	GT	S	PCT
9	1	2	3	+2	2	0	0	0	0	11	9.1

1992-93 statistics:

GP	G	A	TP	+/-	PIM	PP	SH	GW	GT	S	PCT
84	15	28	45	-25	74	1	0	0	2	183	8.2

1993-94 statistics:

GP	G	A	TP	+/-	PIM	PP	SH	GW	GT	S	PCT
59	6	6	12	-9	42	0	0	1	0	109	5.5

1994-95 statistics:

GP	G	A	TP	+/-	PIM	PP	SH	GW	GT	S	PCT
43	9	6	15	-3	24	0	3	1	0	74	12.2

LAST SEASON

Led team in shorthanded goals. Missed three games with an elbow injury.

THE FINESSE GAME

Zamuner doesn't have great speed, but he compensates for it in other ways, including with all-out effort. He is a complementary player, a grinder who can also handle the puck and has some good hand skills. The problem is finding a niche for him. He is not talented enough to be a number one or number two winger, and not good enough defensively to play a checking role against top lines. On a better team (which Tampa Bay isn't — yet), Zamuner could be a penalty killing specialist and be spotted elsewhere.

Zamuner was a good scorer at the minor league level but has not been able to make the same impact in the NHL. He has a decent touch for scoring or passing.

He is fairly alert defensively. He has to be, since he is not a quick enough skater to recover if he is caught napping. Zamuner plays well on Tampa Bay's aggressive penalty killing unit because of his anticipation and work ethic.

THE PHYSICAL GAME

Zamuner has had problems in the past with fitness, until he realized what a big edge he could have with better conditioning. He has good size and uses it effectively. On many nights, he will be the most physically active forward on the Lightning, adding a real spark with his effort.

THE INTANGIBLES

Zamuner needs the confidence to believe he can produce goals at the NHL level. If he does, he will get more ice time and find a more comfortable role. This will be a big season for him, because the team's getting younger and Zamuner isn't.

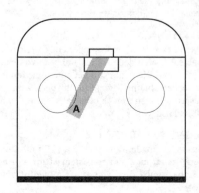

TORONTO MAPLE LEAFS

Players' Statistics 1994-95

POS	NO.	PLAYER	GP	G	A	PTS	+/-	PIM	PP	SH	GW	GT	S	PCTG
C	13	MATS SUNDIN	47	23	24	47	-5	14	9		4	1	173	13.3
L	14	DAVE ANDREYCHUK	48	22	16	38	-7	34	8		2	2	168	13.1
C	7	MIKE RIDLEY	48	10	27	37	1	14	2	2	1	1	88	11.4
C	93	DOUG GILMOUR	44	10	23	33	-5	26	3		1	1	73	13.7
D	23	TODD GILL	47	7	25	32	-8	64	3	1	2		82	8.5
L	24	RANDY WOOD	48	13	11	24	7	34	1	1	2		125	10.4
R	11	MIKE GARTNER	38	12	8	20		6	2	1	1	1	91	13.2
D	15	DMITRI MIRONOV	33	5	12	17	6	28	2				68	7.4
C	32	BENOIT HOGUE	45	9	7	16		34	2		2	1	66	13.6
D	4	DAVE ELLETT	33	5	10	15	-6	26	3		1		84	6.0
C	25	PAUL DIPIETRO	34	5	6	11	-9	10			1	1	60	8.3
R	9	MIKE CRAIG	37	5	5	10	-21	12	1		1		61	8.2
D	34	JAMIE MACOUN	46	2	8	10	-6	75	1				84	2.4
R	28	TIE DOMI	40	4	5	9	-5	159					46	8.7
D	19	*KENNY JONSSON	39	2	7	9	-8	16			1		50	4.0
D	2	GARTH BUTCHER	45	1	7	8	-5	59					24	4.2
L	21	WARREN RYCHEL	33	1	6	7	-4	120					41	2.4
L	10	BILL BERG	32	5	1	6	-11	26			2		57	8.8
D	3	GRANT JENNINGS	35		6	6	-4	43					25	
R	25	TERRY YAKE	19	3	2	5	1	2	1		2		26	11.5
R	12	DIXON WARD	22		3	3	-4	31					15	
R	20	RICH SUTTER	37		3	3	-6	38					39	
C	16	*DARBY HENDRICKSON	8		1	1		4					4	
L	18	KENT MANDERVILLE	36		1	1	-2	22					43	
D	28	*DAVID HARLOCK	1				-1							
R	45	*ZDENEK NEDVED	1					2						
L	22	KEN BAUMGARTNER	2					5					1	
L	43	*KEN BELANGER	3					9					1	
L	8	*TODD WARRINER	5				-3						1	
G	1	*DAMIAN RHODES	13					4						
D	33	*MATT MARTIN	15				2	13					14	
G	29	FELIX POTVIN	36					4						

GP = games played; G = goals; A = assists; PTS = points; +/- = goals-for minus goals-against while player is on ice; PIM = penalties in minutes; PP = power play goals; SH = shorthanded goals; GW = game-winning goals; GT = game-tying goals; S = no. of shots; PCTG = percentage of goals to shots; * = rookie

DAVE ANDREYCHUK

Yrs. of NHL service: 13
Born: Hamilton, Ont.; Sept. 29, 1963
Position: left wing
Height: 6-3
Weight: 220
Uniform no.: 14
Shoots: right

Career statistics:

GP	G	A	TP	PIM
935	448	497	945	704

1991-92 statistics:

GP	G	A	TP	+/-	PIM	PP	SH	GW	GT	S	PCT
80	41	50	91	-9	71	28	0	2	2	337	12.2

1992-93 statistics:

GP	G	A	TP	+/-	PIM	PP	SH	GW	GT	S	PCT
83	54	45	99	+4	56	32	0	4	1	310	17.4

1993-94 statistics:

GP	G	A	TP	+/-	PIM	PP	SH	GW	GT	S	PCT
83	53	45	98	+22	98	21	5	8	0	333	15.9

1994-95 statistics:

GP	G	A	TP	+/-	PIM	PP	SH	GW	GT	S	PCT
48	22	16	38	-7	34	8	0	2	2	168	13.1

LAST SEASON

Second on team in goals, points and power play goals. One of three Leafs to appear in all 48 games.

THE FINESSE GAME

Andreychuk just can't get enough of the game, but defenders have certainly had their fill of him. The big winger uses a very stiff shaft on his long stick, allowing him to lean on it hard in front of the net. He tries to keep his blade on the ice for deflections, and by pushing his 220 pounds on the stick, he makes it almost impossible for a defender to lift it off the ice.

The slowdown game played by most NHL teams helped Andreychuk rise to even greater heights. He has slow feet but a cherry-picker reach, which he uses with strength and intelligence. He is a lumbering skater, but since he works in tight areas, he only needs a big stride or two to plant himself where he wants. He has marvellous hand skills in traffic and can use his stick to artfully pick pucks out of mid-air, slap at rebounds or for wraparounds. He has quick and accurate wrist and snap shots.

From the hash marks in, Andreychuk is one of the most dangerous snipers in the league. On the other four-fifths of the ice, he is a liability. He doesn't finish his checks and he doesn't skate well. He understands the game well enough to position himself, but won't battle anywhere other than right in front of the net. When Doug Gilmour takes an offensive-zone draw, Andreychuk curls in behind him, using the centre as a screen or pick.

Increasingly, Andreychuk is becoming a power play specialist. He needs to play with people who can get him the puck and with people who can skate, to cover up for his skating deficiencies. He gets into occasional slumps when he overhandles the puck. He is at his peak when he works the give-and-go and keeps his legs moving.

Andreychuk's hands are so quick, he can take draws if needed.

THE PHYSICAL GAME

If you're looking for someone to protect his smaller teammates, or to inspire a team with his hitting, then Andreychuk is not the man for you. Andreychuk is a giant shock absorber, soaking up hits without budging or retaliating.

He's tough in his own way, in front of the opponent's net, at least. He is huge and impossible to budge, and with his long arms can control pucks. He isn't dominating, but he is physically prominent within five feet of the crease. He pays the price and knows how to use his talent.

THE INTANGIBLES

Andreychuk suffered from his team's injuries and lineup changes and never seemed comfortable last season. His best work is done alongside Doug Gilmour, but Andreychuk played most of the year with the hard working but less creative Mike Ridley, and his production suffered (he scored a prorated 66 points).

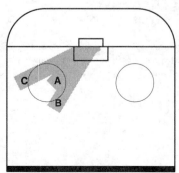

BILL BERG

Yrs. of NHL service: 5
Born: St. Catharines, Ont.; Oct. 21, 1967
Position: left wing
Height: 6-1
Weight: 190
Uniform no.: 10
Shoots: left

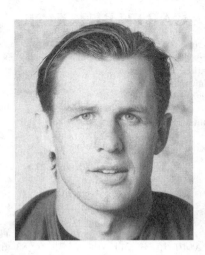

Career statistics:

GP	G	A	TP	PIM
327	41	48	89	327

1991-92 statistics:

GP	G	A	TP	+/-	PIM	PP	SH	GW	GT	S	PCT
47	5	9	14	-18	28	1	0	1	0	60	8.3

1992-93 statistics:

GP	G	A	TP	+/-	PIM	PP	SH	GW	GT	S	PCT
80	13	11	24	+3	103	0	3	2	0	113	11.5

1993-94 statistics:

GP	G	A	TP	+/-	PIM	PP	SH	GW	GT	S	PCT
83	8	11	19	-3	93	0	0	1	0	99	8.1

1994-95 statistics:

GP	G	A	TP	+/-	PIM	PP	SH	GW	GT	S	PCT
32	5	1	6	-11	26	0	0	2	0	57	8.8

LAST SEASON

Missed 16 games with a knee injury.

THE FINESSE GAME

A converted defenseman, Berg has developed into a solid checking forward who can also produce the odd key point. He can finish a play, shoot the puck and make or receive a pass, and he has the skill to make something happen if the checking line creates an offensive opportunity with its pressure, as so often happens. Berg plays the game hard and could produce more offensively, but he is so strong defensively that the Leafs are willing to sacrifice the points. He gets plenty of chances.

He skates well, though he doesn't have a lot of shifty speed. He is strong and effective with his skating and angles well. Berg takes great pride in his penalty killing.

Berg is a character player with quiet leadership, and honest with his efforts. The team comes first and he will do whatever is asked. Players cough up the puck because they know that when Berg is bearing down on them they're going to get hit.

THE PHYSICAL GAME

Berg is an agitator, adding a pesky element to an already sound defensive game.

He has tried at times to bulk up by lifting weights, but oddly the Leafs often prod him to becomes a little leaner (and meaner) to add a step to his fore-check. He is a solid body checker.

He will take a poke in the kisser to get his team a power play. For being as involved as he is, Berg seldom retaliates with a bad penalty. He drives opponents crazy because he never drops his gloves.

THE INTANGIBLES

Last season was a struggle for Berg, who lost his regular linemates Peter Zezel and Mark Osborne and never meshed comfortably with any other combination. He was spotted, but wants more ice time. Berg is an outstanding team player.

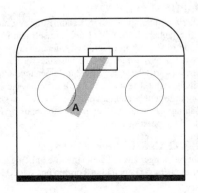

GARTH BUTCHER

Yrs. of NHL service: 11
Born: Regina, Sask.; Jan. 8, 1963
Position: right defense
Height: 6-0
Weight: 200
Uniform no.: 55
Shoots: right

Career statistics:

GP	G	A	TP	PIM
880	49	155	204	2307

1991-92 statistics:

GP	G	A	TP	+/-	PIM	PP	SH	GW	GT	S	PCT
68	5	15	20	+5	189	0	0	0	0	50	10.0

1992-93 statistics:

GP	G	A	TP	+/-	PIM	PP	SH	GW	GT	S	PCT
84	5	10	15	0	211	0	0	2	0	83	6.0

1993-94 statistics:

GP	G	A	TP	+/-	PIM	PP	SH	GW	GT	S	PCT
60	5	12	17	0	148	2	0	0	0	48	10.4

1994-95 statistics:

GP	G	A	TP	+/-	PIM	PP	SH	GW	GT	S	PCT
45	1	7	8	-5	59	0	0	0	0	24	4.2

LAST SEASON

Missed three games with a back injury.

THE FINESSE GAME

Butcher is a quietly effective and consistent defense-man. There are many things he can't do, though. He is not a very good skater (average speed and below-average agility), but he compensates by playing a sound positional game and by not taking low-percentage chances.

Butcher doesn't go for the home-run pass up the middle but makes safe yet creative short plays, off the boards or just after a defender has moved out of position to come to him. He does not panic with the puck and is a natural killing penalties.

Given some room to skate, Butcher will rush the puck and move it smartly, but he won't venture too deep into the attacking zone. His offensive contributions are limited to shots from the right point.

THE PHYSICAL GAME

Butcher's reputation as a fierce competitor and hitter is well established. He will protect himself and is the first one to step up in defense of a teammate. He is only a decent size for an NHL defenseman (or, for that matter, forward) these days, but his demeanour adds a few inches and a few pounds to his frame. He is a willing hitter but not a great puncher. He is very good at goading his rivals, and often stirs up opposing forwards to the point of fury.

THE INTANGIBLES

Butcher no longer has to handle the role of being a top defenseman on a team, and in Toronto has settled into a niche as a reliable defensive defenseman. If he is moved, it will have to be to another defensive-minded team where he can fill his role.

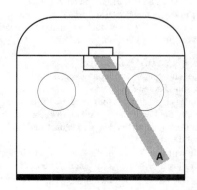

MIKE CRAIG

Yrs. of NHL service: 5
Born: London, Ont.; June 6, 1971
Position: right wing
Height: 6-0
Weight: 180
Uniform no.: 9
Shoots: right

Career statistics:

GP	G	A	TP	PIM
285	56	72	128	444

1991-92 statistics:

GP	G	A	TP	+/-	PIM	PP	SH	GW	GT	S	PCT
67	15	16	31	-12	155	4	0	4	0	136	11.0

1992-93 statistics:

GP	G	A	TP	+/-	PIM	PP	SH	GW	GT	S	PCT
70	15	23	38	-11	106	7	0	0	0	131	11.5

1993-94 statistics:

GP	G	A	TP	+/-	PIM	PP	SH	GW	GT	S	PCT
72	13	24	37	-14	139	3	0	2	0	150	8.7

1994-95 statistics:

GP	G	A	TP	+/-	PIM	PP	SH	GW	GT	S	PCT
37	5	5	10	-21	12	1	0	1	0	61	8.2

tabbed last year as a crucial one for Craig, but given the shortened season we'll highlight this one instead. Craig has a big upside, but hasn't put all of his skills into one tidy, complete package yet.

LAST SEASON

Worst plus-minus on team. Signed as a free agent. Missed eight games with a broken finger.

THE FINESSE GAME

Craig is a choppy skater, but he chops with enthusiasm. Almost everything he does he does with great intensity, Tony Granato style.

Craig has good hands and is tenacious. He can play well with top offensive people because he will do the grunt work for them in the corners and along the boards. With his nice touch, he produces goals when he goes to the front of the net. His wrist shot is especially effective, accurate and quickly unleashed. The problem with Craig continues to be his inconsistency.

His short game is his greatest asset. He is smart and poised through traffic. He can play the power play down low.

THE PHYSICAL GAME

Craig likes to play bigger than he is. He has to continue gaining more strength so he can hold that game through a full schedule — either that or learn to pace himself better, because he tends to wear down in the second half. Much of his effort appears to be wasted. He works hard, but doesn't always work smart. On most nights, though, his effort sparks the bench.

THE INTANGIBLES

Craig will continue to have trouble getting ice time this season — and that will make it hard to improve his game. It could be the beginning of a downward spiral. He has too much talent to let his game slip away, but he has to find the tenacity to earn a spot. We

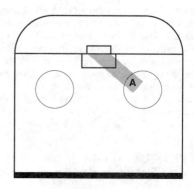

DAVE ELLETT

Yrs. of NHL service: 11
Born: Cleveland, Ohio; Mar. 30, 1964
Position: left defense
Height: 6-1
Weight: 200
Uniform no.: 4
Shoots: done

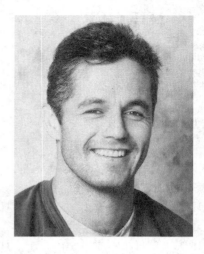

Career statistics:

GP	G	A	TP	PIM
785	139	347	486	782

1991-92 statistics:

GP	G	A	TP	+/-	PIM	PP	SH	GW	GT	S	PCT
79	18	33	51	-13	95	9	1	4	0	225	8.0

1992-93 statistics:

GP	G	A	TP	+/-	PIM	PP	SH	GW	GT	S	PCT
70	6	34	40	+19	46	4	0	1	0	186	3.2

1993-94 statistics:

GP	G	A	TP	+/-	PIM	PP	SH	GW	GT	S	PCT
68	7	36	43	+6	42	5	0	1	1	146	4.8

1994-95 statistics:

GP	G	A	TP	+/-	PIM	PP	SH	GW	GT	S	PCT
33	5	10	15	-6	26	3	0	1	0	84	6.0

LAST SEASON

Missed 15 games with a cracked bone in his foot.

THE FINESSE GAME

It was a frustrating season for this veteran defenseman, who missed five weeks after breaking a bone in his foot while blocking a Brett Hull shot. The injury prevented him from skating, or even riding the bike, making it difficult for him to maintain his aerobic conditioning.

Ellett is a very sound player for someone who was labelled as an offensive defenseman early in his career. He is used in all situations: power play, penalty killing, four-on-four, protecting a lead or helping his team come from behind.

His game has always been powered by his fine skating. He is a graceful mover. His lateral mobility is not great, which is why he's not an elite point man on the power play. He sometimes has trouble getting his shot through.

Ellett started using a shorter stick a few seasons ago and his shots were more accurate and more quickly released. His hand skills are fine too, but instead of using his skills to jump into the offense at every opportunity, he conserves his energy for the defensive part of the ice. He understands the game and is aware of his importance to the team. He is not expected to go end to end, but instead to be steady and move the puck. He is a good passer with a soft touch, and uses his skills to get to the puck, get turned, make the first pass and watch the forwards go.

THE PHYSICAL GAME

Ellett uses his skills to keep himself out of physical situations. By getting to the puck and moving it briskly out of the corner, he can avoid getting crunched. He doesn't have a physical presence and doesn't clear out the front of his net as well as he should for a player of his size. He will tie up players with his long reach.

Ellett keeps himself in top condition and can handle the large amount of ice time the Leafs like to give him.

THE INTANGIBLES

Versatile and a good team player, the classy Ellett has developed into a solid two-way defenseman under coach Pat Burns. He turned his considerable finesse skills to defense first and became a much better all-around defenseman. His point production may tail off into the low 40-point range even if he stays healthy, but he will be used in all situations and because of his reliability will continue to get a ton of ice time.

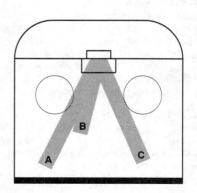

MIKE GARTNER

Yrs. of NHL service: 16
Born: Ottawa, Ont.; Oct. 29, 1959
Position: right wing
Height: 6-0
Weight: 190
Uniform no.: 11
Shoots: right

Career statistics:

GP	G	A	TP	PIM
1208	630	562	1191	1045

1991-92 statistics:

GP	G	A	TP	+/-	PIM	PP	SH	GW	GT	S	PCT
76	40	41	81	+11	55	15	0	6	0	286	14.0

1992-93 statistics:

GP	G	A	TP	+/-	PIM	PP	SH	GW	GT	S	PCT
84	45	23	68	-4	59	13	0	3	1	323	13.9

1993-94 statistics:

GP	G	A	TP	+/-	PIM	PP	SH	GW	GT	S	PCT
81	34	30	64	+20	62	11	5	4	0	275	12.4

1994-95 statistics:

GP	G	A	TP	+/-	PIM	PP	SH	GW	GT	S	PCT
38	12	8	20	0	6	2	1	1	1	91	13.2

LAST SEASON

Record streak of 30 or more goals ended at 15 seasons. Missed 10 games with a collapsed lung and a fractured foot.

THE FINESSE GAME

The usually durable Gartner got taken out early in the season by a hard, clean Bryan Marchment hit that injured his ribs and resulted in a collapsed lung. The rest of the season was downhill for this gifted skater, who is still going strong at age 36.

Gartner still has exceptional speed. If he is not the fastest skater in the NHL anymore, then he is still in the top three. He has flawless technical form — great stride, deep knee bend and excellent posture, which add up to power and speed. He is a human skating machine. Carrying the puck doesn't slow him down and he can still pull away from pursuers.

Gartner may have to learn to add some more crafty moves to his patented drive wide down the wing. As he slows, he can hold up and wait for a trailing teammate, because he still pushes defensemen back with his speed and opens up the ice.

Ever alert to his offensive chances, Gartner is sometimes guilty of hanging a little at the redline, looking for the break into the attacking zone. He can accept a pass in full flight. He has a clever play he uses in which he treats the boards as an extra teammate, giving himself a little pass off the wall or setting up a linemate with a smart feed.

Gartner drives his shot off the wing on the fly or uses a strong wrist shot from closer range. If his lane to the net is blocked, he will curl around behind the net — still at good speed — for a wraparound try. He isn't much of a playmaker. His assists come from teammates smart enough to follow up on his play for rebounds.

THE PHYSICAL GAME

Gartner is wiry and strong. When he doesn't beat a checker cleanly to the outside, he will still manage to squeeze through along the boards and keep going forward with the puck, even if dragged to his knees.

He goes to the net and into the corners for the puck. He has strong arms and wrists to reach into scrums and control the puck. He can flick a puck to the net one-handed. He seldom takes bad penalties. Even with a lot of miles on him, Gartner is very fit.

THE INTANGIBLES

Gartner is one of the most respected players around for his intelligence, talent and work ethic, but his skills are heading for the down side. He desperately wants to win a Stanley Cup, and this season might be his last chance, or close to it. He may return to the 30-goal level.

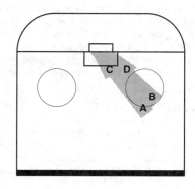

TODD GILL

Yrs. of NHL service: 9
Born: Brockville, Ont.; Nov. 19, 1965
Position: right defense
Height: 6-0
Weight: 180
Uniform no.: 23
Shoots: left

Career statistics:

GP	G	A	TP	PIM
565	52	190	242	806

1991-92 statistics:

GP	G	A	TP	+/-	PIM	PP	SH	GW	GT	S	PCT
74	2	15	17	-22	91	1	0	0	0	82	2.4

1992-93 statistics:

GP	G	A	TP	+/-	PIM	PP	SH	GW	GT	S	PCT
69	11	32	43	+4	66	5	0	2	0	113	9.7

1993-94 statistics:

GP	G	A	TP	+/-	PIM	PP	SH	GW	GT	S	PCT
45	4	23	27	+8	44	2	0	1	0	74	5.4

1994-95 statistics:

GP	G	A	TP	+/-	PIM	PP	SH	GW	GT	S	PCT
47	7	25	32	-8	64	3	1	2	0	82	8.5

LAST SEASON

Led team defensemen in scoring. Second on team in assists.

THE FINESSE GAME

Gill made a complete recovery from a lingering groin/abdominal pull that prevented him from being 100 per cent in 1993-94.

Gill wants to be a leader on the team. He is a gamer, and a player who knows his limitations and seldom tries to do what he can't. He has improved in reading plays, and his maturity has cut down on the mistakes that plagued him in the past.

Gill also has a flair for offense. He has good hockey sense and can do some things with the puck. His passing touch will never make people forget Brian Leetch, and his shot won't impress Al MacInnis, but he has above-average finesse skills in all departments. Gill doesn't like the puck to linger in his own zone. He will carry it out and make smart plays. He has faith in his partners and lets them and the puck do the work.

He isn't afraid to venture deep and use a wrist or snap shot from the left circle. Once in a while he will brave the front of the net (though he has to be darned sure when he tries it). He is smart and talented enough to work the point on the power play on the second unit.

THE PHYSICAL GAME

Gill is a tough, snotty-nosed defenseman with a ton of heart and spunk. He's on the slight side for an NHL defenseman, and through his career he will have to be mindful of conditioning and nutrition to keep up with the grind. And grind is what he has to do to be effec-tive. He will drop the gloves and go if he has to, and he stands up for his teammates, taking on the biggest guy on the ice.

THE INTANGIBLES

Gill has overcome injury woes to become a reliable member of the top four defense corps on a strong defensive team. We predicted a 40-point comeback season for Gill last year, and he nearly made that number despite the lockout-shortened season. He may not lead the team's defense in scoring again, but he's a good bet for another 40. He is a solid competitor and is well respected in the Leafs' locker room.

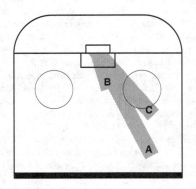

DOUG GILMOUR

Yrs. of NHL service: 11
Born: Kingston, Ont.; June 25, 1963
Position: centre
Height: 5-11
Weight: 185
Uniform no.: 93
Shoots: left

Career statistics:

GP	G	A	TP	PIM
900	314	655	969	813

1991-92 statistics:

GP	G	A	TP	+/-	PIM	PP	SH	GW	GT	S	PCT
78	26	61	87	+25	78	10	1	4	1	168	15.5

1992-93 statistics:

GP	G	A	TP	+/-	PIM	PP	SH	GW	GT	S	PCT
83	32	95	127	+32	100	15	3	2	2	211	15.2

1993-94 statistics:

GP	G	A	TP	+/-	PIM	PP	SH	GW	GT	S	PCT
83	27	84	111	+25	105	10	1	3	1	167	16.2

1994-95 statistics:

GP	G	A	TP	+/-	PIM	PP	SH	GW	GT	S	PCT
44	10	23	33	-5	26	3	0	1	1	73	13.7

LAST SEASON

Led team in shooting percentage. Fourth on team in points. Missed four games with a back injury and a broken nose.

THE FINESSE GAME

Gilmour had two years of great success, but a serious ankle injury in the 1994 playoffs with subsequent bone spurs (requiring surgery on both feet during the off-season), derailed his conditioning. The lockout made matters worse, and Gilmour never regained his excellence of the previous years. Last season he looked like a disaster. He just never had the same kind of jump that characterized his play previously.

A superior leader on ice (he is rather quiet in the dressing room), Gilmour played through the playoffs on an ankle that was so badly injured he would have been sidelined for about six weeks if it were the regular season. Even so, he outscored all but three players whose teams made it to the finals. Younger players look at him and are inspired to work harder.

Gilmour is one of those rare individuals who feels he owes his team and teammates every dollar of his salary ($3 million per year). For a team to have its best player possess that attitude is invaluable. The mark of a great player is that he takes his team upwards with him. Wayne Gretzky has done it, Mario Lemieux has done it, and now Gilmour has.

A creative playmaker, he is one of those rare NHL players who has eschewed the banana blade for a nearly straight model, so he can handle the puck equally well on his forehand or backhand. He will bring people right in on top of him before he slides a little pass to a teammate, creating time and space. He is very intelligent and has great anticipation. He loves to set up from behind the net and intimidates because he plays with such supreme confidence.

Gilmour is a set-up man who needs finishers around him and doesn't shoot much. When he does, he won't use a big slapper, but instead scores from close range either as the trailer or after losing a defender with his subtle dekes and moves. He's not a smooth, gifted skater, but he is nimble and quick.

Gilmour ranks as one of the best face-off men in the NHL and routinely beats big, stronger centres on draws. In his own end, he is very sound positionally.

THE PHYSICAL GAME

Gilmour plays with passion and savvy, challenging bigger opponents regardless of where or when he plays. He puts life into the Leafs with his relentless work ethic. Although he's listed at 185 pounds, he plays at around 165 during the season and has lost up to seven pounds in a single playoff game. Gilmour needs to keep the weight off. His play is effortless at a lighter weight, and he seldom misses a morning skate or an optional practice.

The only drawback to Gilmour's competiveness is that he can become so fierce and intense that he loses his focus. He does not turn the other cheek. He goes into the trenches because that's where the puck is, and that's what he hungers for.

THE INTANGIBLES

Although he will be 32 when the season opens, expect a big bounce-back season from a healthy Gilmour. He has a huge heart, and should regain his status as one of the most reliable and skilled players in the game.

Gilmour provides never-say-die leadership. He often responds with a big shift after his team has been scored upon and will ignite the Leafs and the crowd with an inspirational bump or goal. He will do everything he can to win a game.

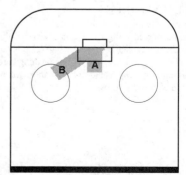

DARBY HENDRICKSON

Yrs. of NHL service: 0
Born: Richfield, Minn.; Aug. 28, 1972
Position: centre/left wing
Height: 6-0
Weight: 185
Uniform no.: 16
Shoots: right

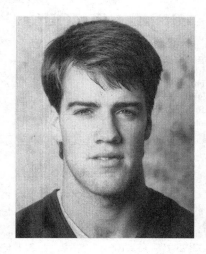

Career statistics:

GP	G	A	TP	PIM
8	0	1	1	4

1994-95 statistics:

GP	G	A	TP	+/-	PIM	PP	SH	GW	GT	S	PCT
8	0	1	1	0	4	0	0	0	0	4	0.0

LAST SEASON
Will be entering first full NHL season. Played 59 games with St. John's (AHL), scoring 16-20 — 36 with 48 PIM.

THE FINESSE GAME
Hendrickson will be an older rookie when he breaks into the NHL full-time, having done tours with the University of Minnesota, the 1994 U.S. Olympic team and Toronto's farm team.

Hendrickson, despite his experience, is a tentative player, and seems afraid to make mistakes. He can take the puck to the net and put it in the net, but he has to have the faith in his skills and playmaking decisions. His development was hampered by his indecision. He was never the player he could be.

At the minor league level, Hendrickson killed penalties and worked on the power play. He is an above-average skater. He has a decent shot and is defensively aware. His game will probably be more heavily weighted towards defense, but he can become a checking winger who can also produce some points.

THE PHYSICAL GAME
Hendrickson is strong and very fit, and takes pride in his conditioning. He doesn't have a mean streak or much of a physical presence.

THE INTANGIBLES
Hendrickson would probably make a better centre, though he played wing for Toronto last season. At present, he is a typical third-line winger. He is coachable and willing to learn, and will be pushing hard for a job in training camp. Hendrickson wants a job in the NHL and wants to improve.

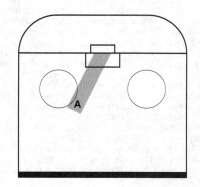

BENOIT HOGUE

Yrs. of NHL service: 7
Born: Repentigny, Que.; Oct. 28, 1966
Position: centre/right wing
Height: 5-10
Weight: 190
Uniform no.: 32
Shoots: left

Career statistics:

GP	G	A	TP	PIM
466	153	194	347	557

1991-92 statistics:

GP	G	A	TP	+/-	PIM	PP	SH	GW	GT	S	PCT
75	30	46	76	+30	67	8	0	5	0	149	20.1

1992-93 statistics:

GP	G	A	TP	+/-	PIM	PP	SH	GW	GT	S	PCT
70	33	42	75	+13	108	5	3	5	0	147	22.4

1993-94 statistics:

GP	G	A	TP	+/-	PIM	PP	SH	GW	GT	S	PCT
83	36	33	69	-7	73	9	5	3	0	218	16.5

1994-95 statistics:

GP	G	A	TP	+/-	PIM	PP	SH	GW	GT	S	PCT
45	9	7	16	0	34	2	0	2	1	66	13.6

LAST SEASON

Acquired from the New York Islanders with third-round pick in 1995 and fifth-round pick in 1996 for Eric Fichaud. One of three NHL players to score on a penalty shot.

THE FINESSE GAME

Hogue's chief asset is his speed. He is explosive, leaving defenders flat-footed with his acceleration. Add to that his anticipation and ability to handle the puck at a high tempo, and the result is an ever-lurking breakaway threat. Hogue is not a great puckhandler or shooter, but he capitalizes on each situation with his quickness and agility. He is a threat to score whenever he is on the ice.

Hogue plays primarily on the left side and even when playing centre will cut to the left wing boards as he drives down the ice. He is not a great playmaker, but he creates scoring chances off his rushes.

He is an excellent, aggressive penalty killer who is a shorthanded threat, and he can also be used on the power play, though he lacks the patience to be as effective as he could be. He is very good on draws. Toronto gave him quite a bit of power play time.

THE PHYSICAL GAME

Hogue is a strong one-on-one player who will use his body to lean on an opponent. He is not a big checker, but he gets involved and uses his speed as a weapon to intimidate. He is a crunch-time player, whether a team needs to protect a lead or create one. He can get into ruts where he takes bad penalties.

THE INTANGIBLES

Hogue needed a change of scenery. Since he did exceptionally well in his first two seasons after going to the Islanders from Buffalo, that might presage a big bounce-back season. But Hogue will have to deal with intense media scrutiny in Toronto and, if he doesn't get off to a quick start, the heat will be on him full blast.

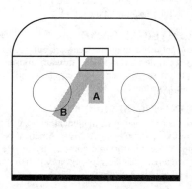

KENNY JONSSON

Yrs. of NHL service: 1
Born: Angelholm, Sweden; Oct. 6, 1974
Position: defense
Height: 6-3
Weight: 195
Uniform no.: 19
Shoots: left

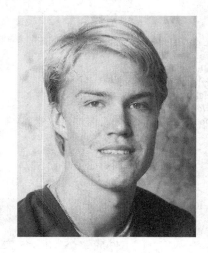

Career statistics:

GP	G	A	TP	PIM
39	2	7	9	16

1994-95 statistics:

GP	G	A	TP	+/-	PIM	PP	SH	GW	GT	S	PCT
39	2	7	9	-8	16	0	0	1	0	50	4.0

LAST SEASON

First NHL season. Missed one game with the flu. Missed one game with a hip injury.

THE FINESSE GAME

The lockout started the season on a stutter-step for Jonsson, who went back to Europe to play when the NHL season was delayed, then played a brief stint in St. John's (AHL) before joining the Leafs. Jonsson never truly hit full stride, and it's tough enough for a young European player to break into the NHL as a defenseman without such roadblocks.

Jonsson reads the ice and passes the puck very well. He can be used in almost every game situation. He kills penalties, works the point on the power play and will become a regular top four defenseman — perhaps as high as a number two.

Jonsson got beaten one-on-one by fellow rookie Jeff Friesen in just his second game, and took a lot of heat in the media. It affected him mentally, until the coaches convinced him that more than a few veterans would get toasted by the speedy Friesen as well. Jonsson did bounce back.

He is a talented skater but part of his adjustment will be learning to protect himself by using the net in his own zone. He tends to leave himself open after passes and gets nailed. Jonsson did improve on that aspect as the season went on.

THE PHYSICAL GAME

Jonsson got off to an impressive start, but wore down as his ice time increased due to team injuries. He needs to get stronger, and it appears he is still filling out with some muscle.

THE INTANGIBLES

Jonsson is a shy and quiet individual, but once he adjusts to living and playing in North America, he will become more comfortable and consistent. He has great potential, but still needs a year or two of adjustment before he's at his best.

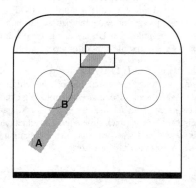

KENT MANDERVILLE

Yrs. of NHL service: 2
Born: Edmonton, Alta.; April 12, 1971
Position: left wing
Height: 6-3
Weight: 207
Uniform no.: 18
Shoots: left

Career statistics:

GP	G	A	TP	PIM
136	8	16	24	102

1991-92 statistics:

GP	G	A	TP	+/-	PIM	PP	SH	GW	GT	S	PCT
15	0	4	4	+1	0	0	0	0	0	14	0.0

1992-93 statistics:

GP	G	A	TP	+/-	PIM	PP	SH	GW	GT	S	PCT
18	1	2	3	-9	17	0	0	1	0	15	6.7

1993-94 statistics:

GP	G	A	TP	+/-	PIM	PP	SH	GW	GT	S	PCT
67	7	9	16	+5	63	0	0	1	0	81	8.6

1994-95 statistics:

GP	G	A	TP	+/-	PIM	PP	SH	GW	GT	S	PCT
36	0	1	1	-2	22	0	0	0	0	43	0.0

LAST SEASON

Missed games with an ankle injury.

THE FINESSE GAME

Manderville knows the game well and understands the role of a checking forward. He's a good skater for his size, gets on the puck quickly, and forces the play.

He has a long stride that covers the ice effortlessly and he is surprisingly quick. He was utilized most effectively by the Leafs as a penalty killer, taking some of the heat off Doug Gilmour and letting that superstar catch his breath once in awhile. Manderville can play wing or centre.

Manderville doesn't have a great scoring touch. He is unselfish and can handle the puck in traffic, though he will almost always give up the shot for the pass. He needs to simply power the puck to the net more to create some offense. One measly assist in 36 games is ridiculous for even the most defense-minded player. Goalies score more.

THE PHYSICAL GAME

Manderville uses his size and speed to great effect on the fore-check. He is not an especially tough player for someone of his size, but perhaps as he gains more ice time and confidence he will become more of a force. After missing some of the 1994 playoffs with a broken wrist, he came back very fit.

THE INTANGIBLES

Manderville is a frustrating player. While he is sound defensively, he could add much more to his game offensively. He lacks the finishing touch.

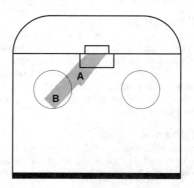

SERGIO MOMESSO

Yrs. of NHL service: 11
Born: Montreal, Que.; Sept. 4, 1965
Position: left wing
Height: 6-3
Weight: 215
Uniform no.: 27
Shoots: left

Career statistics:

GP	G	A	TP	PIM
597	140	178	318	1367

1991-92 statistics:

GP	G	A	TP	+/-	PIM	PP	SH	GW	GT	S	PCT
58	20	23	43	+16	198	2	0	3	0	153	13.1

1992-93 statistics:

GP	G	A	TP	+/-	PIM	PP	SH	GW	GT	S	PCT
84	18	20	38	+11	200	4	0	1	0	146	12.3

1993-94 statistics:

GP	G	A	TP	+/-	PIM	PP	SH	GW	GT	S	PCT
68	14	13	27	-2	149	4	0	1	0	112	12.5

1994-95 statistics:

GP	G	A	TP	+/-	PIM	PP	SH	GW	GT	S	PCT
48	10	15	25	-2	65	6	0	1	0	82	12.2

often he crosses the fine line between toughness and out-of-control play.

LAST SEASON

One of two Canucks to appear in all 48 games. Acquired from Vancouver for Mike Ridley.

THE FINESSE GAME

Momesso is a power forward, but one without the hand skills to do too much damage in the scoring column. He is big and strong and has enough speed to drive defenders back, but he can't make much happen with the extra room he gets.

He knows his game is to go to the net. He can also use a heavy slap shot from the wing, but it is not very accurate. When he does get it on target, he just about knocks the goalie into the cage. Momesso uses his power and balance well in front of the net to create traffic and scrap for loose pucks.

He does a respectable job defensively. He's turned into an ideal third-line winger. Expectations will always be there for Momesso to deliver more, but he seems to have levelled off at the 15- to 20-goal range.

THE PHYSICAL GAME

Momesso's great balance and size make him tough to knock off the puck — and difficult for anyone to withstand one of his punishing hits. He is unpredictable, which gets him plenty of room most nights. He could go ballistic at any moment, and it's not a pretty sight. Two drawbacks: the intensity isn't there every game, and he takes bad penalties.

THE INTANGIBLES

Momesso became a more useful player when his work ethic improved. If he plays a game of controlled aggression, he can be a valuable tempo-changer, but too

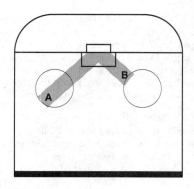

LARRY MURPHY

Yrs. of NHL service: 15
Born: Scarborough, Ont.; Mar. 8, 1961
Position: right defense
Height: 6-2
Weight: 210
Uniform no.: 55
Shoots: right

Career statistics:

GP	G	A	TP	PIM
1152	233	706	945	894

1991-92 statistics:

GP	G	A	TP	+/-	PIM	PP	SH	GW	GT	S	PCT
77	21	56	77	+33	50	7	2	3	0	206	10.2

1992-93 statistics:

GP	G	A	TP	+/-	PIM	PP	SH	GW	GT	S	PCT
83	22	63	85	+45	73	6	2	2	0	230	9.6

1993-94 statistics:

GP	G	A	TP	+/-	PIM	PP	SH	GW	GT	S	PCT
84	17	56	73	+10	44	7	0	4	0	236	7.2

1994-95 statistics:

GP	G	A	TP	+/-	PIM	PP	SH	GW	GT	S	PCT
48	13	25	38	+12	18	4	0	3	0	124	10.5

LAST SEASON

Led team defensemen in scoring for third consecutive season. Tied for fifth among NHL defensemen in scoring. One of three Penguins to appear in all 48 games. Second on team in assists. Traded to Toronto for Dmitri Mironov.

THE FINESSE GAME

Murphy is big and nimble, so strong that other teams' game plans usually involve keeping the puck away from his side of the ice, to prevent him from gearing up behind his goal line. Teams generally try to attack the weaker half of the defense pairing, and that means whoever Murphy is paired with is usually under constant harassment.

He is not the offensive force he was early in his career, because he has concentrated on his defense and has become a better all-around player as a result. He can either rush the puck out of his zone or make the nice first pass that gives his team the jump on the opponents.

Murphy is smart and poised. He will not force bad passes up the middle but will use the boards if that's the safest play. His pinches are well timed, and he has the reach to prevent a lot of pucks from getting by him at the point. His shot selection is intelligent. He loves to shoot, but he won't fire blindly. He will use a low wrist shot rather than a big slap to keep the puck on net. Murphy's positional play is where he has shown the most improvement. He reads plays well and seldom seems to be floundering on the ice.

Murphy's skating is effortless, with good leg extension on his strokes, and he has lateral mobility.

THE PHYSICAL GAME

Murphy does not play a physical game. He will bump his man in front but doesn't make strong takeouts. He prefers to position his body and force the shooter to make a play while he himself goes for the puck or stick. It is the weakest part of his game, and is just adequate.

THE INTANGIBLES

Age (34) and ice time have started to catch up with Murphy, He will be a key man on the point for the Maple Leafs' power plays, and can continue to contribute as a two-way defenseman, but his even-strength points should continue to decline. Under the Leafs' defensive style, Murphy's flaws should be less apparent.

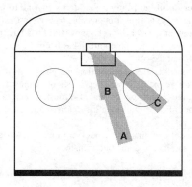

FELIX POTVIN

Yrs. of NHL service: 3
Born: Anjou, Que.; June 23, 1971
Position: goaltender
Height: 6-1
Weight: 183
Uniform no.: 29
Catches: left

Career statistics:

GP	MINS	GA	SO	GAA	A	PIM
154	9018	415	5	2.76	5	12

1991-92 statistics:

GP	MINS	GAA	W	L	T	SO	GA	S	SAPCT	PIM
4	210	2.29	0	2	1	0	8	120	.933	0

1992-93 statistics:

GP	MINS	GAA	W	L	T	SO	GA	S	SAPCT	PIM
48	2781	2.50	25	25	7	2	116	1286	.910	4

1993-94 statistics:

GP	MINS	GAA	W	L	T	SO	GA	S	SAPCT	PIM
66	3883	2.89	34	22	9	3	187	2010	.907	4

1994-95 statistics:

GP	MINS	GAA	W	L	T	SO	GA	S	SAPCT	PIM
36	2144	2.91	15	13	7	0	104	1120	.907	4

LAST SEASON

GAA has been under 3.00 each of his three NHL seasons.

THE PHYSICAL GAME

Potvin is a butterfly goalie with a heart-stopping style. He does things his own way, tradition and technique be darned, but when it works as well as it does for him, it's impossible to argue with it.

Potvin stays square to the puck, keeping his torso upright, and the puck just hits him. Goaltending can be so simple. He taunts shooters by leaving air between his pads, but he has the great reflexes to snap them closed at the last second.

Everything about Potvin's stance looks wrong. He plants his skates so far apart and is so anchored along the goal line that he has almost no lateral mobility and doesn't take away much of the shooter's angle. He is excellent down low, so the book is to shoot high, yet the top corners are the most difficult spots for a shooter to hit, and Potvin just dares anyone to beat him there. He is almost impossible to beat on the first shot. Potvin controls his rebounds well for a butterfly goalie. He can also be comfortable hanging onto the puck for a face-off.

He has excellent anticipation and just seems to get the puck stopped. To beat Potvin, shooters must force him to move side to side, and also must be able to lift the puck. Potvin will take his chances against those odds.

He does not handle the puck or move it much, and he doesn't like to come out of his net.

THE MENTAL GAME

Potvin is as impassive as his mask. He doesn't get excited during a game and his outward calm radiates towards his teammates. He never seems shaken or overly excited. Bad goals and bad games are easily forgotten.

THE INTANGIBLES

Potvin is getting some pressure from Damian Rhodes, who might have been the most improved player on the Leafs last season, but the two were also teammates in the minors and there doesn't seem to be any real challenge for Potvin's ice time. Rhodes just might help keep Potvin sharp, because the Leafs aren't afraid to give Rhodes big games. Potvin needs some improvement in his technique, but the Leafs are understandably leery of messing with success.

MATS SUNDIN

Yrs. of NHL service: 5
Born: Bromma, Sweden; Feb. 13, 1971
Position: right wing/centre
Height: 6-4
Weight: 215
Uniform no.: 13
Shoots: right

Career statistics:

GP	G	A	TP	PIM
371	158	223	381	333

1991-92 statistics:

GP	G	A	TP	+/-	PIM	PP	SH	GW	GT	S	PCT
80	33	43	76	-19	105	8	2	2	1	231	14.3

1992-93 statistics:

GP	G	A	TP	+/-	PIM	PP	SH	GW	GT	S	PCT
80	47	67	114	+21	96	13	4	9	1	215	21.9

1993-94 statistics:

GP	G	A	TP	+/-	PIM	PP	SH	GW	GT	S	PCT
84	32	53	85	+1	60	6	2	4	0	226	14.2

1994-95 statistics:

GP	G	A	TP	+/-	PIM	PP	SH	GW	GT	S	PCT
47	23	24	47	-5	14	9	0	4	1	173	13.3

LAST SEASON

Led team in goals, points, power play goals, game-winning goals and shots. One of three NHL players to score on a penalty shot. Missed one game with a shoulder injury.

THE FINESSE GAME

Sundin reinforced his status as one of the game's premier forwards by stepping into a new team and not only leading them in the regular season, but moving his play up even another notch in the playoffs.

Sundin is a big skater who looks huge as he uses an ultra-long stick that gives him a broad wingspan. For a big man, he is an agile skater, and his balance has improved. He has good lower body strength, supplying good drive for battles along the boards. He doesn't stay checked. He is evasive, and once he is on the fly is hard to stop. Sundin is less effective when he is carrying the puck. His best play is to get up a head of steam, jump into the holes and take a quick shot. He also likes to use his reach, curling around behind the net for a stuff-in goal.

Sundin can take bad passes in stride, either kicking an errant puck up onto his stick or reaching behind to corral it. He has played centre and wing, but makes a much better winger. He isn't a clever stickhandler. Sundin's game is power and speed.

In open ice, Sundin doesn't look fast, but he has ground-eating strides that allow him to cover in two strokes what other skaters do in three or four. He is quick, too, and can get untracked in a heartbeat.

His shot is excellent. He can use a slap shot, one-timer, wrister, or backhand. The only liability to his reach is that he will dangle the puck well away from his body and he doesn't always control it, which makes him vulnerable to a poke check. Sundin's shot and play selection earned him some time on the point on the power play, when some of Toronto's point men were ailing, but he also works well down low.

THE PHYSICAL GAME

Sundin is big and strong. He has shown better attention to off-ice work to improve his strength. His conditioning is excellent — he can skate all night. He has even shown a touch of mean, but mostly with his stick, not his fists.

THE INTANGIBLES

Sundin is becoming a better all-around player with a commitment to the defensive part of his game. He was a bit shy of the veteran talent in Toronto (especially linemate Doug Gilmour), but by the end of the season had assumed a leadership role. He hasn't hit the magic 100-point mark yet (last year's total was a prorated 84 points), but with a healthy Gilmour this season, Sundin could do it. One thing is a sure bet: Sundin hasn't maxed out yet. The best is still to come.

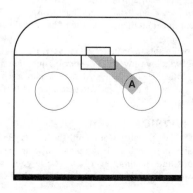

RANDY WOOD

Yrs. of NHL service: 8
Born: Princeton, N.J.; Oct. 12, 1963
Position: left wing
Height: 6-0
Weight: 195
Uniform no.: 24
Shoots: left

Career statistics:

GP	G	A	TP	PIM
550	161	141	302	480

1991-92 statistics:

GP	G	A	TP	+/-	PIM	PP	SH	GW	GT	S	PCT
78	22	18	40	-12	86	7	1	3	0	215	10.2

1992-93 statistics:

GP	G	A	TP	+/-	PIM	PP	SH	GW	GT	S	PCT
82	18	25	43	+6	77	3	2	2	0	176	10.2

1993-94 statistics:

GP	G	A	TP	+/-	PIM	PP	SH	GW	GT	S	PCT
84	22	16	38	+11	71	2	2	5	0	161	13.7

1994-95 statistics:

GP	G	A	TP	+/-	PIM	PP	SH	GW	GT	S	PCT
48	13	11	24	+7	34	1	1	2	0	125	10.4

LAST SEASON

Acquired in waiver draft. Led team in plus-minus. One of three Leafs to appear in all 48 games.

THE FINESSE GAME

The story of Wood's career has always been hard work, speed, intelligence and hands of . . . well, wood. Wood is always around the net, usually barrelling in at top speed, but his trouble is that he can't handle the puck while he is tearing along. He doesn't have great balance either, so he usually ends up plowing into the goalie (which drives opposing teams nuts) or sliding past the net into the boards with nothing to show for all of his hard work.

His determination is such that the Leafs gave him some time on the power play. Wood seemed to score goals at opportune times.

He is constantly jumping into the holes on the attack or coming back to help out defensively. He is a strong penalty killer who checks aggressively and can pick off passes and start shorthanded rushes. He's a constant threat on the ice because of his straightaway speed.

Wood wants to be better offensively. He tries creative plays down low but is better off just ramming and jamming. He is a dedicated, durable player who is always in top condition and can take every shift at top speed.

THE PHYSICAL GAME

Wood will do the dirty work along the boards. He has good size and uses it well, bumping and scrapping for the puck and finishing every check. He gets other teams mad at him because he's always in their face,

and he should take this as a compliment. He's that annoying.

THE INTANGIBLES

The Maple Leafs were pleasantly surprised by Wood's skill level, and seem to be happy if he can produce in the 20-goal range for the next few seasons. It's likely that he can, even at 33, since the guys with the great wheels last longest in the NHL, and Wood is definitely in that category.

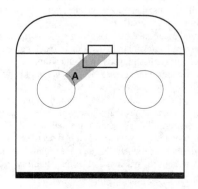

VANCOUVER CANUCKS

Players' Statistics 1994-95

POS	NO.	PLAYER	GP	G	A	PTS	+/-	PIM	PP	SH	GW	GT	S	PCTG
L	10	PAVEL BURE	44	20	23	43	-8	47	6	2	2		198	10.1
C	16	TREVOR LINDEN	48	18	22	40	-5	40	9		1	3	129	14.0
R	9	RUSS COURTNALL	45	11	24	35	2	17	2	2	2		132	8.3
L	14	GEOFF COURTNALL	45	16	18	34	2	81	7		1		144	11.1
C	42	JOSEF BERANEK	51	13	18	31	-7	30	3			1	134	9.7
D	22	JEFF BROWN	33	8	23	31	-2	16	3				111	7.2
L	27	SERGIO MOMESSO	48	10	15	25	-2	65	6		1		82	12.2
C	7	CLIFF RONNING	41	6	19	25	-4	27	3		2		93	6.5
L	23	MARTIN GELINAS	46	13	10	23	8	36	1		4		75	17.3
R	28	*ROMAN OKSIUTA	38	16	4	20	-12	10	6		1		67	23.9
C	20	CHRISTIAN RUUTTU	45	7	11	18	14	29			2		44	15.9
D	21	JYRKI LUMME	36	5	12	17	4	26	3		1		78	6.4
D	44	DAVE BABYCH	40	3	11	14	-13	18	1				58	5.2
D	3	BRET HEDICAN	45	2	11	13	-3	34					56	3.6
C	33	*MIKE PECA	33	6	6	12	-6	30	2		1	1	46	13.0
L	29	GINO ODJICK	23	4	5	9	-3	109					35	11.4
D	5	DANA MURZYN	40		8	8	14	129					29	
R	19	TIM HUNTER	34	3	2	5	1	120					17	17.6
C	15	JOHN MCINTYRE	28		4	4	-3	37					6	
D	34	*JASSEN CULLIMORE	34	1	2	3	-2	39					30	3.3
D	2	*YEVGENY NAMESTNIKOV	16		3	3	2	4					18	
R	9	GARY LEEMAN	10	2		2	-3				1		14	14.3
D	6	*ADRIAN AUCOIN	1	1		1	1						2	50.0
R	20	JOSE CHARBONNEAU	3	1		1							2	50.0
R	36	*DANE JACKSON	3	1		1		4					6	16.7
G	35	KAY WHITMORE	11		1	1		7						
D	24	*SCOTT WALKER	11		1	1		33					8	
G	1	KIRK MCLEAN	40		1	1		4						
D	4	*MARK WOTTON	1				1						2	
R	25	*ALEK STOJANOV	4				-2	13					1	

GP = games played; G = goals; A = assists; PTS = points; +/- = goals-for minus goals-against while player is on ice; PIM = penalties in minutes; PP = power play goals; SH = shorthanded goals; GW = game-winning goals; GT = game-tying goals; S = no. of shots; PCTG = percentage of goals to shots; * = rookie

JOSEF BERANEK

Yrs. of NHL service: 4
Born: Litvinov, Czechoslovakia; Oct. 25, 1969
Position: left wing/centre
Height: 6-2
Weight: 185
Uniform no.: 42
Shoots: left

Career statistics:

GP	G	A	TP	PIM
255	68	73	141	211

1991-92 statistics:

GP	G	A	TP	+/-	PIM	PP	SH	GW	GT	S	PCT
58	12	16	28	-2	18	0	0	1	0	79	15.2

1992-93 statistics:

GP	G	A	TP	+/-	PIM	PP	SH	GW	GT	S	PCT
66	15	18	33	-8	78	1	0	0	0	130	11.5

1993-94 statistics:

GP	G	A	TP	+/-	PIM	PP	SH	GW	GT	S	PCT
80	28	21	49	-2	85	6	0	2	0	182	15.4

1994-95 statistics:

GP	G	A	TP	+/-	PIM	PP	SH	GW	GT	S	PCT
51	13	18	31	-7	30	3	0	0	1	134	9.7

LAST SEASON
Acquired from Philadelphia for Shawn Antoski.

THE FINESSE GAME
Beranek uses all of the ice and his teammates well. He works to get himself into the clear and is usually in a quality scoring area. Although he came up through the Edmonton system as a centre, he is much more suited to the wing where he finds more open ice. He does not have much interest in one-on-one battles in closed spaces. He would rather get the puck, draw a man to him and pass.

Beranek has good hockey vision and the skills and size to finish or be a smart playmaker. He has good hands and a quick wrist shot from the top of the circle in. He will also drive to the net for rebounds. As long as he keeps his feet moving, he is effective.

THE PHYSICAL GAME
Beranek isn't eager to try to beat a defenseman down the boards with the puck, but will try to go to the inside where there is more room. On the wing, he too often allows himself to be steered to the boards where he loses control of the puck. But when he wants to, he can win a corner, come out with the puck, make a pass in front and beat his man back into the slot. He has the size and should initiate more hitting.

THE INTANGIBLES
We touted Beranek as a potential 30-goal scorer two seasons ago, and he came close in the pre-lockout season, but he is starting to show signs of backsliding. He had a dismal playoff (one goal in 11 games), and this year could determine which way he's going to go.

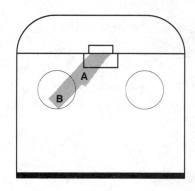

JEFF BROWN

Yrs. of NHL service: 10
Born: Ottawa, Ont.; Apr. 30, 1966
Position: right defense
Height: 6-1
Weight: 204
Uniform no.: 22
Shoots: right

Career statistics:

GP	G	A	TP	PIM
610	145	358	500	410

1991-92 statistics:

GP	G	A	TP	+/-	PIM	PP	SH	GW	GT	S	PCT
80	20	38	58	+8	38	10	0	2	1	214	9.3

1992-93 statistics:

GP	G	A	TP	+/-	PIM	PP	SH	GW	GT	S	PCT
71	25	53	78	-6	58	12	2	3	0	220	11.4

1993-94 statistics:

GP	G	A	TP	+/-	PIM	PP	SH	GW	GT	S	PCT
74	14	52	66	-11	56	7	0	3	1	237	5.9

1994-95 statistics:

GP	G	A	TP	+/-	PIM	PP	SH	GW	GT	S	PCT
33	8	23	31	-2	16	3	0	0	0	111	7.2

LAST SEASON

Led team defensemen in scoring for second consecutive season, despite missing 15 games with cracked bone in wrist. Tied for second on team in assists.

THE FINESSE GAME

Brown is a natural quarterback on the power play. He moves to the left side on the point and likes to glide to the top of the circle to step into a one-timer. Working with a fellow defenseman on the point, instead of a forward (as often happened in St. Louis), gives him more freedom to work the puck low.

Brown's game stems from his skating ability. He has impressive lateral movement and can handle the puck at tempo. He's a very good playmaker for a defenseman, ready to unleash his strong point shot or fake the slap and pass, or headman the pass off a break out of the defensive zone. He sees the ice well and slips perfect passes ahead to speedy wingers like Pavel Bure.

Defensively, Brown's game needs improvement. He has too much hockey sense and too much skill not to be a better player.

THE PHYSICAL GAME

Yes, Brown is an offensive defenseman, but that doesn't mean he should be fishing for the puck in front of the net when he could be dropping someone onto the seat of his pants.

Brown doesn't finish his checks consistently, and he lacks the mean streak needed to be a more dominating player. He has been thrust into a leadership role with the Canucks, a physical team, and has to be willing to take it another step.

THE INTANGIBLES

Brown is not an elite class defenseman, but when he elevates his game he is a B version of Ray Bourque. Thanks to a rapidly developing defense corps in Vancouver, Brown may not be asked to do too much, and he can relax and play his game.

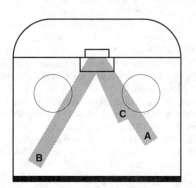

PAVEL BURE

Yrs. of NHL service: 4
Born: Moscow, Russia; Mar. 31, 1971
Position: left wing
Height: 5-11
Weight: 176
Uniform no.: 10
Shoots: left

Career statistics:

GP	G	A	TP	PIM
268	174	146	320	232

1991-92 statistics:

GP	G	A	TP	+/-	PIM	PP	SH	GW	GT	S	PCT
65	34	26	60	0	30	7	3	6	0	268	12.7

1992-93 statistics:

GP	G	A	TP	+/-	PIM	PP	SH	GW	GT	S	PCT
83	60	50	110	+35	69	13	7	9	0	407	14.7

1993-94 statistics:

GP	G	A	TP	+/-	PIM	PP	SH	GW	GT	S	PCT
76	60	47	107	+1	86	25	4	9	0	374	16.0

1994-95 statistics:

GP	G	A	TP	+/-	PIM	PP	SH	GW	GT	S	PCT
44	20	23	43	-8	47	6	2	2	0	198	10.1

LAST SEASON

Led team in goals for second consecutive season. Tied for second on team in assists. Led team in points for second consecutive season. Led team (for second consecutive season) and third in NHL in shots. Tied for team lead in shorthanded goals.

THE FINESSE GAME

Every time Bure touches the puck, fans in his home rink move to the edge of their collective seats. The Russian Rocket's quickness — and his control of the puck at supersonic speed — means anything is possible. He intimidates with his skating, driving back defenders who must play off him or risk being deked out of their skates at the blueline. He opens up tremendous ice for his teammates and will leave a drop pass or, more often, try to do it himself.

Bure's major weakness is his failure to use his teammates better. He will attempt to go through a team one-on-five rather than use his support. Of course, once in a while he can actually do it. That's the scary part. He has great balance and agility and he seems to move equally well with the puck or without it. The puck doesn't slow him down a fraction. The idea of him playing with speedy Alexander Mogilny is just breathtaking, since they will work give-and-go plays to perfection.

Bure doesn't do much defensively. He prefers to hang out at centre ice, and when he is going through a slump he doesn't do the other little things that can make a player useful until the scoring starts to click again. He is a shorthanded threat because of his breakaway speed and anticipation.

His explosive skating comes from his thick, powerful thighs, which look like a speed skater's. Bure is a devotee of the team's hyperbaric chamber, which allows athletes to recover more quickly from injuries and jet leg, and whether it's the gizmo or his conditioning, he can handle two-minute power play shifts.

THE PHYSICAL GAME

Bure is fairly physical for a smallish player, especially in the offensive zone. He gets nasty when frustrated, too.

THE INTANGIBLES

Bure has had his public contract spats with the Canucks, but he should be less sulky with the arrival of Mogilny. Factor in an improving defense and Vancouver could be the team to watch for in 1995-96.

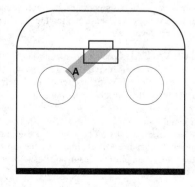

RUSS COURTNALL

Yrs. of NHL service: 11
Born: Duncan, B.C.; June 2, 1965
Position: right wing
Height: 5-11
Weight: 183
Uniform no.: 9
Shoots: right

Career statistics:

GP	G	A	TP	PIM
772	242	365	607	445

1991-92 statistics:

GP	G	A	TP	+/-	PIM	PP	SH	GW	GT	S	PCT
27	7	14	21	+6	6	0	1	1	1	63	11.1

1992-93 statistics:

GP	G	A	TP	+/-	PIM	PP	SH	GW	GT	S	PCT
84	36	43	79	+1	49	14	2	3	2	294	12.2

1993-94 statistics:

GP	G	A	TP	+/-	PIM	PP	SH	GW	GT	S	PCT
84	23	57	80	+6	59	5	0	4	0	231	10.0

1994-95 statistics:

GP	G	A	TP	+/-	PIM	PP	SH	GW	GT	S	PCT
45	11	24	35	+2	17	2	2	2	0	132	8.3

LAST SEASON

Acquired from Dallas for Greg Adams, Dan Kesa and a fifth-round draft pick in 1995. Led team in assists. Third on team in points. Tied for team lead in short-handed goals.

THE FINESSE GAME

Courtnall has jackrabbit speed. He goes straight down the runway, creating fear in the opposition and opening up a lot of room for his teammates. He pushes people back with sheer velocity.

He uses his speed intelligently and puts a lot of pucks in the net or works the give-and-go. He often follows a great play with a good one, and can slip a puck into a tiny hole off the rush. Once a fairly selfish player, he has developed into someone who uses his teammates well. He needs to play on a line with slick skaters, or else he tends to get too far ahead of the play.

Defensively aware, Courtnall uses his speed well defensively and is a shorthanded threat.

THE PHYSICAL GAME

Courtnall is tough for his size. While he tends to stick to the open ice where he can flash and dash, he will make a hit to drive to the net. For the most part, though, he avoids scrums and corner work.

THE INTANGIBLES

Courtnall had his problems with Bob Gainey in Dallas, at one point taking off his equipment and throwing the gear into a trash can after being told he wouldn't dress for a game against Detroit. He seems happy with the move to Vancouver, and produced 18 points in 13 regular season games and 12 points in 11 playoff games with the Canucks. He may be close to a point-per-game player this season if that keeps up, which would mean his production will catch up with his skills — finally.

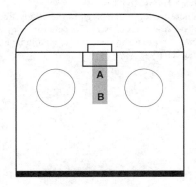

JASSEN CULLIMORE

Yrs. of NHL service: 1
Born: Simcoe, Ont.; Dec. 4, 1972
Position: left defense
Height: 6-5
Weight: 225
Uniform no.: 34
Shoots: left

Career statistics:

GP	G	A	TP	PIM
34	1	2	3	39

1994-95 statistics:

GP	G	A	TP	+/-	PIM	PP	SH	GW	GT	S	PCT
34	1	2	3	-2	39	0	0	0	0	30	3.3

LAST SEASON
First NHL season.

THE FINESSE GAME
Cullimore is big and rangy, and a good skater for his size, who jumps smartly into the play, using a big stride and a big reach. He pinches down the boards and can be found in front of the attacking net at times, but on balance the scales will be tipped heavily on the defensive side in his game.

Cullimore sometimes joins the play when he shouldn't, but is a strong enough skater to get back to his position when play breaks the other way. He is a good passer but not a creative playmaker. He is happier (and better off) making the safe, short pass or chipping the puck off the boards.

Cullimore is intelligent and diligent in his approach to the game, and wants to learn and analyze what he does.

THE PHYSICAL GAME
Cullimore is not tough, not mean, and not a fighter, but he takes his man out effectively along the boards and in the corners. A touch of mean wouldn't hurt him, though, since it would make opponents more wary of him, given his size and ability to move.

THE INTANGIBLES
Cullimore has been compared to the steady Randy Gregg because of his conservative defensive play. His season got off to a slow start due to a groin injury in training camp.

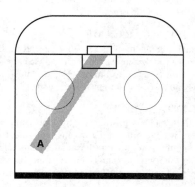

MARTIN GELINAS

Yrs. of NHL service: 6
Born: Shawinigan, Que.; June 5, 1970
Position: left wing
Height: 5-11
Weight: 195
Uniform no.: 23
Shoots: left

Career statistics:

GP	G	A	TP	PIM
368	87	84	171	226

1991-92 statistics:

GP	G	A	TP	+/-	PIM	PP	SH	GW	GT	S	PCT
68	11	18	29	+14	62	1	0	0	0	94	11.7

1992-93 statistics:

GP	G	A	TP	+/-	PIM	PP	SH	GW	GT	S	PCT
65	11	12	23	+3	30	0	0	1	0	93	11.8

1993-94 statistics:

GP	G	A	TP	+/-	PIM	PP	SH	GW	GT	S	PCT
64	14	14	28	-8	34	3	0	1	2	107	13.1

1994-95 statistics:

GP	G	A	TP	+/-	PIM	PP	SH	GW	GT	S	PCT
46	13	10	23	+8	36	1	0	4	0	75	17.3

LAST SEASON

Led team in game-winning goals.

THE FINESSE GAME

Gelinas is a frustrating package. He broke into the league as an all-finesse player, then set himself to the task of learning the defensive game that is much ignored in junior (and especially in the QMJHL, where Gelinas was a scoring star for Hull).

That combination should have made him a better all-around player, but something got lost in the mix: his production. Still, Gelinas seems to have all of the skills to make more of a contribution offensively. He has quickness and can handle the puck while on the go.

He plays more of a grinding game than his physique and his skills might suggest; most of his scoring comes from his fore-checking. He is strong along the boards and in front of the net. He doesn't have a lot of offensive sense, but he works hard. He is a good penalty killer.

THE PHYSICAL GAME

Gelinas is a small player and seems to get himself into situations where he just gets flattened. He isn't intimidated, but he does get wiped out of the play and he has to be smarter about jumping in and out of holes, paying the price only when necessary.

THE INTANGIBLES

Gelinas will be on the bubble again in training camp, but in the right situation could produce a 25-goal season. He has the skills, but not the consistency.

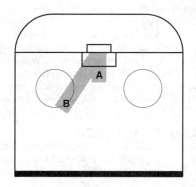

BRET HEDICAN

Yrs. of NHL service: 3
Born: St. Paul, Minn.; Aug. 10, 1970
Position: left defense
Height: 6-2
Weight: 195
Uniform no.: 3
Shoots: left

Career statistics:

GP	G	A	TP	PIM
160	3	31	34	107

1991-92 statistics:

GP	G	A	TP	+/-	PIM	PP	SH	GW	GT	S	PCT
4	1	0	1	+1	0	0	0	0	0	1	100.0

1992-93 statistics:

GP	G	A	TP	+/-	PIM	PP	SH	GW	GT	S	PCT
42	0	8	8	-2	30	0	0	0	0	40	0.0

1993-94 statistics:

GP	G	A	TP	+/-	PIM	PP	SH	GW	GT	S	PCT
69	0	12	12	-7	64	0	0	0	0	88	0.0

1994-95 statistics:

GP	G	A	TP	+/-	PIM	PP	SH	GW	GT	S	PCT
45	2	11	13	-3	34	0	0	0	0	56	3.6

LAST SEASON

Career high in points.

THE FINESSE GAME

Hedican is a confident puck carrier. He happily uses his speed with the puck to drive down the wing and create trouble in the offensive zone. He also varies the attack. He seems to prefer the left wing boards but will also take the right wing route to try to make plays off the backhand.

Hedican is a good enough stickhandler to try one-on-one moves. He is eager to jump into the play and shows signs of becoming an "offenseman," a defender who is down the attacking boards and into the corners as much as he is at the blueline.

Skating is his key asset. He has a nice, deep knee bend and his fluid stride provides good acceleration; each stride eats up lots of ice. His steady balance allows him to go down to one knee and use his stick to challenge passes from the corners. He uses quickness, range and reach to make a confident stand at the defensive blueline.

Hedican knows that if an attacker beats him, he will be able to keep up with him and steer him to bad ice. He is the perfect guy to pick up the puck behind the net and get it to the redline and start the half-court game. He doesn't always just put his head down and go. He will move up the middle and look for a pass to a breaking wing.

THE PHYSICAL GAME

Hedican has decent size but not a great deal of strength or toughness. He won't bulldoze people in front of the net, preferring to tie people up and go for the puck. He is more of a stick checker than a body checker, but will sometimes body a player off the puck at the blueline, control it and make a smart first pass. His preference is to use body positioning to nullify an opponent rather than initiate hard body contact.

THE INTANGIBLES

Hedican's numbers haven't quite matched the flashes of offensive skill he demonstrates, but he is part of a very solid developing defense in Vancouver, and his numbers can be expected to improve sharply over the next few seasons as he gains confidence and experience. He won't lead the team in scoring, but don't be surprised if he's first or second among team defensemen.

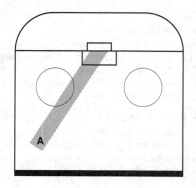

TREVOR LINDEN

Yrs. of NHL service: 7
Born: Medicine Hat, Alta.; Apr. 11, 1970
Position: right wing
Height: 6-4
Weight: 205
Uniform no.: 16
Shoots: right

Career statistics:

GP	G	A	TP	PIM
529	198	229	427	451

1991-92 statistics:

GP	G	A	TP	+/-	PIM	PP	SH	GW	GT	S	PCT
80	31	44	75	+3	99	6	1	6	1	201	15.4

1992-93 statistics:

GP	G	A	TP	+/-	PIM	PP	SH	GW	GT	S	PCT
84	33	39	72	+19	64	8	0	3	0	209	15.8

1993-94 statistics:

GP	G	A	TP	+/-	PIM	PP	SH	GW	GT	S	PCT
84	32	29	61	+6	73	10	2	3	0	234	13.7

1994-95 statistics:

GP	G	A	TP	+/-	PIM	PP	SH	GW	GT	S	PCT
48	18	22	40	-5	40	9	0	1	3	129	14.0

LAST SEASON

Longest active consecutive games-played streak at 372. One of two Canucks to appear in all 48 games. Led team in power play goals. Second on team in goals and points.

THE FINESSE GAME

Not a graceful skater, at times Linden looks very awkward, and he's not as strong on his skates as a player of his size should be. Despite his heavy feet his agility is satisfactory, but he lacks first-step quickness and doesn't have the all-out speed to pull away from a checker. He has a big turning radius.

Linden has a slow release on his shot. He has a long reach, but unlike, say, Dave Andreychuk (who is built along similar lines), his short game is not as effective as it should be. He uses a slapshot off the wing that is released more quickly than his wrist shot.

Linden is unselfish and makes quick, safe passing decisions that help his team break smartly up-ice, often creating odd-man rushes. He seems to lack confidence in his shooting, and when he is the open man on the outnumbered rush he often passes to a covered teammate rather than take the shot himself.

He has improved tremendously in his defensive coverage.

THE PHYSICAL GAME

Linden is big, but usually doesn't play tough, and so doesn't make good use of his size. He will attack the blueline and draw the attention of both defensemen, but will pull up rather than try to muscle through and earn a holding penalty. There are people he should nullify who still seem able to get away from him. He does not skate through the physical challenges along the boards.

If only he would keep his feet moving, Linden would be so much more commanding. Instead, he can be angled off the play fairly easily because he will not battle for better ice. He uses his body more to defend than to help create offense. He will use his range to cut down the ice on a player, then merely stick out his stick to slow him down, rather than throw a shoulder into him.

When Linden is throwing his weight around, he drives to the net and drags a defender or two with him, opening up a lot of ice for his teammates. He creates havoc in front of the net on the power play, planting himself for screens and deflections. When the puck is at the side boards, he's smart enough to move up higher, between the circles, and force the penalty killers to make a decision. If the defenseman on that side steps up to cover him, space will open behind the defenseman; if a forward collapses to cover him, a point shot will open up.

THE INTANGIBLES

Linden is a Group Two free agent and there were differing opinions between owner and general manager as to Linden's worth should the free market drive his value up. Linden will no doubt be pursued, but whether he moves on or stays in Vancouver, he will still be frustrating because he has the ability to deliver more than he usually does. Off the ice, Linden is very likable and a team leader.

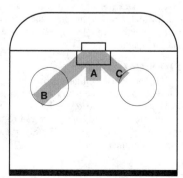

JYRKI LUMME

Yrs. of NHL service: 7
Born: Tampere, Finland; July 16, 1966
Position: right defense
Height: 6-1
Weight: 207
Uniform no.: 21
Shoots: left

Career statistics:

GP	G	A	TP	PIM
434	48	178	226	314

1991-92 statistics:

GP	G	A	TP	+/-	PIM	PP	SH	GW	GT	S	PCT
75	12	32	44	+25	65	3	1	1	0	106	11.3

1992-93 statistics:

GP	G	A	TP	+/-	PIM	PP	SH	GW	GT	S	PCT
74	8	36	44	+30	55	3	2	1	0	123	6.5

1993-94 statistics:

GP	G	A	TP	+/-	PIM	PP	SH	GW	GT	S	PCT
83	13	42	55	+3	50	1	3	3	0	161	8.1

1994-95 statistics:

GP	G	A	TP	+/-	PIM	PP	SH	GW	GT	S	PCT
36	5	12	17	+4	26	3	0	1	0	78	6.4

THE INTANGIBLES

Lumme has improved defensively, but his key value remains his open-ice play and his involvement in the attack.

LAST SEASON

Second among team defensemen in scoring. Missed 12 games with rib and knee injuries.

THE FINESSE GAME

Lumme is one of the Canucks' more mobile defenseman, an accomplished puck-carrier who can rush the puck out of danger and make a smart first pass to start the attack. He likes to gamble a bit offensively, but he has the good skating ability to be able to wheel back into a defensive mode. He became a lower risk defenseman last season.

He plays the right point on the power play. His shot isn't overpowering, but he keeps it low and on net, and he times it well. He has very good hands and is adept at keeping the puck in. He also uses his lateral mobility to slide along the blueline into the centre to quarterback the power play.

Defensively, he uses his hand skills for sweep-and poke-checks. He will challenge at the blueline to try to knock the puck free, but he doesn't always follow through with his body if the poke-check fails.

Lumme is a strong penalty killer because of his range and anticipation.

THE PHYSICAL GAME

Lumme is all finesse. He will take a hit to protect the puck or make a play, but he won't throw himself at anybody. Other teams like to key on Lumme, because if he gets hit often and hard enough, he can be taken out of a game early, depriving the Canucks of a valuable component of their offense.

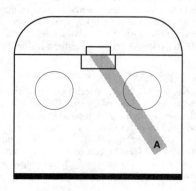

KIRK MCLEAN

Yrs. of NHL service: 8
Born: Willowdale, Ont.; June 26, 1966
Position: goaltender
Height: 6-0
Weight: 177
Uniform no.: 1
Catches: left

Career statistics:

GP	MINS	GA	SO	GAA	A	PIM
404	23451	1267	17	3.24	16	46

1991-92 statistics:

GP	MINS	GAA	W	L	T	SO	GA	S	SAPCT	PIM
65	3852	2.74	38	17	9	5	176	1780	.901	0

1992-93 statistics:

GP	MINS	GAA	W	L	T	SO	GA	S	SAPCT	PIM
54	3261	3.39	28	21	5	3	184	1615	.886	16

1993-94 statistics:

GP	MINS	GAA	W	L	T	SO	GA	S	SAPCT	PIM
52	3128	2.99	23	26	3	3	156	1430	.891	2

1994-95 statistics:

GP	MINS	GAA	W	L	T	SO	GA	S	SAPCT	PIM
40	2374	2.75	18	12	10	1	109	1140	.904	4

LAST SEASON

Second-best GAA of career. Stopped Russ Courtnall on penalty shot.

THE PHYSICAL GAME

McLean stays on his feet more than any goalie in the NHL. He has great lateral movement. Maybe because of his soccer training, his movement and balance are advanced. He is smooth, almost casual, in his post-to-post moves.

McLean makes himself look big in the net because of his positioning and stand-up play. He is very solid technically and has good reflexes. His solid foundation means few bad stretches of play. He will blow the occasional angle, especially on the stick side, but he has a great deal of confidence in his game and does not rattle easily. On occasion, he will stay a little too deep in the crease, but such lapses are rare.

He's good up high, with a quick glove hand. He is strong on his stick and uses it well around the net for jabbing at puckhandlers or breaking up passes. He makes shooters try to be too perfect. McLean does not waste any motion, which makes him seem downright lethargic at times, but the lack of dramatics should not detract from his overall technical skill. There's nothing objectionable about making the job easier, the job is tough enough without adding unnecessary flourishes.

McLean will stand there and let the puck hit him. Even when he is bombarded with shots, the barrage seems to take little out of him. If he does drop down for a save, he is back up quickly for a rebound. He is seldom out of the play. When the siege is over, he is standing calmly with the puck in his mitt for the linesman. He does not showboat.

McLean handles the puck well, again, without much excitement, but enough to help out his team defensively. He is smart with the puck on his forehand and backhand, and recognizes when to move it and when to leave it for his defense.

THE MENTAL GAME

McLean needs some time to get into a game. He can be beaten early, but gets better as the game moves along. He never looks rattled, flustered or out of control.

THE INTANGIBLES

McLean is a classic goalie. He steals wins for his team, and rare is the night when he's the one responsible for losing a game.

McLean was rewarded last season with a five-year, $12.5-million contract. Some players do not handle the pressure of big paychecks. There should be no such struggle for the even-keeled McLean.

ALEXANDER MOGILNY

Yrs. of NHL service: 6
Born: Khabarovsk, Russia; Feb. 18, 1969
Position: right wing
Height: 5-11
Weight: 195
Uniform no.: 89
Shoots: left

Career statistics:

GP	G	A	TP	PIM
381	211	233	444	203

1991-92 statistics:

GP	G	A	TP	+/-	PIM	PP	SH	GW	GT	S	PCT
67	39	45	84	+7	73	15	0	2	0	235	16.5

1992-93 statistics:

GP	G	A	TP	+/-	PIM	PP	SH	GW	GT	S	PCT
77	76	51	127	+7	40	27	0	11	0	360	21.1

1993-94 statistics:

GP	G	A	TP	+/-	PIM	PP	SH	GW	GT	S	PCT
66	32	47	79	+8	22	17	0	7	1	258	12.4

1994-95 statistics:

GP	G	A	TP	+/-	PIM	PP	SH	GW	GT	S	PCT
44	19	28	47	0	36	12	0	2	1	148	12.8

LAST SEASON

Led team in points (for third consecutive season) and shots on goal. Second on team in power play goals, goals, and assists. Acquired from Buffalo for Mike Peca, Mike Wilson and a first-round draft pick.

THE FINESSE GAME

Mogilny will be reunited with Pavel Bure, a teammate from his old Russian national junior team days, and the results should be wonderful and terrible to see — wonderful for the Canucks, and terrible for Vancouver opponents. Skating is the basis of Mogilny's game. He has a burst of speed from a standstill. He hits his top speed in just a few strides. When he streaks down the ice, there is a good chance you'll see something new, something you didn't expect. He is unbelievably quick. Mogilny may hate to fly in a plane but he loves to fly over the ice.

His anticipation sets him apart from other players who are merely fast. He won't skate deeply into his own defensive zone, instead awaiting a turnover and a chance to get a jump on the defenseman, with a preferred move to the outside — but he is not afraid to go inside either, so a defenseman intent on angling him to the boards could just as easily get burned inside.

Mogilny can beat you in so many ways. He has a powerful and accurate wrist shot from the tops of the circles in. He shoots without breaking stride. He can work a give-and-go that is a thing of beauty. He one-times with the best of them. And everything is done at racehorse speed.

THE PHYSICAL GAME

The major knock on Mogilny is that, as good as he is, there always seems to be something left in the tank, that Mogilny doesn't push himself to the limit. He also suffers from a lack of consistency, and no one is ever sure which Mogilny is going to show up. There are nights when he is invisible on the ice, and that is unpardonable for a player of his ability and importance.

Mogilny intimidates with his speed but will also add a physical element. He has great upper body strength and will drive through a defender to the net.

THE INTANGIBLES

Mogilny returned to a healthy state after battling injuries in two of the past three seasons. His return to 60-goal status is just about a certainty given the passion and joy that is sure to return to his game. Mogilny should have many peak seasons left.

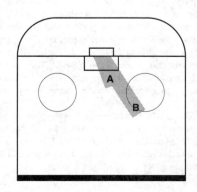

YEVGENY NAMESTNIKOV

Yrs. of NHL service: 0
Born: Arzamis-Ig, Soviet Union; Oct. 9, 1971
Position: defense
Height: 5-11
Weight: 190
Uniform no.: 2
Shoots: right

Career statistics:

GP	G	A	TP	PIM
33	0	8	8	14

1993-94 statistics:

GP	G	A	TP	+/-	PIM	PP	SH	GW	GT	S	PCT
17	0	5	5	-5	10	0	0	0	0	11	0.0

1994-95 statistics:

GP	G	A	TP	+/-	PIM	PP	SH	GW	GT	S	PCT
16	0	3	3	+2	4	0	0	0	0	18	0.0

LAST SEASON
Will be entering first full NHL season.

THE FINESSE GAME
Namestnikov skates well and moves the puck well. Despite those skills, he doesn't have much instinct or inclination for the offensive part of the game. Looking at a defenseman of his size puts one in immediate mind of an offensive defenseman, but Namestnikov concentrates on his own end of the ice.

He reads and reacts quickly to the rush, and can be paired with a more eager partner because Namestnikov will make a smart pass out of the zone and then stay back to take care of business while his partner goes up-ice. He is a good penalty killer.

THE PHYSICAL GAME
Despite his small stature, Namestnikov is a willing and earnest open-ice hitter. His skating gives him the impetus to put more oomph in his checks. He has trouble with attackers down low, where he can be overpowered, but he is a human torpedo when he gets some room. He likes to step up, and while he's not a fighter, he is tough as nails. Namestnikov's face is always festooned with fresh cuts from crashing into people.

THE INTANGIBLES
Namestnikov is something of a rarity in the NHL. He's a small defensive specialist, like Curt Giles of seasons past. He will be a reliable fifth or sixth defenseman. Only his size prevents him from moving up on the depth chart.

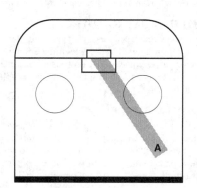

GINO ODJICK

Yrs. of NHL service: 4
Born: Maniwaki, Que.; Sept. 7, 1970
Position: left wing
Height: 6-2
Weight: 205
Uniform no.: 29
Shoots: left

Career statistics:

GP	G	A	TP	PIM
284	35	38	73	1394

1991-92 statistics:

GP	G	A	TP	+/-	PIM	PP	SH	GW	GT	S	PCT
65	4	6	10	-1	348	0	0	0	0	68	5.9

1992-93 statistics:

GP	G	A	TP	+/-	PIM	PP	SH	GW	GT	S	PCT
75	4	13	17	+3	370	0	0	1	0	79	5.1

1993-94 statistics:

GP	G	A	TP	+/-	PIM	PP	SH	GW	GT	S	PCT
76	16	13	29	+13	271	4	0	5	0	121	13.2

1994-95 statistics:

GP	G	A	TP	+/-	PIM	PP	SH	GW	GT	S	PCT
23	4	5	9	-3	109	0	0	0	0	35	11.4

but one the team will live with.

LAST SEASON
Missed 25 games with a groin/abdominal strain.

THE FINESSE GAME
Odjick is a goon who knows that goons are facing extinction in the NHL. To preserve his job, he has added important elements to become more than a one-dimensional player.

His abdominal injury robbed him of most of the strength and toughness that are his hallmarks. He had improved his skating since dropping some weight over the past few seasons, but now conditioning will become a priority.

Odjick's scoring chances come from in tight. He works tirelessly around the net for loose pucks, slamming and jamming. He could use a little more patience, since he gets a lot of room for his first move, but his theory seems to be that three whacks at the puck (which he can get easily) are worth one finesse move (which he might not be able to make anyway).

THE PHYSICAL GAME
Odjick takes cheap penalties. He aggravates, hits late and hits from behind, yet is a legitimate tough guy when the gloves come off. He protects his teammates. He is also strong enough to simply run over people en route to the net.

THE INTANGIBLES
Odjick is a huge favourite with the fans in Vancouver, and the coaches can't help but love the effort he puts into his game and his career. If he continues to work at the little parts of his game, he will make a big impact for seasons to come. His skating remains a major flaw,

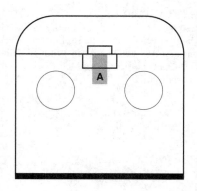

ROMAN OKSIUTA

Yrs. of NHL service: 1
Born: Murmansk, Soviet Union; Aug. 21, 1970
Position: left wing
Height: 6-3
Weight: 229
Uniform no.: 28
Shoots: left

Career statistics:

GP	G	A	TP	PIM
48	17	6	23	14

1993-94 statistics:

GP	G	A	TP	+/-	PIM	PP	SH	GW	GT	S	PCT
10	1	2	3	-1	4	0	0	0	0	18	5.6

1994-95 statistics:

GP	G	A	TP	+/-	PIM	PP	SH	GW	GT	S	PCT
38	16	4	20	-12	10	6	0	1	0	67	23.9

LAST SEASON

First NHL season. Led team and third in NHL in shooting percentage. Tied for second among NHL rookies in goals. Acquired from Edmonton for Jiri Slegr.

THE FINESSE GAME

Oksiuta has a long reach, and he needs it, because he is slow afoot. He is very powerful on his skates and once he is established in front of the net is very tough to budge. Oksiuta has very soft hands and good scoring instincts. He sees the ice well and moves the puck with assurance. The lumbering Soviet could truly become a force on the power play because of his size and touch.

Oksiuta's clunky skating makes him a liability defensively, and keeps him from getting any four-on-four time.

While he is outstanding with the puck, he has to work on his game without the puck to be a factor.

THE PHYSICAL GAME

Oksiuta's conditioning is something he will need to concentrate on. The Canucks are concerned about his life skills, but in the past year he has claimed to have cleaned up his off-ice habits and is dedicating himself to becoming an NHL regular. He has never paid much attention to training before, which is why his progress has been minimal. Oksiuta will take a beating, but doesn't retaliate or initiate. He has dropped some weight, which may help his mobility.

THE INTANGIBLES

Vancouver is willing to make room for Oksiuta as a number two winger, but he has to be willing to work for the job. Like most power forwards, Oksiuta is a long-term project whose best seasons may be a few years away, but he will get the chance to continue to earn — and learn — the job this season.

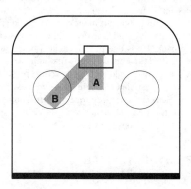

MIKE RIDLEY

Yrs. of NHL service: 10
Born: Winnipeg, Man.; July 8, 1963
Position: centre
Height: 6-1
Weight: 200
Uniform no.: 7
Shoots: left

Career statistics:

GP	G	A	TP	PIM
754	266	419	675	353

1991-92 statistics:

GP	G	A	TP	+/-	PIM	PP	SH	GW	GT	S	PCT
80	29	40	69	+3	38	5	5	3	0	123	23.6

1992-93 statistics:

GP	G	A	TP	+/-	PIM	PP	SH	GW	GT	S	PCT
84	26	56	82	+5	44	6	2	3	0	148	17.6

1993-94 statistics:

GP	G	A	TP	+/-	PIM	PP	SH	GW	GT	S	PCT
81	26	44	70	+15	24	10	2	4	3	144	18.1

1994-95 statistics:

GP	G	A	TP	+/-	PIM	PP	SH	GW	GT	S	PCT
48	10	27	37	+1	14	2	2	1	1	88	11.4

LAST SEASON

Led team in assists and shorthanded goals. Third on team in points. One of three Leafs to appear in all 48 games. Acquired from Toronto for Sergio Momesso.

THE FINESSE GAME

Ridley is a straight-ahead player who much prefers a north-south game to an east-west game. He is a solid two-way centre, smart and strong, and has good offensive instincts to combine with his defensive awareness. He concentrates on defense first. If the opponent has a big centre, then Ridley gets the assignment.

Ridley plays all 200 feet of the ice. He is just as likely to make an important play behind either net. He is effective on face-offs, winning the draw and then swiveling his hip into the opposing centre, buying time for his teammates to get to the puck (technically speaking, he cheats, but he's good at it).

A strong skater who can win one-on-one battles against all but the biggest defensemen, he grinds in the corners and in front of the net. He draws penalties by outworking his opponents in the corners. Ridley never gives up on a play, and is always willing to pay a price for the puck. He is one of the league's best penalty-killers, and worked on Toronto's first unit.

A sneaky passer down low, he scores most of his goals from wrist shots in tight. Ridley doesn't shoot enough. He is extremely accurate, but often holds onto the puck too long. Opponents will always play the pass until he demonstrates he is more willing to fire away.

THE PHYSICAL GAME

Ridley is a crunch-time player. He will protect the puck with his body or work like crazy to get the puck free. He pays the toll in the traffic areas. He is a very disciplined player. For someone as involved as he is, he takes only a tiny number of bad penalties, and should be a Lady Byng candidate. Ridley is always in great physical condition. He has missed few games, but not because he doesn't get hurt. He just plays hurt.

THE INTANGIBLES

Ridley is one of the most dependable forwards in the NHL. Everything he has accomplished in his career — from making the Rangers as a free agent tryout from the University of Manitoba in 1985 — has been done with hard work. That ethic hasn't deserted him for a single shift. A gamer.

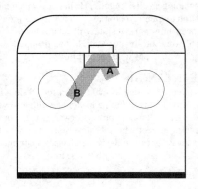

CLIFF RONNING

Yrs. of NHL service: 8
Born: Vancouver, B.C.; Oct. 1, 1965
Position: centre
Height: 5-8
Weight: 175
Uniform no.: 7
Shoots: left

Career statistics:

GP	G	A	TP	PIM
467	144	242	386	187

1991-92 statistics:

GP	G	A	TP	+/-	PIM	PP	SH	GW	GT	S	PCT
80	24	47	71	+18	42	6	0	2	1	216	11.1

1992-93 statistics:

GP	G	A	TP	+/-	PIM	PP	SH	GW	GT	S	PCT
79	29	56	85	+19	30	10	0	2	0	209	13.9

1993-94 statistics:

GP	G	A	TP	+/-	PIM	PP	SH	GW	GT	S	PCT
76	25	43	68	+7	42	10	0	4	1	197	12.7

1994-95 statistics:

GP	G	A	TP	+/-	PIM	PP	SH	GW	GT	S	PCT
41	6	19	25	-4	27	3	0	2	0	93	6.5

LAST SEASON

Missed six games with a groin injury. Was a healthy scratch for the first time in his career.

THE FINESSE GAME

Ronning's forte is not scoring goals but creating chances for his wingers. He lets bigger linemates attract defenders so that he can dipsydoodle with the puck. He's quick, shifty and smart. He likes to work from behind the net, using the cage as a shield and daring defenders to chase him. Much of his game is a dare. He is a tempting target, and even smaller-sized defensemen fantasize about smashing Ronning to the ice, but he keeps himself out of the trouble spots by dancing in and out of openings and finding free teammates.

A quick thinker and unpredictable, Ronning can curl off the wall into the slot, pass to the corners or the point and jump to the net, or beat a defender wide to the top of the circle and feed a trailing teammate coming into the play late.

He puts a lot of little dekes into a compact area. He opens up the ice with his bursts of speed and his fakes. Unless the defense can force him along the wall and contain him, he's all over the ice trying to make things happen.

THE PHYSICAL GAME

No one asks jockeys to tackle running backs. Ronning is built for speed and deception. He is smart enough to avoid getting crunched and talented enough to compensate for his lack of strength. Ronning has skills and a huge heart.

He gets involved with his stick, hooking at a puck-carrier's arm and worrying at the puck in a player's skates. He keeps the puck in his skates when he protects it, so that a checker will often have to pull Ronning down to get at the puck, which creates a power play for the Canucks.

THE INTANGIBLES

Tough in his way, Ronning has excelled at a game that everyone told him he was too small to play. However, he is starting on the downside of his career, and it may be difficult for him to get ice time this season.

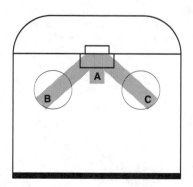

WASHINGTON CAPITALS

Players' Statistics 1994-95

POS	NO.	PLAYER	GP	G	A	PTS	+/-	PIM	PP	SH	GW	GT	S	PCTG
R	12	PETER BONDRA	47	34	9	43	9	24	12	6	3	1	177	19.2
C	90	JOE JUNEAU	44	5	38	43	-1	8	3			1	70	7.1
C	20	MICHAL PIVONKA	46	10	23	33	3	50	4	2	2		80	12.5
D	6	CALLE JOHANSSON	46	5	26	31	-6	35	4		2		112	4.5
L	8	DIMITRI KHRISTICH	48	12	14	26		41	8		2	2	92	13.0
C	22	STEVE KONOWALCHUK	46	11	14	25	7	44	3	3	3		88	12.5
L	10	KELLY MILLER	48	10	13	23	5	6	2		1		70	14.3
C	32	DALE HUNTER	45	8	15	23	-4	101	3		1		73	11.0
R	26	KEITH JONES	40	14	6	20	-2	65	1		4		85	16.5
D	3	SYLVAIN COTE	47	5	14	19	2	53	1		2		124	4.0
D	4	JIM JOHNSON	47		13	13	6	43					46	
D	24	MARK TINORDI	42	3	9	12	-5	71	2		1		71	4.2
C	9	DAVE POULIN	29	4	5	9	2	10		2		1	30	13.3
C	36	MIKE EAGLES	40	3	4	7	-11	48					28	10.7
D	17	*SERGEI GONCHAR	31	2	5	7	4	22					38	5.3
D	29	JOE REEKIE	48	1	6	7	10	97					52	1.9
L	27	CRAIG BERUBE	43	2	4	6	-5	173					22	9.1
R	25	ROB PEARSON	32		6	6	-6	96					34	
D	44	IGOR ULANOV	22	1	4	5	1	29					13	7.7
D	2	*KEN KLEE	23	3	1	4	2	41					18	16.7
C	14	PAT PEAKE	18		4	4	-6	12					30	
R	34	*MARTIN GENDRON	8	2	1	3	3	2					11	18.2
C	41	*JASON ALLISON	12	2	1	3	-3	6	2				9	22.2
D	28	JOHN SLANEY	16		3	3	-3	6					21	
C	23	*KEVIN KAMINSKI	27	1	1	2	-6	102			1		12	8.3
C	15	*JEFF NELSON	10	1		1	-2	2					4	25.0
G	35	*BYRON DAFOE	4											
G	37	*OLAF KOLZIG	14					4						
G	30	*JIM CAREY	28											

GP = games played; G = goals; A = assists; PTS = points; +/- = goals-for minus goals-against while player is on ice; PIM = penalties in minutes; PP = power play goals; SH = shorthanded goals; GW = game-winning goals; GT = game-tying goals; S = no. of shots; PCTG = percentage of goals to shots; * = rookie

JASON ALLISON

Yrs. of NHL service: 0
Born: North York, Ont.; May 29, 1975
Position: centre
Height: 6-3
Weight: 200
Uniform no.: 41
Shoots: right

Career statistics:

GP	G	A	TP	PIM
10	2	2	4	6

1993-94 statistics:

GP	G	A	TP	+/-	PIM	PP	SH	GW	GT	S	PCT
2	0	1	1	+1	0	0	0	0	0	5	0.0

1994-95 statistics:

GP	G	A	TP	+/-	PIM	PP	SH	GW	GT	S	PCT
8	2	1	3	-3	6	2	0	0	0	9	22.2

LAST SEASON
Will be entering first full NHL season.

THE FINESSE GAME
Allison has great hands for passing or shooting, and wonderful patience with the puck. He has more poise and composure than many young players of his comparitive experience. Allison has trouble adjusting to the pace of the NHL game as far as his skating is concerned, but he has the head and instincts of a polished offensive player.

Although he will have to improve his even-strength play to get the ice time he needs to improve, Allison should become a key on the Caps' power play, which was among the best in the NHL last year and will get better with Allison's creativity.

THE PHYSICAL GAME
Allison has good size and has to have the confidence to use his power more. The fact that he is not a very fast skater doesn't give him the range to find and pop people, but he will take his punishment around the net and has a long fuse.

THE INTANGIBLES
The Caps were in a quandary with Allison last season. He was too good to send back to junior, too young to go play in the minors, and too slow to play a regular role with the big club. Allison did go to Portland (AHL) for the playoffs, and went with a good attitude. His numbers (3-8 — 11 in seven games) should give him a confidence boost going into this season.

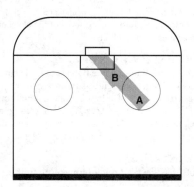

CRAIG BERUBE

Yrs. of NHL service: 7
Born: Calahoo, Alta.; Dec. 17, 1965
Position: left wing
Height: 6-1
Weight: 205
Uniform no.: 27
Shoots: left

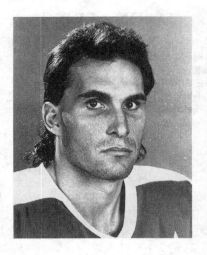

Career statistics:

GP	G	A	TP	PIM
515	35	56	94	1508

1991-92 statistics:

GP	G	A	TP	+/-	PIM	PP	SH	GW	GT	S	PCT
76	6	11	17	-5	264	1	0	1	0	69	8.7

1992-93 statistics:

GP	G	A	TP	+/-	PIM	PP	SH	GW	GT	S	PCT
77	4	8	12	-6	209	0	0	2	0	58	6.9

1993-94 statistics:

GP	G	A	TP	+/-	PIM	PP	SH	GW	GT	S	PCT
84	7	7	14	-4	305	0	0	0	0	48	14.6

1994-95 statistics:

GP	G	A	TP	+/-	PIM	PP	SH	GW	GT	S	PCT
43	2	4	6	-5	173	0	0	0	0	22	9.1

LAST SEASON

Led team in PIM for third consecutive season. Tied for fifth in NHL in PIM. Missed three games with the flu.

THE FINESSE GAME

Berube has limited skills but is proficient enough in all areas not to embarrass himself on the ice. He is a strong and powerful skater, but slow. He is at his best in tight in front of the net, where he can plant himself and force others to try to move him. He does not have the quickness to do much else.

His hand skills are average. He has the intelligence to do something with the puck, and when he drives to the net and slides a backpass to a trailer, he adds the element of surprise as he sets up a screen. He will test goalies now and then by trying a backhand shot. Berube also has the balance and presence of mind to kick a puck up onto his stick blade for a shot.

Most of Berube's goals are generated from his hard work around the net. He is an eager player, but he isn't quick enough to convert most of the chances his big size creates around the net.

THE PHYSICAL GAME

Berube is one of the top five fighters in the league, but that is no longer enough to sustain a player's NHL career. He is a bit of a loose cannon, which makes other players on the ice wary, but he has to be more judicious in his use of muscle or his ice time will become more limited — and it's scarce enough as it is.

THE INTANGIBLES

Berube has been working to make himself a more complete player, but is not doing enough to merit a full-time role. He could become a useful fourth-line winger who chips in 10 goals or so a season, but he has to stay out of the penalty box in order to do so. He can play tough without leaving the ice.

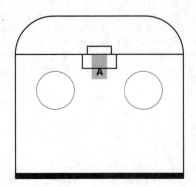

PETER BONDRA

Yrs. of NHL service: 5
Born: Lutsk, Ukraine; Feb. 7, 1968
Position: right wing
Height: 5-11
Weight: 180
Uniform no.: 12
Shoots: left

Career statistics:

GP	G	A	TP	PIM
324	135	120	255	223

1991-92 statistics:

GP	G	A	TP	+/-	PIM	PP	SH	GW	GT	S	PCT
71	28	28	56	+16	42	4	0	3	0	158	17.7

1992-93 statistics:

GP	G	A	TP	+/-	PIM	PP	SH	GW	GT	S	PCT
83	37	48	85	+8	70	10	0	7	0	239	15.5

1993-94 statistics:

GP	G	A	TP	+/-	PIM	PP	SH	GW	GT	S	PCT
69	24	19	43	+22	40	4	0	2	0	200	12.0

1994-95 statistics:

GP	G	A	TP	+/-	PIM	PP	SH	GW	GT	S	PCT
47	34	9	43	+9	24	12	6	3	1	177	19.2

LAST SEASON

Led NHL in goals and shorthanded goals. Led team and fifth in NHL in power play goals. Led team in points, shots and shooting percentage. Missed one game with the flu.

THE FINESSE GAME

Bondra at long last lived up to the expectations the Caps had held for him for four seasons. He is the first Capital ever to lead the NHL in goals, and he did it despite increased checking attention. The difference came in Bondra's willingness to consistently go into the high traffic areas instead of staying on the perimeter.

Bondra's speed is exceptional and he is intelligent on the ice offensively. He accelerates quickly and smoothly and drives defenders back because they have to play off his speed. If he gets hooked to the ice he doesn't stay down, but jumps back to his skates and gets involved in the play again. He has excellent balance and quickness.

He cuts in on the off-wing and shoots in stride. He has a very good backhand shot and likes to cut out from behind the net and make things happen in tight. He mixes up his shots. He will fire quickly or drive in close and deke and wrist a little shot.

Bondra had never killed penalties until this season, and he ended up as the league's top shorthanded threat. He makes other teams' power plays jittery because of his anticipation and breakaway speed.

THE PHYSICAL GAME

Bondra isn't strong, but he will lean on people. He has improved his off-ice conditioning and handled a lot of ice time last season. He doesn't seem to tire. Bondra was much more determined in fighting through checks.

THE INTANGIBLES

Bondra looked like a new player last season. He still tends to be streaky, but his days as a 50-goal scorer (which general manager David Poile once predicted) may have finally arrived. The question is, can he sustain his play over a full season?

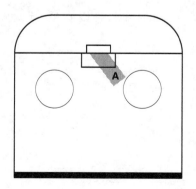

JIM CAREY

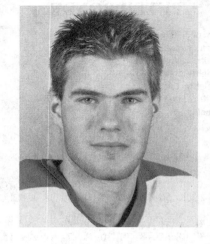

Yrs. of NHL service: 1
Born: Dorchester, Mass.; May 31, 1974
Position: goaltender
Height: 6-2
Weight: 190
Uniform no.: 30
Catches: left

Career statistics:

GP	MINS	G	SO	AVG	A	PIM
28	1604	57	0	2.13	0	0

1994-95 statistics:

GP	MINS	GAA	W	L	T	SO	GA	S	SAPCT	PIM
28	1604	2.13	18	6	3	4	57	654	.913	0

LAST SEASON

First NHL season. Finalist for 1995 Calder and Vezina Trophies. Third in NHL in GAA. Tied for third in NHL in shutouts.

THE PHYSICAL GAME

Carey has great fundamentals and makes goaltending look simple. After a remarkable stretch after his call-up from the AHL — a move that virtually saved the season for the Capitals — he made the game look easy simply by being in the right place and letting the puck hit him. He is similar to Vancouver's Kirk McLean in his economical style.

Carey makes the quality saves. He has an exceptional glove hand. He needs to learn to use his stick more to break up plays around the net, and since he has an aggressive nature, he should take to this part of the game readily.

THE MENTAL GAME

At times Carey gets "that look" in his eyes (one coach says that when he does, you can see clear through to the back of his head), and when he does, he gets erratic.

THE INTANGIBLES

The Caps asked a boy to do a man's job in the playoffs and Carey wasn't quite ready for it, but we don't think he's a one-season wonder. He's got the goods.

SYLVAIN COTE

Yrs. of NHL service: 10
Born: Quebec City, Que.; Jan. 19, 1966
Position: left defense
Height: 5-11
Weight: 185
Uniform no.: 3
Shoots: right

Career statistics:

GP	G	A	TP	PIM
668	84	168	252	331

1991-92 statistics:

GP	G	A	TP	+/-	PIM	PP	SH	GW	GT	S	PCT
78	11	29	40	+7	31	6	0	2	0	151	7.3

1992-93 statistics:

GP	G	A	TP	+/-	PIM	PP	SH	GW	GT	S	PCT
77	21	29	50	+28	34	8	2	3	0	206	10.2

1993-94 statistics:

GP	G	A	TP	+/-	PIM	PP	SH	GW	GT	S	PCT
84	16	35	51	+30	66	3	2	2	0	212	7.5

1994-95 statistics:

GP	G	A	TP	+/-	PIM	PP	SH	GW	GT	S	PCT
47	5	14	19	+2	53	1	0	2	0	124	4.0

LAST SEASON

Second among team defensemen in scoring. Missed one game with an eye laceration.

THE FINESSE GAME

Cote has matured into a solid two-way defenseman. He has good puckhandling skills and can make a pass to his forehand or backhand side with confidence. He overhandles the puck at times, especially in his defensive zone, and when he gets into trouble he seems to struggle with his forehand clearances off the left wing boards.

Cote can do everything in stride. Carrying the puck does not slow him down and he can rush end to end. He is gifted in all of the skating areas — fine agility, good balance, quick stops and starts. He likes to bring the puck up on the power play. He gets a lot on his shot from the point, which causes rebounds, and is the source of most of his assists.

His hockey sense has improved. He can lead a rush or come into the play as a trailer, but he knows enough not to force and to play more conservatively when the situation dictates.

He still needs to improve his defensive reads, but he is working hard at it and his skating helps cover up for most of his lapses. His instincts lag well behind his skill level. Cote can be beaten one-on-one, but it takes a good player to do it.

THE PHYSICAL GAME

Cote is the strength of the Washington defense. He doesn't have great size, but he is a solid hitter who finishes his checks. He isn't mean, however. He will occasionally fall into the trap of playing the puck in-

stead of the man.

THE INTANGIBLES

Cote is part of a strong defense corps in Washington, and when Mark Tinordi is healthy, he can be comfortably slotted into his ideal spot as the number three defenseman (behind Tinordi and Calle Johansson). This means Cote doesn't have to face the other team's top lines, and he can take advantage of his opportunities,

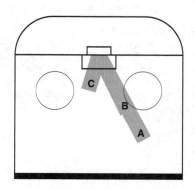

MIKE EAGLES

Yrs. of NHL service: 9
Born: Sussex, N.B.; Mar. 7, 1963
Position: centre
Height: 5-10
Weight: 180
Uniform no.: 36
Shoots: left

Career statistics:

GP	G	A	TP	PIM
600	62	103	165	730

1991-92 statistics:

GP	G	A	TP	+/-	PIM	PP	SH	GW	GT	S	PCT
65	7	10	17	-17	118	0	1	0	0	60	11.7

1992-93 statistics:

GP	G	A	TP	+/-	PIM	PP	SH	GW	GT	S	PCT
84	8	18	26	-1	131	1	0	1	0	67	11.9

1993-94 statistics:

GP	G	A	TP	+/-	PIM	PP	SH	GW	GT	S	PCT
73	4	8	12	-20	96	0	1	0	0	53	7.5

1994-95 statistics:

GP	G	A	TP	+/-	PIM	PP	SH	GW	GT	S	PCT
40	3	4	7	-11	48	0	0	0	0	28	10.7

LAST SEASON

Acquired from Winnipeg with Igor Ulanov for third- and fifth-round draft picks in 1995.

THE FINESSE GAME

Eagles is the prototypical defensive centre. He is on the puck in a hurry when fore-checking, creating turnovers and forcing bad passes. He has never had the touch to convert these chances into scoring attempts, but he can create chaos for the opponents.

Eagles always hustles and hits. If any points come, they are a bonus. He usually concentrates on shutting down the opposing centre on draws. He blocks shots and kills penalties. He can't match up against some of the league's power forwards, but he can keep up with the fleet ones.

THE PHYSICAL GAME

Eagles drives other players to distraction with his dogged pursuit, and he will get the stick up or give a facial massage with his glove. He's no angel.

THE INTANGIBLES

Eagles is a steady, veteran checker, and a coach knows just what he's getting in terms of effort every night. There is no truth to the rumour that the Caps obtained Eagles just because he matches their new sweater crest. (Is any other NHL player named for his team's logo?)

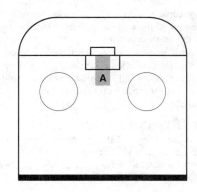

DALE HUNTER

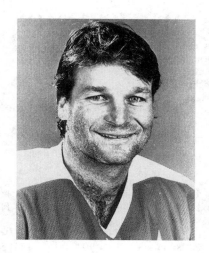

Yrs. of NHL service: 15
Born: Petrolia, Ont.; July 31, 1960
Position: centre
Height: 5-10
Weight: 198
Uniform no.: 32
Shoots: left

Career statistics:

GP	G	A	TP	PIM
1099	286	614	910	3106

1991-92 statistics:

GP	G	A	TP	+/-	PIM	PP	SH	GW	GT	S	PCT
80	28	50	78	-2	205	13	0	4	1	110	25.5

1992-93 statistics:

GP	G	A	TP	+/-	PIM	PP	SH	GW	GT	S	PCT
84	20	59	79	+3	198	10	0	2	0	120	16.7

1993-94 statistics:

GP	G	A	TP	+/-	PIM	PP	SH	GW	GT	S	PCT
52	9	29	38	-4	131	1	0	1	0	61	14.8

1994-95 statistics:

GP	G	A	TP	+/-	PIM	PP	SH	GW	GT	S	PCT
45	8	15	23	-4	101	3	0	1	0	73	11.0

LAST SEASON

Became second player in NHL history to record 900 points and 1,600 PIM for career, joining Gordie Howe. Second to Tiger Williams (3,966) on all-time PIM list. Reached 600-assist milestone. Missed three games with a knee injury.

THE FINESSE GAME

Hunter is canny, and he's a crafty player, especially down low. He doesn't skate well enough to be very effective in open ice, but when the Caps have control of the offensive zone, he digs in deep, setting screens and picks and driving to the net. He is not a big player, but he forces teams to pay attention with his effort.

Hunter is skilled on face-offs. He gets low to the ice, then moves forward and drives back the opposing centre. He never fails to bump his opposite number. He turns his body and grinds it out. And he works at buying time for his linemates by creating time and space with his puck control.

Hunter is a complete player. At this stage of his career he should have settled into a nice role-playing position. The Caps have needed him full-time over the past few seasons, but if they improve their strength up front, Hunter can be more effective by being spotted.

THE PHYSICAL GAME

Hunter knows only one way to play the game. He gets shots in, hits, harasses and does whatever it takes to win. This has been his hallmark from the first day he pulled on an NHL jersey. Look at the few great moments in the Capitals' history — notably their drive to the Stanley Cup semi-finals in 1990 — and Hunter has always been a key-player. The size of the oppo-

nent doesn't matter to him.

THE INTANGIBLES

Hunter still has a lot of heart and hockey left in him. If correctly used, he will be the player making the big plays down the stretch and in the playoffs. He hasn't mellowed one bit.

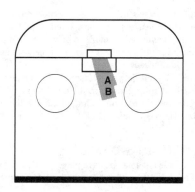

CALLE JOHANSSON

Yrs. of NHL service: 8
Born: Göteborg, Sweden; Feb. 14, 1967
Position: left defense
Height: 5-11
Weight: 205
Uniform no.: 6
Shoots: left

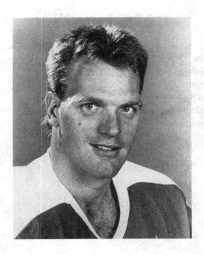

Career statistics:

GP	G	A	TP	PIM
567	61	267	328	321

1991-92 statistics:

GP	G	A	TP	+/-	PIM	PP	SH	GW	GT	S	PCT
80	14	42	56	+2	49	5	2	2	0	119	11.8

1992-93 statistics:

GP	G	A	TP	+/-	PIM	PP	SH	GW	GT	S	PCT
77	7	38	45	+3	56	6	0	0	1	133	5.3

1993-94 statistics:

GP	G	A	TP	+/-	PIM	PP	SH	GW	GT	S	PCT
84	9	33	42	+3	59	4	0	1	0	141	6.4

1994-95 statistics:

GP	G	A	TP	+/-	PIM	PP	SH	GW	GT	S	PCT
46	5	26	31	-6	35	4	0	2	0	112	4.5

LAST SEASON

Led team defensemen in scoring. Fourth on team in points. Missed two games with the flu.

THE FINESSE GAME

Johansson has tremendous legs, notably big, strong thighs that generate the power for his shot and his explosive skating. He makes every move look easy. He is agile, mobile and great at moving up-ice with the play. Speed, balance and strength allow him to chase a puck behind the net, pick it up without stopping and make an accurate pass. He is confident, even on the backhand, and likes to have the puck in key spots.

He is smart offensively. He moves the puck with a good first pass, then has enough speed and instinct to jump up and be ready for a return pass. He keeps the gap tight as the play enters the attacking zone, which opens up more options: he is available to the forwards if they need him for offense, and closer to the puck if it turns over.

Johansson has a low accurate shot that can be tipped. He is unselfish to a fault, often looking to pass when he should use his shot. He plays the right point on the power play, and feasts on one-timers set up for him by Joe Juneau.

He has good defensive instincts and reads plays well. His skating gives him the confidence (maybe overconfidence) to gamble and challenge the puck carrier. He has a quick stick for poke- and sweep-checks.

THE PHYSICAL GAME

Johansson is not an aggressive player, but he is strong and knows what he has to do with his body in the de-fensive zone. This part of the game has not come naturally, but Johansson has worked at it. He is still not an impact player defensively, although he wins his share of the one-on-one battles because he gets so much power from his legs.

THE INTANGIBLES

Johansson recovered well from a serious injury suffered in the 1994 playoffs, and had such a strong season that he was rewarded with a five-year, $5-million contract extension. Easily the team's best offensive defenseman, Johansson is an underrated asset.

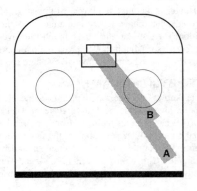

JIM JOHNSON

Yrs. of NHL service: 10
Born: New Hope, Minn.; Aug. 9, 1962
Position: right defense
Height: 6-1
Weight: 190
Uniform no.: 4
Shoots: left

Career statistics:

GP	G	A	TP	PIM
692	22	154	176	1071

1991-92 statistics:

GP	G	A	TP	+/-	PIM	PP	SH	GW	GT	S	PCT
71	4	10	14	+11	102	0	0	1	0	86	4.7

1992-93 statistics:

GP	G	A	TP	+/-	PIM	PP	SH	GW	GT	S	PCT
79	3	20	23	+9	105	1	0	0	0	67	4.5

1993-94 statistics:

GP	G	A	TP	+/-	PIM	PP	SH	GW	GT	S	PCT
61	0	7	7	-7	63	0	0	0	0	49	0.0

1994-95 statistics:

GP	G	A	TP	+/-	PIM	PP	SH	GW	GT	S	PCT
47	0	13	13	+6	43	0	0	0	0	46	0.0

THE INTANGIBLES

Johnson is an outstanding penalty killer and a reliable defenseman who gives you few highs but almost no lows.

LAST SEASON

Missed one game with an arm injury.

THE FINESSE GAME

Johnson plays a strong role as a defensive defenseman, killing penalties and getting the job done against the other team's top scoring lines night after night. He handles his duties with quiet success. He protects the puck well in the defensive zone and makes good outlet passes even when he is forced to his backhand.

Johnson uses his skating more in a defensive role now, positioning himself, getting in and out. He was a bit more offensively inclined in his first few years in the league, and he can still get involved in the attack. If a good play is to be made down deep, Johnson will take the chance, but he won't pinch or pressure unwisely. He has a good wrist shot and makes sure to play the safe play. If he does get caught, he can usually scramble back quickly to return to the play defensively.

His finesse skills are good enough that the Caps used him up front on occasion as a winger.

He blocks shots well and understands the game. He plays an aggressive game in terms of stepping up and forcing the attacker.

THE PHYSICAL GAME

Johnson is an average-size defenseman who picks his spots. He uses most of his weight and strength to control people, and for the most part he can control. He can make the occasional hard thump, but he doesn't go out of his way to try to knock opponents into the 12th row.

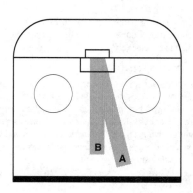

KEITH JONES

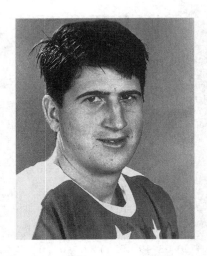

Yrs. of NHL service: 3
Born: Brantford, Ont.; Nov. 8, 1968
Position: right wing
Height: 6-2
Weight: 190
Uniform no.: 26
Shoots: right

Career statistics:

GP	G	A	TP	PIM
179	42	42	81	338

1992-93 statistics:

GP	G	A	TP	+/-	PIM	PP	SH	GW	GT	S	PCT
71	12	14	26	+18	124	0	0	3	0	73	16.4

1993-94 statistics:

GP	G	A	TP	+/-	PIM	PP	SH	GW	GT	S	PCT
68	16	19	35	+4	149	5	0	1	0	97	16.5

1994-95 statistics:

GP	G	A	TP	+/-	PIM	PP	SH	GW	GT	S	PCT
40	14	6	20	-2	65	1	0	4	0	85	16.5

LAST SEASON

Led team in game-winning goals. Missed eight games with a separated shoulder and a bruised foot.

THE FINESSE GAME

Jones is a spark plug. He likes to make things happen by driving to the front of the net and taking a defenseman with him. His skating is adequate, and he uses quick bursts of speed to power himself to and through the traffic areas.

He has decent hands, is an eager finisher and plays well at both ends of the ice. He keeps the game simple and does his job. He isn't very creative, but his efforts churn up loose pucks for teammates smart enough to trail in his wake.

THE PHYSICAL GAME

The Caps throw Jones on the ice whenever the team or the crowd needs a lift. He is energetic and uses his size well. He needs more experience, but is tough and willing to pay a physical price. The Caps could use another couple of players like him. He isn't the biggest player on the ice, but there are nights when you come away thinking he is.

Jones finishes every check in every zone, and sometimes runs around a bit, but he is becoming more responsible defensively.

THE INTANGIBLES

Jones was a scorer at Western Michigan and plays with grit and determination. He has a few rough edges to his game yet, but the Caps are in desperate need of his sandpaper qualities. He has a good future as a two-way winger who can get 15-20 goals a season and who will be a catalyst. He loves the game and knows what he has to do to stay in the lineup.

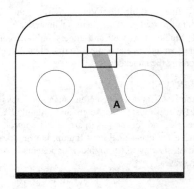

JOE JUNEAU

Yrs. of NHL service: 3
Born: Pont-Rouge, Que.; Jan. 5, 1968
Position: centre
Height: 6-0
Weight: 175
Uniform no.: 90
Shoots: right

Career statistics:

GP	G	A	TP	PIM
216	61	136	249	86

1991-92 statistics:

GP	G	A	TP	+/-	PIM	PP	SH	GW	GT	S	PCT
14	5	14	19	+6	4	2	0	0	0	38	13.2

1992-93 statistics:

GP	G	A	TP	+/-	PIM	PP	SH	GW	GT	S	PCT
84	32	70	102	+23	33	9	0	3	3	229	14.0

1993-94 statistics:

GP	G	A	TP	+/-	PIM	PP	SH	GW	GT	S	PCT
74	19	66	85	+11	41	6	0	2	1	164	11.6

1994-95 statistics:

GP	G	A	TP	+/-	PIM	PP	SH	GW	GT	S	PCT
44	5	38	43	-1	8	3	0	0	0	1	7.1

LAST SEASON

Led team in assists for second consecutive season. Second on team in points. Missed one game with a hip injury. Missed one game with a back injury.

THE FINESSE GAME

Juneau plays at centre, but he seems to gravitate to the left wing and generates most of his scoring chances from there. He varies his play selection. He will take the puck to the net on one rush, then pull up at the top of the circle and hit the trailer late on the next rush.

While the circles are his office, he is not exclusively a perimeter player. Juneau will go into traffic. He is bigger than he looks on the ice. His quick feet and light hands make him seem smaller, because he is so crafty with the puck.

Laterally, Juneau is among the best skaters in the NHL. He has an extra gear that allows him to pull away from people. He does not have breakaway speed, but he has great anticipation and gets the jump on a defender with his first few steps.

Juneau doesn't shoot the puck enough and gets a little intimidated when there is a scramble for a loose puck in front of the net. He is not always willing to sacrifice his body that way. He shoots a tad prematurely. When he could wait and have the goalie down and out, he unloads quickly, because he hears footsteps. His best shot is a one-timer from the left circle.

THE PHYSICAL GAME

Juneau has improved his toughness and willingness to take a hit to make a play, but he is still something of a featherweight. He skates in a hunched-over position, like a human letter "C", and a hit that would other-wise be clean catches him in the face. He plays with a huge protective shield that doesn't appear to get in his way too much unless the puck is right in his feet.

THE INTANGIBLES

Smart, smart, smart. Juneau is also a little moody and isn't the guy to lift a team if things are going poorly. If his team is on a roll, though, Juneau will ride the crest of the wave and pick up bushels of points.

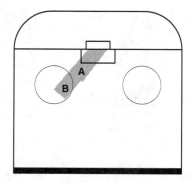

STEVE KONOWALCHUK

Yrs. of NHL service: 3
Born: Salt Lake City, Utah; Nov. 11, 1972
Position: centre
Height: 6-0
Weight: 180
Uniform no.: 22
Shoots: left

Career statistics:

GP	G	A	TP	PIM
145	27	35	62	93

1991-92 statistics:

GP	G	A	TP	+/-	PIM	PP	SH	GW	GT	S	PCT
1	0	0	0	0	0	0	0	0	0	1	0.0

1992-93 statistics:

GP	G	A	TP	+/-	PIM	PP	SH	GW	GT	S	PCT
36	4	7	11	+4	16	1	0	1	0	34	11.8

1993-94 statistics:

GP	G	A	TP	+/-	PIM	PP	SH	GW	GT	S	PCT
62	12	14	26	+9	33	0	0	0	0	63	19.0

1994-95 statistics:

GP	G	A	TP	+/-	PIM	PP	SH	GW	GT	S	PCT
46	11	14	25	+7	44	3	3	3	0	88	12.5

LAST SEASON

Tied career high in assists. Missed penalty shot attempt. Scored first career shorthanded goal.

THE FINESSE GAME

Maybe the Capitals won't miss the retired Dave Poulin so much now that they have his protege. Konowalchuk is just the kind of player coach Jim Schoenfeld loves. He's a digger who has to work hard for his goals, and an intelligent and earnest player who uses every ounce of energy on every shift.

Konowalchuk is so reliable defensively that if the Caps are killing off a 3-on-5 penalty, he will be the forward sent out for the draw. He ties up the opposing centre if he doesn't win the puck drop outright. He uses his feet along the boards as well as his stick.

There is nothing fancy about his offense. He just lets his shot rip and drives to the net. He doesn't have the moves and hand skills to beat a defender one-on-one, but he doesn't care. He'll go right through him.

THE PHYSICAL GAME

Konowalchuk is very strong. He has some snot in him, too, and will aggravate opponents with his constant effort. He doesn't take bad penalties, but often goads rivals into retaliating. He is very fit and can handle a lot of ice time.

THE INTANGIBLES

What's not to like? Good character, good work ethic, good effort. His numbers won't ever be fancy, but neither is his play.

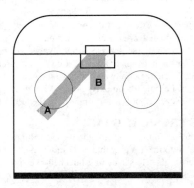

KELLY MILLER

Yrs. of NHL service: 10
Born: Lansing, Mich.; Mar. 3, 1963
Position: left wing/right wing
Height: 5-11
Weight: 196
Uniform no.: 10
Shoots: left

Career statistics:

GP	G	A	TP	PIM
768	155	243	398	379

1991-92 statistics:

GP	G	A	TP	+/-	PIM	PP	SH	GW	GT	S	PCT
78	14	38	52	+20	49	0	1	3	0	144	9.7

1992-93 statistics:

GP	G	A	TP	+/-	PIM	PP	SH	GW	GT	S	PCT
84	18	27	45	-2	32	3	0	3	0	144	12.5

1993-94 statistics:

GP	G	A	TP	+/-	PIM	PP	SH	GW	GT	S	PCT
84	14	25	39	+8	32	0	1	3	0	138	10.1

1994-95 statistics:

GP	G	A	TP	+/-	PIM	PP	SH	GW	GT	S	PCT
48	10	13	23	+5	6	2	0	1	0	70	14.3

LAST SEASON

One of three Capitals to appear in all 48 games. In eight full seasons with Caps, has missed only four of 616 games.

THE FINESSE GAME

If a team doesn't have complete control of the puck in the zone, Miller will come in hard. If they have control, he backs off to the neutral zone. He's smart enough to know the difference, instead of plunging in with a wild fore-check and expending useless energy. Miller may be the best defensive winger in the game.

Miller has never produced the kind of offensive numbers that his skills indicate he could. He has the skating ability, hockey sense and hands to score maybe 30 goals, but he'll never do it because he's always thinking defense. Miller drives to the net on occasion and has a quick release on his shot.

Defensively, there is no weak part to Miller's game. A complete player, he is always in motion. He creates a lot of scoring chances from turnovers. He reads plays when he fore-checks, and either goes to the net or finds a teammate in front with a good short pass. He is one of the best penalty killers around.

THE PHYSICAL GAME

Miller is not very big, but he is strong and durable. His stamina allows him to fore-check hard all night, and he drives opponents batty because he is always on them. There is never a moment's peace when Miller is on the ice.

THE INTANGIBLES

Miller has great work habits, every night. His commit-

ment to the game is remarkable. How he gets overlooked year after year for Selke Trophy consideration confounds us.

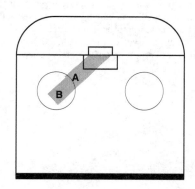

PAT PEAKE

Yrs. of NHL service: 2
Born: Rochester, Mich.; May 28, 1973
Position: centre
Height: 6-0
Weight: 195
Uniform no.: 14
Shoots: right

Career statistics:

GP	G	A	TP	PIM
67	11	22	33	51

1993-94 statistics:

GP	G	A	TP	+/-	PIM	PP	SH	GW	GT	S	PCT
49	11	18	29	+1	39	3	0	1	1	91	12.1

1994-95 statistics:

GP	G	A	TP	+/-	PIM	PP	SH	GW	GT	S	PCT
18	0	4	4	-6	12	0	0	0	0	30	0.0

LAST SEASON

Second NHL season.

THE FINESSE GAME

Peake is among the class of '91. One of the best drafts in ages, it has already produced NHLers Eric Lindros, Pat Falloon, Scott Niedermayer, Scott Lachance and Peter Forsberg.

Although he won't be one of the luminaries of the group, Peake is maturing into a decent prospect. He is an excellent skater with agility and good lateral movement. He has flashed the talent to dominate games. He also has polished playmaking skills and can pass equally well to either side.

Peake has a hard shot and loves to score. He has good hockey vision and creativity.

THE PHYSICAL GAME

Peake is a finesse player who is competitive, but he will have to learn to pay the physical price necessary in the NHL. That is one of the toughest adjustments for any player coming out of junior. He won't have as much time or room to shoot, and he will have to fight for what he wants.

THE INTANGIBLES

Injuries have slowed Peake's development. Last year he was afflicted by mononucleosis, an illness that wasn't diagnosed until he had struggled to play his way through the worst of it. He should get another opportunity to prove himself in training camp.

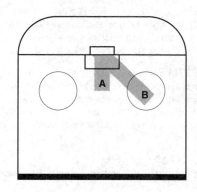

MICHAL PIVONKA

Yrs. of NHL service: 9
Born: Kladno, Czechoslovakia; Jan. 28, 1966
Position: centre/left wing
Height: 6-1
Weight: 198
Uniform no.: 20
Shoots: left

Career statistics:

GP	G	A	TP	PIM
629	170	325	495	388

1991-92 statistics:

GP	G	A	TP	+/-	PIM	PP	SH	GW	GT	S	PCT
80	23	57	80	+10	47	7	4	2	1	177	13.0

1992-93 statistics:

GP	G	A	TP	+/-	PIM	PP	SH	GW	GT	S	PCT
69	21	53	74	+14	66	6	1	5	0	147	14.3

1993-94 statistics:

GP	G	A	TP	+/-	PIM	PP	SH	GW	GT	S	PCT
82	14	36	50	+2	38	5	0	4	0	138	10.1

1994-95 statistics:

GP	G	A	TP	+/-	PIM	PP	SH	GW	GT	S	PCT
46	10	23	33	+3	50	4	2	2	0	80	12.5

LAST SEASON

Third on team in assists and points. Will miss the first three games of the season with a suspension as the result of a playoff incident.

THE FINESSE GAME

Far too streaky a player for someone with his talents, Pivonka gets into funks and gets down on himself, and when that happens he is useless because he doesn't even do the little things well. A reliable player will contribute in any way he can when his scoring touch temporarily deserts him — Pivonka just chucks it.

Pivonka has marvellous skills. On the power play and in four-on-four situations, he takes full advantage of the extra ice. He skates well, with quickness and breakaway speed. He moves the puck quickly and jumps into the play for a give-and-go. His acceleration is outstanding.

He shoots well in stride (a trait of many Europeans), but he is too shy about shooting, usually looking to make the pass first. His stick is always on the ice. It's a small detail, but it allows him to pick up pucks that bounce off other players' sticks or skates.

Pivonka makes a lot of little dekes in tight, forcing a goalie to move his feet, and then he finds the opening.

THE PHYSICAL GAME

On any given night, Pivonka can play a forceful game, hitting and taking hits. Other nights he will be AWOL. It is a frustrating trait because Pivonka has the size and strength to be an on-ice leader, yet he has no consistency.

THE INTANGIBLES

Pivonka essentially became the team's number one centre as he played most of the season with Peter Bondra. The responsibility brought out the best in him. If he (and his linemate) can sustain their production over a full season, Pivonka could score in the 80-point range.

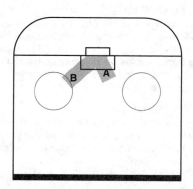

JOE REEKIE

Yrs. of NHL service: 9
Born: Victoria, B.C.; Feb. 22, 1965
Position: left defense
Height: 6-3
Weight: 215
Uniform no.: 29
Shoots: left

Career statistics:

GP	G	A	TP	PIM
430	15	84	99	736

1991-92 statistics:

GP	G	A	TP	+/-	PIM	PP	SH	GW	GT	S	PCT
54	4	12	16	+15	85	0	0	0	1	59	6.8

1992-93 statistics:

GP	G	A	TP	+/-	PIM	PP	SH	GW	GT	S	PCT
42	2	11	13	+2	69	0	0	0	0	53	3.8

1993-94 statistics:

GP	G	A	TP	+/-	PIM	PP	SH	GW	GT	S	PCT
85	1	16	17	+15	156	0	0	0	0	98	1.0

1994-95 statistics:

GP	G	A	TP	+/-	PIM	PP	SH	GW	GT	S	PCT
48	1	6	7	+10	97	0	0	0	0	52	1.9

LAST SEASON

Led team in plus-minus. One of three Caps to appear in all 48 games.

THE FINESSE GAME

Early in his career, Reekie had impressive enough finesse skills that he was tried out as a forward. Knee surgery put an end to that experiment while he was still in the Buffalo system, and he became a dedicated defensive defenseman.

Reekie has an unusual skating style, with a choppy stride, but he is light on his feet for a big man. He has good anticipation, which allows him to gain a step here and there. He will move the puck well out of his own end with a pass, but won't lug it unless he has to.

Reekie seldom cheats in deep, instead sticking to the blueline. He does not see much, if any, power play time, because he doesn't have much zip on his shot. He is a mainstay on the penalty killing unit.

THE PHYSICAL GAME

Reekie has good size and strength, but his restricted range compromises his ability to be an impact hitter. He can play mean, especially in front of the net, and is strong along the boards and in the corners. Because he is slow-footed, he tries to get away with a lot of restraining fouls, but often gets caught.

THE INTANGIBLES

Reekie is a steady, workmanlike defenseman who is an ideal number five. As long as he not asked to do too much, he can be a very useful defenseman in a limited role.

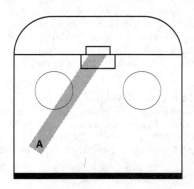

MARK TINORDI

Yrs. of NHL service: 7
Born: Deer River, Alta.; May 9, 1966
Position: left defense
Height: 6-4
Weight: 205
Uniform no.: 24
Shoots: left

Career statistics:

GP	G	A	TP	PIM
441	39	117	156	1136

1991-92 statistics:

GP	G	A	TP	+/-	PIM	PP	SH	GW	GT	S	PCT
63	4	24	28	-13	177	4	0	0	0	93	4.3

1992-93 statistics:

GP	G	A	TP	+/-	PIM	PP	SH	GW	GT	S	PCT
69	15	27	42	-1	157	7	0	2	0	122	12.3

1993-94 statistics:

GP	G	A	TP	+/-	PIM	PP	SH	GW	GT	S	PCT
61	6	18	24	+6	143	1	0	0	0	112	5.4

1994-95 statistics:

GP	G	A	TP	+/-	PIM	PP	SH	GW	GT	S	PCT
42	3	9	12	-5	71	2	0	1	0	71	4.2

LAST SEASON

Acquired from Dallas with Rick Mrozik for Kevin Hatcher. Missed six games with bruised ribs and a sprained knee.

THE FINESSE GAME

Tinordi can play both sides and with any partner. He can be the point man on the power play and he can kill penalties. You can use him in the first minute and in the last minute, when you're trying to protect a lead.

Tinordi doesn't have much in the way of finesse skills, but oh, how he loves to go to the net. He starts out at the point on the power play but doesn't hesitate to crash down low. He is an impact player and a major force on the ice.

He is becoming more effective offensively. He has a big-time point shot, low, hard and accurate, and he also sees the play well and moves his passes crisply. He intimidates when he moves low and bulls his way to the net. He is poised with the puck and will use a wrist shot in deep.

An above-average skater, Tinordi is mobile for his large size. He lacks one-step quickness, but once in gear he has a long stride with good balance and mobility. He can use his long reach well around the net or to take the puck away from a defender. He is a strong penalty killer with good hockey sense.

THE PHYSICAL GAME

Tinordi plays with the throttle wide open and doesn't recognize any other playing style. One of the reasons why he is so susceptible to getting hurt is that he is more concerned with making the play than with protecting himself, and he ends up in vulnerable situa-

tions. A little less reckless abandon would help keep him in one piece, but we're not sure if Tinordi knows how to play that way.

As honest and tough as they come, Tinordi commands respect on the ice. He has too short a fuse, though in recent years he has done a better job of curbing his temper, realizing he is more important to his team on the ice than in the penalty box. He is competitive and fearless.

THE INTANGIBLES

Tinordi has now suffered three season-ending injuries that prevented him from being a factor in the playoffs. His fragility has to be a concern.

It's still tough to gauge this blue-collar Scott Stevens. Tinordi could score 25 goals and have a great season, or 15 and still have a great season, or five and still have a great season. He's that useful in that many ways. He is a crunch-time player. Too bad he's the one who so often ends up crunched.

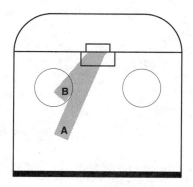

WINNIPEG JETS

Players' Statistics 1994-95

POS	NO.	PLAYER	GP	G	A	PTS	+/-	PIM	PP	SH	GW	GT	S	PCTG
C	10	ALEXEI ZHAMNOV	48	30	35	65	5	20	9		4		155	19.4
L	7	KEITH TKACHUK	48	22	29	51	-4	152	7	2	2	1	129	17.1
R	8	TEEMU SELANNE	45	22	26	48	1	2	8	2	1	1	167	13.2
R	19	NELSON EMERSON	48	14	23	37	-12	26	4	1	1		122	11.5
R	23	IGOR KOROLEV	45	8	22	30	1	10	1		1		85	9.4
C	18	DALLAS DRAKE	43	8	18	26	-6	30			1		66	12.1
D	4	STEPHANE QUINTAL	43	6	17	23		78	3		2		107	5.6
D	27	TEPPO NUMMINEN	42	5	16	21	12	16	2				86	5.8
C	32	MIKE EASTWOOD	49	8	11	19	-9	36					55	14.5
D	3	DAVE MANSON	44	3	15	18	-20	139	2		1		104	2.9
C	25	THOMAS STEEN	31	5	10	15	-13	14	2				32	15.6
D	24	DARRYL SHANNON	40	5	9	14	1	48		1			42	11.9
C	16	ED OLCZYK	33	4	9	13	-1	12	2				56	7.1
C	15	RANDY GILHEN	44	5	6	11	-17	52		1	1		47	10.6
L	34	DARRIN SHANNON	19	5	3	8	-6	14	3		1		26	19.2
L	17	KRIS KING	48	4	2	6		85					58	6.9
D	2	NEIL WILKINSON	40	1	4	5	-26	75					25	4.0
L	75	*MICHAL GROSEK	24	2	2	4	-3	21			1		27	7.4
D	36	GREG BROWN	9		3	3	1	17					12	
C	12	ROB MURRAY	10		2	2	1	2					5	
D	42	OLEG MIKULCHIK	25		2	2	10	12					5	
R	28	*CRAIG MARTIN	20		1	1	-4	19					3	
G	35	*N. KHABIBULIN	26		1	1		4						
G	29	TIM CHEVELDAE	30		1	1		2						
C	47	*TAVIS HANSEN	1											
R	37	JOHN LEBLANC	2											
C	38	LUCIANO BORSATO	4				-1						2	
L	21	RUSS ROMANIUK	6				-3						3	
D	22	BRENT THOMPSON	29				-17	78					16	

GP = games played; G = goals; A = assists; PTS = points; +/- = goals-for minus goals-against while player is on ice; PIM = penalties in minutes; PP = power play goals; SH = shorthanded goals; GW = game-winning goals; GT = game-tying goals; S = no. of shots; PCTG = percentage of goals to shots; * = rookie

TIM CHEVELDAE

Yrs. of NHL service: 5
Born: Melville, Sask.; Feb. 15, 1968
Position: goaltender
Height: 5-11
Weight: 180
Uniform no.: 29
Catches: left

Career statistics:

GP	MINS	GA	SO	GAA	A	PIM
308	17384	1000	10	3.45	16	18

1991-92 statistics:

GP	MINS	GAA	W	L	T	SO	GA	S	SAPCT	PIM
72	4236	3.20	38	23	9	2	226	1978	.886	6

1992-93 statistics:

GP	MINS	GAA	W	L	T	SO	GA	S	SAPCT	PIM
67	3880	3.25	34	24	7	4	210	1897	.889	4

1993-94 statistics:

GP	MINS	GAA	W	L	T	SO	GA	S	SAPCT	PIM
44	2360	3.64	21	17	2	2	143	1212	.882	2

1994-95 statistics:

GP	MINS	GAA	W	L	T	SO	GA	S	SAPCT	PIM
30	1571	3.70	8	16	3	0	97	818	.881	2

LAST SEASON

Fewest wins since rookie season. Stopped Dave Andreychuk on penalty shot.

THE PHYSICAL GAME

Cheveldae doesn't rely on his reflexes — a darned good thing, because he's a pretty slow mover (with the exception of his fairly sharp glove hand). He is a strict angle player who is out at the top of his crease and very aggressive. He doesn't like any wasted motion, which is why he's been able to be one of the league's real workhorses without showing any stress and strain physically.

An average skater at best with limited lateral movement, the key to beating him is to go east-west from dot-to-dot to get him moving from side to side. He allows few soft goals, so the trick is to get him in motion. When he is able to keep his feet, he is so good technically he takes away a huge portion of the net.

Cheveldae is an average to below-average puck-handler, an area where he needs to show improvement, as that skill has become more important to modern goalies. He stops hard-arounds well but prefers to leave the puck for a teammate rather than move it.

He skates boldly out of his net to stickhandle pucks away from charging opponents, but he often seems to have missed communications with his defensive partners on how to handle the puck.

THE MENTAL GAME

Cheveldae is a bounce-back goalie who can shake off a bad goal, period or game and suffer few lingering effects. He is composed — it shows in his physical carriage — and that has a comforting effect on his teammates. Even when facing a barrage, Cheveldae gives the illusion he is in control, not under siege.

THE INTANGIBLES

Cheveldae split his playing time with Russian rookie Nikolai Khabibulin, but the Jets weren't thrilled with his play and will be shopping for a goalie during the off-season. It's unfair to blame Cheveldae for the team's failure to make the playoffs. He didn't have much defense in front of him, and the team had to play the final quarter of the season with the distraction of the possible sale and move of the team.

DALLAS DRAKE

Yrs. of NHL service: 3
Born: Trail, B.C.; Feb. 4, 1969
Position: centre
Height: 6-0
Weight: 170
Uniform no.: 18
Shoots: left

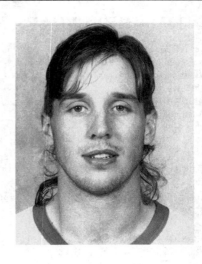

Career statistics:

GP	G	A	TP	PIM
177	39	71	110	172

1992-93 statistics:

GP	G	A	TP	+/-	PIM	PP	SH	GW	GT	S	PCT
72	18	26	44	+15	93	3	2	5	0	89	20.2

1993-94 statistics:

GP	G	A	TP	+/-	PIM	PP	SH	GW	GT	S	PCT
62	13	27	40	-1	49	1	2	3	0	112	11.6

1994-95 statistics:

GP	G	A	TP	+/-	PIM	PP	SH	GW	GT	S	PCT
43	8	18	26	-6	30	0	0	1	0	66	12.1

LAST SEASON

Missed three games with a back injury.

THE FINESSE GAME

Drake has the makings of a solid two-way centre. He is an aggressive fore-checker who is strong along the boards and in front of the net. He's on the small side, so he doesn't stand in and take a bashing, but he'll jump in and out of traffic to fight for the puck or bounce on rebounds.

He is very aware defensively and was named the WCHA's Defensive Player of the Year at Northern Michigan in 1991-92, after leading the league in goals. He isn't very good on draws, but he is aces as a playmaker. He made something of a reputation as a scorer but is better at setting up his wingers.

Drake is quick and powerful in his skating. He'll get outmuscled, but not outhustled. His scoring chances will come in deep.

THE PHYSICAL GAME

Drake gets noticed because he runs right over people. He is limited by his size, but he will give a team whatever he's got. He's feisty enough to get the other team's attention, and he works to keep himself in scoring position.

Good things invariably happen when Drake takes the body. He is a strong penalty killer and fore-checker.

THE INTANGIBLES

Drake's grit and determination set him apart from some finesse players who might take too many nights off. He will earn a regular shift and should be capable of 20 goals once he gets regular ice time.

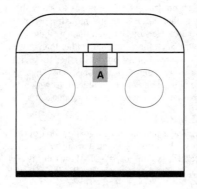

MIKE EASTWOOD

Yrs. of NHL service: 3
Born: Ottawa, Ont.; July 1, 1967
Position: centre
Height: 6-2
Weight: 190
Uniform no.: 32
Shoots: right

Career statistics:

GP	G	A	TP	PIM
124	17	29	46	89

1991-92 statistics:

GP	G	A	TP	+/-	PIM	PP	SH	GW	GT	S	PCT
9	0	2	2	-4	4	0	0	0	0	6	0.0

1992-93 statistics:

GP	G	A	TP	+/-	PIM	PP	SH	GW	GT	S	PCT
12	1	6	7	-2	21	0	0	0	0	11	9.1

1993-94 statistics:

GP	G	A	TP	+/-	PIM	PP	SH	GW	GT	S	PCT
54	8	10	18	+2	28	1	0	2	0	41	19.5

1994-95 statistics:

GP	G	A	TP	+/-	PIM	PP	SH	GW	GT	S	PCT
49	8	11	19	-9	36	0	0	0	0	55	14.5

LAST SEASON

Acquired from Toronto with third-round pick in 1995 for Tie Domi. One of three NHL players to appear in 49 games.

THE FINESSE GAME

With a little more spunk, Eastwood could be a strong third-line centre. His problem is a lack of consistency. He is a big, strong player that coaches always want to get more out of. He has some sparkling games but lacks the confidence and offensive contribution to become an effective everyday player, though Winnipeg gave him some time on their number two line as a right wing with Keith Tkachuk.

Eastwood is sound defensively. He is good on draws and is alert and aware.

Deceptively quick as a skater, he doesn't always want to push himself hard and needs to be urged along by coaches. He kills penalties well.

THE PHYSICAL GAME

Eastwood is strong and doesn't get knocked off the puck, but he doesn't have much presence on the ice and could initiate more contact.

He has to work on his conditioning and off-ice strengthening.

THE INTANGIBLES

The next step is to wring more offense out of Eastwood. If he can bump his numbers up into the 15-goal range, he could become a regular. He has to make a decision and grab a position, otherwise he will be a part-timer.

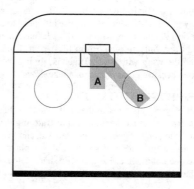

NELSON EMERSON

Yrs. of NHL service: 4
Born: Hamilton, Ont.; Aug. 17, 1967
Position: centre/left wing
Height: 5-11
Weight: 165
Uniform no.: 19
Shoots: right

Career statistics:

GP	G	A	TP	PIM
296	92	154	246	236

1991-92 statistics:

GP	G	A	TP	+/-	PIM	PP	SH	GW	GT	S	PCT
79	23	36	59	-5	66	3	0	2	0	143	16.1

1992-93 statistics:

GP	G	A	TP	+/-	PIM	PP	SH	GW	GT	S	PCT
82	22	51	73	+2	62	5	2	4	0	196	11.2

1993-94 statistics:

GP	G	A	TP	+/-	PIM	PP	SH	GW	GT	S	PCT
83	33	41	74	-38	80	4	5	6	1	282	11.7

1994-95 statistics:

GP	G	A	TP	+/-	PIM	PP	SH	GW	GT	S	PCT
48	14	23	37	-12	26	4	1	1	0	122	11.5

LAST SEASON

Fourth on team in points. One of five Jets to appear in all 48 games. Scored his first career hat trick.

THE FINESSE GAME

On the power play, Emerson can play either point or work down low. He has an excellent point shot, keeping it low, on target and tippable. He is intelligent with the puck and doesn't always fire from the point, but works it to the middle of the blueline and uses screens well. When he carries in one-on-one against a defender, especially on a shorthanded rush, he always manages to use the defenseman to screen the goalie.

Emerson works well down low at even strength. He is mature and creative, with a terrific short game. He has quick hands for passing or snapping off a shot. He likes to work from behind the net, tempting the defense to chase him behind the cage. Speed and puck control are the essence of his game.

He has nice quickness and balance, and he darts in and out of traffic in front of the net. He's too small to do any physical damage. He can use his speed to drive wide on a defenseman, who will think he has Emerson angled off, only to watch him blast past. Emerson played the wing with Keith Tkachuk, giving the Jets an edge because either player can take draws.

THE PHYSICAL GAME

Small players can excel in the NHL, as Theo Fleury, Mark Recchi and Emerson demonstrate night after night. Emerson has good skating balance, and that will give him a little edge to knock a bigger player off-stride once in a while. He will work hard defensively but has to play a smart, small man's game to avoid getting pasted.

THE INTANGIBLES

Emerson will never be a star, but he will rack up 70-80 points a season and will give the Jets a strong second line once their big guns are healthy. He is a top-notch, two-way forward.

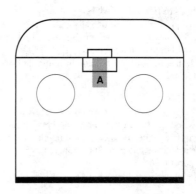

MICHAL GROSEK

Yrs. of NHL service: 1
Born: Vyskov, Czechoslovkia; June 1, 1975
Position: left wing
Height: 6-2
Weight: 180
Uniform no.: 75
Shoots: right

Career statistics:

GP	G	A	TP	PIM
27	3	2	5	21

1993-94 statistics:

GP	G	A	TP	+/-	PIM	PP	SH	GW	GT	S	PCT
3	1	0	1	-1	0	0	0	0	0	4	0.0

1994-95 statistics:

GP	G	A	TP	+/-	PIM	PP	SH	GW	GT	S	PCT
24	2	2	4	-3	21	0	0	1	0	27	7.4

LAST SEASON

First NHL season. Missed 24 games with a fractured foot and a separated shoulder.

THE FINESSE GAME

Grosek is a bundle of talent whose first shot at an NHL job was derailed by two serious injuries. He uses his speed and size to create some room, and is genuinely tough.

He is still very young and has an eagerness to succeed at the NHL level. He is an excellent stickhandler, good enough to play his off (left) wing as well as the right. He doesn't have a great shot, but he intimidates with his speed and drives to the net. With more confidence, his release may improve.

Defensively, Grosek's game needs help.

THE PHYSICAL GAME

Grosek has a wild streak and thinks he's a physical player. Instead of using his speed to make things happen, he will start running around looking for people to hit. He will learn to pick his spots.

THE INTANGIBLES

This upcoming season should be counted as Grosek's true rookie season. He is still only 20 years old and has a lot of potential. He is a sleeper, but should get a shot because the Jets want more size on the wings.

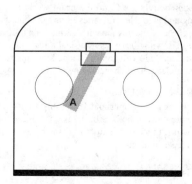

KRIS KING

Yrs. of NHL service: 7
Born: Bracebridge, Ont.; Feb. 18, 1966
Position: left wing
Height: 5-11
Weight: 210
Uniform no.: 17
Shoots: left

Career statistics:

GP	G	A	TP	PIM
486	46	54	100	1329

1991-92 statistics:

GP	G	A	TP	+/-	PIM	PP	SH	GW	GT	S	PCT
79	10	9	19	+13	224	0	0	2	0	97	10.3

1992-93 statistics:

GP	G	A	TP	+/-	PIM	PP	SH	GW	GT	S	PCT
78	8	11	19	+4	203	0	0	1	0	74	10.8

1993-94 statistics:

GP	G	A	TP	+/-	PIM	PP	SH	GW	GT	S	PCT
83	4	8	12	-22	205	0	0	1	0	86	4.7

1994-95 statistics:

GP	G	A	TP	+/-	PIM	PP	SH	GW	GT	S	PCT
48	4	2	6	0	85	0	0	0	0	58	6.9

LAST SEASON

One of five Jets to appear in all 48 games.

THE FINESSE GAME

King is a checking winger, a role that can wear on a player night after night, but he brings enthusiasm and hustle to every shift. He has to play that way to stay in the NHL, because he doesn't have much in the way of skills. He will generate some scoring chances with his speed but can't do much with the puck at tempo. He's more intent on chasing the puck carrier. He will create turnovers but doesn't do much with the puck when he gets it. Most of his scoring chances will be garbage goals off the scrums in front from his hard work.

A superb crunch-time player, whether protecting a lead or needing a big play in overtime, he'll do his utmost to deliver. He is a gamer.

THE PHYSICAL GAME

King is strictly peasant stock on a team of aristocrats. But somebody's got to do the grunt work, and he's willing and able. He's relentless along the boards and in the corners, and anyone who has his back to King or his head down will pay the physical price. King takes no prisoners. He will fight if needed, but his reputation as a clean, hard checker is no secret.

THE INTANGIBLES

King brings sandpaper and leadership to a team in desperate need of both. Still, he is a third-line player who will find ice time harder to come by as the team gets deeper in talent.

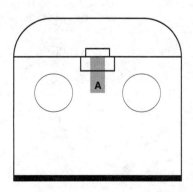

IGOR KOROLEV

Yrs. of NHL service: 3
Born: Moscow, Russia; Sept. 6, 1970
Position: right wing
Height: 6-1
Weight: 187
Uniform no.: 23
Shoots: left

Career statistics:

GP	G	A	TP	PIM
192	18	55	73	70

1992-93 statistics:

GP	G	A	TP	+/-	PIM	PP	SH	GW	GT	S	PCT
74	4	23	27	-1	20	2	0	0	0	76	5.3

1993-94 statistics:

GP	G	A	TP	+/-	PIM	PP	SH	GW	GT	S	PCT
73	6	10	16	-12	40	0	0	1	0	93	6.5

1994-95 statistics:

GP	G	A	TP	+/-	PIM	PP	SH	GW	GT	S	PCT
45	8	22	30	+1	10	1	0	1	0	85	9.4

LAST SEASON
Acquired from St. Louis in waiver draft.

THE FINESSE GAME
Korolev improved his play after adjusting to the move from St. Louis. He frequently found himself playing on the top line with Alexei Zhamnov (one of the game's most underrated players) and Teemu Selanne. With the attention focused on Selanne, he often had room on the left side. Korolev likes to trail the play, following up the speed of his linemates. He gets open and gets his chances.

Unfortunately, Korolev doesn't have a great shot. He is either so unaccustomed to handling the responsibility of scoring (he was an afterthought with the Blues), or he just doesn't have the instinct. He's a good one-on-one player.

Korolev is a very good skater. He doesn't have exceptional speed, but he's quick and balanced. He lacks consistency.

THE PHYSICAL GAME
Korolev is solidly built to take hits. He doesn't initiate, but checkers often bounce off him because he is sturdy.

THE INTANGIBLES
Korolev played with Zhamnov in Russia, and the Jets obviously hoped the old magic would immediately return when they were united. It took 10 or 12 games, but even when they started clicking, it wasn't exactly magic. Perhaps if Korolev comes into camp with the idea that the team will be relying on him in an important role, he will be better prepared.

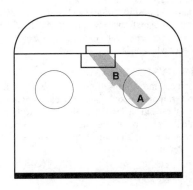

DAVE MANSON

Yrs. of NHL service: 9
Born: Prince Albert, Sask.; Jan. 27, 1967
Position: left defense
Height: 6-2
Weight: 202
Uniform no.: 3
Shoots: left

Career statistics:

GP	G	A	TP	PIM
606	76	182	258	1937

1991-92 statistics:

GP	G	A	TP	+/-	PIM	PP	SH	GW	GT	S	PCT
79	15	32	47	+9	220	7	0	2	0	206	7.3

1992-93 statistics:

GP	G	A	TP	+/-	PIM	PP	SH	GW	GT	S	PCT
83	15	30	45	-28	210	9	1	1	1	244	6.1

1993-94 statistics:

GP	G	A	TP	+/-	PIM	PP	SH	GW	GT	S	PCT
70	4	17	21	-14	191	1	0	0	0	180	2.2

1994-95 statistics:

GP	G	A	TP	+/-	PIM	PP	SH	GW	GT	S	PCT
44	3	15	18	-20	139	2	0	1	0	104	2.9

LAST SEASON

Second on team in PIM. Missed one game with a bruised kidney.

THE FINESSE GAME

Defensively, Manson could be ranked among the top rearguards in the league. He has all of the physical tools to be there, but he's his own worst enemy. He needs more maturity and patience. He will often leave his position to support his defense partner, even when his partner has things under control and doesn't need the help. This simply results in a hole on the left side of the ice.

Manson's best scoring weapon is a one-timer from the point. He is smart and effective on the power play, because he will mix up his shot with a big fake and freeze. But there isn't much that's subtle about Manson. His game is power.

A very good skater for a big player, he jumps into the play eagerly (sometimes too eagerly — he will get caught out of position up-ice) and can make a 360 degree turn in a small space with the puck. He will gamble down deep and is canny enough to use an accurate wrist shot when he is in close.

THE PHYSICAL GAME

Manson can throw himself off his game. He will lose control, run after people and take bad penalties. He patrols the front of his net well, can hit to hurt and intimidates players into getting rid of the puck faster than they want to. They flinch from even the threat of a Manson bodycheck.

THE INTANGIBLES

Manson knows his shortcomings and wants to be a better player. Offensively, though, it's unlikely he will score more than 30-40 points. He is a key part of a Winnipeg team that is trying to get tougher, and he should fit right in.

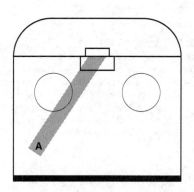

OLEG MIKULCHIK

Yrs. of NHL service: 1
Born: Minsk, USSR; June 27, 1964
Position: right defense
Height: 6-2
Weight: 200
Uniform no.: 42
Shoots: right

Career statistics:

GP	G	A	TP	PIM
29	0	3	3	29

1993-94 statistics:

GP	G	A	TP	+/-	PIM	PP	SH	GW	GT	S	PCT
4	0	1	1	-2	17	0	0	0	0	3	0.0

1994-95 statistics:

GP	G	A	TP	+/-	PIM	PP	SH	GW	GT	S	PCT
25	0	2	2	+10	12	0	0	0	0	5	0.0

LAST SEASON

First NHL season. Second on team in plus/minus. Spent part of season with Springfield (AHL), scoring 5-6 — 21 in 50 games with 59 PIM. Missed three games with a fractured toe.

THE FINESSE GAME

Mikulchik is an older "rookie." He is a mid-size defenseman who takes the body well enough and gets in the way.

He is a good passer and has quick feet. He was acquired (as a free agent) to help out the farm team, but has clawed his way up the depth chart. He has good hockey sense and can play on both special teams. He won't get a lot of points, but uses his finesse skills defensively to move the puck out of his zone quickly. The Jets forwards love playing with him, because he is one of the better passing defensemen on the team and they will get the puck in the flat while they're moving.

THE PHYSICAL GAME

Mikulchik isn't a physical force, but he's big and uses his range well. He is a solid checker, although he doesn't put anyone into the seats because he doesn't have much of a mean streak.

THE INTANGIBLES

Mikulchik figures to be among the Jets' top six backliners this season. He isn't a top three, but he's a solid number four.

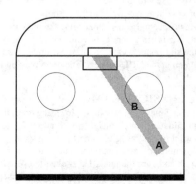

TEPPO NUMMINEN

Yrs. of NHL service: 7
Born: Tampere, Finland; July 3, 1968
Position: left defense
Height: 6-1
Weight: 190
Uniform no.: 27
Shoots: right

Career statistics:

GP	G	A	TP	PIM
473	42	169	211	193

1991-92 statistics:

GP	G	A	TP	+/-	PIM	PP	SH	GW	GT	S	PCT
80	5	34	39	+15	32	4	0	1	0	143	3.5

1992-93 statistics:

GP	G	A	TP	+/-	PIM	PP	SH	GW	GT	S	PCT
66	7	30	37	+4	33	3	1	0	0	103	6.8

1993-94 statistics:

GP	G	A	TP	+/-	PIM	PP	SH	GW	GT	S	PCT
57	5	18	23	-23	28	4	0	1	0	89	5.6

1994-95 statistics:

GP	G	A	TP	+/-	PIM	PP	SH	GW	GT	S	PCT
42	5	16	21	+12	16	2	0	0	0	86	5.8

LAST SEASON

Led team in plus-minus. Second among team defensemen in scoring. Missed one game with the flu. Missed five games with a knee injury.

THE FINESSE GAME

Numminen's agility and anticipation make him look much faster than he is. He is graceful with a smooth change of direction, and he never telegraphs what he is about to do. His skating makes him valuable on the first penalty-killing unit. He will not get caught out of position and is seldom bested one-on-one. His knee injury (suffered in February) took away some of his skating ability last year.

Numminen is not afraid to give up the puck on a dump and chase rather than force a neutral zone play if he is under pressure. He would rather dish off than rush with the puck, and he is a savvy passer, moving the puck briskly and seldom overhandling it. He is not a finisher. He will join the play but not lead it. Most of his offense is generated from point shots.

He is uncannily adept at keeping the puck in at the point, frustrating oppoents who try to clear it out around the boards. One of the most underrated defensemen in the NHL, he gets little press playing with the Jets.

THE PHYSICAL GAME

Numminen plays an acceptable physical game. He can be intimidated, which makes him a target for teams who want to neutralize his smart passing game. He'll employ his body as a last resort but would rather use his stick and gain the puck. He is even-tempered and not at all nasty. Playing with a big, brave defenseman

(like Dave Manson) gets him some room.

THE INTANGIBLES

Numminen is being asked to be a number one defenseman, but is not quite in the class of most teams' number one defenders. He is capable of playing a strong all-around game and scoring 50 points if he stays healthy, but is best suited as a number two or three defenseman.

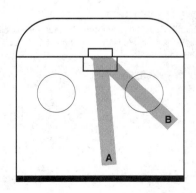

TEEMU SELANNE

Yrs. of NHL service: 3
Born: Helsinki, Finland; July 3, 1970
Position: right wing
Height: 6-0
Weight: 181
Uniform no.: 13
Shoots: right

Career statistics:

GP	G	A	TP	PIM
180	123	111	234	69

1992-93 statistics:

GP	G	A	TP	+/-	PIM	PP	SH	GW	GT	S	PCT
84	76	56	132	+8	45	24	0	7	0	387	19.6

1993-94 statistics:

GP	G	A	TP	+/-	PIM	PP	SH	GW	GT	S	PCT
51	25	29	54	-23	22	11	0	2	0	191	13.1

1994-95 statistics:

GP	G	A	TP	+/-	PIM	PP	SH	GW	GT	S	PCT
45	22	26	48	+1	2	8	2	1	1	167	13.2

LAST SEASON

Second on team in power play goals. Tied for team lead in shorthanded goals. Tied for second on team in goals. Third on team in assists and points. Served two-game suspension for slashing. Missed one game with a knee injury.

THE FINESSE GAME

Although Selanne appeared to have recovered well from his Achilles tendon surgery, he was hampered by patella tendinitis (inflammation in the left knee), which limited his practice time. Selanne wasn't close to 100 per cent most of the season. He lacked his old touch with the puck, but knowing that the Jets needed him, he had the knee "frozen" and kept playing through the pain.

Selanne's skating is such a major part of his game that his recuperation from his ailments will determine his future. Before the injury, his skating was exceptional. He had Porsche turbo speed. He got down low and then simply exploded past defensemen, even when he started from a standstill. He got tremendous thrust from his legs and had quick feet. Acceleration, balance, it was all there — all in the past tense until proven otherwise.

Everything you could ask for in a shot is there as well. Selanne employs all varieties of attacks. He and Alexei Zhamnov work especially well weaving back and forth, with Zhamnov setting up Selanne with a one-timer from the low right circle. Selanne is constantly in motion. If his first attempt is stopped, he'll pursue the puck behind the net, make a pass and circle out again for a shot. He is almost impossible to catch and is tough to knock down because of his balance. He will set up on the off-wing on the power play and can score on the backhand. His shot is not especially hard, but it is quick and accurate.

Selanne doesn't just try to overpower with his skating, he also outwits opponents. He has tremendous hockey instincts and vision, and is as good a playmaker as a finisher. He is able to lift little passes to teammates over defenders' blades, so the puck hits flat for the recipient.

THE PHYSICAL GAME

Teams set out to bump and grind Selanne from the first shift. If the Jest get a little deeper, some of the checking pressure can be taken off the top line, but for the time being, Selanne will have to fight his way through the junk. When the referees are slow on the whistle, he takes matters into his own hands, usually with his stick. He is one of the toughest young players in the league, European or otherwise.

THE INTANGIBLES

Selanne's future hinges on his injury. Expect him to have a very slow first half, or first few months after his return. Not only do the Jets need him, but the NHL does, too. Despite his painful ailment, Selanne played in what might have been the last game played in Winnipeg last season — a meaningless event, except to the fans. That kind of commitment is hard to find in a pro athlete these days.

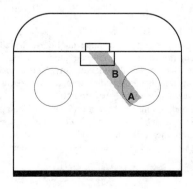

BRENT THOMPSON

Yrs. of NHL service: 3
Born: Calgary, Alta.; Jan. 9, 1971
Position: left defense
Height: 6-2
Weight: 200
Uniform no.: 22
Shoots: left

Career statistics:

GP	G	A	TP	PIM
110	1	9	10	324

1991-92 statistics:

GP	G	A	TP	+/-	PIM	PP	SH	GW	GT	S	PCT
27	0	5	5	-7	89	0	0	0	0	18	0.0

1992-93 statistics:

GP	G	A	TP	+/-	PIM	PP	SH	GW	GT	S	PCT
30	0	4	4	-4	76	0	0	0	0	27	0.0

1993-94 statistics:

GP	G	A	TP	+/-	PIM	PP	SH	GW	GT	S	PCT
24	1	0	1	-1	81	0	0	0	0	9	11.1

1994-95 statistics:

GP	G	A	TP	+/-	PIM	PP	SH	GW	GT	S	PCT
29	0	0	0	-17	78	0	0	0	0	16	0.0

LAST SEASON

Only Jets skater with 25 or more games played to fail to get a point. Acquired from Los Angeles for the rights to Ruslan Batyrshin and a second-round draft pick in 1996.

THE FINESSE GAME

One of the reasons why Thompson is so effective in his own end is that he wants to spend precious little time there. He has the strength and quickness to go after the puck, and the intelligence to know when to skate it out, when to look for a man breaking through the middle or when to make a safe dump off the boards.

Thompson uses all of his skills in the defensive mode and seldom gets involved in the action at the other end of the ice. He would be perfectly happy with one point a year if his plus/minus were in double digits (on the plus side, not the minus, as it was last year). He has a decent shot from the point but won't score many points.

THE PHYSICAL GAME

Thompson is big, tough and mean. Injuries have been part of the reason why his development has been slower than expected. When healthy, he is a force on the blueline, banging bodies around and clearing out the crease — a goalie's best friend.

Conditioning has been a problem for Thompson. He has put on 25 pounds over the past few seasons — although the NHL media guide still lists him at his draft weight of 175 — and most of it is muscle.

THE INTANGIBLES

The Jets need Thompson to help toughen up their defense. They will put up with his lack of offense — they have enough skilled players for that — but need him to bring his physical presence to the ice every night.

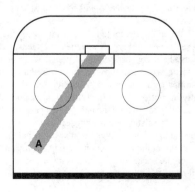

KEITH TKACHUK

Yrs. of NHL service: 3
Born: Melrose, Mass.; Mar. 28, 1972
Position: left wing
Height: 6-3
Weight: 218
Uniform no.: 7
Shoots: left

Career statistics:

GP	G	A	TP	PIM
232	94	97	191	636

1991-92 statistics:

GP	G	A	TP	+/-	PIM	PP	SH	GW	GT	S	PCT
17	3	5	8	0	28	2	0	0	0	22	13.6

1992-93 statistics:

GP	G	A	TP	+/-	PIM	PP	SH	GW	GT	S	PCT
83	28	23	51	-13	201	12	0	2	1	199	14.1

1993-94 statistics:

GP	G	A	TP	+/-	PIM	PP	SH	GW	GT	S	PCT
84	41	40	81	-12	255	22	3	3	1	218	18.8

1994-95 statistics:

GP	G	A	TP	+/-	PIM	PP	SH	GW	GT	S	PCT
48	22	29	51	-4	152	7	2	2	1	129	17.1

LAST SEASON

Led team in PIM and tied for team lead in shorthanded goals. One of five Jets to appear in all 48 games; has played in 199 consecutive games. Second on team in assists and points. Tied for second on team in goals.

THE FINESSE GAME

In only his third NHL season, Tkachuk has joined the ranks of the league's top power forwards. Like Brendan Shanahan, Adam Graves and Kevin Stevens, Tkachuk is at his best when he uses his power and scoring touch in tight. The scary thing is that Tkachuk is better than they were at an earlier age.

In front of the net, Tkachuk will bang and crash, but he also has soft hands for picking pucks out of skates and flicking strong wrist shots. He can also kick at the puck with his skates without going down. He has a quick release. He looks at the net, not down at his stick, and finds the openings.

Tkachuk keeps growing, and there are times when he looks awkward, as if all the components were sprouting at different times. He has improved his one-step quickness and agility. He is powerful and balanced, and often drives through bigger defensemen.

Tkachuk plays with Nelson Emerson, but often takes the draws. When he doesn't win outright, he will tie up the opposing centre and fight for the puck.

THE PHYSICAL GAME

Tkachuk is a rugged scrapper who will pay the price, as his PIM total — first on the team — illustrates. On nights when his game is on, he can dictate the physical tempo of a game with his work in the corners and along the boards, a rare gift for so inexperienced a player. He has to play that way every night.

He is too valuable to lose in poor trade-offs. Tkachuk isn't intimidated by the size or reputation of his foe. He gets under a lot of skins, and gets into battles on the ice and at the benches. He will yap and aggravate.

THE INTANGIBLES

Tkachuk was named the youngest captain in the NHL for his grit, heart and maturity. He will be in the 50-goal range in a season or two. This hard-nosed winger was one of the most attractive Group Two free agents during the off-season, but the cash-strapped Jets have the right to match and can't afford to lose him.

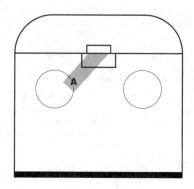

NEIL WILKINSON

Yrs. of NHL service: 6
Born: Selkirk, Man.; Aug. 16, 1967
Position: left defense
Height: 6-3
Weight: 180
Uniform no.: 2
Shoots: right

Career statistics:

GP	G	A	TP	PIM
317	11	49	60	599

1991-92 statistics:

GP	G	A	TP	+/-	PIM	PP	SH	GW	GT	S	PCT
60	4	15	19	-11	97	1	0	0	0	95	4.2

1992-93 statistics:

GP	G	A	TP	+/-	PIM	PP	SH	GW	GT	S	PCT
59	1	7	8	-50	96	0	1	0	0	51	2.0

1993-94 statistics:

GP	G	A	TP	+/-	PIM	PP	SH	GW	GT	S	PCT
72	3	9	12	+2	114	1	0	0	0	72	4.2

1994-95 statistics:

GP	G	A	TP	+/-	PIM	PP	SH	GW	GT	S	PCT
40	1	4	5	-26	75	0	0	0	0	25	4.0

LAST SEASON

Worst plus-minus on team. Missed six games with a back injury.

THE FINESSE GAME

Wilkinson is solid in most areas of the game, though nothing really stands out. He carries the puck, but wouldn't be categorized as a rushing defenseman. He will play back, but his defensive reads are in serious need of improvement. He does not complete easy passes and doesn't have much of a shot.

Wilkinson is an average skater and has some difficulty with his foot speed when backskating. He is vulnerable to outside speed. He has to learn to angle his man to the boards.

He has a good attitude and will try anything the coaching staff asks, but he is a high risk defenseman.

THE PHYSICAL GAME

Wilkinson is tall and gives the impression that he will be more of a bruiser, but his checks aren't that jarring. He will play tough and help his teammates. He is not a great fighter, but he will give it a go if provoked. Because he isn't a good skater, he can't hit a moving target.

THE INTANGIBLES

Wilkinson will get more ice time with Winnipeg, which is looking to toughen up its overall team and add size to the blueline corps. Because of his size, the Jest will also expect more from Wilkinson than they'll get.

ALEXEI ZHAMNOV

Yrs. of NHL service: 3
Born: Moscow, Russia; Oct. 1, 1970
Position: centre
Height: 6-1
Weight: 187
Uniform no.: 10
Shoots: left

Career statistics:

GP	G	A	TP	PIM
177	81	127	208	140

1992-93 statistics:

GP	G	A	TP	+/-	PIM	PP	SH	GW	GT	S	PCT
68	25	47	72	+7	58	6	1	4	1	163	15.3

1993-94 statistics:

GP	G	A	TP	+/-	PIM	PP	SH	GW	GT	S	PCT
61	26	45	71	-20	62	7	0	1	1	196	13.3

1994-95 statistics:

GP	G	A	TP	+/-	PIM	PP	SH	GW	GT	S	PCT
48	30	35	65	+5	20	9	0	4	0	155	19.4

LAST SEASON

Finalist for 1995 Lady Byng Trophy. Led team and tied for third in NHL in goals; one of only five players with 30 or more. Led team and third in NHL in points. Led team in power play goals, game-winning goals, shots and shooting percentage. Led team in assists for second consecutive year. One of five Jets to appear in all 48 games.

THE FINESSE GAME

Zhamnov appears fully recovered from his back injury of a season ago. The Russian's game is puck control. He can carry it at top speed or work give-and-gos with his favourite linemate, Teemu Selanne, another player coming off a serious injury.

Zhamnov is a crafty playmaker and is not too unselfish. While he will look first to set up Selanne's one-timer or to spring his right winger on a breakaway, he also has an accurate if not overpowering shot. As well, he can blast off the pass, or manoeuvre until he has a screen and then wrist it. On the power play, he can dart in and out in front of the goalie, using his soft hands for a tip.

He also kills penalties on the second unit, a credit to his quickness and overall hockey sense. Defensively, he is very sound. He is a dedicated backchecker and never leaves the zone too quickly.

THE PHYSICAL GAME

Zhamnov will bump to prevent a scoring chance or go for a loose puck, but body work is not his forte. He is strong and fights his way through traffic in front of the net to get to a puck. He needs to do a better job of tying up the opposing centre on face-offs, since he wins few draws cleanly.

THE INTANGIBLES

Because he plays in Winnipeg (and at that, is overshadowed by Selanne), Zhamnov doesn't get much ink, but he gets a lot of ice. And he's got world-class talent. We said in last year's *HSR* that a healthy Zhamnov could score 100 points. His prorated total for an 84-game season is 113 points. Enough said.

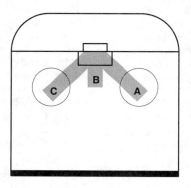

PLAYER INDEX

Player Index